PRACTICAL RAY TRACING IN C

Author's Note

This book is the second in a series of books from Wiley dealing with the exciting field of imaging on a PC. The first book, *Practical Image Processing in C*, introduced the creation, manipulation, and storage of digitized images. This book discusses the creation of photo-realistic imaging using ray tracing. If you have enjoyed these titles, keep your eyes open for the next in this series of C imaging books by this author and published by John Wiley & Sons, Inc.

PRACTICAL RAY TRACING IN C

Craig A. Lindley

JOHN WILEY & SONS, INC.
New York   Chichester   Brisbane   Toronto   Singapore

Library of Congress Cataloging-in-Publication Data

Lindley, Craig A.
    Practical ray tracing in C / Craig A. Lindley
       p. cm.
    Includes bibliographical references and index.
    ISBN 0-471-57301-9 (acid-free paper : book/disk set)
     1. Computer graphics.   2. C (Computer program language).
   I. Title.

T385.L5585   1992
006.6—dc20   92-30223
                                                  CIP

Printed in the United States of America

10 9 8 7 6 5 4 3 2 1

This book is dedicated to those people whose quest
for knowledge lights the pathway to the future.

Trademarks and Copyrights

About the Author

Craig A. Lindley is the founder and president of Clockwork Software, an imaging consulting company which specializes in developing multimedia products. Prior to this, he worked as a software engineer/scientist for such companies as Hewlett-Packard, IBM/Rolm, NASA's Jet Propulsion Labs, and TRW. He has written three books, including *Practical Image Processing in C* for John Wiley & Sons, and has over 24 technical publications to his credit as well as numerous invention disclosures with IBM.

Recently, an art gallery sold some of his ray-traced images produced with the techniques presented in this book. He hopes to pursue the sale of more images as time goes on.

Important Note

No patent liability is assumed with respect to the use of the information contained herein. While every precaution has been taken in the preparation of this book, the publisher and author assume no responsibility for errors or omissions. Neither is a liability assumed for damages resulting from the use of the information contained herein.

Contents

Introduction   *3*
Software Environment and Development Tools   *5*
PC Display Adapters   *10*
   Modes and Resolutions   11
   Hardware Palettes and Color Modes   13
   Video Memory Organization   18
   Image Palette Generation   24
   VESA   25   ~~Bad~~   *PCI good*
      THE VESA SOFTWARE INTERFACE   *27*
   VGA/SuperVGA Function Library   43
   Gamma Correction   56
   32K-Color Modes   59
Conclusions   *60*

Introduction   *65*
General Concepts   *66*

Figures

Program Listings

Preface

The magic that created the image on the front cover of this book is a computer graphics technique called "ray tracing" and is the focus of this book. If you think about it, you'll realize that you probably have seen ray-traced images before. Once you've read this book, you'll realize that you haven't seen anything yet. With the proliferation of affordable, powerful desktop PCs and workstations, you'll soon see greater use of ray tracing in all forms of visual media. In this book we'll participate in this visual revolution by bringing the concepts of ray tracing out from the folds of academia into the hands of the people who are just now able to put it to use—people who can use the techniques to their fullest advantage; people interested in and involved in presentation graphics, such as engineers, computer programmers, graphic artists, or CAD designers. Like any true art form, ray tracing can produce an image of almost anything you can imagine—you are not bound by physical reality. With this book as your guide, your imagination is your only limit.

What Is Ray Tracing?

Ray tracing is a method for the generation of photo-realistic three-dimensional images using the principles of geometric optics. Ray tracing models, albeit simply, the interaction of light and objects within a scene, making possible many of the effects that increase the realism of images: perspective, shadowing, reflection, refraction, and texturing are a few examples. These effects provide the depth information to the viewer's brain that enhances the three-dimensional effects contained in a two-dimensional image.

Ray tracing is useful when you want to view a realistic image of something that either:
1. You do not want to make a physical model of due to cost, size, or other constraints; or
2. You do not have direct access to.

Ray tracing finds applications in advertising (product promotions and logos, for example), architecture (including virtual reality), art (as on the front cover of this book), CAD

(Computer Aided Design, especially in the mechanical field), and entertainment (science-fiction movies and graphics on MTV).

Ray tracing is not, however, a graphics panacea. We will discuss the limitations and problems associated with ray tracing along with its advantages throughout this book.

What Is in This Book and Why Should I Buy It?

Although ray tracing is one of the simplest three-dimensional graphical rendering techniques available, learning it can be at first a little overwhelming. After all, how many people are familiar with concepts such as "geometric optics" and "vector mathematics"? The information that is publicly available about ray tracing generally focuses on advanced rather than introductory topics. Even introductory books (I'm aware of two at the time of this writing) treat the subject as if the reader already knew the topic. Having undertaken the study of ray tracing and suffered through the learning process, I came to the conclusion that a new introductory book was necessary. Further, I felt that this book should talk in detail about basic ray-tracing techniques without skipping over the parts that everyone is supposed to already understand, because everyone doesn't. This book answers many of the "Why does it work this way?" questions I had while I was learning the basic techniques.

In essence, this book has two audiences: the technical audience and the artistic audience. To best address both audiences, I have organized this book into three parts:

- Part One. The Science of Ray Tracing
- Part Two. The Art of Ray Tracing
- Part Three. Additional Information

Part One is for the technical reader, Part Two for the artistic user, and Part Three for both audiences. A more complete picture of ray tracing can be formed, however, if the book is read in its entirety.

Part One. The Science of Ray Tracing

Part One discusses the basic theories behind ray tracing. To illustrate the concepts presented, I have provided a basic yet functional ray tracer with its full C code implementation for discussion, study, and experimentation. Other topics discussed in Part One include VGA and Super-VGA programming, vector mathematics, parametric ray equations, ray/object intersections, color quantization, and graphic image file formats. This section is intended for more technical readers.

Like my other books, this book focuses more on the practical aspects of ray tracing than on the theories involved. The technical portions of this book assume a general knowledge of C programming along with some assembly language programming experience for the 80X86 family of Intel processors. Most of the software provided in this book is designed to be used as stand-alone application programs, so understanding the detailed operation is not strictly necessary (except by those readers who feel compelled to understand how something works to use it). In all cases, the code is well documented and should be easy for even a beginner to understand.

Some math is required to fully comprehend how ray tracing works. This book assumes the reader has some working knowledge of algebra and some trigonometry, just as it assumes some C programming experience. This book does not pretend to teach these skills. The small amount of specialized math required for a complete understanding of the processes involved will be discussed in detail. *Note:* The math is presented for those individuals who want to understand, in detail, how ray tracing works. Others who just want to know how to use a ray tracer or who want only an overview of the capabilities of current generation ray tracers do not need to study or understand the math presented.

Part Two. The Art of Ray Tracing

Part Two emphasizes the practical applications of a ray tracer. Here we'll use a full-featured ray-tracing program called DKBTrace (all of the C source code for this program is also provided on the companion disks). We present the operation and capabilities of DKBTrace in a series of tutorial exercises that acquaint the user with the program's basic function. Further exercises will touch on the more advanced techniques. Finally, when the reader is fully prepared, some of the image models shown in the "Gallery of Images" (following page 314) will be discussed in depth. You can modify these models to create art of your own design. Part Two also discusses the use of photography to capture ray-traced images on film, along with a discussion of various uses of ray-traced imagery.

Part Three. Additional Information

Part Three contains information of a more generalized nature that will be of interest to all readers of this book. Included in this section are a glossary and a section of Further Reading for readers seeking more information.

Required Equipment

To use the ray-tracing code provided in this book to its full potential the following equipment is necessary:

1. An IBM-compatible PC (preferably with a 286, 386, or 486 processor) *with a VGA graphics adapter and color monitor.* A numeric co-processor is not absolutely required, but it will allow some of the more complex image renderings to finish within your lifetime.
2. An ASCII editor of your choice. Borland's Sidekick is extremely useful for this purpose.
3. A Borland/Turbo C compiler version 2.0 or later. The code can be made to work with other brands of C compilers as well. The use of the Microsoft C compiler, for example, will be discussed. *Note:* A compiler is required only if you wish to modify any of the code provided. Executable versions of the most important programs in the book are available on the companion disks and can be used immediately without any program development (except if you require the DKBTrace ray tracer to run on an 8088 machine—more on this later).

Ray tracing requires an impressive amount of computing power to perform. The rendering of complex images can bring even the most powerful PC or workstation to its knees. Some of the images in the "Gallery of Images" required more than thirty hours to render on a 33 MHz 486 PC. For this reason, the more powerful the computer put to the task the better. If a numeric co-processor is available, that's better yet. Anyone seriously considering the production of complex ray-traced images would find a numeric co-processor worth the investment in both time and money, especially since the prices of numeric co-processors have fallen so much recently.

All code has been extensively tested on both an IBM PS2 Model 70 (20 MHz 386 processor) with 2 megabytes of RAM, an 80387 numeric co-processor, and a VGA graphics adapter and a Gateway 2000 33 MHz i486 with 8 megabytes of RAM and SuperVGA capability. You can execute the DKBTrace ray-tracing code as provided on the companion disks on any IBM-compatible PC with a 286, 386, or 486 processor. With a little bit of effort (a recompilation of the source code), you can make the code work on even the original 4.77 MHz 8088 machine, although for performance reasons this is not recommended. (See the file IBM.MAK on the companion disk for details.) The images must be displayed, however, on a VGA-equipped PC. *Neither CGA nor EGA graphics adapters are supported by the code in this book. A VGA graphics adapter is absolutely required.* We will discuss the reasons for this in Chapter 1.

The companion disks included with this book contain all of the source code developed in the book along with some images from the "Gallery of Images." I should mention that the DKBTrace ray-tracer code (also on the companion disks) has been ported to many different computer environments including the IBM PC, the Amiga, the MAC, the VAX, and the UNIX environments. Documentation exists on the companion disks for some of these ports although they are not discussed in this book. *Please note:* The DKBTrace code on the companion disks is also available free of charge on Internet via an anonymous ftp. It can be found in the /pub/dkbtrace directory on alfred.ccs.carleton.ca for those who have Internet access. However, the tools and image models developed in this book for use with DKBTrace are available only on the companion disks.

The most important goal of this book is to introduce you to the fascinating world of ray tracing. You will find that ray tracing not only has many tangible uses but that it also provides hours of entertainment. I hope you have lots of fun designing and producing your own original ray-tracing masterpieces. Happy Imaging.

CRAIG A. LINDLEY

Manitou Springs, Colorado

Acknowledgments

First and foremost I must acknowledge my wife Heather's contribution to this book. Even though this is the third book of mine that she has had to proofread, she did not complain. Somehow she managed to squeeze in the proofreading between gardening, weaving, and pampering me. I could not have done this without her help and support.

David Buck, the genius behind the DKBTrace ray-tracing program deserves very special recognition. He graciously allowed me to include his program with this book. Without DKB-Trace this would have been just another dry computer book. With his DKBTrace program readers can immediately begin experimenting with an incredibly capable ray tracer to produce images to be proud of. David Buck has done a real service to the computer graphics industry by giving his time and energy so that more people can experiment with ray tracing. Thanks, David. I, for one, have learned a lot from your work.

I would also like to thank Paul Bame at Hewlett-Packard for answering some of my initial questions about ray tracing and for providing me with information on the subject. It was those long discussions with Paul (and Ida Newcomer) over margaritas at Henri's that got me interested in ray tracing.

William Ives, the PC whiz kid at HP, also needs to be acknowledged for helping me conceptualize an object-oriented approach to ray-tracer design. He showed me how C++ techniques could be implemented in ANSI standard C. Thanks Bill.

Wolfgang Stuerzlinger needs to be thanked for writing the octree color quantization code and placing it in the public domain where I found it and modified it for use in this book. Thank you Wolfgang.

I would also like to thank Diane Cerra and Terri Hudson of John Wiley & Sons for helping me with the business of book publishing and the Hewlett-Packard Company for providing me with the opportunity to write another book. Finally, I would like to thank those people who directly and/or indirectly convinced me that it was time to strike out on my own. Thank you everyone.

All images in this book were designed and rendered by me on my IBM-compatible PC in my messy little office in the Colorado mountains. Each image is truly an original that no one would claim, except me.

C.A.L.

PART ONE

THE SCIENCE OF RAY TRACING

Rarely are our creative efforts admired for what we as creators consider most admirable.

—Jeff Duntemann

1

Background Information

Make haste slowly.
—Augustus

In this chapter you will learn about:
- **The software development tools and processes necessary to use the code in this book**
- **Why a VGA display adapter is required for serious imaging work**
- **VGA display adapters, their modes, and resolutions**
- **SuperVGA graphic hardware extensions to standard VGA**
- **What VESA is and what it attempts to do**
- **The code required to interface a graphics application program with a VGA/Super-VGA display adapter**
- **Gamma correction for accurate image display**
- **Enhanced 32,768-color modes available on some SuperVGA hardware**

Introduction

It is an unfortunate fact of life that a certain amount of background investigation is required before delving into any new subject area. It doesn't even matter what the subject is: a little study is always necessary to acquaint yourself with the technology, the vocabulary unique to the subject, and the tools with which to manipulate the technology that makes the subject possible. Once you understand the background information, higher-level concepts will make much more sense. The background information is the foundation on which you build your greater understanding.

The subject of ray tracing is no different. Ray tracing is complex enough to require the understanding of a wide range of subject areas before all the pieces will come together and begin to make sense. It is analogous to the book publishing process. As an author you don't really need to understand all aspects of book production (typesetting, printing, etc.) to write a book, although you may write a better book if you do. With computer graphics in general, it's not absolutely necessary but it helps to understand the complete scope of the problem from the lowest-level graphic primitive to the high-level algorithms. In this way you can determine more accurately where, when, and if trade-offs must be made.

In this first chapter we spend some time discussing subjects not directly related to ray tracing, namely, the software development environment and PC display adapters. These discussions are not major treatises on the subjects, which could fill complete volumes of their own, rather they provide the information you will need to understand subsequent discussions in this book and to understand the software provided.

It must be noted that the primary target of the software provided in this book (also referred to as "code" throughout the book) is the IBM PC and compatible computers. Only PC display adapters will be described. Space does not allow the discussion of the hundreds of other display adapter devices available in the computer industry. However, DKBTrace, the ray-tracing program provided in this book (and available in source form on the companion disks), has been ported to many disparate computer environments including the Amiga computer, the MAC, VAX machines, Next computers, standard UNIX workstations, and X11 workstations. Some of the information required for performing these ports of DKBTrace is included. The other code provided in this book (the simple ray tracer and the various tools) has been run only on IBM compatibles. Porting this code to one of these other environments should not, however, be a serious problem given the proper motivation.

As mentioned in the Preface, this book does not try to teach programming. Therefore, only the aspects of the programming languages used in this book will be discussed. There is no generalized coverage of computer programming, as a working knowledge of C and assembler programming is an expected prerequisite. See the list of books provided in the Further Reading section of Part Three for more information on programming.

There is one more important note on processor performance. Ray tracing is a numerically intensive computational activity. Complex imagery can consume *any* PC put to this task. The more horsepower available for ray tracing the better. While all of the programs developed for and provided with this book (with the exception of the protected-mode version of DKBTrace) can be made to run on the original 4.77 MHz IBM PC (a VGA graphics adapter will be required to display the results, however), the results will be available much sooner on a 20 MHz 80386 processor with numeric co-processor, and even sooner with a 50 MHz 486.

Please bear with me while we discuss these necessary topics. If you must begin the study of ray tracing immediately, skip ahead to Chapter 2 now. You can come back to the information in this chapter when the need arises. If you are not, however, an experienced graphics programmer on the IBM PC (or compatible) platform, I suggest you spend the time reading this chapter; your time will not be wasted.

Software Environment and Development Tools

This section touches on many subjects, most of which are not directly applicable to the topic of ray tracing. This is both unfortunate and necessary, however. Unfortunate in that this section is a catchall for the discussion of many disparate subjects, but also necessary because we must establish a baseline understanding of these non-ray-tracing topics before we can proceed. It is important that we discuss software development early because we will be getting directly into code in the following sections of this chapter. Practical books are like that.

Note: Throughout these discussions, we refer to many program files. To find out where these files reside on the companion disks, please consult the Companion Disks section in Part Three. Almost all files on the companion disks are compressed to save space and therefore must be decompressed before they can be used. Instructions for decompressing the files are in the Companion Disks section.

Before beginning we need to make some distinctions between code written by the author and code that is part of the DKBTrace ray-tracing package written by David Buck and others. Code written by the author will be generically referred to as the "tools" code. All code that is part of the DKBTrace package will be referred to as "DKBTrace" code. We use these terms to describe the two types of code throughout this book. Regardless of its origin, all code discussed in this book (including the DKBTrace and tools code) is available in C source code form on the companion disk. This should make your experimentation with ray tracing as effortless and fun as possible. This large body of source code is a very valuable commodity. Pieces of the code can be used for many different graphics applications, some of which will be suggested throughout this book.

The DKBTrace code consists of the C source code for the ray tracer, major documentation files, and make files (make files contain instructions on how application programs are to be constructed) for utilizing the source code in many different computing environments (including the IBM PC, the Amiga, the MAC, VAX machines, UNIX workstations, etc.). Included are three executable versions of the DKBTrace ray tracer:

1. dkbno87.exe. This is a real-mode version of the ray tracer for use with PCs that do not have a numeric co-processor installed. As supplied, a 286 or greater processor is required to run this program. DKBTrace must be recompiled in order to run on an 8088/8086 processor. See the file on the companion disks "ibm.mak" for details.
2. dkb.exe. This is a real-mode version of the ray tracer for use with PCs that have a numeric co-processor installed. Same caveats as above.
3. dkbpro.exe. This is a protected-mode version of the ray tracer for use with PCs that have a numeric co-processor installed. This version can *only* be run on computers that have an 80286, 80386, or 80486 processor. This version can be used to ray trace very complex image models because it is not limited to the 640K of memory that the real-mode versions are. In other words, it has access to all extended memory available in your computer. Two megabytes of extended RAM minimum is required to use this program; it will, however, will use all extended RAM it finds. Also, it will use portions of your hard disk for virtual memory if your images are really complex. See the files "dkbpro.doc" and "dkbmod.doc" on the companion disks for more information on the protected-mode version of DKBTrace.

Given the availability on the companion disks of these executable versions of the DKB-Trace program along with executable versions of the tools code that supports DKBTrace, no software development is required to begin experimentation with ray tracing. Rebuilding (editing, compiling, and linking) DKBTrace will be necessary only if you make changes to the source code for your own uses. A make file is included for use with Microsoft C (or Borland/Turbo C with a little work) to rebuild the real-mode versions of DKBTrace when and if that becomes necessary. (There is a brief discussion of make files later in this section.) Complete instructions are provided in the DKBTrace documentation for rebuilding and/or porting the code to different computing environments. Executable versions of DKBTrace for other computers are available over the Internet, as mentioned in the Preface.

The code for the tools was developed and tested using the IDE (Integrated Development Environment) in Borland C, simply because this is the author's favorite programming environment. The tools code comprises the majority of the code presented and discussed in this book. The tools code includes:

1. A VGA/SuperVGA function library with VESA SuperVGA support
2. A very simple ray-tracer program for illustrating the concepts involved
3. Three different color quantizing programs
4. A PCX and GIF graphics file function library and file viewer

You may need to modify these tools slightly if they have to run in a different computing environment or with a different compiler. Here again, software development may not be required at all because executable versions of all of the major tools exist on the companion disks.

In terms of the computer equipment you need to utilize the programs in this book, the minimum requirements are as follows:

1. IBM AT or compatible computer. An IBM PC can be made to work but the DKB-Trace program will have to be recompiled.
2. VGA graphics/display adapter.
3. 640K of memory.
4. MSDOS 2.0 or newer, with MSDOS 5.0 recommended.

This configuration will run every program in this book except the protected-mode version of DKBTrace, which requires extended memory to operate. To generate and display 256-color images in resolutions higher than 320 by 200 resolution requires a SuperVGA card instead of a standard VGA card. The SuperVGA card should have a minimum of 512K bytes of video RAM (Random Access Memory) with 1 megabyte being preferred. One megabyte of video memory is necessary for the display of 256 colors at a resolution of 1024 by 768 and for the 800 by 600 resolution 32,768 (32K)-color mode. The SuperVGA card should be VESA compatible to run the tools code as provided (modifications to the tools code for non-VESA-compliant graphics adapters will be discussed). The significance of VESA will be discussed in the next section. Finally, if 32K colors are desired in 640 by 480 or 800 by 600 resolutions, a Sierra Hicolor DAC (digital to analog converter) coupled with a Tseng Labs ET-4000 based SuperVGA card is required. For performance considerations, the faster the computer the better, because ray tracing consumes lots of CPU (Central Processing Unit) cycles. A numeric co-processor chip installed in your computer will help the performance a good deal. Even better is an 80486 processor with an internal numeric co-processor. It doesn't matter much computing horsepower you have for ray tracing, you will never think your computer is fast enough. However, the results will be worth waiting for. Trust me!

Given the required display adapter hardware as just discussed, the DKBTrace program and the tools code provided are capable of generating, processing, and displaying beautiful ray-traced images in each of the following formats:

| 320 by 200 | 640 by 480 | 800 by 600 | 1024 by 768 | —in 256 colors |
| | 640 by 480 | 800 by 600 | | —in 32K colors |

The higher-resolution images can take a long time to generate but are visually stunning when finished. See the "Gallery of Images" for some examples.

All of the programs in this book are designed to run under MSDOS (or PCDOS) from the DOS command line prompt. Running under MSDOS places severe memory limits on all of these programs. Special considerations and/or trade-offs were made during program design to allow execution under MSDOS. The color quantizer programs from Chapter 4, for example, had to be designed to make multiple passes over the ray-traced image data it uses as its input, instead of keeping all of the image data in memory at one time. In other words, we traded reduced memory usage for multiple passes over the image data. This reduced the color quantizer programs' performance, but it allows them to run under MSDOS. Similarly, many of the other tools programs (which process and display the imagery) operate on the image data a raster line at a time to reduce memory consumption. The moral to this story is to try and have as much free memory available in your system as possible when these programs are run. The more memory available, the faster some of these programs will run. MSDOS 5.0 is the recommended version of the operating system because by loading itself in high memory it gives application programs (which DKBTrace and tools programs are) the most memory possible. An adventurous soul might try porting the programs in this book to the Window 3.X environment not only to solve the memory problems but also to add a nice Graphical User Interface (GUI).

All of the tools code is written with clarity, not speed, in mind. All source code is heavily commented for ease of understanding by even a beginning C programmer and is also discussed at length in the accompanying text. All of the tools code appears in a consistent format to make it as readable as possible. In terms of C coding style, we have avoided forward references through the use of include files containing function prototypes and through the ordering of functions within files. This results in PASCAL-like C code with the "main" function at the end instead of the beginning of the C source file. We have used ANSI function prototypes throughout to allow the compiler to catch parameter type, number, and ordering problems. There aren't many stand-alone 80X86 assembler code files in this book. There is, however, some embedded assembly code within some of the C source files (see the file "vga.c," for example). We intentionally kept the amount of assembler code to a minimum to enhance portability and understandability. What little assembly code there is will be discussed in the appropriate context.

To make the tools code as portable as possible between ANSI C compilers, we provided all of the graphics support required for operation as part of the tool package. In other words, we use none of the native and nonportable graphics support provided by the compiler vendors.

You can therefore avoid any portability problems. It should take very little effort to port the C tools code to any other PC-based ANSI C compiler. *Note*: All of the tools code is compiled using the small memory model unless otherwise noted.

Borland C's Integrated Development Environment (IDE) was used exclusively for all of the tool programs developed in this book. Its speed, flexibility, user interface, debugger, and "project make" facility allow applications to be produced quickly and errors to be found and fixed quickly. Project make, although not a full UNIX-style Make program (a make file of program build instructions is feed to a Make program which causes the application program to be built), is sufficient for keeping the object modules that make up an application organized and up to date with little thought required from the user. Be sure to see the Borland and/or Turbo C Users Guide manuals for a complete description of the project make facility in your specific programming environment. Although the project make facility performs the same function in both the Borland C and Turbo C environments, its usage is slightly different in each environment. In Turbo C, the project make file is an ASCII file like that shown below, which is built with an editor. In Borland C, the project file is built within the IDE and is not viewable otherwise. Borland C's project make supports automatic dependency checking, which eliminates the need for the include file dependencies to be listed explicitly in the project make file.

An example project make file for use with Turbo C is shown below for purpose of discussion. This happens to be the project make file for the simple ray-tracing program given in Chapter 3. It is called "ttrace.prj" and is available on the companion disks.

```
attrib      (struct.h trace.h)
light       (struct.h trace.h mymem.h vectors.h)
linklist    (struct.h trace.h mymem.h)
output      (struct.h trace.h errors.h)
plane       (struct.h trace.h mymem.h vectors.h)
rays        (struct.h trace.h vectors.h)
sphere      (struct.h trace.h mymem.h vectors.h)
trace       (struct.h trace.h)
```

The name of an executable file produced by a project make file is the filename of the project make file without the .prj extension. In other words, the executable file that is generated by this project make file will be named "ttrace.exe."

Project make understands, via built-in rules, that any filename listed in a project make file without an extension is a C file. It inherently knows also that it must compile a C file before it can be linked with other files. The line in the project make file shown above containing "trace" illustrates both of these rules. Further, this same line says the trace.c file depends on the include files, struct.h and trace.h. In other words, if the time stamp (the date and time when the file was last modified) on any of the include files is newer than trace.c (indicating a modification of the include files that may affect how trace.c works), trace.c must be recompiled before it can be linked.

Other files could also be listed in a project make file such as library files (.lib extension) and object files (.obj extension). These files would be linked with the "ttrace.obj" file produced by the compiler to form a complete program. The project make file takes care of the whole process automatically.

The same project make file for use in the Borland C programming environment would just be a list of the C files that make up the finished executable program. This list would be built within the IDE using the project make editor. As above, the output executable file is given the name of the project make file. The project make file for use with Borland C is included on the companion disks and is called "btrace.prj."

In other, more traditional, programming environments, including the Borland/Turbo C command line environments, the organization of files that make up a complete application is handled by a Make program. Make reads a file (typically called "Makefile" in the DOS or UNIX environments) of application build specifications, including which files make up the application program, what dependencies exist between the component pieces of the application, and rules on how those pieces are made. When Make is executed it examines all pieces of the application program (just as described above for project make) and it builds (compiles or assembles) the pieces that are out of date and links the complete application together into a finished product, all without user intervention. Make files can also perform many other functions (any function that can be executed from the command line prompt) including copying files, renaming files, deleting files, and so on. Some people even use make files to assist in document processing.

Generating make files is a tedious process because of the unforgiving syntax required, but once they are correct they save time and can prevent the many types of common build errors that people make when the process is performed manually. To continue with the example above, the following is a traditional make file for use with Microsoft C. This file is included on the companion disks and is called "trace.mak." *Note*: There are many possible variations of a make file that would have the same outcome. The make file shown below is just one possible make file configuration.

```
# Make file for A First Ray-Tracer Program
# written by Craig A. Lindley

CSwitch  = /c /Zpil /G2 /Ox
LnkSwitch = /CO /MAP

attrib.obj:    attrib.c struct.h trace.h
               cl $(CSwitch) attrib.c

light.obj:     light.c struct.h trace.h mymem.h vectors.h
               cl $(CSwitch) light.c

linklist.obj: linklist.c struct.h trace.h mymem.h
               cl $(CSwitch) linklist.c

output.obj:    output.c struct.h trace.h errors.h
               cl $(CSwitch) output.c

plane.obj:     plane.c struct.h trace.h mymem.h vectors.h
               cl $(CSwitch) plane.c

rays.obj:      rays.c struct.h trace.h vectors.h
               cl $(CSwitch) rays.c
```

(continued)

```
sphere.obj:    sphere.c struct.h trace.h mymem.h vectors.h
               cl $(CSwitch) sphere.c

trace.obj:     trace.c struct.h trace.h
               cl $(CSwitch) trace.c

trace.exe:     attrib.obj light.obj linklist.obj output.obj plane.obj rays.obj sphere.obj trace.obj
               link $(LnkSwitch) attrib+light+linklist+output+plane+rays+sphere+trace,trace,trace,\
                               graphics.lib+slibce.lib
```

To help alleviate the headaches involved in the production of traditional make files, Borland includes a utility program with its compilers called "prj2mak.exe." This program builds a traditional make file from the information contained in a project make file. The resultant make file can be executed successfully by Borland's Make program and many other varieties of Make programs.

Note: All project make files included on the companion disks are for use with Borland C. They will have to be converted manually for use with Turbo C or other C compilers.

PC Display Adapters

Because the output of the ray-tracing process is a visual image, the means of viewing the result is extremely important. In fact, the quality and capability of the display hardware (adapter card and monitor) is the single most important item to consider in a computer system to be used for ray tracing or any kind of imaging/image processing (followed closely by high performance and large amounts of disk space and memory, etc.).

A graphics adapter is the hardware circuitry internal to a PC that gives it the capability of displaying graphic images in addition to text. Graphic images are composed of a series of dots and lines that can be placed anywhere in the display area of the attached monitor. Graphics frees the programmer of the constraints placed upon him or her by the text mode of operation. When the term "graphics adapter" is used, it implies the availability of both text and graphics modes of operation. In industry, the term "display adapter" may imply text modes only. In this book, both terms are used to mean the same thing: the ability to display both text and graphics.

The graphics display capabilities of IBM PCs and compatibles have steadily increased over the years. The first graphics display adapter, the Color Graphics Adapter (CGA), could display a 320- by 200-pixel resolution screen in four colors or a 640 by 200 resolution screen in two colors. Contrast that with VGA (Video Graphics Array) display technology, which can support screen resolutions of 640 by 480 in 16 colors or 320 by 200 in 256 colors, and with SuperVGA technology, which can display images with resolutions up to 1024 by 768 with 256 colors (and sometimes with 32,768 colors). Advances in graphics display technology have been driven by:

1. Lower hardware costs, especially DRAM memory chips
2. The demand for Graphical User Interfaces (GUIs)
3. Imaging and desktop publishing applications

The trend toward high-resolution and higher-performance graphics hardware is not abating. Already, VGA is being eclipsed. Megapixel resolution display hardware with true color capabilities (8 bits per color per pixel = 24 bits/pixel) is already appearing on the market at a reasonable cost. Hardware with a 1280 by 1024 display will probably be standard equipment on the personal computers and workstations of the mid-1990s. Spatial and color resolution of this magnitude will provide photographic-quality image display on the desktop. High-resolution ray-traced imagery at these resolutions will be spectacular to look at, but will take hours or days of computer time to produce given the current processor and algorithmic technology.

In the IBM and compatible world, there are no fewer than 11 display adapter standards available at this time:

1. MDA (Monochrome Display Adapter).
2. HGA (Hercules Graphics Adapter).
3. CGA (Color Display Adapter).
4. The display adapter in the IBM PC Jr.
5. EGA (Enhanced Graphic Adapter).
6. MCGA (Multi Color Graphics Array), which is available on some low-end IBM PS/2 computers.
7. VGA (Video Graphics Array), which is available for just about any IBM-compatible computer.
8. 8514/A graphics. This is a graphics adapter with graphics co-processor support. This was one of the first successful "intelligent" graphics cards available from IBM. IBM's earlier attempt at an intelligent graphics card was the PGA (Professional Graphics Adapter), which never gained much support and was subsequently discontinued.
9. XGA. This is IBM's latest graphics standard, which competes directly with Super-VGA. In some modes, 65,535 colors are available simultaneously on the screen. Maximum resolution is the same as SuperVGA.
10. SuperVGA. This is a generic term referring to any graphics adapter that has a super set of standard VGA modes. Typically, SuperVGA devices can display higher-resolution images then standard VGA, with up to 256 colors possible.
11. TIGA—Texas Instruments Graphics Architecture. This is a processor-independent graphics standard. Typically, TIGA-based graphics adapters utilize one of the high-performance Texas Instruments digital signal processors such as the 34010 or 34020 processors. The on-board graphics processor qualifies a TIGA board as an intelligent graphics card.

It is interesting to note that most of the display standards on the above list were developed and promoted by IBM Corporation.

Modes and Resolutions

High-quality image display demands a certain minimum acceptable level of graphics adapter functionality. Certainly a fixed, four-colors-on-the-screen-at-a-time graphics adapter such as the CGA does not provide acceptable performance for anything but black-and-white or two-color images. The display of color images in their true color with the CGA adapter is poor at best. The question becomes, what is the minimum graphics adapter functionality required for

	Resolution	Colors	CGA	PCJr	EGA	MCGA	VGA	Super VGA
1.	320 by 200	4	*	*	*	*	*	*
2.	640 by 200	2	*	*	*	*	*	*
3.	160 by 200	16	*					
4.	320 by 200	16		*	*		*	*
5.	320 by 200	256				*	*	*
6.	640 by 200	4		*				
7.	640 by 200	16			*		*	*
8.	640 by 350	2			*		*	*
9.	640 by 350	4			*			
10.	640 by 350	16			*		*	*
11.	640 by 400	256						*
12.	640 by 480	2				*	*	*
13.	640 by 480	16					*	*
14.	640 by 480	256						*
15.	800 by 600	16						*
16.	800 by 600	256						*
17.	1024 by 768	16						*
18.	1024 by 768	256						*
19.	Configurable Palette			*	*	*	*	*
20.	Configurable Color Registers					*	*	*

Notes:
1. A configurable palette allows the collection of colors displayed on a screen to be selected from a larger number of possible colors.
2. A color register is configurable if its individual RGB (Red, Green, and Blue) components can be altered with software.

Figure 1.1   Common Display Adapter Graphics Capabilities

acceptable (a subjective criteria) image display? Figure 1.1 details the graphics capabilities of the most common display adapters to help in determining just what acceptable means. The text modes available on the various display adapters are not as important as the graphics modes for ray-tracing applications and are therefore not shown in the table, nor do they affect our minimum requirement decisions.

To display color images, you need configurable palettes and color registers. The RGB components of the color registers must be set directly to provide the proper color balance for realistic image display. Although the EGA provides 16 simultaneous colors out of a palette of

64, its lack of configurable color registers makes it of limited usefulness in ray-tracing applications. You can use dot dithering to increase the number of apparent colors an EGA can display, but at the expense of lowering the display resolution. Since photo realism is the goal of the ray-tracing process, trading resolution for pseudocolors on a display monitor does not seem a suitable trade-off.

From the discussion above it should be obvious that a VGA graphics adapter is a minimum requirement for acceptable ray-traced image display. VGA has all of the capabilities required for the imaging work done in this book. *Note*: Standard VGA has the *minimum* capability required for experimentation with ray tracing. Anything less than VGA capability will not produce satisfactory results. Capabilities beyond standard VGA, however, are desirable. For this reason, all of the programs in this book assume the existence of a VGA adapter. VGA will be required to utilize the programs in this book. There is no support for graphics display adapters of less then VGA capability. Support is provided for the more capable SuperVGA, however. For example, the ray-tracing code and tools provided in this book support the following VGA/SuperVGA capabilities:

1. Spatial resolutions of 320 by 200, 640 by 480, 800 by 600, and 1024 by 768 with 256 colors
2. 32,768 colors in 640 by 480 and 800 by 600 resolutions

A VGA/SuperVGA adapter is standard equipment on most modern PCs and is also available from many manufacturers as a plug-in card for older PCs. An investment in a VGA/SuperVGA adapter and required analog monitor (fixed frequency for VGA or multisync for SuperVGA) is a prerequisite for any serious ray tracing or imaging work to be done on PC and PC-compatible computers.

Hardware Palettes and Color Modes

A palette is the set of paints used by a painter to paint a scene. These paints are, by necessity, only a subset of all possible colors that could be present in a scene. Although in nature colors may appear infinite to the eye, painters approximate the full range of colors with a finite subset of paint colors. In computer graphics terms, the palette is the collection of colors available for simultaneous display on a color monitor. Various graphics adapters use different mechanisms for placing colors on a screen. Three such arrangements are shown in Figures 1.2, 1.3, and 1.4. Each will be given a short discussion.

Figure 1.2 shows the palette configuration for the 16-color VGA modes. This arrangement, referred to as the "planar" organization, breaks up the video memory into four distinct bit planes of memory, hence the name. The 4 bits of data stored in the video memory planes (1 bit in each of 4 bytes) form an index into the palette data structure. The 4 video data bits result in 16 possible color index values ranging from 0 to 15. Entries in the palette structure are 8 bits wide and refer to one of 256 color registers. Perhaps more importantly, each of the color registers has adjustable red, green, and blue (RGB) color components. Given that each of the color components uses 6 bits of information, there are a total of 2^{18} different colors available. This works out to be 262,144 different color possibilities, 16 of which can be displayed simultaneously (commonly referred to as 16 of 256K colors). To display VGA graphics requires an

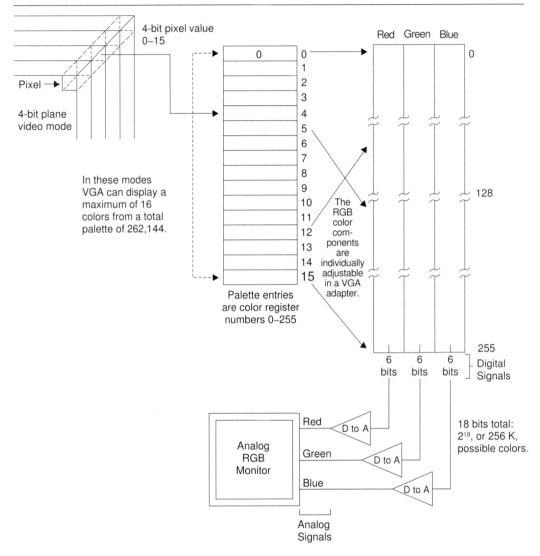

Note: D to A is digital to analog converter.

Figure 1.2   Planar Memory Configuration—VGA 16-Color Modes

analog monitor with RGB inputs. An analog monitor accepts analog input signals, as opposed to the digital one used with EGA. Analog input signals are necessary to convey the wide range of color information available with VGA. Analog inputs are infinitely adjustable and hence provide the fine color control required. This makes VGA more expensive than EGA (both the graphics adapter itself and the monitor), but the increased color capabilities make up for the incremental price difference.

In either the EGA or VGA case, as changes are made to the content of the palette, all pixels mapped to the index being changed will automatically assume the new color. Once a screen is painted with an image, you can produce bizarre special effects by altering the color numbers stored in the palette. This technique is referred to as "color cycling" and will be the subject of a future book. Some of these effects are quite striking and can create the effect of depth and/or movement.

Figure 1.3 illustrates the palette mechanism used for all 256-color VGA and SuperVGA modes. Actually, it would be more accurate to say it shows the lack of palette mechanism used

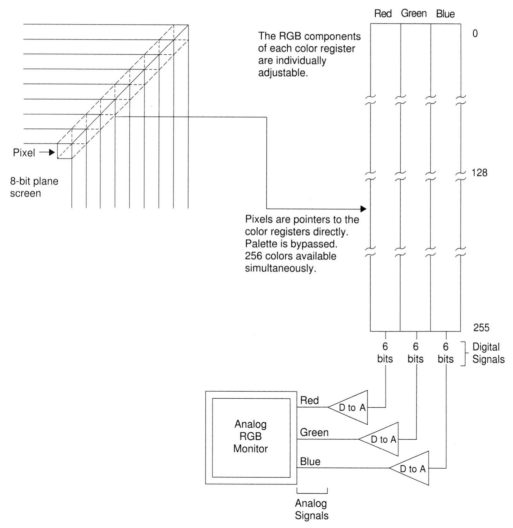

Figure 1.3   VGA/SuperVGA 256-Color Modes

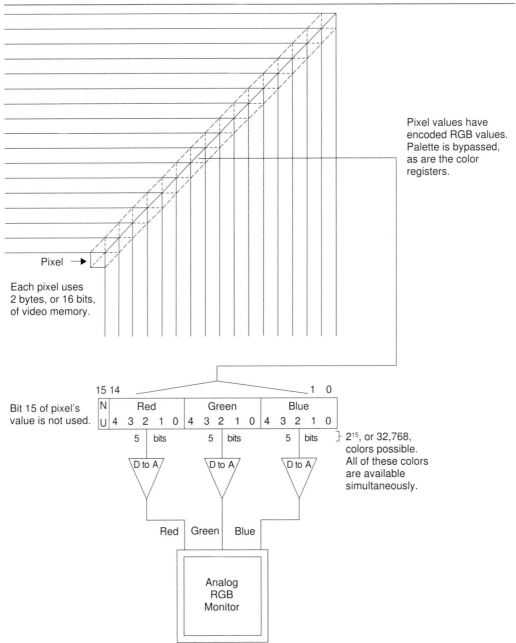

Pixel values have encoded RGB values. Palette is bypassed, as are the color registers.

Pixel →

Each pixel uses 2 bytes, or 16 bits, of video memory.

Bit 15 of pixel's value is not used.

2^{15}, or 32,768, colors possible. All of these colors are available simultaneously.

Figure 1.4   SuperVGA 32,768-Color Modes

for these modes. In the 256-color modes, the display memory is set up much differently than in the planar modes discussed previously. This is sometimes referred to as the "packed pixel" mode because all of the bits that make up a pixel's value are contained in the same byte of memory. Eight bits of video data are used in the 256-color modes. This allows a pixel to take on any value from 0 to 255. In this mode, the palette mechanism is bypassed completely and the video data value (pixel value) indexes a color register directly. A video pixel value of 10 takes on the color defined by the RGB values of color register 10, and so on. Using this graphics mode, an image can be displayed with 256 different colors out of a total of 262,144 possible. Also, any one of the 256 colors can be any of the 262,144.

Figure 1.4 illustrates the color selection mechanism used for the special 32K-color modes provided by the Sierra Hicolor DAC (Digital to Analog Converter) that is available on some SuperVGA cards (Diamond SpeedStar+, for example) at the time of this writing. In the hicolor modes, neither a palette nor color registers are used. Instead, 2 adjacent bytes of display memory are concatenated together to form a 16-bit pixel value. The layout of the display memory is in "little endian" format. That is, the least significant byte portion of the value is stored at the lower address and the most significant byte at that address plus one. Once these bytes are concatenated into a single 16-bit word, they are viewed by the Hicolor DAC as a set of three color components of 5 bits each, with the most significant bit unused. Five bits for each color component results in 32 possible color intensity values per color component, ranging from 0 through 31. Three sets of 32 intensity levels results in 32,768 possible colors on the screen at the same time. This is not true color (8 bits per color per pixel for a total of 16.7 million simultaneous colors), but somewhat better than 256 colors. This color data format is referred to in the industry as the 5-5-5 TARGA format. The following diagram illustrates the process:

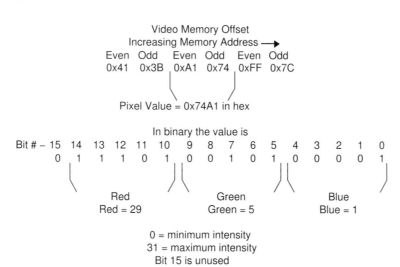

Video Memory Organization

The discussion above centered on how the graphics adapter fetches pixel values out of video memory and subsequently displays them with the appropriate colors. The other half of the process that we need to discuss is how the processor (the term processor, microprocessor, and CPU will be used throughout this book to mean the same thing: the main computing element within most personal computers) puts the pixel values into video memory in the first place. After all, the end result of all graphics applications is the output of pixel values to video memory; the display hardware does the rest.

To understand how video memory is accessed by the processor, you must understand a little about the segmented architecture of the Intel processors. The 8088/86 processor model, forced by the use of MSDOS regardless of the actual processor your computer has, can be characterized as follows:

1. The processor has the ability to address 1 megabyte of memory total in 64K byte segments.
2. Four special 16-bit segment registers are used to manage the segmented memory architecture. They are the DS (data segment register), the CS (code segment register), the SS (stack segment register), and finally the ES (extra segment register).
3. Segments start on paragraph boundaries. A paragraph is 16 bytes in length. A paragraph boundary is any address evenly divisible by 16.
4. "segment:offset" is the notation used to identify a memory location. Segment points to the start of an area of memory, and the offset contains the difference between the start segment address and the address of interest. Since segments can overlap, each memory location can be identified by more than one segment:offset pair. In other words, each segment:offset specifies a unique memory location; other segment:offset pairs may also specify the same location. Since the offset is a 16-bit quantity, each segment is a maximum 64K bytes in length.
5. To convert from an address specified in segment:offset notation to an actual 20-bit address as utilized by the processor when reading or writing memory, the segment value should be shifted 4 bits to the left (one hex digit) and the offset should be added to it. For example, the hex address 4E75:0221 in segment:offset notation has a 20-bit address of 4E971 hex. To convert the other way from a 20-bit address (sometimes referred to as a physical address) to segment:offset notation, mask off all but the last 4 bits of the physical address and this becomes the offset. Shift the physical address 4 bits to the right, throwing away those bits that fall off the end, and this value becomes the segment value. To continue with the previous example, the physical address 4E971 hex becomes 4E97:0001 in segment:offset notation. Note that the addresses 4E75:0221 and 4E97:0001 refer to the same actual memory location.

In actuality, the segmented architecture of the Intel processors (while executing in real mode, which is forced by MSDOS) is not ideally suited for the creation and manipulation of graphic images. Almost all of the images produced by the ray tracers detailed in this book required more memory than can be contained in a single data segment. Additional code is required to access image data that cross segment boundaries. This extra code extracts a performance penalty for the Intel processors while operating in real mode. Protected-mode operation of the Intel processors elevates many of the segment problems. It is not available, however, under MSDOS without a lot of extra effort with DOS extenders. The Motorola 680X0 series of processors, with their large linear address space, would be a better choice for a ray-trace/graphics engine. However, since the Intel processors are ubiquitous in the PC world, we will focus on them for our purposes.

When IBM laid out the memory map for the original PC, it wisely reserved the memory between A0000 hex and BFFFF hex for use as video display memory. IBM assumed that 128K bytes of display memory would be more than would ever be needed. In addition to setting aside this space for the video memory, IBM also positioned the video BIOS (Basic Input/Output System code) at address C0000 hex in the processor's memory map. Display adapters utilize the video display memory space in different ways depending on which video mode they are operating in. The original IBM monochrome display adapter, for example, used 4K of memory beginning at physical address B0000 hex for its text buffer. The original CGA display adapter's 16K buffer was located at B8000 hex. EGA and VGA adapters begin their buffers exclusively at address A0000 hex unless they are emulating one of the earlier video modes. For compatibility reasons, EGA, VGA, and all known SuperVGA adapters utilize only a single 64K segment of video memory beginning at address A0000 hex for processor access. This allows for dual monitor operation. An EGA, VGA, or SuperVGA adapter/monitor combination can reside and operate in the same computer along with a monochrome adapter/monitor.

Direct video memory accessibility worked quite well as long as the total amount of video memory needed for a given video mode was less than a full segment (64K bytes) in size. Things got complex when this segment size was exceeded and video memory paging became necessary. The table below summarizes the amount of video memory required for the VGA and SuperVGA modes utilized in this book. The table is ordered by increasing memory requirements.

Resolution	Memory Required	Number of Colors
320 by 200	64,000	256
640 by 480	307,200	256
800 by 600	480,000	256
640 by 480	614,400	32,768
1024 by 768	786,432	256
800 by 600	960,000	32,768

You can see from this table that in order to utilize any of the last three video modes you need a SuperVGA card with 1 Meg of video memory. *Note*: To utilize the 32K-color modes requires a SuperVGA adapter with a Sierra Hicolor DAC. This table implicitly illustrates how many bank switches would be required to map the complete video memory through a single 64K segment.

Only the 320 by 200 resolution video mode uses little enough memory to be accessed directly through the segment at A000 address A0000 hex. All other video modes require paging or bank switching on the part of the graphics adapter to allow the processor to access all of the video memory. In other words, the graphics adapter, on command from the host processor, bank switches pages of the video memory into the memory map of the processor. Whichever page is currently switched in becomes accessible to the processor through the single segment at address A000 hex. The processor writes into the selected video memory through a movable window at segment A000.

With the entire video memory for the 320 by 200 mode available to the processor, it is a simple matter to access it; that is, to read and write pixel values into it. The assembler code shown in Listing 1.1 provides simple functions for putting (writing) and getting (reading) pixel values. We have included this code on the companion disks in a file called "vgagraph.asm." You can link it with other Borland/Turbo C or Microsoft C code when you use the small memory model. Both of the assembler functions are described below.

The "PutPixel256" function places a pixel on the 320 by 200 resolution (video mode 13 hex) display by directly accessing the VGA video memory. The video memory organization for mode 13 hex is a linear array of 64,000 bytes located at segment A000 hex in the PC's memory map. To place a pixel directly, you need to calculate where in the 64,000 bytes of VGA memory the pixel resides and store the value of the color index there. The address calculation is as follows:

VGA memory address = x coordinate (Column) + (320 * y coordinate(Row))

This address calculation is actually the offset into the video segment of the pixel's location. With the segment and offset of the pixel known, it is a simple task to store the color index value there. You must, of course, have the VGA graphics adapter in mode 13 hex before you can use this function.

The operation of "GetPixel256" is similar to "PutPixel256" except that the color index value of the pixel located at "Col" and "Row" is retrieved from video memory and returned to the calling program instead of being written into the memory. You calculate the location of the specified pixel within the VGA memory in an identical manner to that shown above.

If you are interested in performing the same function in C, see Listing 1.2. This code is also on the companion disks in the file "vgagraph.c."

Ideally, the next example would show the same pixel read/write functions, only for a higher-resolution 256-color mode. Unfortunately, because of the nonstandard paging required to access the whole of video memory in the higher-resolution modes, any example would be SuperVGA-card specific. In other words, it would run only on the SuperVGA card for which it was designed and therefore would not be useful as a general purpose example program. We do not give a higher-resolution example for this very reason. See the "Further Reading" section of Part Three for books and articles that deal with SuperVGA graphics adapters. A VESA-compatible graphics adapter solves this problem, as you will see shortly.

Listing 1.1   320 by 200 256-Color Mode Assembler Functions

The following is the contents of the file "vgagraph.asm."

```
; VGA Mode 13 hex--256 color 320 by 200 functions
;
_TEXT    segment byte public 'CODE'
         DGROUP   group _DATA,_BSS
         assume   cs:_TEXT,ds:DGROUP,ss:DGROUP
_TEXT    ends
```

```
_DATA    segment word public 'DATA'
;
_DATA    ends

_BSS     segment word public 'BSS'
;
_BSS     ends
;
;
_TEXT    segment byte public 'CODE'
;
;320 by 200 256-Color Mode Routines
;
; Procedure _PutPixel256
;
; This procedure is used to directly access the video memory when a VGA or
; MCGA graphics adapter is in the 256-color mode 13 hex. This function sets
; the pixel in the specified Column and Row to the specified Color.
;
; CALL:   callable from C.
; PROTOTYPE: void PutPixel256 (unsigned Col, unsigned Row, unsigned Color);
; INPUT:  all parameters passed to this function are on the stack. The
;         stack should contain the following: Color at [bp+8], Row
;         at [bp+6] and the Col at [bp+4] for the small memory model.
; OUTPUT: the specified pixel on the VGA screen is modified.
; USES:   and destroys ax,bx,cx,dx registers
;
      Public _PutPixel256
;
_PutPixel256     proc      near
;
      push     bp
      mov      bp,sp
      mov      cx,[bp+8]            ;get pixel color in cl reg
      mov      ax,[bp+6]            ;get Row #
      mov      bx,[bp+4]            ;get Col #
;
;compute the address of the pixel in the video buffer
;
      mov      dx,320              ;each pixel is one byte
      mul      dx                  ;find offset
      add      bx,ax               ;bx = x + 320 * y
      mov      ax,0A000H           ;seg of video buffer
      mov      es,ax               ;es:bx pts at pixel in buffer
      mov      es:[bx],cl          ;update the pixel
      pop      bp
      ret
;
_PutPixel256     endp
;
```

(continued)

Listing 1.1 *(continued)*

```
; Procedure _GetPixel256
;
; This procedure is used to directly access the video memory when the VGA or
; MCGA is in the 256 color mode 13 hex. This function returns the color value
; of the pixel located at the specified Column and Row position on the
; screen.
;
; CALL:   callable from C.
; PROTOTYPE: unsigned GetPixel256 (unsigned Col, unsigned Row);
; INPUT:  all parameters passed to this function are on the stack. The
;         stack should contain the following: Row at [bp+6] and
;         the Col at [bp+4] for the small memory model.
; OUTPUT: the specified pixel on the VGA screen is returned in ax.
;         The index of the color register 0..255 is returned.
; USES:   and destroys ax,bx,cx,dx registers
;
      Public _GetPixel256
;
_GetPixel256      proc        near
;
      push        bp
      mov         bp,sp
      mov         ax,[bp+6]             ;get Row #
      mov         bx,[bp+4]             ;get Col #
;
;compute the address of the pixel in the video buffer
;
      mov         dx,320               ;each pixel is one byte
      mul         dx                   ;find offset
      add         bx,ax                ;bx = x + 320 * y
      mov         ax,0A000H            ;seg of video buffer
      mov         es,ax                ;es:bx pts at pixel in buffer
      mov         al,es:[bx]           ;get the pixels value
      xor         ah,ah                ;mask most significant byte
      pop         bp
      ret
;
_GetPixel256      endp

;
_TEXT      ends
      end
```

Note, both these function names must have a prepended underscore so that they appear as C
functions to the C compiler.

Listing 1.2   320 by 200 256-Color Mode C Functions

The following is the contents of the file "vgagraph.c."

```c
#include <dos.h>  /* this must be included for FP_SEG and FP_OFF */

void PutPixel256 (unsigned Col, unsigned Row, unsigned Color)  {

  unsigned char far *VideoMemPtr;
  unsigned PixelAddress;

  /*
  Calculate the address of the pixel's location using the same algorithm
  as above.
  */
  PixelAddress = Col + (320 * Row);

  /*
  Build a far pointer to the required address in video memory with
  the segment of the video memory and the offset to the pixel's address.
  */
  FP_SEG(VideoMemPtr) = 0xA000;
  FP_OFF(VideoMemPtr) = PixelAddress;

  /* Store the value of the pixel at that address */
  *VideoMemPtr = (unsigned char) Color;
}

unsigned GetPixel256 (unsigned Col, unsigned Row)  {

  unsigned char far *VideoMemPtr;
  unsigned PixelAddress;

  /*
  Calculate the address of the pixel's location using the same algorithm
  as above.
  */
  PixelAddress = Col + (320 * Row);

  /*
  Build a far pointer to the required address in video memory with
  the segment of the video memory and the offset to the pixel's address.
  */
  FP_SEG(VideoMemPtr) = 0xA000;
  FP_OFF(VideoMemPtr) = PixelAddress;

  /* Return the value of the pixel at that address */
  return(*VideoMemPtr);
}
```

Image Palette Generation

To display a ray-traced image, you must either force the image to be displayed with the colors from a preset (and possibly fixed) palette that most closely match the required colors or generate and install a palette of colors that reflect the color content of the actual image.

The first of these techniques is rarely successful aesthetically but is necessary when only a fixed palette is available. To find the closest match between a pixel's RGB value in an image and the RGB values of the colors within the palette, you generally calculate an error function. This function returns a value for each palette entry that describes how close the pixel's color is to the palette entry color. The palette entry that has the smallest error value is the closest color. The technique is to loop through each of the entries in the default palette and calculate the error function. You can select the palette entry that exhibits the minimum error for use in place of the actual color.

Whenever you enter any graphics video mode, the video BIOS for that mode sets up a default color palette. Since you may be using the algorithm above with this default palette to display a ray-traced image, you may want to know the contents of the default palette. The default palette setup at initialization time for the 320 by 200 256-color mode (mode 13 hex) contains the following colors. (This information was excerpted from the IBM PS/2 Hardware Interface Technical Reference manual.)

a. The first 16 color registers are loaded with values corresponding to the CGA and EGA colors.
b. The second 16 color registers are loaded with evenly spaced gray shades.
c. The final 216 color registers contain values based on a hue, saturation, and intensity model tuned to provide a usable, generic color set that covers a wide range of color values.

Even when you know what the colors in the default palette are, you can seldom use them to display an image as effectively as the algorithms discussed next. For this reason, we do not provide an example of this technique. The program "mquan.exe" described in Chapter 4, however, uses a variation of this technique. You can examine that code if you want to see how to implement this method.

The second method of image/palette matching is called "color quantization." Actually, color quantization refers to a class of algorithms that builds the optimal color palette that most accurately reflects the colors in the original image. In other words, the collection of colors, the palette, that is used to display the ray-traced imagery is determined from the actual colors in the image. This is in contrast to displaying the image with the closest colors in a preset palette, as discussed above. Extracting the palette information from the image results in a much more realistic image display. Chapter 4 presents the color quantization algorithms used for palette selection.

With either palette/image matching technique, adjustability of the color registers in the display adapter is an absolute necessity. This is one area in which the VGA/SuperVGA adapter with its adjustable color registers is vastly superior to the EGA. With the fixed colors available with the EGA, color images cannot be displayed accurately. In all cases when using EGA, the palette used to display an image is the "closest fit" to the fixed colors that are available. This results in color distortion in the displayed image. VGA, in contrast, allows the color registers to be set to colors that accurately display the ray-traced image.

VESA

With the introduction of the VGA (Video Graphics Array in IBM parlance) graphics adapter integrated into the IBM PS/2 series of computers in 1987, IBM established a new level of graphics capabilities in personal computers. Along with a spatial resolution higher than EGA (640 by 480), VGA allowed the simultaneous display of more colors (256 colors in a single video mode) than was previously possible. Another important but underrated improvement with VGA was the advent of the square pixel. Before VGA, the pixels displayed on the PC were not square because the resolution of the screen was not an exact multiple of the 4:3 aspect ratio standardized in all TVs and computer monitors. Square pixels allow geometric objects to be displayed without distortion and without the processing overhead necessary to correct the aspect ratio in order to remove the spatial distortion. Everyone has seen what was supposed to be a circle displayed on a computer monitor that looked more like an ellipse. This is an example of the spatial distortion that is caused by nonsquare pixels.

The graphics capabilities of the PC equipped with a VGA graphics adapter reached a new high as software applications began taking advantage of the VGA hardware's capabilities. Over time, however, the newness of VGA began to wear off. Display chip manufacturers figured out how to clone VGA chip sets (with no help from IBM) by reverse engineering IBM's VGA. These manufacturers became so good at producing standard VGA chips that they all began adding enhancements of their own. Most enhancements took the form of even higher resolutions, though some manufacturers added hardware cursor support and hardware bitblit (bitbliting is the ability to move and/or transform video data quickly from one portion of video memory to another without host processor support). During this time IBM was typically silent about its direction in future VGA graphics enhancements. IBM has since attempted to standardize its 8514/A and the XGA graphics standards.

Without a standard to conform to, the VGA chip vendors were free to implement their super set of standard VGA functions anyway they saw fit. Each of these vendors extended standard VGA in what they felt was a logical manner. Unfortunately, no two vendors' logic was exactly the same. The chip vendors knew, however, what consumers wanted. Once consumers had tasted the increased capabilities offered with VGA there was no going back. Instead, they wanted higher resolutions and more colors at, of course, lower cost. The VGA chip vendors were more than willing to oblige. The chip manufacturers seemingly independently arrived at a set of specifications for the super set of standard VGA functionality that has become known today as SuperVGA.

In retrospect it seems obvious where enhancements needed to be made. In terms of resolution, 640 by 480 just was not high enough for photographic-quality imagery or graphical user interfaces (GUIs), which were just beginning to get popular. The idea of the square pixel ushered in quietly with VGA was so popular that all new higher-resolution SuperVGA modes had to meet this requirement. Trading off video memory requirements and monitor costs, while retaining the square pixel, resulted in almost all chip manufacturers adopting the 800 by 600 and 1024 by 768 resolutions. In terms of colors, since everyone thought that 256 simultaneous colors on the screen were now essential, all the new high-resolution modes support both 16 and 256 colors.

Surprisingly, almost all SuperVGA chip sets ended up with approximately the same functionality. The problem that developed was that although most chip sets had the same functionality, there was no standard means of programming them. All of the chip sets understood standard VGA requirements (mode numbers, register addresses, register bit functions, etc.), so that one driver within an application program could talk to any of the SuperVGA cards while operating in standard VGA modes. If an application tried to utilize any of the actual SuperVGA modes, though, this commonality ended and the application programmer was forced to talk in specific ways to each different SuperVGA chip set. In other words, each chip set required specific programming when any of its higher-resolution modes were utilized. Even such basic things as the mode numbers for the various modes differed from one chip set to the next. Pity the poor applications' developer who had to write and maintain a unique device driver for each possible SuperVGA card or chip set. The cost of acquiring the necessary expertise on each chip set to write the individual device drivers was high. In some cases this meant that 10 to 50 different device drivers had to be written to allow an application to function with the various SuperVGA display adapters. (To get an idea of the type and complexity of the code required to support multiple SuperVGA cards, examine the file "ibm.c" on the companion disks. It contains the very minimal SuperVGA support provided by the DKBTrace ray tracer.) The generation of a large number of device drivers placed a severe burden on the small developer. More and more development time was spent on the device drivers, leaving less time for writing and testing the actual applications.

With the advent of Microsoft's Windows and its device independence, some of the programming burden for support of the display device has been removed from the application's developer (at the expense of the Windows learning curve, however). The SuperVGA board vendor has become responsible for writing a Windows-compatible device driver for its board. Once the vendor-written device driver is installed, application programs are free to use as much of its inherent capabilities as they have use for. This indeed is a step in the right direction. Unfortunately, many other environments for the PC exist (much to Microsoft's dismay) in which SuperVGA modes are or would be beneficial. For example, non-Windows DOS applications are still being developed, and there is a growing number of UNIX implementations for the PC. In these environments the idiosyncrasies of the individual SuperVGA cards must still be addressed. This is why VESA came into being.

It didn't take the manufacturers of VGA chip sets and graphics adapters long to realize what the lack of a standard was doing to SuperVGA acceptance. While technically superior to standard VGA, SuperVGA was slow to be supported because of the complexity noted above. Chip manufacturers had a lot of money tied up in SuperVGA development, and the slowness of SuperVGA acceptance was directly affecting their bottom lines. In an attempt to promote SuperVGA, these manufacturers and vendors formed the Video Electronics Standards Association, or VESA. Their charter was to define a software interface that was backwards compatible with the existing SuperVGA hardware and that application programmers could utilize to hide the details of the underlying, incompatible hardware. With a software interface of this type accepted by the adapter designers, application programmers could once again write one VESA-compliant driver for their products and have it run on SuperVGA hardware from many manufacturers. This frees the application developer from having to have specific knowledge of the graphics adapter manufacturer or chip set utilized. The VESA organization work culminated with a specification entitled "VESA VGA BIOS Extension Proposal" in April of 1989. This specification was subsequently updated in October of 1989, in June of 1990, and most recently in October of 1991. Finally, SuperVGA had a specification. With the VESA BIOS extensions in place, the problems associated with not having a standard (mode numbers, initialization requirements, video memory organization, register bit assignments, standard and extended port usage, and segment mapping—also referred to as video memory paging or bank switching) seemed to go away. In reality, the problems did not go away completely, but at least they were handled in a standard manner.

Using the VESA software programming interface, you can determine the capabilities of the graphics adapter, the level of VESA support, the status of the adapter (including the current video mode), the modes supported by the adapter, specific information about the capabilities supported in each mode, and you can save and restore the complete state of the adapter. The VESA specification is backwards compatible with VGA and thus supports VGA, the standard SuperVGA extensions, and OEM (original equipment manufacture)-specific extensions to SuperVGA. In addition, the VESA specification standardized the display timing requirements of computer monitors, which has allowed the proliferation of the low-cost, analog monitors that have made SuperVGA a success today. All in all, VESA has been primarily responsible for SuperVGA's success. Their efforts should be applauded.

The VESA Software Interface. The VESA interface is implemented as a set of extensions to the video BIOS available through software interrupt 10 hex (16 decimal). The VESA interface is built directly into some display adapters and in others is implemented as a device driver or as a terminate and stay resident (TSR) program that is loaded when the computer boots. Either way, the actual implementation is immaterial. You can access the VESA extensions as you do any other video BIOS function. That is, the processor's registers are loaded with values that determine which BIOS function is requested and with other parameters pertinent to the requested function. You then execute software interrupt 10 hex to perform the requested BIOS function. Upon completion, control is returned to the calling program. Certain video BIOS functions return results and/or error codes. These values are passed back from the BIOS in the processor registers also. As a simple illustrative example, consider the following C function, which places the graphics adapter into mode 13 hex (the 320 by 200 256-color mode) by calling the video BIOS:

```
#include <dos.h>            /* has the definitions of the REGS union */

#define VIDEO 0x10          /* equate for the video BIOS number */

void SetVideoMode13H (void) {

  union REGS regs;          /* declare an instance of the REGS */

  regs.h.ah = 0;            /* set video mode is function zero */
  regs.h.al = 0x13;         /* set video mode 13 hex */
  int86(VIDEO,&regs,&regs); /* perform the video BIOS call */
                            /* to change the video mode */
}
```

In this example, the "Set Video Mode" function code of zero is stored in the processor's "ah" register. ("ah" is the upper 8 bits of the 16-bit "ax" register. That is why in the code above it is referenced with a ".h." Full 16-bit registers are referenced with a ".x," as will be seen.) The requested video mode number, in this case 13 hex, is placed in the "al" register. In actuality, these values are placed in the REGS union until the "int86" function is executed. At execution time, the register values are copied from the REGS union into the processor's registers and software interrupt 10 hex is performed. The value of the processor's registers on completion of the video BIOS call are copied back into the REGS union. In this case, however, the "Set Video Mode" function does not return any information to the calling program, so no use is made of the data passed back.

VESA BIOS extension functions are accessed in a similar, equally simple, manner. In the VESA case, the code passed in the "ah" register to the video BIOS is 4F hex. 4F hex identifies the BIOS function request for VESA SuperVGA support. The requested VESA function number is passed in the "al" register. Upon return from any of the VESA BIOS functions, *status* is returned in both halves of the "ax" register. The function call was successful if the "ah" register is equal to zero and a failure if "ah" is equal to any other value. Additionally, if the "al" register contains 4F hex on return, the requested VESA function is supported. Any other value indicates the requested function was not supported.

In total, the VESA SuperVGA specification defines nine functions, zero through eight. Many of these functions, however, have numerous subfunctions, which greatly expands the VESA BIOS functionality. All of the functions and subfunctions are described in Figure 1.5. For our purposes in this book, only two of the VESA functions are used, although information on all of the functions is provided. Function zero is used to determine whether a VESA-compliant graphics adapter is present, and function two is used to select the SuperVGA modes once it is known a VESA device exists. With VESA, 15-bit mode numbers are used instead of the 7-bit numbers used with standard VGA. Since VGA modes are a subset of the VESA SuperVGA modes, you can use function two to select any video mode supported by the display adapter, not just the SuperVGA modes. Figure 1.6 shows the VESA-defined SuperVGA modes and the associated mode numbers. *Please note*: if the SuperVGA adapter you have is not VESA compatible, you will have to change some of the code in the VGA function library discussed later in this chapter before you can use it.

Once the display adapter is placed in the required video mode via VESA function zero, you can use the normal video BIOS functions "Write Graphics Pixel" and "Read Graphics Pixel" to read and write pixel data to the display. This may be somewhat slower than the direct video access afforded by the VESA interface, but with ray tracing and image processing in general, the time spent in calculations dwarfs the time spent reading and writing pixels. For this reason the BIOS read and write functions were deemed fast enough, and they are definitely simpler to implement.

For those readers interested in exploring the capabilities of their VESA-compatible display adapter at a low level, the program shown in Listing 1.3 provides a vehicle. This program first queries the display adapter to see if it is in fact VESA compliant by polling for the Global SuperVGA Information. If it is VESA compatible, the Global Information is displayed to the user. This information includes the VESA signature (VESA, of course), the VESA version number (either 1.0, 1.1, or 1.2), and a pointer to the supported video modes. After the display of the Global Information, additional information is requested from the VESA adapter and displayed for each possible VESA video mode. The mode information is decrypted from the

All processor registers are preserved across the VESA calls except those that are explicitly utilized and shown below.

1. Function 0. **Return SuperVGA Global Information**

Input Parameters:
> ah = 4F hex   VESA function identifier
> al = 0   Function 0 ID
> es:di = ptr to 256 byte buffer

Output Parameters:
> ax = status—See discussion in text

Operation:
The purpose of this function call is to provide information to the calling program about the general capabilities of the SuperVGA environment. This function fills an information block structure at the address specified in es:di. The size of the information block is 256 bytes.

2. Function 1. **Return SuperVGA Mode Information**

Input Parameters:
> ah = 4F hex   VESA function identifier
> al = 1   Function 1 ID
> cx = Requested mode number
> es:di = ptr to 256 byte buffer

Output Parameters:
> ax = status

Operation:
This function returns information about a specific SuperVGA mode in a ModeInfoBlock structure. See Figure 1.7.

3. Function 2. **Set VGA/SuperVGA Video Mode**

Input Parameters:
> ah = 4F hex   VESA function identifier
> al = 2   Function 2 ID
> bx = Requested mode number

The requested mode number is in bits 0..14 of the "bx" register. Bit 15 determines whether the video memory is cleared when the requested video mode is entered. If this bit is a zero, the video memory is cleared. If a one, video memory is not cleared.

Output Parameters:
> ax = status

Operation:
This function causes the video adapter to enter a specified video mode. The mode number is contained in the bx register.

Figure 1.5   VESA-Defined SuperVGA Functions   *(continued)*

4. Function 3. **Return the Current Video Mode**

Input Parameters:

> ah = 4F hex   VESA function identifier
> al = 3   Function 3 ID

Output Parameters:

> ax = status
> bx = current video mode

Operation:

This function returns the current video mode in the bx register.

5. Function 4. **Save/Restore SuperVGA Video State**
   Subfunction 0. **Return State Buffer Size**

Input Parameters:

> ah = 4F hex   VESA function identifier
> al = 4   Function 4 ID
> cx = requested states
> dl = 0   Return state buffer size
>   subfunction code

This function returns the amount of memory required by the calling program to hold the SuperVGA state information. Knowing the state buffer size is important because when the state is saved, it will be stored in a buffer of this size. Bits within the "cx" register determine what portion(s) of the Super-VGA adapter's state are to be saved or restored and therefore how much host memory will be required. If bit 0 is set, the size of the buffer necessary to hold the hardware state is returned. If bit 1 is set, the size of the buffer necessary to hold the video BIOS data is returned. If bit 2 is set, the size of the buffer necessary to hold the DAC state is returned. And finally, if bit 3 is set, the size of the buffer necessary to hold the SuperVGA state is returned. See the VESA specification for more details.

Output Parameters:

> ax = status
> bx = number of 64 byte blocks to hold state

6. Function 4. **Save/Restore SuperVGA Video State**
   Subfunction 1. **Save SuperVGA Video State**

Input Parameters:

> ah = 4F hex   VESA function identifier
> al = 4   Function 4 ID
> cx = requested states, see above
> dl = 1   Save SuperVGA video state
>   subfunction code
> es:bx = pointer to buffer of required size

Figure 1.5   *(continued)*

Output Parameters:
> ax = status
> and buffer contains video state info

Operation:
Execution of this function causes the specified portions of the video state to be saved in a user-defined buffer.

7. Function 4. **Save/Restore SuperVGA Video State**
   Subfunction 2. **Restore SuperVGA Video State**

Input Parameters:
> ah = 4F hex   VESA function identifier
> al = 4   Function 4 ID
> cx = requested states, see above
> dl = 2   Restore SuperVGA video state
>   subfunction code
> es:bx = pointer to buffer of required size
>   filled with state information

Output Parameters:
> ax = status
> and video state is restored

Operation:
This function restores portions of the video state from the user-defined buffer.

8. Function 5. **CPU Video Memory Window Control**
   Subfunction 0. **Select Video Window**

Input Parameters:
> ah = 4F hex   VESA function identifier
> al = 5   Function 5 ID
> bh = 0   Select video window
>   subfunction code
> bl = Window selected. Window A=0, Window B=1
> dx = Window position in video memory
>   in window granularity units

Output Parameters:
> ax = status

Operation:
This function call sets the position of the specified window in video memory. This function allows direct access to the hardware paging registers.

Figure 1.5 *(continued)*   *(continued)*

9. Function 5. **CPU Video Memory Window Control**
    Subfunction 1. **Return Video Window Memory**

Input Parameters:

ah = 4F hex   VESA function identifier
al = 5   Function 5 ID
bh = 1   Return video window memory
               subfunction code
bl = Window selected. Window A=0, Window B=1

Output Parameters:

ax = status
dx = Window position in video memory
       in window granularity units

Operation:
This function returns the position of the specified window in video memory.

10. Function 6. **Get/Set Logical Scanline Length**
     Subfunction 0. **Set Scanline Length**

Input Parameters:

ah = 4F hex   VESA function identifier
al = 6   Function 6 ID
bl = 0   Set Scanline Length
             subfunction code
cx = Desired width in pixels

Output Parameters:

ax = status
bx = Bytes/Scanline
cx = Actual pixels per Scanline
dx = Maximum number of Scanlines

Operation:
This function sets the length of a logical scanline. It allows an application to set up a logical video memory buffer that is wider than the displayed area. Function 7 is then used to set the starting position that is to be displayed.

11. Function 6. **Get/Set Logical Scanline Length**
     Subfunction 1. **Get Scanline Length**

Input Parameters:

ah = 4F hex   VESA function identifier
al = 6   Function 6 ID
bl = 1   Get Scanline Length
             subfunction code

Figure 1.5 *(continued)*

Output Parameters:

 ax = status
 bx = Bytes/Scanline
 cx = Actual pixel per Scanline
 dx = Maximum number of Scanlines

Operation:
See description above.

12. Function 7. **Get/Set Display Start**
  Subfunction 0. **Set Display Start**

Input Parameters:

 ah = 4F hex VESA function identifier
 al = 7   Function 7 ID
 bh = 0   Reserved and must be 0
 bl = 0   Set Display Start
       subfunction code
 cx = First displayed pixel in Scanline
 dx = First displayed Scanline

Output Parameters:

 ax = status

Operation:
This function selects the pixel to be displayed in the upper left corner of the display from the logical page. It is used to pan and scroll around logical screens that are larger than the displayed screen. This function finds use in double buffering schemes typically used in animation.

13. Function 7. **Get/Set Display Start**
  Subfunction 1. **Get Display Start**

Input Parameters:

 ah = 4F hex VESA function identifier
 al = 7   Function 7 ID
 bl = 1   Get Display Start
       subfunction code

Output Parameters:

 ax = status
 bh = 0
 cx = First displayed pixel in Scanline
 dx = First displayed Scanline

Figure 1.5 *(continued)*   *(continued)*

14. Function 8. **Get/Set DAC Palette Control**
    Subfunction 0. **Set DAC Palette Width**

Input Parameters:

> ah = 4F hex   VESA function identifier
> al = 8   Function 8 ID
> bl = 0   Set DAC Palette Width
>   subfunction code
> bh = Bits of color/primary. Standard VGA is 6

Output Parameters:

> ax = status
> bh = Current bits/primary.

Operation:

This function sets the operating mode of DAC palettes that are configurable.

15. Function 8. **Get/Set DAC Palette Control**
    Subfunction 1. **Get DAC Palette Width**

Input Parameters:

> ah = 4F hex   VESA function identifier
> al = 8   Function 8 ID
> bl = 1   Get DAC Palette Width
>   subfunction code

Output Parameters:

> ax = status
> bh = Current bits/primary.

Figure 1.5   *(continued)*

Graphics Modes

Resolution	Number of Colors	VESA Mode Number
640 by 400	256	100 hex
640 by 480	256	101 hex
800 by 600	16	6A hex or 102 hex
800 by 600	256	103 hex
1024 by 768	16	104 hex
1024 by 768	256	105 hex
1280 by 1024	16	106 hex
1280 by 1024	256	107 hex

Text Modes

Characters/Line	Number of Lines	VESA Mode Number
80	60	108 hex
132	25	109 hex
132	43	10A hex
132	50	10B hex
132	60	10C hex

The extended text modes defined above were added in version 1.1 of the VESA specification.

Graphics Modes

Resolution	Colors	Bits/Color (R:G:B)	VESA Mode Number
320 by 200	32K	(5:5:5)	10D hex
320 by 200	64K	(5:6:5)	10E hex
320 by 200	16.8M	(8:8:8)	10F hex
640 by 480	32K	(5:5:5)	110 hex
640 by 480	64K	(5:6:5)	111 hex
640 by 480	16.8M	(8:8:8)	112 hex
800 by 600	32K	(5:5:5)	113 hex
800 by 600	64K	(5:6:5)	114 hex
800 by 600	16.8M	(8:8:8)	115 hex
1024 by 768	32K	(5:5:5)	116 hex
1024 by 768	64K	(5:6:5)	117 hex
1024 by 768	16.8M	(8:8:8)	118 hex
1280 by 1024	32K	(5:5:5)	119 hex
1280 by 1024	64K	(5:6:5)	11A hex
1280 by 1024	16.8M	(8:8:8)	11B hex

The extended graphics modes defined above were added in version 1.2 of the VESA specification.

Figure 1.6 VESA-Defined SuperVGA Modes

Three important VESA data structures are shown in this figure. They are shown in C structure form. *Note*: These structures contain the definitions as of version 1.2 of the VESA specification. The first, "VgaInfoBlock," is used with function 0 to return the global information about the video adapter. The "ModeInfoBlock" structure is filled in by a call to function 1 that is a request for information about a specified video mode. The final data structure detailed here is internal to the "ModeInfoBlock" information. It is a 16-bit word of mode attribute data (called, strangely enough, "ModeAttributes").

```
struct VgaInfoBlock    {
  unsigned char        VESASignature[4]; These 4 bytes should contain the characters VESA.
  unsigned int         VESAVersion;      High byte major:Low byte minor version number
  unsigned char far *OEMStringPtr;       This points at a manufacturer's name
  unsigned char        Capabilities[4];  Capabilities of the device
  unsigned       far *VideoModePtr;      This points to a list of supported
                                         video modes. List is terminated by
                                         a word of FFFF hex.
  unsigned int         TotalMemory;      # of 64K memory blocks
  unsigned char        Reserved[242];    Unused area in structure
};

struct ModeInfoBlock   {
  unsigned int  ModeAttributes;          See below
  unsigned char WinAAttributes;          Window A attributes
  unsigned char WinBAttributes;          Window B attributes
  unsigned int  WinGranularity;          Window granularity
  unsigned int  WinSize;                 Window size
  unsigned int  WinASegment;             Window A start segment
  unsigned int  WinBSegment;             Window B start segment
  (far *WinFunctPtr)();                  Pointer to Window function
  unsigned int  BytesPerScanLine;        Bytes per scan line
/*
  The remainder of this structure was optional until version 1.2
  of the VESA specification. It is now mandatory. It contains extended
  information on the video mode
*/
  unsigned int  XResolution;             Horizontal resolution
  unsigned int  YResolution;             Vertical resolution
  unsigned char XCharSize;               Character cell width
  unsigned char YCharSize;               Character cell height
  unsigned char NumberOfPlanes;          Number of video memory planes
  unsigned char BitsPerPixel;            Bits per pixel
  unsigned char NumberOfBanks;           Number of banks of video memory
  unsigned char MemoryModel;             Memory model type
  unsigned char BankSize;                Bank size in kilo bytes
  unsigned char NumberOfImagePages;      Number of images
  unsigned char Reserved;                Reserved for page function
  unsigned char RedMaskSize;             Size of direct color red mask in bits
  unsigned char RedFieldPosition;        Bit position of lsb of red mask
  unsigned char GreenMaskSize;           Size of direct color green mask in bits
```

Figure 1.7 Important VESA Data Structures

```
    unsigned char GreenFieldPosition;     Bit position of lsb of green mask
    unsigned char BlueMaskSize;           Size of direct color blue mask in bits
    unsigned char BlueFieldPosition;      Bit position of lsb of blue mask
    unsigned char RsvdMaskSize;           Size of direct color reserved mask in bits
    unsigned char RsvdFieldPosition;      Bit position of lsb of reserved mask
    unsigned char DirectColorModeInfo;    Direct color mode attributes
    unsigned char Reserved[216];          Unused portion of ModeInfoBlock
};


The Mode Attributes information:

                    Bits of the Mode Attribute 16-bit word.
         15  14  13  12  11  10  9   8   7   6   5   4   3   2   1   0
         |_____ unused _____|   |   |   |   |   |
                     Mode type_____|   |   |   |   |
                       Text=0  Graphics=1                  |   |   |   |
                     Monochrome/Color_____|   |   |   |
                        Monochrome=0  Color=1                      |   |   |
                     BIOS output functions supported_____|   |   |
                        No=0  Yes=1                                   |   |
                     Reserved _____|   |
                                                                           |
                     Mode supported in hardware_____|
                        No=0  Yes=1
```

Figure 1.7 *(continued)*

VESA data structures into English for ease of understanding. You can use this stand-alone program as presented or enhance it to provide more detailed VESA information. See the VESA exploration program shown in Listing 1.3 for examples of how some of these functions are utilized.

If you would like to see the entire VESA specification for SuperVGA, you can order it directly from the VESA association at the following address:

VESA
2150 North First Street, Suite 360
San Jose, CA 95131-2020
Phone: (408) 435-0333
Fax: (408) 435-8225

Examples of VESA usage appear in the next section of this chapter.

Listing 1.3 VESA Exploration Program

The following is the contents of the file "vesa.c."

```
/*************************************************************/
/***                      "vesa.c"                       ***/
/***          VESA Video Adapter Exploring Program       ***/
/***                         for                         ***/
/***                  "A First Ray Tracer"               ***/
/***       from the book "Practical Ray Tracing in C"    ***/
/***             written in Borland/Turbo C 2.0          ***/
/***                         by                          ***/
/***                  Craig A. Lindley                   ***/
/***                                                     ***/
/***         Ver: 1.0    Last Update: 03/10/92           ***/
/*************************************************************/

/*
NOTE this program has not been updated to the latest version
of the VESA specification. It supports version 1.1 in its
present form.
*/

#include <stdio.h>
#include <dos.h>
#include <conio.h>

#define VIDEOINT            0x10
#define VESAFUNCTIONID      0x4F

/* Define the VESA functions and sub functions */
#define RETURNSUPERVGAINFO          0
#define RETURNSUPERVGAMODEINFO      1
#define SETSUPERVGAVIDEOMODE        2
#define RETURNCURRENTVIDEOMODE      3

#define SAVERESTORESUPERVGASTATE    4
#define   RETURNSTATEBUFFERSIZE     0
#define   SAVESUPERVGAVIDEOSTATE    1
#define   RESTORESUPERVGAVIDEOSTATE 2

#define CPUVIDEOMEMWINDOWCONTROL    5
#define   SELECTSUPERVGAMEMWINDOW   0
#define   RETURNSUPERVGAMEMWINDOW   1

#define SETGETLOGICALSCANLINELENGTH 6
#define SETGETDISPLAYSTART          7

/* Now the VESA defined extended graphics SuperVGA modes */
#define MG640x400x256       0x100
#define MG640x480x256       0x101
#define MG800x600x16        0x102
#define MG800x600x256       0x103
```

```
#define MG1024x768x16        0x104
#define MG1024x768x256       0x105
#define MG1280x1024x16       0x106
#define MG1280x1024x256      0x107

/* Now the VESA defined extended text modes */
/* VESA version 1.1 only */
#define MT80x60              0x108
#define MT132x25             0x109
#define MT132x43             0x10A
#define MT132x50             0x10B
#define MT132x60             0x10C

static unsigned char GLOBALINFO[256];  /* Global adapter info */
static unsigned char MODEINFO[256];    /* Local mode info */

/* Format of the GLOBALINFO information */
struct VgaInfoBlock   {
  unsigned char      VESASignature[4];
  unsigned char      VESAVersion;
  unsigned char      VESARevision;
  unsigned char far *OEMStringPtr;
  unsigned char      Capabilities[4];
  unsigned      far *VideoModePtr;
};

/* Format of the MODEINFO information */
struct ModeInfoBlock   {
  unsigned int  ModeAttributes;
  unsigned char WinAAttributes;
  unsigned char WinBAttributes;
  unsigned int  WinGranularity;
  unsigned int  WinSize;
  unsigned int  WinASegment;
  unsigned int  WinBSegment;
  (far *WinFunctPtr)();
  unsigned int  BytesPerScanLine;

  /* the remainder of this structure is optional */

  unsigned int  XResolution;
  unsigned int  YResolution;
  unsigned char XCharSize;
  unsigned char YCharSize;
  unsigned char NumberOfPlanes;
  unsigned char BitsPerPixel;
  unsigned char NumberOfBanks;
  unsigned char MemoryModel;
  unsigned char BankSize;
};
```

(continued)

Listing 1.3   *(continued)*

```
/*
This function tests whether the video adapter supports a specified
video mode. If not, this function just returns. If the mode is
supported, the information from the ModeInfoBlock is printed for
inspection.
*/

int TestVESAMode(char *ModeName, unsigned int Mode)    {

  union REGS regs;
  struct ModeInfoBlock *VgaPtr;

  clrscr();
  printf("Testing for VESA mode: %s\n",ModeName);

  /* Call VESA function 1 to get mode info */
  regs.h.ah = VESAFUNCTIONID;
  regs.h.al = RETURNSUPERVGAMODEINFO;
  regs.x.cx = Mode;
  _ES =        FP_SEG(MODEINFO);
  regs.x.di = FP_OFF(MODEINFO);
  int86(VIDEOINT,&regs,&regs);
  if ((regs.h.al != VESAFUNCTIONID) || (regs.h.ah != 0))  {
    printf("Display mode 0x%X not supported\n",Mode);
    getch();
    return(-1);
  }
  /* Get a pointer to the MODEINFO data and then print entries */
  VgaPtr = (struct ModeInfoBlock *)&MODEINFO;
  printf("Display mode %s number 0x%X supported\n",ModeName,Mode);
  printf("  Mode attributes 0x%X breaks down as follows:\n",VgaPtr->ModeAttributes);
  printf("    Mode %s supported in hardware\n",(VgaPtr->ModeAttributes & 1) ? "is":"is not");
  printf("    Extended info %s available for this mode\n",(VgaPtr->ModeAttributes & 2) ? "is":"is not");
  printf("    BIOS output functions %s supported\n",(VgaPtr->ModeAttributes & 4) ? "are":"are not");
  printf("    Display mode is %s\n",(VgaPtr->ModeAttributes & 8) ? "color":"monochrome");
  printf("    %s mode\n",(VgaPtr->ModeAttributes & 16) ? "Graphics":"Text");
  printf("  Window A attributes: 0x%X  Window B attributes: 0x%X\n",
          VgaPtr->WinAAttributes,VgaPtr->WinBAttributes);
  printf("  Window Granularity: 0x%X\n",VgaPtr->WinGranularity);
  printf("  Window Size: 0x%X\n",VgaPtr->WinSize);
  printf("  Window A Segment: 0x%X  Window B Segment: 0x%X\n",
          VgaPtr->WinASegment,VgaPtr->WinBSegment);
  printf("  Window Function Ptr: %Fp\n",VgaPtr->WinFunctPtr);
  printf("  Bytes/scanline: %d\n",VgaPtr->BytesPerScanLine);
  printf("The rest of these structure members are optional\n");
  printf("  X Resolution: %d  Y Resolution: %d\n",
          VgaPtr->XResolution,VgaPtr->YResolution);
  printf("  X Char Size: %d  Y Char Size: %d\n",
          VgaPtr->XCharSize,VgaPtr->YCharSize);
  printf("  Number of planes: %d\n",VgaPtr->NumberOfPlanes);
```

```
  printf("  Bits/Pixel: %d\n",VgaPtr->BitsPerPixel);
  printf("  Number of banks: %d\n",VgaPtr->NumberOfBanks);
  printf("  Memory model: %d\n",VgaPtr->MemoryModel);
  printf("  Bank size: %d\n",VgaPtr->BankSize);
  printf("\nPress <Enter> to continue, ^C to abort\n");
  getchar();
  return(0);
}


/*
This function first checks for the presence of a VESA-compliant display
adapter and if one is not found, exits. If the adapter is compliant,
the information from the VGA info block is printed.
*/

void main (void)   {

  union REGS regs;
  struct VgaInfoBlock *VgaPtr;
  unsigned Index;
  unsigned far *ModePtr;

  clrscr();
  printf("VESA-Compliant Video Adapter Exploration Program\n");
  printf(" from the book, \"Practical Ray Tracing in C\"\n");
  printf(" written by Craig A. Lindley\n\n");

  /* Determine if a VESA-compliant video adapter is present */
  regs.h.ah = VESAFUNCTIONID;
  regs.h.al = RETURNSUPERVGAINFO;
  _ES =       FP_SEG(GLOBALINFO);
  regs.x.di = FP_OFF(GLOBALINFO);
  int86(VIDEOINT,&regs,&regs);
  if ((regs.h.al != VESAFUNCTIONID) || (regs.h.ah != 0))  {
     printf("Display Adapter not VESA compliant\n");
     exit(-1);
  }
  printf("\n\nDisplay Adapter is VESA compliant\n\n");
  /* Make a pointer to the GLOBALINFO structure info */
  VgaPtr = (struct VgaInfoBlock *)&GLOBALINFO;

  /* Print the VESA signature */
  printf("  Signature is: ");
  for (Index=0; Index < 4; Index++)
    printf("%c",VgaPtr->VESASignature[Index]);
  printf("\n");

  /* Print the VESA version number */
  printf("  Version Number: %d.%d \n",VgaPtr->VESAVersion,
          VgaPtr->VESARevision);

  /* Print the supported mode numbers */
```

(continued)

Listing 1.3   *(continued)*

```
printf("  Supported VESA modes are (in hex):\n   ");
ModePtr = VgaPtr->VideoModePtr;
while(*ModePtr != 0xFFFF)
  printf("%X  ",*ModePtr++);

printf("\n\nPress <Enter> to continue, ^C to abort\n");
getchar();

/* Now test for the various supported video modes */
/* First the extended graphics modes */
TestVESAMode("MG640x400x256"  ,MG640x400x256);

TestVESAMode("MG640x480x256"  ,MG640x480x256);
TestVESAMode("MG800x600x16"   ,MG800x600x16);
TestVESAMode("MG800x600x256"  ,MG800x600x256);
TestVESAMode("MG1024x768x16"  ,MG1024x768x16);
TestVESAMode("MG1024x768x256" ,MG1024x768x256);
TestVESAMode("MG1280x1024x16" ,MG1280x1024x16);
TestVESAMode("MG1280x1024x256",MG1280x1024x256);

/* Now test for the extended text modes */
TestVESAMode("MT80x60" ,MT80x60);
TestVESAMode("MT132x25",MT132x25);
TestVESAMode("MT132x43",MT132x43);
TestVESAMode("MT132x50",MT132x50);
TestVESAMode("MT132x60",MT132x60);

regs.h.ah = VESAFUNCTIONID;
regs.h.al = SETSUPERVGAVIDEOMODE;
regs.x.bx = 0x13;
int86(VIDEOINT,&regs,&regs);
if ((regs.h.al != VESAFUNCTIONID) || (regs.h.ah != 0))  {
   printf("Display Adapter not VESA compliant\n");
   exit(-1);
}
printf("\n\nNow in mode 13 hex\n\n");
getchar();
regs.h.ah = VESAFUNCTIONID;
regs.h.al = SETSUPERVGAVIDEOMODE;
regs.x.bx = 3;
int86(VIDEOINT,&regs,&regs);
if ((regs.h.al != VESAFUNCTIONID) || (regs.h.ah != 0))  {
   printf("Display Adapter not VESA compliant\n");
   exit(-1);
}
printf("Back to normal text mode\n");
while(1)
   ;
}
```

VGA/SuperVGA Function Library

As noted earlier in this chapter, the programs in this book do not use any of the graphics functions provided by the compiler manufacturers. This gives the programs much more portability between the various software development environments. To accomplish this feat, we provide all of the graphics functions required by the tool programs in this book locally. All of these functions are grouped together and collectively referred to as the "VGA/SuperVGA Function Library." This function library consists of 13 functions (callable from C application programs) that provide the required graphic services. Some of these functions set and return video modes, others manipulate the VGA color registers and read/write pixel values. The VGA/SuperVGA library functions are shown in Listing 1.4 and are described in detail in Figure 1.8.

Listing 1.4   VGA Function Library

The following is the contents of the file "vga.h."

```
/************************************************************/
/***                     "vga.h"                        ***/
/***       VGA/SuperVGA Graphic Adapter Header File     ***/
/***     from the book "Practical Ray Tracing in C"     ***/
/***          written in Borland Turbo C 2.0            ***/
/***                        by                          ***/
/***               Craig A. Lindley                     ***/
/***                                                    ***/
/***        Vers: 1.0   Last Update: 12/12/91           ***/
/************************************************************/

#define VESAFUNCTIONID 0x4F            /* VESA function identifier */

#define MAXNUMCOLREGS 256             /* max number of color registers */
#define MAXCOLREGVAL   63
#define MAXCOLS      1024
#define MAXROWS       768
/*
The following define the VGA 256 color modes. The first is a standard VGA
mode whereas all others are VESA SuperVGA modes.
*/
#define Mode320x200  0x13             /* 320x200  256 color VGA video mode */
#define Mode640x400  0x100            /* 640x400  256 color VESA video mode */
#define Mode640x480  0x101            /* 640x480  256 color VESA video mode */
#define Mode800x600  0x103            /* 800x600  256 color VESA video mode */
#define Mode1024x768 0x105            /* 1024x768 256 color VESA video mode */

#ifndef __BYTE
#define __BYTE
typedef unsigned char BYTE;
#endif
```

(continued)

Listing 1.4   *(continued)*

```c
#ifndef __ColorRegister
#define __ColorRegister
typedef struct {
    BYTE Red;                    /* RGB components of color */
    BYTE Green;                  /* register */
    BYTE Blue;
} ColorRegister;
#endif

/* VGA C Function Prototypes */
void SetTextMode (void);
void CheckForVESA (void);
unsigned GetstandardVideoMode(void);
void SetStandardVideoMode (unsigned Mode);
int  GetVESAVideoMode(void);
int  SetVESAVideoMode (unsigned Mode, unsigned ClearVMemFlag);
int  SelectVideoMode(unsigned Width, unsigned Height,
                     unsigned ClearVMemFlag);
void SetAColorReg (unsigned RegNum, unsigned Red,
                   unsigned Green,  unsigned Blue);
void GetAColorReg (unsigned RegNum, unsigned *Red,
                   unsigned *Green, unsigned *Blue);
void SetPixelValue (unsigned Col, unsigned Row, unsigned Value);
unsigned GetPixelValue (unsigned Col, unsigned Row);
void SetAllColorRegs (ColorRegister *Palette);
void GetAllColorRegs (ColorRegister *Palette);
```

The following is the contents of the file "vga.c."

```c
/*********************************************************/
/***                   "vga.c"                       ***/
/***       VGA/SuperVGA Graphic Adapter Functions    ***/
/***     from the book "Practical Ray Tracing in C"  ***/
/***           written in Borland/Turbo C 2.0        ***/
/***                      by                         ***/
/***             Craig A. Lindley                    ***/
/***                                                 ***/
/***       Vers: 1.0  Last Update: 12/12/91          ***/
/*********************************************************/

#include <stdio.h>
#include <process.h>
#include <dos.h>
#include "misc.h"
#include "vga.h"

static union REGS regs;

/* Start of VGA/SuperVGA functions */
```

```
/*
This function restores the text mode of operation after the display
adapter has been in the graphics mode. This function should always
be called when a graphic program exits.
*/

void SetTextMode( void )  {

  regs.h.ah = 0;                  /* set video mode function # */
  regs.h.al = 3;                  /* 80x25 text 16 color */
  int86(VIDEO,&regs,&regs);
}


/*
This function determines if a VESA-compliant video adapter is present.
If so, it returns to the calling program. If not, it outputs an error
message and terminates program operation. If this message is received
by the user it is an indication that either the display adapter is not
VESA compliant or that the TSR that makes it so has not been loaded.
If neither is the case, the function "SelectVideoMode" will have to
be rewritten to make the appropriate video mode selections using the
mode numbers for the specific display adapter.
*/

void CheckForVESA (void)  {

  unsigned char GLOBALINFO[256];

  /* Determine if a VESA-compliant video adapter is present */
  regs.h.ah = VESAFUNCTIONID;
  regs.h.al = 0;                 /* return SuperVGA mode function */
  _ES =       FP_SEG(GLOBALINFO);
  regs.x.di = FP_OFF(GLOBALINFO);
  int86(VIDEO,&regs,&regs);
  if ((regs.h.al != VESAFUNCTIONID) || (regs.h.ah != 0))  {
    SetTextMode();
    printf("\nDisplay adapter not VESA compliant !!!\n");
    printf("See text for details\n\n");
    exit(-1);
  }
}


/*
These functions get/set the video mode from the VGA
video controller. The first two functions deal with
standard VGA devices whereas the second two deal with
VESA SuperVGA devices.
*/

unsigned GetStandardVideoMode(void)  {
```

(continued)

Listing 1.4   *(continued)*

```
  regs.h.ah = 0x0F;            /* request the current video mode */
  int86(VIDEO,&regs,&regs);
  return(regs.h.al);           /* return it to caller */
}


void SetStandardVideoMode(unsigned Mode)  {

  regs.h.ah = 0;               /* set mode function code */
  regs.h.al = Mode;            /* this is the requested mode */
  int86(VIDEO,&regs,&regs);    /* ask nicely */
}


int GetVESAVideoMode(void)  {

  regs.h.ah = VESAFUNCTIONID;           /* request SuperVGA function */
  regs.h.ah = 0x03;                     /* return video mode cmd */
  int86(VIDEO,&regs,&regs);             /* execute request and check result */
  if ((regs.h.al != VESAFUNCTIONID) || (regs.h.ah != 0))
    return(-1);                         /* if error return -1 */
  else
    return(regs.x.bx);                  /* else return video mode to caller */
}


int SetVESAVideoMode(unsigned Mode, unsigned ClearVMemFlag)  {

  unsigned TempMode;

  TempMode = Mode & 0x7FFF;             /* clear bit 15 to clear memory */
  if (!ClearVMemFlag)                   /* if request to not clear memory */
    TempMode |= 0x8000;                 /* set bit 15 to indicate no clear */

  regs.h.ah = VESAFUNCTIONID;           /* request SuperVGA function */
  regs.h.al = 0x02;                     /* set video mode cmd */
  regs.x.bx = TempMode;                 /* this is the requested mode */
  int86(VIDEO,&regs,&regs);             /* ask nicely */
  if ((regs.h.al != VESAFUNCTIONID) || (regs.h.ah != 0))
    return(-1);                         /* if error return -1 */
  else
    return(0);                          /* else return 0 */
}

/* Set a VESA-compatible VGA card into an appropriate 256-color mode. */
int SelectVideoMode(unsigned Width, unsigned Height,
                    unsigned ClearVMemFlag)  {

  int ReturnCode = 0;

  if ((Width <= 320) && (Height <= 200))
    ReturnCode = SetVESAVideoMode(Mode320x200,ClearVMemFlag);
```

```
   else
   if ((Width <= 640) && (Height <= 400))
     ReturnCode = SetVESAVideoMode(Mode640x400,ClearVMemFlag);
   else
   if ((Width <= 640) && (Height <= 480))
     ReturnCode = SetVESAVideoMode(Mode640x480, ClearVMemFlag);
   else
   if ((Width <= 800) && (Height <= 600))
     ReturnCode = SetVESAVideoMode(Mode800x600,ClearVMemFlag);
   else
     ReturnCode = SetVESAVideoMode(Mode1024x768, ClearVMemFlag);

   return(ReturnCode);
}

/* Set an individual VGA color register */
void SetAColorReg(unsigned RegNum, unsigned Red,
                  unsigned Green,  unsigned Blue)  {

  union REGS regs;

  /*
  With graphics mode set, we can load a color register
  in the DAC.
  */

  /* set a Color Register */
  regs.h.ah = 0x10;
  regs.h.al = 0x10;
  regs.x.bx = RegNum;
  regs.h.dh = Red;
  regs.h.ch = Green;
  regs.h.cl = Blue;
  int86(VIDEO,&regs,&regs);
}

/* Get the color components of a VGA color register */
void GetAColorReg(unsigned RegNum, unsigned *Red,
                  unsigned *Green, unsigned *Blue)  {

  union REGS regs;
  /*
  With graphics mode set, we can read a color register
  from the DAC.
  */

  /* get a Color Register's components */
  regs.h.ah = 0x10;
  regs.h.al = 0x15;
  regs.x.bx = RegNum;
```

(continued)

Listing 1.4   *(continued)*

```
  int86(VIDEO,&regs,&regs);
  /* store the returned values at the pointers */
  *Red   = regs.h.dh;
  *Green = regs.h.ch;
  *Blue  = regs.h.cl;
}


/*
Set and get the color value of the specified pixel on the VGA screen. These
functions will work regardless of current video mode. That is why they
are used here.
*/
void SetPixelValue(unsigned Col, unsigned Row, unsigned Value)  {

  /* set a graphic pixel */
  regs.h.ah = 0x0C;
  regs.h.al = Value;
  regs.x.bx = 0;
  regs.x.dx = Row;
  regs.x.cx = Col;
  int86(VIDEO,&regs,&regs);
}


unsigned GetPixelValue(unsigned Col, unsigned Row)  {

  /* set a graphic pixel */
  regs.h.ah = 0x0D;
  regs.x.bx = 0;
  regs.x.dx = Row;
  regs.x.cx = Col;
  int86(VIDEO,&regs,&regs);
  regs.h.ah = 0;
  return(regs.x.ax);
}


/*
Set all 256 color registers
*/
void SetAllColorRegs(ColorRegister *Palette) {

  /* set a block of Color Registers */
  regs.h.ah = 0x10;
  regs.h.al = 0x12;
  regs.x.bx = 0;
  regs.x.cx = MAX256PALETTECOLORS;
  _ES = FP_SEG(Palette);
  regs.x.dx =FP_OFF(Palette);
  int86(VIDEO,&regs,&regs);
}
```

```
/*
Read all 256 color registers
*/
void GetAllColorRegs(ColorRegister *Palette) {

    /* set a block of Color Registers */
    regs.h.ah = 0x10;
    regs.h.al = 0x17;
    regs.x.bx = 0;
    regs.x.cx = MAX256PALETTECOLORS;
    _ES = FP_SEG(Palette);
    regs.x.dx =FP_OFF(Palette);
    int86(VIDEO,&regs,&regs);
}
```

The VGA function library is made up of functions written in C with a small amount of embedded assembly language code. All of these functions are in the file "vga.c" on the companion disks.

1. Set the text video mode of operation.

Prototype:

> void SetTextMode(void);

Operation:

This simple function uses the video BIOS to place the display adapter back into the 80-character by 25-line 16-color text mode (video mode 3). Calling this function is useful at the termination of any graphics program that has changed the video mode to put the computer back into normal text mode.

2. Check for the presence of a VESA-compliant video adapter.

Prototype:

> void CheckForVESA(void);

Operation:

This function makes sure the display adapter on the computer in which this code is running is VESA compliant. This function is called within every tools program before an attempt is made to change the video mode. If the display adapter is VESA compatible, this function returns to the calling program immediately without returning any results. If the display adapter is found not to be VESA compliant, this function promptly and absolutely terminates the operation of the program with an error message and an exit code of -1. This was done because most of the functions in this library expect a VESA display adapter and there is no point in continuing execution without one. If

Figure 1.8 The VGA Library Functions

(continued)

the code in this library is modified (as will be discussed shortly) to run with a non-VESA display adapter, the call to this function within the applications programs must be removed.

This function operates by calling VESA function zero to see if a VESA device exists. The call is made through the video BIOS interrupt 10 hex. Before the video interrupt is executed, the proper parameters are set up in the REGS union, including a pointer to a buffer area into which the "VgaInfoBlock" information will be returned if a VESA device exists. The parameters returned in the "ax" register on completion of the video interrupt are used to determine if a VESA device is present or not. If the "al" register contains 4F hex and the "ah" register contains a zero, then the display adapter is VESA compliant. Any other values returned indicate no VESA device exists and cause this function to abruptly terminate.

3. Get the current video mode (standard VGA method).

Prototype:

> unsigned GetStandardVideoMode(void);

Operation:

"GetStandardVideoMode" returns the number of the current video mode being used. Note this is a call directly to the standard VGA BIOS and therefore will not return the correct video mode number if the display happens to be in one of the SuperVGA modes. Currently, there are 20 defined video modes for PC-compatible computers with a standard VGA adapter: modes 0 through 13 hex. Not all of these modes are available on all computers, however. For our use in this book, only one standard VGA mode is important, the 320 by 200 256-color mode 13 hex.

This function, along with most others in this VGA/SuperVGA function library, operates by placing the correct values for the function call number and required parameters to support the function call into the processor registers and executing a call (actually a software interrupt) to the video BIOS. In the case of the "GetStandardVideoMode" function, the value returned in the "al" register is the current video mode. This value is passed back to the calling code via the return statement.

4. Set the video mode (standard VGA method).

Prototype:

> void SetStandardVideoMode(unsigned Mode);

Operation:

This function sets a display adapter to any of its supported video modes (the mode number is specified in the parameter "Mode") including the SuperVGA modes. It is the converse of the function discussed immediately above. You cannot use this function to set the video modes on a VESA-compliant SuperVGA display adapter (using the VESA mode numbers anyway). You must do that with the "SetVESAVideoMode" function described below. If you know the manufacturer-specific mode numbers for a SuperVGA card, you can in most cases use them with this function to set the video mode.

5. Get the current video mode (VESA method).

Prototype:

> int GetVESAVideoMode(void);

Figure 1.8 *(continued)*

Operation:

This function is similar to the "GetStandardVideoMode" function above except that it can only be called with a VESA-compliant display device. It returns the current video mode regardless of whether the display is operating in a VGA or SuperVGA mode. The results of the BIOS call are checked for errors. If an error is encountered in the execution of this function it is probably because the graphics adapter is not VESA compatible. In this case, this function returns a -1 error code instead of a mode number.

6. Set the video mode (VESA method).

Prototype:

> int SetVESAVideoMode(unsigned Mode, unsigned ClearVMemFlag);

Operation:

This function is used to set the video mode in a VESA-compatible display adapter. It can be used to set all video modes, both standard VGA and SuperVGA. The mode number desired is passed in the "Mode" parameter. In addition, the "ClearVMemFlag" parameter determines whether the video memory is cleared when the mode is changed. If this flag is FALSE or zero, the video memory is not modified. If, however, it is TRUE or nonzero, the video memory is cleared when the mode is changed. In most cases, the video memory should be cleared when changing the video mode, otherwise strange screen displays can result.

This function accesses the VESA BIOS extensions through the video BIOS. A -1 error code is returned if the VESA function call fails. A zero is returned when no errors are encountered.

7. Select an appropriate 256-color video mode.

Prototype:

> int SelectVideoMode(unsigned Width, unsigned Height,
>   unsigned ClearVMemFlag);

Operation:

This function selects the appropriate 256-color mode given the Width and Height parameters it is passed. The lowest-resolution video mode that can completely display an image of the specified Width and Height is selected. The "ClearVMemFlag" is also passed into this function. It operates as discussed above. As written, this function will work only on a VESA-compatible display adapter. If you must modify this function to work on non-VESA-compatible display adapters, you must replace each call to "SetVESAVideoMode" within this function with a call to the "SetStandardVideoMode" function. The mode numbers used with each call to "SetStandardVideoMode" would be those pertinent to your display adapter and to the resolution required. For example, for the Diamond Speed-Star+ SuperVGA card, this function would be rewritten as follows:

```
    int SelectVideoMode(unsigned Width, unsigned Height,
                        unsigned ClearVMemFlag)  {


  if ((Width <= 320) && (Height <= 200))
    SetStandardVideoMode(0x13);
  else
  if ((Width <= 640) && (Height <= 400))
```

Figure 1.8 *(continued)*   *(continued)*

```
      SetStandardVideoMode(0x2F);
   else
   if ((Width <= 640) && (Height <= 480))
     SetStandardVideoMode(0x2E);
   else
   if ((Width <= 800) && (Height <= 600))
     SetStandardVideoMode(0x30);
   else
     SetStandardVideoMode(0x38);

   return(0);
}
```

In this case, the "ClearVMemFlag" parameter would be ignored and a bogus value of zero would always be returned, indicating a successful operation.

8. Set an individual VGA color register.

Prototype:

> void SetAColorReg(unsigned RegNum, unsigned Red,
>   unsigned Green, unsigned Blue);

Operation:

RegNum is the number indicating which of the 256 color registers is to be manipulated, and Red, Green, and Blue are the color components that should be given to that register. Each component can range in value from 0 to 63. RGB components of 0, 0, and 0 result in black, whereas components 63, 63, and 63 are white. If all three color components are equal in value, the result is a shade of the color gray.

9. Get the color components of a VGA color register.

Prototype:

> void GetAColorReg(unsigned RegNum, unsigned *Red,
>   unsigned *Green, unsigned *Blue);

Operation:

RegNum is a number indicating which of the 256 color registers is to be read. Red, Green, and Blue are pointers to locations in which the specified color register's color component values should be stored. This function performs the converse operation of the function above. It returns the RGB components of a specified color register each in the range 0..63.

10. Set a pixel to a color value.

Prototype:

> void SetPixelValue(unsigned Col, unsigned Row, unsigned Value);

Where:

"Col" and "Row" specify the location of the pixel on the screen to be modified and "Value" indicates the number of the color register to be assigned to that pixel. For the 256-color modes, the range of values for "Value" is 0..255.

Figure 1.8   *(continued)*

Operation:

This function writes pixels to the display by calling the standard video BIOS function "Write Pixel Value." "SetPixelValue" will work for any graphics video mode regardless of resolution or the number of colors. It will not work, however, for the 32K-color modes. A special version of this function will be provided for the 32K-color case later in this chapter. The parameters that are passed into this function are placed into the appropriate processor registers and the video BIOS software interrupt 10 hex is called to write the actual pixel value to video memory and, therefore, the screen.

11. Get a pixel's color value.

Prototype:

    unsigned GetPixelValue(unsigned Col, unsigned Row);

Where:

"Col" and "Row" specify the location of the pixel on the screen to read the value from. For the 256-color modes, the range of values returned by this function is 0..255.

Operation:

This function is the converse of the one discussed directly above. It returns the number of the color register associated with the specified pixel instead of setting the value. All caveats discussed above apply here also.

12. Set all color register values at once.

Prototype:

    void SetAllColorRegs(ColorRegister *Palette);

Where:

"Palette" is a pointer to an array of 256 "ColorRegister" values. A "ColorRegister" is a 3-byte data structure with a byte each of Red, Green, and Blue, in that order. "Palette" then points at a data structure that is 768 bytes in length total. The values stored at "Palette" are transferred into color registers 0 through 255 in the video digital to analog converter (DAC).

Operation:

This function is used to change the values of all of the color registers simultaneously. It is handy when a new color palette has been calculated and needs to be installed or when a palette has been read from a graphics file and needs to be installed to display the contained image in the correct colors. See the color quantization program "mquan.c" in Chapter 4 for an example.

This function also works by calling the video BIOS (are you surprised?). The only thing new here is the use of the "FP_SEG" and "FP_OFF" macros to get the segment and offset values of the array of "ColorRegister" values that "Palette" points at. Their use, however, is straightforward and shown in the listing.

13. Get all color register values at once.

Prototype:

    void GetAllColorRegs(ColorRegister *Palette);

Figure 1.8   *(continued)*   *(continued)*

Where:
"Palette" is a pointer to an array of 256 3-byte storage locations where the color register values should be stored. "Palette" then points at an area of memory 768 bytes in length. The values stored at "Palette" are transferred from color registers 0 through 255 in the video DAC.

Operation:
This function reads all of the color registers and stores their values in a user-defined area of memory. It performs a complimentary operation to the function discussed just above.

Figure 1.8   *(continued)*

The functions in this VGA/SuperVGA function library are used in many of the tools programs in this book. To utilize these functions, an application program would need to include the files "misc.h," "pcx.h," and "vga.h" in its code and then be linked with the file "vga.obj" produced by the compiler when the VGA function library was compiled. You can handle this automatically by placing the filename "vga.c" in your project make file.

The "misc.h" file contains some miscellaneous type definitions and error code definitions needed by the function library. This simple file is shown in Listing 1.5. *Note*: The order of the include files within an application program is significant. Improper ordering will result in compilation errors. The correct ordering of these files can be seen in any of the tools programs. The correct ordering is "misc.h," then "vga.h," then "pcx.h," and finally "gif.h." Of course, if any of these include files are not needed by an application, you can omit them.

Listing 1.5   The "misc.h" Include File

The following is the contents of the file "misc.h."

```
/***********************************************************/
/***                    "misc.h"                     ***/
/***         Miscellaneous item include file          ***/
/***     for Image Processing/Ray Tracing Functions    ***/
/***      from the book "Practical Ray Tracing in C"    ***/
/***         written in Borland/Turbo C 2.0           ***/
/***                      by                          ***/
/***             Craig A. Lindley                     ***/
/***                                                  ***/
/***        Vers: 1.0   Last Update: 01/06/92         ***/
/***********************************************************/
```

```
/* Define new types */
#ifndef __BYTE
#define __BYTE
typedef unsigned char BYTE;
#endif

#ifndef _CompletionCode_
#define _CompletionCode_
typedef int CompletionCode;
#endif

#define TRUE        1
#define FALSE       0

#define VIDEO     0x10

/* Common Macros */
#define MIN(a,b)  ((a)>(b)) ? (b):(a)
#define MAX(a,b)  ((a)>(b)) ? (a):(b)
#define SQUARE(x) (x)*(x)

#define MAXSCREENWIDTH              1024
#define MAXBYTESPERSCAN    MAXSCREENWIDTH
#define MAXSCREENHEIGHT             768
#define MAXPALETTECOLORS            16
#define MAX256PALETTECOLORS        256

/* Error Bit Definitions */
#define NoError          0
#define EBadParms       -1
#define EFileNotFound   -2
#define EOpeningFile    -3
#define EReadFileHdr    -4
#define ENotPCXFile     -5
#define ECorrupt        -6
#define EWrtFileHdr     -7
#define EWrtOutFile     -8
#define EReadScanLine   -9
#define EWrtScanLine   -10
#define EPCCFile       -11
#define EGraphics      -12
#define ENoMemory      -13
#define EWrtExtPal     -14
#define ENotGIFFile    -15
#define EReadRowNum    -16
#define EReadData      -17
```

Gamma Correction

The shading models used within ray-tracing programs mix colors in a linear fashion to best simulate the physical mixing of light within a scene. This makes the color calculations simpler to use and faster to execute. Unfortunately, the computer monitors (and normal TV sets for that matter) on which these images will be displayed do not have a linear relationship between the numerical value of the data in a color register and the resultant luminance (brightness) of the display. This problem is caused by the phosphors used to coat the screens in cathode ray tubes (CRTs). These phosphors exhibit a nonlinear excitation versus brightness curve. To compensate for this nonlinearity, we need to introduce a gamma correction factor. Gamma correction attempts to establish a linear relationship between the stimulus given a monitor and the corresponding brightness. With the correct gamma correction factor, a near-linear relationship between stimulus and brightness for a monitor can be established, with the result being a more accurately displayed image.

The television industry has acknowledged the need for gamma correction for many years and has built a gamma correction factor of approximately 2.222 into television cameras to correct for the TV's nonlinear CRT. In other words, gamma correction has been applied at the source instead of having to be compensated for within individual TV sets.

Of course, since the type and formulation of phosphor used in computer monitors vary from CRT to CRT, so does the required gamma correction factor. There is no single gamma correction factor that can be universally applied to all monitors. In fact, gamma correction factors of 1.8 to 2.6 are typical, with 2.222 being most common. The amount of correction that your computer monitor requires depends on the manufacturer. Consult the relevant documentation for a possible answer. If you cannot determine the correction number from the documentation, experiment to find the best results.

Note: Since most color CRTs use three electron guns of the same design, and the three color phosphors (red, green, and blue) exhibit similar excitation characteristics, generally, the same gamma correction factor can be applied to each color channel. You can use either of the following formulas to calculate gamma corrected data given the linear input data and a gamma correction factor:

Corrected Value = exp(ln(Value)/Gamma correction factor)

or a simpler but equivalent formula:

Corrected Value = pow(Value,1.0/Gamma correction factor)

The code fragment shown below can be used to generate a table of gamma corrected values and in fact was used to prepare Figure 1.9. This code fragment is available on the companion disks in the file called "gamma.c."

```c
#include <stdio.h>
#include <math.h>

#define MAXINPUTVALUE   255         /* maximum value in the input domain */
#define MAXOUTPUTVALUE  63          /* maximum desired output value */
#define GAMMA ((double) 2.2222)     /* gamma correction value */
```

```
/*
This function will calculate a set of gamma corrected data values given
the maximum value of the input data, the maximum desired output value,
and the gamma correction factor.
*/
void main (void)    {

  double Value;
  int i;

  for (i=0; i < MAXINPUTVALUE+1; i++)   {    /* for each input value */
    if ((i % 20) == 0)                       /* format 20 entries/line */
      printf("\n");
    Value = MAXOUTPUTVALUE * pow((double) i/(double) MAXINPUTVALUE, (double) 1.0/GAMMA);
    printf("%2d,",(int)floor(Value));
  }
}
```

For our uses later in this book, gamma corrected data will be required. We use gamma correction in Chapter 4 when we discuss the color quantization techniques. We use a table of values instead of calculating the corrected values at run time for performance reasons. Because gamma correction calculations require floating-point numbers, they can take a significant amount of time to execute. By precalculating the values and placing them in a table ahead of time, you can perform a quick table lookup at run time without any floating-point calculation overhead being necessary.

Three tables are shown in Figure 1.9. Each is arranged as an array of bytes. The input data is used as an index into the byte array from where the output, gamma corrected data, is fetched. The first table uses 256 input values to produce 64 gamma corrected output values. The second table also uses 256 input values, but the output domain is limited to 32 output values. The third table is used to gamma correct 64 input values by producing 64 gamma corrected output values. All tables were calculated using a gamma of 2.222. Chapter 4 describes the need for these tables. See the *Raster Graphics Handbook* by Conrac Corporation for further discussion of gamma correction.

All of the color quantization programs of Chapter 4 invoke gamma correction as part of their normal operation. The gamma correction tends to make the ray-traced images brighter and more uniform in illumination. At times, however, images are more interesting when gamma correction is not used. Images displayed without gamma correction seem to have a wider dynamic range of illumination, resulting in a wider range of colors; from darker darks to lighter lights. For this reason, the color quantization programs "mquan.exe" and "oquan.exe" of Chapter 4 have a command line switch "-c" which disables gamma correction. When quantizing and saving your images, you should view them with and without gamma correction to see which you like better. The "Gallery of Images" section in the middle of the book has an example of an image quantized with and without gamma correction. The differences are obvious.

256 input values 0..255 with a maximum output value of 63

```
unsigned char Gamma256x64Table[] = {
        0,  5,  7,  8,  9,10,11,12,13,13,14,15,15,16,17,17,18,18,19,19,
       20,20,20,21,21,22,22,22,23,23,24,24,24,25,25,25,26,26,26,27,
       27,27,27,28,28,28,29,29,29,29,30,30,30,31,31,31,31,32,32,32,
       32,33,33,33,33,34,34,34,34,34,35,35,35,35,36,36,36,36,36,37,
       37,37,37,38,38,38,38,38,39,39,39,39,39,40,40,40,40,40,40,41,
       41,41,41,41,42,42,42,42,42,42,43,43,43,43,43,44,44,44,44,44,
       44,45,45,45,45,45,45,46,46,46,46,46,46,47,47,47,47,47,47,47,
       48,48,48,48,48,48,49,49,49,49,49,49,49,50,50,50,50,50,50,50,
       51,51,51,51,51,51,51,52,52,52,52,52,52,52,53,53,53,53,53,53,
       53,53,54,54,54,54,54,54,54,55,55,55,55,55,55,55,55,56,56,56,
       56,56,56,56,56,57,57,57,57,57,57,57,57,58,58,58,58,58,58,58,
       58,59,59,59,59,59,59,59,60,60,60,60,60,60,60,60,60,61,61,
       61,61,61,61,61,61,62,62,62,62,62,62,62,62,63
};
```

256 input values 0..255 with a maximum output value of 31

```
unsigned char Gamma256x32Table[] = {
        0,  2,  3,  4,  4,  5,  5,  6,  6,  6,  7,  7,  7,  8,  8,  8,  8,  9,  9,  9,
        9,10,10,10,10,10,11,11,11,11,11,12,12,12,12,12,12,13,13,13,
       13,13,13,13,14,14,14,14,14,14,14,15,15,15,15,15,15,15,15,16,
       16,16,16,16,16,16,16,17,17,17,17,17,17,17,17,17,18,18,18,
       18,18,18,18,18,18,19,19,19,19,19,19,19,19,19,19,19,20,20,20,
       20,20,20,20,20,20,20,20,21,21,21,21,21,21,21,21,21,21,21,21,
       22,22,22,22,22,22,22,22,22,22,22,22,23,23,23,23,23,23,23,23,
       23,23,23,23,23,24,24,24,24,24,24,24,24,24,24,24,24,24,24,25,
       25,25,25,25,25,25,25,25,25,25,25,25,25,26,26,26,26,26,26,
       26,26,26,26,26,26,26,26,27,27,27,27,27,27,27,27,27,27,27,27,
       27,27,27,27,28,28,28,28,28,28,28,28,28,28,28,28,28,28,28,28,
       29,29,29,29,29,29,29,29,29,29,29,29,29,29,29,29,29,30,30,
       30,30,30,30,30,30,30,30,30,30,30,30,30,30,31
};
```

64 input values 0..63 with a maximum output value of 63

```
unsigned char Gamma64x64Table[] = {
        0,  9,13,16,18,20,21,23,24,26,27,28,29,30,32,33,34,34,35,36,
       37,38,39,40,40,41,42,43,43,44,45,45,46,47,47,48,48,49,50,50,
       51,51,52,53,53,54,54,55,55,56,56,57,57,58,58,59,59,60,60,61,
       61,62,62,63
};
```

Notes:
1. A gamma correction factor of 2.222 was used to generate these tables.
2. To access the data in these tables, use the following convention:

    Corrected Value = GammaXXTable[Input Value];

Figure 1.9   Gamma Correction Tables

32K-Color Modes

As mentioned previously in this chapter, with certain SuperVGA hardware it is possible to display 32,768 simultaneous colors in certain video resolutions. This gives these SuperVGA users the same color capabilities as some of the higher-end graphics boards at a much lower cost. From experimental measurements we know that the human visual system (the eye/brain combination) is capable of distinguishing approximately 350,000 colors. Any natural scene we look at is made up of many colors, both striking and subtle. The eye/brain system uses the dominant colors to convey the image information to our brains, where the image is perceived. The more subtle aspects of color in the perceived image enhance the details of an image, but they are not absolutely necessary for recognition. The brain will fill in details that appear to be missing in order to make sense of an image. In terms of traditional computer graphics, the availability of a large number of colors can help to make up for lack of spatial resolution on a display device. For example, a low-resolution (nonvertical or nonhorizontal) line drawn on a computer monitor will generally have the "jaggies." Jaggies make the line appear more like a stair step than a straight line. Jaggies result from a phenomena called "aliasing," which we describe in the next chapter. Techniques called "anti-aliasing" can be used to visually smooth out the jaggies in a line even on a low-resolution display. Anti-aliasing works by selecting the proper colors to display the line. The more colors available, the better the results of anti-aliasing will be.

While the human visual system is capable of distinguishing a large color space, most computers and monitors are not capable of producing anywhere near that many unique colors. As we have seen, the maximum number of simultaneously displayable colors available on a standard VGA/SuperVGA graphics adapter is 256—less than one-thousandth of the number of colors the eye can perceive. Yet, by optimally choosing the dominant 256 colors, you can produce an accurate, visually acceptable image.

Graphics adapters that are referred to as "true color" have the capability to display the full gamut of colors perceivable by humans. These adapters typically utilize 24 bits (some utilize 32 bits) of image data per pixel, generally broken down into 8 bits each of red, green, and blue color information. True-color graphics adapters can theoretically display 16.8 million colors (2^{24}) but, unfortunately, are expensive. The higher cost is due to the large amount of fast video memory required and to the fact that for performance reasons they usually contain an onboard processor for the execution of graphic primitives. A 1024 by 768 true-color image, for example, would require 2.35 megabytes of video memory. Eventually, when the hardware prices of these true-color adapters drop, true-color capabilities will be available to more PC users. Until that time, however, most people will have to be satisfied with the color capabilities of VGA/SuperVGA.

The incorporation of the Sierra Hicolor DAC into a SuperVGA adapter is an interim solution to the color limitation problem. As mentioned, this gives the capability of displaying 32,768 (32K) colors on the screen at one time. At this time, however, the incorporation of the hicolor DAC is extremely dependent on the VGA/SuperVGA hardware. It will work only on special VGA/SuperVGA boards. The graphics board must have the hicolor DAC engineered in to take advantage of the hicolor modes. While this is unfortunate for older SuperVGA adapters, almost all new adapters have the required interface to the hicolor DAC chip. The code provided in this section is definitely hardware dependent. It will work only with a Super-VGA adapter that is based upon the Tseng Labs ET-4000 chip set, which is interfaced to the Sierra Hicolor DAC. While this violates the philosophy of using generally applicable example code in this book, it does illustrate the techniques required to use the hicolor modes. Hopefully, these techniques will be adaptable to other SuperVGA hardware combinations as they become available.

To get an idea of the improvements in image quality because of the increased number of colors available, examine image sequence two in the "Gallery of Images" (following page 314). Image (a) shows a full spectrum color gradient applied to a sphere and displayed in 256 colors. We produced this display with the color quantizer program "mquan.exe" described in Chapter 4. Note the wide banding that results from the color quantization process. Because of the limited number of colors available, colors that are similar (in terms of hue and intensity) are assigned the same value, with the result being bands of identical colors. Image (b) is the same image data display in the 32K-color mode (the actual number of unique colors is unknown). We produced this display with the color quantizer program "hquan.exe" described in Chapter 4. Notice that even with 32,768 colors available there is still visible banding, but the bands are much smaller. A true-color display of this same image would have perfectly smooth color transitions without any bands at all.

Two of the hicolor modes are important to the programs in this book. They are the 640 by 480 and the 800 by 600 32K-color modes. To utilize these for a graphics application, you need the following four basic functions:

1. A function to check for the existence of a Sierra Hicolor DAC
2. A function to put the VGA chip set into the required modes for 32K-color operation
3. A function to write a pixel to the screen
4. A function to read a pixel from the screen

These four functions for the Tseng Labs/Sierra Hicolor DAC hardware combination are shown in Listing 1.6. They are very similar to the functions discussed earlier in the VGA function library. With the background you now have, the operation of these functions should be obvious. These functions are included in the file "hicolor.c" on the companion disks. If an application's program wishes to use these functions, it should include the file "hicolor.h" in its source code and then be linked with "hicolor.obj" in addition to the application's code.

Conclusions

With the information presented in this chapter on the software development environment, processes, and tools, in addition to that on PC graphics adapters, you should have the background necessary to apply what you have learned to basic computer graphics problems. You can apply the code presented in this chapter to image processing in general and ray tracing specifically. You may find other uses for the code presented in addition to those discussed in the text. Once you understand this background information, you will be ready for the information on ray tracing presented in Chapter 2.

Listing 1.6 32K Hicolor Code

Note: This code works only on a SuperVGA card utilizing a Sierra HiColor DAC and the Tseng Labs ET-4000 chip set.

The following is the contents of the file "hicolor.h."

```
/************************************************************/
/***                  "hicolor.h"                     ***/
/***             32K color include file               ***/
/***          for 32K color access functions          ***/
/***      from the book "Practical Ray Tracing in C"   ***/
/***          written in Borland/Turbo C 2.0          ***/
/***                      by                          ***/
/***              Craig A. Lindley                     ***/
/***                                                  ***/
/***       Ver: 1.0    Last Update: 01/04/92          ***/
/************************************************************/

/* Function prototypes for the hicolor functions */
int CheckForSierraDAC1 (void);
int CheckForSierraDAC2 (void);
int SetHicolorVideoMode (unsigned Mode);
void PutPixel32K (unsigned Width, unsigned Col,
                  unsigned Row, unsigned Color);
unsigned GetPixel32K (unsigned Width, unsigned Col,
                      unsigned Row);
```

The following is the contents of the file "hicolor.c."

```
/************************************************************/
/***                  "hicolor.c"                     ***/
/***          32K color support code for the          ***/
/*** Tseng Labs ET-4000 chip set and Sierra Hicolor DAC ***/
/***    Tested on the Diamond SpeedStar+ SuperVGA card  ***/
/***      from the book "Practical Ray Tracing in C"   ***/
/***          written in Borland/Turbo C 2.0          ***/
/***                      by                          ***/
/***              Craig A. Lindley                     ***/
/***                                                  ***/
/***       Ver: 1.0    Last Update: 12/12/91          ***/
/************************************************************/

#include <stdio.h>
#include <dos.h>              /* contains REGS union definition */
#include "hicolor.h"

/*
This is one method for checking for the existence of the Sierra
Hicolor DAC. It uses a call to the Tseng Labs BIOS for the ET-4000
```

(continued)

Listing 1.6   *(continued)*

```
chip. This function returns a zero if the DAC is detected or a -1
otherwise.
*/

int CheckForSierraDAC1 (void)    {

  union REGS regs;

  /* Check for Sierra Hicolor DAC by querying the ET4000 BIOS. */
  regs.h.ah = 0x10;               /* Get DAC type function code */
  regs.h.al = 0xF1;
  int86(0x10,&regs,&regs);        /* ask the BIOS */
  if (regs.x.ax != 0x10)          /* return if function not supported */
    return(-1);
  if (regs.h.bl == 1)             /* if hicolor DAC */
    return(0);
  else
    return(-1);                     /* normal DAC */
}


/*
This is a second technique for determining the presence of the DAC
by directly checking for its presence instead of asking the Tseng
BIOS. This technique was excerpted from the Sierra Semiconductor
application notes.  See application note for details of operation.
*/

#define PEL_MASK     0x3C6    /* palette pixel read mask port address */
#define PEL_ADDR_REG 0x3C8    /* palette address register port address */

int CheckForSierraDAC2 (void)    {

  unsigned i, new_cmd;

  inp(PEL_ADDR_REG);          /* reset command register flag */
  for(i=0; i<4; i++)          /* read 4 times to set flag */
    inp(PEL_MASK);
  outp(PEL_MASK,0xFF);        /* put test pattern in command register */
  inp(PEL_ADDR_REG);          /* reset command register flag */
  outp(PEL_MASK,0x00);        /* put test pattern in PEL */
  for(i=0; i<4; i++)          /* read 4 times to set flag */
    inp(PEL_MASK);
  new_cmd = inp(PEL_MASK);    /* read back the test pattern */
  outp(PEL_MASK,0x00);        /* put command register in known state */
  outp(PEL_MASK,0xFF);        /* put PEL in known state */
  if (new_cmd == 0x00)        /* check for hicolor DAC */
    return(-1);               /* none found */
  else
    return(0);                /* got one */
}
```

```
/*
The following function attempts to place the Sierra Hicolor DAC and VGA
hardware into the 32K video mode passed to it as a parameter. The currently
supported modes with mode numbers are:

  640x350 is mode 0x2D, 640x480 is mode 0x2E,
  640x400 is mode 0x2F, 800x600 is mode 0x30.

This function returns a zero if successful or a -1 otherwise.
*/

int SetHicolorVideoMode (unsigned Mode)    {

  union REGS regs;

  regs.x.ax = 0x10F0;          /* Hicolor setmode function number */
  regs.h.bl = Mode;            /* mode number to set */
  int86(0x10,&regs,&regs);     /* ask the BIOS */
  return((regs.x.ax == 0x10) ? 0:-1);   /* 0 for success: -1 for failure */
}

/*
This function writes a pixel to the screen of specified color at a
specified location when the graphics adapter is in a hicolor video mode.
*/

void PutPixel32K (unsigned Width, unsigned Col, unsigned Row, unsigned Color)    {

  unsigned far *VideoMemPtr;
  unsigned Bank;
  unsigned long PixelAddress;
  /*
  Calculate the address of the pixel's location using a modification
  of the algorithm used for the 320 by 200 mode earlier. In this case,
  the width of the raster line in pixels is necessary to calculate the
  address of the pixel of interest because each row of raster data occupies
  twice that number of bytes. The Col parameter is multiplied by two because
  each pixel uses two bytes.
  */
  PixelAddress = (Col << 1) + ((Width << 1) * (unsigned long) Row);

  /*
  The upper 16 bits of the PixelAddress contains the number of the
  64K bank which contains the pixel of interest.
  */
  Bank = PixelAddress >> 16;
  /*
  The appropriate bank must be selected by the processor before the
  pixel data can be accessed. The ET-4000 uses a separate read and
  write bank. The upper nibble written to the bank select port is
```

(continued)

Listing 1.6 *(continued)*

```
the read bank number whereas the lower nibble is the write bank
number. Both are set in this code when the bank numbers are
written.
*/
outp(0x3CD, (Bank << 4) | Bank);

/*
Build a far pointer to the required address in video memory with
the segment of the video memory and the offset to the pixel's address.

*/
FP_SEG(VideoMemPtr) = 0xA000;
FP_OFF(VideoMemPtr) = (unsigned)(PixelAddress & 0xFFFF);

/* Store the value of the pixel at that address */
*VideoMemPtr = Color;
}


/*
This function reads and returns the value of a pixel from the screen at a
specified location when the graphics adapter is in a hicolor video mode.
*/

unsigned GetPixel32K (unsigned Width, unsigned Col, unsigned Row)    {

  unsigned far *VideoMemPtr;
  unsigned Bank;
  unsigned long PixelAddress;

  /* Calculate the address of the pixel's location as above. */
  PixelAddress = (Col << 1) + ((Width << 1) * (unsigned long) Row);

  /* Calculate the correct bank */
  Bank = PixelAddress >> 16;
  /* Select the appropriate read and write banks */
  outp(0x3CD, (Bank << 4) | Bank);

  /* Build a far pointer */
  FP_SEG(VideoMemPtr) = 0xA000;
  FP_OFF(VideoMemPtr) = (unsigned)(PixelAddress & 0xFFFF);

  /* Return the value of the pixel at that address */
  return(*VideoMemPtr);
}
```

Introduction to Ray-Tracing Theory

Learning is not attained by chance, it must be sought for with ardor and attended to with diligence.

—Abigail Adams

In this chapter you will learn about:
- **What ray tracing is**
- **How ray tracing fits into the family of computer graphics techniques**
- **Vectors, rays, and vector mathematics**
- **Parametric equations of lines**
- **Ray/object intersection techniques for quadric surfaces**
- **Shading, shadows, reflection, refraction, transparency, texture mapping, and fog**
- **Some classic solutions to problems with ray tracing**

Introduction

Photo realism is something that computer graphics scientists have been striving for for decades. As computers have become more powerful and graphical hardware I/O devices more prevalent, photo realism has been achieved. No one fails to be impressed when they learn how much of what they see in modern science-fiction movies is actually computer graphics. What used to require painstaking model building and matte painting can now be modeled with computers in such detail that it is virtually indistinguishable from reality. Yet computer graphics scientists continue their pursuit of still better techniques to simulate visual reality. Many are finding, however, that as simple as nature sometimes appears, accurate simulations of natural processes (in this case the interaction of light with objects) on a computer require complicated algorithms and tremendous computer power. Still, they continue their quest.

The technique of ray tracing resulted from the endless pursuit for photo realism. Once dismissed as an abysmally inefficient computer graphics technique that could never be of any use, ray tracing has since gathered quite a following. The reasons for this are threefold:

- First, and possibly most important, the concepts of ray tracing are simple enough to be understood by anyone interested in the technique, not only by a computer graphics scientist.
- Second, the inefficiency issues of ten years ago are not nearly as important today. With computer performance increasing at such an incredible rate, as it has done recently, inefficiency can be countered with raw computing horsepower. In addition, new techniques have been incorporated into ray-tracing programs to increase their efficiency.
- Third, the ray-tracing algorithm itself allows the incorporation of many visual effects in a straightforward manner. Adding the same effects into other three-dimensional computer graphics techniques is much more difficult, if not impossible. The reasons for this will become evident.

This chapter presents the *basic theories* of ray tracing. As such, this is the substantive chapter in this book. Where you draw the line between basic and advanced techniques is somewhat subjective, however. The goal here is to present enough theory to allow you to construct a basic ray-tracing program of your own design and to provide enough foundation information so that you can understand the current ray-tracing literature. You must read and understand the information in this chapter before you can tackle advanced ray-tracing topics. Concepts such as texture mapping, ray-tracing acceleration techniques, and distributed ray tracing will only be mentioned in this chapter, as they fall more into the category of advanced ray-tracing techniques. Pointers to the definitive papers that describe the advanced techniques are provided both in this chapter and in the section on "Further Reading" in Part Three.

We first discuss general ray-tracing concepts to give you an overall idea of how the process works. A description of basic vector mathematics follows, which will be necessary to understand and implement the ray-tracing algorithms. Next will come a somewhat theoretical explanation of rays, ray/object intersections, and shading. Finally, we discuss some of the real-life problems inherent with ray tracing. Chapter 3 will reinforce the theory presented here by implementing a simple (but brute force) ray tracer that puts the basic theory presented in this chapter into practice.

General Concepts

The intent of this section is to provide you with an intuitive feeling for how the process of ray tracing works. Once you have a sense for that, the actual theory is somehow more palatable. As a practical book, providing a general description of how ray tracing works is what we are after and is all most people will ever want or need. For those readers who want the gory details, we will provide them following the discussion of the general concepts.

Ray tracing's reason for existence is to produce photo-realistic imagery. A photo-realistic image is one in which the interplay of light and shadows with three-dimensional objects closely resembles what would be found in nature. One of ray tracing's biggest advantages over other three-dimensional rendering techniques is the simplicity with which effects such as shadows, reflections, and transparency can be incorporated. The reason ray tracing can produce photo-realistic images with these visual effects is because the tracing of rays simulates light. In other words, ray tracing models the interaction of light rays and objects using principles of geometric optics. The rules used for light ray/object interaction are simplified from those of nature but are still close enough to provide realistic results. Ray-tracing programs such as the two presented in this book assume that light rays travel only in straight lines through homogeneous media and interact with objects only at their surfaces. Properties of light such as diffraction, phase, polarization, wavelength, and attenuation over distance are not taken into consideration. Modeling many of these phenomena is still pushing the state of computer graphics art. Once simplified models can be identified, these effects may also be incorporated into ray-tracing programs.

Ray tracing is an example of a class of graphics algorithms referred to as point sampling algorithms. These algorithms determine the visibility of a surface (object) using a finite number of sample points and then make assumptions about the points in between. Ray tracing is thus an approximation of reality. Other algorithms in this class are the Z-buffer algorithm, the painters' algorithm, and the scanline algorithm. All of these algorithms are involved with hidden surface determination and removal. The other major class of algorithms is referred to as continuous algorithms. These are not approximations; they try to determine visibility continuously over entire surfaces. These calculations, as you might well imagine, are very time consuming and not suitable for implementation on a PC at this time.

Two problems arise as a result of ray tracing's point sampling heritage: performance and aliasing. Performance is an issue because as the number of points evaluated for ray/object intersection increases so does the computation time. Unfortunately (for those of us with limited computing power), as the number of points evaluated increases so does the realism of the image. Additionally, the use of many light sources within a scene can also cause severe performance bottlenecks.

Aliasing is a problem that must be faced by every sampling system, be it graphical or electrical. Aliasing is an undesirable artifact arising from the inability to reconstruct the original signal from its discrete samples. The severity of the aliasing problem is directly related to the frequency of the signal being sampled and the sampling rate. If the sampling rate or frequency is high enough, aliasing is not a problem. However, as the sampling frequency nears that of the signal being sampled, undesirable low-frequency signal components are created that are not part of the signal being sampled. These undesirables are called aliases.

In imaging terms, when you use a point sampling process like ray tracing to produce images with fine detail (high-frequency content), some of that detail will be masked by aliases. This results in many different varieties of image distortion, including the dreaded "jaggies," that must be dealt with in order to produce photo-realistic imagery. Aliasing artifacts in still ray-traced images are bad enough, but when animation of the still images is required the problems are compounded due to temporal aliasing. Rendering an image with higher resolution (higher-frequency sampling) helps, but it does not solve the problem completely. Graphical techniques used to combat aliasing problems are called "anti-aliasing" techniques. We describe some techniques for anti-aliasing and performance improvement later in this chapter. Using the DKBTrace ray tracer discussed in Part Two of this book, you can see the improvement in image quality you can have by applying anti-aliasing.

To construct a ray-traced image, you begin by defining a three-dimensional scene. A scene consists of light source(s) and object(s). Each object is given an assigned location and attributes that define its shape and surface properties (color, reflectivity, texture, etc.). With the scene defined, you must next establish the view geometry (the topic of a future section). Briefly, the viewing geometry specifies where in three-dimensional space the viewer's eye will be located (where the scene will be viewed from), the direction the eye will be looking, the orientation of the eye, and the field of view the eye will have. The eye views the three-dimensional scene though a hypothetical window in space called the "view plane." The view

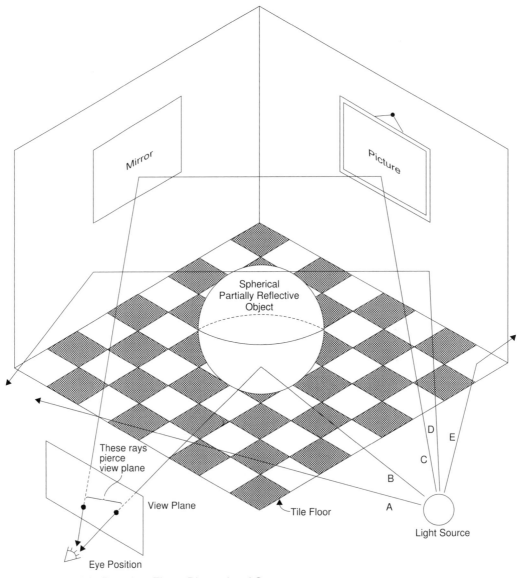

Figure 2.1   Light Rays in a Three-Dimensional Scene

plane will be mapped to the computer's monitor, and that is where the eye sees the ray-traced scene. No matter where the eye is located or how it is positioned, the view plane always lies between the eye and the objects in the three-dimensional scene. Figure 2.1 shows a scene with objects, a light source, and the eye's position established.

It seems intuitive that to trace light rays we should begin at the light source(s), generate rays that would enter the scene, and see which ones pierce the view plane after bouncing through the scene and are therefore visible to the eye. This approach, sometimes referred to as forward ray tracing, is workable but *very* computationally expensive. To accurately render a scene would require that you generate and trace billions (and billions) of light rays with only a very small percentage having the correct trajectory to ultimately pass through the view plane. An image generated in this manner would require months if not years of PC computation time to complete.

A small alteration in thinking will produce a technique that although still computationally expensive is much more efficient than forward ray tracing. This technique is known in the literature by many names, including ray casting, backward ray tracing, and reverse ray tracing. The idea is to reverse the tracing of rays by starting at the eye location and generating a ray that will pass through each pixel of the view plane on its way out into the three-dimensional scene. As this ray strikes objects in the scene, the pixel through which the ray passed takes on the color of the closest intersected object. If the point of intersection between the ray and the closest object has an unobscured view of a light source, the point of intersection is not in shadow; it is fully illuminated by the light source. If, however, any objects in the scene lie between the point of intersection and the light source, the object at that point is in shadow and its corresponding pixel's intensity is diminished accordingly. A pseudocode description of the complete ray-tracing process is shown below. You may be able to understand it better than the description you have just read.

Procedure Ray Trace

```
Begin
  For each row of the image
    For each column of the image
      Generate a ray from the eye's location through the pixel at (column,row)
      For each object in 3D universe
        Calculate ray/object intersection
        If intersection occurred
          If intersection time t is the smallest yet (object is closest to eye)
            Save this new intersection time
          EndIf
        EndIf
      EndFor
      If intersection occurred
        Calculate point of intersection of ray with closest object
        Calculate normal to object's surface at point of intersection
        For each light source in 3D universe
          Generate a ray from the point of intersection to light source
          For each object in 3D universe except the one initially intersected
            Calculate light ray/object intersection
            If no intersection occurred, point of intersection is not in shadow
              Calculate pixel's color value and intensity as a function of this light source
```

```
            EndIf
         EndFor
       EndFor
     Else no intersections with objects occurred
        Set pixels color and intensity to that of the background
     EndIf
     Color pixel on screen and/or save pixel data to a file
   EndFor { column }
 EndFor { row }
End
```

Determining an object's color at the point of intersection would be easy if not for the fact that an object can be reflective and/or refractive in addition to having a texture. Actually, ray-traced images without these effects are usually uninteresting to look at. The color at the point of ray/object intersection becomes a function of the object's color, the color of the light source (and sometimes the distance from the intersection), and any contributions made via reflection or refraction. For example, study ray C in Figure 2.1. A ray shot from the eye into this scene would first intersect the mirror on the wall. A mirror being a perfectly reflecting surface has no real color of its own. The color perceived by the eye in the mirror is that reflected from the picture on the opposite wall and the illumination provided by the light source. If the light source is a color other than white, it, too, plays a part in the color of the reflected picture as seen by the eye. As you might expect, the calculation of color is a recursive process. The name given to this process is "shading." Every time a reflective or refractive object is intersected by the eye ray, an additional set of rays must be generated. Each of the additional rays must then be traced back to each light source to determine its contribution to the object's color. Because the process is recursive, what results is (the automatic creation of) a ray tree in which each branch describes the components that make up the object's color. (*Note*: You must place a limit on the depth of recursion or else an image with many reflective/refractive surfaces would never be completed. The limit can either be some fixed number, like five or ten recursion levels, or be a function of how much of a contribution the additional color information represents. Once a threshold is crossed in which the additional rays don't make a significant contribution to the final color, recursion is terminated.) The color contributions at the leaves of the tree are evaluated and passed back up the tree. Each contribution figures into the final color of the object and the color of the pixel with which it is associated.

This description has attempted to present the somewhat involved process of ray tracing in simple terms. If it did not completely sink in on the first reading, try reading the description again. Look around your current surroundings and try to imagine the path of the light rays entering your eyes. Then, visualize a grid in front of your face. Notice that you perceive only a part of the whole three-dimensional scene through each portion of the grid or view plane. Using these physical/mental aids may help you understand the process. Now for a change of pace, sharpen your pencils and get ready for the math class "Vectors 101," which is about to begin.

Vectors and Vector Mathematics

In this section we discuss the specialized mathematics required for performing ray tracing. This math is specialized only in that it isn't typically used by computer programmers on a daily basis.

As you will see, however, the math is not at all difficult. The basic mathematics discussed here is used by all ray-tracing programs, not just the ones presented in this book. Additionally, this same mathematics finds use in many areas of physics and is taught as part of first-year college physics courses. For some, the information presented will be a review; for others it will be an entirely new subject area. Later discussions will assume the knowledge presented here.

The "vector" is the foundation on which ray tracing is based. Vectors are quantities that have both magnitude (size) and direction. Vectors are used extensively in engineering and physics to express such things as force, velocity, acceleration, electric field strength, and magnetic induction. Two- and three-dimensional vectors find widespread use in many branches of science. For our purposes, a vector will always be a three-dimensional quantity with components (both magnitude and direction) in the X, Y, and Z directions. Unless explicitly stated otherwise, all vectors are assumed to have an origin at 0,0,0 and extend some distance in each of the X, Y, and Z directions. Visualize a vector as an arrow with its tail at the origin and its head at some X, Y, and Z coordinates. Vectors with an implied common origin are sometimes referred to as "positional vectors." Although vectors can be expressed and manipulated in polar coordinate form, we shall use the Cartesian coordinate system exclusively in our discussions. Because of the implied origin, only three numbers are required to specify a vector completely. In this book we shall indicate a vector with the following notation:

$$<V_X, V_Y, V_Z>$$

where V_X is the component of the vector along the X axis, V_Y is the component along the Y axis, and V_Z is the component along the Z axis. From these component values it is possible to determine the vector's magnitude and the direction it is pointing.

In the following section we discuss the vector operations that find use in ray tracing. These operations include vector addition, subtraction, scaling, normalizing, and three varieties of multiplication.

Vector Addition

The most basic operation that can be applied to vectors is vector addition. Vector addition in three dimensions is accomplished by adding together the individual components of the vectors. For example, given two three-dimensional vectors, Vector A <3,4,5> and Vector B <6,7,8>, their vector sum is <9,11,13> because:

    Sum of X components = 3 + 6 = 9
    Sum of Y components = 4 + 7 = 11
    Sum of Z components = 5 + 8 = 13

It is important to realize that vector addition is both commutative and associative. For those who do not remember what this means, just remember that the order or the grouping used to add vectors doesn't matter, the sum is always the same. Graphically, you can picture vector addition by placing the tail of one vector at the head of the other and drawing a line between them. This new line or vector represents the sum of the vectors. Vector addition is illustrated in two dimensions in Figure 2.2. While you can easily picture the addition process in two dimensions, it works exactly the same in three.

Vector Addition

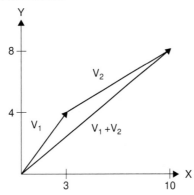

If V_1 is <3,4> and V_2 is <7,4> the sum is :

$$3 + 7 = 10$$
$$4 + 4 = 8 \qquad \text{or } <10,8>$$

Vector Subtraction

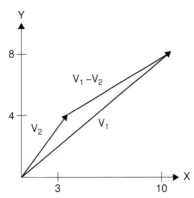

If V_1 is <10,8> and V_2 is <3,4> the difference $V_1 - V_2$ is then:

$$10 - 3 = 7$$
$$8 - 4 = 4 \qquad \text{or } <7,4>$$

$V_2 - V_1$ is then:

$$3 - 10 = -7$$
$$4 - 8 = -4 \qquad \text{or } <-7,-4>$$

a vector pointing in the opposite direction.

Vector Scaling

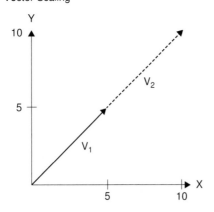

If V_1 is <5,5> and the scaling factor k is 2, the new vector V_2 is then:

$$5*2$$
$$5*2 \qquad \text{or } <10,10>$$

Figure 2.2   Vector Operations Illustrated

Vector Magnitude and Unit Vectors.

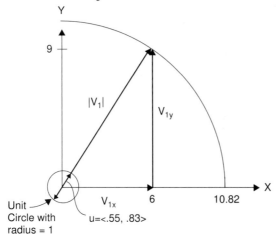

If V_1 is <6,9> its magnitude is then:

$$|V_1| = \sqrt{6^2 + 9^2} = 10.82$$

Its unit vector, u, is then:

$$u = \frac{6}{10.82} , \frac{9}{10.82}$$

$$u = <.55, .83>$$

Vector Dot Product

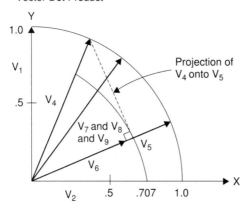

If all vectors are unit vectors:
$$V_1 \text{ dot } V_2 = |V_1| |V_2|^* \cos \theta$$

If V_1 is at 90° to V_2 then:
$$V_3 = V_1 \text{ dot } V_2 = 0$$

If V_4 is at 45° to V_5 then:
$$V_6 = V_4 \text{ dot } V_5 = |V_4| |V_5| \cos 45°$$
$$V_6 = .707$$

If V_7 is at 0° to V_8 then:
$$V_9 = V_7 \text{ dot } V_8 = |V_7| |V_8| \cos \theta°$$
$$V_9 = 1.0$$

Vector Cross Product

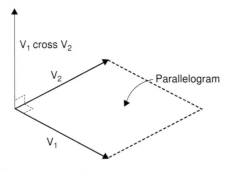

V_1 cross V_2 is perpendicular to the plane formed from V_1 and V_2.

Right-hand rule determines direction of cross product.

$$V_1 \text{ cross } V_2 <> V_2 \text{ cross } V_1$$

$$V_1 \text{ cross } V_2 = -V_2 \text{ cross } V_1$$

Figure 2.2 *(continued)*

Vector Subtraction

Vector subtraction is very similar to vector addition. In fact, you can perform vector subtraction with an addition process by adding the negative of one vector to another vector. A negative of a vector is a vector with equal magnitude but in the opposite direction (the signs of each of the component values are reversed). We, however, will perform vector subtraction by subtracting the individual components of the involved vectors, which is the same thing. To continue with the previous example, the result of subtracting Vector A <3,4,5> from Vector B <6,7,8> yields <3,3,3> because:

> Difference of X components = 6 − 3 = 3
> Difference of Y components = 7 − 4 = 3
> Difference of Z components = 8 − 5 = 3

A two-dimensional vector subtraction is shown also in Figure 2.2. To subtract two vectors graphically, we draw both vectors originating from their common origin and then draw a new resultant vector representing their difference from the head of one vector to the other. As before, the three-dimensional vector subtraction works in an identical manner to the two-dimensional example. *Note*: The order in which vectors are subtracted is important. In other words,

$$V_1 - V_2 \text{ does not equal } V_2 - V_1$$

When the order of the vectors is reversed, the magnitude of the result is the same but the direction is opposite.

Vector Scaling

Another important vector operation is scaling. When a vector is scaled, its length or magnitude (to be defined shortly) is changed by some factor, but its direction remains unaffected. Scaling is a vector multiplication operation in which a vector is multiplied by a scaler. A scaler is a nonvector quantity; a single real number. If we are given a vector, V_1, and a scale factor "k" we can write the scaled vector result V_2 as:

$$V_2 = kV_1$$

where V_2 has the magnitude of k times the magnitude of V_1. V_2 points in the same direction as V_1 if k is positive and if k is negative, in the opposite direction. To perform a scaling operation in three dimensions, we perform the scaling on each of the individual components as follows:

$$V_{2X} = kV_{1X}$$
$$V_{2Y} = kV_{1Y}$$
$$V_{2Z} = kV_{1Z}$$

If k had a value of 2 and V_1 was <3,4,5>, V_2 would equal <6,8,10>.

Vector Magnitude

Since the discussion above has continually referred to the concept of a vector's magnitude, it is time magnitude was defined. As mentioned, a vector's magnitude refers to its length. Vector magnitude is indicated symbolically as:

$$|V|$$

the absolute value symbol. This is appropriate because a vector's magnitude is always a positive quantity. Again reverting to a two-dimensional analogy as shown in Figure 2.2, it becomes obvious that a vector V is really the hypotenuse of a right triangle defined by its X and Y components. As we were taught in school, Pythagoras's theorem can be used to calculate the hypotenuse of a right triangle given the lengths of its two sides. Therefore,

$$|V| = \sqrt{(X^2 + Y^2)}$$

Extending this concept to three dimensions and assuming the vector originates at the origin, the magnitude of a three-dimensional vector is thus:

$$|V| = \sqrt{(V_X^2 + V_Y^2 + V_Z^2)}$$

If the vector is an odd one that does not originate at the origin, we can still calculate its magnitude by subtracting the vector's components from its origin as follows:

$$|V| = \sqrt{((V_X - V_{X0})^2 + (V_Y - V_{Y0})^2 + (V_Z - V_{Z0})^2)}$$

Unit Vectors and Normalization

A vector of magnitude one is called a unit vector. Unit vectors are used extensively in ray tracing (and elsewhere) to describe direction without regard for magnitude. The process for converting a vector into a unit vector is called "normalization." Normalization is accomplished by first calculating the magnitude of the vector and then dividing each vector component by that magnitude. To convert vector V $<V_X, V_Y, V_Z>$ into a unit vector (to extract its direction information), you would perform the following calculations:

$$|V| = \sqrt{(V_X^2 + V_Y^2 + V_Z^2)}$$

unit vector $U = < V_X/|V|, V_Y/|V|, V_Z/|V| >$

For example, if we had a vector $<10, -29, 13>$, its magnitude would be 33.32. When converted to a unit vector to distill its direction, its unit vector would be $<+0.30, -0.87, +0.39>$.

A unit vector swept 360 degrees traces a unit circle in two dimensions. If swept in three dimensions, a unit sphere results.

Now that we have described the basic vector mathematical operations, we can go on to the higher-order vector operations.

Vector Dot Product

Earlier, we introduced vector scaling. Scaling is one form of vector multiplication in which a vector is multiplied by a scaler quantity with the result being a vector with different magnitude. Two other vector multiplication methods find use in ray tracing. These are vector "dot product" and vector "cross product." A dot product multiplies two vectors with the result being a scaler. A cross product multiplies two vectors also but returns a new vector instead of a scaler. Let's look at the details.

A dot product indicates the degree to which two vectors point in the same direction. Mathematically, a dot product is defined as:

A dot B = |A||B| cos Theta (where 0 <= Theta <= PI)

assuming the origin of both vectors coincide. If vectors A and B are perpendicular, their dot product will equal zero, indicating that the vectors have no directional components in common. However, if vector A equals vector B, their dot product is equal to the magnitude of either vector squared. That is because the two vectors have exactly the same direction. Like vector addition, dot products are also commutative. Thus:

A dot B = B dot A

An interesting property of dot products is that if vectors A and B are unit vectors, the dot product represents the cosine of the angle between them. Under these conditions, the dot product will range in value from zero (unit vectors are perpendicular) to one (unit vectors have identical direction). Dot products are most easily calculated as the sum of products of the vectors' components, as follows:

Vector A < A_X,A_Y,A_Z >
Vector B < B_X,B_Y,B_Z >

A dot B = $A_X*B_X + A_Y*B_Y + A_Z*B_Z$

Dot products are used extensively in ray tracing during calculations of shading, as we shall see later.

Vector Cross Product

The final method of vector multiplication we are interested in is called a cross product. As mentioned, a cross product multiplies two vectors and returns a new vector. This new vector has a magnitude equal to the area of the parallelogram described by the original vectors. Three dimensions must be used to graphically illustrate cross products because the resulting vector is perpendicular to the plane described by the original two vectors. A cross product is shown in Figure 2.2. Mathematically, a cross product is defined as:

A cross B = |A||B| sin Theta (where 0 <= Theta <= PI)

The right-hand rule can be used to determine the direction of a cross product. If you point the index finger of your right hand in the direction of one of the vectors and wrap your fingers in the direction of the other, your thumb will point in the direction of the resultant vector. By studying Figure 2.2, you should see that:

A cross B does not equal B cross A

but instead:

A cross B = −B cross A

In other words, since cross products are not commutative like many of the previous vector operations, you must pay attention to the order in which vector cross products are performed. We will calculate cross products using the following algorithm:

Vector A $< A_X, A_Y, A_Z >$
Vector B $< B_X, B_Y, B_Z >$
Vector C $< C_X, C_Y, C_Z > = $ A cross B

$C_X = A_Y*B_Z - A_Z*B_Y$
$C_Y = A_Z*B_X - A_X*B_Z$
$C_Z = A_X*B_Y - A_Y*B_X$

Cross products find use in ray tracing when calculating a normal to a surface given two vectors that define a plane. In other sciences, vector cross products describe torque, angular momentum, and the flow of electromagnetic energy.

In the basic ray-tracing program described in the next chapter, we implement all vector operations with C macros. This makes the code readable while eliminating the overhead of function calls. This is a form of code optimization. These vector macros are contained in the file "vectors.h" on the companion disks and are shown for illustration in Listing 2.1. A program can utilize the vector macros by including the file of macros during the compilation process.

Listing 2.1 Vector Operation Macros

The following is the contents of the file "vectors.h."

```
/**********************************************************/
/***                   "vectors.h"                   ***/
/***            Vector Manipulation Macros            ***/
/***                      for                         ***/
/***             "A First Ray Tracer"                 ***/
/***      from the book "Practical Ray Tracing in C"  ***/
/***            written in Borland/Turbo C 2.0        ***/
/***                       by                         ***/
/***               Craig A. Lindley                   ***/
/***                                                  ***/
/***        Ver: 1.0    Last Update: 03/10/92         ***/
/**********************************************************/

/*
Various Vector manipulation MACROS
*/

/* Vector Add: a + b = c */
#define VAdd(a, b, c) {(c).X=(a).X+(b).X; (c).Y=(a).Y+(b).Y; (c).Z=(a).Z+(b).Z;}

/* Vector Subtract: c = a - b */
#define VSub(a, b, c) {(c).X=(a).X-(b).X; (c).Y=(a).Y-(b).Y; (c).Z=(a).Z-(b).Z;}

/* Vector Negate: b = -a */
#define VNegate(a, b) {(b).X=-(a).X; (b).Y=-(a).Y; (a).Z=-(a).Z;}

/* Vector Scale: b = k * a */
#define VScale(a, k, b) {(b).X=(a).X*(k); (b).Y=(a).Y*(k); (b).Z=(a).Z*(k);}
```

(continued)

Listing 2.1 *(continued)*

```
/* Vector Dot Product: c = a dot b */
#define VDot(a, b, c) {c=(a).X*(b).X+(a).Y*(b).Y+(a).Z*(b).Z;}

/* Vector Cross Product: c = a cross b */
/* c must be different than a and b */
#define VCross(a,b,c) {(c).X=(a).Y*(b).Z-(a).Z*(b).Y; \
                       (c).Y=(a).Z*(b).X-(a).X*(b).Z; \
                       (c).Z=(a).X*(b).Y-(a).Y*(b).X;}

/* Vector Length: l = len(a) */
#define VLength(a, l) {l=√((a).X*(a).X+(a).Y*(a).Y+(a).Z*(a).Z);}

/* Vector Normalize: u = |a| */
#define VNormalize(a,u) {VTemp=√((a).X*(a).X+(a).Y*(a).Y+(a).Z*(a).Z);\
                         (u).X=(a).X/VTemp;\
                         (u).Y=(a).Y/VTemp;\
                         (u).Z=(a).Z/VTemp;}
```

Viewing Geometry

Before we can begin to fire rays out into our three-dimensional universe in an attempt to create a ray-traced image, we must first set up our viewing geometry. Viewing geometry determines the relationship between the position of the viewer's eye and the objects in our image. Basically, it determines what portion of the image the eye will be able to see and with what orientation. The field of view into our universe in both the horizontal and vertical directions is also determined during view geometry setup. The viewing geometry defines the view port into the three-dimensional world. Finally, by proper selection of viewing parameters it is possible for the viewing geometry to compensate for nonsquare pixels on the computer monitor.

There are many ways to define the viewing geometry for ray-tracing programs. The one explained here is used in both of the ray tracers presented in this book. We use it because of its flexibility and simplicity. As we shall see, changes to the viewing parameters and therefore the viewing geometry can create an almost unlimited number of unique views of the objects in our three-dimensional universe. Additionally, clever manipulation of the viewing parameters can result in unusual special effects. We shall touch upon some of these special effects shortly.

As we mentioned earlier, rays are shot from the eye position through a view plane (mapped over the pixels on the computer monitor) into "object space" where they may or may not intersect objects defined in our universe. When a ray does intersect an object, the pixel that corresponds to this ray takes on the color of the object it intersected (simplistic explanation, the details will be filled in later in this chapter). The relationship between the position of the viewer's eye and the view plane can be visualized as shown in Figure 2.3(a). As shown, the viewing volume can be represented as a sideways pyramid with the view plane as its base and the eye's position as its apex. This viewing pyramid is sometimes referred to as the viewing

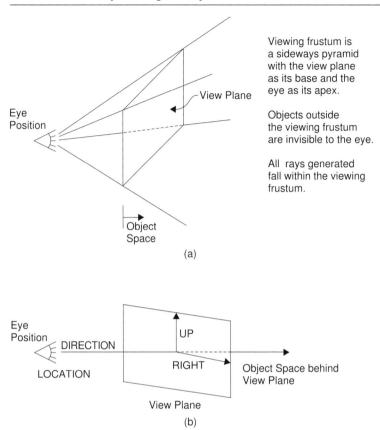

Viewing frustum is
a sideways pyramid
with the view plane
as its base and the
eye as its apex.

Objects outside
the viewing frustum
are invisible to the eye.

All rays generated
fall within the viewing
frustum.

Eye
Position

View Plane

Object
Space

(a)

Eye
Position

DIRECTION

LOCATION

UP

RIGHT

Object Space behind
View Plane

View Plane

(b)

Figure 2.3   Viewing Frustum and Viewing Geometry

frustum. Only objects or portions of objects within the frustum can be seen by the viewer's eye. Those objects or portions of objects outside the frustum are invisible to the viewer. While ray tracing is being performed, no rays are ever generated that lie outside of the viewing frustum. For this reason, object clipping is never required because the rays define the complete field of view. Other graphical techniques require clipping to keep the extents of the objects from leaving the view port. Object space, where the objects in the three-dimensional universe exist, is on the opposite side of the view plane from the viewer.

For our use, the view plane is the entire screen of the computer monitor. The three-dimensional objects visible within the frustum are projected onto the view plane (computer monitor) and the viewer sees them there as a two-dimensional representation of the three-dimensional image. The purpose of the remainder of this section is to mathematically describe the relationship between the eye position, the view plane, and the three-dimensional objects. These relationships make up the viewing geometry.

We shall use four vectors to define our viewing geometry:

1. *LOCATION*. Location defines where the eye is located in three-dimensional space. The eye's location is specified in the same coordinate space in which the objects are defined. By convention within this book, the eye's location is on the positive Z axis.
2. *DIRECTION*. Direction defines a vector from the location of the eye through the exact middle of the view plane regardless of the direction the eye is looking. Additionally, the magnitude of this vector determines the distance between the eye's position and the view plane.
3. *UP*. Up is a vector within the view plane that begins at the center (of the view plane) and points toward the top center edge of the view plane.
4. *RIGHT*. Right is a vector within the view plane that begins at the center (of the view plane) and points toward the right center edge of the view plane.

The relationships of these vectors is shown in Figure 2.3(b). Armed with these four vectors we can generate the unique rays that we require to trace our image. We will need some of the vector math discussed previously to do so.

Every raster graphics display can be thought of as an array of pixel values. The higher the spatial resolution of the display, the greater the number of pixels in the array. For PC-compatible graphics adapters, the pixels are numbered left to right in the horizontal direction and top to bottom in the vertical direction. The pixel whose location is specified by the screen coordinates (0,0) occupies the upper left corner of the display whereas the pixel at (X_{Max}, Y_{Max}) is at the lower right corner. The values of X_{Max} and Y_{Max} depend on the display mode and therefore the resolution being utilized.

For our ray-tracing activities, we require the equation of a ray that originates at the eye and passes through a specified pixel on its way to object space. The first step in this process is to convert the screen coordinates for a specified pixel into a resolution-independent number relative to the center of the display that takes into consideration that Y values increase toward the bottom of the screen. Said another way, given a pixel location specified in screen coordinates, we must convert it to a number that is relative to the center of the screen (relative screen coordinate 0,0) and resolution independent. The conversion we will use results in relative coordinates that span the range –0.5 to +0.5 in both the X and Y directions, where –0.5 in the X direction is the left side of the screen and +0.5 is the right. In the Y direction, +0.5 specifies the top of the screen. As mentioned before, 0,0 represents the center of the screen. These conversions are performed as follows:

$$Screen_X = \frac{Pixel_X - Display\ Width/2}{Display\ Width}$$

$$Screen_Y = \frac{(Display\ Height-1) - Pixel_Y - Display\ Height/2}{Display\ Height}$$

When higher-resolution images are being created, the converted coordinates of adjacent pixels become closer together while remaining within the specified range. The converted screen coordinates express the deviation of a pixel's location from the center of the screen.

Next, the horizontal and vertical fields of view are determined by scaling the Screen$_X$ and Screen$_Y$ values by the UP and RIGHT vectors, respectively. As the magnitude of UP and/or RIGHT increase, each pixel will contain more image information per pixel in the corresponding direction, resulting in a larger viewing frustum. Because the UP and RIGHT vectors lie in the view plane (coplanar vectors), we add them together to determine the location where the ray from the eye's LOCATION would pierce the view plane. The final step in this ray-generation process is to add the DIRECTION vector to the vector calculated immediately above. This results in the ray we desire from the eye position through the screen into object space. Of course, the ray's direction should be converted to a unit vector, and the ray's origin must be set to the eye's location before the ray is used in any subsequent calculations. Every ray shot into the three-dimensional universe is generated in this manner.

Most ray-tracing programs generate an image a pixel at a time in standard raster order from left to right and top to bottom. This is not a requirement, it is just expedient. This is usually accomplished by using nested loops; the outer loop for the row or Y value and the inner loop for the column or X value. The X and Y values at any point in time would be subjected to the coordinate transform described above and a ray through that point would be generated. This ray would be checked for intersection with all objects in object space. (We will postpone the discussion of ray/object intersection until later in this chapter.)

As hinted at above, this model for viewing geometry is very flexible. It is so because it doesn't mandate that the UP, RIGHT, and DIRECTION vectors are at right angles to each other (mutually orthogonal). These vectors can be used in expected ways with predictable results or in unexpected ways that distort the resultant view. Some rather bizarre spatial distortion effects are possible by manipulating the UP and RIGHT vectors. When used in their normal manner, these vectors (along with the magnitude of the DIRECTION vector) control the horizontal and vertical field of view and the object space orientation, and they can be used to correct for aspect ratio problems.

A narrow field of view (the magnitude of the UP and RIGHT vectors less than one) results in a telephoto-like view of object space. Conversely, magnitudes greater than one result in a wide angle view of things. The ratio of the magnitudes of these two vectors is also important. When display modes that exhibit square pixels are utilized, the ratio of these vectors determines the field of view, as discussed. In this case, their ratio should be one. If a display mode is utilized with nonsquare pixels, modifying the UP and RIGHT ratio can correct the spatial distortion that results. In other words, square pixels can be simulated on a display that has nonsquare pixels. This means that a displayed sphere that would appear ellipsoidal when displayed with nonsquare pixels will in fact look round as expected. VGA video mode 13 hex (320 by 200 resolution with 256 colors) is an example of a video mode infected with nonsquare pixels (all EGA graphics modes suffer from the same problem). On a 13-inch monitor, a mode 13 hex pixel would be approximately 0.027 inches wide and 0.036 inches tall. If a sphere is rendered in this mode without correction, it will appear flattened vertically—wider than it is tall. To compensate for this phenomena, you can lengthen the RIGHT vector from the normal magnitude of 1.00 to 1.3333 (0.036″/0.027″ is 1.333). Now, more image information will be contained per pixel in the horizontal direction than in the vertical direction and the spatial aberration will disappear.

The magnitude of the DIRECTION vector also figures into the calculation of the field of view. For this reason, you can use the UP and RIGHT vectors for aspect ratio correction if required and use the magnitude of the DISTANCE vector to control field of view.

You can also produce other effects by manipulating the UP and RIGHT vectors. To turn an image completely upside down, the UP vector, which is usually specified as <0 1 0>, is changed to <0 –1 0>. Along the same vein, image left and right can be reversed by changing the RIGHT vector, usually <1 0 0> (or <1.333 0 0>) to <–1 0 0> (or <–1.333 0 0>).

Much of the time you spend designing ray-traced imagery will be spent fine tuning the viewing geometry to get the exact view you desire. You will have to go through much experimentation before you will feel completely comfortable with the interaction of the viewing parameters. After a time, however, it will become intuitive. We will take up viewing geometry again in the next chapter and in Part Two of this book.

Parametric Equations of Rays

As the name ray tracing suggests, the ray is the basis for this technique. A ray is an extension of the vector discussed earlier. A ray has both a direction and an origin. As you will recall, a positional vector had an implied origin at 0,0,0 of our three-dimensional coordinate system. A ray has a stated origin not necessarily at the coordinate system origin. A ray is made up of two vectors: one describing its direction and one describing its origin. Given a starting point (the ray's origin) and the ray's direction, it is possible to calculate the trajectory of a ray given only how long the ray has been moving in the specified direction. If we indicate time as "t," the trajectory of a ray becomes:

Trajectory of Ray R = direction * t + origin

which more mathematically is described as:

$R(t) = R_d*t + R_o$ for $t > 0$

with R(t) describing a set of points that make up the ray's trajectory. Of course, this equation must be stated in three dimensions to be of interest to us. Thus, the equation of a point through which a ray passes in three dimensions as a function of t becomes:

$$P_X = X_d*t + X_o$$
$$P_Y = Y_d*t + Y_o$$
$$P_Z = Z_d*t + Z_o$$

where the ray's direction is described by the vector $<X_d,Y_d,Z_d>$ and its origin by the vector $<X_o,Y_o,Z_o>$. We will use this explicit form of the parametric ray equation (parametric because it is a function of parameter t) throughout this text. *Note*: You should use unit vectors for the direction of a ray during all calculations.

As you might have surmised, ray tracing involves a lot of checks to determine if rays and objects intersect. Using the above parametric equation of a ray it is relatively simple to determine if an intersection occurs between simple shapes (shapes defined by quadratic equations, for example) and a ray. In the ray tracer presented in the next chapter, intersection checks between rays and spheres and rays and planes will be required. For that reason, we present those intersection calculations below. Following that, we present a general solution for ray/quadric surface intersection, even though it is not utilized in the example ray tracer. *Note:* Any surface whose equation is a quadratic in variables X, Y, and Z is called a quadric surface. For other ray/shapes intersection calculations, see the book *An Introduction to Ray Tracing.* Information about this book appears in the "Further Reading" section of Part Three.

Ray/Sphere Intersection Calculations

To determine if a ray intersects a sphere, the parametric ray equation is substituted into the equation of a sphere and then solved. This results in a second order quadratic equation that can easily be solved. To see how this is done, consider an equation for a sphere S as:

$$(X_s-X_c)^2 + (Y_s-Y_c)^2 + (Z_s-Z_c)^2 = Radius^2$$

which describes a sphere as a collection of surface points X_s, Y_s, Z_s centered at X_c, Y_c, Z_c with radius of Radius. What we need to determine is if our ray intersects this sphere at its surface. To do this, let us substitute the explicit form of the ray equation into the sphere equation as follows:

$$(X_d*t + X_o - X_c)^2 + (Y_d*t + Y_o - Y_c)^2 + (Z_d*t + Z_o - Z_c)^2 = Radius^2$$

A half page of algebra can easily prove that the above equation reduces to:

$$A*t^2 + B*t + C = 0$$

where:

A= $X_d^2 + Y_d^2 + Z_d^2$ which equals one, because the ray's direction vector was normalized (i.e., it was a unit vector).

B= $2*(X_d*(X_o-X_c) + Y_d*(Y_o-Y_c) + Z_d*(Z_o-Z_c))$

C= $(X_o-X_c)^2 + (Y_o-Y_c)^2 + (Z_o-Z_c)^2 - Radius^2$

You probably recognize the above equation as a quadratic equation with roots that can be determined with the formula:

$$\frac{-B \pm \sqrt{B^2 - 4*A*C}}{2*A}$$

Given the fact that A equals one, we can simplify and solve the above equation as follows:

$$t_1 = \frac{-B + \sqrt{B^2 - 4*C}}{2}$$

$$t_2 = \frac{-B - \sqrt{B^2 - 4*C}}{2}$$

where the quantity:

$$B^2 - 4*C$$

is referred to as the determinant. If the determinant is negative, denoting imaginary roots, the ray is presumed to miss the sphere completely. If real roots (positive roots) are returned, the smallest positive root determines the closest intersection between the ray and the sphere—the intersection closest to the eye's LOCATION. This is the intersection we are interested in. If you think about it, only three possible ray/sphere scenarios exist:

1. The ray misses the sphere completely.
2. The ray intersects the sphere tangentially which results in only a single root.
3. The ray passes through the sphere. That is, it enters and then exits. This results in two positive roots, one smaller than the other.

Remember, the solution to this equation is the time parameter t in the ray equation. When t is known, it can be substituted back into the ray equation to find the coordinates of point P, the point of intersection between the ray and the sphere. Once you have established the point of intersection, another important item you must determine is the surface normal at the point of intersection. A normal is a vector that generally points away from the surface in such a manner as to be perpendicular to some point on the surface. A surface normal is used to help determine the optical properties at the point of intersection. How a surface normal is used as part of the ray-tracing process will be discussed later. For now, we will concentrate on how the surface normal for a sphere is calculated.

Consider the ray/sphere intersection shown in Figure 2.4. It shows a ray striking a sphere at point P. To calculate the normal N at P we simply subtract the coordinates of point P on the surface from the coordinates of the sphere's center. With this done, we have created a new ray with its origin at the center of the sphere and extending to the sphere's surface at point P. Since only the direction of this normal is what we are interested in, we will convert the direction portion of this ray to a unit vector. We can do this by dividing each component of this vector by its magnitude. We already know the magnitude of the vector because we have the radius of the sphere. Thus, the normal calculations are as follows:

$$X_N = \frac{X_P - X_C}{\text{Radius}}$$

$$Y_N = \frac{Y_P - Y_C}{\text{Radius}}$$

$$Z_N = \frac{Z_P - Z_C}{\text{Radius}}$$

You may be wondering why our normal vector does not originate at point P and point perpendicularly out into space instead of originating at the sphere's center and just reaching the sphere's surface. While it is helpful to visualize a normal that points from the surface outward, the subsequent calculation we will perform depends only on the direction of the normal, not its origin. For this reason it is unnecessary to translate the normal's origin from the center of the sphere to the surface at point P. It is important, however, that the normal points the way it does—out of the sphere. This direction is assumed during all further calculations.

As we have seen, only the specifications of the ray (its origin and direction) and the specifications of the sphere (its location and radius) are required to determine ray/sphere intersection. Given that an intersection exists, the surface normal at the point of intersection is easily calculated.

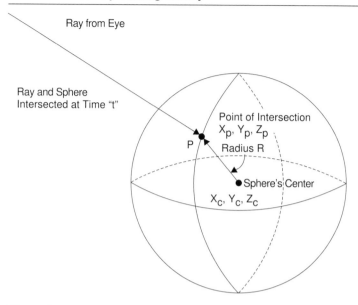

Ray from Eye

Ray and Sphere
Intersected at Time "t"

Point of Intersection
X_p, Y_p, Z_p

P

Radius R

Sphere's Center
X_c, Y_c, Z_c

Figure 2.4   Ray/Sphere Intersection

Ray/Plane Intersection Calculations

The next primitive quadric shape we shall consider is the plane. A plane is a geometric entity that divides the space through which it passes in two. A plane, unlike a sphere, continues on infinitely; that is, it is unbounded. A sphere in contrast is bounded. The method used to calculate ray/plane intersection is very similar to that used for ray/sphere intersection. We begin with the equation of a plane, which is defined as:

$$AX + BY + CZ + D = 0$$

In total, four numbers define a plane: A, B, C, and D. The first three of these numbers, A, B, and C, define a unit vector normal to the plane. By definition, therefore, $A^2 + B^2 + C^2$ must equal one. *Note*: A vector that is normal to a plane at one point is normal to the plane at all points. The factor D in the above equation defines the distance of the plane from the coordinate system origin at 0,0,0. To calculate the intersection we again substitute the explicit form of the ray parametric equation into the plane equation and solve again for t as follows:

$$A*(X_d*t + X_o) + B*(Y_d*t + Y_o) + C*(Z_d*t + Z_o) + D = 0$$

then:

$$t = \frac{-(A*X_o + B*Y_o + C*Z_o + D)}{A*X_d + B*Y_d + C*Z_d}$$

If the denominator of this equation is equal to zero, the ray and the plane are parallel or lie in the same plane, and no intersection occurs; calculations can stop at this point. If the denominator is nonzero, calculations must continue. If the denominator is greater than zero, the normal of the plane is pointing in the same direction as the ray and may have to be reversed for later use.

The solution to this equation, the parameter t, is calculated in a straightforward manner as it is a linear equation with all variables known. A, B, C, and D define the plane, whereas X_d, Y_d, Z_d, X_o, Y_o, and Z_o are defined by the ray. If t is less than zero, no intersection occurs and calculations can again be halted. If t is a positive number, an intersection has been found. The point of intersection is then calculated by substituting the value of t back into the ray equation and solving for P. As mentioned above, the surface normal for the plane may not be pointing in the appropriate direction. Usually we want the normal to point back toward the origin of the ray. The backwards normal condition is indicated when the denominator of the equation above evaluates to a number greater than zero. To reverse the direction of the normal it must be negated. Vector negation was discussed previously.

General Ray/Quadric Surface Intersection Calculations

Even though both the sphere and the plane are examples of quadric surfaces, the solutions given above did not treat them in a general manner as such. Instead, each solution was unique and somewhat optimized for the shape involved; not general purpose at all. In this section, we present a generalized solution to the complete family of quadric surfaces. Using this approach it is possible to ray trace any of the quadric surfaces, including the sphere, the plane, the ellipsoid, the cylinder, the cone, the hyperboloid, and the paraboloid. Due to the generality of this approach, you can handle sphere and plane intersections using the quadric solution presented, although the previously presented solutions would probably execute faster because they are less complex.

The generalized quadratic formula describing the quadric family of surfaces is given as:

$$A*X^2 + B*Y^2 + C*Z^2 + D*X*Y + E*X*Z + F*Y*Z + G*X + H*Y + I*Z + J = 0$$

This formula implies that all possible quadric surfaces at all possible locations in space and all possible orientations can be defined with just ten numbers (defining parameters), A through J. As you shall see shortly, this is a very powerful concept.

To proceed, we again substitute the parametric equation of a ray into the generalized quadratic equation above. After a couple of pages of algebra, we can reduce the equation to the form:

$$A_c*t^2 + B_c*t + C_c = 0$$

where:

$$A_c = A*X_d^2 + B*Y_d^2 + C*Z_d^2 + D*X_d*Y_d + E*X_d*Z_d + F*Y_d*Z_d$$

$$B_c = 2*A*X_o*X_d + 2*B*Y_o*Y_d + 2*C*Z_o*Z_d + D*X_o*Y_d + D*Y_o*X_d + E*X_o*Z_d + \qquad E*Z_o*X_d$$
$$+ F*Y_o*Z_d + F*Z_o*Y_d + G*X_d + H*Y_d + I*Z_d$$

$$C_c = A*X_o^2 + B*Y_o^2 + C*Z_o^2 + D*X_o*Y_o + E*X_o*Z_o + F*Y_o*Z_o + G*X_o + H*Y_o +$$
$$I*Z_o + J$$

We then use the determinant $B_c^2 - 4*A_c*C_c$ to determine if an intersection exists. Simply, if this value is less than zero, no intersection exists between the specified ray and the quadric surface and the calculations can be terminated at this point. If a solution does exist, it is found by solving the quadratic formula for the two possible roots t_1 and t_2.

$$t_1 = \frac{-B_c - \sqrt{B_c^2 - 4*A_c*C_c}}{2*A_c}$$

$$t_2 = \frac{-B_c + \sqrt{B_c^2 - 4*A_c*C_c}}{2*A_c}$$

The second root, t_2, needs to be solved only if t_1 is less than zero. The root we are interested in is the smallest positive one.

The calculation of the normal for the generalized quadric surface requires a bit of calculus to prove. Since this is outside the scope of this discussion we will not describe it here. Suffice it to say that the normal is the partial derivative of the generalized quadratic formula given at the start of this section with respect to X, Y, and Z. In other words:

$$N_X = 2*A*X + D*Y + E*Z + G$$
$$N_Y = 2*B*Y + D*X + F*Z + H$$
$$N_Z = 2*C*Z + E*X + F*Y + I$$

To calculate the normal, we must know the coordinates of the point of intersection between the ray and the quadric surface. Since we now have the solution for the parameter t (either t_1 or t_2), we can substitute it back into the parametric ray equation and solve as follows:

$$P_X = X_d*t + X_o$$
$$P_Y = Y_d*t + Y_o$$
$$P_Z = Z_d*t + Z_o$$

By substituting the values of P_X, P_Y, and P_Z for X, Y, and Z in the normal equation above and providing the values of A, B, C, D, E, F, G, H, and I from the equation of the quadric surface being used, we can calculate the surface normal. *Please note*: The calculated surface normal will not be normalized. It must be converted to a unit vector before it is used in any subsequent calculations. Also, as was cautioned above, the calculated surface normal may be pointing in the direction of the ray instead of back toward the origin of the ray as is usually required. If the dot product of the unit normal and the ray's direction vector is greater than zero, this is the case. Under these conditions, the normal should be negated to point in the correct direction just as before.

Quadric Shape Definitions

Ten numbers, A through J, are used to define all of the quadric surfaces. Even fewer numbers are required if we make a few simplifying assumptions about the quadric shapes. If we assume, for example, that all surfaces are created at the origin (0,0,0) and that all are of size one (sphere's radius is one, cylinder's radius is one, a cone's a, b, and c axes' lengths are one, etc.), the quadric surfaces can be defined as shown in Figure 2.5.

Surface	Implemented Equation	Parameters									
		A	B	C	D	E	F	G	H	I	J
Sphere	$X^2 + Y^2 + Z^2 - 1 = 0$	1	1	1	0	0	0	0	0	0	-1
Cylinder along											
X	$Y^2 + Z^2 - 1 = 0$	0	1	1	0	0	0	0	0	0	-1
Y	$X^2 + Z^2 - 1 = 0$	1	0	1	0	0	0	0	0	0	-1
Z	$X^2 + Y^2 - 1 = 0$	1	1	0	0	0	0	0	0	0	-1
Cone along											
X	$-X^2 + Y^2 + Z^2 = 0$	-1	1	1	0	0	0	0	0	0	0
Y	$X^2 - Y^2 + Z^2 = 0$	1	-1	1	0	0	0	0	0	0	0
Z	$X^2 + Y^2 - Z^2 = 0$	1	1	-1	0	0	0	0	0	0	0
Plane in											
YZ axis	$X = 0$	0	0	0	0	0	0	1	0	0	0
XZ axis	$Y = 0$	0	0	0	0	0	0	0	1	0	0
XY axis	$Z = 0$	0	0	0	0	0	0	0	0	1	0
Paraboloid along											
X	$Y^2 + Z^2 - X = 0$	0	1	1	0	0	0	-1	0	0	0
Y	$X^2 + Z^2 - Y = 0$	1	0	1	0	0	0	0	-1	0	0
Z	$X^2 + Y^2 - Z = 0$	1	1	0	0	0	0	0	0	-1	0
(one sheet) Hyperboloid along											
X	$-X^2 + Y^2 + Z^2 - 1 = 0$	-1	1	1	0	0	0	0	0	0	-1
Y	$X^2 - Y^2 + Z^2 - 1 = 0$	1	-1	1	0	0	0	0	0	0	-1
Z	$X^2 + Y^2 - Z^2 - 1 = 0$	1	1	-1	0	0	0	0	0	0	-1

Figure 2.5   Quadric Surfaces—Equations and Parameters

Sometimes it is desirable to define a quadric surface (an ellipsoid or hyperboloid of two sheets, for example) with specific location and specific geometrical properties instead of defining it with the assumptions listed above. The process of determining the ten defining parameters, A through J, is a bit more complex, but it is still possible to do with the procedure outlined below. The following steps illustrate how this is done.

1. From a math reference book, get the defining equation of the quadric shape you desire to model. For example, the equation for an ellipsoid centered at the origin is:

$$\frac{X^2}{a^2} + \frac{Y^2}{b^2} + \frac{Z^2}{c^2} = 1$$

This equation was taken from *Calculus and Analytic Geometry* by George B. Thomas, Jr. The letters a, b, and c represent the axes of the ellipsoid in the X, Y, and Z directions, respectively. To displace the ellipsoid from the origin, the defining equation is modified as follows:

$$\frac{(X-X_c)^2}{a^2} + \frac{(Y-Y_c)^2}{b^2} + \frac{(Z-Z_c)^2}{c^2} = 1$$

2. Substitute into the above equation your specific values for X_c, Y_c, and Z_c, the location of the ellipsoid's center, and values for the axes a, b, and c.
3. Simplify the resulting equation as far as possible. For the ellipsoid example, the simplified result will look something like:

$$4*X^2 + Y^2 + 9*Z^2 - 48*X - 18*Y + 36*Z - 315 = 0$$

4. Match the coefficients in the equation directly above to the defining parameters in the generalized quadratic equation listed previously. This pairing results in A = 4, B = 1, C = 9, D = 0, E = 0, F = 0, G = −48, H = −18, I = 36, and J = −315 for the ellipsoid example.
5. Use these defining parameters to define your ellipsoid quadric shape. By the way, these ten numbers define an ellipsoid positioned at 6, 9, −2 with axes of 12, 24, and 8, respectively.

Other quadric shapes can be defined just as easily.

Shading

In the previous sections of this chapter, we have discussed view geometry (which allows us to control what is within the field of view of the eye), eye ray generation (which uses the view geometry to construct rays originating at the eye's position that pierce the view plane and extend into the three-dimensional object space), and ray/object intersections (which allow us to determine what, if anything, our eye rays intersect). The final missing piece of the ray-tracing puzzle is "shading." Shading is the process by which color is assigned to the objects the eye ray intersects and how that color information is interpreted for display on a computer monitor.

A bit of warning may be necessary here. Shading concepts are the most complex part of ray tracing. The shading model used to describe the interaction of light with surfaces of various materials and attributes can be very complex indeed. This is especially true if the shading model takes into consideration the frequency of the light and the angles of intersection. The complexity of shading points out how hard it is to simulate (model) nature within a computer. Light/surface intersection has many subtle properties that must be simulated accurately for an image to appear real. The human eye/brain system uses these subtle cues to make determinations about what it is looking at. When the cues are missing, the brain can sometimes fill in but a loss of realism is perceived. Luckily, some very clever means of simulating light surface interactions have been developed that are much less costly in computer terms to implement than a full simulation. Some of these techniques are based on geometric optics and physics while others were arrived at empirically. The Phong specular reflection model is an example of a shading technique arrived at empirically. We will discuss Phong shading shortly.

Please keep in mind what shading is and what it is not. The purpose of shading is to calculate the color and intensity of light leaving a surface and traveling back to the eye for subsequent viewing. The color of the light perceived by the eye is a combination of the object's surface color, the color of any light reflected by the object, and the color of any light transmitted through the object. Shading is not hidden surface removal. The fact that an eye ray always intersects the object closest to it means that shading will be applied only to surfaces guaranteed to be in the foreground and visible to the viewer. Shading is never applied to obscured objects or obscured portions of objects—obscured, of course, from the viewer's perspective.

As if it isn't bad enough that calculating shading for a scene is difficult and imprecise, after the calculations are done, we find that current PC computer graphics systems don't have the full gamut of colors necessary to display what was calculated. We must make trade-offs in the shading process and even more in the display process. We can partially remedy the limited color availability during display with color quantization, which is discussed in depth in Chapter 4. (See Chapter 4 for all further discussions of the display side of the shading problem.)

To make ray-tracing programs independent of display hardware, colors are usually specified in RGB (Red, Green, and Blue) coordinates with each color component expressed as a floating-point number in the range zero to one. This allows a near infinite number of color possibilities. A color component value of zero indicates darkness (no intensity), whereas a value of one indicates maximum intensity (independent of the actual values used by a graphics display system for minimum and maximum intensity levels). The RGB color system is an additive system such that the absence of color, as indicated by R=G=B=0, indicates black, and colors are built by adding color component values. For example, R=1 G=B=0 specifies pure red of maximum intensity. All colors that have equal color component values represent a shade of gray. Maximum and equal color component values of R=G=B=1 represent white. An RGB color value of I*R,I*G,I*B when I is between zero and one is considered a shade of the color RGB of intensity I. Therefore, shades of gray can also be considered shades of the color white. The additive nature of the RGB color system is utilized throughout our description of the shading process.

As we discuss the shading process, keep in mind that as we trace light rays within a scene to arrive at a representative pixel color and intensity for display, both the direction of the rays and the surface properties must be taken into consideration. The meaning and significance of this statement will hopefully become clear as the discussion proceeds.

When light rays (photons of light, actually) interact with a surface of an object, shading tells us how much light is passed or "propagated" from the surface back toward the viewer. Propagation can be broken down into two major components: specular propagation and diffuse propagation. Specularly propagated light is directionally oriented, whereas diffusely propagated light is light that goes equally in all directions with no relationship to the incident light's direction. Both specular and diffuse propagation must be thought about in terms of reflection and transmission. Reflection is what happens when you look in the mirror or admire your face reflected in a newly waxed automobile. Transmission is what happens when you look through a transparent or semi-transparent surface. The light that arrives at your eye is transmitted through the surface of the object. Looking through a glass window or staring at a fish in a clear stream are examples of transmission of light. In total, therefore, there are four light propagation possibilities to consider in a complete shading model. These are sometimes referred to in the graphics literature as the four light transport modes.

To complicate matters further, all four of these transport mechanisms should be considered both for light coming directly from a light source and for light coming from other objects within a scene. In total then, eight sources of light could be considered when trying to decide the color of each and every pixel in a ray-traced image. As you might expect, this would be exceedingly time-consuming. The Hall shading model described in *An Introduction to Ray Tracing* attempts to take most of the eight light propagation modes into consideration and is therefore very complex. Most ray-tracing programs make simplifications to this type of shading model. These simplifications trade off computation time for accuracy. The visual result of these simplifications is an image that is not exact, but close enough for general use. Some of the simplifications typically made to complex shading models are:

1. *The removal of frequency-dependent terms.* In real light/surface interaction, the frequency of the light factors into how the light plays on an object. A prism, for example, works because light bends differing amounts, depending on its frequency components. The omission of frequency-dependent terms from the shader equation means prisms cannot be modeled and other subtle lighting effects will be lost.

2. *Interobject reflections and transmissions ignored.* Interobject reflections and transmissions aid in the illumination of most scenes. Because many objects reflect light diffusely, they contribute some undirected light to other objects in a scene. Some of this light finds its way back to the eye and is therefore visible to the viewer. How best to handle this contribution to scene illumination is still a matter of much debate. One way to handle the calculations for indirect illumination within a scene is through a technique called "radiosity." Radiosity uses the laws of conservation of energy to figure out how much energy in terms of light would be radiated from a surface. The techniques of radiosity are beyond the scope of this book and are still for the most part research issues.

    Because of the difficulty involved in calculating indirect illumination from other objects within a scene, most basic shading models replace the interobject contributions to lighting with an "ambient light" term. Without something to replace the indirect illumination naturally occurring in a scene, all objects not directly illuminated by a light source would be black and generally invisible. The incorporation of an ambient term provides a small amount of light within a scene, which makes obscured objects visible and therefore simulates, very crudely, light reflected and transmitted by other objects.

3. *Distance.* As most everyone (technical people, anyway) is aware, light traveling through space is attenuated as the square of the distance. That is, light traveling twice as far is one-quarter as intense. Some shading models do not take the distance between the light source and objects nor the distance between objects that provided reflected light to another object into consideration. While this sounds like a serious omission, it really doesn't matter as long as all objects within a scene are placed a similar distance from the light sources. When distance is taken into consideration by dividing the calculated light intensities by the distance squared, the lighting effects seem somewhat harsh. For this reason, the $1/d^2$ is often softened to $1/(d+d_o)$, where d_o is a suitably chosen constant less than d. The visual effect of this minor change to reality is much more pleasing to look at. However, the shaders used in most basic ray-tracing programs ignore distance completely.

With all of these items left out of the shading model, you may be asking yourself what remains. Of course, this varies from implementation to implementation but in general most basic shaders consider:

- Ambient lighting
- Diffuse reflection
- Specular reflection
- Specular transmission (refraction)

We discuss the contribution of each of these light transport mechanisms below.

Ambient Lighting

As mentioned, ambient lighting is a contrivance that is meant to compensate for interobject indirect illumination. This method appears natural without requiring excessive calculations. Rays of ambient light within a scene can be envisioned to strike an object's surface from all directions and reflect off in all directions. The intensity of the ambient light reflected to the eye is independent of the direction to the viewer or the direction to the light source(s). Ambient lighting contribution can be calculated in one of two ways. First, by application of the formula:

$$I_a = k_a * I_l$$

where I_l is the intensity of the ambient light source and k_a is the ambient absorbation constant. The constant k_a determines how much of the ambient light will be reflected from the surface. The problem with this method of calculation is that the ambient light reflected from an object's surface is a function of the light's color, not the object's color. You can get a more realistic effect by using a different ambient light calculation. In this case:

$$I_a = k_a * I_o$$

where I_o represents the color of the object's surface and k_a determines how much of the surface's color should be visible with ambient lighting. A typical value of k_a is 0.4. With this method, objects within a scene illuminated only by ambient light will show a darker intensity (or shade) of their true color.

The equation above is for monochromatic (single color) light. To make use of it and the other equations within this section, you must apply it to all three RGB color components separately. The color version of this formula would then become:

$$I_{aRed} = k_{aRed} * I_{oRed}$$
$$I_{aGreen} = k_{aGreen} * I_{oGreen}$$
$$I_{aBlue} = k_{aBlue} * I_{oBlue}$$

More simplistic shaders make the absorbation constants k_{aRed}, k_{aGreen}, and k_{aBlue} equal, even though it is well known that most surface materials absorb differing frequencies of light (different colors of light) at different levels. Reality notwithstanding, this simplification is generally made.

Diffuse Reflection

Diffusely reflected light reflects in all directions with equal intensity. The theory that explains this phenomena is that as a photon of light hits a surface with diffuse reflective properties, it is temporarily absorbed by the surface. The increase in energy experienced by the atoms in the surface is momentarily heightened but cannot be sustained. Eventually the surface gives up a photon to lower its energy level back to a stable state. The photon emitted from the surface takes off in a random direction unrelated to the angle of incidence of the incoming photon. The contribution of diffusely reflected light to a surface will appear the same regardless of the position of the viewer. For this reason, the direction to the viewer's eye does not enter into the calculations. What is important is the relationship between a ray from the surface to the light source and the surface normal. The amplitude of the diffusely reflected light is proportional to the cosine of the angle between the incident light and the normal. This relationship is referred to as "Lambert's Law." If the light ray L and the normal N are both unit vectors, the cosine of the angle between them is their dot product. Further, if N dot L is less than or equal to zero, the surface faces away from the light source and therefore receives no contribution of light from it.

Since not all of the light that impinges a surface is diffusely reflected, another absorbation constant, k_d, is introduced. Therefore, the monochromatic equation for the contribution of diffuse reflection to the total shading equation is:

$$I_d = I_l * k_d * \cos \text{Theta} = I_l * k_d * N \text{ dot } L$$

For scenes illuminated with multiple light sources, the sum of all diffuse contributions (from all light sources) should be used. Multiple light sources are treated as if each source were the only light source within a scene and the individual contributions from each are summed together.

Just as before, the monochromatic equation above needs to be solved three times to be used with the RGB color model. Also, k_d would have different values of absorbation for each of the three colors. In practice, many shaders will simulate the differing values of k_d by introducing the color of the surface being shaded into the equation as follows:

$$k_{dRed} = k_d' * I_{oRed}$$
$$k_{dGreen} = k_d' * I_{oGreen}$$
$$k_{dBlue} = k_d' * I_{oBlue}$$

where k_d' is a single absorbation constant used in all three cases and I_o is the color of an object's surface. Intuitively, this makes sense in that the amount of light absorbed by a surface depends on both the color of the light and the color of the surface. For example, if white light is diffusely reflected off a red surface, the reflected light will appear red because the blue and green components of the light will have been absorbed (filtered out) by the surface. By essentially multiplying the color of the light by the color of the surface in these calculations, the filtering effects work as would be expected.

Specular Reflection

Specular reflection is exhibited by smooth surfaces. If a surface is smooth enough, specular highlights will appear. A specular highlight appears on the surface of the object as a small bright patch of light that is the color of the light being reflected. The smoother the surface, the tighter the highlight appears. The highlights do not take on the color of the surface because the photons of light that impinge the surface are not absorbed and re-emitted by the surface as they were in the case of diffuse reflection. Instead, they immediately bounce off the hard surface at an angle of reflection equal to the angle of incidence; it works just like a billiard ball bouncing off the side of a billiard table or a rock thrown at a shallow angle into a still lake.

Unlike diffuse reflections, the contribution of specular reflection to a surface's color as perceived by a viewer is highly directional. To understand how specular reflections work, you must consult Figure 2.6(a). Specular highlights are caused by a light source being reflected off a surface directly into the viewer's eye. The angle between the reflection of the light source (R) and the ray to the viewer (V) determines how much of a contribution to a surface's color specular reflections make. When the vectors R and V coincide exactly, the maximum effect occurs. As these vectors diverge in direction, the effect is diminished. As before, the dot product is used to determine how closely R and V coincide, because it is the angle between them that interests us. *Note*: For the dot product comparison to work, both R and V must be unit vectors. But how is R arrived at? For a given ray/object intersection we will have the point of intersection P and the view vector V. From these, we can calculate the surface normal N by knowing the type of object intersected. We then generate the ray L from the point of intersection to light source L. Given this information and the fact that vectors R, N, and L would all be in the same plane and the fact that the angle of incidence equals the angle of reflection, the reflected unit vector R can be calculated from (I'll spare you the algebra):

$$R = 2*N*(L \text{ dot } N) - L$$

assuming the vector orientations shown in the figure.

Now that we have both vectors V and R, we can determine the maximum intensity of the specular highlight for the point being shaded. But as mentioned before, the size of the highlight is a function of surface smoothness, not just the geometry of the viewer and the reflection angles. Typically, the Phong reflection model is used to adjust for this phenomena. With the Phong model, a new factor n is introduced, which characterizes the surface material. The larger the value of n, the higher polish a surface has. If n equaled infinity, the surface would be perfectly smooth. Incorporating the Phong model into the equation for specular reflection yields the following:

$$I_s = I_l * k_s * (R \text{ dot } V)^n$$

A large value of n makes the specular highlight fall off very quickly as the eye ray direction diverges from the reflected light. This causes tighter specular highlights on smoother surfaces, as we expect. Note that the Phong model is based not on physics but on empirical observations. The visual result is very close to what occurs in nature but requires much less computation to arrive at. The specular absorbation constant, k_s, is a function of the surface material and should be broken into three constants for each of the RGB calculations. In more complex shading models, these absorbation constants would vary with the angle of incidence of the light rays.

A model for specular reflection that is based on theory and not empirical data is the "Torrance-Sparrow" model. This model is based on the concept that all surfaces are made up of

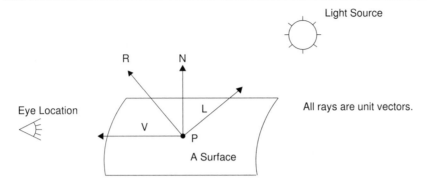

V is a ray to the eye.
N is the surface normal.
L is a ray to the light source.
R is a ray reflected from the light source.
P is the point of intersection.

(a)

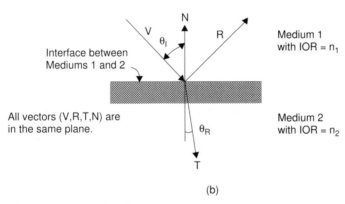

(b)

Figure 2.6 Shading Rays

"microfacets." These microfacets are tiny, flat, perfect reflectors. In rough surfaces, these microfacets are positioned randomly such that incident light would bounce around on the surface for quite a while before being reflected off. This would result in the reflected light taking on more of the object's surface color. Highly polished surfaces would have the microfacets aligned such that incident light would reflect immediately off the surface and its color would remain unaffected by the surface color. Intuitively, you can understand how calculating these effects would be more time-consuming then the Phong technique just presented.

Specular Transmission

The final light transport mechanism that we will examine is specular transmission, which is the phenomena whereby light arrives at a point on the surface of an object by passing through the object. For this to happen, of course, the object cannot be opaque to light; it must be somewhat transparent for the light to travel through it. When we look through transparent objects we find that in general the light rays will have bent. This phenomena is called "refraction" and is observed wherever light passes between mediums of differing density. The light bends because the speed of light through the differing media changes. The amount of bend is related to the difference in density of the media involved. This is the effect you see when you view fish in water. The fish are never really where you think they are because the light rays are bent when you see them.

To describe refraction mathematically, we must assign to each medium an "index of refraction," or IOR. The IOR measures the speed of light through the media in relation to the speed through an empty vacuum. Air has an IOR of almost exactly one. Water has an IOR of 1.333 and glass can have an IOR in the range of approximately 1.46 to 1.66, depending on its formulation. The bending of the light happens at the interface or junction between the two media involved. See Figure 2.6(b). "Snell's Law" relates the angle of incidence to the angle of refraction as follows:

$$\frac{\sin \text{Theta}_I}{\sin \text{Theta}_R} = \frac{n_2}{n_1} = n_{21}$$

The direction of the transmitted ray T can then be defined as:

$$T = n_{12}*V + (n_{12}*C - \sqrt{(1 + (n_{12}{}^2*(C^2 - 1)))}) * N$$

where C = V dot N. Note that T would not be a unit vector and would have to be normalized before being used. If the quantity $(1 + n_{12}{}^2*(C^2 - 1))$ is less than zero, it indicates a condition referred to as "total internal reflection," or TIR. TIR occurs when light passes from a dense medium to one that is less dense at a shallow angle. If the angle is under a certain threshold, the incident light rays do not bend and pass through the media but reflect off the internal surfaces and back out the way they came. In this case, ray T does not exist and does not contribute to the point being shaded.

In terms of the overall shading equation, the lighting contribution of specular transmission is of the same form as specular reflection and can be expressed as:

$$I_{st} = I_l*k_{st}*(T \text{ dot } V)^{n'}$$

where all of the terms in this equation are analogous to their specular counterparts. This equation shows that transmitted light can cause highlights just as reflected light can.

Combining the lighting contribution of the four light transport mechanisms just discussed, we can produce a shading equation for use within a ray-tracing program. A shading equation for a single light source that incorporates ambient lighting, diffuse reflection, specular reflection, and specular transmission is of the form:

$$I = \frac{I_l}{d + d_o} * (k_d*(L \text{ dot } N) + k_s*(R \text{ dot } V)^n + k_{st}*(T \text{ dot } V)^{n'}) + k_a*I_a$$

where all terms have been previously identified. As mentioned, some shaders do not take distance into consideration, which would lead to a simplification of the equation above. You can also eliminate other terms in this equation if you don't need them for a specific application. You can apply the practical adjustments we discussed to the various terms in this equation as well.

Recursive Shading

The color assigned to a point on a surface struck by an eye ray is a combination of:

1. The interaction of light rays emanating from all light sources within a scene and the surface material. These interactions are governed by the shading equation and are referred to in this text as local shading.
2. Any contributions made by the reflection of light onto the eye ray.
3. Any contributions made by the transmission of light through a surface and into the eye ray.

Since the process begins at the eye and moves backwards through a scene, at any point in the overall shading computation there are always two unknowns, the reflected and transmitted contributions, which prohibit solving for the illumination of the point under consideration. To eliminate this Catch-22-like situation, we can calculate the shading of a point on a surface by the recursive application of the shading model which, as mentioned, builds a ray tree of contributing illumination sources. A ray tree, like other tree structures, contains a root node, intermediate nodes, branches, and leaves. The root node of this tree is the point being shaded and that viewable by the eye. Each branch contains contributions to the overall illumination of the surface, with the contributions growing less important percentage-wise as you go deeper into the ray tree. The leaf nodes of the tree contain the initial lighting contributions from which the surface shading can be derived. The shading to be applied to a point on the surface is the summation of the lighting contributions contained in the ray tree. The depth of the tree is a function of the recursion depth and must somehow be limited to allow the shading calculations to conclude. This is especially important in a scene that contains many reflective or transmissive surfaces, as the recursion could go on for quite a while taking all of the reflected and refracted rays into consideration. As mentioned, either a threshold of lighting contribution (this technique is referred to as adaptive tree depth) or a hard-coded recursion level is typically used to terminate recursion. When the recursion starts to unwind, the color (lighting) contributions calculated at the deepest levels bubble up toward the root of the tree and are combined with color (lighting) contributions calculated elsewhere in the tree. The final result is a color to be assigned to the first object intersected by the eye ray. At each juncture the light (or color) calculated by local shading is augmented by the contribution of reflected and refracted light. For reflected light:

$$Color_p = Color_s + \text{Reflection Coefficient} * Color_{\text{Reflected Ray}}$$

In other words, the color of a point P, Color$_p$, is a combination of the local shading contribution, Color$_s$, plus the contribution from a reflected ray weighted by how reflective the surface at point P is. If the surface is completely nonreflective, no reflected ray will be traced and no contribution will be added. If, however, the surface has a nonzero reflection coefficient, you must trace the reflected ray and consider its contribution to the surface shading. For transmitted or refracted light:

$$\text{Color}_p = (1 - \text{Transmission Coefficient}) * \text{Color}_s +$$
$$\text{Transmission Coefficient} * \text{Color}_{\text{Transmitted Ray}}$$

In this case, the transmission coefficient determines how transparent an object's surface is, with zero meaning opaque and one meaning totally transparent. If a surface is opaque, no transmission ray will be traced and no lighting contribution will be added. But, as in the case above, if a surface has a nonzero transmission coefficient, you must trace the refracted ray as it contributes to the color of the surface.

Shading concepts are the hardest part of ray tracing to understand. It is natural that a recursive solution be applied to shading. But, recursive processes in general take time to understand and fully appreciate. The simple ray tracer presented in the next chapter shows how recursion is used within the shading function to calculate reflected ray contributions to an object's color. To keep the ray tracer simple, we did not implement transmission of light, but if we had, it would be implemented as discussed here.

Other Ray-Tracing Effects

What we have described so far are the shading effects that are at the heart of every ray-tracing program. Using the composite shading model provided, you can ray trace objects of any color and with many surface material attributes, including shininess, reflectivity, and refractivity. One thing that is missing, however, is surface textures. Surface textures add real interest to ray-traced images. The point sampling nature of ray tracing makes it easy for you to add many textural effects. For example, bit-mapped images can be applied to surfaces; you can make surfaces look bumpy, dented, or even covered by waves. In general, any surface attribute can be made to vary algorithmically over the surface to provide an almost unlimited number of unique visual effects. These types of textures are called "procedural textures." Some of them have an analog in nature and others don't. Because of the vast number of effects possible, we provide only an overview here of how the various textures can be produced. The DKBTrace program discussed in Part Two of this book provides an almost unlimited number of unique textures with which to experiment. We will show some of these in the example images of Part Two. You can examine the source code that DKBTrace uses for texturing (in the file "textures.c") to see how they are implemented if you are so inspired.

The process for applying a texture to a surface is generally referred to in the literature as "texture mapping." In more specific terms, texture mapping is a process that adds surface detail without modeling it as part of the surface's geometry. Two general categories of textures can be defined: coloration textures and surface perturbation textures. Coloration textures change the color of a surface in some controlled manner without affecting surface geometry. Examples of coloration textures include color gradients, bit maps, and the simulation of various mineral colors like granite. Surface perturbation textures, as the name suggests, add character to a surface by simulating physical features such as bumps, dents, or wrinkles so that they appear to be part of the surface's geometry. The judicious application of noise can generate many textures to modify the value of a surface attribute. The noise function used is not just any noise, but one with three well-defined traits:

1. It is continuously defined in three-dimensional space. That is, when given any X, Y, and Z three-dimensional coordinate value, it returns the value of the noise there.
2. If two points in three-dimensional space are close together, the noise values returned are also close together.
3. If two points in three-dimensional space are far apart, the noise values returned will be uncorrelated.

Given such a noise function, it is easy to produce many of the coloration textures. Instead of using a fixed color for an object's surface during shading, you can pass the three-dimensional coordinates of the point of intersection of an eye ray and a surface to a noise function. The noise value returned is used to determine the color to be assigned to the surface at that point. Many times, a color map will be available that describes how colors for a particular texture are to vary with the value of the noise. Generally, three linear interpolations are performed to arrive at the actual color: one for the red, one for the green, and one for the blue color components. This RGB value is used to color the point of intersection. Normal shading then proceeds using the calculated color for the point on the surface. By subsequent application of shading to the calculated surface point, you can, for example, have shiny and reflective granite colored objects.

Surface perturbation textures work slightly differently. Here, a noise function is used to perturb the surface normal at the point of intersection in a pseudorandom fashion. This variation in the surface normal results in the visual impression that the surface itself is perturbed. The noise function used for these types of textures is slightly different than that used above. Instead of returning the value of the noise at a three-dimensional location, it returns a small magnitude directional vector. This noise vector is added to the surface normal with regular vector addition, and a new value of the normal results. Once the new normal is converted to a unit vector, you can use it within the shading calculations as described previously. The shading applied to this textured surface will give the impression of an irregular surface, and hence add to the surface's character. *Note:* There is nothing that would prevent the simultaneous use of both a coloration and a surface perturbation texture on a single surface. The use of both texture types can add real character to a ray-traced image.

Bit maps or image maps are a special type of coloration texture. Bit maps are a two-dimensional array of values that contain some kind of image. When a bit map is used as a texture, the image contained within it is projected on a surface(s) pixel by pixel. There are many ways to project a bit map onto an object's surface. One technique requires the coordinates of the point of intersection in terms of a local coordinate system relative to the surface being shaded. Local coordinates are typically specified by (u,v) with both u (the horizontal component) and v (the vertical component) ranging in value from zero to one. It is as if the object being shaded were flattened out into a plane and a two-dimensional coordinate system were overlaid. The point of intersection is converted into local coordinates through a process called "inverse mapping." Many techniques exist for inverse mapping; most of these depend on the shape of the object being shaded. The book *Introduction to Ray Tracing* mentioned previously contains some of the many inverse mapping techniques available.

The next step in the process of using a bit map as a coloration texture is to get the image into a two-dimensional array of values (usually byte values). The image would typically be read from disk and stored into the array. Each image would have a specified width and height expressed in pixels. Now, instead of thinking about the image in terms of its maximum width and height, we need to think about it in terms of the local coordinate system. In other words, the upper left corner of the image would be given the coordinates of (0,0) and the lower right the coordinates of (1,1). The conversion from the original coordinate system to local coordinates is simple; simply divide the pixel's original coordinates by the image width in the horizontal direction and the image height in the vertical direction, respectively. To convert the other way, from local coordinates to original image coordinates, use multiplication instead of division. The actual mapping process can be summarized in the following steps:

1. Once you have determined the point of intersection between the eye ray and the surface being shaded, use inverse mapping to get the local coordinates of the intersection on the object.

2. Multiply the local horizontal u coordinate by the image width to arrive at a horizontal pixel coordinate within the bit map array, and multiply the local vertical v coordinate by the image height to arrive at a vertical pixel coordinate. *Note*: Since local coordinates are specified in real (floating-point) numbers, the calculated pixel coordinates will have to be truncated to integers before you can use them to access the bit map array. Then fetch the RGB color components from the bit map array and return them as the color of the surface being shaded.

3. A more accurate method of retrieving the bit map data would be to use the fractional pixel addresses (instead of truncating them to integers) to interpolate the color value from the bit map data. You can use a simple two-dimensional linear interpolation with great result. Said another way, since the calculated pixel addresses will lie between the actual pixel addresses in the bit map array, the proximity to real pixel addresses should be used to weigh and therefore calculate the color value to return. The closer the calculated pixel address is to a real pixel address, the larger the influence the real pixel's value should have on the calculated pixel's value.

For more information on procedural textures, you can consult the paper "An Image Synthesizer," by Ken Perlin. This paper is available in the proceedings of the SIGGRAPH '84. Another paper of interest is "A Survey of Texture Mapping," by Paul Heckbert. This paper was published in the *IEEE Computer Graphics and Applications* magazine in November of 1986.

Another interesting effect you can produce during the shading process is "fog." Fog can easily be simulated as a colored entity that obscures our view of a scene as its density increases. For objects near the viewer, the presence of fog has little or no effect. For objects far from the viewer, nothing can be seen except the fog. For objects lying between near and far, the density of the fog determines how much can be seen, with nearer objects most visible and farther objects less visible. Again, you can use a linear interpolation to merge the color of the fog into the color of a shaded object in proportion to the distance the object is from the viewer.

You would have to perform this interpolation after you finish the shading operation for a point. That is, the point's color must already be established. You can incorporate fog into a ray tracer using the following steps:

1. Establish three fog parameters: the distance from the viewer in which the fog should begin taking effect, the distance from the viewer in which the fog should completely obscure the scene, and the color of the fog (usually light gray, dark blue, or black).

2. From the known distance to the object being shaded (the intersection time t), calculate a fractional value that ranges from zero to one. This will be used to determine the mix of object color to fog color at the point being shaded. This fractional value should be zero for all distance less than the fog begin distance, and it should equal one when the distance equals the fog obscure distance. Between these two thresholds, the fractional value should increase linearly.

3. The new color (C_n) to be assigned to the surface would be its color as calculated with shading (C_s) plus the fraction calculated above times the fog color (C_f) minus the shaded color. In terms of an equation:

$$C_n = C_s + \text{fraction} * (C_f - C_s)$$

Even with all of the effects detailed thus far in this chapter, most ray-traced images lack complete visual reality. One of the reasons for this is that not all lighting phenomena are taken into consideration, especially in simple, brute-force ray-tracing programs. Effects such as gloss (blurred reflection), translucency (blurred refraction), depth of field, soft shadows (penumbras), and motion blur can be added to a ray tracer without much increase in effort. Images rendered without these visual effects are characterized by sharp shadows, sharp reflections, and sharp focus. When you provide these effects, you dramatically increase the image's realism.

These effects are generally incorporated into ray-tracing programs using a technique called "distributed" or "probabilistic" ray tracing. If you are interested in knowing how these techniques work, see the paper "Stochastic Sampling and Distributed Ray Tracing," by Robert L. Cook, which describes distributed ray tracing in detail. This paper is included in the book *An Introduction to Ray Tracing*.

Some Problems with Ray Tracing

Ray tracing with all of its inherent advantages as a three-dimensional graphics technique is not without problems of its own. As previously mentioned, performance is of major concern as well as aliasing. Certain implementation issues can also cause problems during ray tracing even though they are not directly attributable to the ray-tracing algorithm itself. We briefly discuss each of these problems in this section. We also provide the classic solutions to them.

Performance Problems and Solutions

Anyone who has ray traced complex imagery knows how long the process can take. The resistor maze image shown in the "Gallery of Images" required over 27 hours of computer time to render on a 33 MHz 486 computer system. If this image were attempted on a slower PC or a

PC without a numeric co-processor to speed the floating-point calculations, it could require a week of computer time to produce. The use of floating-point numbers within ray-tracing programs is (probably) unavoidable because of the range and accuracy of the numbers required. Some industrious individual might be able to put together a fixed-point ray tracer of some type, which would help performance considerably. For the most part, however, floating-point implementation of ray-tracing programs is ubiquitous, so ray-tracing acceleration techniques must focus attention elsewhere in trying to increase ray-tracing performance.

Before attempting to increase the performance of any software, you must first determine what portions of the software consume the most amount of execution time. In most cases, 10 percent of the software consumes 90 percent of the execution time. Under these conditions, it is obvious where the optimization time should be spent—on the 10 percent of the code consuming the most time.

The majority of the time spent ray tracing is tied up in ray/object intersection testing. Some estimates run as high as 95 percent for the total amount of time spent checking for intersections. This being the case, you can assume (correctly) that shading and other miscellaneous required data manipulations that occur during the ray-tracing process require very little time to perform—less than 5 percent. It makes sense then to concentrate optimization efforts on ray/object intersection testing. Actually, you can take two different approaches (singularly or in combination) to achieve better ray-tracing performance:

1. Make the ray/surface intersection routines faster; and/or
2. Reduce the total number of rays that need to be traced, therefore reducing the total number of intersection checks that must be performed.

The second approach has the best prospects for dramatically increasing ray-tracing performance. Up until this point, we have described "exhaustive ray tracing." This refers to a brute-force technique (common to all basic ray tracers) where all rays generated are tested against all objects within a scene. This results in a lot of wasted time and computational energy because not all rays intersect all objects. Two optimization techniques are popular in helping to reduce the number of unnecessary ray/object intersection calculations. They are the bounding volume and spatial subdivision techniques.

The bounding volume technique surrounds complex objects within a three-dimensional scene with a simpler object that requires a less complicated intersection routine to check. The idea is that if a ray does not pierce the bounding volume, then it cannot possibly intersect any of the objects within the bounding volume and therefore intersection tests with the contained objects need not be performed. If the bounding volume contains ten objects, for example, the single failed intersection test with the bounding volume would replace the ten intersection tests that would otherwise be required. Of course, if the ray did pierce the bounding volume, a total of eleven intersection tests would be needed—one for the bounding volume and one each for the ten objects contained within it. The simpler the bounding volume, the simpler and therefore the faster the intersection test. For this reason, many ray-tracing programs use spheres as bounding volumes.

An extension to this technique that again increases performance is called "hierarchical bounding volumes." With this technique, all complex objects within a scene are surrounded by bounding volumes. All of the individual bounding volumes are then further surrounded by other bounding volumes in such a manner that eventually the complete scene is enveloped in nested bounding volumes. As rays are tested for intersection with the largest bounding volume and rejected, large numbers of individual intersection tests can be avoided. As an intersection is detected with a bounding volume, a test with each of the contained bounding volumes must be performed. As soon as an intersection test fails, no further tests are necessary on it or any other contained bounding volumes for the specified ray. The prospects for increasing ray-tracing performance using this technique should be obvious.

Spatial subdivision is another technique for minimizing the number of ray/object intersection tests performed during ray tracing. This technique divides three-dimensional space into individual rectangular volume elements called "voxels" and assigns to them pointers to objects that contain them. When a ray is fired into object space, only the objects that contain voxels that are intersected by the ray need to be tested for intersection against the ray. Again, this results in many fewer ray/object intersection tests.

Readers interested in the details of these techniques should investigate the books and articles listed in the "Further Reading" section of Part Three. As an aside, the DKBTrace program of Part Two uses bounding volumes as a performance enhancement technique. The rendering speed improvements when using bounding boxes are impressive, to say the least.

Aliasing Problems and Solutions

Anyone familiar with computer graphics has seen the effects that aliasing has on image quality. Aliasing artifacts create regular, repeatable patterns of distortion within an image that the human brain, unfortunately, is very good at discerning. Increasing the resolution with which an image is rendered goes a long way toward reducing the problem, but it does not eliminate it altogether. Even the highest-resolution image will show some aliasing effects when enlarged. Two types of aliasing effects are important with ray-traced imagery. They are spatial aliasing (spatial referring to space) and temporal aliasing (temporal referring to time). For single images, only spatial aliasing is important. For images to be used in animation sequences, both aliasing phenomena are important. Both phenomena are caused by inadequate sampling.

Spatial aliasing is responsible for the visual aberration of jaggies. It is caused by sampling via a uniform grid of pixels at too low a rate. Spatial aliasing can also be responsible for obscuring small objects within a scene. If an object is small enough, it may fall between two rays and never be seen in the finished ray-traced image. Temporal aliasing is seen when ray-traced images are used in animation. Examples of temporal aliasing in real life are the rolling screens seen on television whenever TVs or computer monitors are shown, and the slowly backward rolling of wheels seen when vehicles are moving in the forward direction. Both of these phenomena are caused by events that are happening too fast to be accurately recorded (sampled) on film. In terms of ray tracing, temporal aliasing can show up as small objects that come and go between frames or that jump from position to position. Obviously, these effects can be very distracting (the human eye/brain system is very adept at detecting this type of visual phenomena) and must be dealt with for professional-looking animations. We discuss techniques to combat both types of aliasing next.

Supersampling is a general class of techniques where multiple rays are generated for each pixel in an image. The actual color to be assigned to a pixel is the average of all of the colors returned by tracing the rays associated with the pixel. Usually a set number of rays per pixel are used and these are arranged in a regular grid (typically eight rays for the corners and sides of the pixel and one for the middle). Although this technique does improve image quality, it does so by trading off image rendering time. All of the additional rays traced and averaged per pixel require additional computation time. Also, many of the additional rays traced per pixel are not needed when areas of uniform illumination are being shaded.

Adaptive supersampling attempts to optimize anti-aliasing by generating extra rays only when they are actually needed. In this case, maybe five rays per pixel will be used initially. The colors returned by tracing these five rays are examined to see how much difference in color is detected over the pixel area. If a difference larger than some threshold is detected, the portion of the pixel that had the largest difference will again be subdivided into five more pixels that will be traced. This is a recursive process that continues until the color differences detected are all under the difference threshold. When recursion terminates, the color values are weighted and summed and the actual pixel color is assigned. As you can see, this technique generates extra rays only when they are required and is therefore a much more efficient anti-aliasing technique than plain supersampling.

The regular gridlike arrangement of rays traced with the supersampling techniques causes aliasing effects of its own. In other words, it substantially reduces aliasing effects in the original image while adding aliasing effects of its own. A technique called "stochastic ray tracing" breaks with the gridlike sampling and scatters the traced rays with a specific distribution. This is basically the same technique as "distributed ray tracing" described earlier and used to provide imaging effects like motion blur and soft shadows. With the proper scattering distribution, aliasing effects in an image are converted to random noise, which is much less objectionable to the eye. Still, with this technique many more rays than necessary may be used in areas of uniform illumination. So stochastic ray tracing is not the be all and end all anti-aliasing technique for ray tracing. Hybrid techniques are being developed that algorithmically determine how many rays are required and then properly scatter those rays to combat aliasing. Such techniques combine efficiency with anti-aliasing.

Precision Problems and Solutions

The final problem to be aware of when implementing a ray-tracing program is numeric precision. As mentioned, this is not a problem with ray tracing but a problem when using floating-point numbers in general. The problem arises when comparisons are made between floating-point numbers that are very close in value. If, for example, a division is performed with floating-point numbers such as 2.000/2.000, the result returned may be 0.9999999995 instead of the 1.0 we would expect. If we were comparing the result of this division to 1.0, the test would fail every time, even though the numbers are effectively equal. To correct this problem, all comparisons should be performed by subtraction of the two numbers instead of by direct comparison. If the result of the subtraction is less than some small number, epsilon, then the numbers are considered equal. In other words, comparisons of the form:

$$\frac{2.000}{2.000} = 1.0$$

should be replaced with the comparison:

$$\text{fabs}\left(\frac{2.000}{2.000} - 1.0\right) <= \text{epsilon}$$

to work correctly. In this comparison "fabs" is the floating-point absolute value function. The value assigned to epsilon might be a constant 0.000001, but it may have to vary depending on the size of the numbers being compared. If minute numbers are being compared, this value of epsilon may in fact be too large. If large numbers are being compared, an epsilon of 1.0 may be okay.

Inexact floating-point number comparisons can cause ray/object intersection tests to act erratically if the above cautions are not taken into consideration. For example, a light ray shot from the point of intersection on an object's surface to a light source for shadow detection may determine the object itself is obscuring the light source and place the point in shadow. In other words, an object may seem to be shadowing itself. This problem can be seen visually as dark specs on the surface of an object and is sometimes referred to as "digital acne." Other inexact comparisons may cause a ray to miss an object completely, even though it should have intersected it. By carefully structuring the numerical comparisons, you could avoid such problems. Any good book on numerical methods can help you avoid this and other problems when working with floating-point numbers.

Conclusions

We have discussed basic ray-tracing theories in this chapter. We have presented information about basic ray-tracing concepts, the properties of vectors, mathematical operations on vectors, parametric equations of rays, ray/object intersections, shading of surfaces, and some problems associated with ray tracing. For the technical reader, it is hoped that you have gained a firm enough understanding of the basic concepts that you are ready to try your hand at designing your own simple ray-tracing program. It is quite a thrill when you get a ray tracer of your own design to work for the first time. For those who want to learn more about advanced ray-tracing techniques, the book *An Introduction to Ray Tracing* is highly recommended. With the background material presented in this book, you should now be much more able to understand the body of advanced ray-tracing material available in the literature.

For the less technical reader, it is hoped you gained an appreciation for the complexities involved with ray tracing and understand more about the subject in general. What you have learned should help you in composing your ray-traced images and understanding what you see when the results are not quite what you expected.

Theory for theory's sake is less important than theory for application's sake. Let's put the theory described in this chapter to use in building a simple ray tracer in the next chapter. The ray tracer we present is simple enough to get your arms all the way around yet capable enough to produce some beautiful images. Without further ado, let's get started. This is where the fun begins.

3

A First Ray-Tracer Program

The art of being wise is the art of knowing what to overlook.
—William James

In this chapter you will learn about:

- **Converting the basic ray-tracing theory into practice**
- **Practical matters involved in implementing a ray-tracing program**
- **How to use the C programming language to write object-oriented code similar to C++**

Introduction

With ray-tracing basics and vector math behind us, we can now put together a basic but functional ray tracer. Although not nearly as capable a ray tracer as DKBTrace, which is discussed in Part Two of this book, the program we shall build nevertheless illustrates all that a ray tracer needs to do to be functional. This basic ray tracer

- Allows you to position sphere and plane objects anywhere in the three-dimensional universe
- Allows multiple light sources, each with its own color
- Has an infinitely variable viewpoint within the three-dimensional universe
- Is object oriented in design
- Is easily extendible
- Has user definable surface properties including:
  ambient lighting
  diffuse lighting
  Phong specular highlights
  reflection (including mirrored images)
- Has the ability to create beautiful images of adjustable resolution

Our basic ray tracer utilizes the same viewing geometry as DKBTrace. This means that simple images produced with this program can be rendered with DKBTrace with equivalent results. We will refer to this basic ray-tracer program hereafter as TRACE.

What TRACE Does

Before we jump into the technical discussion of how TRACE works, let's first describe at a high level what TRACE does. Our purpose might best be served by describing TRACE's inputs and output. Inputs are provided by the user, and TRACE generates the output from the inputs. *Note*: In order to keep the code clean, uncluttered, and easily understandable, TRACE performs little error checking on operator input. For this reason, the user must beware.

TRACE Program Inputs—specified in "trace.c" file

- A specification for the color of the background in RGB color, each component in the range 0.0 to 1.0
- Viewpoint information including:
  1. The viewpoint location
  2. The direction of view
  3. The up and right vectors
- Object specification including:
  1. Shape
  2. Location
  3. Surface properties
- Light source(s) specification including:
  1. Location
  2. Color
- Image characteristics including:
  1. Resolution of image

TRACE Program Outputs

- Output data file in "dump" RGB format. We will describe this format in detail in Chapters 4 and 5. For now, it is important just to know that this is the output file format required by the other tools in this book and will be used to post process the image produced by the TRACE program.

With the exception of the image resolution information, all user input is specified via floating-point numbers. The image resolution information is input as integers.

All scene information is hard coded into the "trace.c" file shown in Listing 3.12 (page 150), mostly in the form of parameters to functions. If you change the scene, you must recompile the "trace.c" program, relink it with the other files that make up the ray tracer, and execute it again. This sounds cumbersome, but it is workable as a demonstration vehicle.

You can render images created with TRACE at any resolution you desire. TRACE does not have any inherent limits on the complexity of the images that can be produced, other than memory. You can generate very high-resolution images, with lots of objects and many, many light sources. However, as the complexity and resolution of an image increases, so does the time required to generate it. TRACE is a brute-force ray-tracing program that does not include any acceleration techniques to reduce the number of rays traced. Therefore, complex imagery will require a lot of time to generate. You have been warned!

The TRACE program has a single output, a data file in the "dump" format. In order to see the image contained in the data file, you must post process the image file via a color quantization program such as "mquan.exe" from Chapter 4. This program crunches the image data into something palatable by a VGA graphics adapter—more on this program later.

As the TRACE program runs, it will display the current row number it is calculating on the screen as an indication of current status and to indicate the program is running. The beginning and ending of the program's execution is time tagged to give you an idea of how long the ray tracing took. You can stop the TRACE program by pressing any keyboard key while it is running.

In summary, TRACE takes operator inputs from the "trace.c" file and generates an image file as output. You must use a separate program to view the actual result.

Data Structures—Program Structure

One of the goals of writing TRACE was to make it easily extendible so an interested reader could use it to try out various advanced ray-tracing techniques that it does not implement. This requirement demanded an object-oriented implementation. A C++ implementation was considered but rejected for the more ubiquitous C. We felt this material would reach a greater audience as a result. It is possible, with proper design, to write object-oriented C without the need for C++. We did so by using the concepts of data hiding and inheritance in this implementation along with the concept of objects. As a testimony to the object-oriented success of this implementation, it is possible to add new object shapes (such as cones or general quadrics) by:

1. Defining a data structure for the new shape
2. Modifying one existing data structure
3. Providing a file of code for the new shape that
   - Knows how to calculate the ray/object intersection
   - Knows how to calculate a normal on the object's surface at the point of intersection
   - Knows how to print the new object's data structure
   - Knows how to dynamically allocate memory for the new object and initialize it with user-specified parameters

When this code for a new object is provided, it will effortlessly integrate with the original ray-tracing code without needing any other change. The beauty of this object-oriented approach is apparent only if you first attempt a non-object-oriented implementation.

While the purpose of this book is not to teach object-oriented programming techniques, it provides useful insight to compare a more traditional C approach with an object-oriented approach. This short digression will allow you to appreciate the trade-offs involved and the gains to be made. For the sake of discussion, consider that all three-dimensional objects in our ray tracer are linked together with a linked list and that we desire during debugging to print out the contents of each object's data structure. We will want to traverse the linked list from its beginning to its end, identifying each object on the list and calling the correct print function for the object's type. To identify each object, you traditionally put a tag (usually an enumerated type) into the data structure with a unique value for each defined object type. If you disregard the complications involved in even linking objects of various types, the following code fragment illustrates how a print operation might be performed:

```
while (ListObjectPtr)  {
   switch(ListObjectPtr -> Tag) {
      case Sphere:
         PrintSphere((SPHERE*) ListObjectPtr);
         break;
      case Plane:
         PrintPlane((PLANE*) ListObjectPtr);
         break;
      .
      .
      .
   }
   ListObjectPtr = ListObjectPtr -> Next;
}
```

The important concept here is that every time an object from the linked list is accessed, a switch statement must be utilized, first to identify the type of object being pointed at and then to cast ListObjectPtr to the proper type before using it. This would not be so bad except the list of objects is always being traversed during the normal operation of the ray tracer to find intersections, calculate shadow objects, and so on. This approach not only produces unpleasant code, it also produces code that must be modified every time a new object type is added. As an example, if we were to add a cylinder to our basic shapes, each switch statement would have to be modified to incorporate the cylinder. This makes for error-prone modifications to the ray tracer.

In contrast, consider an object-oriented approach that embeds functions (which would be called methods in object-oriented languages) into the data structures (which would be called classes) for the objects. In other words, each object's data structure would contain functions (actually pointers to functions) that:

1. Know how to calculate an intersection between itself and a ray given as input
2. Know how to calculate the normal to this object given the point of intersection with the ray
3. Know how to print out the contents of its internal data structure

The incorporation of the function pointers cleans up the code completely. The code fragment shown earlier for printing the objects on a linked list is reduced to:

```
while (ListObjectPtr)  {
  ListObjectPtr->Print(ListObjectPtr);
  ListObjectPtr = ListObjectPtr->Next;
}
```

Nice, huh? Notice that no messy switch statement or pointer type casting is required. Notice also that if we decided to add a new cylinder shape, this print function would not need to change at all because it has no knowledge of the shape being printed. It only knows (and needs to know) how to call the print function embedded within the object being pointed at by ListObjectPtr. The object's print function knows how to print out the important information about itself. The same technique comes into play when a ray tracer attempts to calculate ray/object intersection or to calculate the surface normal at the point of intersection. For example, the code wishing to calculate the normal makes a call to the intersection calculation function embedded with an object and passes to it the ray to check. Again, the calling code has no (and needs no) information about the object on which the ray/object intersection check is being performed, so new object types can easily be added without affecting this code's operation.

C++ aficionados will recognize this approach as exactly that taken by C++. In C++, all methods are passed a hidden parameter "this," which is a pointer to the object the method was called on. In our implementation, when we say

    ListObjectPtr->Print(ListObjectPtr);

we are explicitly passing a pointer to the object to the Print function, which accomplishes exactly the same result. How the object-oriented approach is utilized in this ray tracer will become clear as we discuss the actual implementation.

We begin with an examination of the data structures that we shall use in the ray tracer. Please examine Listing 3.1 throughout this discussion. This file is called "struct.h" on the companion disks. We will describe the ray-tracing program's data structures in detail because they are so important to the understanding of the implementation.

The most basic data structures are defined first. These are:

1. The VECTOR
2. The COLOR
3. The RAY

We show these names in uppercase to indicate they each represent a type-defined structure.

A VECTOR, as discussed in the previous chapter, is a structure that contains three floating-point double numbers. These numbers contain the vector's X, Y, and Z component values. A VECTOR can describe any point in three-dimensional space and can describe a RAY with an assumed origin.

A COLOR is also a structure of three double values, one each for the Red, the Green, and the Blue (or RGB) components of a color. This ray-tracer program uses the additive RGB color system exclusively. The range of values for any color component is between 0.0 and 1.0. The use of double values results in a near-infinite number of color possibilities being described by the COLOR structure.

A RAY contains two VECTOR structures: one describes the origin of the ray relative to the origin of the coordinate system, and the second indicates the RAY's direction. A RAY's direction vector is generally a unit vector, as described in the last chapter. By definition, a unit vector has a length of one.

The next structure defined is the VIEWPOINT. This structure contains all of the information necessary to locate and orient the position of the viewer in our ray tracer. The VIEW-

Listing 3.1 General Data Structure Definitions

The following is the contents of the file "struct.h."

```
/************************************************************/
/***                     "struct.h"                    ***/
/***             Data Structure Definitions            ***/
/***                        for                        ***/
/***                 "A First Ray Tracer"              ***/
/***      from the book "Practical Ray Tracing in C"   ***/
/***            written in Borland/Turbo C 2.0         ***/
/***                         by                        ***/
/***                 Craig A. Lindley                  ***/
/***                                                   ***/
/***       Ver: 1.0    Last Update: 03/10/92           ***/
/************************************************************/

/* Define a three-dimensional vector */
typedef struct  {
  double X;                     /* X, Y , Z components */
  double Y;
  double Z;
} VECTOR;

/* Define a color structure */
typedef struct  {
  double Red;                   /* RGB components of a color */
  double Green;
  double Blue;
} COLOR;

/* Define a ray */
typedef struct  {
  VECTOR Origin;                /* a ray has an origin and direction */
  VECTOR Direction;
} RAY;

/* Define the position and direction of our viewpoint */
typedef struct  {
  VECTOR Location;           /* Where our eye is */
  VECTOR Direction;          /* Which direction we are looking */
  VECTOR Up;                 /* Which direction is up */
  VECTOR Right;              /* Which direction is to the right of us */
} VIEWPOINT;

/* Define the display environment */
typedef struct  {
  unsigned DisplayWidth;
  unsigned DisplayHeight;
} DISPLAY;
```

(continued)

Listing 3.1   *(continued)*

```c
/* All objects have a set of these surface properties */
typedef struct  {
  COLOR  Color;             /* color of object in RGB */
  double Ambient;           /* ambient factor */
  double Diffuse;           /* diffuse factor */
  double Brilliance;        /* brilliance factor */
  double Specular;          /* specular RGB */
  double Roughness;         /* specular coefficient */
  double Reflection;        /* reflection 0.0 - 1.0 */
} SURFACE;

/* All currently defined object types */
enum ObjectType {NoTAnObject,Light,Sphere,Plane};

/* Define sphere specific info */
struct ASphere  {
  VECTOR  Center;           /* Its location */
  double  Radius;           /* Its radius */
  double  Radius2;          /* Its radius squared */
};

/* Define plane specific info */
struct APlane  {
  VECTOR  Normal;           /* Its defining normal */
  double  Distance;         /* Distance from origin */
};

/* Define light source specific info */
struct ALight  {
  VECTOR  Center;           /* Its location */
};

/* The generic object definition */
typedef struct AnObject  {
  struct AnObject *Next;    /* ptr to next object in list */
  enum   ObjectType Type;   /* object type for debugging */

  /* function pointers for operations on objects */
  double (*Intersect)(struct AnObject *, RAY *);
  VECTOR (*Normal)(struct AnObject *, VECTOR);
  void   (*Print)(struct AnObject *);

  SURFACE Properties;       /* object's properties */
  union  {
    struct ASphere S;       /* object specific info goes here */
    struct APlane  P;
    struct ALight  L;
  } ObjSpecific;
} OBJECT;
```

POINT is also referred to as the eye point and/or the camera point in ray-tracing literature. It is called the camera point because our simple viewing model simulates a pin-hole camera. The ray tracer that we shall construct in this chapter uses the same viewing geometry as DKBTrace. Therefore, VIEWPOINT contains the same parameters, and these parameters function the same in both programs. The first VECTOR in VIEWPOINT is the Location. Location defines where the "eye" is in relation to the origin of the coordinate system. The VIEWPOINTs defined in this book generally place the Location somewhere on the negative Z axis (with our left-handed coordinate system). The Direction VECTOR determines which way the eye is looking. With Location typically specified on the -Z axis, Direction is generally specified in the +Z direction, toward the objects in the scene. Direction is sometimes referred to as the gaze direction in other ray-tracing programs.

The Up and the Right VECTORs determine the orientation of the VIEWPOINT. Figuratively speaking, it is the orientation of your head while viewing the ray-traced scene. Up determines which direction is above your head and is typically specified as a VECTOR <0.0 1.0 0.0> (*Note*: This is the same vector notation described in Chapter 2 and utilized throughout this book). This Up VECTOR means your head is upright and that it is aligned with the positive Y axis. If Up were specified as <0.0 -1.0 0.0>, the image being viewed would appear upside down, as if you were standing on your head while viewing or holding a photograph upside down.

The Right VECTOR has two functions. First, it determines what direction will be to the right of the VIEWPOINT (your head). Right would generally be specified as <1.0 0.0 0.0>, indicating the +X axis is coincident with what would be on the viewer's right. The second use of the Right VECTOR is to compensate for "aspect ratio" distortion, as described in Chapter 2. As mentioned there, this compensation is necessary only when the display device does not have square pixels.

The DISPLAY structure contains information about the image to be rendered. By changing the DisplayWidth and DisplayHeight values, you can alter the resolution of the ray-traced image. The TRACE program will adapt to any resolution specified in the DISPLAY structure without any other changes being required.

SURFACE describes the properties of the surface for each object used by this ray tracer. It could be said that each object inherits these SURFACE properties. The entries, which have been described earlier, are color, ambient lighting, diffuse lighting, brilliance, specular reflection, roughness, and reflection coefficients.

The enumerated type "ObjectType" assigns a unique value to each possible object used by this ray tracer. An "ObjectType" entry is made in each object's data structure. This was done for debugging purposes because it allows for quick identification of objects when traversing the linked list of objects. An object type tag is not actually required during the execution of the TRACE program.

Next, the "ASphere" structure is defined. This structure contains specific information about an object of type sphere. The minimum sphere-specific information that must be maintained to define a sphere is:

1. Its location in three-dimensional space. This information is contained in the Center vector. The center of the sphere has a specific X, Y, and Z coordinate.

2. Its radius. This determines how big the sphere is. You'll notice that the square of the radius is also maintained here. Having this value precalculated and stored speeds the ray/sphere intersection calculation somewhat.

The structure "APlane" contains plane-specific information. To define a plane fully requires:

1. Its defining Normal vector
2. Its distance from the coordinate axis origin

The "ALight" structure defines the light-source-specific information. Only the location of the light source specified by the X, Y, and Z location of its center is required at this time. All light sources utilized by this ray-tracing program are point sources. If light sources were defined to have size, like a sphere, you would have to include other light-source-specific information in the "ALight" structure.

The final and most important data structure is the OBJECT. All objects utilized by this ray tracer are held internally in an OBJECT structure during program operation. The OBJECT definition is one of the few areas in this program that would need modification if new object types were added. You would have to place the object-specific attributes of a new object in the object-specific union contained in OBJECT. No other changes would be required. The other entries in the OBJECT data structure include:

1. Next, which is a pointer to another OBJECT. This field is used to place OBJECTs into a singly linked list for ease of manipulation by the ray tracer.
2. Type, which contains an identifier of the OBJECT's type. As mentioned, this is used during debugging only. At this time, a light source has a type of 1, a sphere has a type of 2, and a plane has a type of 3. These values come from the object type enumeration.
3. Intersect, which is a pointer to a function that accepts a pointer to an object (this object) and a pointer to a RAY and returns the parameter T of the ray/object intersection, if there is one. Examine the listing to see how the function pointers are declared.
4. Normal, which is a pointer to a function that accepts a pointer to this object and a vector describing the point of intersection between this object and a RAY and returns the normal of that point as a vector.
5. Print, which is a pointer to a function that accepts a pointer to this object and prints the contents of this object's data structure.
6. Properties, which contain the surface attributes of this object.
7. As mentioned, any object-specific data is contained in the object-specific union.

The important thing to understand about this OBJECT data structure is that it has sufficient intelligence by itself to interact with the ray tracer. Once an object data structure has been defined, the ray tracer has little need to differentiate between objects. To this ray tracer an object is an object is an object.

Two linked lists, "ObjectList" and "LightList," are used to organize the objects in this ray tracer. "ObjectList" contains all of the objects in the three-dimensional scene to be ray traced. "LightList" is the list of light sources for the scene. Because all objects are of type

OBJECT, it is easy to link them together and, once linked, very easy to traverse the lists and process the OBJECTs. The file "linklist.c," which contains the link list function, is shown in Listing 3.2. This file contains three simple functions:

1. "AddToList," which accepts a pointer to a pointer to a list of objects and a pointer to an object. This function links the object to the beginning of the specified singly linked list. The function utilizes the simple linked list concepts taught in beginning data structure classes. This function is used to add objects to the "ObjectList" and light sources to the "LightList."

2. "FreeList" accepts a pointer to a pointer to a list. It frees the dynamically allocated memory associated with each OBJECT on the specified list. When all OBJECT memory has been freed, the list pointer is set to NULL, indicating an empty list, and the number of objects that have been freed is returned.

3. "PrintList" is used for debugging purposes only. It accepts a pointer to a list of OBJECTs as input and traverses the list, printing out OBJECT information for each OBJECT on the list. Notice how simple this function is. If invoked as:

> PrintList(ObjectList);

a detailed dump of all OBJECTs on the ObjectList will be printed to the screen. If invoked as:

> PrintList(LightList);

all light source information is printed. Similar to "FreeList," "PrintList" returns the number of OBJECTs found on the specified list.

Listing 3.2 Linked List Functions

The following is the contents of the file "linklist.c."

```
/*************************************************************/
/***                    "linklist.c"                     ***/
/***               Linked List Functions                 ***/
/***                        for                          ***/
/***                "A First Ray Tracer"                 ***/
/***       from the book "Practical Ray Tracing in C"    ***/
/***            written in Borland/Turbo C 2.0           ***/
/***                        by                           ***/
/***                  Craig A. Lindley                   ***/
/***                                                     ***/
/***         Ver: 1.0    Last Update: 03/10/92           ***/
/*************************************************************/

#include <stdio.h>
#include <stdlib.h>
#include "mymem.h"
#include "struct.h"
#include "trace.h"

/*
Given a ptr to the ptr to the list and a ptr to an object,
```

(continued)

Listing 3.2 *(continued)*

```
add the object at the head of the list.
*/
void AddToList (OBJECT **ListPtr, OBJECT *Item)    {

  if (*ListPtr == NULL)    {
    *ListPtr = Item;
    Item->Next = NULL;
  }
  else    {
    Item->Next = *ListPtr;
    *ListPtr = Item;
  }
}


/*
Given a ptr to ptr to the list, traverse the list deleting each
object on the list. Return the number of objects deleted.
*/
unsigned FreeList (OBJECT **ListPtr)    {

  OBJECT *TempPtr;
  unsigned Number = 0;

  while (*ListPtr)    {
    Number++;
    TempPtr = *ListPtr;
    *ListPtr = (*ListPtr)->Next;
    free (TempPtr);
  }
  ListPtr = NULL;
  return (Number);
}


/*
Given a ptr to a list, traverse the list and print out the
information about each object on the list. The function called to
print an object is contained in the object itself. Return the number
of objects in the list.
*/
unsigned PrintList (OBJECT *ListPtr)    {

  unsigned Number = 0;

  while (ListPtr)    {
    Number++;
    ListPtr->Print(ListPtr);
    ListPtr = ListPtr->Next;
  }
  return (Number);
}
```

Two more include files, "vectors.h" and "trace.h," shown in Listings 3.3 and 3.4 respectively, provide the remainder of the foundation required to discuss the internal workings of this ray tracer. Discussed in Chapter 2, the file "vectors.h" contains C macros that implement the most common vector math operations. The file "trace.h" is simply an include file of other common macros and function prototypes for all of the ray-tracer functions. We include "trace.h" in all C files that make up the TRACE ray-tracer program. We include "vectors.h" in all C files where vector mathematics is required.

Listing 3.3 Vector Math Macros

The following is the contents of the file "vectors.h."

```
/**********************************************************/
/***                  "vectors.h"                      ***/
/***            Vector Manipulation Macros              ***/
/***                     for                            ***/
/***              "A First Ray Tracer"                  ***/
/***     from the book "Practical Ray Tracing in C"     ***/
/***          written in Borland/Turbo C 2.0            ***/
/***                      by                            ***/
/***               Craig A. Lindley                     ***/
/***                                                    ***/
/***        Ver: 1.0    Last Update: 03/10/92           ***/
/**********************************************************/


/*
Various Vector manipulation MACROS
*/

/* Vector Add: a + b = c */
#define VAdd(a, b, c) {(c).X=(a).X+(b).X; (c).Y=(a).Y+(b).Y; (c).Z=(a).Z+(b).Z;}

/* Vector Subtract: c = a - b */
#define VSub(a, b, c) {(c).X=(a).X-(b).X; (c).Y=(a).Y-(b).Y; (c).Z=(a).Z-(b).Z;}

/* Vector Negate: b = -a */
#define VNegate(a, b) {(b).X=-(a).X; (b).Y=-(a).Y; (a).Z=-(a).Z;}

/* Vector Scale: b = k * a */
#define VScale(a, k, b) {(b).X=(a).X*(k); (b).Y=(a).Y*(k); (b).Z=(a).Z*(k);}

/* Vector Dot Product: c = a dot b */
#define VDot(a, b, c) {c=(a).X*(b).X+(a).Y*(b).Y+(a).Z*(b).Z;}

/* Vector Cross Product: c = a cross b */
/* c must be different than a and b */
#define VCross(a,b,c) {(c).X=(a).Y*(b).Z-(a).Z*(b).Y; \
                       (c).Y=(a).Z*(b).X-(a).X*(b).Z; \
                       (c).Z=(a).X*(b).Y-(a).Y*(b).X;}
```

(continued)

Listing 3.3   *(continued)*

```
/* Vector Length: l = len(a) */
#define VLength(a, l) {l=sqrt((a).X*(a).X+(a).Y*(a).Y+(a).Z*(a).Z);}

/* Vector Normalize: u = |a| */
#define VNormalize(a,u) {VTemp=sqrt((a).X*(a).X+(a).Y*(a).Y+(a).Z*(a).Z);\
                          (u).X=(a).X/VTemp;\
                          (u).Y=(a).Y/VTemp;\
                          (u).Z=(a).Z/VTemp;}
```

Listing 3.4   "trace.h" Include File

The following is the contents of the file "trace.h."

```
/*************************************************************/
/***                    "trace.h"                      ***/
/***       Misc. Definitions and Function Prototypes   ***/
/***                      for                          ***/
/***             "A First Ray Tracer"                  ***/
/***    from the book "Practical Ray Tracing in C"     ***/
/***          written in Borland/Turbo C 2.0           ***/
/***                       by                          ***/
/***               Craig A. Lindley                    ***/
/***                                                   ***/
/***        Ver: 1.0    Last Update: 03/10/92          ***/
/*************************************************************/

/* Define a new BYTE type */
#ifndef __BYTE
#define __BYTE
typedef unsigned char BYTE;
#endif

#define TRUE        1
#define FALSE       0

#define BIG         1e10
#define EPSILON     1e-03
#define MAXRECURSELEVEL 5

/* Max width of the display row is set at 640 pixels */
#define MAXLINEWIDTH 640

/* Common Macros */
#define MIN(a,b)  ((a)>(b)) ? (b):(a)
#define MAX(a,b)  ((a)>(b)) ? (a):(b)
#define SQUARE(x)  (x)*(x)
```

```
/* Declarations of lists and other globals used in ray tracer */
extern OBJECT *ObjectList;
extern OBJECT *LightList;
extern DISPLAY Display;
extern VIEWPOINT View;
extern COLOR BackGround;
extern double VTemp;

/* Function prototypes for linked listed */
void AddToList (OBJECT **ListPtr, OBJECT *Item);
unsigned FreeList (OBJECT **ListPtr);
unsigned PrintList (OBJECT *ListPtr);

/* Function prototypes for attributes */
void PrintSurfaceAttrib (OBJECT *ObjectPtr);
void SetSurfaceAttrib (OBJECT *ObjectPtr,
                       double Red, double Green, double Blue,
                       double Ambient, double Diffuse, double Brilliance,
                       double Specular, double Roughness, double Reflection);

/* Function prototypes for objects */
OBJECT *MakeSphere (double X, double Y, double Z, double Radius);
OBJECT *MakePlane  (double A, double B, double C, double D);
OBJECT *MakeLight  (double X, double Y, double Z,
                    double Red, double Green, double Blue);

/* Miscellaneous Function Prototypes */
void ParseCmdLine(short argc, char *argv[]);
void Trace (RAY *Ray, COLOR *Color);
void DoRayTrace(void);
double MakeLightRay (OBJECT *LightPtr, VECTOR Point, RAY *Ray);
COLOR GetLightColor (OBJECT *LightPtr, OBJECT *ObjectPtr, RAY *Ray,
                     double Distance);

/* Function prototypes for file output */
int OpenOutputFile (char *FileName, unsigned IWidth, unsigned IHeight);
int CloseOutputFile (void);
int WritePixelColor (COLOR *Color, unsigned Col);
```

Detailed File Descriptions

The preceding discussion has attempted to illustrate the data structures and program structures used in the TRACE program. With this basis, we can now discuss each of the component C files that make up the ray tracer. We will point out how the data structure drove the code design where appropriate. We will first discuss the five files that form the support function for the main ray-tracer program "trace.c." We will deal with "trace.c" last, since it ties together all of the ray-tracing code in the other files and because it contains the "main" function of the TRACE program.

We previously pointed out that the functions required for each object type were contained in separate files. This was not a requirement of the object-oriented design but rather an implementation convenience. Specifically, these files contain a ray/object intersection function, a normal calculation function, an object print function, and an object creation function. The files "sphere.c" and "plane.c" are those files for the sphere and plane objects, respectively. Ray/object intersection and normal calculation algorithms for these shapes have been discussed. The algorithms coded into these files are strict conversions into C code of the mathematics discussed in Chapter 2. No surprises here. For this reason we need no additional discussion of these concepts. We will, however, discuss the object creation functions further.

The object creation functions "MakeSphere" (shown in Listing 3.5) and "MakePlane" (shown in Listing 3.6) are remarkably similar. This is due again to the object-oriented nature of this design. Both functions begin by dynamically allocating space for the object from the heap via a call to "malloc." Both functions "malloc" the same amount of memory because spheres and planes are both specialized types of OBJECTs. If the memory allocation was successful, the memory is cleared to all zeros with a call to the "memset" C function. If unsuccessful, these functions return a NULL pointer to the calling program.

Next, function pointers are stored in the OBJECT for ray/object intersection calculations, normal calculations, and for OBJECT data structure printing. Remember, each OBJECT carries around these three function pointers so it knows how to perform these operations on itself when requested to do so. Of course, the sphere OBJECTs and plane OBJECTs are assigned a different set of three function pointers. That is because their different shapes require unique operations to be performed on them.

Listing 3.5   Sphere Functions

The following is the contents of the file "sphere.c."

```
/*********************************************************/
/***                    "sphere.c"                   ***/
/***              Sphere Object Functions            ***/
/***                       for                       ***/
/***               "A First Ray Tracer"              ***/
/***      from the book "Practical Ray Tracing in C" ***/
/***           written in Borland/Turbo C 2.0        ***/
/***                        by                       ***/
/***                 Craig A. Lindley                ***/
/***                                                 ***/
/***        Ver: 1.0    Last Update: 03/10/92        ***/
/*********************************************************/

#include <stdio.h>
#include <stdlib.h>
#include "mymem.h"
#include <math.h>
#include "struct.h"
#include "trace.h"
#include "vectors.h"
```

```
/*
The following sphere intersection function is based upon the
substitution of the 3D parametric equation of a line into the formula
for a sphere. See text for details.
*/
double SphereIntersect (OBJECT *This, RAY *Ray)  {

  double B, C, Discrim, t0, t1;

  /* Don't need to calculate the A term as Ray is a unit vector */
  /* Calculate the B term */
  B = 2 *((Ray->Direction.X * (Ray->Origin.X - This->ObjSpecific.S.Center.X)) +
          (Ray->Direction.Y * (Ray->Origin.Y - This->ObjSpecific.S.Center.Y)) +
          (Ray->Direction.Z * (Ray->Origin.Z - This->ObjSpecific.S.Center.Z)));

  /* Calculate the C term */
  C = SQUARE(Ray->Origin.X - This->ObjSpecific.S.Center.X) +
      SQUARE(Ray->Origin.Y - This->ObjSpecific.S.Center.Y) +
      SQUARE(Ray->Origin.Z - This->ObjSpecific.S.Center.Z) -
      This->ObjSpecific.S.Radius2;

  /*
  Calculate the discriminant. If discriminant not positive
  then the ray does not hit the sphere. Return a t of 0.
  */
  Discrim = (SQUARE(B) - 4*C);
  if (Discrim <= EPSILON)
    return(0.0);

  /*
  Solve the quadric equation for the roots of the equation.
  You remember the roots are (-B +/- sqrt(B**2 - 4*A*C)) / 2A.
  */
  Discrim = sqrt(Discrim);
  t0 = (-B-Discrim) * 0.5;
  /*
  If t0 is positive we are done. If not, we must calculate
  the other root t1.
  */
  if (t0 > EPSILON)
    return(t0);

  t1 = (-B+Discrim) * 0.5;
  if (t1 > EPSILON)
    return(t1);

  return(0.0);
}
```

(continued)

Listing 3.5   *(continued)*

```c
/*
The following function returns a unit normal to a sphere.
Given the point of intersection of a ray and the sphere.
*/

VECTOR SphereNormal (OBJECT *This, VECTOR Point)  {

  VECTOR Normal;

  VSub(Point,This->ObjSpecific.S.Center,Normal);
  VNormalize(Normal,Normal);
  return(Normal);
}


/* A function to print the contents of a sphere object */
void SpherePrint (OBJECT *This)  {

  printf("\n\nSphere centered at <X=%g,Y=%g,Z=%g> with radius of %g\n",
         This->ObjSpecific.S.Center.X,
         This->ObjSpecific.S.Center.Y,
         This->ObjSpecific.S.Center.Z,
         This->ObjSpecific.S.Radius);
  PrintSurfaceAttrib(This);
}


/* Declare an object of type sphere */
OBJECT *MakeSphere (double X, double Y, double Z, double Radius)   {

  OBJECT *ObjectPtr = NULL;

  ObjectPtr = malloc(sizeof(OBJECT));
  if (ObjectPtr != NULL)  {
    memset(ObjectPtr,'\0',sizeof(OBJECT));
    ObjectPtr->Type = Sphere;
    /* Assign functions for intersection, normal, and printing */
    ObjectPtr->Intersect = SphereIntersect;
    ObjectPtr->Normal    = SphereNormal;
    ObjectPtr->Print     = SpherePrint;
    ObjectPtr->ObjSpecific.S.Center.X = X;
    ObjectPtr->ObjSpecific.S.Center.Y = Y;
    ObjectPtr->ObjSpecific.S.Center.Z = Z;
    ObjectPtr->ObjSpecific.S.Radius   = Radius;
    ObjectPtr->ObjSpecific.S.Radius2  = SQUARE (Radius);
    AddToList(&ObjectList,ObjectPtr);
  }
  return(ObjectPtr);
}
```

Listing 3.6   Plane Functions

The following is the contents of the file "plane.c."

```
/**********************************************************/
/***                   "plane.c"                  ***/
/***             Plane Object Functions           ***/
/***                      for                     ***/
/***               "A First Ray Tracer"           ***/
/***     from the book "Practical Ray Tracing in C"  ***/
/***          written in Borland/Turbo C 2.0      ***/
/***                      by                      ***/
/***                Craig A. Lindley              ***/
/***                                              ***/
/***        Ver: 1.0    Last Update: 03/17/92     ***/
/**********************************************************/

#include <stdio.h>
#include <stdlib.h>
#include "mymem.h"
#include <math.h>
#include "struct.h"
#include "trace.h"
#include "vectors.h"

/*
The following plane intersection function is based upon the
substitution of the 3D parametric equation of a line into the formula
for a plane. See text for details.
*/
double PlaneIntersect (OBJECT *This, RAY *Ray)  {

  double Vd, Vo, T;

  /*
  Calculate the dot product of the plane's normal and the
  ray's direction.
  */
  VDot(This->ObjSpecific.P.Normal,Ray->Direction,Vd);

  if (Vd <= EPSILON)          /* ray is parallel to plane. No intersection */
    return(0.0);              /* return t=0 */

  VDot(This->ObjSpecific.P.Normal,Ray->Origin,Vo);
  Vo += This->ObjSpecific.P.Distance;
  Vo *= -1.0;

  T = Vo/Vd;
  if (T < 0.0)                /* intersection behind ray origin */
    return(0.0);             /* return t=0 */
  return(T);                 /* else return t */
}
```

(continued)

Listing 3.6 *(continued)*

```
/*
The following function returns a unit normal to a plane. The normal to
the plane is that given in its definition.
*/

VECTOR PlaneNormal (OBJECT *This, VECTOR Point)  {

  VECTOR Normal;

  Normal.X = This->ObjSpecific.P.Normal.X;
  Normal.Y = This->ObjSpecific.P.Normal.Y;
  Normal.Z = This->ObjSpecific.P.Normal.Z;
  return(Normal);
}

/* A function to print the contents of a plane object */
void PlanePrint (OBJECT *This)  {

  printf("\n\nPlane's normal is: <A=%g,B=%g,C=%g> with distance D=%g\n",
         This->ObjSpecific.P.Normal.X,
         This->ObjSpecific.P.Normal.Y,
         This->ObjSpecific.P.Normal.Z,
        -1.0*This->ObjSpecific.P.Distance);
  PrintSurfaceAttrib(This);
}

/* Declare an object of type plane */
OBJECT *MakePlane (double A, double B, double C, double D)   {

  OBJECT *ObjectPtr = NULL;

  ObjectPtr = malloc(sizeof(OBJECT));
  if (ObjectPtr != NULL)  {
    memset(ObjectPtr,'\0',sizeof(OBJECT));
    ObjectPtr->Type = Plane;
    /* Assign functions for intersection, normal and printing */
    ObjectPtr->Intersect = PlaneIntersect;
    ObjectPtr->Normal    = PlaneNormal;
    ObjectPtr->Print     = PlanePrint;
    ObjectPtr->ObjSpecific.P.Normal.X = A;
    ObjectPtr->ObjSpecific.P.Normal.Y = B;
    ObjectPtr->ObjSpecific.P.Normal.Z = C;
    ObjectPtr->ObjSpecific.P.Distance = -D;
    /* Make the normal in case it wasn't entered that way */
    VNormalize(ObjectPtr->ObjSpecific.P.Normal,ObjectPtr->ObjSpecific.P.Normal);
    AddToList(&ObjectList,ObjectPtr);
  }
  return(ObjectPtr);
}
```

Once the function pointers are assigned, the OBJECT-specific information is filled in from parameters passed to the "MakeSphere" and "MakePlane" functions. After the OBJECT is completely initialized, the linked list function "AddToList" is called to add the OBJECT onto the global list of OBJECTs called, surprisingly enough, "ObjectList." Finally, both of these OBJECT creation functions return a pointer to the newly created OBJECT to the code that called them. You need this pointer because it is a handle to the new OBJECT. This handle is used to initialize the surface properties of the new OBJECT. Calls to the OBJECT creation functions are always followed by calls to the "SetSurfaceAttrib" function, as shown below:

```
ObjectPtr = MakeSphere(-37.5,-30.0,-15.5,20);
SetSurfaceAttrib(ObjectPtr,1.0,0.0,0.0,0.3,0.7,1.0,0.0,0.0,0.0);
```

Calling "SetSurfaceAttrib" initializes the SURFACE portion of the OBJECT's data structure with the nine attribute values that are passed as parameters. The handle returned by the OBJECT creation functions identifies which OBJECT's SURFACE parameters are to be initialized. The SURFACE parameters for all OBJECTs are the same regardless of the shape. Actual use of the "SetSurfaceAttrib" function can be seen in the file "trace.c" shown in Listing 3.12 (see pages 150–152). The "SetSurfaceAttrib" function itself can be seen in Listing 3.7 and is contained in the file "attrib.c."

The OBJECT print functions for spheres and planes are also very similar and very simple. They are included in the file of object functions for debugging purposes only. When an OBJECT is instructed to print itself, it first prints its OBJECT-specific data (which was initialized by the OBJECT creation functions) and then calls the function "PrintSurfaceAttrib," shown also in the listing, to print out the complete SURFACE data. The "PrintSurfaceAttrib" function needs only a pointer to an OBJECT to print out the appropriate OBJECT's data.

The code in the file "output.c" produces the output file from the TRACE program. The output file contains the numerical data that results from the ray-tracing process. This output file is in a format that is identical to the "dump" image format produced by the DKBTrace program. This output data file will be feed to a color quantizer program for display of the actual ray-traced image. Color quantization is necessary because the TRACE program produces 8 bits of color information for each of the RGB color components. This results in a total of 24 bits of color or 16.8 million possible colors. The color quantization reduces this extreme number of colors to the most important 256 for display on a VGA graphics adapter. Three functions comprise the "output.c" file shown in Listing 3.8.

The first function, "OpenOutputFile," attempts to open a binary file of the specified name for writing the ray-tracer output data. The first entry made in this file will be a header that contains the width and height of the image data to follow. For a 320 by 200 resolution image, the header consists of the numbers 320 followed by 200, both expressed as 16-bit integers. The color quantizer program needs this information to post process the ray-tracer data correctly. If the file is opened and the header write is successful, "OpenOutputFile" returns the "NoError" code. An appropriate error code will be returned if either operation fails. The second function, "CloseOutputFile," does what its name implies. It closes the output data file after all the data has been written to the file.

Most of the real work is done by the function "WritePixelColor." This function is called once for each calculated pixel. It accepts a COLOR structure that contains the RGB color

Listing 3.7   Surface Attribute Code

The following is the contents of the file "attrib.c."

```
/*************************************************************/
/***                    "attrib.c"                       ***/
/***            Object Attribute Functions               ***/
/***                       for                           ***/
/***               "A First Ray Tracer"                  ***/
/***     from the book "Practical Ray Tracing in C"      ***/
/***           written in Borland/Turbo C 2.0            ***/
/***                       by                            ***/
/***                 Craig A. Lindley                    ***/
/***                                                     ***/
/***         Ver: 1.0    Last Update: 03/10/92           ***/
/*************************************************************/

#include <stdio.h>
#include <stdlib.h>
#include "struct.h"
#include "trace.h"

/* A function to print the surface attributes of an object */
void PrintSurfaceAttrib (OBJECT *This)  {

  printf("Surface Attributes:\n");
  printf(" Object's Color: Red=%g, Green=%g, Blue=%g\n",
          This->Properties.Color.Red, This->Properties.Color.Green,
          This->Properties.Color.Blue);
  printf(" Ambient=%g, Diffuse=%g, Brilliance=%g, Specular=%g, Roughness=%g\n",
          This->Properties.Ambient,    This->Properties.Diffuse,
          This->Properties.Brilliance, This->Properties.Specular,
          This->Properties.Roughness);
  printf(" Reflectivity=%g\n",This->Properties.Reflection);
}

void SetSurfaceAttrib (OBJECT *This, double Red, double Green, double Blue,
                       double Ambient, double Diffuse, double Brilliance,
                       double Specular, double Roughness, double Reflection)  {

  This->Properties.Color.Red   = Red;
  This->Properties.Color.Green = Green;
  This->Properties.Color.Blue  = Blue;
  This->Properties.Ambient     = Ambient;
  This->Properties.Diffuse     = Diffuse;
  This->Properties.Brilliance  = Brilliance;
  This->Properties.Specular    = Specular;
  This->Properties.Roughness   = Roughness;
  This->Properties.Reflection  = Reflection;
}
```

Listing 3.8   Output File Producing Code

The following is the contents of the file "output.c."

```
/*************************************************************/
/***                     "output.c"                      ***/
/***             Pixel Output Code Functions             ***/
/***                        for                          ***/
/***               "A First Ray Tracer"                  ***/
/***      from the book "Practical Ray Tracing in C"     ***/
/***            written in Borland/Turbo C 2.0           ***/
/***                         by                          ***/
/***                 Craig A. Lindley                    ***/
/***                                                     ***/
/***         Ver: 1.0    Last Update: 03/10/92           ***/
/*************************************************************/

#include <stdio.h>
#include "struct.h"
#include "trace.h"
#include "errors.h"

/* Create three buffers for the storage of the pixel colors */
static BYTE Red[MAXLINEWIDTH];
static BYTE Green[MAXLINEWIDTH];
static BYTE Blue[MAXLINEWIDTH];

static FILE *ImageFile;
static unsigned LineNumber;

/* Data file header definition for the raw data file */
static struct {
  unsigned Width;
  unsigned Height;
} Hdr;

/*
Open the output raw data file in preparation for writing the pixel
color values to disk.
*/
int OpenOutputFile (char *FileName, unsigned IWidth, unsigned IHeight)  {

  /* Attempt to open the output file for writing */
  if (!(ImageFile = fopen(FileName,"wb")))
    return(EOpeningFile);

  /* Fill in and write the raw image header */
  Hdr.Width  = IWidth;
  Hdr.Height = IHeight;

  if (fwrite(&Hdr,sizeof(Hdr),1,ImageFile) != 1)
    return(EWrtFileHdr );
```

(continued)

Listing 3.8 *(continued)*

```
  LineNumber = 0;
  return(NoError);
}

/* Close the output file */
int CloseOutputFile(void)  {

  return(fclose(ImageFile));
}

int WritePixelColor (COLOR *Color, unsigned Col)   {

  /*
  Look at the calculated color value and clip if necessary
  so that it remains in the range 0.0 .. 1.0. If color value is
  greater than 1.0 then it becomes 1.0.
  */

  Color->Red   = (Color->Red   > 1.0) ? 1.0 : Color->Red;
  Color->Green = (Color->Green > 1.0) ? 1.0 : Color->Green;
  Color->Blue  = (Color->Blue  > 1.0) ? 1.0 : Color->Blue;

  /*
  Break up the color into components and store in
  appropriate buffer awaiting write to disk. Color is
  converted from floating-point double value into a BYTE
  value in the range 0 .. 255. The color passed in is constrained
  to the range 0 .. 1.
  */
  Red[Col]   = (BYTE)(255.0 * Color->Red);
  Green[Col] = (BYTE)(255.0 * Color->Green);
  Blue[Col]  = (BYTE)(255.0 * Color->Blue);

  /* Check to see if a disk write is required */
  if (Col == (Hdr.Width - 1))  {
    /* First write the line number to the file */
    if(fwrite(&LineNumber,sizeof(unsigned),1,ImageFile) != 1)   {
      fclose(ImageFile);
      return(EWrtScanLine);
    }
    LineNumber++;
    /*
    Now write the Red then the Green then the Blue data
    to the file
    */
    if (fwrite(Red,Hdr.Width,1,ImageFile) != 1)  {
      fclose(ImageFile);
      return(EWrtScanLine);
    }
```

```
    if (fwrite(Green,Hdr.Width,1,ImageFile) != 1)   {
      fclose(ImageFile);
      return(EWrtScanLine);
    }
    if (fwrite(Blue,Hdr.Width,1,ImageFile) != 1)   {
      fclose(ImageFile);
      return(EWrtScanLine);
    }
  }
  return(NoError);
}
```

components of the pixel along with the column number associated with this pixel. Before the pixel color data can be written to the output file, it must be converted from its floating-point representation to an 8-bit byte. This is done in two steps. First, the RGB components are constrained into the range 0.0 to 1.0. This is necessary because the additive nature of the shading model used in TRACE can produce color values slightly outside this range of values. After the RGB values are properly constrained, they are converted into BYTE values in the range 0 to 255 and separated into three different buffers in preparation for writing to the disk file. The column number passed as a parameter to this function determines where in the buffer the pixel's color component value belongs.

Calls to "WritePixelColor" continue uninterrupted until a full raster row of data has been accumulated. When this happens, it is time to write the data to the output file. In accordance with dump file format, the line number (row number) must be written to the output file preceding the row data. After the current row number is written to the output file, it is incremented for the next row data write. The row data is then written to the output file with the Red row data first, followed by the Green row data, and then the Blue row data. With all the row data written to disk, this function will again accumulate the calculated color data into the buffers without further writes until the next complete row has been collected. This function returns "NoError" if all went well and "EWrtScanLine (Error Writing Scan Line) if any problems were encountered. All error codes are contained in the file "errors.h" and shown in Listing 3.9.

Up until this point, all of the code discussed has dealt with the TRACE program's structure and very little with actual ray-tracing concepts. The discussion from this point forward, however, deals with ray tracing.

The "light.c" code shown in Listing 3.10 contains all of the code for creating light sources, creating light rays from OBJECTs to the light sources, and for performing shadowing calculations. The function "MakeLight" is very similar to the other OBJECT creation functions discussed recently. It accepts the location, in X, Y, and Z coordinates, of the point light source and the RGB components of the light source's color as input parameters. If the creation of the light source is successful, it will be linked onto the global linked list of light sources called "LightList."

Listing 3.9   TRACE Error Codes

The following is the contents of the file "errors.h."

```
/************************************************************/
/***                      "errors.h"                   ***/
/***                 Output Error Codes                ***/
/***                        for                        ***/
/***              "A First Ray Tracer"                 ***/
/***      from the book "Practical Ray Tracing in C"   ***/
/***            written in Borland/Turbo C 2.0         ***/
/***                        by                         ***/
/***                 Craig A. Lindley                  ***/
/***                                                   ***/
/***        Ver: 1.0    Last Update: 03/10/92          ***/
/************************************************************/

#define __ERRORS              /* indicate this file loaded */

/* Error bit definitions from graphics code */
#define NoError           0
#define EBadParms        -1
#define EFileNotFound    -2
#define EOpeningFile     -3
#define EReadFileHdr     -4
#define ENotPCXFile      -5
#define ECorrupt         -6
#define EWrtFileHdr      -7
#define EWrtOutFile      -8
#define EWrtScanLine     -9
#define EPCCFile        -10
#define EGraphics       -11
#define ENoMemory       -12
#define EWrtExtPal      -13
```

You'll notice that a light source is an OBJECT much like a sphere or a plane. Its required memory is created dynamically, it is tagged with an object type in a similar fashion, its OBJECT-specific features are initialized, and its SURFACE properties (in this case just its color) are filled in as described earlier for the other OBJECT creation functions. Note, however, that the function pointers for the intersection, the normal calculation, and the printing functions are not used for light source OBJECTs. The only other major difference is that the fully initialized light source OBJECT is linked onto a separate list of light sources instead of being linked onto the "ObjectList." A separate linked list for light sources is not strictly necessary but was done to increase the performance of the TRACE program by reducing the search time for normal OBJECTs and light sources.

Listing 3.10   Light Source Code

The following is the contents of the file "light.c."

```
/***********************************************************/
/***                    "light.c"                      ***/
/***          Light Ray / Light Source Code            ***/
/***                     for                           ***/
/***               "A First Ray Tracer"                ***/
/***     from the book "Practical Ray Tracing in C"    ***/
/***          written in Borland/Turbo C 2.0           ***/
/***                     by                            ***/
/***               Craig A. Lindley                    ***/
/***                                                   ***/
/***       Ver: 1.0    Last Update: 03/10/92           ***/
/***********************************************************/


#include <stdio.h>
#include <stdlib.h>
#include <math.h>
#include "mymem.h"
#include "struct.h"
#include "trace.h"
#include "vectors.h"


/*
The following two functions are used in testing for shadow. They
calculate information about light ray/object intersections.
*/
double MakeLightRay (OBJECT *LightPtr, VECTOR Point, RAY *Ray)  {

  double DistanceT;

  /*
  Create a ray from the point of intersection to this light source.
  Ray origin is the point. Ray direction is direct ray from center
  of light source to point. Since both rays are positional, the new
  ray is just the difference between the other rays.
  */
  Ray->Origin = Point;

  VSub(LightPtr->ObjSpecific.L.Center,Point,Ray->Direction);
  /*
  Find and return the length or distance of this ray. Make unit vector of
  direction.
  */
  VLength(Ray->Direction,DistanceT);
  VNormalize(Ray->Direction,Ray->Direction);
  return(DistanceT);
}
```

(continued)

Listing 3.10 *(continued)*

```c
COLOR GetLightColor (OBJECT *LightPtr, OBJECT *ObjectPtr, RAY *Ray,
                     double Distance)  {

  OBJECT *ShadowObjPtr;
  COLOR   Color;
  double  DistanceT;

  /* Assume light source is obscured by some object */
  Color.Red = Color.Green = Color.Blue = 0.0;

  /*
  Traverse the object list looking for obscuring object. Do not test
  to see if object itself is obscuring the light source.
  */
  ShadowObjPtr = ObjectList;
  while (ShadowObjPtr)  {
    if (ShadowObjPtr != ObjectPtr)  {
      DistanceT = ShadowObjPtr->Intersect(ShadowObjPtr,Ray);
      /*
      If an intersection is found and it is between the light and
      the object and not past it then return black for color.
      */
      if ((DistanceT > EPSILON) && (DistanceT < Distance))
        return(Color);
    }
    ShadowObjPtr = ShadowObjPtr->Next;
  }
  /*
  If we got here, no objects obscure the light from the specified
  light source to the intersection point. Therefore, return the
  colors specified for the light source.
  */
  Color.Red   = LightPtr->Properties.Color.Red;
  Color.Green = LightPtr->Properties.Color.Green;
  Color.Blue  = LightPtr->Properties.Color.Blue;
  return(Color);
}

/* Declare a light source */
OBJECT *MakeLight (double X, double Y, double Z,
                   double Red, double Green, double Blue)   {

  OBJECT *ObjectPtr = NULL;

  ObjectPtr = malloc(sizeof(OBJECT));
  if (ObjectPtr != NULL)  {
    memset(ObjectPtr,'\0',sizeof(OBJECT));
    ObjectPtr->Type = Light;
    ObjectPtr->ObjSpecific.L.Center.X = X;
```

```
   ObjectPtr->ObjSpecific.L.Center.Y = Y;
   ObjectPtr->ObjSpecific.L.Center.Z = Z;
   ObjectPtr->Properties.Color.Red   = Red;
   ObjectPtr->Properties.Color.Green = Green;
   ObjectPtr->Properties.Color.Blue  = Blue;
   AddToList(&LightList,ObjectPtr);
 }
 return(ObjectPtr);
}
```

The function "MakeLightRay" generates a RAY from the point of intersection of an OBJECT and an eye RAY to a specified light source. The function aids in determining if the specified light source adds to the illumination of the intersected OBJECT at the point of intersection. To make this determination, "MakeLightRay" accepts as parameters a pointer to a light source OBJECT, a point VECTOR, and a pointer to where the calculated RAY will be stored. This function calculates the RAY and returns it to the calling code. The origin of this RAY begins at the point of intersection and points at the specified light source. The direction of this light ray is determined by the vector subtraction of the center of the light source (its position in three-dimensional space) and the point of intersection. As you will recall, subtraction of two positional VECTORs yields a third VECTOR that spans the distance between the heads of the two input VECTORs. This new VECTOR describes the direction of the RAY that we are interested in and also the distance between the intersected OBJECT and the light source. Figure 3.1 illustrates these concepts. The intersection distance or length of this VECTOR is important for the shadow calculations described shortly and for this reason, it is returned by the "MakeLightRay" function. The final operation performed is to normalize the direction VECTOR. This is required because all RAYs utilized in the TRACE program have a unit direction VECTOR.

Note: The ray generated by this function could pass directly through the object it originates from on its way from the intersection point to the light source. A check for this condition is not important here, however, because this function will never be called by the shader (described shortly) if the light source is behind the object. All RAYs calculated by this function will therefore be valid ones.

The final function in this file is "GetLightColor." The purpose of this function is to determine if some OBJECT within our ray-traced image (our simulated three-dimensional universe) lies between the point of intersection and the light source. The idea here is that if some OBJECT does lie on this path, the specified light source will be prevented from contributing its light to the point being shaded. In other words, the point being shaded will be in the shadow of the obscuring OBJECT from the specified light source's perspective. Refer to Figure 3.1 again for a pictorial illustration of this concept. To perform these checks, the "ObjectList" is traversed, an OBJECT at a time, and an intersection calculation between the OBJECT from the list and the previously calculated light RAY is performed. The variable "DistanceT" will

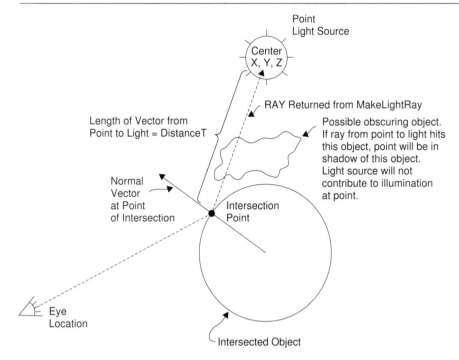

Figure 3.1   MakeLightRay Function Operation

be set to the distance along the RAY to the point of intersection with the OBJECT if an inter-section exists. If no intersection with the current OBJECT occurs, the linked list of OBJECTs is traversed further to the next OBJECT and intersection is checked again. Traversing "ObjectList" will continue until either all OBJECTs on the list have been tested for intersec-tion or until one of the OBJECTs lies between the point of intersection and the light source. When an intersection is detected, the distance to the intersection is compared to the length of the light RAY calculated by "MakeLightRay" to determine if an obscuring intersection has occurred. If an intersection did occur but is past the OBJECT, it is of no importance.

If no obscuring OBJECTs are located, the COLOR returned by this function will be that of the specified light source. If an obscuring OBJECT was found, the color of black (R=G=B=0.0) is returned because the point is in shadow.

Almost all of the ray-tracing theory discussed in Chapter 2 is embodied in the file "rays.c" shown in Listing 3.11. For this reason, this is the largest of the files that make up the TRACE ray-tracing program. The discussion of the code in "rays.c" will make more sense if we perform it backwards, from the end to the beginning. In this manner, we will traverse from the highest level of discussion toward increasing levels of detail. If you understand the mater-ial presented in this file, you are well on your way to understanding all of the ray-tracing tech-niques presented in this program. Do not be discouraged if you don't absorb all of the pre-sented information on the first reading. After some thought, the concepts should become clear, especially with the lucid explanation that follows.

Listing 3.11 The Main Ray-Tracing Code

The following is the contents of the file "rays.c."

```
/**************************************************************/
/***                    "rays.c"                         ***/
/***          Ray Creation and Shading Functions         ***/
/***                      for                            ***/
/***              "A First Ray Tracer"                   ***/
/***      from the book "Practical Ray Tracing in C"     ***/
/***            written in Borland/Turbo C 2.0           ***/
/***                       by                            ***/
/***                Craig A. Lindley                     ***/
/***                                                     ***/
/***        Ver: 1.0    Last Update: 03/10/92            ***/
/**************************************************************/

#include <stdio.h>
#include <stdlib.h>
#include <math.h>
#include <conio.h>
#include <time.h>
#include "struct.h"
#include "trace.h"
#include "vectors.h"

/*
Global variables used throughout this file and program
*/
DISPLAY Display;
VIEWPOINT View;
COLOR BackGround;
static unsigned RecurseLevel;
static unsigned Ver = 1;
static unsigned Rev = 0;
double VTemp;               /* temp variable used by macros */


/* Definition of the two major lists we will use */
OBJECT *ObjectList;         /* list of objects */
OBJECT *LightList;          /* list of light sources */


/*
Shade the point at which the ray strikes the object.
*/
void Shade(OBJECT *ObjectPtr, RAY *Ray, VECTOR Normal,
           VECTOR Point, COLOR *Color)  {

  double K, Ambient, Diffuse, Specular, DistanceT;
  RAY LightRay;
  RAY ReflectedRay;
```

(continued)

Listing 3.11   *(continued)*

```
OBJECT *LightSourcePtr;
COLOR LightColor, NewColor;

/*
Calculate the reflected ray R from the normal N and incoming ray V. The
formula for the reflected ray is generally:
                          R = 2(V dot N)N - V
assuming V points away from the point of intersection, which it
does not do in our model since the ray originates at the eye. We
must therefore reverse V to correspond to our model. To do this,
we must scale V by -1.0. The result is then:
                          R = -2N(V dot N) + V
which is the formula we will use here.

The reflected ray is that which will be traced to find color contributions
to the point being shaded if the surface being shaded is reflective. The
reflected ray starts at Point and has a direction away from the surface.
*/
VDot(Ray->Direction,Normal,K);
K *= -2.0;

ReflectedRay.Origin = Point; /* structure copy */

ReflectedRay.Direction.X = K * Normal.X + Ray->Direction.X;
ReflectedRay.Direction.Y = K * Normal.Y + Ray->Direction.Y;
ReflectedRay.Direction.Z = K * Normal.Z + Ray->Direction.Z;
/*
We do not have to normalize the reflected ray because
both V and N were unit vectors. The calculated reflected
ray is then automatically a unit vector.
*/
/*
Start the calculation of the color with the ambient contribution.
This is light that is everywhere in a scene.
*/
Ambient = ObjectPtr->Properties.Ambient;
Color->Red   = ObjectPtr->Properties.Color.Red   * Ambient;
Color->Green = ObjectPtr->Properties.Color.Green * Ambient;
Color->Blue  = ObjectPtr->Properties.Color.Blue  * Ambient;

/*
Now we must traverse the LightList to find the contribution
of each light source to the pixel color we are calculating.
*/
LightSourcePtr=LightList;  /* get us a ptr to list of sources */
while (LightSourcePtr)  {  /* for each source */
  /*
  Generate a ray from Point to light source of interest. DistanceT
  is the length of the ray from Point to light source. Call
```

```
    GetLightColor to see if there are any blocking objects along this
    ray.
    */
    DistanceT  = MakeLightRay(LightSourcePtr,Point,&LightRay);
    LightColor = GetLightColor(LightSourcePtr,ObjectPtr,&LightRay,DistanceT);

    /* Check to see if our object faces the light */
    VDot(Normal,LightRay.Direction,Diffuse);
    if ((Diffuse > 0.0) && (ObjectPtr->Properties.Diffuse > 0.0)) {
      Diffuse = pow(Diffuse,ObjectPtr->Properties.Brilliance) *
                  ObjectPtr->Properties.Diffuse;
      Color->Red   += (LightColor.Red   * ObjectPtr->Properties.Color.Red   * Diffuse);
      Color->Green += (LightColor.Green * ObjectPtr->Properties.Color.Green * Diffuse);
      Color->Blue  += (LightColor.Blue  * ObjectPtr->Properties.Color.Blue  * Diffuse);
    }
    /*
    Note: usually the specular component is calculated by seeing how
    the incident ray V lines up with the reflected light ray.
    The closer they are to being equal, the bigger contribution
    made to the color of the object at Point. In our case, we will
    do the same thing by comparing how the reflected incident ray
    calculated above and called ReflectedRay lines up with the
    LightRay. This requires less computation because ReflectedRay and
    LightRay already point in the same direction. This works because the
    angle between the two sets of rays is the same.
    */
    VDot(ReflectedRay.Direction,LightRay.Direction,Specular);
    /* add highlight */
    if ((Specular > 0.0) && (ObjectPtr->Properties.Specular > 0.0)) {
      Specular = pow(Specular,ObjectPtr->Properties.Roughness) *
      ObjectPtr->Properties.Specular;
      Color->Red   += (LightColor.Red   * Specular);
      Color->Green += (LightColor.Green * Specular);
      Color->Blue  += (LightColor.Blue  * Specular);
    }
    LightSourcePtr = LightSourcePtr->Next;
  }
  /* Now consider reflection */
  K = ObjectPtr->Properties.Reflection;
  if (K > 0.0)  {
    RecurseLevel++;
    Trace(&ReflectedRay,&NewColor);
    Color->Red   += NewColor.Red   * K;
    Color->Green += NewColor.Green * K;
    Color->Blue  += NewColor.Blue  * K;
    RecurseLevel--;
  }
}
```

(continued)

Listing 3.11 *(continued)*

```c
/*
Create a Ray from the eye position through the display
at CurX, CurY.
*/
void MakeRay (unsigned CurX,  unsigned CurY, RAY *Ray)    {

  double ScrnX, ScrnY;
  VECTOR TempV1, TempV2;

  /* Convert the X Coordinate to be a double from -0.5 to 0.5 */
  ScrnX  = (CurX - (double) Display.DisplayWidth / 2.0) /
           (double) Display.DisplayWidth;

  /* Convert the Y Coordinate to be a double from -0.5 to 0.5 */
  ScrnY  = (((double)(Display.DisplayHeight -1) - CurY) -
             (double) Display.DisplayHeight / 2.0) /
             (double) Display.DisplayHeight;

  VScale (View.Up,     ScrnY, TempV1);
  VScale (View.Right, ScrnX, TempV2);
  VAdd (TempV1, TempV2, Ray->Direction);
  VAdd (View.Direction, Ray->Direction, Ray->Direction);
  VNormalize (Ray->Direction, Ray->Direction);
  Ray->Origin.X = View.Location.X;
  Ray->Origin.Y = View.Location.Y;
  Ray->Origin.Z = View.Location.Z;
}


/*
Given a ray from the eye position through the screen, trace that ray
into the 3D universe to see what it intersects, if anything. Call
shader to figure out the color of what is hit.
*/
void Trace (RAY *Ray, COLOR *Color)   {

  double T, MinT, NormalDir;
  OBJECT *MinObjectPtr;
  OBJECT *ObjectPtr;
  VECTOR Point;
  VECTOR Normal;

  /* Initialize color to black */
  Color->Red = Color->Green = Color->Blue = 0.0;

  /* Recursion limit check */
  if (RecurseLevel > MAXRECURSELEVEL)
    return;

  MinT = BIG;
  MinObjectPtr = NULL;
  ObjectPtr = ObjectList;
```

```
      /*
      What objects does this ray intersect?  T is the parameter of
      the intersection. A T of 0.0 means nothing was intersected
      by Ray
      */
      while(ObjectPtr)  {
        T = (ObjectPtr->Intersect(ObjectPtr,Ray));
        if ((T > EPSILON) && (T < MinT))  {
          /* Save ptr to closest object intersected */
          MinT = T;
          MinObjectPtr = ObjectPtr;
        }
        ObjectPtr = ObjectPtr->Next;
      }
      /* if nothing was intersected, return background color */
      if (MinT == BIG )  {
        Color->Red   = BackGround.Red;
        Color->Green = BackGround.Green;
        Color->Blue  = BackGround.Blue;
        return;
      }
      /*
      If we get here, we know that our Ray has intersected an object
      use the parameter MinT to calculate the point of intersection.
      */
      Point.X = MinT * Ray->Direction.X + Ray->Origin.X;
      Point.Y = MinT * Ray->Direction.Y + Ray->Origin.Y;
      Point.Z = MinT * Ray->Direction.Z + Ray->Origin.Z;
      /*
      Now find the normal to the intersected object at the point
      of intersection.
      */
      Normal = MinObjectPtr->Normal(MinObjectPtr, Point);
      /*
      Check to see if Normal is pointing toward Ray. If not
      we must reverse the direction of the Normal.
      */
      VDot(Normal,Ray->Direction,NormalDir);
      if (NormalDir > 0.0)
        VNegate(Normal,Normal);

      /* Shade this point */
      Shade(MinObjectPtr,Ray,Normal,Point,Color);
}


/*
This function provides help in the advent of operator error. Program
terminates after help is given
*/
```

(continued)

Listing 3.11 *(continued)*

```c
void ShowHelp( void )  {

  printf("Trace is invoked as follows:\n\n");
  printf("Usage: trace [-l]<cr>\n");
  printf("  -l or L renders the larger 320x200 pixel image\n");
  exit(1);
}

/*
Parse the command line to see if larger image format is
required.
*/
void ParseCmdLine(short argc, char *argv[])  {

  unsigned ArgIndex;

  /* Assume we'll render a small 80x50 pixel image with 256 colors */
  Display.DisplayWidth  = 80;
  Display.DisplayHeight = 50;

  printf("\n\nA First Ray Tracer Program - Version: %d.%d\n",Ver,Rev);
  printf("from the book \"Practical Ray Tracing in C\"\n");
  printf("Written by Craig A. Lindley\n\n");

  /* parse all command line arguments */
  for (ArgIndex=1; ArgIndex < argc; ArgIndex++)  {
    if (*argv[ArgIndex] != '-')      /* if not a cmd line switch */
      ShowHelp();                    /* then it's an error */
    else {                           /* it's a cmd line switch */
      switch (*(argv[ArgIndex]+1)) { /* parse the cmd line switch */
        case 'h':
        case 'H':
          ShowHelp();
          break;
        case 'l':
        case 'L':
          /* Select the large image format */
          Display.DisplayWidth  = 320;
          Display.DisplayHeight = 200;
          break;
        default:
          printf("Error - invalid cmd line switch encountered\n");
          ShowHelp();
      }
    }
  }
}
```

```
/*
Perform the actual ray tracing of the scene described in the
file "trace.c."
*/
void DoRayTrace(void)  {

  unsigned X, Y;
  RAY Ray;
  COLOR Color;

  time_t timer;
  struct tm *tblock;

  /* Initialize the recurselevel to zero */
  RecurseLevel = 0;

  /* Open the output file for this image */
  OpenOutputFile("ray.raw",Display.DisplayWidth,Display.DisplayHeight);

  /* get the time the ray tracing was started */
  timer = time(NULL);

  /* converts date/time to a structure */
  tblock = localtime(&timer);

  printf("\nBegin Ray Trace on %s",asctime(tblock));
  printf("Tracing Row\n");          /* print the identifier */

  /* Do the ray tracing pixel by pixel, line by line */
  for (Y = 0; Y < Display.DisplayHeight && (!kbhit()); Y++)    {
    printf("%4d",Y);                /* print the current row */
    for (X = 0 ; X < Display.DisplayWidth ; X++) {
      MakeRay (X,Y,&Ray);           /* calculate eye ray for this pixel */
      Trace (&Ray, &Color);         /* trace it through the scene */
      WritePixelColor(&Color,X);    /* output pixel color to disk */
    }
  }
  /* get the time the ray tracing was completed */
  timer = time(NULL);

  /* converts date/time to a structure */
  tblock = localtime(&timer);

  printf("\nEnd Ray Trace on %s\n",asctime(tblock));
  CloseOutputFile();
  FreeList(&ObjectList);     /* return memory */
  FreeList(&LightList);
}
```

Let us begin the discussion with the function "DoRayTrace." This function performs the ray tracing of the image described in the file "trace.c." No parameters are passed to "DoRayTrace" as it takes all of its inputs from global data set up before it is called. The first item of business is to initialize the "RecurseLevel" variable to zero. As discussed in Chapter 2, the calculations for reflective surfaces use recursion. We maintain a count of the recursion level as a way to limit the number of levels for image rendering time and stack space considerations. Currently, the limit is set at five levels of recursion by the macro constant "MAXRECURSE-LEVEL," defined in the file "trace.h."

Next, we open the output data file that will contain the calculated ray-traced data (in "dump" file format). By default, the name given to this file will be "ray.raw." The "Display-Width" and "DisplayHeight" values that will control the resolution of the image to be ray traced are passed along with the filename to the "OpenOutputFile" function. As mentioned previously, these values will be placed in a header and written to the output data file to help identify the file's contents to later color quantization programs.

Execution continues with the display of a few status messages, along with the time the ray tracing was initiated. On completion of this function's execution, the time is again displayed. We did this so you could easily figure out how long it took to generate your ray-traced image.

Now the real ray tracing begins. Two nested "for" loops control the ray tracing on a line-by-line and pixel-by-pixel basis. The outer loop controls which row of screen data is being generated. The inner loop controls which pixel of the row is being generated. You'll notice that if you hit a key on the keyboard the ray tracing will be aborted. This allows a quick termination of a lengthy ray-trace session. You should note, however, that there are no provisions to salvage the partial file of data. Once a ray trace is aborted, the data is useless. Notice that the extents of these loops are controlled by the resolution parameters DisplayWidth and Display-Height. As the resolution specified by these parameters increases, so does the number of passes through these loops. For a 320 by 200 resolution image (the default large image used in this program), a total of 64,000 passes are made, one for each pixel. For a 640 by 480 image, 307,200 pixels are calculated. For a 1024 by 768 image, 786,432 pixels are calculated. You can start to appreciate why ray tracing high-resolution images takes such a long time.

Ray tracing proceeds a pixel at a time. Please review the basic ray-tracing algorithm in Chapter 2 if you have any uncertainties about how this code segment works. As you will recall, we shoot a RAY from our eye position (VIEWPOINT) through a pixel on the screen out into our imaginary three-dimensional universe to see what it hits, if anything. We determine what color to make the pixel on the screen based on what the RAY hit. This process is accomplished with the following three functions:

1. "MakeRay," which generates the RAY from the VIEWPOINT through the pixel being calculated
2. "Trace," which traces the RAY through our three-dimensional scene and returns the COLOR of what was hit
3. "WritePixelColor," which writes the calculated pixel COLOR to the output file

Sounds simple, doesn't it? This pixel-by-pixel process continues until all pixels in all rows of the image have been calculated. "DoRayTrace" then terminates by outputting the ray trace end time and message, closing the output file, and freeing all of the memory allocated to OBJECTs and light sources defined in the scene just ray traced. At this point, a data file called "ray.raw" should exist in the current directory. This file contains the ray-traced image data in numerical form. A color quantization program could then be executed with the following command line:

    mquan ray.raw <Enter>

to display the actual image.

The function "MakeRay" implements the viewing geometry or model for this ray tracer. TRACE uses, by no small coincidence, the same view geometry as does the DKBTrace ray tracer. This allows any images created with TRACE to be rendered by DKBTrace with basically the same result. To understand viewing geometry, see Chapter 2. To understand how it is implemented in the TRACE program, stay tuned.

The viewing geometry describes the way in which the VIEWPOINT parameters interact to determine how the viewer (of a ray-traced image) sees the objects within a three-dimensional scene. Manipulation of the VIEWPOINT parameters allows infinite ways of viewing the three-dimensional scene. To picture how this works, imagine yourself sitting in front of your computer's monitor with your eyes positioned directly in front of the center of the screen. Think of the monitor's screen as a grid of pixels (similar to a wire mesh) each defined by an X and a Y coordinate. Imagine some objects behind the monitor's screen that show themselves through the grid. Now, sweep your eyes left to right, starting at the top and continuing to the bottom of the screen. In some portions of the grid, you would see portions of the objects within the scene. In others, you would see just the background behind the objects. Also, some of the objects will appear brighter than other objects. This has to do with the position of the object in relation to the light sources illuminating the scene and the surface properties of the individual objects.

The process just described is ray tracing. When the eye looks through one of the cells in the grid out into the scene it is just as if a ray had been shot from the eye's position through a pixel on the screen and into the scene. The color of the cell the eye sees is determined by the laws of geometric optics; the same laws that govern ray tracing. The difference between these two conceptual processes is that in actual ray tracing, instead of your eye directly perceiving the color of an object, the screen pixel is set to the object's color and your eye sees that. To understand how this process is performed by a computer requires a discussion of Figure 3.2. Please examine this diagram now.

As we discussed earlier, four VECTORs define the VIEWPOINT. They are Location, Direction, Up, and Right and are shown in this figure. Location is the position in Cartesian coordinates of where the eye is located. Direction is a VECTOR that starts at Location and always points to the center of the view plane simulated by the computer monitor. In other words, regardless of the actual direction of view into the scene, this simulated screen will always be placed directly centered on the viewing direction. The Up VECTOR originates at the center of this screen and points upwards toward the middle of the top edge of the screen. The Right VECTOR also starts at the screen's center but points to what would be the center of the right edge. The Up and Right VECTORs therefore determine the orientation of the OBJECTs the eye sees. As we have seen in Chapter 2, these VECTORs also control the relative fields of view in both the horizontal and vertical directions.

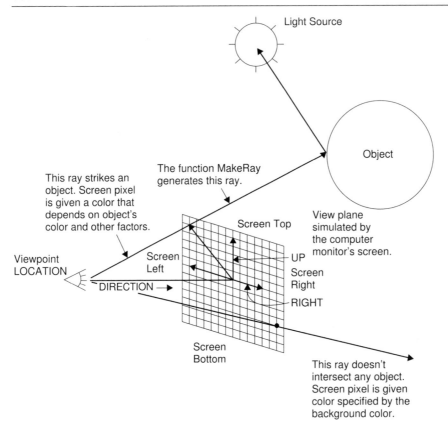

Figure 3.2   VIEWPOINT Diagram

The function "MakeRay" uses all four of the VIEWPOINT VECTORs in addition to the current pixel's X and Y coordinates to generate a RAY from the VIEWPOINT through the pixel and out into the scene. The first step in this process is to convert the X and Y values of the pixel into floating-point numbers in the range -0.5 to +0.5. This conversion is resolution-independent. That is, the converted value will always lie in that range regardless of the resolution of the image being rendered. This conversion is straightforward, but note the added complication when calculating "ScrnY" due to the fact that Y screen coordinates start at zero at the top of the screen and grow progressively more positive when moving toward the bottom.

After the "ScrnX" and "ScrnY" values are calculated, you can use them to scale the Right and Up VECTORs, respectively. If the Up VECTOR points straight up and the Right VECTOR points directly right, and if they are both unit VECTORs in the plane of the view plane, then the two calls to "VScale" form a two-dimensional vector on the screen from the center to an X coordinate of the pixel and from the center to the Y coordinate of the same pixel. Adding these two vectors together yields a vector from the center of the screen directly to the pixel to be rendered. Adding this vector to the viewing Direction VECTOR yields a VECTOR from the eye through the specified pixel and onward. This VECTOR is then normalized and saved as the new RAY's direction. The RAY's origin is set equal to the eye's location. In this way, a new eye RAY is formed and returned from "MakeRay."

As discussed earlier, the Up and Right vectors control the field of view. As these VECTORs take on lengths greater than one (they need not be unit VECTORs), the distance represented by each increment of direction becomes greater. You can use this fact in many ways, the most common being aspect ratio correction and field of view determination, as discussed. Because of the flexibility of this viewing model, you can use the Up and Right VECTORs to alter images drastically. You can produce some rather bizarre special effects simply by changing the relationship of the Up and Right VECTORs. Until this point, we have always assumed that these VECTORs are at right angles to each other. ("Orthogonal" is the term for this relationship.) Nothing in the view model dictates this, however. Try rendering an image with differing angles between the Up and the Right VECTORs for some interesting effects. *Note*: The VIEWPOINT is described in terms of the same coordinate system as that used by the OBJECTs in the scene.

Once you have generated a RAY with "MakeRay," you must trace its path into the scene to see what happens. The function "Trace" does this. It accepts a RAY (generated by "MakeRay") as an input parameter and returns a pointer to a COLOR structure that contains the RGB components of the corresponding pixel. How the color is calculated is described next.

The first operation that "Trace" performs is to set the COLOR structure to be returned to zeros—the color black. Since the RGB color system is additive, colors are built by adding the individual RGB components. Lack of color is black (R=G=B=0.0), whereas the sum of all colors is white (R=G=B=1.0). See the "RGB Color Tables" section of Part Three for a table of colors and their corresponding RGB values.

Next, the level of recursion is checked. If the maximum level has already been exceeded, meaning that no further reflective rays will be traced, this function immediately returns with COLOR set to black. This indicates that the ray just traced makes no lighting contribution. When the color black is added to any other color by the code that calls "Trace," it will have no effect, as zero added to any number is still the number.

If we haven't exceeded the recursion level, "Trace" proceeds to test for intersections between the input RAY and all OBJECTs defined in our three-dimensional scene. "Trace" does this by traversing the "ObjectList" and executing the intersection calculation on each OBJECT. As intersections are found, the minimum distance in terms of the parameter T and a pointer to the intersected OBJECT are saved. Remember, we are interested only in the closest intersection to the viewer, as that is the surface that will be visible. This operation performs hidden surface removal on a point-by-point basis. After "Trace" has traversed the "ObjectList," two scenarios can exist. First, it is possible that the RAY did not intersect any of the OBJECTs in our scene. In this case, COLOR is set equal to the background color and "Trace" returns. In the second scenario, an OBJECT has been intersected and there is much more work to do.

Since the origin and the direction of the RAY are known and the parameter T is known also, the actual point of intersection can be calculated with the explicit equation of a RAY provided in Chapter 2 and shown next:

> Point.X = MinT * Ray->Direction.X + Ray.Origin.X
> Point.Y = MinT * Ray->Direction.Y + Ray.Origin.Y
> Point.Z = MinT * Ray->Direction.Z + Ray.Origin.Z

What we have done here is to plug the parameter T (called MinT) back into the equation and solve for the point of intersection, Point. With the point of intersection now known, we need to calculate a normal VECTOR to the surface of the intersected object that passes through Point. We do this by calling the normal function for the intersected OBJECT and passing Point. *Note*: It is unimportant what type of OBJECT has been intersected; by calling the normal function through the intersected OBJECT, we are guaranteed that the proper normal calculation procedure will be performed. The appropriate normal VECTOR is calculated and returned. A check is placed into the trace function's code to determine if the newly calculated normal points in the direction of the intersecting RAY. If not, the normal is negated to point back at the RAY. This check and possible correction, although not strictly necessary in our simple ray tracer, will become more important if the ray tracer is extended. The correction is sometimes applied during plane calculations if the defining normal for the plane was incorrectly entered. The final operation of "Trace" is to call the shader function "Shade" to determine the color of the surface (and therefore the color of the pixel being calculated) at the point of intersection.

"Shade" is the most complex function in the entire TRACE program. This is where the laws of optics are combined with the surface properties of OBJECTs to determine realistic color. Remember, shading has nothing to do with shadows, only with the calculation of color. To perform shading requires the surface attributes of the intersected OBJECT, the RAY which intersected it, the normal of the OBJECT at the point of intersection, and the actual point of intersection. All these are combined to calculate a single pixel's color. Everything we know about this intersection is shown diagrammatically in Figure 3.3.

The first operation that "Shade" performs is the calculation of the reflection RAY R. As shown in Figure 3.3, this is the RAY along which light reflected from somewhere else in the scene would contribute to the color at Point if this OBJECT were at all reflective, and it would be seen by the eye. To calculate the reflected RAY R given the incidence ray V and the normal N, we will utilize the idea that the angle of incidence equals the angle of reflection. Since all of these VECTORs are in the same plane, the formula for reflection will be:

$$R = -2 * N * (V \text{ dot } N) + V$$

Note: This is a different formula for reflected ray calculation than given in Chapter 2 because the direction of the view ray V is reversed. If you substitute -V into the equation above, you will get the formula from Chapter 2.

It is interesting to note that this property of reflection has been known since the time of Euclid with a formal proof performed by Christian Huygens in 1678. Note also, that if all involved VECTORs are unit VECTORs, the calculated reflected RAY will also be a unit VECTOR.

Now that we have calculated this reflected RAY we can begin to calculate our pixel's color using as our starting point the simplified illumination equation:

$$I = I_l * (k_d * (L \text{ dot } N) + k_s * (R \text{ dot } V)^{Roughness}) + I_o * k_a$$

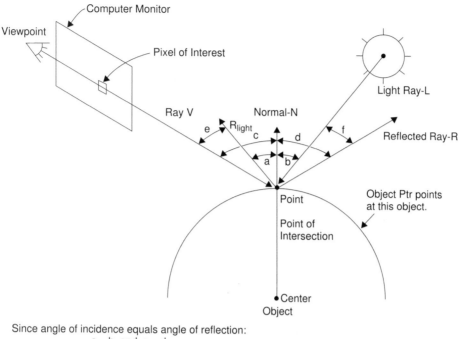

Since angle of incidence equals angle of reflection:
a = b and c = d

Figure 3.3 Shading Information Diagram

which was described in Chapter 2. As you will recall, this equation must be solved for each of the three R, G, and B color components. We start by calculating the ambient light contribution to the pixel's color. The ambient term is the final term in the equation above. The color of the pixel is initially set equal to the OBJECT's RGB components multiplied by the ambient light absorbation constant k_a, which is one of the SURFACE properties stored for each OBJECT. *Note*: The ambient light contribution to our pixel's color is independent of any light sources defined in our scene and also independent of the direction to the viewer. Providing ambient lighting in a scene is a simplification of nature that we allow because calculating the actual interaction of light between surfaces is difficult. This simplification provides realistic imagery with simple calculations.

Once we have calculated the ambient lighting, we must separately consider the diffuse contribution from each light source. To calculate the total diffuse lighting contribution, we traverse the "LightList" and calculate the contribution of each light source independently; each time we add that contribution to the final pixel's color. In preparation, we call "MakeLightRay" to generate a RAY from the point of intersection to the currently selected light source and "Get-LightColor" to look for obscuring OBJECTs that would place the point in shadow. We can calculate the diffuse component of the lighting by performing a dot product between the light RAY's direction and the surface normal to determine if the OBJECT faces the light. Remember, if the RAY's direction VECTOR and the normal VECTOR are unit VECTORs, the dot product is the cosine of the angle between them. Thus, if the cosine returns a negative number, the light source is more than ± 90 degrees from the normal and therefore cannot contribute to the OBJECT's illumination. If the OBJECT does not face the light source, no diffuse contribution is added. If the OBJECT does face the light and if the OBJECT being shaded has a diffuse surface parameter greater than zero, we need to add a diffuse contribution from this light source. The portion of the illumination equation for diffuse lighting is:

$$I_d = I_1 * (k_d * (L \text{ dot } N))$$

but we will make a couple of small modifications to this formula to make the results more realistic. (We described such modifications in Chapter 2.) First, we add a new term "Brilliance," which is used to limit the effect of the diffuse light. In other words, "Brilliance" increases the impact of the diffuse lighting near the normal (and reduces its contribution quickly as the angle from the normal increases), thus adding a more realistic lighting effect. "Brilliance" is incorporated into the diffuse lighting calculations by modifying the above formula to yield:

$$I_d = I_1 * (k_d * (L \text{ dot } N)^{Brilliance})$$

Remember, this illumination formula is for a single monochromatic light source. In reality, we must apply the formula three times, once for each of the color components of the light source, each time using a different diffuse absorbation constant k_d. In our simplified shading model we will assume the existence of a single diffuse coefficient (contained in the SURFACE definition portion of each OBJECT) and approximate the absorbation characteristics by multiplying by the OBJECT's real color. The process for calculating the diffuse lighting contribution to a pixel can be illustrated succinctly with the pseudocode that follows:

```
Perform dot product of normal and light RAY
if dot product is greater than zero and OBJECT has nonzero diffuse coefficient then
    Diffuse = dot product ^ Brilliance * diffuse coefficient
    Red contribution   = Red component of light   * Red component of OBJECT   * Diffuse
    Green contribution = Green component of light * Green component of OBJECT * Diffuse
    Blue contribution  = Blue component of light  * Blue component of OBJECT  * Diffuse
```

This is the tact taken in the TRACE ray-trace program.

The reflective properties of an object depend on the smoothness of its surface. The smoother the surface, the more it will act like a mirror. A rough surface will diffuse light in all directions due to minute microfacets on the surface. When a surface reaches a certain smoothness, bright highlights will appear. These highlights take on the color of the light source near their center but quickly fade to the OBJECT's color at the edges. Those highlights are formed when the incident ray, V from the previous figure, lines up with the reflection of the light RAY. The closer these RAYs line up, the better the approximation is to a perfect reflector. These highlights are referred to as specular reflections. We will use the Phong reflection model, described in Chapter 2, to calculate the specular highlights. The portion of our illumination equation that describes specular reflection is:

$$I_{sp} = I_1 * (k_s * (R_{light} \text{ dot } V)^{Roughness})$$

which is surprisingly similar to the equation used for diffuse lighting. Again, for implementation reasons, we will slightly change the way we apply this formula. The change we make is to
calculate the dot product between the previously calculated reflected RAY R and the actual
light RAY L. This has exactly the same effect as calculating the dot product between the viewing RAY V and the reflected light RAY R$_{light}$. We did this because we will need the reflected
ray R in the reflection calculations that come next. That way, we calculate only one reflected
RAY, and it can be used in two different places in the code. You can see the specular reflection
calculations in the listing. *Note*: The larger the "Roughness" value, the smoother the surface
appears. In reality, the specular coefficient k$_s$ also depends on the surface material, but we do
not take that fact into consideration in this program.

After we consider the ambient lighting contribution, the diffuse lighting contribution,
and the specular contribution for each light source, the final factor that can contribute to a
pixel's color depends on the reflective properties of the OBJECT's surface. If the OBJECT
being shaded is at all reflective, reflections off other OBJECTs in the scene can contribute
greatly to its color. Picture a highly reflective silver ball on a bright red piece of paper. The
portion of the ball that faces the red paper (the bottom) will reflect the red color and will
appear red. Very little of the ball's silver color will be evident; the reflected color will dominate. If the ball is somewhat less reflective, less of the reflected red color will be visible and
the ball will retain more of its natural silver color. In the case where the ball is totally nonreflective, the reflected color will not be evident at all. The final portion of the "Shade" function
determines how the OBJECT's reflectivity helps determine its color.

As we have discussed, the calculation of reflection is recursive in nature. If OBJECT A's
color depends on reflection from OBJECT B, OBJECT B's color may also depend on reflection from OBJECT C, and so on. Two basic techniques are typically used to determine just
how far this recursion process should go, and they have been described in Chapter 2. Remember, performing recursive shading calculations can be time-consuming for a computer. It is for
this reason that we need to limit recursion. Again, our goal is to produce a reasonable approximation of a photo-realistic image in a reasonable amount of time. As soon as an image looks
good enough, we need go no further.

The actual reflection contribution is simple to calculate, and the calculation is performed
only if a surface has a nonzero reflection coefficient. When an OBJECT is reflective, the
"RecurseLevel" variable is incremented and "Trace" is called again, this time using the previously calculated reflected RAY R (remember that "Trace" originally called "Shade," which
now recursively calls "Trace" again for the reflected ray). When "Trace" returns with the new
color (the color contribution from the reflected ray), its color components are added to the
composite color for the point being shaded, as weighted by the reflection coefficient. An
OBJECT that is a perfect mirror would have a coefficient of 1.0. You can see that the larger
the reflection coefficient, the more the light reflected onto the surface contributes to the surface's color. After the color contribution is summed, the recursion level is decremented and
the "Shade" function returns.

The final file that makes up the TRACE program defines the actual three-dimensional
scene that will be ray traced. This file is called "trace.c" and is shown in Listing 3.12. You can
see the image described in the file in the "Gallery of Images." Please keep the content of this
image in your mind as we finish our discussion of the ray tracer.

Listing 3.12   The Scene-Defining Code

The following is the contents of the file "trace.c."

```
/***********************************************************/
/***                      "trace.c"                    ***/
/***          Ray Trace Scene Definition File          ***/
/***                        for                        ***/
/***               "A First Ray Tracer"                ***/
/***      from the book "Practical Ray Tracing in C"   ***/
/***          written in Borland/Turbo C 2.0           ***/
/***                         by                        ***/
/***               Craig A. Lindley                    ***/
/***                                                   ***/
/***        Ver: 1.0    Last Update: 03/10/92          ***/
/***********************************************************/

#include "struct.h"
#include "trace.h"

/*
Make up some color and surface definitions
*/
/*      Color            Red Green Blue components */
#define BLACK              0.000,0.000,0.000
#define GOLD               0.800,0.498,0.196
#define MEDIUMFORESTGREEN  0.419,0.556,0.137
#define MIDNIGHTBLUE       0.184,0.184,0.304
#define ORANGE1            1.000,0.160,0.000
#define ORANGE2            1.000,0.350,0.000
#define COPPER             0.840,0.160,0.000
#define GREEN1             0.450,0.910,0.000
#define BLUE               0.000,0.000,1.000
#define RED                1.000,0.000,0.000
#define GREEN              0.000,1.000,0.000
#define PURPLE1            0.870,0.000,1.000
#define PURPLE3            0.820,0.000,0.820

#define SURFACE 0.3,0.7,20.0,0.9,100.0,0.65

/*
A First Ray-Tracer Program
*/

void main(short argc, char *argv[])  {

  OBJECT *ObjectPtr;

  ParseCmdLine(argc,argv);

  /* Initialize our ray-tracer's universe */
```

```
/* Set the BackGround color */
BackGround.Red   = 0.0;
BackGround.Green = 0.0;
BackGround.Blue  = 0.0;

/* Set up the eye data */
View.Location.X =   0.0;    /* set the eye's location */
View.Location.Y =  -5.0;
View.Location.Z = -110.0;
View.Direction.X =  0.0;    /* and gaze direction */
View.Direction.Y = -0.05;
View.Direction.Z =  1.0;
View.Up.X        =  0.0;    /* up is above the eye on +Y axis */
View.Up.Y        =  1.0;
View.Up.Z        =  0.0;
View.Right.X     =  1.333; /* right is to the right correcting for */
View.Right.Y     =  0.0;    /* aspect ratio. */
View.Right.Z     =  0.0;

/* Make some objects */
ObjectPtr = MakeSphere(0,0,0,25);
SetSurfaceAttrib(ObjectPtr,GOLD,SURFACE);

ObjectPtr = MakeSphere(-37.5,-30.0,-15.5,20);
SetSurfaceAttrib(ObjectPtr,MEDIUMFORESTGREEN,SURFACE);

ObjectPtr = MakeSphere(52.5,-17.5,-18.0,20);
SetSurfaceAttrib(ObjectPtr,ORANGE1,SURFACE);

ObjectPtr = MakeSphere(-57.5,12.5,0.0,15);
SetSurfaceAttrib(ObjectPtr,COPPER,SURFACE);

ObjectPtr = MakeSphere(12.5,-32.5,-14.0,15);
SetSurfaceAttrib(ObjectPtr,COPPER,SURFACE);

ObjectPtr = MakeSphere(47.5,17.5,20.0,15);
SetSurfaceAttrib(ObjectPtr,PURPLE1,SURFACE);

ObjectPtr = MakeSphere(-32.5,32.5,35.0,15);
SetSurfaceAttrib(ObjectPtr,GREEN1,SURFACE);

ObjectPtr = MakeSphere(17.5,30.0,47.5,20);
SetSurfaceAttrib(ObjectPtr,GOLD,SURFACE);

ObjectPtr = MakeSphere(62.5,0.0,-77.5,20);
SetSurfaceAttrib(ObjectPtr,BLUE,SURFACE);

ObjectPtr = MakeSphere(0.0,-30.0,-100.0,20);
SetSurfaceAttrib(ObjectPtr,RED,SURFACE);
```

(continued)

Listing 3.12 *(continued)*

```
ObjectPtr = MakeSphere(-62.5,0.0,-77.5,20);
SetSurfaceAttrib(ObjectPtr,GREEN,SURFACE);

ObjectPtr = MakeSphere(-45.0,-18.5,0.0,15);
SetSurfaceAttrib(ObjectPtr,ORANGE2,SURFACE);

ObjectPtr = MakeSphere(40.0,-18.5,0.0,15);
SetSurfaceAttrib(ObjectPtr,PURPLE3,SURFACE);

ObjectPtr = MakeSphere(-75.0,100.0,-50.0,40);
SetSurfaceAttrib(ObjectPtr,ORANGE2,SURFACE);

/* Back drop */
ObjectPtr = MakePlane(0,0,-1,-200);
SetSurfaceAttrib(ObjectPtr,MIDNIGHTBLUE,0.3,0.7,1.0,0.0,0.0,0.0);

/* Floor */
ObjectPtr = MakePlane(0,1,0,-50);
SetSurfaceAttrib(ObjectPtr,BLUE,0.3,0.7,1.0,0.0,0.0,0.0);

/* Make some light sources */
MakeLight(65,100,-100,1.0,1.0,1.0);

DoRayTrace();

}
```

The first part of this file symbolically defines constants for the surface properties utilized in the code and for various colors. Each color #defined on the listing represents the RGB components of the color. These constants are defined because it is much easier to think of a color by name than by its RGB components. The SURFACE define will be used to describe all spheres in the example ray-traced image. The breakdown of this define results in surfaces with the following characteristics:

Ambient coefficient = 0.3
Diffuse coefficient = 0.7
Brilliance coefficient = 20.0
Specular coefficient = 0.9
Roughness coefficient = 100.0
Reflectivity coefficient = 0.65

The definition of the ray-traced scene begins in the "main" function. The only variable used is a pointer to an OBJECT, which will be used to set surface attributes for each OBJECT. Program operation begins by calling "ParseCmdLine" to see if the user has requested the larger 320 by 200 image instead of the normal 80 by 50 pixel resolution. A "-l" specified on the command line will select the larger image format. Any other command line switch specified will result in program termination with a short help message. Following command line parsing, our scene is defined. First, the background color is set to black. Next, the VIEW-POINT VECTORs are initialized. Then, the 14 spheres that make up the majority of our scene are defined. "MakeSphere" is called each time to specify the sphere's location and radius. The OBJECT pointer returned by "MakeSphere" is then used by "SetSurfaceAttrib" to set the color and surface properties of the newly defined spheres. Two planes are then defined: one as the backdrop and one as a floor, if you will. The planes are defined by the defining normal and the distance from the origin. "SetSurfaceAttrib" is also used to set the surface properties of both planes. Finally, a single light source is created to illuminate the scene. You perform the actual ray tracing with the call to "DoRayTrace."

Even though we have not yet discussed the DKBTrace ray tracer in any depth, you may want to see how it can generate the same example image that the TRACE program in this chapter generates. In the TRACE program, the definition of the image to be ray traced is hard coded in C in the file "trace.c." With DKBTrace, an image is described using a scene description language. The image description shown in Listing 3.13 will cause DKBTrace to generate the exact same image as the TRACE program did. In Part Two of this book, we discuss DKBTrace and its scene description language in detail. Listing 3.13 may make more sense to you after reading Part Two.

Listing 3.13   DKBTrace Image Model of TRACE Image

The following is the contents of the file "trace.dat."

```
{ DKBTrace version of trace.c }

INCLUDE "colors.dat"            { standard includes for color }
INCLUDE "shapes.dat"            { for shapes and }
INCLUDE "textures.dat"          { for textures }

DECLARE Copper  = COLOR RED 0.84 GREEN 0.04 BLUE 0.15
DECLARE Orange1 = COLOR RED 1.00 GREEN 0.16 BLUE 0.00
DECLARE Orange2 = COLOR RED 1.00 GREEN 0.35 BLUE 0.00
DECLARE Purple1 = COLOR RED 0.87 GREEN 0.00 BLUE 1.00
DECLARE Purple2 = COLOR RED 1.00 GREEN 0.14 BLUE 1.00
DECLARE Purple3 = COLOR RED 0.82 GREEN 0.00 BLUE 0.82
DECLARE Green1  = COLOR RED 0.45 GREEN 0.91 BLUE 0.00
DECLARE Brown1  = COLOR RED 0.52 GREEN 0.19 BLUE 0.00

VIEW_POINT
   LOCATION  < 0  -5 -110 >
   DIRECTION < 0 -0.05  1 >
   UP  < 0  1  0 >
   RIGHT < 1.33333 0 0 >
END_VIEW_POINT
```

(continued)

Listing 3.13 *(continued)*

```
OBJECT
   SPHERE  <0.0  0.0  0.0> 20 END_SPHERE
   TRANSLATE  <65  100  -100 >
   TEXTURE
     COLOUR White
     AMBIENT 1.0
     DIFFUSE 0.0
   END_TEXTURE
   COLOUR White
   LIGHT_SOURCE
END_OBJECT

{ Add the backdrop to the picture }
OBJECT
   PLANE < 0 0 -1 > -200 END_PLANE
   TEXTURE
     COLOR MidnightBlue
     AMBIENT 0.3
     DIFFUSE 0.7
     BRILLIANCE 1.0
   END_TEXTURE
END_OBJECT

{ Define the ground }
OBJECT
  PLANE < 0 1 0 > -50 END_PLANE
   TEXTURE
     AMBIENT 0.3
     DIFFUSE 0.7
     BRILLIANCE 1.0
     COLOR Blue
   END_TEXTURE
END_OBJECT

DECLARE SphereTex = TEXTURE
  REFLECTION 0.65
  BRILLIANCE 20.0
  PHONG 0.9
  PHONGSIZE 100
END_TEXTURE

OBJECT { Sphere 1 }
  SPHERE < 0 0 0 > 25 END_SPHERE
  TEXTURE
    SphereTex
    COLOR Gold
  END_TEXTURE
END_OBJECT
```

```
OBJECT { Sphere 2 }
  SPHERE < -37.5 -30 -15.5 > 20 END_SPHERE
  TEXTURE
    SphereTex
    COLOR MediumForestGreen
  END_TEXTURE
END_OBJECT

OBJECT { Sphere 3 }
  SPHERE < 52.5 -17.5 -18 > 20 END_SPHERE
  TEXTURE
    SphereTex
    COLOR Orange1
  END_TEXTURE
END_OBJECT

OBJECT { Sphere 4 }
  SPHERE <-57.5 12.5 0 > 15 END_SPHERE
  TEXTURE
    SphereTex
    COLOR Copper
  END_TEXTURE
END_OBJECT

OBJECT { Sphere 5 }
  SPHERE < 12.5 -32.5 -14 > 15 END_SPHERE
  TEXTURE
    SphereTex
    COLOR Copper
  END_TEXTURE
END_OBJECT

OBJECT { Sphere 6 }
  SPHERE < 47.5 17.5 20 > 15 END_SPHERE
  TEXTURE
    SphereTex
    COLOR Purple1
  END_TEXTURE
END_OBJECT

OBJECT { Sphere 7 }
  SPHERE <-32.5 32.5 35 > 15 END_SPHERE
  TEXTURE
    SphereTex
    COLOR Green1
  END_TEXTURE
END_OBJECT
```

(continued)

Listing 3.13   *(continued)*

```
OBJECT { Sphere 8 }
  SPHERE < 17.5 30 47.5 > 20 END_SPHERE
  TEXTURE
    SphereTex
    COLOR Gold
  END_TEXTURE
END_OBJECT

OBJECT { Sphere 9 }
  SPHERE < 62.5 0 -77.5 > 20 END_SPHERE
  TEXTURE
    SphereTex
    COLOR Blue
  END_TEXTURE
END_OBJECT

OBJECT { Sphere 10 }
  SPHERE < 0 -30 -100 > 20 END_SPHERE
  TEXTURE
    SphereTex
    COLOR Red
  END_TEXTURE
END_OBJECT

OBJECT { Sphere 11 }
  SPHERE <-62.5 0 -77.5 > 20 END_SPHERE
  TEXTURE
    SphereTex
    COLOR Green
  END_TEXTURE
END_OBJECT

OBJECT { Sphere 12 }
  SPHERE <-45 -18.5 0 > 15 END_SPHERE
  TEXTURE
    SphereTex
    COLOR Orange2
  END_TEXTURE
END_OBJECT

OBJECT { Sphere 13 }
  SPHERE <40 -18.5 0 > 15 END_SPHERE
  TEXTURE
    SphereTex
    COLOR Purple3
  END_TEXTURE
END_OBJECT
```

```
OBJECT { Sphere 14 }
  SPHERE <-75 100 -50 > 40 END_SPHERE
  TEXTURE
    SphereTex
    COLOR Orange2
  END_TEXTURE
END_OBJECT
```

Conclusions

In this chapter we have discussed in detail the operation of the basic ray-tracing program called TRACE. We have seen how to convert the theory from Chapter 2 into a working program and how theory must sometimes be tempered by practical considerations. We have also seen that an object-oriented approach to the implementation resulted in a very clean program structure that will allow us to incorporate extensions easily to the basic ray tracer.

As we pointed out in this chapter, the TRACE program does not render the actual ray-traced image but instead produces a file of numeric data that contains the image. In the next chapter we will discover how this numeric data is turned into a beautiful, full-color image and displayed on your computer's monitor.

Color Quantization and Display of Image Data

The ability to simplify means to eliminate the unnecessary so that the necessary can speak.

—Hans Hofmann

In this chapter you will learn:

- Why color quantization is necessary for display of image data
- Why color quantization techniques are becoming a thing of the past
- Three different methods for performing color quantization with a complete implementation of each
- How the median cut algorithm works
- How the octree algorithm works
- How quantization to 32K colors can be performed
- What "autodisplay" images are, how they work, and how they relate to the other supported graphics image file formats
- What the "dump" file format is
- How to save the images you create in either of two popular graphics image file formats for distribution or later display (We discuss the file formats themselves in the next chapter.)

Introduction

The production of ray-traced images as described in this book is basically a three-step process. First, the artist/designer conceptualizes the image and expresses it in the form of a data file that is submitted to the ray-tracing program. In the second step of this process, the ray-tracing program reads the input data file, does the ray tracing, and produces an output data file that contains the actual image data. The final step is the display of the ray-traced image on a computer monitor. We discuss the concepts and thought processes that go into the first step throughout Part Two of this book. We discussed how a ray-tracing program works in depth in Chapters 2 and 3. The step necessary to convert an image data file into something displayable on a computer monitor is the focus of this chapter.

Initially, you may think that the display of the ray-traced imagery would be a trivial problem in comparison to the technical complexity required in generating the image in the first place. This initial impression, however, is not correct—at least not yet. If ray-traced images always contained fewer colors than your computer graphics adapter and monitor (or other output device for that matter) were capable of displaying, the display of these images would indeed be trivial. Unfortunately, given current graphics adapter technology, if this were the case (the images had fewer colors than the typical output devices), the images themselves would probably be visually boring or completely garish because of the lack of fine gradations of color, especially where object shading is concerned.

The ideal situation would be if your computer's graphics adapter and monitor were capable of displaying the full gamut of colors produced by the ray-tracing program. Since most ray tracers (including the two in this book) produce what is referred to as "true-color" images utilizing 24 bits of color information per pixel, your graphics adapter would need to display all possible colors expressible in 24 bits on the screen at the same time. This works out to be an impressive 16.8 million colors. True-color display allows images to be displayed without any visible color edges. The vast number of colors available allows completely smooth color transitions to be made. As the number of simultaneously displayable colors is reduced, color banding occurs. The banding occurs because the color transitions become drastic enough that your eyes detect the visible edges. As we noted in Chapter 1, true-color graphics adapters are still too expensive for most people and for this reason are not yet universally available. Given the rapidly falling prices of computer hardware (and the rising value per dollar invested), it probably will not be long until most computers sold have true-color capability. Until that time, however, we must utilize what we have access to in the fullest way possible.

The problem then, with today's VGA/SuperVGA-capable computers, is that the images produced by ray-tracing programs and other imaging applications and devices (including color scanners and color video digitizers) contain many more colors than can be displayed simultaneously. As we have seen, typical SuperVGA hardware is capable of displaying 256 colors in resolutions up to 800 by 600 or 1024 by 768. With the addition of a special color palette/digital to analog converter (DAC) chip, some of these SuperVGA adapters can directly display 32,768 colors in resolutions up to 800 by 600. The shortage of colors becomes acute when we are required to display images that could contain up to 16.8 million colors (typically much fewer) on an output device capable of only 256 or 32K colors. Just how are the 256 (or 32K) most important colors in an image chosen so that the displayed image looks like it is supposed to? This process is called "color quantization," and it deals not only with how the most important colors in an image are picked but also with how the colors from the original image are mapped to these selected colors so as to represent the full range of colors necessary for accurate image display. In the future, color quantization techniques will not be necessary. For now, however, they are standard equipment in every imaging tool box.

Many different algorithms exist for performing color quantization. The best-known algorithms are:

1. *Uniform Quantization.*
   This technique divides the three-dimensional RGB color space into equal volumes and uses the mean color values in these volumes to display an image. In other words, the image is displayed with a fixed, full range, color palette that was not derived from its content. Colors from the original image are displayed with the closest color found in the fixed palette. We discussed this method briefly in Chapter 1.
2. *Popularity Quantization.*
   The most frequently occurring colors in an image are used to display the image.
3. *Median Cut Quantization.*
   This technique chooses the colors for display of the image so that each color represents approximately the same number of pixels in the original image.
4. *Octree Quantization.*
   This technique tries to maintain the full range of colors within an image by merging similar colors together and replacing them with their mean color value.

In our case, of course, quantization down to 256 colors is the goal.

Some of these quantization techniques work well for some types of images and terribly for others. Some require massive amounts of memory to implement. Still others are slow in execution because of the computations involved in the reduction of colors. In this chapter, we present three different color quantization methods: the median cut, the octree, and a 32K-color quantization method. The 32K-color quantization method is a brute-force approach that doesn't quite fit into any of the algorithmic categories we've listed. These three color quantization methods were chosen because, in general, they provide the highest quality imagery. We offer three different methods so that you can choose which works best (i.e., provides the highest quality image production) for your specific imaging applications. Each of these quantization methods solves the color reduction problem in a unique way and is interesting in and of itself.

When viewed from a high level, each of these color quantization programs appears very similar. Each is executed from the DOS prompt, each utilizes a simple command line interface with various command line switches to control its operation, each reads an image file in "dump file format," each performs processing on the data for color reduction, and each finally displays the resultant image on the computer monitor. Additionally, two of the three programs allow you to save the displayed quantized image in three different output file formats (the autodisplay, GIF, and PCX formats). (We discuss the dump input file format later in this chapter, with a continuing explanation in Chapter 5. We will defer the detailed examination of graphics file formats until Chapter 5.)

It is only when you start looking closer do the differences in these programs become apparent. In this chapter, we will examine the details of each algorithm's implementation closely.

By necessity, this chapter contains a lot of code. This code is built on much of the code developed in Chapter 1, and you may find the descriptions there useful. We present the quantization techniques in order of decreasing complexity. The first and most complex of the algorithms is the median cut algorithm implemented in the "mquan.exe" program. Next, we describe octree quantization along with its "oquan.exe" realization. Finally, the "hquan.exe" program implements a technique for quantizing an image for display with 32K colors. For reasons to be explained, the "oquan.exe" program does not allow you to save images displayed in 32K colors.

Note: The programs presented in this chapter were developed for the display of ray-traced images, but their usefulness does not end there. Any type of true-color imaging data that is available in dump file format or that can be converted into this format can be quantized and displayed with these programs. This means that you can also use these programs to process images produced by color scanners or color video digitizers. In addition, the ability to convert other types of true-color data into dump file format allows you to import the data into the DKBTrace ray-tracing program as an "IMAGEMAP texture." We cover the use of imagemaps in Part Two of this book. Techniques for image data file conversions will be examined in Chapter 5.

When you use any of the color quantization techniques presented, you will see accurate, full-color images displayed on the VGA monitor after a gratifyingly short period of processing time.

Median Cut Color Quantization

The median cut color quantization algorithm is probably the most widely used quantization technique in the graphics/imaging industry, even though it is one of the most complex of the algorithms to implement. The reason for its popularity is the quality of the images it produces. This algorithm works remarkably well regardless of the image content. Some of the other color quantization algorithms may produce equal or better quality images for a given image but none consistently produces the quality of images produced with the median cut algorithm. We included an implementation of this algorithm in this book for just that reason. The other two quantization techniques are presented for that unique image that may look better when quantized with a different method.

The structure used for implementating all of the color quantization programs is basically the same. The "mquan.exe" program presented in this section is a model for the other two programs that follow. For this reason, we discuss it in more depth than the others. Do not worry, the discussions of the quantization algorithms have the same level of treatment in each case. The additional discussion in this section is for issues that are peripheral to the actual color quantization methods. Specifically, we discuss the simple command line user interface used in each of these programs as well as the "dump file format" and "autodisplay" file creation.

The code that performs the median cut color quantization is shown in Listing 4.1 and is contained in the files "mquan.prj" and "mquan.c" on the companion disks. Please refer to this listing during the discussion to follow.

Listing 4.1   The MQUAN Color Quantization Program

The following describes the contents of the file "mquan.prj," even though this file itself is not directly viewable outside of the Borland environment. To build the "mquan" program, you must have access to the following C files (either in the current directory or by way of an explicit path): "vga.c," "pcx.c," "gif.c," and "mquan.c." The include files "misc.h," "vga.h," "pcx.h," and "gif.h" must also be available. Most of these files with the exception of "pcx.h," "gif.h," and "mquan.c" have been shown and described previously. We show "mquan.c" below, and we discuss "pcx.h" and "gif.h" in Chapter 5.

The following is the contents of the file "mquan.c."

```
/*********************************************************/
/***                   "mquan.c"                     ***/
/***         Median Cut Color Quantizer Program      ***/
/***              produces 256-color images          ***/
/***      from "dump" format color image data files  ***/
/***      from the book, "Practical Ray Tracing in C" ***/
/***            written in Borland/Turbo C 2.0        ***/
/***                       by                        ***/
/***              Craig A. Lindley                    ***/
/***                                                 ***/
/***        Ver: 1.0    LastUpdate: 12/14/91         ***/
/*********************************************************/

#include <stdio.h>
#include <conio.h>
#include <dos.h>
#include <process.h>
#include <string.h>
#include <alloc.h>
#include "misc.h"
#include "vga.h"
#include "gif.h"
#include "pcx.h"

/*
Memory allocation bits used to keep track of how much far heap memory
has been allocated by this program.
*/

#define RGBMEM        1
unsigned MemoryAlloc = 0;               /* variable used to keep track */

#define SQUARE(x)     (x)*(x)
#define COLLEVELS     32                /* number of brightness levels */
#define NUMAXIS       3                 /* num of axes in RGB cube */

/* Local global variables */
/*
Data file structure information
*/
```

```
static struct {
   unsigned Width;
   unsigned Height;
} Hdr;

static unsigned Ver = 1;
static unsigned Rev = 0 ;
static unsigned ImageWidth;
static unsigned ImageHeight;
static unsigned long ImagePixels;
static int MaxValue;

/* Single row buffers for reading raw data */
static BYTE RedRowBuf[MAXCOLS];
static BYTE GreenRowBuf[MAXCOLS];
static BYTE BlueRowBuf[MAXCOLS];

/*
RGBCube: Three-dimensional array implemented in such a way as to work well
on a machine that has trouble with objects greater than 64K.  The indices
into this array are the color components, rgb, normalized to fit in
the range defined by COLLEVELS.  The values in the array are frequency counts
of the particular color.  The array is set up here to be an array of pointers
to smaller 2-dimensional arrays, so no object is greater than 64K.
*/

static unsigned long far *RGBCube[COLLEVELS];
static unsigned NumBoxes;
static unsigned Verbose;
static unsigned CorrectGamma;
static unsigned GenComFile;
static unsigned GenGIFFile;
static unsigned GenPCXFile;
static unsigned InstallColors;

/* Gamma correction table - GAMMA = 2.222 */
static BYTE GammaTable[] =   {
    0, 9,13,16,18,20,21,23,24,26,27,28,29,30,32,33,
   34,34,35,36,37,38,39,40,40,41,42,43,43,44,45,45,
   46,47,47,48,48,49,50,50,51,51,52,53,53,54,54,55,
   55,56,56,57,57,58,58,59,59,60,60,61,61,62,62,63
};

/*
Boxes: Structure holding the unsorted generated color boxes.  Includes the
low and high value along each axis of RGBCube, and the number of elements
in the box.
*/

struct Box  {
   unsigned Lo[3];
   unsigned Hi[3];
```

(continued)

Listing 4.1 *(continued)*

```
   unsigned long NumElements;
}  Boxes[MAXNUMCOLREGS];

/*
Sorted version of Boxes.
*/

struct Box SBoxes[MAXNUMCOLREGS];

/*
ColRegs: Holds the determined values of the color registers.
*/
ColorRegister ColRegs[MAXNUMCOLREGS];

/*
SColRegs: Sorted version of ColRegs.
*/

ColorRegister SColRegs[MAXNUMCOLREGS];


/* beginning of program functions */

/*
This function will output the message string passed to it if the Verbose
option variable is set true.
*/

void Message(char *String)  {
   if (Verbose)
      printf("%s",String);
}

/*
This function deallocates all far heap memory that has been allocated
*/

void DeAllocMemory( void )  {

   register unsigned Index;

   /* test MemoryAlloc bit to see what was allocated then dispose */

   Message("Deallocating program memory\n");

   if (MemoryAlloc & RGBMEM)
      for (Index=0; Index < COLLEVELS; Index++)
         if (RGBCube[Index] != NULL)
            farfree((char far *) RGBCube[Index]);
```

```
}

/*
Allocate all memory for the entire program. The MemoryAlloc variable is
used to keep track of all memory that has been allocated from the far
heap. That way DeAllocMemory can give it all back to the system when the
program terminates.
*/

unsigned AllocMemory( void )  {

   register unsigned Index;

   Message("Allocating program memory\n");

   /* create COLLEVELS number of pointer to 2-D arrays */

   /*
   Set the initial values of the RGBCube sub-array pointers to NULL,
   so we can do proper checks later to see if they have been allocated
   or not.
   */

   for (Index=0; Index < COLLEVELS; Index++)
      RGBCube[Index] = NULL;

   for (Index=0; Index < COLLEVELS; Index++)  {
      RGBCube[Index] = (unsigned long far *) farcalloc(COLLEVELS*COLLEVELS,
        (unsigned long) sizeof(unsigned long));

      if (RGBCube[Index] == NULL)  {
         printf("RGBCube memory allocation failed\n");
         printf("\t only %ld bytes of memory available\n",farcoreleft());
         DeAllocMemory();
         return(FALSE);
      }
      /* clear it to all zeros */
      _fmemset((char far *) RGBCube[Index],'\0',
               COLLEVELS*COLLEVELS*sizeof(unsigned long));
   }
   MemoryAlloc |= RGBMEM;               /* indicate success */

   return(TRUE);
}


/*
This function sets the indices to the numbers of the other axis after
a main axis has been selected.
*/
```

(continued)

Listing 4.1   *(continued)*

```c
void OtherAxes(unsigned MainAxis, unsigned *Other1, unsigned *Other2)  {
   switch (MainAxis)  {
   case 0:
     *Other1 = 1;
     *Other2 = 2;
     break;
   case 1:
     *Other1 = 0;
     *Other2 = 2;
     break;
   case 2:
     *Other1 = 0;
     *Other2 = 1;
   }
}


/*
This function takes an index value into the Boxes array, and shrinks the
specified box to tightly fit around the input color frequency data (e.g.,
there are no zero planes on the sides of the box).
*/

void Shrink(unsigned BoxIndex)  {

   unsigned axis,aax1,aax2;
   register unsigned ind[3], flag;

   /* Along each axis: */

   for (axis=0; axis < NUMAXIS; axis++)  {
     OtherAxes(axis,&aax1,&aax2);

    /* Scan off zero planes on from the low end of the axis */
    flag = 0;
    for (ind[axis]=Boxes[BoxIndex].Lo[axis];
         ind[axis] <= Boxes[BoxIndex].Hi[axis]; ind[axis]++)  {
      for (ind[aax1]=Boxes[BoxIndex].Lo[aax1];
           ind[aax1] <= Boxes[BoxIndex].Hi[aax1]; ind[aax1]++)  {
        for (ind[aax2]=Boxes[BoxIndex].Lo[aax2];
             ind[aax2] <= Boxes[BoxIndex].Hi[aax2]; ind[aax2]++)
          if (RGBCube[ind[0]][ind[1]*COLLEVELS+ind[2]])  {
            flag=1;
            break;
          }
        if (flag) break;
      }
     if (flag) break;
    }
    Boxes[BoxIndex].Lo[axis] = ind[axis];
```

```
        /* Scan off zero planes from the high end of the axis */
        flag = 0;
        for (ind[axis]=Boxes[BoxIndex].Hi[axis];
            ind[axis]+1 >= Boxes[BoxIndex].Lo[axis]+1; ind[axis]--)  {
          for (ind[aax1]=Boxes[BoxIndex].Hi[aax1];
              ind[aax1]+1 >= Boxes[BoxIndex].Lo[aax1]+1; ind[aax1]--)  {
            for (ind[aax2]=Boxes[BoxIndex].Hi[aax2];
                ind[aax2]+1>=Boxes[BoxIndex].Lo[aax2]+1; ind[aax2]--)
              if (RGBCube[ind[0]][ind[1]*COLLEVELS+ind[2]])  {
                flag = 1;
                break;
              }
            if (flag) break;
          }
          if (flag) break;
        }
        Boxes[BoxIndex].Hi[axis] = ind[axis];
      }
}


/*
This function selects the optimum colors from the color frequency data,
using the Median Cut algorithm.  It prints the number of colors used at
its termination.
*/

void SelectColorBoxes( void )  {

    register unsigned SelectedBox, c;
    register unsigned ind[3], Max, axis, TargetBox, k;
    unsigned aax1,aax2;
    unsigned long LongMax, PlaneSum, ElementSum;

    /*
    Initialize the first and only box in the array to contain the entire RGBCube,
    then discard unused zero planes surrounding it.
    */

    for (c=0; c < NUMAXIS; c++)  {
      Boxes[0].Lo[c] = 0;
      Boxes[0].Hi[c] = COLLEVELS-1;
    }
    Boxes[0].NumElements = ImagePixels;
    NumBoxes = 1;

    Shrink(0);

    /* Perform the following until all color registers are used up */
```

(continued)

Listing 4.1   *(continued)*

```
while(NumBoxes < MAXNUMCOLREGS)  {
  /*
  Pick the box with the maximum number of elements that is not a single
  color value to work with.  It will be the box we will split.
  */

  LongMax = 0;
  SelectedBox = 1000;
  for (c=0; c < NumBoxes; c++)  {
    if ((Boxes[c].NumElements > LongMax) &&
        ((Boxes[c].Lo[0] != Boxes[c].Hi[0]) ||
         (Boxes[c].Lo[1] != Boxes[c].Hi[1]) ||
         (Boxes[c].Lo[2] != Boxes[c].Hi[2])))  {
      LongMax = Boxes[c].NumElements;
      SelectedBox = c;
    }
  }

  /*
  If we couldn't find any box that was not a single color, we don't
  need to assign any more colors, so we can terminate this loop.
  */

  if (SelectedBox == 1000)
    break;

  /* Choose the longest axis of the box to split it along */

  axis = 0;
  Max = Boxes[SelectedBox].Hi[axis] - Boxes[SelectedBox].Lo[axis];
  for (k=1; k < NUMAXIS; k++)  {
    if (Max < (c=(Boxes[SelectedBox].Hi[k]-Boxes[SelectedBox].Lo[k])))  {
      Max = c;
      axis = k;
    }
  }

  /*
  Check to see if any of our previously assigned boxes have zero elements
  (may happen in degenerate cases), if so, reuse them.  If not, use the
  next available box.
  */

  TargetBox = NumBoxes;
  for (c=0; c < NumBoxes; c++)  {
    if (Boxes[c].NumElements == 0)  {
      TargetBox = c;
      break;
    }
  }
```

```
OtherAxes(axis,&aax1,&aax2);
if (Boxes[SelectedBox].Hi[axis] != Boxes[SelectedBox].Lo[axis])  {

   /*
   Sum planes of box from low end until the sum exceeds half the total
   number of elements in the box.  That is the point where we will
   split it.
   */

   ElementSum = 0;
   for (ind[axis]=Boxes[SelectedBox].Lo[axis];
        ind[axis] <= Boxes[SelectedBox].Hi[axis]; ind[axis]++)  {
      PlaneSum = 0;
      for (ind[aax1]=Boxes[SelectedBox].Lo[aax1];
           ind[aax1] <= Boxes[SelectedBox].Hi[aax1]; ind[aax1]++)
         for (ind[aax2]=Boxes[SelectedBox].Lo[aax2];
              ind[aax2] <= Boxes[SelectedBox].Hi[aax2]; ind[aax2]++)
            PlaneSum += RGBCube[ind[0]][ind[1]*COLLEVELS+ind[2]];
         ElementSum += PlaneSum;
         if (ElementSum > Boxes[SelectedBox].NumElements/2)
           break;
   }
   /*
   If we did not exceed half the total until we added the last plane
   (such as in a case where the last plane contains the bulk of the data
   points), back up so we do not create the new box as a degenerate box.
   */

   if (ind[axis] == Boxes[SelectedBox].Hi[axis])  {
      ind[axis]--;
      ElementSum -= PlaneSum;
   }


   /*
   The new box has most of the data the same as the old box, but its low
   extent is the index above the point where we needed to split, and its
   number of elements is the total number of elements in this whole box,
   minus the number in the planes we just summed.
   */

   for (c=0; c < NUMAXIS; c++)  {
      Boxes[TargetBox].Lo[c] = Boxes[SelectedBox].Lo[c];
      Boxes[TargetBox].Hi[c] = Boxes[SelectedBox].Hi[c];
   }
   Boxes[TargetBox].Lo[axis] = ind[axis]+1;
   Boxes[TargetBox].NumElements = Boxes[SelectedBox].NumElements -
                                  ElementSum;

   /*
   The high extent of our old box is now cut off at the plane we just
   split at and the number of elements in it is the number we just
   summed.
   */
```

(continued)

Listing 4.1   *(continued)*

```
        Boxes[SelectedBox].Hi[axis] = ind[axis];
        Boxes[SelectedBox].NumElements = ElementSum;

        /* Discard zero planes around both our new boxes */

        Shrink(SelectedBox);
        Shrink(TargetBox);

        /*
        If we used the top box in our list, we have to increment the
        total number of boxes used, to make ready for the use of the next
        free box.
        */

        if (TargetBox == NumBoxes)
           NumBoxes++;
      }
   }

   /* show number of display colors to be used if requested to */
   if (Verbose)
      printf("%d colors will be used for display of the image\n",NumBoxes);
}

/*
This function calculates the actual color register values for each box,
based on the weighted distribution of data in the box.  It then sorts the
color registers by brightness (using a calculation described by the VGA
technical reference for calculating brightness).
*/

void SortColors( void )  {

   register unsigned Index,c,flag,temp,r,b,g;
   unsigned indices[MAXNUMCOLREGS];
   unsigned long weightedcolor[MAXNUMCOLREGS],rsum,bsum,gsum,tmp;

   for (Index=0; Index < NumBoxes; Index++)  {

      /* Calculate a weighted sum of the color values in the box */

      rsum = bsum = gsum = 0;
      for (r=Boxes[Index].Lo[0]; r<=Boxes[Index].Hi[0]; r++)
         for (b=Boxes[Index].Lo[1]; b<=Boxes[Index].Hi[1]; b++)
            for (g=Boxes[Index].Lo[2]; g<=Boxes[Index].Hi[2]; g++)  {
               tmp = RGBCube[r][b*COLLEVELS+g];
               rsum += r*tmp;
               bsum += b*tmp;
               gsum += g*tmp;
            }
```

```
      /* Pick the actual color for that box based on the weighted sum */

      ColRegs[Index].Red   = rsum/Boxes[Index].NumElements;
      ColRegs[Index].Blue  = bsum/Boxes[Index].NumElements;
      ColRegs[Index].Green = gsum/Boxes[Index].NumElements;
   }
   /*
   Set up for an index sort of the brightness by first calculating the
   weighted brightness of each color (based on the calculation described
   in the VGA manual).
   */

   for (Index=0; Index < NumBoxes; Index++)  {
      indices[Index] = Index;
      weightedcolor[Index] = ColRegs[Index].Red  *30 +
                             ColRegs[Index].Blue *11 +
                             ColRegs[Index].Green*59;
   }

   /*
   Do a bubble sort of the weighted colors via indices. Sort is done in
   ascending order.
   */

   flag = 1;
   while (flag)  {
      flag = 0;
      for (Index=0; Index < NumBoxes-1; Index++)
         if (weightedcolor[indices[Index]] > weightedcolor[indices[Index+1]])  {
            temp = indices[Index];
            indices[Index] = indices[Index+1];
            indices[Index+1] = temp;
            flag = 1;
         }
   }

   /*
   Remap the boxes and the color registers into SBoxes and SColRegs via the
   sorted indices found above.
   */

   for (Index=0; Index < NumBoxes; Index++)  {
      SColRegs[Index].Red   = ColRegs[indices[Index]].Red;
      SColRegs[Index].Blue  = ColRegs[indices[Index]].Blue;
      SColRegs[Index].Green = ColRegs[indices[Index]].Green;
      SBoxes[Index].NumElements = Boxes[indices[Index]].NumElements;
      for (c=0; c < NUMAXIS; c++)  {
         SBoxes[Index].Hi[c] = Boxes[indices[Index]].Hi[c];
         SBoxes[Index].Lo[c] = Boxes[indices[Index]].Lo[c];
      }
   }
}
```

(continued)

Listing 4.1   *(continued)*

```
/*
This function maps the raw image pixel data from the raw data file into the
new color map we've come up with in the SColRegs array.
*/

int DisplayImageData(char *FileName )  {

   FILE *ImageFile;
   unsigned Row, Col;
   register unsigned c,k,goodindex, PixVal;
   unsigned long minerror,error;
   unsigned RowNum, Red, Green, Blue;
   register int ReturnCode,r,b,g,i;

   /*
   Set the RGBCube array to a value that can't be a color register index
   (MAXNUMCOLREGS*2) so we can detect when we hit on a part of the array that
   is not included in a color box.
   */

   for (c=0; c < COLLEVELS; c++)
      for (k=0; k < COLLEVELS*COLLEVELS; k++)
        RGBCube[c][k] = MAXNUMCOLREGS*2;

   /*
   Fill the boxes in the RGBCube array with the index number for that box, so
   we can tell what box a particular color index into the RGBCube array is in
   by a single access.
   */

   for (i=0; i < NumBoxes; i++)
     for (r=SBoxes[i].Lo[0]; r <= SBoxes[i].Hi[0]; r++)
       for (b=SBoxes[i].Lo[1]; b <= SBoxes[i].Hi[1]; b++)
          for (g=SBoxes[i].Lo[2]; g <= SBoxes[i].Hi[2]; g++)
            RGBCube[r][b*COLLEVELS+g] = i;

   /*
   Rescan the raw image file so that it can now be displayed.
   */

   printf("\nPass 2\n");
   if (Verbose)
      printf("Reading file: %s\n",FileName);

   /* Attempt to open the file */
   if (!(ImageFile = fopen(FileName,"rb")))   {
      printf("File %s not found in Pass 2!\n",FileName);
      ReturnCode = EFileNotFound;
      goto ErrorExit;
   }
```

```
/* Read in the header */
if (fread(&Hdr,sizeof(Hdr),1,ImageFile) != 1)   {
   ReturnCode = EReadFileHdr;
   goto ErrorExit;
}

/*
Now attempt to read the raw image file into three
separate buffers: Red, Green, & Blue a row at a time.
*/

for (Row=0; Row < ImageHeight; Row++)   {
   if (fread(&RowNum,sizeof(unsigned),1,ImageFile) != 1)   {
     printf("\nError reading image row number !\n");
     ReturnCode = EReadRowNum;
     goto ErrorExit;
   }

   /* Now read a line of red data */
   if (fread(RedRowBuf,ImageWidth,1,ImageFile) != 1)   {
     printf("\nError reading red data in Pass 2!\n");
     ReturnCode = EReadData;
     goto ErrorExit;
   }

   /* Now read a line of green data */
   if (fread(GreenRowBuf,ImageWidth,1,ImageFile) != 1)   {
     printf("\nError reading green data in Pass 2!\n");
     ReturnCode = EReadData;
     goto ErrorExit;
   }

   /* Now read a line of blue data */
   if (fread(BlueRowBuf,ImageWidth,1,ImageFile) != 1)   {
     printf("\nError reading blue data in Pass 2!\n");
     ReturnCode = EReadData;
     goto ErrorExit;
   }

   /*
   For each RGB triplet in this row of image data. Scale values
   accordingly.
   */
   for (Col=0; Col < ImageWidth; Col++) {
     Red   = RedRowBuf[Col]   > 3;
     Green = GreenRowBuf[Col] > 3;
     Blue  = BlueRowBuf[Col]  > 3;

     /*
     If this particular color is inside one of the boxes,
     assign the color index for this pixel to the value at that
```

(continued)

Listing 4.1   *(continued)*

```
          spot in the cube.
          */
          if (RGBCube[Red][(Blue*COLLEVELS)+Green] != MAXNUMCOLREGS*2)   {
            PixVal = RGBCube[Red][Blue*COLLEVELS+Green];
            SetPixelValue(Col,Row,PixVal);
          }
          else  {
            /*
            Otherwise, we need to scan the array of colors to find which is
            the closest to our prospective color.
            */

            goodindex = 0;
            minerror = SQUARE(Red-SColRegs[goodindex].Red)+
                       SQUARE(Blue-SColRegs[goodindex].Blue)+
                       SQUARE(Green-SColRegs[goodindex].Green);
          /*
          Scan all color registers to find which has the smallest error
          when it is used for this pixel.
          */

          for (k=1; k < NumBoxes; k++)  {
            error = SQUARE(Red-SColRegs[k].Red)+
                    SQUARE(Blue-SColRegs[k].Blue)+
                    SQUARE(Green-SColRegs[k].Green);
            if (error < minerror)  {
              minerror = error;
              goodindex = k;
            }
          }

        /* Assign that register to this pixel */
        SetPixelValue(Col,Row,goodindex);
        }
      }
    }
  /* Normal function exit point */
  printf("\n");
  fclose(ImageFile);
  return(0);

ErrorExit:
  fclose(ImageFile);
  return(ReturnCode);

}

/*
The purpose of this function is to partially make up
for the normalization of pixel values performed previously.
The values in the color registers are scaled upwards toward
```

```
the maximum value of 63 to increase image brightness. Then, if
requested, the color data is gamma corrected.
*/

void ScaleColRegisters(void)  {

   register unsigned Index;
   register unsigned Temp;

   /* Find the maximum value of any RGB component value */
   MaxValue = -1;
   for (Index = 0; Index < MAXNUMCOLREGS; Index++)  {
      if (SColRegs[Index].Red > MaxValue)
        MaxValue = SColRegs[Index].Red;
      if (SColRegs[Index].Green > MaxValue)
        MaxValue = SColRegs[Index].Green;
      if (SColRegs[Index].Blue > MaxValue)
        MaxValue = SColRegs[Index].Blue;
   }
   /* Scale all color register components accordingly */
   for (Index = 0; Index < MAXNUMCOLREGS; Index++)  {

      /* temp used to prevent overflow of BYTE value */
      Temp = SColRegs[Index].Red * (unsigned) MAXCOLREGVAL;
      Temp /= MaxValue;
      if (CorrectGamma)
        SColRegs[Index].Red = GammaTable[Temp];
      else
        SColRegs[Index].Red = Temp;

      Temp = SColRegs[Index].Green * (unsigned) MAXCOLREGVAL;
      Temp /= MaxValue;
      if (CorrectGamma)
        SColRegs[Index].Green = GammaTable[Temp];
      else
        SColRegs[Index].Green = Temp;

      Temp = SColRegs[Index].Blue * (unsigned) MAXCOLREGVAL;
      Temp /= MaxValue;
      if (CorrectGamma)
        SColRegs[Index].Blue = GammaTable[Temp];
      else
        SColRegs[Index].Blue = Temp;
   }
}

/*
This function produces an executable .COM file for display of the
digitized color image. It writes a small code segment followed by
the 256-color register value followed by the image data to the
specified file.
*/
```

(continued)

Listing 4.1 *(continued)*

```c
void WriteComFile(char *FileName)  {

    FILE *OutPutFile;
    char     String[80];
    unsigned Index, PixelValue, Col, Row;
    BYTE FileCode[] =
      {0xB4,0x0F,0xCD,0x10,0xA2,0x37,0x01,0xB4,0x00,0xB0,0x13,0xCD,0x10,
       0xB8,0x12,0x10,0xBB,0x00,0x00,0xB9,0x00,0x01,0xBA,0x38,0x01,0xCD,
       0x10,0xB9,0x00,0xFA,0xBE,0x38,0x04,0xB8,0x00,0xA0,0x8E,0xC0,0xBF,
       0x00,0x00,0xF3,0xA4,0xB4,0x00,0xCD,0x16,0xB4,0x00,0xA0,0x37,0x01,
       0xCD,0x10,0xC3,0x00};


    if (!strchr(FileName,'.'))  {       /* is there an ext ? */
       strcpy(String,FileName);         /* copy filename to buffer */
       FileName = String;               /* FileName now points at buffer */
       strcat(FileName,".com");         /* if not add .com ext */
    }
    /* open the output file */

    if ((OutPutFile = fopen(FileName,"wb")) == NULL)  {
       SetTextMode();
       DeAllocMemory();
       printf("Cannot open Image .COM file\n");
       exit(1);
    }

    /* write code segment to the file */
    for (Index=0; Index < sizeof(FileCode); Index++)
       if (fputc(FileCode[Index],OutPutFile) != FileCode[Index])  {
          SetTextMode();
          DeAllocMemory();
          printf("Error writing Image .COM code seg\n");
          exit(1);
       }

    /* now write the color register rgb values to the file */
    for (Index = 0; Index < MAX256PALETTECOLORS; Index++)  {
       if (fputc(SColRegs[Index].Red,OutPutFile) != SColRegs[Index].Red)  {
          SetTextMode();
          DeAllocMemory();
          printf("Error writing Image .COM red color reg\n");
          exit(1);
       }
       if (fputc(SColRegs[Index].Green,OutPutFile) != SColRegs[Index].Green)  {
          SetTextMode();
          DeAllocMemory();
          printf("Error writing Image .COM green color reg\n");
          exit(1);
       }
```

```
         if (fputc(SColRegs[Index].Blue,OutPutFile) != SColRegs[Index].Blue)   {
            SetTextMode();
            DeAllocMemory();
            printf("Error writing Image .COM blue color reg\n");
            exit(1);
         }
      }
   /* now write the actual image data to the file */
   for (Row=0; Row < 200; Row++)
      for (Col=0; Col < 320; Col++)  {
         PixelValue = GetPixelValue(Col,Row); /* read the value from display */
         fputc(PixelValue,OutPutFile);
      }

   fclose(OutPutFile);
}


/*
Pass 1 through the data reads the raw data file, scales the raw
data, and builds the RGBCube.
*/

int ProcessPass1(char *FileName)   {

   FILE *ImageFile;
   register unsigned Row, Col;
   unsigned RowNum, NumColors, c,k;
   unsigned Red, Green, Blue;
   int ReturnCode;

   printf("\nPass 1\n");
   if (Verbose)
      printf("Reading file: %s\n",FileName);

   /* attempt to allocate required memory for RGBCube */
   if (!AllocMemory())  {
      printf("\nMemory allocation error in Pass 1!\n");
      ReturnCode = ENoMemory;
      goto ErrorExit;
   }

   /* Attempt to open the file */
   if (!(ImageFile = fopen(FileName,"rb")))   {
      printf("File %s not found in Pass 1!\n",FileName);
      ReturnCode = EFileNotFound;
      goto ErrorExit;
   }

  /* Read in the header */
  if (fread(&Hdr,sizeof(Hdr),1,ImageFile) != 1)   {
     printf("Error reading image header in Pass 1!\n",FileName);
```

(continued)

Listing 4.1 *(continued)*

```
      ReturnCode = EReadFileHdr;
      goto ErrorExit;
   }
/* Make local copies of image parameters */
ImageWidth  = Hdr.Width;
ImageHeight = Hdr.Height;
ImagePixels = (unsigned long) ImageWidth * ImageHeight;
/*
Now scan complete image scaling the RGB values from
the range 0..FF to 0..1F by right shifting three bits.
Each row of raw data is comprised of a RowNum and then
a row of RGB color values.
*/

Message("Reading Line:   0");
for (Row=0; Row < ImageHeight; Row++)   {

   if (fread(&RowNum,sizeof(unsigned),1,ImageFile) != 1)   {
     printf("\nError reading image row number in Pass 1!\n");
     ReturnCode = EReadRowNum;
     goto ErrorExit;
   }
   if (Verbose)
     printf("\b\b\b%3d",RowNum);    /* output row number to display */

   /* Now read a line of red data */
   if (fread(RedRowBuf,ImageWidth,1,ImageFile) != 1)   {
     printf("\nError reading red data in Pass 1!\n");
     ReturnCode = EReadData;
     goto ErrorExit;
   }

   /* Now read a line of green data */
   if (fread(GreenRowBuf,ImageWidth,1,ImageFile) != 1)   {
     printf("\nError reading green data in Pass 1!\n");
     ReturnCode = EReadData;
     goto ErrorExit;
   }

   /* Now read a line of blue data */
   if (fread(BlueRowBuf,ImageWidth,1,ImageFile) != 1)   {
     printf("\nError reading blue data in Pass 1!\n");
     ReturnCode = EReadData;
     goto ErrorExit;
   }

   /*
   For each RGB triplet in this row of image data. Scale values
   accordingly.
   */
```

```
        for (Col=0; Col < ImageWidth; Col++)  {
          Red   = RedRowBuf[Col]   > 3;
          Green = GreenRowBuf[Col] > 3;
          Blue  = BlueRowBuf[Col]  >3;

          /* Add one to the count of pixels with that color */
          (RGBCube[Red][(Blue*COLLEVELS)+Green])++;
        }
    }
    /*
    Count and print the number of unique colors in the input by scanning the
    RGBCube array and looking for nonzero frequencies.
    */

    NumColors = 0;
    for (c=0; c < COLLEVELS; c++)
      for (k=0; k < COLLEVELS*COLLEVELS; k++)
        if (RGBCube[c][k])
          NumColors++;

    if (Verbose)
       printf("\n%d unique colors in image data\n",NumColors);

    if (Verbose)
      printf("Pass 1 completed.\n\n");

    /* Normal function exit point */
    fclose(ImageFile);
    return(NoError);

ErrorExit:
    printf("\n");
    DeAllocMemory();
    fclose(ImageFile);
    return(ReturnCode);

}

/*
This function provides help in the advent of operator error. Program
terminates after help is given
*/

void ShowHelp( void )  {

  printf("\nThis program quantizes, displays, and saves a 256-color image.\n");
  printf("It is invoked as follows:\n\n");
  printf("Usage: mquan [-c -g -h -i -p -v -x] infilename [outfilename]<cr>\n");
  printf("  -c inhibit gamma correction\n");
  printf("  -g create a GIF output file\n");
  printf("  -h or ? show help\n");
```

(continued)

Listing 4.1 *(continued)*

```
  printf("  -i prevents the color reg values from being installed\n");
  printf("  -p create PCX output file\n");
  printf("  -v displays program progress information\n");
  printf("  -x create executable display program\n");
  printf(" outfilename is name given to generated display file(s).\n\n");
  exit(1);
}

/* main quantizer program */

void main(short argc, char *argv[])  {

   unsigned FileNameCounter, ArgIndex;
   char    *ImageFileName;
   char    *OutputFileName;

   clrscr();
   printf("MQUAN -- Median Cut Color Quantizer Program.  Ver: %d.%d\n",Ver,Rev);
   printf("from the book \"Practical Ray Tracing in C\"\n");
   printf("Written by Craig A. Lindley\n\n");
   printf("This program converts 16.8 million 24-bit color images\n");
   printf("in dump format to 256-color images for display on a VGA\n");
   printf("equipped computer\n\n");

   /* install default options */
   Verbose       = FALSE;            /* don't be wordy */
   GenComFile    = FALSE;            /* don't generate a .COM file */
   GenGIFFile    = FALSE;            /* don't generate a GIF file */
   GenPCXFile    = FALSE;            /* don't generate a PCX file */
   InstallColors = TRUE;            /* install calculated colors */
   CorrectGamma  = TRUE;            /* do gamma correction */

   /* parse all command line arguments */

   FileNameCounter = 0;                  /* count of user-specified filenames */
   for (ArgIndex=1; ArgIndex < argc; ArgIndex++)  {
      if (*argv[ArgIndex] != '-')  {   /* if not a cmd line switch */
                                       /* must be a filename */
         if (*argv[ArgIndex] == '?')   /* help requested ? */
           ShowHelp();
         if (FileNameCounter > 2)       /* only two filenames allowed */
           ShowHelp();                  /* if more then error exit */
         if (FileNameCounter == 0)
           ImageFileName = argv[ArgIndex];  /* save input image filename */
         else
           OutputFileName = argv[ArgIndex]; /* save output image filename */

         FileNameCounter++;            /* inc count for error check */
      }
      else  {                          /* it's a cmd line switch */
        switch (*(argv[ArgIndex]+1))  {  /* parse the cmd line */
```

```
          case 'c':
          case 'C':
            CorrectGamma = FALSE;
            break;
          case 'g':
          case 'G':
            GenGIFFile = TRUE;
            break;
          case 'h':
          case 'H':
            ShowHelp();
            break;
          case 'i':
          case 'I':
            InstallColors = FALSE;
            break;
          case 'p':
          case 'P':
            GenPCXFile = TRUE;
            break;
          case 'v':
          case 'V':
            Verbose   = TRUE;
            break;
        case 'x':
        case 'X':
            GenComFile = TRUE;
            break;
        default:
            printf("Error - invalid cmd line switch encountered\n");
            ShowHelp();
        }
    }
}
if (FileNameCounter < 1)  {
    printf("Error - input filename required\n");
    ShowHelp();
}
if ((GenComFile | GenGIFFile | GenPCXFile) && (FileNameCounter != 2))  {
    printf("Error - input and output filename required\n");
    ShowHelp();
}

if (ProcessPass1(ImageFileName) == NoError)   {
  Message("Selecting optimum color palette\n");
  SelectColorBoxes();
  SortColors();

  /* Check for VESA compliance */
  CheckForVESA();
  /* display the resultant color image with the proper palette */
  SelectVideoMode(ImageWidth,ImageHeight,TRUE);
```

(continued)

Listing 4.1 *(continued)*

```
DisplayImageData(ImageFileName);
/*
If we want real colors InstallColors is TRUE. If we want pseudocolors
for special effects, InstallColors is FALSE. In this case
we must call GetAllColorRegs to store the default RGB values of the
color registers into the SColReg array.
*/

if (InstallColors)  {
  ScaleColRegisters();
  SetAllColorRegs(SColRegs);
}
else
  GetAllColorRegs(SColRegs);

if (GenGIFFile)  {
  /*
  Create a 256-color GIF file of displayed image. Assumes
  single bit plane with one byte per pixel.
  */
  WriteGIFFile(OutputFileName,ImageWidth,ImageHeight,
                            ImageWidth,ImageHeight,0,0);
}
if (GenPCXFile)  {
  /*
  Create a 256-color PCX file of displayed image. Assumes
  single bit plane with one byte per pixel.
  */
  WritePCXFile(OutputFileName, ImageWidth, ImageHeight);
}
if (GenComFile && (ImageWidth <= 320))  {
  /* create an executable file for display of color image */
  WriteComFile(OutputFileName);
}
}
/* prepare to return to dos */
getch();
SetTextMode();
DeAllocMemory();
}
```

We can summarize the operation of the "mquan" program in a single statement: The "mquan" program is an implementation of the median cut color quantization algorithm for execution on a PC running the MSDOS operating system. Its operation is directed by command line arguments (command line switches) passed to it when the program is executed. The "mquan" program makes two passes over the "dump image file" formatted data. One pass is to build the required data structures and perform the color reduction. The second pass is to display the image on the computer monitor. Gamma correction is applied to the displayed image if not inhibited by a command line switch. Once the image is displayed, various types of output files can be created if the user requests them. The possible output files are the PCX, GIF, and "autodisplay" files. After creation of the output files, the program waits, with the quantized image displayed on the computer screen, for the user to terminate its operation by pressing a keyboard key. At that time, the image is erased and control is returned to DOS.

The Dump Image File Format

Each of the color quantization programs presented expects its input data in the "dump" format. This format is produced by the simple ray-tracing program presented in Chapter 3 and the DKBTrace ray tracer discussed in Part Two of this book. We use this format extensively in this book because it is so simple to read and write. A dump formatted image file consists of a file header followed by the image's raster data. The file header contains just two 16-bit entries: the image width and the image height, in that order. Both of these quantities are expressed in little endian byte order (see Chapter 1 for details). The image width determines how many bytes make up a raster line of data. The image height tells how many raster lines of image data are contained in the file. A single raster line of data is made up of a 16-bit raster line row number followed by three image-width byte arrays of color data—first red, then green, then blue. This format contains 24 bits (3 bytes) of color information per pixel of image data. You can see the technique used within the "mquan" program for parsing a dump formatted file in the function "ProcessPass1" of Listing 4.1. In this function, the dump file is opened and the image header is read into a "Hdr" structure. Then the program loops through the image, image height number of times, each time reading the row number then reading the whole raster line of RGB data. Individual pixels of image data are built from a byte of data from each of the three arrays of color component data as shown.

We showed an example of writing a dump file in Listing 3.8 of the previous chapter. Generalized Dump file I/O functions are provided in the next chapter. Remember, any true-color image data that can be put into this simple data file format can be quantized and displayed with the programs in this chapter.

A Simple Command Line Interface

Most programs with the complexity of those presented in this chapter provide options for tailoring their operation to the user's requirements. All of the programs provided here are controlled by parameters called command line switches, which are passed to them when they are executed from the DOS prompt. The usage of the "mquan" program can be diagrammatically illustrated as follows:

```
mquan [-c -g -h -i -p -v -x ?] InFilename [OutFilename]
```

All of the command line switches, shown in the brackets and preceded by a dash, control the operation of the program. All of the items in brackets [] are optional. Figure 4.1 gives a brief description of what each of the available command line switches does. In the simplest case,

Program usage:

    mquan [-c -g -h -i -p -v -x ?] InFilename [OutFilename]

The OutFilename is optional, as are all the command line switches.

-c   This switch inhibits gamma correction of the color data.

-g   The inclusion of this switch results in the generation of a GIF image file from the image displayed on the VGA monitor. When this switch is included on the command line, an output filename without extension is required. The name of the produced GIF image file will be "OutFilename.gif."

-h   This switch causes the program to display a concise help screen describing the operation of the "mquan" program and each of the command line switches. The program terminates immediately after the help screen is displayed.

-i   This switch prohibits the installation of the calculated color palette during image display. The resultant image is displayed with colors unrelated to its color content. This switch is used as a special effect to produce images with wild coloring.

-p   The inclusion of this switch results in the generation of a PCX image file from the image displayed on the VGA monitor. When this switch is included on the command line, an output filename without extension is required. The name of the produced PCX image file will be "OutFilename.pcx."

-v   This option turns on the verbose flag in the code, which causes the program to report its progress. In the verbose mode, the steps required to process the image will be displayed.

-x   This option causes a COM file to be created that will display the color image when executed. This feature is referred to as "autodisplay" and will be discussed in detail later in this chapter. When this switch is included on the command line, an output filename without extension is required. The name of the autodisplay program will become "OutFilename.com." This option can be used only with 320 by 200 resolution 256-color images.

Any and all of the command line switches (except the requests for help that terminate program operation after help is given) can be used singly or together for a combined effect. You must separate each switch from the previous switch by a space. Switches can be specified in either upper- or lowercase. It is possible to execute the program without specifying any switches. This will result in the display of a color image without any optional processing or output files.

Figure 4.1   MQUAN Program Command Line Switches

the "mquan" program can be executed with only a single input filename specified. In this case, the default values of all program options will be used for the production of the specified image. *Note*: The specified input image must be in the "dump" file format previously discussed. No output files are created by default. If the "mquan" program is executed without the required input filename or with a question mark instead of a filename, it will output a short screen of help text and terminate. The help text reminds the user of the legal command line switches and provides a brief description of what each does.

    Parsing of the command line within the "mquan" program is performed in the "main" function. The "argc" and "argv" values provided by the C compiler's run time environment are accessed to determine which if any of the command line switches are present. Since "argc" contains the number of user-specified items on the command line, it is used to loop through each of these items and parse them one at a time. If a dash is not the first character in a command line item, this item must be either a request for help (if it is a question mark) or a filename. If a filename is found, the count of filenames is incremented for subsequent error checking. If the filename count exceeds two, an error has been detected and "mquan" terminates by calling "ShowHelp." As the input and output filenames are identified, pointers are saved to each of them for later access. The first filename encountered is expected to be the input filename and the second, the optional output filename.

If a dash is detected as the first character, the command line item is assumed to be a command line switch. In this case, a switch statement is used to parse the character following the dash to see which command line switch it represents. An individual case within the switch statement exists for each legal command line switch. *Note*: Both upper- and lowercase entries vector to the same case statement, so both upper- and lowercase user input is acceptable. If an illegal command line switch is detected, "ShowHelp" is called after an appropriate error message is displayed. The program then terminates within the "ShowHelp" function.

The process of parsing the command line entries continues until no more entries remain or an error is detected. If the "argc" loop successfully terminates, two additional checks are made on the user's inputs. First, a check is made to see if the single required filename has been entered. Finally, if the user had specified that one (or more) output files were to be created, this code verifies that two filenames were indeed supplied instead of just one. A failure of either of these checks terminates program execution and displays the help message.

Output Image Files

This program can produce three very different output files. First, if the "-g" command line switch is used when the program is executed, a 256-color GIF image file will be produced from the image on the display. If the "-p" command line switch is used, a 256-color PCX image file will be produced. The "v256.exe" program, given at the end of the next chapter, can be used to display these image files at any time. You can also use any other PCX/GIF file viewer capable of displaying 256-color high-resolution images to display the produced images. Since we would be getting ahead of ourselves if we described the PCX and GIF file formats in this chapter, we will postpone that discussion until Chapter 5. Because the "autodisplay" file format is unique to this book and is definitely nonstandard, we will discuss it next. For now, you must just use the code to write both the PCX and the GIF files in the "mquan" program as presented. Chapter 5 will shed light on these file formats and the code required to read and write them.

An autodisplay file is created with the "-x" command line switch. As mentioned, autodisplay files can be created only for 320 by 200 resolution 256-color images. It would be difficult but possible to extend this concept to higher-resolution images, but we will leave that to you. In its present form, an "autodisplay" file is a unique file type that contains a small code segment, the 256 color register values, and the raster data for a 320 by 200 color image. This file is organized into DOS "COM" file format and given the filename specified by the user. Having a COM file means that you can directly execute the file by typing its name at the DOS prompt or by including it within a batch file. Autodisplay files will display the contained 320 by 200 resolution image immediately, in full color, when the file is executed. Please refer to the code for the autodisplay program shown in Listing 4.2 during the short discussion to follow.

Listing 4.2   The Autodisplay Program

The following is the contents of the file "imagecom.asm."

```
;320x200 Color Image Display Program
;
;NOTE: this program will only work with a VGA video adapter
;
;written by  Craig A. Lindley
;Vers: 1.0   Last Update: 06/21/89
;
;This program produces a .COM file which when executed will display a
;320x200 256-color image originally produced by the ray tracer.
;
VIDEO             EQU    10H         ;video BIOS interrupt code
KEYBOARD          EQU    16H         ;keyboard BIOS interrupt code
;
IMAGESIZE         EQU    64000       ;320x200 image size in bytes
RGBSIZE           EQU    256*3       ;number of rgb bytes
GETVIDEOMODE      EQU    0FH         ;BIOS function code
SETVIDEOMODE      EQU    00H         ;BIOS function code
SET256COLORMODE   EQU    13H         ;320x200 256-color video mode
SETCOLREGBLOCK    EQU    1012H       ;BIOS function/sub function code
VGAMEMSEG         EQU    0A000H      ;segment of VGA display memory
GETKEY            EQU    00H         ;wait for key function code
;
;
CSEG    SEGMENT  PARA  PUBLIC  'CODE'
        ASSUME  CS:CSEG,DS:CSEG,SS:CSEG,ES:CSEG ;set by loader
;
        ORG     100H                ;com file org location
;
;NOTE: when transcribing the addresses listed in the list file to the
;      procedure WriteComFile be sure to reverse the order of the address
;      bytes otherwise the resultant .COM image file will not execute.
;
;Start of the display program
;
Start   proc    near

        mov     ah,GETVIDEOMODE   ;get the current video mode
        int     VIDEO             ;result in AL register
        mov     VMode,al          ;save video mode
;
        mov     ah,SETVIDEOMODE   ;set video mode function code
        mov     al,SET256COLORMODE;to special VGA mode
        int     VIDEO             ;do it
;
        mov     ax,SETCOLREGBLOCK ;prepare to load all 256 color regs
        mov     bx,0              ;starting with reg 0
        mov     cx,256            ;all 256 registers
        mov     dx,offset ColorRegs  ;point at rgb[256] data
                                  ;assumes es=cs
```

```
        int     VIDEO               ;load the registers
;
        mov     cx,IMAGESIZE        ;number of bytes to move
        mov     si,offset ImageData  ;source of data to move
                                    ;assume ds=cs
        mov     ax,VGAMEMSEG        ;dest of data to be moved is VGA
        mov     es,ax              ;memory. es[di] = A000:0000
        mov     di,0
        rep     movsb              ;move the image data
;
        mov     ah,GETKEY          ;wait for key press
        int     KEYBOARD           ;ask BIOS
;
        mov     ah,SETVIDEOMODE    ;set video mode function code
        mov     al,VMode           ;to original mode
        int     VIDEO              ;do it
;
        ret                        ;ret to dos
;
Start   endp
;
;Program Data Area - stored in code segment cs
;
VMode       DB      0           ;storage for original video mode
ColorRegs   DB      RGBSIZE   DUP(0);256 rgb triads
ImageData   DB      IMAGESIZE DUP(0);image data storage 64000 bytes
;
CSEG    ENDS
        END     Start
```

The code portion of an "autodisplay" program file is comprised of 23 lines of assembler code. The bulk of the file is comprised of color register data and image raster data. All "autodisplay" COM files are exactly 64,824 bytes in length because the raster data is always the same size and is uncompressed. You can best understand the operation of this code by examining the pseudocode below:

Function AutoDisplay

```
Begin
  Get the current video mode by asking the BIOS
  Save the current video mode in memory
  Set the video mode to mode 13H the 320 by 200 256-color mode.
  Copy the RGB values for all 256 color registers from the
    file into the VGA color registers.
  Set the CX register to the number of bytes of raster data
    stored in the file that will be moved to VGA video memory.
  Set DS:SI registers to point at the raster data in the file.
  Set ES:DI registers to point at VGA video memory located
    at A000:0000.
```

```
    Block move the raster data to video memory.
    Wait for user to hit a key (keyboard polled via BIOS).
    Get original video mode from memory.
    Restore original video mode.
End
```

The function of this code should be obvious and requires little further explanation. You can observe the operation of this code by executing one of the COM files in the "galley" directory on the companion disks. For a nice change of pace, try executing one of these autodisplay files from your computer's "autoexec.bat" file. Then, each time you turn your computer on, you will be greeted with a ray-traced image to start off your day.

The function "WriteComFile" within the "mquan" program is what creates the autodisplay file. In this function, the object code generated by assembling the autodisplay program (Listing 4.2) is hard coded into the array "FileCode." The sequence of events necessary to create an executable autodisplay program are as you would expect. First, an output file is opened in binary mode with the name specified by the user on the command line and the extension ".com" supplied by the program. The executable code is then written from the "FileCode" array to the file. The color register data is then written to the file. The RGB components of color register 0 are written to the file followed by color registers 1, 2, and so on until color register 255 is written. Finally, the image raster data is read directly from the VGA display with the function "GetPixelValue" and written to the file. The data is written in normal raster format from the top of the display to the bottom. After the raster data is written, the autodisplay file is closed, which completes the creation process.

There are no other new techniques in this code that we need to discuss. You move data into the VGA video memory by the same technique that we described in Chapter 1 when we discussed the VGA video memory access.

The Median Cut Algorithm

Note: The median cut algorithm is the brainchild of Paul Heckbert and was published in *Computer Graphics Magazine* in 1982. See the "Further Reading" section of Part Three for the specifics of this article.

During the color quantization process, the median cut algorithm tries to assign colors such that each assigned color represents approximately the same number of pixels in the original image. Intuitively, this provides an explanation of why this algorithm seems to be universally applicable. It searches for and finds 256 regions within the total color space defined by an image that represent approximately the same number of pixels. Regions within the color space in which pixel colors are clustered are assigned many unique color values. Regions that contain few pixels are gathered together and assigned a single color value. This makes sense in that regions of the color space that contain only a few pixels are not very important in the display of the image. Regions that contain lots of pixels are important and the use of accurate colors for display of these pixels is much more important to the resultant image quality.

In order to quantify the colors contained in an image, as required for the quantization process, you need a three-dimensional color histogram. Because each color component value can range from 0 to 255, an ideal three-dimensional histogram could be implemented as a three-dimensional array (with Red, Green, and Blue indices) declared as follows:

    unsigned long RGBCube[256][256][256];

The data stored in each array entry is the count of pixels within the original image that had the specific RGB color value. For example, if a Red pixel value (1,0,0) were detected, the entry in the RGBCube array corresponding to that value would be incremented as follows:

    RGBCube[1][0][0]++;

Unfortunately, an array of this type would require over 67 megabytes of memory to implement. An array type of unsigned long (requiring 4 bytes for each entry) is required to count the number of pixels within the image that had the color specified by the array indices. A data type of unsigned short (maximum value of 65,535) is insufficient because it is possible in the higher resolutions supported by this program for a short value to overflow. In other words, there may be more than 65,535 pixels within a single image that have the exact same RGB value. This is true especially in 1024 by 768 images, which have a total pixel count of 786,432.

Typically, images produced by a ray-tracing program or by a color digitizer contain less than 5,000 unique colors. In this case, the "RGBCube" declared above would have 5,000 or fewer nonzero entries. These entries, when totaled, would equal the number of pixels within the image. Once it is realized that the "RGBCube" is a rather sparse array, you can use various techniques to reduce its voracious appetite for memory.

The method chosen for this implementation is to prescale the RGB data such that it occupies the range from 0 to 31 instead of 0 to 255. This is done by shifting the color component values 3 bits to the right. In effect, this scaling groups the eight closest shades of each color together. This causes distortion in the color quantization process as a trade-off for reduced memory consumption. The bottom line, however, is that we are attempting to reduce images with vast numbers of colors down to 256 colors. (With the maximum resolution of the images we will be quantizing being 1024 by 768, the maximum number of colors possible is 786,432. That would mean every pixel in the image was a different color, which is highly unlikely.) This color reduction causes considerable amounts of color distortion. The additional amount of distortion we are introducing as a side effect of this implementation is negligible by comparison. The new declaration of the RGBCube could then become:

    unsigned long RGBCube[32][32][32];

which would require a mere 128K of memory to implement. While this is a worthwhile reduction in memory, we still have a problem with an array of this size on a PC (running real-mode MSDOS) because the array size exceeds 64K. To circumvent this problem, we declare the RGBCube as:

    unsigned long far *RGBCube[32];

RGBCube is then an array of 32 far pointers to unsigned long values. To form the complete RGBCube, you must initialize these pointers within the "AllocMemory" function to point to two-dimensional arrays of unsigned longs. These two-dimensional arrays are only 4,096 bytes in length and therefore solve our memory problem. To access a single entry within the RGBCube, you can use the following mechanism:

RGBCube[Red][(Blue*32)+Green]

The function "ProcessPass1" in the listing shows how the three-dimensional color histogram, RGBCube, is built. Basically, as the RGB components of each pixel's value are identified, they are used as the indices into the RGBCube. The value in the RGBCube at these indices is incremented each time a pixel of this color is found. After the complete image is read and processed, each nonzero entry in the RGBCube represents a unique color in the original image.

Once the RGBCube is built, you can apply the median cut algorithm to the color data contained within it. To do this, you use a data structure called a "Box." A Box is defined as follows:

```
struct Box {
  unsigned short Lo[3];
  unsigned short Hi[3];
  unsigned long NumElements;
};
```

One Box exists for each color in the final image. In this case, an array of 256 Boxes will be used. The array "Lo" within the Box contains the lower extremes of the RGB color component values contained within this Box, while "Hi" contains the upper extreme. "NumElements" contains the number of image pixels that fall within this Box; that is, within the range of the RGB values contained within the Box. The median cut algorithm attempts to divide the RGBCube into 256 regions (Boxes) of nearly equal pixel counts. This function is performed within the "SelectColorBoxes" function. Initially, a single Box, Box[0], is created, which spans the complete RGBCube. This is accomplished by setting the "Lo" entries to 0, the "Hi" entries to 31 (COLLEVELS-1), and the "NumElements" to the total number of pixels in the image being quantized. Then for each of 256 Boxes, a search is made through the currently utilized Boxes for the Box that contains the highest "NumElements" count. Within this Box, the Hi and Lo values of each color component are subtracted to determine the color that has the largest spread of values. The color with the largest delta is considered the major axis. This is the axis along which this Box will be split. Next, the number of pixels contained within this Box is summed from the low to the high end of the Box along the major axis. The process is stopped when the sum exceeds one-half the total number of pixels in the Box (NumElements/2). This Box is then split into two Boxes along the major axis at the point where one-half the pixel count was detected. Thus, Box[0] is split into Box[0] and Box[1], with each containing approximately the same number of pixels. In this case, they each would contain half the total number of image pixels. This process continues until 256 Boxes of approximately equal pixel counts are identified.

Once all the Boxes are identified, you then must determine the single color that will be used for display of the pixel values that fall within the region of the color space defined by each Box. The "SortColors" function performs this operation. The single color used for each

Box is the weighted average of the color component values multiplied by the color counts (from RGBCube) and divided by the total number of pixels contained within this Box. Once a single color is identified for each Box, the luminance (or brightness) value of these colors is calculated. The luminance values (calculated from the simple NTSC formula shown in the listing) of each color are used to sort the color values into increasing brightness. The end result of this process is the creation of the "SColRegs" array, which contains the 256 sorted color values. These color values are moved into the VGA's DAC after scaling and gamma correction (see the "ScaleColRegisters" function). These are the colors that will be used to display the quantized image.

The final process that needs to be performed is a mapping between the original pixels' RGB values and the new RGB values to be used for image display. This is one of the first operations performed by the "DisplayImageData" function within the "mquan" program. Here, the RGBCube is reused. Its initial function has been fulfilled and therefore the color histogram data that it contains is no longer required. The RGBCube will now be used to implement the mapping function. The RGB color components of a pixel from the original image will be used as indices into the RGBCube. The value fetched from the RGBCube will be the color index value to display the pixel with; thus the mapping.

Before this can be done, however, the RGBCube must be prepared with the mapping function. The first step in this process is to initialize every entry in the RGBCube to some out-of-range value so we can determine if we hit a portion of the RGBCube not contained within a Box. Next, nested loops access each Box, assigning a single unique color index value to all colors encompassed by the Box. Now that the mapping function has been established, we perform pass two over the image data. As each pixel in the original data is identified, its RGB components are scaled then applied as indices to the RGBCube and a color index is returned. If the index is valid, the pixel is displayed with the color described by this color index (the palette of 256 colors that will be transferred to the DAC). If, however, the index is not valid (the out-of-range, initialization value was returned), a search is made through the color register values to determine the closest color with which to display this pixel. The color that exhibits the smallest error is used for the display.

In summary, the process of quantizing image data and converting it to a format suitable for display on a VGA/SuperVGA graphics adapter can be described by a four-step process. The first step is the sampling of the image to determine its color distribution. The result of this step is a three-dimensional color histogram (the RGBCube in our implementation) that is needed in step two.

The second step in this process is "colormap selection." Here, the optimal 256 colors required to display the color image are extracted from the input color distribution (or histogram) provided in step one. This color distribution is the content of the original image.

In the third step, a mapping is established between all colors that made up the original image and the closest colors contained in the color map. The mapping function is usually stored in a quantization table (the RGBCube is reused in this implementation) to speed the processing in step four. In other words, the mapping between the many thousands of colors in the original image and the 256 colors that will be used to display the image is developed.

After the colormap has been selected in step two and the quantization table is created in step three, the fourth and final step of the process is image quantization and display. In this step, each pixel of the original image is passed through the quantization table (thereby mapping it to the correct color register for display) and is then written to the VGA/SuperVGA adapter. Installation of the correct 256-color palette is the final step in the display process.

Note: Because the installation of the color palette is the last operation performed, the image displayed on the computer's monitor during the majority of the quantization process will be in false, random colors. When the color palette is finally installed, the image on the screen will instantly be displayed in its correct colors.

Overall Program Operation

The steps that the "mquan.exe" program goes through to process full-color images are best illustrated with the pseudocode shown below. As you will see, many more steps are required in practice to provide a usable program than were described in our theoretical discussion.

```
Begin
  Display the startup message
  Parse command line switches and set the appropriate global variables
  Output error messages and display help if required

  Pass One—Read the image data file
    Allocate memory for the RGBCube
    Scale input data while building the color histogram (RGBCube)
      for the image.
    Calculate the number of unique colors in the image.
    Perform the median cut algorithm to divide the color space into
      256 regions of approximately equal pixel counts.
    Calculate the color to be used for the display of all colors
      mapped within a region. Repeat for all 256 regions.

  Check for the presence of a VESA-compatible VGA/SuperVGA adapter. Abort
    program operation if one is not found.
  Select the video mode required for the display of this image. Computer is
    now in the appropriate graphics mode.

  Pass Two—Reread the image data file
    Pass every pixel in the image data through the RGBCube for color mapping.
    Write the color index value returned from RGBCube to the display adapter
      at the appropriate location.

  Scale and gamma correct the color palette values in "SColRegs."
  Move these values into the VGA/SuperVGA's DAC.
  Process any output file requests.
  Wait for the user to hit a key to terminate the image display.
  Select the text mode.
  Free the memory associated with the RGBCube.
  Return to DOS with an exit code.
End
```

The production of quantized color images is not a trivial task. This program, by necessity, is the most complex presented in this book with the exception of DKBTrace. Over 3,500 lines of C are required to quantize and display the color images. The results, for the most part, are quite spectacular in terms of color quality and color selection.

You can achieve an interesting effect by changing the code within the "mquan" program to reduce the number of colors used for image quantization and display. For example, you may want to reduce the number of colors to 16. To do this, add the statement "#define MAXNUM-COLREGS 16" to the program and recompile it. Notice the effect this change has on image quality. Lowering the number of available colors has a drastic impact on the realism of ray-traced images.

Octree Color Quantization

The second method of color quantization we discuss is called "octree color quantization." The program that implements this quantization algorithm, "oquan.exe," has the same features as did "mquan.exe." Namely, it quantizes 24-bit-per-pixel images in the "dump" format with resolutions up to and including 1024 by 768 down to 256 colors for display and/or saving in a standard graphics file format. The structures of these two programs are almost identical. Only the color quantization algorithm is different. In both cases, two passes over the image data are required to quantize the colors and to display the resultant image.

The octree quantization code contained in the "oquan.exe" program was written for the most part by Wolfgang Stuerzlinger and placed in the public domain. We have taken Wolfgang's code, added a few enhancements, and then manipulated it into the form you see in Listing 4.3. It is contained in the files "oquan.prj" and "oquan.c" on the companion disks. Please refer to this listing during the discussion to follow.

How It Works

To understand how octree quantization works, you must first understand what an octree is. An octree is a treelike data structure used to manage the RGB color space. It is like a binary tree except that a total of three decision variables are used instead of one. The number of decision variables determines how many links are required in each node of a tree. A binary tree, for example, with a single decision variable has 2^1, or two, links per node. A quad tree with two decision variables would require four links per node. An octree requires eight links for each node, or 2^3. The three decision variables utilized are the red, green, and blue (RGB) color component values of a node. For 24-bits-per-pixel images, we will use an octree of depth eight because all 16.8 million possible colors can be managed with an octree of this size (eight levels of octree nodes with eight links leaving each node is 8^8 or 16.8 million). Fortunately, we never need to build the whole octree; only those portions of it that represent the colors of the image being quantized are needed. An octree is a perfect structure for managing the RGB color space because it allows quick identification of similar colors. The deeper you are in the tree, the closer together the color values are in RGB space. This is important in the reduction of the octree, as we shall show.

A key to understanding how an octree is used to manage the color space is to master how the color components are used (in this implementation anyway) to maneuver around the octree. As mentioned, the deeper you are into the octree (the further from the root), the closer the colors become to one another. You can achieve this organization of colors at a finer and finer level by examining the color component values in a bit-wise manner from most to least significant bit as you go deeper into the tree. It is no accident that each color component value is in the range 0 to 255 and expressed in 8 bits and that there are eight levels in the octree structure. During the construction and traversal of the octree, you can find the position of the nodes representing the various colors by following the links from the root node toward the leaves. Which link to follow or which branch to take from each node is calculated as follows:

Branch = TESTBIT(RGB.Red,   MAXDEPTH—Depth) * 4 +
                TESTBIT(RGB.Green, MAXDEPTH—Depth) * 2 +
                TESTBIT(RGB.Blue,   MAXDEPTH—Depth);

where TESTBIT is a macro that tests the bit position specified by the second argument of the value specified by the first argument. TESTBIT returns a zero value if the specified bit position is cleared or a one value if it is set. The value being tested is not modified in any way.

As you can see, the depth within the tree determines which bit of each color component is tested. After the required bits are tested, the results are weighted by color and combined into the "Branch" variable. Branch is a number from zero to seven that determines by which link (of the eight within the node) to exit this node. Links are implemented as an array of pointers to other nodes. Branch is the index into the array of pointers. It should be obvious that each of the 16.8 million possible colors would map to a unique node within an octree using this branching method. Fortunately, most imagery does not contain anywhere near that number of colors.

With node branching behind us, we can now discuss how octree color quantization works. Basically, the process starts out with a color table (which we shall refer to as the color palette from now on) of size 256 (an array of 256 color register values) that has all RGB entries initialized to zero. As the image to be quantized is read, each unique color is added into the color palette. When all 256 entries in the palette are filled, colors that are similar are merged together and replaced by their mean or average color value. This process continues until the complete image has been read. At no time during this process are there more than 256 entries in the color palette. The colors remaining in the palette are those that will be used to display the quantized image. Once the color palette is built, the image is again read and displayed in the colors contained within this palette.

In practice, the process is a bit more complex than just described; so what else is new? In reality, three steps are required to perform the complete process. Steps one and two are performed during pass one over the image data, and step three is performed during pass two. These steps are:

1. Building the octree from the image data
2. Building the color palette from the octree
3. Mapping the original colors from the image into their new representatives while in the process of displaying the image

We discuss these steps next. We describe both the theory and the implementation of that theory in the "oquan" program.

Listing 4.3   The OQUAN Color Quantization Program

The following describes the contents of the file "oquan.prj," even though this file itself is not directly viewable outside of the Borland environment. To build the "oquan" program, you must have access to the following C files (either in the current directory or by way of an explicit path): "vga.c," "pcx.c," "gif.c," and "oquan.c." The include files "misc.h," "vga.h," "pcx.h," and "gif.h" must also be available. Most of these files with the exception of "pcx.h," "gif.h," and "oquan.c" have been shown and described previously. We show "oquan.c" below, and we discuss "pcx.h" and "gif.h" in Chapter 5.

The following is the contents of the file "oquan.c."

```
/**********************************************************/
/***                  "oquan.c"                        ***/
/***          Octree Color Quantizer Program           ***/
/***              produces 256-color images            ***/
/***      from "dump" format color image data files    ***/
/***      from the book, "Practical Ray Tracing in C"   ***/
/***          written in Borland/Turbo C 2.0            ***/
/***                      by                            ***/
/***      Wolfgang Stuerzlinger and Craig A. Lindley    ***/
/***                                                    ***/
/***          Ver: 1.0    Last Update: 12/18/91         ***/
/**********************************************************/

/*
This code implements the algorithm described in the article
"A Simple Method for Color Quantization: Octree Quantization" by
Michael Gervautz, Werner Purgathofer from the book "Graphic Gems"
edited by Andrew Glassner. This code was originally written
and placed in the public domain by Wolfgang Stuerzlinger. The
code was subsequently modified for use in the PC environment by
the author.
*/

#include <stdio.h>
#include <conio.h>
#include <dos.h>
#include <process.h>
#include <string.h>
#include <alloc.h>
#include <math.h>
#include "misc.h"
#include "vga.h"
#include "gif.h"
#include "pcx.h"

/*
Miscellaneous Defines
*/
#define TESTBIT(a,i) (((a)&(1<<(i)))>(i))
#define MAXCOLOR 256          /* max number of colors */
#define MAXDEPTH 7            /* max depth of octree - 1 */
```

(continued)

Listing 4.3 *(continued)*

```c
/*
Data Structure Definitions
*/

struct ColorSum {
  unsigned long R;
  unsigned long G;
  unsigned long B;
};

typedef struct Node * OCTREE;

struct Node {                  /* an octree node data structure */
  unsigned Leaf;
  unsigned Level;
  unsigned ColorIndex;
  unsigned Children;
  unsigned long ColorCount;
  struct ColorSum RGBSum;
  OCTREE NextReduceable;
  OCTREE Next[8];
};

static struct {                /* dump file header */
  unsigned Width;
  unsigned Height;
} Hdr;


static unsigned Ver = 1;
static unsigned Rev = 0;
static unsigned ImageWidth;
static unsigned ImageHeight;
static unsigned Verbose;
static unsigned GenComFile;
static unsigned GenGIFFile;
static unsigned GenPCXFile;
static unsigned InstallColors;
static unsigned CorrectGamma;

/*
Gamma correction table for Gamma = 2.222. The 256 input entries map
to 64 possible outputs. See Chapter 1 of the text for information
on how this table was created.
*/
unsigned char GammaTable[] = {
 0, 5, 7, 8, 9,10,11,12,13,13,14,15,15,16,17,17,18,18,19,19,
20,20,20,21,21,22,22,22,23,23,24,24,24,25,25,25,26,26,26,27,
27,27,27,28,28,28,29,29,29,29,30,30,30,31,31,31,31,32,32,32,
32,33,33,33,33,34,34,34,34,34,35,35,35,35,36,36,36,36,36,37,
```

```
37,37,37,38,38,38,38,38,39,39,39,39,39,40,40,40,40,40,40,41,
41,41,41,41,42,42,42,42,42,42,43,43,43,43,43,44,44,44,44,44,
44,45,45,45,45,45,45,46,46,46,46,46,46,47,47,47,47,47,47,47,
48,48,48,48,48,48,49,49,49,49,49,49,49,50,50,50,50,50,50,50,
51,51,51,51,51,51,51,52,52,52,52,52,52,52,53,53,53,53,53,53,
53,53,54,54,54,54,54,54,54,55,55,55,55,55,55,55,55,56,56,56,
56,56,56,56,56,57,57,57,57,57,57,57,57,58,58,58,58,58,58,58,
58,59,59,59,59,59,59,59,59,60,60,60,60,60,60,60,60,61,61,
61,61,61,61,61,61,61,62,62,62,62,62,62,62,62,63
};

/* Single row buffers for reading raw data */
static BYTE RedRowBuf[MAXCOLS];
static BYTE GreenRowBuf[MAXCOLS];
static BYTE BlueRowBuf[MAXCOLS];


/* Variables used in the octree method */
static unsigned Size;
static unsigned ReduceLevel;
static unsigned LeafLevel;
static ColorRegister Palette[MAXCOLOR];
static OCTREE Tree;
static OCTREE ReduceList[MAXDEPTH + 1];
static unsigned NumNodes = 0;
static unsigned MaxNodes = 0;

/* beginning of program functions */
/*
This function returns the color index of the color that most closely
matches the color passed to it. This function can only be called after
the Octree is built.
*/
unsigned Quantize(OCTREE Tree, ColorRegister TheColor)  {

  if (Tree->Leaf)
    return(Tree->ColorIndex);
  else
    return(Quantize(Tree->Next[
            TESTBIT(TheColor.Red,  MAXDEPTH - Tree->Level) * 4 +
            TESTBIT(TheColor.Green,MAXDEPTH - Tree->Level) * 2 +
            TESTBIT(TheColor.Blue, MAXDEPTH - Tree->Level)],TheColor));
}

/*
This function traverses the octree assigning a unique color index
value to each leaf node. It also calculates the RGB color components
to be used in the leaf nodes by averaging. Finally, it copies the
RGB color value for the leaf node into the Palette array.
*/
void InitPalette(OCTREE Tree, unsigned *Index)    {
```

(continued)

Listing 4.3   *(continued)*

```
  unsigned Ind;

  if (Tree != NULL)  {
     if (Tree->Leaf || Tree->Level == LeafLevel)  {
        Palette[*Index].Red   = (BYTE)(Tree->RGBSum.R / Tree->ColorCount);
        Palette[*Index].Green = (BYTE)(Tree->RGBSum.G / Tree->ColorCount);
        Palette[*Index].Blue  = (BYTE)(Tree->RGBSum.B / Tree->ColorCount);

        Tree->ColorIndex = *Index;
        Tree->Leaf = 1;
        *Index = *Index + 1;
     }
     else  {
        for (Ind=0; Ind < 8; Ind++)
           InitPalette(Tree->Next[Ind],Index);
     }
  }
}


/*
The purpose of this function is to transform the color register values
in the range 0..255 to 0..63 as required for the RAM DAC. If gamma
correction is enabled, the data is gamma corrected and scaled
simultaneously.
*/

void ScaleColRegisters(void)  {

   register unsigned Index;
   register unsigned Temp;

   /* Scale all color register components accordingly */
   for (Index = 0; Index < MAXCOLOR; Index++)    {
      /* temp used to prevent overflow of BYTE value */

      if (CorrectGamma)
        Palette[Index].Red = GammaTable[Palette[Index].Red];
      else {
        Temp = Palette[Index].Red * (unsigned) MAXCOLREGVAL;
        Temp /= 255;
        Palette[Index].Red = Temp;
      }

      if (CorrectGamma)
        Palette[Index].Green = GammaTable[Palette[Index].Green];
      else {
        Temp = Palette[Index].Green * (unsigned) MAXCOLREGVAL;
        Temp /= 255;
        Palette[Index].Green = Temp;
      }
```

```
      if (CorrectGamma)
        Palette[Index].Blue = GammaTable[Palette[Index].Blue];
      else {
        Temp = Palette[Index].Blue * (unsigned) MAXCOLREGVAL;
        Temp /= 255;
        Palette[Index].Blue = Temp;
      }
    }
}

/*
This function is called whenever a new node needs to be allocated.
*/
void NewandInit(OCTREE *Tree, unsigned Depth)  {

  *Tree = (struct Node *) calloc(1,sizeof(struct Node));
  if (*Tree == NULL)  {
     printf("Error: out of memory");
     exit(ENoMemory);
  }
  NumNodes++;
  if (NumNodes > MaxNodes)
    MaxNodes = NumNodes;

  (*Tree)->Level = Depth;
  (*Tree)->Leaf = (Depth >= LeafLevel);
  if ((*Tree)->Leaf)
     Size++;
}

/*
Get a pointer to the next node to be reduced.
*/
void GetReduceable(OCTREE *Node)    {

  unsigned NewReduceLevel;

  NewReduceLevel = ReduceLevel;
  while (ReduceList[NewReduceLevel] == NULL) /* find a level with a node */
     NewReduceLevel--;                       /* to reduce */
  *Node = ReduceList[NewReduceLevel];        /* return ptr to that node */
  ReduceList[NewReduceLevel] =               /* update linked list of reducible */
        ReduceList[NewReduceLevel]->NextReduceable;
}                                            /* nodes. */

/*
This function links a node that has been determined to be
reducible into a linked list of reducible nodes at the same
depth level in the octree.
*/
void MakeReduceable(unsigned Level, OCTREE Node)  {
```

(continued)

Listing 4.3   *(continued)*

```
  Node->NextReduceable = ReduceList[Level];
  ReduceList[Level] = Node;
}

/*
This function recursively frees memory associated with the node
it is pointing at and all nodes under it (its siblings).
*/
void KillTree(OCTREE *Tree)    {

  register unsigned Index;

  if (*Tree == NULL)
    return;
  for (Index=0; Index < 8; Index++)
    KillTree(&((*Tree)->Next[Index]));

  NumNodes--;
  free(*Tree);
  *Tree = NULL;
}

/*
This function performs the reduction of the octree.
*/
void ReduceTree(void)  {

  OCTREE Node;
  register unsigned Index, Depth;

  GetReduceable(&Node);              /* get ptr to deepest node needing reduction */
  Node->Leaf = 1;                    /* change it from intermediate node to leaf */
  Size = Size - Node->Children + 1;  /* reduce number of leaves by the number of children.*/
  Depth = Node->Level;

  for (Index=0; Index < 8; Index++)  /* free memory occupied by children */
    KillTree(&(Node->Next[Index]));

  if (Depth < ReduceLevel)  {        /* if depth of reduced node is less */
    ReduceLevel = Depth;             /* than current reduce level, reduce */
    LeafLevel = ReduceLevel + 1;     /* reduce level and leaf level to */
  }                                  /* deepest intermediate (non leaf) node. */
}

/*
This function builds the octree from the pixel color values passed
to it.
*/
void InsertTree(OCTREE *Tree, ColorRegister RGB, unsigned Depth)  {
```

```
   unsigned Branch;

  if (*Tree == NULL)
     NewandInit(Tree,Depth);
  (*Tree)->ColorCount++;
  (*Tree)->RGBSum.R += (unsigned long) RGB.Red;
  (*Tree)->RGBSum.G += (unsigned long) RGB.Green;
  (*Tree)->RGBSum.B += (unsigned long) RGB.Blue;
  if (((*Tree)->Leaf == FALSE) && (Depth < LeafLevel))  {
     Branch = TESTBIT(RGB.Red,  MAXDEPTH - Depth) * 4 +
              TESTBIT(RGB.Green,MAXDEPTH - Depth) * 2 +
              TESTBIT(RGB.Blue, MAXDEPTH - Depth);
     if ((*Tree)->Next[Branch] == NULL)  {
        (*Tree)->Children++;
        if ((*Tree)->Children == 2)    /* any node with 2 or more children */
           MakeReduceable(Depth,*Tree);/* is candidate for reduction */
     }
     InsertTree(&((*Tree)->Next[Branch]),RGB,Depth + 1);
  }
}

/*
This function will output the message string passed to it if the Verbose
option variable is set true.
*/
void Message(char *String)  {
   if (Verbose)
      printf("%s",String);
}

/*
This function makes a pass over the image data and calls
InsertTree which builds the octree from each pixel.
*/
int GenOctree(char *FileName, OCTREE *Tree)  {

   FILE *ImageFile;
   register unsigned Row, Col;
   unsigned RowNum;
   int ReturnCode;
   ColorRegister RGB;

   Size = 0;                          /* initialize variables */
   ReduceLevel = MAXDEPTH;
   LeafLevel = ReduceLevel + 1;

   /* Attempt to open the file */
   if (!(ImageFile = fopen(FileName,"rb")))  {
      printf("\nFile %s not found in Pass 1\n",FileName);
      ReturnCode = EFileNotFound;
      goto ErrorExit;
   }
```

(continued)

Listing 4.3   *(continued)*

```
/* Read in the header */
if (fread(&Hdr,sizeof(Hdr),1,ImageFile) != 1)    {
    printf("Error reading image header in Pass 1\n",FileName);
    ReturnCode = EReadFileHdr;
    goto ErrorExit;
}

/* Store the actual image dimensions */
ImageWidth  = Hdr.Width;
ImageHeight = Hdr.Height;
/*
Now scan complete image building the octree.
*/
Message("Reading Line:    0");
for (Row=0; Row < ImageHeight; Row++)    {
  if (fread(&RowNum,sizeof(unsigned),1,ImageFile) != 1)    {
      printf("\nError reading image row number in Pass 1!\n");
      ReturnCode = EReadRowNum;
      goto ErrorExit;
  }
  if (Verbose)
    printf("\b\b\b%3d",RowNum);    /* output row number to display */

  /* Now read a line of data */
  if (fread(RedRowBuf,ImageWidth,1,ImageFile) != 1)    {
    printf("\nError reading red data in Pass 1 !\n");
    ReturnCode = EReadData;
    goto ErrorExit;
  }

  /* Now read a line of green data */
  if (fread(GreenRowBuf,ImageWidth,1,ImageFile) != 1)    {
    printf("\nError reading green data in Pass 1 !\n");
    ReturnCode = EReadData;
    goto ErrorExit;
  }

  /* Now read a line of blue data */
  if (fread(BlueRowBuf,ImageWidth,1,ImageFile) != 1)    {
    printf("\nError reading blue data in Pass 1 !\n");
    ReturnCode = EReadData;
    goto ErrorExit;
  }

  /* For each pixel in raster line of image data */
  for (Col=0; Col < ImageWidth; Col++) {
    RGB.Red   = RedRowBuf[Col];    /* RGB is the pixel's color value */
    RGB.Green = GreenRowBuf[Col];
    RGB.Blue  = BlueRowBuf[Col];
```

```
      InsertTree(Tree,RGB,0);          /* insert color into octree */
      if (Size > MAXCOLOR - 1)         /* max number of colors */
        ReduceTree();                  /* reduce tree if more than 256 colors */
    }                                  /* (256 leaf nodes) exist. */
  }
  if (Verbose)  {
    printf("\nPass 1 complete.\n");
    printf("MaxNodes = %d\n\n",MaxNodes);
    delay(1000);
  }
  /* Normal function exit point */
  fclose(ImageFile);
  return(NoError);

ErrorExit:
  printf("\n");
  fclose(ImageFile);
  return(ReturnCode);
}

/*
Pass one processing consists of building the octree and building
the color palette.
*/
int ProcessPass1(char *FileName)  {

  unsigned Index;
  int      ReturnCode;

  printf("\nPass1\n");
  if (Verbose)
    printf("Reading file: %s\n",FileName);

  /* Initialize all of the Palette memory to zeros. */
  memset(Palette,'\0',sizeof(Palette));

  Tree = NULL;
  ReturnCode = GenOctree(FileName,&Tree);  /* read through the file */

  Index = 1;                       /* entry 0 is left black */
  InitPalette(Tree,&Index);        /* on return Index is # of colors */

  if (Verbose)
    printf("%d colors used for image.\n",Index);

  return(ReturnCode);
}

/*
This function maps the original image pixel data from the image file into the
new color map we've come up with.
*/
```

(continued)

Listing 4.3   *(continued)*

```
int ProcessPass2(char *FileName )
{
   FILE *ImageFile;
   register unsigned Row, Col, PixVal;
   unsigned RowNum;
   int ReturnCode;
   ColorRegister RGB;

   /*
   Rescan the raw image file so that it can now be displayed.
   */

   printf("\nPass 2\n");

   /* Attempt to open the file */
   if (!(ImageFile = fopen(FileName,"rb")))   {
      printf("File %s not found in Pass 2\n",FileName);
      ReturnCode = EFileNotFound;
      goto ErrorExit;
   }

  /* Read in the header */
  if (fread(&Hdr,sizeof(Hdr),1,ImageFile) != 1)   {
      ReturnCode = EReadFileHdr;
      goto ErrorExit;
   }

   /*
   Now attempt to read the raw image file into three
   separate buffers: Red, Green & Blue a row at a time.
   */

   for (Row=0; Row < ImageHeight; Row++)   {
      if (fread(&RowNum,sizeof(unsigned),1,ImageFile) != 1)   {
        printf("\nError reading image row number !\n");
        ReturnCode = EReadRowNum;
        goto ErrorExit;
      }

      /* Now read a line of red data */
      if (fread(RedRowBuf,ImageWidth,1,ImageFile) != 1)   {
        printf("\nError reading red data in Pass 2 !\n");
        ReturnCode = EReadData;
        goto ErrorExit;
      }

      /* Now read a line of green data */
      if (fread(GreenRowBuf,ImageWidth,1,ImageFile) != 1)   {
        printf("\nError reading green data in Pass 2 !\n");
        ReturnCode = EReadData;
```

```
            goto ErrorExit;
        }

        /* Now read a line of blue data */
        if (fread(BlueRowBuf,ImageWidth,1,ImageFile) != 1)   {
          printf("\nError reading blue data in Pass 2!\n");
          ReturnCode = EReadData;
          goto ErrorExit;
        }

        /*
        For each RGB triplet in this row of image data look up the
        pixel value.
        */
        for (Col=0; Col < ImageWidth; Col++)  {
          RGB.Red   = RedRowBuf[Col];
          RGB.Green = GreenRowBuf[Col];
          RGB.Blue  = BlueRowBuf[Col];

          PixVal = Quantize(Tree,RGB);/* select which color is best */
          SetPixelValue(Col,Row,PixVal);  /* from Octree and display pixel */
        }                                  /* in that color */
    }
    /* Normal function exit point */
    printf("\n");
    fclose(ImageFile);
    return(NoError);

ErrorExit:
    fclose(ImageFile);
    return(ReturnCode);
}

/*
This function produces an executable .COM file for display of the
digitized color image. It writes a small code segment followed by
the 256-color register value followed by the image data to the
specified file. This can only be done with 320x200 resolution
images.
*/

void WriteComFile(char *FileName)   {

    FILE *OutPutFile;
    char     String[80];
    register unsigned Index, PixelValue, Col, Row;
    BYTE FileCode[] =          /* executable object code */
      {0xB4,0x0F,0xCD,0x10,0xA2,0x37,0x01,0xB4,0x00,0xB0,0x13,0xCD,0x10,
       0xB8,0x12,0x10,0xBB,0x00,0x00,0xB9,0x00,0x01,0xBA,0x38,0x01,0xCD,
       0x10,0xB9,0x00,0xFA,0xBE,0x38,0x04,0xB8,0x00,0xA0,0x8E,0xC0,0xBF,
```

(continued)

Listing 4.3 *(continued)*

```
      0x00,0x00,0xF3,0xA4,0xB4,0x00,0xCD,0x16,0xB4,0x00,0xA0,0x37,0x01,
      0xCD,0x10,0xC3,0x00};


  if (!strchr(FileName,'.'))  {       /* is there an ext ? */
     strcpy(String,FileName);         /* copy filename to buffer */
     FileName = String;               /* FileName now points at buffer */
     strcat(FileName,".com");         /* if not add .com ext */
  }
  /* open the output file */
  if ((OutPutFile = fopen(FileName,"wb")) == NULL)  {
     printf("Cannot open Image .COM file\n");
     exit(1);
  }


  /* write code segment to the file */
  for (Index=0; Index < sizeof(FileCode); Index++)
     if (fputc(FileCode[Index],OutPutFile) != FileCode[Index])  {
        SetTextMode();
        printf("Error writing Image .COM code seg\n");
        exit(1);
     }


  /* now write the color register rgb values to the file */
  for (Index = 0; Index < MAX256PALETTECOLORS; Index++)  {
     if (fputc(Palette[Index].Red,OutPutFile) != Palette[Index].Red)  {
        SetTextMode();
        printf("Error writing Image .COM red color reg\n");
        exit(1);
     }
     if (fputc(Palette[Index].Green,OutPutFile) != Palette[Index].Green)  {
        SetTextMode();
        printf("Error writing Image .COM green color reg\n");
        exit(1);
     }
     if (fputc(Palette[Index].Blue,OutPutFile) != Palette[Index].Blue)  {
        SetTextMode();
        printf("Error writing Image .COM blue color reg\n");
        exit(1);
     }
  }
  /* now write the actual image data to the file */
  for (Row=0; Row < 200; Row++)
     for (Col=0; Col < 320; Col++)  {
        PixelValue = GetPixelValue(Col,Row); /* read the value from display */
        fputc(PixelValue,OutPutFile);
     }


  fclose(OutPutFile);
}
```

```
/*
This function provides help in the advent of operator error. Program
terminates after help is given
*/


void ShowHelp( void )  {

  printf("\nThis program quantizes, displays, and saves a 256-color image\n");
  printf("using the Octree algorithm. It is invoked as follows:\n\n");
  printf("Usage: oquan [-c -g -h -i -p -v -x] infilename [outfilename]<cr>\n");
  printf("  -c inhibits gamma correction\n");
  printf("  -g create GIF output file\n");
  printf("  -h or ? show help\n");
  printf("  -i prevents the color reg values from being installed\n");
  printf("  -p create PCX output file\n");
  printf("  -v displays program progress information\n");
  printf("  -x create executable display program\n");
  printf("  outfilename is name given to generated display file(s).\n\n");
  exit(EBadParms);
}


/* Main Octree Quantizer Program */

int main(short argc, char *argv[])  {

   unsigned FileNameCounter, ArgIndex;
   char     *ImageFileName;
   char     *OutputFileName;
   int      ReturnCode;

   clrscr();
   printf("OQUAN -- Octree Color Quantizer Program.  Ver: %d.%d\n",Ver,Rev);
   printf("from the book \"Practical Ray Tracing in C\"\n");
   printf("Code written by Wolfgang Stuerzlinger and Craig A. Lindley\n\n");
   printf("This program converts 16.8 million 24-bit color images\n");
   printf("in dump format to 256-color images for display on a SuperVGA\n");
   printf("equipped computer\n\n");

   /* install default options */
   Verbose      = FALSE;               /* don't be wordy */
   GenComFile   = FALSE;               /* don't generate a .COM file */
   GenGIFFile   = FALSE;               /* don't generate a GIF file */
   GenPCXFile   = FALSE;               /* don't generate a PCX file */
   InstallColors = TRUE;               /* install calculated colors */
   CorrectGamma  = TRUE;               /* do gamma correction */

   /* parse all command line arguments */

   FileNameCounter = 0;                /* count of user-specified filenames */
   for (ArgIndex=1; ArgIndex < argc; ArgIndex++)  {
      if (*argv[ArgIndex] != '-')  {   /* if not a cmd line switch */
                                       /* must be a filename */
```

(continued)

Listing 4.3   *(continued)*

```
        if (*argv[ArgIndex] == '?')    /* help requested ? */
          ShowHelp();
        if (FileNameCounter > 2)       /* only two filenames allowed */
          ShowHelp();                  /* if more then error exit */
        if (FileNameCounter == 0)
          ImageFileName = argv[ArgIndex];  /* save input image filename */
        else
          OutputFileName = argv[ArgIndex]; /* save output image filename */

        FileNameCounter++;             /* inc count for error check */
      }
      else {                           /* it's a cmd line switch */
        switch (*(argv[ArgIndex]+1)) {/* parse the cmd line */
          case 'c':                    /* don't do gamma correction */
          case 'C':
            CorrectGamma = FALSE;
            break;
          case 'g':
          case 'G':
            GenGIFFile = TRUE;
            break;
          case 'h':
          case 'H':
            ShowHelp();
            break;
          case 'i':
          case 'I':
            InstallColors = FALSE;
            break;
          case 'p':
          case 'P':
            GenPCXFile = TRUE;
            break;
          case 'v':
          case 'V':
            Verbose    = TRUE;
            break;
         case 'x':
          case 'X':
            GenComFile = TRUE;
            break;
         default:
            printf("Error - invalid cmd line switch encountered\n");
            ShowHelp();
        }
      }
    }
  if (FileNameCounter < 1)  {
    printf("Error - input filename required\n");
    ShowHelp();
```

```
}
if ((GenComFile | GenGIFFile | GenPCXFile) && (FileNameCounter != 2))   {
   printf("Error - input and output filename required\n");
   ShowHelp();
}
/*
In pass one, preprocess the image data to build the Octree
for quantization.
*/
if ((ReturnCode = ProcessPass1(ImageFileName)) == NoError)   {

   /* Check for VESA compliance */
   CheckForVESA();

   /* Select the proper video mode for image display */
   SelectVideoMode(ImageWidth,ImageHeight,TRUE);
   /*
   If we want real colors InstallColors is TRUE. If we want pseudocolors
   for special effects, InstallColors is FALSE. In this case
   we must call GetAllColorRegs to store the default RGB values of the
   color registers into the Palette array.
   */
   if (InstallColors)   {
      ScaleColRegisters();
      SetAllColorRegs(Palette);
   }
   else
      GetAllColorRegs(Palette);

   /*
   Pass two maps the pixel codes from the image to the closest color
   found in the Octree. The complete image is read again and each
   pixel is looked up and converted separately.
   */
   ProcessPass2(ImageFileName);
   /*
   Check each of the output file options.
   */
   if (GenGIFFile)
     /*
     Create a 256-color GIF file of displayed image. Assumes
     single bit plane with one byte per pixel.
     */
     WriteGIFFile(OutputFileName,ImageWidth,ImageHeight,
                               ImageWidth,ImageHeight,0,0);

   if (GenPCXFile)
     /*
     Create a 256-color PCX file of displayed image. Assumes
     single bit plane with one byte per pixel.
     */
```

(continued)

Listing 4.3   *(continued)*

```
        WritePCXFile(OutputFileName, ImageWidth, ImageHeight);

    if (GenComFile && (ImageWidth <= 320))
      /* create an executable file for display of color image */
      WriteComFile(OutputFileName);

    /*
    Free the memory occupied by the Octree
    */
    KillTree(&Tree);

    /* prepare to return to dos */
    getch();                    /* wait for the user to hit a key */
    SetTextMode();              /* restore a normal text video mode */
    return(NoError);
  }
  else  {
    SetTextMode();
    return(ReturnCode);
  }
}
```

Building the Octree

As with most code used to manipulate tree structures, much of the code in the "oquan" program is recursive, including the code that builds the octree from the image data. As mentioned, only the sections of the octree that contain colors from the image are built. In other words, no octree nodes are created for colors not contained in the image. Every color within the image, however, is inserted into the octree at depth eight and is an exact representation of the color. The function "InsertTree" builds a leaf node for each unique color. Any intermediate nodes required to support this leaf node are also created. Whenever the number of unique colors at the leaf level exceeds 256, the octree must be reduced, and any intermediate node that has more than one child node is a candidate for reduction. As the octree is built node by node by "InsertTree," the nodes eligible for reduction are linked together. A separate linked list is maintained for each depth level of the octree. An array of pointers to nodes called "ReduceLevel" contains an entry for each level of the octree that has reducible nodes.

Reduction takes place from the bottom of the octree up toward the root because the colors at greater depths are closer together. When all reducible nodes at a level have been reduced, you proceed to the reducible nodes at the next higher level. Because an intermediate node contains all of the color and color count information for the portion of the octree below it (totals for all of its children nodes), reduction is no more complex than marking the intermediate node as a leaf, deleting all of its children nodes, and performing some additional cleanup. The function "ReduceTree" in the listing performs this task.

The "GenOctree" function called within the "ProcessPass1" function reads and processes the input "dump" format image file. After successfully opening the input file and reading the file header, this function reads the image data a raster line at a time. Individual raster lines are then broken down into individual pixel values, each with its own 24-bit RGB value. This RGB value is passed to the "InsertTree" function to build the octree. Finally when "Size," which is the number of leaf nodes, exceeds 256, a call is made to "ReduceTree" to compact the octree. At the completion of the "GenOctree" function, the octree is fully built and contains no more than 256 leaf nodes.

Building the Color Palette

The other operation performed by the "oquan" program during pass one is the building of the color palette. The function "InitPalette" performs this operation, also recursively. "InitPalette" performs a depth-first traversal of the octree in search of leaf nodes. Those leaf nodes represent the colors that will be used for display of the quantized image. Whenever a leaf node is found, you must perform three operations. First, you must calculate the actual RGB value for this node by dividing the individual color component sum counts by the total number of pixels that mapped to this node. In other words, the average value of all of the pixel colors that mapped to this node will be used for their display. The second operation is to move the calculated color value for this leaf node into the palette (the array of 256 color register values) at the next empty slot. The color values contained in the palette will eventually be transferred to the DAC within the VGA/SuperVGA graphics adapter. The final operation within "InitPalette" is to assign a color index value to the leaf node that corresponds to the position in the color palette of its calculated color. This color index is the value given to a pixel displayed with this RGB color.

Mapping the Image Colors

With the octree built and the color palette initialized, the final operation to be performed is the mapping of the original image data to the newly identified representative colors within the palette that will be used for display. The simple function "Quantize" performs this task. When given a pointer to the octree and a color value from the original image, this function recursively traverses the octree looking for either an exact color match or the closest representative color within the octree. The traversal terminates when a leaf node is encountered. The path from the root to the node of interest is found using the branch calculations described earlier. When the correct leaf node is identified, the color index value from the node, assigned previously, is returned. This value becomes the new pixel value, replacing the pixel's original color.

Overall Program Operation

The "oquan" program has the same structure as the "mquan" program described in the previous section. It utilizes the same command line interface and command line parameters and has all of the same output file options. Because of these similarities, the "main" functions within both programs are amazingly similar. The following pseudocode should give you an idea of the flow of execution within this program.

```
Begin
  Display the startup message
  Parse command line switches and set the appropriate global variables
  Output error messages and display help if required
  Pass One—Read the image data file
    Build the octree from the image data
    Build the color palette from the octree
  Check for the presence of a VESA-compatible VGA/SuperVGA adapter. Abort
    program operation if one is not found.
  Select the video mode required for the display of this image. Computer is now in
    graphics mode
  Scale and gamma correct the color palette values
  Move the color palette values into the VGA/SuperVGA's DAC.
  Pass Two—Reread the image data file
    Pass every pixel in the image data to the "Quantize" function
    Write the pixel value returned to the display adapter at the appropriate position
  Process any output file requests
  Wait for the user to hit a key to terminate the image display
  Select the text mode
  Return to Dos with an exit code
End
```

Advantages and Disadvantages of the Octree Quantization Method

The major advantages of this method of color quantization over the median cut algorithm are memory usage and performance. Memory usage is reduced because the number of nodes within the octree is independent of both the total number of pixels in an image and the number of unique colors in an image. The number of nodes depends only on the size of the color palette being quantized. Unfortunately, when this implementation is run on a PC under MSDOS, the nodes must be dynamically allocated and freed to be able to fit within the 640K memory limit. In other words, you must constantly reuse the node memory. There is a severe performance penalty due to this implementation (and operating system), not due to the algorithm itself. If this code were ported to a different environment, under Windows perhaps on a PC or under UNIX on a workstation, the virtual memory support would preclude freeing the node memory and would result in much higher performance.

In terms of other performance issues such as node insertion and tree traversal, the octree method scores better than most other color quantization methods. In general, the octree color quantization method should execute faster than other methods while producing similar results in image quality.

Other Uses

You could also use this quantization method to map an image to a predetermined fixed-color palette. For example, you could use it to map an image to a palette that was not derived from the actual image data. In this case, the RGB values of the 256 fixed-color palette entries could be used to build an octree. The image data could then be fed to the "Quantize" function and it would return the color index of the "closest" of the colors contained in the fixed palette. You could use this technique within a ray-tracing program, for example, to provide a pseudocolor display of the ray-traced image while it is in the process of being generated. This would give the user an idea of what the finished image would look like even though the colors would not be exact. Of course, to see the finished image quantized to 256 colors, you would have to post process the output file of the ray tracer with a program such as "oquan" described here.

32K-Color Quantization

We have seen in the preceding sections of this chapter how much effort is needed to convert a true-color, 16.8 million-color image into one viewable in 256 colors. In the implementation of both the median cut and octree quantization methods presented earlier, two passes over the image data were necessary. The first pass built the required data structures and performed the required algorithmic computations on the color data. The second pass mapped the raw image data (read again from the image file) into the color map determined in the first pass and displayed the resultant image. Granted, two passes over the image data were made necessary only by the memory limitations of the PC (running under MSDOS). The algorithms themselves, however, are complicated and time-consuming to execute. The fact that 640K of PC memory was barely enough in which to run these algorithms is a further hint of their complexity.

The color quantization method presented in this section gives a glimpse of why quantization techniques will soon be a thing of the past; gone the way of the dinosaur, so to speak. As display adapters provide more and more colors, the need for color quantization diminishes. As you will see, the algorithms themselves become simpler when more colors are available. When true-color display adapters become affordable and ubiquitous, the need for color quantization will disappear completely. With a true-color display adapter, all 24 bits of color information (1 byte each of red, green, and blue) per pixel will be written directly into the display memory without any preparatory processing being required. A step in that direction is the 32K-color code presented here. This code is shown in Listing 4.4 and is contained in the files "hquan.prj" and "hquan.c" on the companion disks. When "hquan.exe" executes, it produces a vivid color image in a single pass over the image data. It operates very quickly because no color palette reduction or processing is required.

The fact that this program operates in a single pass is an indication of its simplicity. The following steps describe the color quantization performed:

1. Reduction of the color data from 8 to 5 bits. This data reduction causes the eight closest shades of color to be grouped into a single shade. This still causes color distortion in the produced image, but the distortion is much less than with either of the two previous algorithms (not because of the algorithms, only because of the number of colors available). This quantization method results in the use of 32,768 unique colors out of a possible 16.8 million. The other algorithms target 256 unique colors only.
2. Gamma correction of the resultant 5-bit data as described in Chapter 1.
3. The writing of the data to a properly initialized video display adapter.

Of course, each of the three color components must be treated in an identical manner. That is, you must use the three-step process shown here with each of the three color components of each pixel.

Listing 4.4   The HQUAN Color Quantization Program

The following describes the contents of the file "hquan.prj," even though this file itself is not directly viewable outside of the Borland environment. To build the "hquan" program, you must have access to the following C files (either in the current directory or by way of an explicit path): "hicolor.c," "vga.c," and "hquan.c." The include files "misc.h," "vga.h," and "hicolor.h" must also be available. All of these files with the exception of "hquan.c" have been shown and described previously. We show "hquan.c" below.

The following is the contents of the file "hquan.c."

```
/**********************************************************/
/***                    "hquan.c"                    ***/
/***            32K-Color Quantizer Program          ***/
/***    for SuperVGA boards with ET-4000 chip set and ***/
/***              Sierra Hicolor DAC                  ***/
/***    from the book, "Practical Ray Tracing in C"   ***/
/***          written in Borland/Turbo C 2.0          ***/
/***                       by                        ***/
/***                Craig A. Lindley                  ***/
/***                                                  ***/
/***        Ver: 1.0   Last Update: 12/16/91          ***/
/**********************************************************/

#include <stdio.h>
#include <conio.h>
#include <dos.h>
#include <process.h>
#include "misc.h"
#include "vga.h"
#include "hicolor.h"

#define HMAXCOLS 800        /* max number of columns in a single raster */
                            /* for the resolutions supported */
/* Local global variables */

/* Dump file header structure */
static struct {
   unsigned Width;
   unsigned Height;
} Hdr;

static unsigned Ver = 1;
static unsigned Rev = 0;
static unsigned ImageWidth;
static unsigned ImageHeight;

/* Single row buffers for reading raw data */
static BYTE RedRowBuf[HMAXCOLS];
static BYTE GreenRowBuf[HMAXCOLS];
static BYTE BlueRowBuf[HMAXCOLS];
```

```
/*
Gamma correction table for Gamma = 2.222. The 256 input entries map
to 32 possible outputs. See Chapter 1 of the text for information
on how this table was created.
*/
static BYTE GammaTable[] = {
 0, 2, 3, 4, 4, 5, 5, 6, 6, 6, 7, 7, 7, 8, 8, 8, 8, 9, 9, 9,
 9,10,10,10,10,10,11,11,11,11,11,12,12,12,12,12,12,13,13,13,
13,13,13,13,14,14,14,14,14,14,14,15,15,15,15,15,15,15,15,16,
16,16,16,16,16,16,16,17,17,17,17,17,17,17,17,17,18,18,18,
18,18,18,18,18,18,19,19,19,19,19,19,19,19,19,19,19,20,20,20,
20,20,20,20,20,20,20,20,21,21,21,21,21,21,21,21,21,21,21,21,
22,22,22,22,22,22,22,22,22,22,22,22,23,23,23,23,23,23,23,23,
23,23,23,23,23,24,24,24,24,24,24,24,24,24,24,24,24,24,24,25,
25,25,25,25,25,25,25,25,25,25,25,25,26,26,26,26,26,26,26,
26,26,26,26,26,26,26,26,27,27,27,27,27,27,27,27,27,27,27,27,
27,27,27,27,28,28,28,28,28,28,28,28,28,28,28,28,28,28,28,28,
29,29,29,29,29,29,29,29,29,29,29,29,29,29,29,29,29,29,30,30,
30,30,30,30,30,30,30,30,30,30,30,30,30,30,31
};


/*
This function performs all of the work in this program. It attempts
to read the dump file whose name is passed as a parameter.
One pass is made over the image data. Color quantization and
display of the image takes place simultaneously.
*/
int Display32KColorImage(char *FileName)   {

    FILE *ImageFile;
    register unsigned Row, Col;
    unsigned RowNum, PixelColor;
    int ReturnCode = EGraphics;

    /* Attempt to open the file */
    if (!(ImageFile = fopen(FileName,"rb")))   {
        printf("\nFile %s not found !\n",FileName);
        ReturnCode = EFileNotFound;
        goto ErrorExit;
    }

    /* Read in the header */
    if (fread(&Hdr,sizeof(Hdr),1,ImageFile) != 1)   {
        printf("Error reading image header !\n",FileName);
        ReturnCode = EReadFileHdr;
        goto ErrorExit;
    }

    /* Store the actual image dimensions from the header */
    ImageWidth  = Hdr.Width;
    ImageHeight = Hdr.Height;
```

(continued)

Listing 4.4   *(continued)*

```
if (((ImageWidth == 640) && (ImageHeight == 480)) ||
    ((ImageWidth == 800) && (ImageHeight == 600)))   {

  /* If we get here the image can be displayed in 32K-color mode */
  /* Now select the proper mode */
  if (ImageWidth == 640)
    SetHicolorVideoMode(0x2E);       /* 640x480x32K color mode */
  else
    SetHicolorVideoMode(0x30);       /* 800x600x32K color mode */

  /* Read the image data line by line */
  for (Row=0; Row < ImageHeight; Row++)   {
    if (fread(&RowNum,sizeof(unsigned),1,ImageFile) != 1)   {
      printf("\nError reading image row number !\n");
      ReturnCode = EReadRowNum;
      goto ErrorExit;
    }

    /* Now read a line of data */
    if (fread(RedRowBuf,ImageWidth,1,ImageFile) != 1)   {
      printf("\nError reading red data !\n");
      ReturnCode = EReadData;
      goto ErrorExit;
    }

    /* Now read a line of green data */
    if (fread(GreenRowBuf,ImageWidth,1,ImageFile) != 1)   {
      printf("\nError reading green data !\n");
      ReturnCode = EReadData;
      goto ErrorExit;
    }

    /* Now read a line of blue data */
    if (fread(BlueRowBuf,ImageWidth,1,ImageFile) != 1)   {
      printf("\nError reading blue data !\n");
      ReturnCode = EReadData;
      goto ErrorExit;
    }

    /*
    With a byte each of RGB data, gamma correct the data
    and format it in TARGA 5-5-5 format for the DAC.
    */
    for (Col=0; Col < ImageWidth; Col++)  {
      PixelColor  =  GammaTable[RedRowBuf[Col]];
      PixelColor <<= 5;
      PixelColor |= (GammaTable[GreenRowBuf[Col]]);
      PixelColor <<= 5;
      PixelColor |= (GammaTable[BlueRowBuf[Col]]);
      PutPixel32K(ImageWidth,Col,Row,PixelColor);
    }
```

```
        }
        /* If we get here, image is on the display in 32K colors */
        /* Normal function exit point */
        fclose(ImageFile);
        return(NoError);
    }

ErrorExit:
    fclose(ImageFile);
    return(ReturnCode);
}


/*
This function provides help in the advent of operator error. Program
terminates after help is given
*/

void ShowHelp(void)  {

    printf("\nThis program quantizes and displays a 32K-color image.\n");
    printf("It works with either 640x480 or 800x600 resolution true-color images.\n");
    printf("It is invoked as follows:\n\n");
    printf("Usage: hquan [-h] infilename <cr>\n");
    printf("  -h or ? show help\n");
    exit(1);
}

/* main quantizer program */

void main(short argc, char *argv[])  {

    unsigned FileNameCounter, ArgIndex;
    char    *ImageFileName;

    clrscr();
    printf("HQUAN -- 32K-Color Quantizer Program.  Ver: %d.%d\n",Ver,Rev);
    printf("from the book \"Practical Ray Tracing in C\"\n");
    printf("Written by Craig A. Lindley\n\n");
    printf("This program converts 16.8 million, 24-bit, color images\n");
    printf("in dump format to 32K-color images for display on a SuperVGA\n");
    printf("equipped computer with a Sierra Hicolor DAC\n\n");
    delay(3500);                        /* pause so user can read message */

    /* parse all command line arguments */
    FileNameCounter = 0;                /* count of user-specified filenames */
    for (ArgIndex=1; ArgIndex < argc; ArgIndex++)  {
        if (*argv[ArgIndex] != '-') {  /* if not a cmd line switch */
                                        /* must be a filename */
            if (*argv[ArgIndex] == '?')     /* help requested ? */
                ShowHelp();
            if (FileNameCounter > 1)        /* only one filename allowed */
                ShowHelp();                 /* if more then error exit */
            ImageFileName = argv[ArgIndex];/* save input image filename */
```

(continued)

Listing 4.4   *(continued)*

```
      FileNameCounter++;            /* inc count for error check */
    }
    else {                          /* it's a cmd line switch */
      switch (*(argv[ArgIndex]+1))  { /* parse the cmd line */
        case 'h':
        case 'H':
          ShowHelp();
          break;
        default:
          printf("Error - invalid cmd line switch encountered\n");
          ShowHelp();
      }
    }
  }
  /* Check for presence of Sierra Hicolor DAC */
  if (CheckForSierraDAC1() != NoError)  {
    printf("Sierra Hicolor DAC not found - aborting !\n\n");
    exit(EGraphics);
  }

  /* Attempt to display the image in 32K colors */
  if (Display32KColorImage(ImageFileName) != NoError)  {
    SetTextMode();
    printf("Image corrupt or non-supported resolution !\n\n");
  }
  else {                        /* image displayed wait for user */
    getch();
    /* prepare to return to text mode and Dos */
    SetTextMode();
  }
}
```

As to the mechanics of this implementation, they are very similar to the previous two implementations and for this reason the similarities need no further discussion. We examine the issues that are unique to the 32K-color operation below.

The first thing you must determine before this program attempts to display an image in 32K colors is whether a hicolor DAC (see Chapter 1 for details) is present. You can determine this (within the "main" function) with a call to the "CheckForSierraDAC1" function. As discussed in Chapter 1, this function returns a "NoError" or zero return code if a hicolor DAC is detected. This program terminates if the call to "CheckForSierraDAC1" determines no Sierra hicolor DAC is present in this system, as it is impossible to display a 32K-color image without one. Once the DAC is known to exist, a call to "Display32KColorImage" performs the image display. It is very similar to the "ProcessPass2" code in the previous sections with three important differences. First, since only 640 by 480 and 800 by 600 resolution images are supported with the current generation of 1 megabyte SuperVGA cards, a check is made to determine if the image to be displayed is of a supported resolution (this code could easily be adapted to display 1024 by 768 images when 2 megabyte SuperVGA cards become available—details to follow shortly). The width information contained in the "dump" input file header is examined to determine the image resolution. If the image contained in the dump file is not in a supported resolution, this function "Display32KColorImage" terminates with an "EGraphics" error return code.

Assuming all is well, the second difference in this code from the previous implementations is the selection of a hicolor video mode via a call to "SetHicolorVideoMode." We discussed this function in detail also in Chapter 1. The image width information from the dump file header is used to select the proper hicolor mode number. If the image is in 640 by 480 format, a mode number of 0x2E is passed to "SetHicolorVideoMode." A mode number of 0x30 is passed if an 800 by 600 image is to be displayed.

Once all of these preliminaries are satisfied, the ray-traced image data file (in dump format) is read a raster line at a time as in each of the previous two implementations. The third and final difference in this code comes to light here. As the individual pixel color component values from the raster line are parsed, they are scaled and gamma corrected simultaneously by judicious selection of the values in the gamma table. The 5-bit gamma corrected color components are then converted to the 5-5-5 TARGA format (a single 16-bit integer value with the 5 bits of red data occupying bits 10–14, the green data in bits 5–9, and the blue data in bits 0–4. The most significant bit, bit 15, is unused). The TARGA-formatted pixel value is then written to the video display at the specified Column and Row position with a call to "PutPixel32K." *Note*: This function requires the width of the raster line to be passed as a parameter. The "ImageWidth" variable (derived from the image file header) satisfies that need.

This program "hquan.exe" is for viewing 32K-color images only. No options are given for saving the displayed image because neither of the two graphics image file formats described in this book supports 32K-color images. Only the more complex image file formats such as TIFF would be capable of containing a 32K-color image. For information on the TIFF image files, please see my previous book, *Practical Image Processing in C*. At the current time, if you wish to save an image for subsequent viewing, it will have to be quantized into 256 colors via one of the two previous color quantization programs, "mquan.exe" or "oquan.exe," and saved in either PCX or GIF file formats.

To enhance this program to display 1024 by 768 32K-color images, you will need to do the following:

1. Have a SuperVGA card with 2 megabytes of video memory with a Sierra Hicolor DAC.
2. Change the #define constant "HMAXCOLS" in Listing 4.4 from 800 to 1024. Symbolically, you can do this by changing all references to HMAXCOLS in the code to "MAXCOLS," as MAXCOLS is already defined to be 1024.
3. Change the if statement that selects the hicolor video mode to a "switch" statement that will select the correct mode number for each of the three image resolution possibilities. At the time of this writing, the video mode number for the Tseng ET-4000 chip set to support 1024 by 768 32K-color images is unknown.

With these changes and a recompilation, "hquan.exe" should be capable of 640 by 480, 800 by 600, and 1024 by 768 32K-color image display.

Conclusions

We have presented a lot of color quantization information and code in this chapter. Three different color quantization algorithms have been implemented in their entirety as stand-alone DOS programs. You should be able to use these programs in displaying the ray-traced images produced in the second part of this book. Also, as noted, you can use them with other types of imaging data as well.

In the next chapter, we will see how GIF and PCX files are structured and how to develop code to read and write these important graphics file formats. We will fill in the details of these and other file formats skipped over in this chapter.

5

Graphics File Formats and Functions

Too much of a good thing can be wonderful.
—Mae West

In this chapter you will learn:

- **The difference between vector and raster graphics**
- **Which graphics file formats are considered the standards in the IBM PC world**
- **How "raw" graphics files are organized**
- **How "dump" graphics files are organized**
- **What it takes to read and write true-color dump files**
- **How PCX graphics files are organized**
- **What it takes to read and write 256-color PCX files**
- **How GIF graphics files are organized**
- **What it takes to read and write 256-color GIF files**
- **How the "v256" program can display both PCX and GIF 256-color image files**
- **Some simple file conversion possibilities**

Introduction

A ray-traced image's value is in its aesthetic appeal. These images become useful when they are put into a form that can be manipulated by other application programs. In order for this to

221

occur, you must put the image data into a "standard form" that other applications can interpret and use. When a ray-traced image can be exported into a paint program, a desktop publishing program, or a film recorder, it can be incorporated into presentations, slide shows, reports, newsletters, prints, and posters. It can even be used to make custom coffee mugs or T-shirts. Photography is another way for ray-traced images to be used outside of the computer environment. (We will discuss photography in Part Two of this book.)

As you are probably starting to realize after reading Chapters 2, 3, and 4, it is a long journey from the initial inspiration for an image to the finished product. Along the way, the information that makes up the image changes form many times. Initially, it is expressed in either a computer program (as it was in Chapter 3) or as an ASCII image description (as used in the DKBTrace program of Part Two) maintained in a computer disk file. Eventually, after much processing (the actual ray-tracing process and subsequent color quantization) it becomes available in a form suitable for display on a color monitor. Each step in this process uses disk files to communicate with the next step in the process. In other words, the ASCII image description file is fed to the ray tracer, which outputs a "dump" formatted image output file. This dump file then provides the input to a color quantization program that outputs some kind of "standard" graphics file for end use. So, as you can see, even though a discussion of graphics file formats is not directly related to the subject of ray tracing, knowing something about the file formats utilized in the overall process of image production will definitely come in handy. Further, knowledge of image file formats can be useful in many areas of computer graphics besides ray tracing. Even though you may not need all of the detailed information on file formats contained in this chapter on a daily basis, you will at least have access to the information when you do need it.

We will provide information on four different file formats in this chapter:

1. The "raw" image file format used for storage of 24-bit-per-pixel image data. This can be considered an intermediary file format, not an end use format.
2. The "dump" image file format also used for storage of 24-bit-per-pixel image data. Dump files can be both an intermediary and end use file format. Dump formatted files are generally more convenient for application programs to manipulate than are raw files.
3. The "PCX" file format for storage (with compression) of quantized and palettized images. This is a standard end use file format.
4. The "GIF" file format also for storage (with compression) of quantized and palettized images. This, too, is a standard end use file format.

We have picked these file formats for inclusion because they are widely used within the IBM PC world. Many other file formats including TIFF, IFF, RIFF, TARGA, and others also find use with ray tracing (including the DKBTrace program), but they are not quite as ubiquitous and are therefore not included here. See the book *Practical Image Processing in C* published by John Wiley & Sons, Inc. for detailed information on TIFF and other file formats.

The two most important standard end use graphics file formats we will be concerned with in this chapter are the PCX format and the GIF format which are supported by almost all desktop publishing programs. We give both the PCX and GIF graphics file formats an in-depth discussion later in this chapter. This discussion includes a look at the format of the files in addition to the compression methods unique to each (in PCX files, RLE compression is used; in GIF files, LZW compression is used). We provide C code to read and write both of these file formats. This code is in the form of a library of functions easily linked into other applications. We also include a 256-color PCX/GIF file viewer program called "v256" which can display properly formatted images in either format. The "v256" program is an example of how the graphics library functions are used in an application program. Finally, we discuss a simple PCX-to-GIF file conversion program called "pcx2gif," along with other file conversion ideas.

One caveat is necessary before the discussion continues. *The code provided in this chapter assumes the existence of a VGA/SuperVGA graphics display adapter in an IBM PC-compatible computer; CGA and EGA display adapters are not supported and therefore neither CGA- and/or EGA-created PCX files nor GIF files are supported. Further, the code provided supports only single-plane, 8-bit-per-pixel, 256-color images.* This is the type of image produced by the color quantization programs of Chapter 4 and therefore fulfills our requirements completely. With the code in this chapter you will be able to produce 256-color PCX and GIF files in the following resolutions: 320 by 200, 640 by 400, 640 by 480, 800 by 600, and 1024 by 768 (assuming a SuperVGA adapter with 1 megabyte of memory). These files can be imported by any application program that understands high-resolution PCX and GIF files.

Vector and Raster Formats

In general, you can categorize graphics programs by how image data is stored and displayed. Two categories exist: "raster" format and "vector" format. Raster format is comprised of a series of picture elements, or pixels, that cover a complete display area. Raster displays are usually generated by the periodic sweeping of an electron beam over an imaging surface with a predetermined pattern (a video camera, for example). The pixels that make up a rasterized image do not necessarily relate to each other; the concept of shape is not inherent in a raster image. Raster images are often used for presentation graphics, where artistic considerations and image quality are important.

The main advantages of raster format are:

1. It is easy to output data from a raster input device (i.e., a video digitizer or scanner) on a raster output device such as a computer monitor or graphics printer.
2. The display of raster data is usually faster than the display of vectored data because raster devices do the display and thus a vector-to-raster conversion does not have to be performed.

Vector format, on the other hand, involves the use of directed line segments instead of pixels to make up an image. A vector image is made up of shapes, which are made up of line segments. Connectedness and hierarchy are the cornerstones of vector images. With vector-formatted image data, it is easy to determine what component line segments make up any object. Vector images are used primarily in CAD applications where precision scaling and element relationships are important. AutoCAD is an example of a program that utilizes vector graphics. Map generation and manipulation is another important application area for vector images. The relationship of objects on a map (all storm drains in a city, for example) and the ability to view only selected objects or collections of objects is often very useful.

It is easy to output vector images to a plotter because a plotter is a vector type device. Vector images can also be converted via software to raster format for display and/or hard copy with a printer. Although the conversion from raster to vector is much harder to achieve, it is now being performed successfully in some application programs.

We will not discuss vector formats further in this book because they are not used in ray-traced image applications. Instead, we will focus on the raster graphics file formats that are used in the ray-tracing applications in this book and in the graphics industry at large.

Raw Image File Format

Raw image files are the most basic of all graphics data files possible. This is because they contain nothing but image data—no format information of any kind. For this reason, only application programs that know the context in which they were created can use them; otherwise, they are indecipherable. In the context of this book, a raw image file actually consists of three separate files—one each for the red, green, and blue color components of the image data. Each of these files utilizes 8-bit values for the color components. This results in an aggregate 24 bits per pixel of color information spread out over the three files. Typically, within the IBM PC realm that uses three-character filename extensions, the raw files would be called "filename.r8" for the red color data, "filename.g8" for the green, and "filename.b8" for the blue data. On other computer systems without the three-character filename extension limit, the red color component data file might be called "filename.red8," for example. Raw data files contain image raster data ordered from left to right and top to bottom of the image.

Some public domain and shareware programs utilize raw data files. The "PICLAB" image processing software from the "Stone Soup Group" is an example. The DKBTrace ray-tracing program will also produce raw image files when instructed to do so. More often than not, however, raw image files are used as an intermediate file format internal to an imaging application and not used as an external image exchange medium. A color video digitizer or flat bed scanner (which makes multiple passes over an image to create color) might write raw image files to disk to save memory as the digitization process progressed, but then it would combine them into some standard graphics file format for export to other application programs.

Most applications that can be envisioned for raw image files access the files in a purely sequential manner as a mass storage medium. Random access to individual pixel data within the raw files would generally not be required but could be implemented if so desired. To get at the 24-bit-per-pixel data within the raw image files, you would have to access all three color component files. The individual byte values (three, one in each file) that make up the 24-bit pixel value would need to be located and then read or written as appropriate for the application.

To use raw image files within an application program, you need four basic functions. First, you need an open function to open the three color component files for either binary read or write access as required. You would then use a pixel write function to write the RGB component values of a specified pixel into the appropriate raw data files. A pixel read function would gather the next sequential RGB component values from the three files and concatenate them into a single pixel value, which it would then return. Finally, you would need a close function to close all three of the raw data files when the access was completed. Because these functions for raw image files are so straightforward and application-specific, we provide no code for them.

Dump Image File Format

"Dump" image files differ from the raw image files discussed previously in that all of the (24 bits per pixel) color information is contained in a single file instead of being spread out among three files. As indicated in Chapter 4, a dump formatted image file consists of a file header followed by image raster data. The file header contains two entries: the image width and the image height. The image width determines how many bytes make up a raster line of data. The image height tells how many raster lines of image data are contained in the file. A single raster line of data is made up of a row number followed by three image-width byte arrays of color data; red then green then blue.

Having all of the image information in a single file is more convenient from the application program's (and programmer's) point of view, but it can result in rather large image files. The size of a dump file in bytes is calculated as follows:

$$\text{Size (bytes)} = \text{Header Size} + \text{Raster Size} + \text{Row Number Size}$$
$$= 4 + (\text{ImageWidth} * 3 * \text{ImageHeight}) + 2 * \text{ImageHeight}$$

Note: The size of the dump file is a function only of the resolution of the contained image and not the image content. This is because dump files are not compressed in any manner. The table that follows shows the size of the dump file produced with the image resolutions used in this book.

Image Resolution	Dump File Size
320 by 200	192,404
640 by 400	768,804
640 by 480	922,564
800 by 600	1,441,204
1024 by 768	2,360,836

Dump files are popular because they contain enough format information for many imaging application programs to decipher them, but they are not so complex that only a rocket scientist can understand them.

Listing 5.1 provides simple code to read and write dump formatted image files. This code is contained in the file "dumpio.c" on the companion disks. We provide four C functions for dealing with dump files. The operation and use of these functions is detailed in Figure 5.1. The "main" function within "dumpio.c" is a test program. It exercises the other functions within the file to verify their operation. The test copies a dump formatted input file, pixel by pixel, to a new dump formatted output file. The test is successful when the output file is identical to the input file. You must remove the "main" function when you use this code in your application programs.

With the ability to read and write dump files on a pixel-by-pixel basis (using the code in "dumpio.c"), many applications suggest themselves, including:

1. The ability to cut out a smaller image from a larger one.
2. The ability to perform some rudimentary image processing on the image data as it is moved between files. This could include image brightening or darkening by adding or subtracting a constant value from each pixel's color components. Selective color replacement would also be possible.

3. Two images could be combined on the fly to create a new image.
4. With some clever code, text could be placed onto an image by placing the text characters into the output file a pixel at a time.

The image processing possibilities offered are endless.

1. **Open a dump file for sequential I/O.**

Prototype:

> int OpenDumpFile (char *FileName, char Mode,
>   unsigned *IWidth, unsigned *IHeight);

Where:
1. FileName is a pointer to a NULL terminated ASCII filename.
2. Mode is a single ASCII character representing the mode in which the dump file should be opened. The two legal modes are 'r' for read only and 'w' for write only. Upper- or lowercase mode characters are accepted.
3. IWidth and IHeight are pointers to unsigned integers. If the dump file is opened for read access, the unsigned integers at which IWidth and IHeight point will be filled in with the width and height values of the image contained in the dump file. This information is retrieved from the dump file header. If the file is opened for write access, IWidth and IHeight should point at the width and height values to be stored in the header of the newly created dump output file.

Operation:
If this function opens a file for write access, the file is opened in binary write mode, a dump file header structure is filled in with the specified width and height values, and then it is written to disk. Finally, the "OutRowNumber" and "OutColumnNumber" variables are initialized as required to guarantee that writing of pixel data begins at the correct position in the color buffers. When this function opens a file for read access, the file is opened in the binary read mode, then the dump header file is read from the file, and the width and height information is passed back to the calling program. The "InColumnNumber" variable is then set equal to the image width so that the first attempt to read a pixel value from the file will fill the color buffers from disk. This function returns the value of "NoError" if all is well and some other error code as defined in "misc.h" if an error occurs.

2. **Close a dump file.**

Prototype:

> int CloseDumpFile (char Mode);

Where:
1. Mode is a single ASCII character representing the dump file to be closed. The three legal mode values are 'r,' which indicates that only the read file should be closed, 'w,' which indicates that only the write file should be closed, and 'a,' which indicates that both the read and the write files should be closed. Upper- or lowercase mode characters are accepted.

Figure 5.1   Dump File I/O Functions   *(continued)*

Operation:
This function uses a C switch statement to process the mode value passed in as a parameter to this function. This function returns the value of "NoError" if all is well and some other error code as defined in "misc.h" if an error occurs.

3. Read the next sequential pixel value from a dump file.

Prototype:
> int ReadPixel (ColorRegister *Color);

Where:
1. Color is a pointer to a 3-byte RGB value that is to be filled in with the pixel color information read from the dump file.

Operation:
Color information is read from a dump file a raster line at a time. As you will recall, a single raster line is composed of three arrays of color information: red, green, and blue. The color information from a single raster line of the image is read into three separate buffers. A byte from each buffer is combined together to form the pixel value that is returned by a call to this function. The "InColumn-Number" variable is used to keep track of where in the buffers the next sequential byte of pixel data should be retrieved from, and if the buffer needs to be reloaded from disk. When a dump file is opened for reading, InColumnNumber is initialized to the width of the image, which forces a read of data from the disk file the first time this function is called. This function returns the value of "NoError" if all is well and some other error code from "misc.h" if an error occurs.

4. Write the next sequential pixel value to a dump file.

Prototype:
> int WritePixel (ColorRegister *Color);

Where:
1. Color is a pointer to a 3-byte RGB value that contains the pixel color information to be written to the dump file.

Operation:
This function performs the inverse operation to the function discussed above. This function divides the pixel information passed to it into three separate color components and stores them in the appropriate buffer. When it is determined the buffers contain a complete raster line of data, the buffers are written to disk along with the raster line row number as required in the dump format. In this case, "OutColumnNumber" keeps track of when the buffers are full and therefore when the disk writes need to occur. As before, this function returns the value of "NoError" if all is well and some other error code if an error occurs.

Figure 5.1 *(continued)*

Listing 5.1 Dump File I/O Functions

The following is the contents of the file "dumpio.c."

```c
/*************************************************************/
/***                    "dumpio.c"                    ***/
/***        Dump format Input/Output functions        ***/
/***      from the book "Practical Ray Tracing in C"  ***/
/***            written in Borland/Turbo C 2.0        ***/
/***                        by                        ***/
/***              Craig A. Lindley                    ***/
/***                                                  ***/
/***        Ver: 1.0    Last Update: 01/06/92         ***/
/*************************************************************/

#include <stdio.h>
#include <stdlib.h>
#include <ctype.h>
#include "misc.h"
#include "vga.h"

/* Data file header definition for the dump data file */
struct Hdr {
  unsigned Width;
  unsigned Height;
};

/*
Create a separate set of variables for dump file input and
dump file output on the chance that input and output occur
simultaneously. Six local buffers for the storage of the pixel
color data will be established. Three for input and three for
output. Buffers are each 1024 bytes in size to accommodate the
largest raster lines supported by this code.
*/

/* Input Variables */
static FILE *InputDumpImageFile;
static struct Hdr InHdr;
static unsigned InRowNumber;
static unsigned InColumnNumber;
static BYTE RedIn   [MAXCOLS];
static BYTE GreenIn [MAXCOLS];
static BYTE BlueIn  [MAXCOLS];

/* Output Variables */
static FILE *OutputDumpImageFile;
static struct Hdr OutHdr;
static unsigned OutRowNumber;
static unsigned OutColumnNumber;
static BYTE RedOut   [MAXCOLS];
static BYTE GreenOut [MAXCOLS];
```

```
static BYTE BlueOut [MAXCOLS];

/*
Open the dump file in preparation for sequential reading or writing
the pixel values from or to disk. The Mode determines the mode in
which the file is opened.
*/
int OpenDumpFile (char *FileName, char Mode,
                  unsigned *IWidth, unsigned *IHeight)  {

  Mode = toupper(Mode);                  /* make mode uppercase for compare */

  if (Mode == 'W')  {                    /* if file opened for writing */
    /* Attempt to open the output file for writing */
    if (!(OutputDumpImageFile = fopen(FileName,"wb")))
      return(EOpeningFile);

    /* Fill in and write the dump image header */
    OutHdr.Width  = *IWidth;
    OutHdr.Height = *IHeight;

    if (fwrite(&OutHdr,sizeof(struct Hdr),1,OutputDumpImageFile) != 1)
      return(EWrtFileHdr );

    OutRowNumber = 0;                    /* start write with row number zero */
    OutColumnNumber = 0;                 /* start write at 1st buff position */

  }
  else if (Mode == 'R')  {               /* if file opened for reading */
    /* Attempt to open the output file for reading */
    if (!(InputDumpImageFile = fopen(FileName,"rb")))
      return(EOpeningFile);

    /* Attempt to read the dump file header */
    if (fread(&InHdr,sizeof(struct Hdr),1,InputDumpImageFile) != 1)
      return(EReadFileHdr );

    /* Retrieve and return the image parameters from the header */
    *IWidth  = InHdr.Width;
    *IHeight = InHdr.Height;

    InColumnNumber = InHdr.Width;        /* prime the pump for disk read */
  }
  else                                   /* if bad mode specified */
    return(EBadParms);

  return(NoError);
}

/*
This function closes the specified dump files after access.
*/
int CloseDumpFile(char Mode)  {
```

(continued)

Listing 5.1   *(continued)*

```
    int ErrorCode;

  Mode = toupper(Mode);                    /* make mode uppercase for compare */

  switch(Mode)  {
    case 'R':                              /* close request on input file */
      if ((ErrorCode = fclose(InputDumpImageFile)) != 0)
        return(ErrorCode);
      break;

    case 'W':                              /* close request on output file */
      if ((ErrorCode = fclose(OutputDumpImageFile)) != 0)
        return(ErrorCode);
      break;

    case 'A':                              /* close request on all files */
      ErrorCode  = fclose(InputDumpImageFile);
      ErrorCode |= fclose(OutputDumpImageFile);
      if (ErrorCode != NoError)
        return(ErrorCode);
      break;
    default:
      return(EBadParms);
  }
  return(NoError);
}

/* Read the next sequential pixel from the input dump file. */

int ReadPixel (ColorRegister *Color)  {

  /* Check to see if a disk read is required */
  if (InColumnNumber == InHdr.Width)  {

    /* Yes a disk read is required. Reset ColumnNumber to zero */
    InColumnNumber = 0;

    /* First read the row number from the file and discard */
    if(fread(&InRowNumber,sizeof(unsigned),1,InputDumpImageFile) != 1)  {
      fclose(InputDumpImageFile);
      return(EReadScanLine);
    }
    /*
    Now read the Red then the Green then the Blue data
    from the file.
    */
    if (fread(RedIn,InHdr.Width,1,InputDumpImageFile) != 1)  {
      fclose(InputDumpImageFile);
      return(EReadScanLine);
    }
```

```
   if (fread(GreenIn,InHdr.Width,1,InputDumpImageFile) != 1)  {
     fclose(InputDumpImageFile);
     return(EReadScanLine);
   }

   if (fread(BlueIn,InHdr.Width,1,InputDumpImageFile) != 1)  {
     fclose(InputDumpImageFile);
     return(EReadScanLine);
   }
 }
 /* Retrieve and return the pixel's color data from the buffers */
 Color->Red   = RedIn  [InColumnNumber];
 Color->Green = GreenIn[InColumnNumber];
 Color->Blue  = BlueIn [InColumnNumber++];
 return(NoError);
}

/* Write the next sequential pixel value to the output dump file. */

int WritePixel (ColorRegister *Color)  {

 /*
 Break up the pixel into its color components and store in
 appropriate buffer awaiting write to disk.
 */
 RedOut   [OutColumnNumber]   = Color->Red;
 GreenOut [OutColumnNumber]   = Color->Green;
 BlueOut  [OutColumnNumber++] = Color->Blue;

 /* Check to see if a disk write is required */
 if (OutColumnNumber == OutHdr.Width)  {

   /* Yes a disk write is required. Reset OutColumnNumber to zero */
   OutColumnNumber = 0;

   /* First write the row number to the file */
   if(fwrite(&OutRowNumber,sizeof(unsigned),1,OutputDumpImageFile) != 1)  {
     fclose(OutputDumpImageFile);
     return(EWrtScanLine);
   }
   OutRowNumber++;
   /*
   Now write the Red then the Green then the Blue data
   to the file.
   */
   if (fwrite(RedOut,OutHdr.Width,1,OutputDumpImageFile) != 1)  {
     fclose(OutputDumpImageFile);
     return(EWrtScanLine);
   }

   if (fwrite(GreenOut,OutHdr.Width,1,OutputDumpImageFile) != 1)  {
```

(continued)

Listing 5.1   *(continued)*

```
        fclose(OutputDumpImageFile);
        return(EWrtScanLine);
    }

    if (fwrite(BlueOut,OutHdr.Width,1,OutputDumpImageFile) != 1)  {
        fclose(OutputDumpImageFile);
        return(EWrtScanLine);
    }
  }
  return(NoError);
}

/*
A small driver program to test the dumpio.c code. It copies one dump
format file to another. It uses the full error checking provided by
the functions. To use this code the filenames specified in the
"OpenDumpFile" calls should be changed to names of your files. To
convert this code into a function code library, a header file called
"dumpio.h" should be created which has function prototypes for:
"OpenDumpFile," "ReadPixel," "WritePixel," and "CloseDumpFile."
*/
void main(void)  {

  unsigned ImageWidth, ImageHeight;
  unsigned long TotalPixels;
  ColorRegister PixColor;

  /* Open the input and the output dump files */
  if (OpenDumpFile("colors.dis",'r',&ImageWidth,&ImageHeight) != NoError)
    exit(-1);
  if(OpenDumpFile("temp.dis",'w',&ImageWidth,&ImageHeight) != NoError)
    exit(-1);

  /* Calculate total pixels in image to copy */
  TotalPixels = (unsigned long) ImageWidth * ImageHeight;

  while(TotalPixels--)  {
    if (ReadPixel(&PixColor)  != NoError)
      exit(-1);

    if (WritePixel(&PixColor) != NoError)
      exit(-1);
  }
  /* Close both the input and the output file */
  if (CloseDumpFile('a') != NoError)
    exit(-1);
}
```

The PCX Graphics File Format

This file format was one of the earliest attempts in the PC industry to store and standardize graphics images. A standard file format was necessary both to allow the movement of images between applications and to provide file compression to save disk space used for image storage. The PCX graphics file format is an example of a method used in industry that became a standard by default. Because it has been around for such a long time, the PCX graphics file format is probably supported by more graphics application programs than all other (IBM PC-compatible) graphics file formats combined. Please realize, the file formats discussed in this chapter up to this point (the raw and the dump file formats) were for storage of 24-bit-per-pixel image data. The graphics file formats discussed from this point on are for storage of "quantized" and "palettized" images, which require no more than 8 bits of information per pixel. The PCX format is an end use format because it is understood by many application programs.

The following discussion touches on how CGA and EGA files are encoded differently

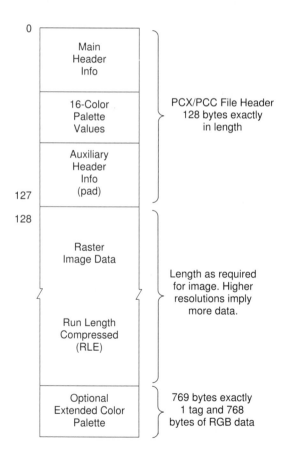

Figure 5.2 PCX/PCC File Structure

than VGA files as well as how multiple-bit-plane images are stored within the PCX file format. It is left to you, however, to implement the changes to the code required for CGA/EGA support. The result of not including CGA/EGA support in this code is that PCX images created for/by these graphics adapters will not be displayed correctly by the PCX function library or the "v256" program provided. The reasons will become obvious when we discuss PCX palettes.

The PCX graphics file format is not very flexible with regard to the information it can contain. The file format is rigid, with a file header of fixed length followed by the raster image data, optionally followed by an extended palette structure. Figure 5.2 shows the layout of a typical PCX file. As we will show, a PCC file is simply a subset (or cutout) of a PCX file.

The simplicity of this file format makes the code required to support PCX easy to understand, develop, and use. The PCX function library code is contained in two files on the companion disks, "pcx.h" and "pcx.c." Both of these files are shown in Listing 5.2 (page 241). Please refer to this listing during the discussion to follow. Figure 5.4 (page 252) provides a description of all of the functions contained within the PCX function library. All information about the structure and format of PCX files was derived from documentation provided by ZSoft Corporation for the PC PaintBrush program.

The PCX File Header

The best way to describe the PCX file format is to describe the contents of the header portion of the file. The header contains the information necessary to allow correct interpretation of the raster data that follows it. Without the header, the image data could not be deciphered. As shown here, the header is 128 bytes in length and is made up of the following data structures:

```
/* The PCX file header */
struct PCXFileHeader  {
   BYTE      Header;             /* marks file as PCX file */
   BYTE      Version;            /* 0 = version 2.5 */
                                 /* 2 = 2.8 with palette info */
                                 /* 3 = no palette info 2.8 or 3.0 */
                                 /* 5 = 3.0 with palette info */
   BYTE      Encode;             /* File encoding mode */
   BYTE      BitPerPix;          /* Bits per pixel */
   unsigned X1;                  /* Picture dimensions inclusive */
   unsigned Y1;
   unsigned X2;
   unsigned Y2;
   unsigned Hres;               /* Graphics adapter Horiz    resolution */
   unsigned Vres;               /* Graphics adapter Vertical resolution */
};

   struct PCXInfo  {
   BYTE      Vmode;              /* Ignore should always be zero */
   BYTE      NumOfPlanes;        /* Number of bit planes */
   unsigned BytesPerLine;        /* Bytes Per Line in picture */
   BYTE      unused[60];         /* fills out header to 128 bytes */
};
```

```
/* The PCX complete file structure */
struct PCX_File  {
    struct PCXFileHeader  PCXHeader;
    ColorRegister         Palette[MaxPaletteColors]; /* Max size of 48 bytes */
    struct PCXInfo        Info;
};
```

The structure "PCX_File" represents the complete header portion of a PCX file. Internal to this structure, the structure "PCXHeader" represents what is referred to as the "Main Header Info" in Figure 5.2, the "Palette," which is an array of 16 color registers with each register containing 1 byte each of red, green, and blue color information, and the "Info" structure, which contains the auxiliary file information. Notice how the "Info" structure is padded to make the entire header exactly 128 bytes in length.

Each of the individual fields within the PCX header plays an important role in characterizing the contained image. The functions of some of the header fields are not intuitively obvious, as they are based on historical perspectives that today escape us. Also, various manufacturers of PCX-generating programs may use these fields in proprietary ways for their specific applications. Worse yet, other PCX programs ignore the file header completely, assuming all imported PCX files were previously written out by their application (and therefore decipherable because of the known context) as if no other PCX-producing programs existed. This means code designed to read PCX files must do the best it can in deciphering so-called "standard" PCX files produced by some application programs. Additionally, code written to produce PCX files must accurately and completely build the PCX file header so other applications have the ability to decode the resultant image files correctly. We discuss next the content of the PCX file header fields as utilized by the code in this book.

The "Header" field in the PCX file header is used to determine if a file is a legitimate PCX or PCC file. The value of this field must be equal to 10 decimal for the file to be considered a PCX file. Most PCX readers will reject a file if the "Header" byte is incorrect.

The "Version" field provides the PCX revision level used to encode the contained image. The major revision levels are:

Version	PCX software revision
0	version 2.5
2	version 2.8 with palette
3	version 2.8 or 3.0 without palette
5	version 3.0 with palette

The PCX code provided in this chapter will read and write only version 3.0 files that contain palette information.

The "Encode" field determines if the raster image data is RLE (run length encoded) or byte packed. If the image is RLE encoded, the value of this field will be nonzero. Otherwise, if the value is zero, the image data is byte packed. For all practical purposes, every PCX file is RLE encoded to save space during image storage. See the section "Run Length Encoded (RLE) Compression" (page 239) for a detailed description of RLE encoding.

The field "BitPerPix" determines how many bits per pixel per bit plane are used in the image. In 16-color, four-bit-plane VGA images, the value of this field is one. A related field, NumOfPlanes, in this case would be set to four. In 256-color images, "BitPerPix" would be eight and "NumOfPlanes" would be one. Remember, only the 256-color images are supported with this code.

The fields "X1," "Y1," "X2," and "Y2" delineate the dimensions of the raster image contained in the PCX file. In PCX files, X1 and Y1 always equal zero, and X2 and Y2 equal the maximum X and Y pixel values available for a display adapter in a given display mode. In other words, PCX files fill a complete display screen. PCC files, on the other hand, have X1 and Y1 values greater than or equal to zero and X2 and Y2 values less than or equal to the maximum display resolution. PCC images are partial images that do not necessarily fill a full display screen. PCC images are not supported by the PCX function library because it is not always possible to tell what resolution VGA screen to use to display a partial screen image from the values contained in the fields X1, Y1, X2, and Y2. Correct interpretation of the two fields described next, "Hres" and "Vres," would eliminate this problem if they were correctly maintained by all PCX application programs. Unfortunately, they are not. For example, one version of Microsoft's PC PaintBrush always stores the value of 75 hex into X2 and Y2 regardless of the display mode the display adapter is in. These unrelated values do not help determine the proper display adapter mode required to display the contained PCC image.

The fields "Hres" and "Vres" should always contain the resolution of the display adapter required to display the raster image. In the PCX function library, these fields are maintained correctly for all PCX images written. These fields are ignored when a PCX file is read with the PCX function library.

The last PCX header field is "BytesPerLine." This value is the number of uncompressed data bytes necessary to contain a full scan line (row of data from the screen) of image data. For images with "BitPerPix" equal to one that are 640 pixels wide (640 by 200 and 640 by 480 images), "BytesPerLine" is equal to 80 (640 pixels/8 pixels per byte). For 256-color images with "BitPerPix" equal to eight, "BytesPerLine" is equal to the width of the raster line. A 1024 by 768 image would have "BytesPerLine" equal to 1,024.

PCX File Palettes

Palette information is stored in a PCX file so an application that reads the PCX image data can display it in the colors in which it was originally created and therefore meant to be displayed. Without palette information, an image would have to be displayed with a default palette provided by the application program. The colors in the default palette may not reflect those of the original image. In fact, displaying an image with a default palette may ruin the beauty of the image completely. Imagine a beautiful ray-traced image with blue sky and white/gray clouds displayed with an orange sky—not very appealing. Saving the palette information within the PCX file allows applications other than that on which an image was created to display the image correctly and accurately.

It is important to understand the distinction between the palette information stored in a PCX file and the hardware palette mechanism used by the VGA display adapter. Chapter 1 told us a palette is no more than a collection of colors that are used to display an image and that can be displayed simultaneously. Images with 256 colors require a 256-color palette. The palette information in a PCX file tells us the correct color components (what percentages of red, green, and blue make up the desired color) of each color that should be available for the image display. There must be one palette entry in the PCX file for each unique color used in the raster image. The order of the palette entries in the PCX file determines the pixel value required to display the described color. For example, a pixel value of 0 should be displayed in the color specified by the 0th palette entry (i.e., the first palette entry). A pixel value of 15 will be displayed in the color specified by the 15th palette entry, and so on.

To display a 256-color PCX image correctly, you must build a palette for the VGA/SuperVGA graphics adapter and load the color registers within the DAC with the RGB components of the required colors. The color information for building the palette is read from the PCX file. Only when the palette of colors that the VGA graphics adapter uses matches that contained in the PCX file can an image be displayed in its proper colors.

Two different palette mechanisms are utilized in PCX files. The original palette mechanism was built into the header of the file. This palette is used for images that contain up to 16 colors for display. This palette structure has room for 16 color register values, composed of a byte of red, green, and blue color information. The total space allotted for this palette structure in the PCX file header is therefore 48 bytes (16 color register values times 3 bytes each). How the palette information is interpreted depends on which graphics adapter you are using.

For 16-color VGA images, the first 16 color registers are set to the colors described by the RGB components in the PCX file's palette structure. The hardware palette, which as you remember is nothing more than a table with which to index the color registers, is set up in sequential order starting at 0 and ending at 15. An image pixel value of 0 will select color register 0, which most of the time is black. A pixel value of 15 will select the color in color register 15, and so on. We described loading RGB values into the VGA color registers in Chapter 1.

An EGA display adapter is capable of displaying 16 colors on the screen simultaneously out of a total palette of 64 colors. The format of a color descriptor is:

r'g'b' R G B

where the R, G, and B bits are referred to as the base color bits, and r', g', and b' are the alternate color bits. If a color component byte has any of the even bits set, then the base color bit is considered on. If any of the odd bits are set, the alternate color bit is on. If both even and odd bits are set, both the base and the alternate bits are on. To determine which of the 64 possible colors a palette entry refers to, you must apply this rule for each of the RGB bytes in a PCX file's palette entry. For example, if the hex values of the RGB components equal 55, AA, and FF respectively, the color descriptor would equal:

	Descriptor	r'	g'	b'	R	G	B	
Red	= 55 => odd bits only	1			0			alternate bit set
Green	= AA => even bits only		0			1		base bit set
Blue	= FF => even and odd			1			1	both set
Total Color Value		1	0	1	0	1	1	= Color 43

The EGA palette for this PCX palette entry would then be set to color 43. *Note*: An equally valid RGB palette entry for this same color would be 01, 02, 03 hex. This satisfies the same criteria with the even and the odd bits. Think about it.

For four-color CGA images, the red component of the first palette entry divided by 16 is the background color (0 through 15) and the red component of the second palette entry divided by 32 is the CGA palette identifier (0 through 7, although standard CGA supports only palettes 0 through 3). The remainder of the palette data is ignored.

A different palette mechanism must be used within a PCX file whenever more than 16 colors are required to display an image. This alternative palette mechanism is referred to as an "extended palette." With the PCX file header being of a fixed length and format, and the palette storage area within the header limited to 48 total bytes, an entirely new palette area must be allocated in a PCX file whenever more than 16 colors are required. All 256-color images as used in this book require an "extended palette."

The extended palette is an additional data structure appended to the end of a PCX file after the raster image data. The format of this data structure is as follows:

```
struct ExtendedPalette {
   BYTE ExtendedPalette;
   ColorRegister Palette[Max256PaletteColors]; /* Max size of 768 bytes */
};
```

The first field in this structure is a tag that identifies the extended palette. This tag is always equal to decimal 12 for a valid extended palette structure. Following the tag are storage locations for 256 3-byte RGB entries—768 bytes total. These RGB entries are transferred directly into the VGA/SuperVGA's 256 color registers within the DAC when the extended palette structure is read from a PCX file. The PCX function library supports the extended palette both in reading and writing PCX files.

The concept of the extended palette illustrates how confining a graphics file format with a fixed structure really is. The extended palette had to be tacked onto the end of the PCX file structure because otherwise it would completely change the fixed format of PCX image files. A change of this magnitude would make the new PCX files unreadable by all existing applications, effectively making them obsolete. This would create a serious problem for all application programs supporting PCX files. Placing the extended palette structure at the end of the file means all application programs that understand extended palettes can find them, and those applications that do not understand them can ignore them.

Although this scheme works, it can cause a problem in PCX file readers. The "v256" program presented at the end of this chapter suffers from just such a problem. That is, the absence or presence of an extended palette is not known until all of the raster image data has already been read from the file. Because the raster data is moved directly onto the video display as it is read, the image is displayed in bizarre colors (from the default palette of the display mode) until the presence of the extended palette structure is verified and its contents read and stored in the VGA adapter. Only after the complete image is written to the screen will the VGA palette be modified to the colors required by the image. And only then will the image be displayed in the proper colors. Of course, extra code could be written that would seek to the end of the PCX file and determine the existence of the extended palette structure before image display is begun. With the extended palette information available first, the image could be displayed in its true colors as it was being read from the PCX file.

What would happen if the PCX file format needed to be extended again? The new extension would also have to be placed at the end of the file for the reasons previously stated. The 769-byte backup from the end of the PCX file to find the extended palette would no longer work; the offset would be wrong. From this discussion, we hope you understand the implications and the limitations of fixed file formats. The GIF format (to be discussed next) was designed to prevent this type of problem.

To conclude this discussion of PCX file palettes, we need to bring up one more important point: the RGB component values contained in a PCX file's palette (as it is stored in the file on disk) are *four times* their actual value. In other words, the range of color component values stored in the PCX file is 0 to 255, whereas the VGA color register values must be in the range 0 to 63. For this reason, when the PCX library functions read a PCX file, the palette color values are divided by four before being loaded into the VGA color registers. Conversely, the color register values are multiplied by four before being placed in a PCX palette structure in preparation for being written to a PCX file. The reason for scaling the color values in this fashion is an anachronism left over from the way EGA PCX files were handled.

Run Length Encoded (RLE) Compression

The need for data compression becomes obvious when you realize how much storage is required for an image. As an example, 307,200 bytes of storage are required for a 640 by 480 256-color image as produced by a ray-tracing program. A page scanner with a 300 DPI (dots per inch) resolution in both the horizontal and vertical directions utilizing 8 bits per pixel can produce a file in excess of 8 megabytes in size. See Figure 5.3 for information on the storage requirements of various bit-mapped images. It does not take many image files of this size to fill up the largest hard disk.

Although the amount of compression achieved by the RLE method depends on the image file, it typically reduces the storage requirement by one-half to three-quarters. This is a significant reduction from such a simple compression method. Other compression methods with higher compression are available (Huffman and LZW algorithms, for example), but they suffer from substantial computational overhead (see the discussion of LZW format in the sec-

The table below indicates the total number of bytes required for storage of an uncompressed image at the specified resolution.

Resolution in dots/inch (DPI)	Bits per Sample			
	1	4	8	24
72	60,588	242,352	484,704	1,454,112
150	262,969	1,051,875	2,103,750	6,311,250
300	1,051,875	4,207,500	8,415,000	25,245,000

Notes:
1. The data assumes all images are 8.5 × 11 inches.
2. The horizontal and vertical resolutions are the same.

Figure 5.3 Storage Requirements of Bit-Mapped Images

ond half of this chapter for more information). RLE compression is a reasonable trade-off between image size and compression/expansion complexity.

In RLE compression, each row of image data is compressed separately. If there are multiple bit planes in an image, the compressed data consists of a row from each of the component planes. The PCX format supports up to four bit planes. The order of these bit planes is "BGRI"—the blue row data, followed by the green row data, followed by the red row data, and finally the row intensity data. RLE compression cannot span a scanline, but it can and does span the color components of a scanline. If the image does not use multiple bit planes (as is the case with images in this book), the image data is the index into the palette for each pixel value on the scanline. Row data is compressed by replacing a repetitive sequence of bytes by a repeat count byte and a data byte. A repeat count byte is identified by having its two most significant bits set to ones. Its lower 6 bits specify a repeat count value from 1 to 63 for the data byte that follows. If a data byte has both of its high-order bits set, then it, too, must be encoded as a repeat count byte and a data byte. The pseudocode for RLE compression is as follows:

Function CompressScanLine

```
Calculate the total number of bytes to compress
Repeat
   Get input data byte character
   Increment input pointer
   Set repeat count to a 1
   While next input data byte is a match and
         the maximum repeat count of 63 is not exceeded and
         there is more input data bytes to compress

       Increment the repeat count
   EndWhile
   If the repeat count is greater than 1 or
      the character has 2 MSBs set then
      Set two MSBs in repeat count
      Write repeat count to the output file
   Endif
   Write the data byte to the file
Until All bytes compressed
End
```

C code that implements the RLE compression is contained in the function "CompressScanLine" from the PCX function library. We show this function in Listing 5.2. An assembler language version of "CompressScanLine" called "Pack" is also shown in Listing 5.3. "Pack" is included on the companion disks as file "compress.asm" but is not utilized in this book. We included it to show two different ways of accomplishing the same thing. It is slightly faster but less portable than the C version.

Because the PCX function library is able to read as well as write PCX image files, you need an analogous RLE expansion function. The function that implements RLE expansion is called "ExpandScanLine." The pseudocode for the expansion process is shown on page 252.

Listing 5.2   The PCX Library Functions

The following is the contents of the file "pcx.h."

```
/*************************************************************/
/***                      "pcx.h"                        ***/
/***                  PCX include file                   ***/
/***              for PCX access functions               ***/
/***     from the book "Practical Ray Tracing in C"      ***/
/***             written in Borland/Turbo C 2.0          ***/
/***                        by                           ***/
/***                 Craig A. Lindley                    ***/
/***                                                     ***/
/***        Vers: 1.0   Last Update: 12/13/91            ***/
/*************************************************************/

#define MAXSCREENWIDTH              1024
#define MAXBYTESPERSCAN    MAXSCREENWIDTH
#define MAXSCREENHEIGHT             768
#define MAXPALETTECOLORS            16
#define MAX256PALETTECOLORS         256

/* PCX File Structures and Defines */

#define PCXHdrTag        10     /* tag in valid PCX file */
#define MaxRepCount      63     /* max # of repeat bytes */
#define PCX256ColorTag   12     /* tag for extended palette in PCX file */

struct PCXFileHeader   {

   BYTE      Header;              /* marks file as PCX file */
   BYTE      Version;            /* 0 = version 2.5 */
                                 /* 2 = 2.8 with palette info */
                                 /* 3 = no palette info 2.8 or 3.0 */
                                 /* 5 = 3.0 with palette info */
   BYTE      Encode;             /* File encoding mode */
   BYTE      BitPerPix;          /* Bits per pixel */
   unsigned X1;                  /* Picture dimensions inclusive */
   unsigned Y1;
   unsigned X2;
   unsigned Y2;
   unsigned Hres;                /* Graphics adapter Horiz    resolution */
   unsigned Vres;                /* Graphics adapter Vertical resolution */
};

struct PCXInfo   {

   BYTE      Vmode;              /* Ignore should always be zero */
   BYTE      NumOfPlanes;        /* Number of bit planes */
   unsigned BytesPerLine;        /* Bytes Per Line in picture */
   BYTE      unused[60];         /* fills out header to 128 bytes */
};
```

(continued)

Listing 5.2 *(continued)*

```
struct PCX_File  {

   struct PCXFileHeader PCXHeader;
   ColorRegister        Palette[MAXPALETTECOLORS]; /* Max size of 48 bytes */
   struct PCXInfo       Info;
};

/* Extended palette data structure for 256-color PCX files */

struct ExtendedPalette  {

   BYTE ExtendedPalette;
   ColorRegister Palette[MAX256PALETTECOLORS]; /* Max size of 768 bytes */
};


/* PCX C Function Prototype Declarations */
void DisplayPCXFile (char *FileName, int Verbose);

void WritePCXFile (char *FileName, unsigned MaxX, unsigned MaxY);
```

The following is the contents of the file "pcx.c."

```
/***********************************************************/
/***                  "pcx.c"                    ***/
/***            PCX Function Library             ***/
/***    from the book "Practical Ray Tracing in C"   ***/
/***         written in Borland/Turbo C 2.0      ***/
/***                   by                        ***/
/***            Craig A. Lindley                 ***/
/***                                             ***/
/***     Vers: 1.0   Last Update: 03/11/92       ***/
/***********************************************************/

#include <stdio.h>
#include <string.h>
#include <process.h>
#include <conio.h>
#include <dos.h>
#include "misc.h"
#include "vga.h"
#include "pcx.h"

/* Externally Accessible Global Variables */
struct   PCX_File PCXData;        /* PCX File Hdr Variable */
unsigned ImageWidth, ImageHeight;
```

```
/* Variables global to this file only */
static FILE    *PCXFile;        /* file handle */
static BYTE    ScanLine[MAXBYTESPERSCAN];
static struct  ExtendedPalette Color256Palette;


/* Start of Functions */
/*
This function opens an image file and attempts to read the
PCX header information.
*/
CompletionCode ReadPCXFileHdr (char *FileName, int Verbose)  {

   char      String[80];

   if (!strchr(FileName,'.'))  {       /* is there an ext ? */
       strcpy(String,FileName);        /* copy filename to buffer */
      FileName = String;               /* FileName now points at buffer */
      strcat(FileName,".pcx");         /* if not add .pcx ext */
   }
   /* try to open the PCX file */
   if ((PCXFile = fopen(FileName,"rb")) == NULL)  {

      printf("PCX file: %s not found\n",FileName);
      return(EFileNotFound);
   }
   /* try to read the file header record */
   if (fread(&PCXData,sizeof(struct PCX_File),1,PCXFile) != 1)  {
      printf("Error reading PCX file header\n");
      return(EReadFileHdr);
   }
   /* check to make sure it's a PCX file */
   if (PCXData.PCXHeader.Header != PCXHdrTag)  {

      printf("Error not a PCX file\n");
      return(ENotPCXFile);
   }
   /* Yep, we've got a PCX file OK. Display info if requested */
   if (Verbose)  {

      clrscr();
      printf("PCX Image Information for file: %s\n\n",FileName);
      printf("\tVersion: %d\n", PCXData.PCXHeader.Version);
      printf("\tCompression: %s\n",
             PCXData.PCXHeader.Encode == 0 ? "None":"RLE");
      printf("\tBits Per Pixel: %d\n",PCXData.PCXHeader.BitPerPix);
      printf("\tX1: %d\n",PCXData.PCXHeader.X1);
      printf("\tY1: %d\n",PCXData.PCXHeader.Y1);
      printf("\tX2: %d\n",PCXData.PCXHeader.X2);
      printf("\tY2: %d\n",PCXData.PCXHeader.Y2);
      printf("\tHoriz Resolution: %d\n",PCXData.PCXHeader.Hres);
```

(continued)

Listing 5.2   *(continued)*

```
      printf("\tVert  Resolution: %d\n",PCXData.PCXHeader.Vres);
      printf("\tVMode: %d\n",PCXData.Info.Vmode);
      printf("\tNumber of Planes: %d\n",PCXData.Info.NumOfPlanes);
      printf("\tBytes Per Scan Line One Plane: %d\n",PCXData.Info.BytesPerLine);
      printf("\nHit <Enter> to proceed - ^C to abort\n");
      getchar();                         /* wait for operator input */
   }
   return(NoError);
}


static CompletionCode ExpandScanLine (FILE *InFile)  {

   register short CharRead;
   unsigned       InPtr,RepCount;
   unsigned       BytesToRead;

   BytesToRead = PCXData.Info.NumOfPlanes * PCXData.Info.BytesPerLine;

   InPtr = 0;                            /* initialize input ptr */
   do  {

      CharRead = getc(InFile);           /* read a byte from the file */
      if (CharRead == EOF)               /* error should never read EOF */
         return(FALSE);                  /* abort picture */

      if ((CharRead & 0xC0) == 0xC0) { /* a repeat tag ? */

         RepCount = CharRead & ~0xC0;  /* repeat 1..63 */
         CharRead = getc(InFile);       /* read byte to repeat */
         if (CharRead == EOF)           /* error should never read EOF */
            return(FALSE);              /* abort picture */

         while (RepCount--)             /* expand byte */
            ScanLine[InPtr++] =         /* RepCount times */
               CharRead;
      }
      else                              /* just a byte of data */
         ScanLine[InPtr++] = CharRead; /* store in buffer */
   } while (InPtr < BytesToRead);       /* expand a full scan line */
/*
When we get here, we have an array, ScanLine, which is composed of
NumOfPlanes sections each BytesPerLine long. For a 256-color VGA image,
it is 1 plane of 320, 640, 800, or 1024 bytes. For a 256-color image,
the ScanLine contains one line of raster data. Return an indication
that this operation went smoothly.
*/

   return(TRUE);
}
```

```
/*
This function reads and displays a 256-color PCX file.
*/

void DisplayPCXFile (char *FileName, int Verbose)
{
   register unsigned ScanNum;            /* scan line being expanded
                                            and displayed */
   register unsigned ColNum, Index;      /* pixel being read */
   int       PCXError;

   if ((PCXError = ReadPCXFileHdr(FileName,Verbose)) != NoError)
      exit(PCXError);

   /* Header has been read, now we are ready to display the PCX image */
   /* PCC files cannot be displayed */

   if ((PCXData.PCXHeader.X1 != 0) || (PCXData.PCXHeader.Y1 != 0))
   {
      printf("Error PCC file not PCX file\n");
      exit(EPCCFile);
   }

   /* Copy image specs to local storage */
   ImageWidth  = PCXData.PCXHeader.Hres;
   ImageHeight = PCXData.PCXHeader.Vres;

   /* Select the correct video mode if VESA device else abort */
   CheckForVESA();
   SelectVideoMode(ImageWidth,ImageHeight,TRUE);

    /* proceed to unpack and display the PCX file */
   for (ScanNum=0; ScanNum < ImageHeight; ScanNum++)  {
     if (ExpandScanLine(PCXFile) != TRUE)  {
       printf("Scanline corrupt in PCX file\n");
       exit(ECorrupt);
     }
     for (ColNum=0; ColNum < ImageWidth; ColNum++)
       SetPixelValue(ColNum,ScanNum,ScanLine[ColNum]);
   }
   /* Now read the extended palette structure from the end of the file */

   if (fread(&Color256Palette,sizeof(struct ExtendedPalette),1,PCXFile) == 1)
     /* Extended palette read ok. Now check tag. */
    if (Color256Palette.ExtendedPalette == PCX256ColorTag)  {
      for(Index=0; Index < MAX256PALETTECOLORS; Index++)  {
        Color256Palette.Palette[Index].Red   >= 2;
        Color256Palette.Palette[Index].Green >= 2;
        Color256Palette.Palette[Index].Blue  >= 2;
      }
      SetAllColorRegs((ColorRegister *) &(Color256Palette.Palette));
```

(continued)

Listing 5.2   *(continued)*

```
     }
   fclose(PCXFile);
}

/*
The following functions create a PCX file from a raster image
on the display and write it to disk.
*/

CompletionCode WritePCXHdr(char *FileName, unsigned BitsPerPixel,
   unsigned MaxX,  unsigned MaxY, unsigned Planes,
   unsigned BytesPerLine)  {
   unsigned    Index;
   char        String[80];

   if (!strchr(FileName,'.'))  {         /* is there an ext ? */
                                         /* if not ... */
      strcpy(String,FileName);           /* copy filename to buffer */
      FileName = String;                 /* FileName now points at buffer */
      strcat(FileName,".pcx");           /* add .pcx ext */
   }

   if ((PCXFile = fopen(FileName,"w+b")) == NULL)
      return (EFileNotFound);

   /* initialize the PCX file header info */
   PCXData.PCXHeader.Header    = PCXHdrTag;
   PCXData.PCXHeader.Version   = 5;
   PCXData.PCXHeader.Encode    = 1;
   PCXData.PCXHeader.BitPerPix = BitsPerPixel;
   PCXData.PCXHeader.X1        = 0;
   PCXData.PCXHeader.Y1        = 0;
   PCXData.PCXHeader.X2        = MaxX-1;
   PCXData.PCXHeader.Y2        = MaxY-1;
   PCXData.PCXHeader.Hres      = MaxX;
   PCXData.PCXHeader.Vres      = MaxY;
   PCXData.Info.Vmode          = 0;
   PCXData.Info.NumOfPlanes    = Planes;
   PCXData.Info.BytesPerLine   = BytesPerLine;

   /*
   Initialize the 16-color palette structure in the PCX file data.
   This 16-color palette will be written to the PCX file even though
   the images are 256-color images containing an extended palette.
   The extended palette will be written at the end of the PCX raster data.
   */

   for (Index = 0; Index < MAXPALETTECOLORS; Index++)  {
      PCXData.Palette[Index].Red   = 0;
```

```
      PCXData.Palette[Index].Green = 0;
      PCXData.Palette[Index].Blue  = 0;
   }

   /* clear the unused area at the end of the PCX header */
   memset(&PCXData.Info.unused,'\0',sizeof(PCXData.Info.unused));

   /* now write the file header to the physical file */
   if (fwrite(&PCXData,sizeof(struct PCX_File),1,PCXFile) != 1)
      return(EWrtFileHdr);

   return(NoError);
}

static CompletionCode CompressScanLine(FILE *OutFile)  {

   register unsigned OutPtr,RepCount,RepChar;
   register unsigned BytesToWrite;

   BytesToWrite = PCXData.Info.NumOfPlanes * PCXData.Info.BytesPerLine;

   OutPtr = 0;                          /* ptr to data to compress */
   do  {

      RepChar = ScanLine[OutPtr++];     /* get byte to start compression */
      RepCount = 1;                     /* byte seen once at this point */
      while ((ScanLine[OutPtr]==RepChar) &&
             (RepCount < MaxRepCount)      &&
             (OutPtr < BytesToWrite))  {
        RepCount++;                     /* count all repetitions of char */
        OutPtr++;                       /* bump ptr and check again */
      }

      /*
      Repeat sequence found or if chars has either or both MSBs set
      than must process as a repetition count and char sequence.
      */

      if ((RepCount > 1) || (RepChar > 0xBF))  {
         RepCount |= 0xC0;              /* set two MSBs */
         if (putc(RepCount,OutFile) == EOF) /* write count to file */
            return(FALSE);             /* if error return error */
      }
      if (putc(RepChar,OutFile) == EOF)/* write char to file */
         return(FALSE);                /* if error return error */
   } while (OutPtr < BytesToWrite);    /* until all bytes in scan
                                          are compressed */
   return(TRUE);                       /* indicate operation successful */
}
```

(continued)

Listing 5.2   *(continued)*

```
/*
This function writes a PCX file to disk from the image currently
being displayed on the monitor. The image data is read directly
off of the screen and the palette information is read from the
DAC.
*/

void WritePCXFile (char *FileName, unsigned MaxX, unsigned MaxY)  {

   register unsigned ScanLineNum, PixelNum, Index;
   int PCXError;

   /* write out PCX header and palette */
   if ((PCXError = WritePCXHdr(FileName, 8, MaxX, MaxY, 1, MaxX)) != NoError)
     exit(PCXError);

   ImageWidth = MaxX;
   ImageHeight = MaxY;

/*
At this point we will read the displayed image from the screen a scanline
at time. For 256-color images there is only a single bit plane
so the data read from the screen is placed directly into the ScanLine array
for compressing.
*/

   for (ScanLineNum=0; ScanLineNum < ImageHeight; ScanLineNum++)  {
     for (PixelNum=0; PixelNum < ImageWidth; PixelNum++)
       ScanLine[PixelNum] = GetPixelValue(PixelNum,ScanLineNum);

     if (CompressScanLine(PCXFile) != TRUE) /* compress a complete scan */
       exit(EWrtScanLine);
   }
   /*
   Write an extended palette record to the file after the
   raster data. Read the 256 color register RGB values and
   store them in the Color256Palette structure before writing
   them to the PCX file. This structure is tagged to assure validity.
   */

   Color256Palette.ExtendedPalette = PCX256ColorTag;
   GetAllColorRegs((ColorRegister *) &(Color256Palette.Palette));

   for (Index = 0; Index < MAX256PALETTECOLORS; Index++)  {
     Color256Palette.Palette[Index].Red   <<= 2;
     Color256Palette.Palette[Index].Green <<= 2;
     Color256Palette.Palette[Index].Blue  <<= 2;
   }
   /*
   With all of the color register values read, write the
```

```
    extended palette structure to the PCX file.
    */

    if (fwrite(&Color256Palette,
                sizeof(struct ExtendedPalette),1,PCXFile) != 1)  {
      fclose(PCXFile);                      /* close the completed PCX file */
      exit(EWrtExtPal);
    }
    /* file has been written prepare to close up shop */

    fclose(PCXFile);                        /* close the completed PCX file */
}
```

Listing 5.3   An Assembler Language RLE Encoder

The following is the contents of the file "compress.asm."

```
; PACK - A RLE Compression Routine callable from Turbo C
;
; written by Craig A. Lindley
; last update: 01/07/92
;
;
_TEXT     segment byte public 'CODE'
      DGROUP group _DATA,_BSS
      assume cs:_TEXT,ds:DGROUP,ss:DGROUP
_TEXT     ends

_DATA     segment word public 'DATA'
;
_DATA     ends

_BSS     segment word public 'BSS'
;
_BSS     ends
;
;
_TEXT     segment     byte public 'CODE'
;
;Scan Line Compression
;
; Procedure _Pack
;
```

(continued)

Listing 5.3 *(continued)*

```
; This procedure compresses a raster line of image data into the RLE
; encoding used by PCX graphics files. In this encoding, a repeat
; byte sequence is compressed into a repeat count followed by the byte
; to be repeated. A maximum repeat of 63 is all that is allowed because a
; repeat count byte is identified by having its most significant two bits
; set high. This also means that any single char with a value above 0BFH
; also will be encoded as a repeat count (C1) followed by the bytes value so
; the bytes value will not be misinterpreted as a repeat count.
;
; CALL:    callable from C.
; PROTOTYPE: unsigned Pack (BYTE far *, BYTE far *, unsigned Count)
; INPUT:   all parameters passed to this function are on the stack. The
;          stack should contain the following: Count at [bp+12], Output buf seg
;          at [bp+10], Output buf offset at [bp+8], Input buf seg at [bp+6]
;          and the Input buf offset at [bp+4].
; OUTPUT: the number of bytes in the packed output buffer returned in ax.
; USES:    ax,bx,cx,dx,es,si,di registers
;
      Public _Pack
;
_Pack       proc      near
;
      push    bp
      mov     bp,sp
      push    si
      push    di
;
      mov     si,[bp+4]        ;load parms from the stack
      mov     ds,[bp+6]        ;ptr to buffer to pack
      mov     di,[bp+8]
      mov     es,[bp+10]       ;ptr to packed buffer
      mov     dx,[bp+12]       ;size of buffer to pack
;
;when we get here the actual RLE encoding is performed
;
      cld                      ;move ptrs forward in memory
pack1:
      lodsb                    ;get byte from input buffer
      mov     bl,al            ;save in bl
      mov     cx,1             ;char rep count is 1
      dec     dx               ;dec # of input bytes to process
;
pack2:
      cmp     dx,0             ;all input bytes compressed ?
      je      pack3            ;jump if so
      cmp     cx,63            ;at max block size ?
      je      pack3            ;jump if so
      cmp     bl,[si]          ;look at next byte
      jne     pack3            ;jump if not same
```

```
        inc     si              ;bump input ptr to next byte
        dec     dx              ;now one less
        inc     cx              ;byte same so bump rep count
        jmp     short pack2     ;try for another match
;
;we are now ready to place compressed items in the output buffer
;
pack3:
        cmp     cx,1            ;rep count > 1 ?
        ja      pack5           ;jump if so
        cmp     al,0BFH         ;char > BFH ?
        ja      pack5           ;jump if so
;
;when we get here we have a single byte to place in the output buffer with
;a value less than C0H.
;
pack4:
        stosb                   ;put byte in output buffer
        cmp     dx,0            ;any more input chars ?
        jne     pack1           ;if so go back and start over
        jmp     short pack6     ;get ready to exit if no more
;
;when we get here, we must process a repeat count followed by a repeat byte
;
pack5:
        push    ax              ;save rep byte
        mov     al,cl           ;rep count to al
        or      al,0C0H         ;set the 2 msbits
        stosb                   ;store rep count in output buffer
        pop     ax              ;get byte back
        jmp     short pack4     ;now output the byte
;
;we're done and ready to exit
;
pack6:
        mov     ax,di           ;get output ptr
        sub     ax,[bp+8]       ;calc # of bytes in output buf
        pop     di              ;restore regs and exit
        pop     si
        pop     bp
        ret
;
_Pack   endp
;
_TEXT   ends
        end
```

Function ExpandScanLine

```
Calculate the number of expanded bytes expected
Repeat
   Read data byte from file
   If two MSBs set then it's a repeat tag
      Mask off the two MSBs to get repeat count
      Get next data byte from file
      Store this byte count number of times in output buffer
   Else its actual data byte
      Store data byte in output buffer
   Endif
Until all bytes are expanded
```

Single-plane images get different treatment than multiple-bit-plane images. Actually, single-plane images require much less processing and can therefore be compressed and expanded much faster. See the function "WritePCXFile" for details. All 256-color images are single-plane images. All standard 16-color VGA images utilize four bit planes.

The PCX Function Library

The PCX function library consists of six PCX functions, only two of which are meant to be called externally by an application program. The other four functions are utilized within the PCX function library. Figure 5.4 shows the external functions and gives a short description of their operation. The operation of the nonexternal functions in the library should be discernible from the comments in the listing.

---

1. **Display a PCX file on the VGA/SuperVGA graphics adapter.**

Prototype:
      void DisplayPCXFile (char *FileName, int Verbose);

Where:
1.   FileName is a pointer to a NULL terminated ASCII filename.
2.   Verbose is a variable that determines whether detailed image information contained in the PCX file header should be displayed. If TRUE, the image information will be displayed in textual form before the image is displayed. See the function "ReadPCXFileHdr" in Listing 5.2 for an idea of what PCX file information will be displayed.

Operation:
This function loads and displays a PCX image from a disk file. All parameters required for proper image display are taken from the header read from the PCX image file. The image data is taken directly from the file and placed onto the VGA/SuperVGA display; no intermediate image buffer is utilized. Any errors encountered in the execution of this function will terminate program operation and will provide an exit code to explain the problem. The error codes are defined in the file "misc.h" and discussed in Chapter 1.

Figure 5.4   The PCX Function Library

2. **Write a PCX file from the image currently being displayed on the VGA/Super-VGA display.**

Prototype:
>   void WritePCXFile(char *FileName, unsigned MaxX, unsigned MaxY);

Where:
1.   FileName is a pointer to a NULL terminated ASCII filename.
2.   MaxX and MaxY are the dimensions of the image to be written out as a PCX file. They should always equal the resolution of the VGA/SuperVGA mode used to display the image.

Operation:
This function creates a PCX file from the image currently being displayed on the VGA monitor. It writes out the PCX file header followed by the raster data and the extended palette structure. A single-plane, 8-bit-per-pixel format image is always used for the 256-color images dealt with in this book.

Figure 5.4   *(continued)*

Example Usage of the PCX Function Library

Actually, we used the PCX function library in Chapter 4 to save ray-traced images in PCX file format. As a prerequisite for using these PCX functions, an application program must include the header files "misc.h," "vga.h," and "pcx.h" during compilation. With these files included, a call to "WritePCXFile" in the application program (linked with "pcx.obj," of course) is all that is needed to produce a 256-color PCX file of the image displayed on the VGA/SuperVGA graphics adapter. The parameters passed to the "WritePCXFile" function were described earlier and are enumerated in Figure 5.5 for reference.

An example of using the PCX library functions to display a PCX file is shown in the last portion of this chapter in the discussion of the "v256" PCX/GIF file viewing program. Please refer directly to Listing 5.5 to see what is required. Displaying a PCX image file is as trivial as writing a PCX file. (We showed examples of writing PCX files in the color quantization programs in Chapter 4.) In both cases, only a single line of code is required within an application program to read or write a PCX file from/to the display adapter using the PCX function library.

Resolution	Colors	MaxX	MaxY
320 by 200	256	320	200
640 by 400	256	640	400
640 by 480	256	640	480
800 by 600	256	800	600
1024 by 768	256	1024	768

Figure 5.5   "WritePCXFile" Function Call Parameters

The GIF Graphics File Format

In this section, we describe the GIF (pronounced "jif") graphics file format. GIF, which stands for "Graphics Interchange Format," is the copyrighted property of CompuServe Corporation of Columbus, Ohio. CompuServe grants a nonexclusive, royalty-free license for the use of the GIF format in computer software. In return, the company requires an acknowledgment within the software and/or the printed documentation accompanying the software that GIF belongs to them. The "v256" PCX/GIF file viewer program discussed later in this chapter displays the required copyright notice when it is first executed. This program, therefore, satisfies CompuServe's licensing requirements.

Most of the information about the GIF graphics file format presented in this chapter was extracted from the GIF specification, version "89a," and dated 1990. This specification is available directly from CompuServe at the following address:

CompuServe Incorporated
Graphics Technology Department
5000 Arlington Center Blvd.
Columbus, OH 43220

The specification is also available on-line from many computer bulletin boards and network services that have a graphics special interest group. This specification is also available from numerous sources via the Internet.

GIF is becoming increasingly popular as an exchange medium for computer imagery of all varieties. GIF readers (also called viewers) are now available for most computer systems from PCs to mainframes, in addition to UNIX workstations. Files created on one machine are viewable on another because GIF's design is hardware independent. A possible reason for GIF's popularity is that it is a relatively simple file format to read and write and, because of its use of LZW compression, the image files are quite compact. Although the GIF format is more complex than the PCX format discussed previously, it is still much simpler to understand and use than TIFF (Tagged Image File Format). This simplicity allows application programs to include GIF capabilities with relatively little effort. A TIFF reader, in contrast, can take a person year of effort to develop.

The complexity associated with GIF files is due to the LZW compression/expansion. LZW stands for Lempel-Ziv and Welsh, the people who originally developed and later extended this extremely clever file compression scheme. This algorithm is so clever that Sperry Corporation has patented it. The company was able to do so because Welsh worked at Sperry when he added his enhancements to the basic algorithm. Fortunately, so far, Sperry has not tried to enforce its patent. If it did, it would affect most file compression programs, because so many of them use LZW as the basis of their operation.

LZW compression differs substantially from the RLE compression discussed previously in that LZW is bit-oriented while RLE (as implemented for PCX files) is byte-oriented. This difference increases the implementation complexity of LZW while at the same time achieving greater file compression. Without exception, a ray-traced image saved in GIF format will be smaller than the same image saved in PCX format. Sometimes the difference in compressed file size is amazing.

To understand how GIF files work, you must understand both the structure of GIF files and how LZW compression/expansion works. We cover both of these topics in detail in this chapter. The GIF code presented is in the form of a function library to be linked with an application program. To use the GIF function library, an application program would have to include the files "misc.h" and "gif.h" in its source code and would need to place the file "gif.c" in its make file. The "v256" program shown and discussed later is an example of how this is done.

In keeping with the functionality required by our ray-tracing application and with that provided by the PCX function library presented earlier, *the GIF code in this chapter supports only 256-color, single-plane, 8-bit-per-pixel images*. Just as before, the GIF function library allows the 256-color image currently displayed on the computer monitor to be saved as a GIF file. Further, it can read and display a properly formatted 256-color GIF file on the computer monitor. You must also understand that even though we took the information used to develop the GIF function library from the "89a" version of the GIF specification, this function library reads and writes only "87a" GIF files. We did this intentionally and in concurrence with the GIF specification. The reason was that we didn't need any of the extensions provided in the "89a" version of the specification. The "89a" version of GIF minus the extensions equals approximately the "87a" version of GIF, and this is what we used. Listing 5.4 (on pages 257–272) shows the code for the GIF function library.

For the purpose of discussion, the terms "encoder" and "compressor" mean the same thing; they refer to a program that accepts a data stream of pixel (color index) values, compresses them using the LZW algorithm, and outputs a data stream of compressed, coded data. A "decoder" or "expander," two terms that we will also use synonymously, is a program that accepts a data stream of coded data, expands it using the LZW algorithm, and outputs a data stream of pixel values. This compression/expansion process is said to be "lossless" because the pixel data out after expansion equals, bit for bit, the pixel data before compression. In other words, output equals input exactly.

Note: All multiple-byte integer values used within the GIF format are expressed in "little endian" format. (See Chapter 1 for an explanation of little endian format.) You would need to consider this if you port the GIF function library code to a different computer that used a "big endian" processor (MC680X0, for example). A big endian processor would have to swap the bytes in all 16-bit integer values as they were read or written to a file to be compatible with the GIF specification. However, since the LZW compressed data is byte-oriented, the byte persuasion of the host processor does not matter.

GIF File Structure

The GIF file structure, as defined in the "89a" version of the specification, is much more flexible than the PCX file structure. Provisions are made for the storage of application-specific information within the GIF file that GIF file readers can successfully ignore if they do not understand it. This illustrates an important difference between these two file formats: the GIF file structure can be extended by an application program in a manner fully consistent with the specification, but, as we saw earlier, PCX files cannot be expanded without making all previously existing PCX readers obsolete.

GIF was originally designed as an on-line protocol for transmission of raster graphics data. One of GIF's design goals was hardware independence—the ability to use GIF files on many different types of computer systems without regard to how the image was created or originally displayed. When the GIF protocol is used on-line, it must be encapsulated into some error-free protocol (transport layer service) because GIF itself has no provisions for error detection and/or correction. Errors that make their way into a GIF data stream can have a catastrophic effect on image retrieval.

A GIF data stream or file (from now on referred to as a GIF data stream) consists of a sequence of protocol blocks and data subblocks. Figure 5.6 summarizes the blocks defined in the "89a" version of the GIF specification. To completely master the GIF format, you must understand:

1. The number of times a specific block type can occur in the data stream
2. The order in which the blocks must occur
3. Which blocks are mandatory and which are optional

The labels used to identify labeled blocks fall into three ranges:

    0x00 through 0x7F—Graphics Rendering Blocks, except for 0x3B, the Trailer
    0x80 through 0xF9—Control Blocks
    0xFA through 0xFF—Special Purpose Blocks

Also, some blocks are unlabeled.

Block Type	Presence in file	Occurrences in file	Label	Type
Application Extension*	Optional	0 or more	0xFF	SPB
Comment Extension*	Optional	0 or more	0xFE	SPB
Global Color Table	Optional	once	none	UB
Graphics Control Extension*	Optional	0 or more	0xF9	CB
Header	Required	once	none	UB
Image Descriptor*	Optional	0 or more	0x2C	GRB
Local Color Table	Optional	0 or more	none	UB
Logical Screen Descriptor*	Required	once	none	UB
Plain Text Extension*	Optional	0 or more	0x01	GRB
Trailer	Required	once	0x3B	SPB

Where:
1. SPB indicates a Special Purpose Block.
2. UB indicates an Unlabeled Block.
3. CB indicates a Control Block.
4. GRB indicates a Graphics Rendering Block.
5. * indicates a new or revised block in the 89a version.

Figure 5.6   GIF Block Summary

Listing 5.4   The GIF Library Functions

The following is the contents of the file "gif.h."

```
/***********************************************************/
/***                      "gif.h"                      ***/
/***                  GIF Header File                  ***/
/***               for GIF access functions            ***/
/***       from the book "Practical Ray Tracing in C"   ***/
/***            written in Borland/Turbo C 2.0         ***/
/***                        by                         ***/
/***                  Craig A. Lindley                 ***/
/***                                                   ***/
/***         Vers: 1.0   Last Update: 01/04/92         ***/
/***********************************************************/

#define BITSPERCOLOR        6
#define GLOBALCOLORTBL      0x80
#define LOCALINTERLACEFLAG 0x40
#define GLOBALCOLORTBLSIZE   8
#define GIFHDRTAG         "GIF87a"        /* tag in valid GIF file */

/* GIF File Structures and Defines */

typedef struct   {
   ColorRegister Palette[MAX256PALETTECOLORS]; /* Max size of 768 bytes */
} ColorTable;

struct GIFHeader   {
  char Hdr[6];
};

struct LogicalScreenDescriptor   {
   unsigned LogicalScreenWidth;   /* logical screen width */
   unsigned LogicalScreenHeight;
   BYTE     PackedField;
   BYTE     BackGroundIndex;
   BYTE     AspectRatio;
};

struct ImageDescriptor   {
   char     ImageSeparator;
   unsigned ImageLeftPosition;
   unsigned ImageTopPosition;
   unsigned ImageWidth;
   unsigned ImageHeight;
   BYTE     PackedField;
};

struct TheTrailer   {
  BYTE  Length;
```

(continued)

Listing 5.4   *(continued)*

```
  char  Trailer;
};


/* Function Declarations */
void DisplayGIFFile (char *FileName, unsigned Verbose);

void WriteGIFFile (char *FileName,
                   unsigned ScreenWidth, unsigned ScreenHeight,
                   unsigned ImageWidth,  unsigned ImageHeight,
                   unsigned ImageTop,    unsigned ImageLeft);
```

The following is the contents of the file "gif.c."

```
/*********************************************************/
/***                    "gif.c"                      ***/
/***        Special 256-Color GIF Function Library   ***/
/***      from the book "Practical Ray Tracing in C" ***/
/***           written in Borland/Turbo C 2.0        ***/
/***                       by                        ***/
/***                Craig A. Lindley                 ***/
/***                                                 ***/
/***        Vers: 1.0   Last Update: 03/04/92        ***/
/*********************************************************/

/*
This code is loosely based on that presented in the June 1990
issue of Dr. Dobbs Journal, in an article by Shawn M. Regan
entitled "LZW Revisited." The errors in the original code
have been corrected and many changes have been made.
*/

#include <stdio.h>
#include <string.h>
#include <process.h>
#include <conio.h>
#include <dos.h>
#include <alloc.h>
#include "misc.h"
#include "vga.h"
#include "gif.h"

/* Global Definitions */
#define BITSPERPIXEL            8
#define MINBITS      (BITSPERPIXEL+1)
#define MAXBITS                12    /* 9 - 12 bits used for 8-bit images */
#define TABLESIZE             5003    /* Prime # greater than 2^MAXBITS */
#define HASHING_SHIFT            5
#define CLEARCODE              256    /* Code to flush the string table */
```

```
#define EOICODE                257    /* End of Information code */
#define FIRSTCODE              258    /* First code_value */
#define EXPBUFSIZE             255    /* Size of GIF data block buffer */
#define EXPBUFBITS    (EXPBUFSIZE<<3) /* Size of above in bits */
#define COMPBUFSIZE            255    /* Size of GIF data block buffer */
#define COMPBUFBITS (COMPBUFSIZE<<3)  /* Size of above in bits */
#define MAXCODEVAL(n)        (1<<(n)) /* Max code value macro */
#define FLUSHCODE     (MAXCODEVAL(MAXBITS+1)) /* signals time to flush */


/* Variables global to this file and used in the GIF format */
static FILE *GIFFile;
unsigned TheImageTop;                 /* top offset of image on screen */
unsigned TheImageLeft;                /* left offset of image */
unsigned TheImageWidth;               /* width  in pixels of image */
unsigned TheImageHeight;              /* height in pixels of image */
struct LogicalScreenDescriptor ScnDesc;
struct ImageDescriptor ImgDesc;
ColorTable GlobalColorTbl;


/* Variable used for the LZW compression and expansion */
static unsigned NumOfBits;            /* current # of bits in code */
static unsigned NextCode;
static unsigned MaxCode;              /* current max code value */
static unsigned NextBitPos;           /* next free bit position */
static BYTE ExpandBuf[EXPBUFSIZE];    /* for expansion for disk read */
static int   BytesLeftInBlock;        /* bytes left in block just read */
static BYTE CompressionBuf[COMPBUFSIZE+3];
static unsigned ScanLine;             /* scan line of raster image */
static unsigned Pixel;                /* pixel in scan line */


/* Pointers to arrays required for compression and expansion */
static unsigned far *prefix_code;
static BYTE     far *append_character;
static int      far *code_value;      /* hash table of code values */
static BYTE     far *decode_stack;    /* array holds decoded string */

static unsigned Mask[4] =             /* values to mask 9, 10, 11, and */
  { 0x01FF, 0x03FF, 0x07FF, 0x0FFF }; /* 12-bit codes */


/*
This function deallocs all memory from the far heap that has
currently been allocated. If the memory pointers are NULL, no
memory has been allocated for the corresponding array.
*/
static void DeAllocMem(void)  {

  if (prefix_code != NULL)        farfree(prefix_code);
  if (append_character != NULL)   farfree(append_character);
  if (code_value != NULL)         farfree(code_value);
  if (decode_stack != NULL)       farfree(decode_stack);
}
```

(continued)

Listing 5.4 *(continued)*

```c
/*
This function allocs the memory for the required arrays from the
far heap. The same memory is allocated for compression and expansion
although not actually necessary.
*/
static unsigned AllocMem(void)   {

  /*
  Set all pointers to null so we can tell whether the alloc
  was successful or not.
  */
  prefix_code = NULL;
  append_character = NULL;
  code_value = NULL;
  decode_stack = NULL;

  prefix_code = (unsigned far *)
    farcalloc((unsigned long) TABLESIZE, (unsigned long) sizeof(unsigned));
  append_character = (BYTE far *)
    farcalloc((unsigned long) TABLESIZE, (unsigned long) sizeof(BYTE));
  code_value = (int far *)
    farcalloc((unsigned long) TABLESIZE, (unsigned long) sizeof(int));
  decode_stack = (BYTE far *)
    farcalloc((unsigned long) TABLESIZE, (unsigned long) sizeof(BYTE));

  /* Make sure all allocs were successful */
  if (!prefix_code || !append_character ||
      !code_value  || !decode_stack)  {
    DeAllocMem();
    printf("Error not enough memory for GIF arrays\n");
    return(FALSE);
  }
  return(TRUE);                /* everything is ok */
}


/*
This function is used in LZW expansion to return the next NumOfBits code
from the input file. It handles the blocking utilized in the GIF
spec. When the expansion buffer is depleted of data, this function
reads in the next block from the disk.
*/

static unsigned InCode(void)   {

  register unsigned BitPos, BytesToMove, Index;
  register unsigned BytePos;
  register unsigned long ExtractWord;
  register int TheChar;

  BitPos = NextBitPos & 7;      /* bits used in current byte of buffer */
  BytePos= NextBitPos > 3;      /* byte in buffer with free bits */
```

```
    if ((NextBitPos + NumOfBits) >= EXPBUFBITS)    {  /* at end of buf ? */
      BytesToMove = EXPBUFSIZE - BytePos;              /* if so move last */
      for (Index = 0; Index < BytesToMove; Index++)  /* bytes to beg of next */
          ExpandBuf[Index] = ExpandBuf[Index+BytePos];/* buffer. */
      while (Index < EXPBUFSIZE)   {                  /* fill rest of buf */
          if (BytesLeftInBlock == 0)    {             /* from disk */
            BytesLeftInBlock = getc(GIFFile);         /* read block count */
            if (BytesLeftInBlock == EOF)              /* if EOF read - abort */
              return(EOICODE);
            if (BytesLeftInBlock == 0)                /* remember to process */
              break;                                  /* last few bytes in */
          }                                           /* ExpandBuf */
          TheChar = getc(GIFFile);                    /* read data from block */
          if (TheChar == EOF)
              return(EOICODE);
          ExpandBuf[Index++] = TheChar;
          BytesLeftInBlock--;
      }
      BitPos = NextBitPos = NextBitPos & 7;
      BytePos= 0;
    }
    /* When we get here, we have a code to return */
    ExtractWord = ((unsigned long) ExpandBuf[BytePos]) |
                  ((unsigned long) ExpandBuf[BytePos+1] << 8) |
                  ((unsigned long) ExpandBuf[BytePos+2] << 16);
    ExtractWord >= BitPos;
    NextBitPos += NumOfBits;
    return(ExtractWord & Mask[NumOfBits-MINBITS]);
}


/*
This function sets one pixel of the raster image each time it is
called. It remembers its location in the image each time it is called.
*/
static void OutPixel(unsigned Color)    {

  SetPixelValue(Pixel+ImgDesc.ImageLeftPosition,
                ScanLine+ImgDesc.ImageTopPosition,
                Color);
  Pixel++;
  if (Pixel == ImgDesc.ImageWidth)   {
    Pixel = 0;
    ScanLine++;
  }
}


/*
This function initializes the code_value array and various variables
necessary for the LZW compressor and expander to work. This is called
initially and then whenever the CLEARCODE is output or received.
*/
```

(continued)

Listing 5.4   *(continued)*

```c
static void InitTable(void)   {

  register unsigned Index;

  /* Initialize the string table first */
  for (Index = 0; Index < TABLESIZE; Index++)
    code_value[Index] = -1;

  NumOfBits= MINBITS;
  NextCode = FIRSTCODE;
  MaxCode  = MAXCODEVAL(MINBITS);
}


/*
Decode a string from the string table, storing it in a buffer.
The buffer can then be output in reverse order by the expansion
program.
*/
static BYTE far *DecodeCodes(BYTE far *Buffer, unsigned Code)
{
   int Count = 0;

   while(Code >= FIRSTCODE )  {
      *Buffer++ = append_character[Code];
      Code = prefix_code[Code];
      if (Count++ >= TABLESIZE )  {
         printf("Error during code expansion\n");
         exit(ECorrupt);
      }
   }
   *Buffer = Code;
   return(Buffer);
}

static void ExpandFile (void)   {

   unsigned NewCode;
   unsigned OldCode;
   unsigned Character;
   BYTE far *Sp;                  /* decode stack stack pointer */

   ScanLine = 0;                  /* initialize where in raster image */
   Pixel = 0;                     /* to store expanded pixel data */
   memset(ExpandBuf,'\0',sizeof(ExpandBuf)); /* clear buffer */
   BytesLeftInBlock = 0;          /* bytes left in block just read */
   NextBitPos = EXPBUFBITS;       /* prime the pump for disk read */
   Character = getc(GIFFile);     /* read bits per pixel then throw away */
   InitTable();
```

```
    while ((NewCode = InCode()) != EOICODE)  {

        if (NewCode == CLEARCODE)  {/* clear string table */
            InitTable();
            OldCode = InCode();
            if (OldCode == EOICODE)
              break;
            Character = OldCode;
            OutPixel(OldCode);
            continue;
        }
        if (NewCode >= NextCode)  { /* check for special case */
            *decode_stack=Character;
            Sp=DecodeCodes(decode_stack+1,OldCode);
        }
        else
            Sp=DecodeCodes(decode_stack,NewCode);

        Character = *Sp;            /* output decoded string in reverse */
        while (Sp >= decode_stack)
          OutPixel(*Sp--);

        if (NextCode <= MaxCode) {  /* add to string table if not full */
                                    /* if full do not add anything */
            prefix_code[NextCode] = OldCode;
            append_character[NextCode++] = Character;
            if ((NextCode == MaxCode) && (NumOfBits < MAXBITS)) {
                MaxCode = MAXCODEVAL(++NumOfBits);
            }
        }
        OldCode=NewCode;
    }
}


static CompletionCode ReadGIFFileHdr (char *FileName, int Verbose)
{
    char   String[80];
    char *GIFStr = GIFHDRTAG;           /* GIF tag */
    struct GIFHeader GIFHeader;

    if (!strchr(FileName,'.'))  {       /* is there an ext ? */
        strcpy(String,FileName);        /* copy filename to buffer */
        FileName = String;              /* FileName now points at buffer */
        strcat(FileName,".gif");        /* if not add .gif ext */
    }
    /* try to open the GIF file */
    if ((GIFFile = fopen(FileName,"rb")) == NULL) {
        printf("GIF file: %s not found\n",FileName);
        return(EFileNotFound);
    }
```

(continued)

Listing 5.4 *(continued)*

```
   /* try to read the file header record */
   if (fread(&GIFHeader,sizeof(GIFHeader),1,GIFFile) != 1) {
      printf("Error reading GIF file header\n");
      fclose(GIFFile);
      return(EReadFileHdr);
   }
   /* check to make sure it's a GIF file */
   if (strncmp((char *)(&(GIFHeader.Hdr)),GIFStr,4) != 0)  {
      printf("Error not a GIF file\n");
      fclose(GIFFile);
      return(ENotGIFFile);
   }
   /* Read in the Logical Screen Descriptor */
   if (fread(&ScnDesc,sizeof(ScnDesc),1,GIFFile) != 1)  {
      printf("Error reading LSD\n");
      fclose(GIFFile);
      return(ECorrupt);
   }
   /* Yep, we've got a GIF file OK. Display info if requested */
   if (Verbose)  {
      memset(String,'\0',sizeof(String));
      memcpy(String,&(GIFHeader.Hdr),6);
      clrscr();
      printf("GIF Image Information for file: %s\n\n",FileName);
      printf("\tVersion: %s\n",String);
      printf("\tLogical Screen Width:  %d\n", ScnDesc.LogicalScreenWidth);
      printf("\tLogical Screen Height: %d\n", ScnDesc.LogicalScreenHeight);
      printf("\tPacked Field: 0x%Xd\n",ScnDesc.PackedField);
      printf("\tBackground Color Index: %d\n",ScnDesc.BackGroundIndex);
      printf("\tAspect Ratio: %d\n",ScnDesc.AspectRatio);
   }
   if ((ScnDesc.PackedField & GLOBALCOLORTBL) == 0)  {
      printf("Error no global color table in file\n");
      fclose(GIFFile);
      return(ECorrupt);
   }
   if ((ScnDesc.PackedField & 7) != 7)  {
      printf("Error only 256 color images supported\n");
      fclose(GIFFile);
      return(ECorrupt);
   }
   if (fread(&GlobalColorTbl,sizeof(GlobalColorTbl),1,GIFFile) != 1)  {
      printf("Error reading GCT\n");
      fclose(GIFFile);
      return(ECorrupt);
   }
   return(NoError);
}
```

```
/*
This function reads and displays the 256-color GIF file.
*/
void DisplayGIFFile (char *FileName, unsigned Verbose)
{
    int      Error, AChar;
    register unsigned Index;

    if (!AllocMem())                   /* alloc the required arrays */
      exit(ENoMemory);

    if ((Error = ReadGIFFileHdr(FileName,Verbose)) != NoError)
      exit(Error);

    /* Header has been read, now read image info */
    if (fread(&ImgDesc,sizeof(ImgDesc),1,GIFFile) != 1)  {
      SetTextMode();
      printf("Error reading ID\n");
      fclose(GIFFile);
      exit(ECorrupt);
    }
    if (Verbose)  {
      printf("\nImage Descriptor Information for file: %s\n\n",FileName);
      printf("\tImage Separator: %c\n",ImgDesc.ImageSeparator);
      printf("\tImage Left Position: %d\n", ImgDesc.ImageLeftPosition);
      printf("\tImage Top  Position: %d\n", ImgDesc.ImageTopPosition);
      printf("\tImage  Width: %d\n", ImgDesc.ImageWidth);
      printf("\tImage Height: %d\n", ImgDesc.ImageHeight);
      printf("\tPacked Field: 0x%Xd\n",ImgDesc.PackedField);
      printf("\nHit <Enter> to proceed - ^C to abort\n");
      getchar();                       /* wait for operator input */
    }

    if (ImgDesc.ImageSeparator != ',')  {
      SetTextMode();
      printf("Image separator expected\n");
      fclose(GIFFile);
      exit(ECorrupt);
    }

    if ((ImgDesc.PackedField & LOCALINTERLACEFLAG) != 0)  {
      SetTextMode();
      printf("Only non-interlaced images supported\n");
      fclose(GIFFile);
      exit(ECorrupt);
    }

    /* Check for VESA compliance */
    CheckForVESA();
```

(continued)

Listing 5.4 *(continued)*

```
    /* Select the appropriate video mode for display of image. */
    SelectVideoMode(ScnDesc.LogicalScreenWidth,
                   ScnDesc.LogicalScreenHeight,TRUE);


    /* Scale the color registers from 0..255 to 0..63 */
    for (Index = 0; Index < 256; Index++)  {
      GlobalColorTbl.Palette[Index].Red   >= 2;
      GlobalColorTbl.Palette[Index].Green >= 2;
      GlobalColorTbl.Palette[Index].Blue  >= 2;
    }
    SetAllColorRegs((ColorRegister *) &GlobalColorTbl);

    /* Proceed to unpack and display the GIF file */
    ExpandFile();

    /* Read the trailer of the file */
    AChar = getc(GIFFile);
    if ((AChar != ';') && (AChar != 0x21))  {
       SetTextMode();
       printf("Error reading trailer or multiple images in GIF file\n");
       fclose(GIFFile);
       exit(ECorrupt);
    }
    fclose(GIFFile);
    DeAllocMem();
}


/*
The following routines create a GIF file from the displayed
raster image and write it to disk.
*/


/*
Output a variable length code. This code packs the Code value into
the current number of bits in the CompressionBuf array. When a full
block (COMPBUFSIZE) has been accumulated it will be written to disk.
When FLUSHCODE is given, the data in CompressionBuf is written to the
disk in a somewhat smaller block.
*/

static CompletionCode OutCode(unsigned Code)  {

   register unsigned BitPos;
   register unsigned BytePos;
   register unsigned long MergeWord;

   BitPos = NextBitPos & 7;      /* bits used in current byte of buffer */
   BytePos= NextBitPos > 3;      /* byte in buffer with free bits */
```

```
    if (Code != FLUSHCODE)   {      /* no flush, just normal operation */
      if (BitPos == 0)    {         /* if buffer happens to be byte aligned */
        CompressionBuf[BytePos]   = Code;      /* store lower 8 bits of Code */
        CompressionBuf[BytePos+1] = Code > 8;  /* store upper bits of Code */
      }
      else   {                      /* not so lucky no byte alignment */
        MergeWord = (((unsigned long) Code) << BitPos) |
                  CompressionBuf[BytePos];
        CompressionBuf[BytePos]   = MergeWord;       /* store lower  bits */
        CompressionBuf[BytePos+1] = MergeWord > 8;  /* store middle bits */
        CompressionBuf[BytePos+2] = MergeWord > 16;/* store upper  bits */
      }
      NextBitPos += NumOfBits;            /* add in current code bit size */
      /*
      Now check to see if we have filled the buffer and must write it to
      the disk.
      */
      if (NextBitPos >= COMPBUFBITS)  { /* is the buffer full ? */
        putc(COMPBUFSIZE,GIFFile);      /* write the block size */
        if (fwrite(CompressionBuf,COMPBUFSIZE,1,GIFFile) != 1)
          return(EWrtScanLine);
        BytePos= NextBitPos > 3;        /* byte in buffer with free bits */
        BytePos -= COMPBUFSIZE;         /* calc # of bytes over COMPBUFSIZE */
        NextBitPos = (BytePos << 3) +   /* calc # of bits to carry over */
                  (NextBitPos & 7);
        /* Copy end of buffer to beginning */
        CompressionBuf[0] = CompressionBuf[COMPBUFSIZE];
        CompressionBuf[1] = CompressionBuf[COMPBUFSIZE+1];
        CompressionBuf[2] = CompressionBuf[COMPBUFSIZE+2];
      }
    }
    else   {                            /* flush code received */
      if (BitPos != 0)                  /* if we have started using new byte */
        BytePos++;                      /* must include it in final block */
      putc(BytePos,GIFFile);            /* write the block size */
      if (fwrite(CompressionBuf,BytePos,1,GIFFile) != 1)
          return(EWrtScanLine);         /* and the block */
    }
    return(NoError);
}


/*
This function gets one pixel of information from the raster image
each time it is called. It remembers its location in the image each
time it is called.
*/
static unsigned GetByte(void)   {

  unsigned RetChar;
```

(continued)

Listing 5.4   *(continued)*

```
  RetChar = GetPixelValue(Pixel+TheImageLeft,ScanLine+TheImageTop);
  Pixel++;
  if (Pixel == TheImageWidth)  {
    Pixel = 0;
    ScanLine++;
    if (ScanLine == TheImageHeight)
      RetChar = EOF;
  }
  return(RetChar);
}


/*
This is the hashing routine. This code probes with the hash at
Index to see if either the entry is empty or if it is filled with
the data we are looking for. If the initial hash Index is
occupied, we will try again for an empty Index by incrementing.
*/
static int FindMatch(unsigned Code, unsigned Character)  {

  register unsigned Index, Offset;

  Offset = 1;
  Index = (Code ^ (Character << HASHING_SHIFT)) % TABLESIZE;

  while(TRUE) {
    if (code_value[Index] == -1)      /* if entry is empty return Index */
      return(Index);
    if (prefix_code[Index] == Code &&/* if entry is our data return also */
       append_character[Index] == Character)
      return(Index);
    Index += Offset;                      /* not empty nor our data so we */
    Offset += 2;                          /* must probe again */
    if (Index >= TABLESIZE)               /* must keep Index within bounds */
      Index -= TABLESIZE;
  }
}


/*
This function performs the actual LZW compression of the raster data.
See text for details of its operation.
*/
static void CompressFile(void)  {

  register unsigned Code;
  register int Character;
  register unsigned Index;

  ScanLine = 0;                           /* initialize where in raster image */
  Pixel = 0;                              /* to fetch pixel data from */
```

```
    InitTable();                              /* initialize variables */
    memset(CompressionBuf,'\0',sizeof(CompressionBuf)); /* clear buffer */
    NextBitPos = 0;                           /* initialize to start at buf beg */
    putc(BITSPERPIXEL,GIFFile);               /* output initial # of bits used */
    OutCode(CLEARCODE);                       /* output clear code */

    Code=GetByte();                           /* get first pixel of data */

    /*
    This is the main compression loop. When the table is full we try
    to increment the code size.
    */
    while((Character = GetByte()) != EOF)   {
       Index=FindMatch(Code,Character);
       if (code_value[Index] != -1)
          /*
          When we get here, Code/Character combo has been found in
          the table. We must fetch the Code value for this combo.
          */
          Code = code_value[Index];
       else {
          /*
          When we get here, the Code/Character combo in not in the
          table so we must add it. NextCode is assigned to this combo.
          */
          OutCode(Code);                            /* send out current code */
          code_value[Index]      = NextCode++;   /* add to table */
          prefix_code[Index]     = Code;
          append_character[Index] = Character;
          /*
          If the next Code to go out will exceed the number of bits we
          are currently using, we must bump to the next larger number
          of bits.
          */
          if ((NextCode-1) == MaxCode) {/* next code needs more bits ? */
             if (NumOfBits < MAXBITS) { /* any more bits to use ? */
                MaxCode = MAXCODEVAL(++NumOfBits);  /* yes, add one more */
             }
             else {                     /* no more bits to use */
                OutCode(CLEARCODE);      /* output clear code and flush */
                InitTable();            /* the string table and start */
             }                          /* over with MINBITS again. */
          }
          Code = Character;
       }
    }
    /* Finish up the rest of the file output */
    OutCode(Code);                      /* Output the final code */
    OutCode(EOICODE);                   /* Output the End of Info code */
    OutCode(FLUSHCODE);                 /* Flush the compressed data to disk */
}
```

(continued)

Listing 5.4   *(continued)*

```
/*
This function opens the GIF file for output and writes the required
GIF header, the Logical Screen Descriptor, the palette of 256 colors
which make up the Global Color Table and the image descriptor. The file
is then ready for the LZW compressed image data.
*/
static CompletionCode WriteGIFHdr(char *FileName,
                          unsigned ScreenWidth,  unsigned ScreenHeight,
                          unsigned ImageLeftPos, unsigned ImageTopPos,
                          unsigned ImageWidth,   unsigned ImageHeight,
                          unsigned BackGround,   unsigned Aspect)   {

  char    String[80];
  char    *GIFStr = GIFHDRTAG;            /* GIF tag */
  BYTE    PackedF;
  register unsigned Index;

  if (!strchr(FileName,'.'))             /* is there an ext ? */
  {                                      /* if not ... */
     strcpy(String,FileName);            /* copy filename to buffer */
     FileName = String;                  /* FileName now points at buffer */
     strcat(FileName,".gif");            /* add .gif ext */
  }
  /* attempt to open the file for binary writing */
  if ((GIFFile = fopen(FileName,"wb")) == NULL) {
     SetTextMode();
     printf("Could not open output GIF file\n");
     return (EWrtOutFile);
  }

  /* now write the GIF tag to the file */
  if (fwrite(GIFStr,strlen(GIFStr),1,GIFFile) != 1) {
     SetTextMode();
     printf("Error writing GIF file header\n");
     fclose(GIFFile);
     return(EWrtFileHdr);
  }
  /* Initialize the logical screen descriptor (LSD) */
  ScnDesc.LogicalScreenWidth  = ScreenWidth;
  ScnDesc.LogicalScreenHeight = ScreenHeight;

  /*
  Indicate a global color table, 8-bit color, 6 bits per primary
  color and that colors are not sorted.
  */
  PackedF = 0;
  PackedF |= GLOBALCOLORTBL;
  PackedF |= ((BITSPERCOLOR-1) << 4);
  PackedF |= (GLOBALCOLORTBLSIZE-1);
  ScnDesc.PackedField = PackedF;
```

```
ScnDesc.BackGroundIndex = BackGround;
ScnDesc.AspectRatio = Aspect;

/* now write the LSD to the file */
if (fwrite(&ScnDesc,sizeof(ScnDesc),1,GIFFile) != 1) {
   SetTextMode();
   printf("Error writing LSD to file\n");
   fclose(GIFFile);
   return(EWrtOutFile);
}

/* Read all 256 color registers from the DAC */
GetAllColorRegs((ColorRegister *) &GlobalColorTbl);

/* Scale the color registers from 0..63 to 0..255 */
for (Index = 0; Index < 256; Index++)  {
  GlobalColorTbl.Palette[Index].Red    <<= 2;
  GlobalColorTbl.Palette[Index].Green  <<= 2;
  GlobalColorTbl.Palette[Index].Blue   <<= 2;
}

/* now write the global color table (GCT) to the file */
if (fwrite(&GlobalColorTbl,sizeof(GlobalColorTbl),1,GIFFile) != 1) {
   SetTextMode();
   printf("Error writing GCT to file\n");
   fclose(GIFFile);
   return(EWrtOutFile);
}
/*
Build the image descriptor without any local color table image
is written noninterlaced
*/
ImgDesc.ImageSeparator    = ',';
ImgDesc.ImageLeftPosition = ImageLeftPos;
ImgDesc.ImageTopPosition  = ImageTopPos;
ImgDesc.ImageWidth        = ImageWidth;
ImgDesc.ImageHeight       = ImageHeight;
ImgDesc.PackedField       = 0;

/* now write the image descriptor (ID) to the file */
if (fwrite(&ImgDesc,sizeof(ImgDesc),1,GIFFile) != 1) {
   SetTextMode();
   printf("Error writing ID to file\n");
   fclose(GIFFile);
   return(EWrtOutFile);
}
/* If we get here, all is well */
return(NoError);
}
```

(continued)

Listing 5.4 *(continued)*

```c
/*
This function writes a GIF file to disk from the raster image currently
being displayed on the monitor.
*/
void WriteGIFFile (char *FileName,
                   unsigned ScreenWidth, unsigned ScreenHeight,
                   unsigned ImageWidth,  unsigned ImageHeight,
                   unsigned ImageTop,    unsigned ImageLeft)  {

    int Error;
    struct TheTrailer ATrailer;

    if (!AllocMem())
      exit(ENoMemory);

    /* write out GIF header and palette */
    if ((Error = WriteGIFHdr(FileName,  ScreenWidth, ScreenHeight,
                             ImageLeft, ImageTop,
                             ImageWidth,ImageHeight,0,0)) != NoError)
      exit(Error);

    /* Record the parameters globally */
    TheImageTop    = ImageTop;
    TheImageLeft   = ImageLeft;
    TheImageWidth  = ImageWidth;
    TheImageHeight = ImageHeight;

    CompressFile();            /* compress the image data */

    /* Finish up by writing a trailer to the GIF file */
    ATrailer.Length = 0;
    ATrailer.Trailer = ';';

    /* now write the trailer to the file */
    if (fwrite(&ATrailer,sizeof(ATrailer),1,GIFFile) != 1) {
      SetTextMode();
      printf("Error writing trailer to the file\n");
      fclose(GIFFile);
      exit(EWrtOutFile);
    }

    /* file has been written, prepare to close up shop */
    fclose(GIFFile);           /* close the completed GIF file */
    DeAllocMem();              /* free up the memory */
}
```

What follows is a verbal description of the "grammar" of the GIF protocol. A pictorial version of this grammar can be found in the GIF specification. All italicized items refer to an actual block type defined in the GIF specification. We itemize all GIF blocks in Figure 5.7.

A GIF data stream is made up of, first, a single required "*GIF header*" block, followed by a single required instance of a "*Logical Screen Descriptor*" (LSD), optionally followed by a single "*Global Color Table*" (GCT), followed by zero or more occurrences of image data records, and finally terminated with a single required "*GIF Trailer*." Image data records consist of either a graphics block or a special purpose block. A graphics block is made up of an

1. Header Block

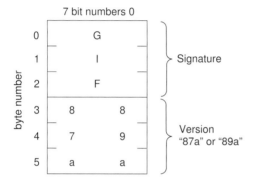

2. Logical Screen Descriptor (LSD) block

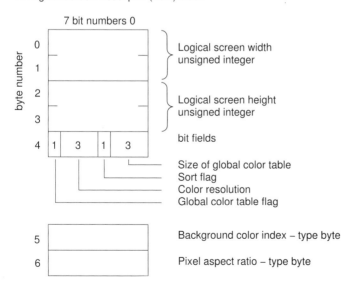

Figure 5.7 GIF File Structure Blocks   *(continued)*

3. Global and Local Color Table blocks

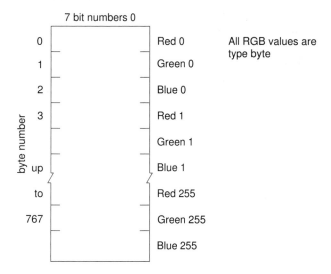

4. Image Descriptor (ID) block

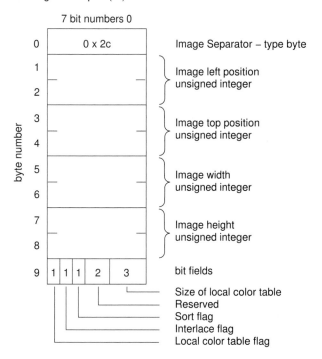

Figure 5.7   *(continued)*

optional "*Graphics Control Extension*" (GCE) followed by a mandatory graphics rendering block. A graphics rendering block contains either a table-based image or a "*Plain Text Extension*" (PTE). A table-based image block consists of an "*Image Descriptor*" (ID), an optional "*Local Color Table*" (LCT), and the mandatory image data compressed in LZW format. A special purpose block is either an "*Application Extension*" (AE) or a "*Comment Extension*" (CE).

5. Table-Based Image Data block

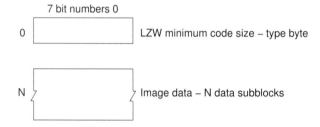

6. Graphics Control Extension block

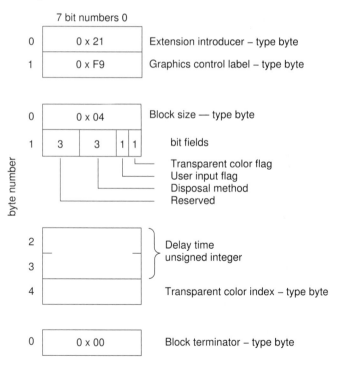

Figure 5.7 *(continued)*

(continued)

7. Comment Extension block

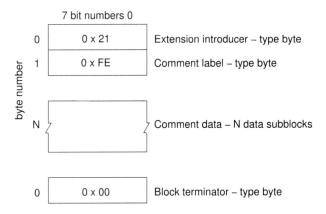

7 bit numbers 0

byte number		
0	0 x 21	Extension introducer – type byte
1	0 x FE	Comment label – type byte
N		Comment data – N data subblocks
0	0 x 00	Block terminator – type byte

8. Plain Text Extension block

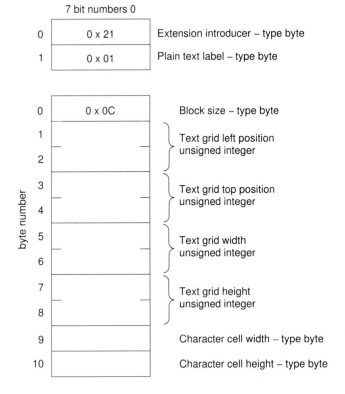

7 bit numbers 0

byte number		
0	0 x 21	Extension introducer – type byte
1	0 x 01	Plain text label – type byte
0	0 x 0C	Block size – type byte
1		Text grid left position unsigned integer
2		
3		Text grid top position unsigned integer
4		
5		Text grid width unsigned integer
6		
7		Text grid height unsigned integer
8		
9		Character cell width – type byte
10		Character cell height – type byte

Figure 5.7   *(continued)*

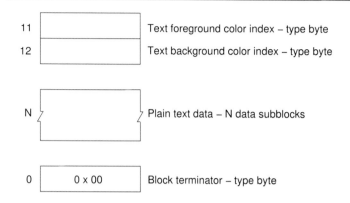

11   Text foreground color index – type byte

12   Text background color index – type byte

N   Plain text data – N data subblocks

0   0 x 00   Block terminator – type byte

9. Application Extension block

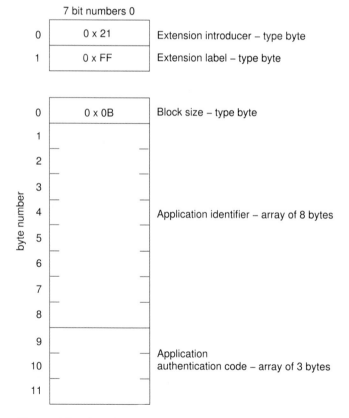

7 bit numbers 0

0   0 x 21   Extension introducer – type byte

1   0 x FF   Extension label – type byte

0   0 x 0B   Block size – type byte

byte number

4   Application identifier – array of 8 bytes

Application
authentication code – array of 3 bytes

Figure 5.7   *(continued)*

(continued)

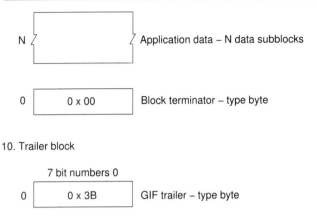

N — Application data – N data subblocks

0 — 0 x 00 — Block terminator – type byte

10. Trailer block

7 bit numbers 0

0 — 0 x 3B — GIF trailer – type byte

Figure 5.7 *(continued)*

As indicated, the first required block in a GIF data stream is the "GIF header." As you can see, it consists of 6 bytes of character data. The signature portion should always contain the uppercase ASCII character string "GIF" and the version should either be the three-character string "87a" or "89a," as previously discussed. By reading (or attempting to read) the GIF header, a GIF reader program can determine if the file is indeed a GIF file and whether it can process and display the image contained within it.

A "Logical Screen Descriptor" (LSD) block must always immediately follow the header block. The purpose of the information within this block is to define the attributes of the display onto which the image will be rendered. The Logical Screen Width within the LSD defines how many pixels wide the logical screen must be to display the image. The Logical Screen Height defines the height of the logical screen. Byte 4 of the LSD contains a packed bit field that contains four different items of information. The most significant bit of the byte, if set, indicates the presence of a "Global Color Table" (GCT) in the file immediately following the LSD. If a GCT is present, the background index entry in the LSD is valid and indicates the color index value to be used as the background color. The next 3 bits indicate the "Color Resolution" available in the image. This is the number of bits per primary color minus 1. In our case, this value is always 6 minus 1, or 5, because the VGA/SuperVGA DAC utilizes 6 bits per primary color, and this is how the image was created. The next bit of the bit field is the "Sort Flag." If set, it indicates the GCT is sorted in order of decreasing color importance. In other words, the colors that are used more frequently in the image are located at the beginning of the GCT, while less frequent colors are stored toward the end. If this bit is cleared, no sorting of the color in the GCT has taken place. The final 3 bits of the bit field are called the "Size of the Global Color Table" and are used to calculate the number of entries in the GCT. The number of entries is the number 2 raised to the Size of the GCT plus 1 power. For 256-color images, the Size of the GCT would be 7, and 2^8 (7 plus 1) would be 256.

Byte 5, the "Background color index" has already been mentioned. You should note, however, that if the GCT flag is cleared, indicating no GCT in the GIF file, this entry is meaningless.

The final entry in the LSD is the "Pixel Aspect Ratio." This is an approximation of the aspect ratio of a pixel in the original image. This aspect ratio is calculated by dividing a pixel's width by its height. If this value is zero, no pixel aspect ratio information is given. If a nonzero value is given, it indicates the aspect ratio of a pixel over the range 4:1 to 1:4 in increments of 1/64th. Please see the GIF specification for additional information. The GIF function library of this chapter always writes this field as a zero.

If a GCT is present in a GIF file, it will be next in the data stream. A GCT is a series of 3-byte RGB values representing the color contained in the image. A GCT is used by images that do not have a Local Color Table (LCT) associated with them. A GCT is also required for use with "Plain Text Extensions." The format of an LCT and a GCT are the same. The presence of an LCT in the GIF file always overrides the GCT. The LCT, however, has a scope that is limited to a single image. When an LCT goes out of scope, a GCT (if present) again regains its prominence. The total size of the GCT in bytes is 3 times 2 raised to the Size of GCT plus 1 power. For 256-color images with 256 GCT entries, the GCT is 768 bytes in length.

Each image in a GIF data stream is made up of an "Image Descriptor" (ID), an optional LCT, and the image data. You must be able to display each image within the logical screen defined in the LSD. The contents of the ID are contained in a 10-byte block. The ID contains information necessary to understand and process the image data that follows it. The first ID field is the "image separator," which always has the value of 0x2C, the ASCII code for a comma. This value is used when parsing a GIF file to validate the presence of more than one ID and therefore more than one image within the file. The fields "Image left position," "Image top position," "Image width," and "Image height" are coordinates within the logical screen and are expressed in pixels. Byte 9 of the ID is another packed bit field. It contains information about the LCT that is analogous to that contained in the LSD for the GCT and explained above. The only new item is the single bit called the "Interlace Flag." If this bit is set, it indicates the image is interlaced. An interlaced image is one that is displayed in four passes. Interlaced images allow the general content of the image to be ascertained immediately during display by staggering raster lines over the whole display screen. As the four passes over the image are made, more and more of the image becomes visible. Interlacing is useful when images are displayed as they are being received over a modem or network. Instead of being displayed as sequential raster lines of image data starting at the top of the screen (this is how noninterlaced images are displayed), raster lines are displayed in the following order:

Pass One —every eighth raster line, starting at line 0
Pass Two —every eighth raster line, starting at line 4
Pass Three —every fourth raster line, starting at line 2
Pass Four —every second raster line, starting at line 1

After all four of these passes are made, the complete image is present on the display. If the Interlace Flag is cleared, the image is considered noninterlaced and displayed sequentially. Finally, two bits within this bit field, bits 3 and 4, are reserved for future use.

The next GIF block type contains the LZW compressed image data. This is called a "Table-Based Image Data" block. This block consists of a single byte of data indicating the LZW minimum code size in bits (in the case of 8-bit pixel data, the minimum code size is 9 bits) followed by whatever number of data subblocks are required to contain the LZW compressed image data. These subblocks are at most 256 bytes long, with the first byte being the number of bytes within the subblock. How LZW is deblocked and decoded will be the subject of a later discussion. The image data is in the form of color index values that must be in range of the active color table, either an LCT or GCT. It is the color index values that the LZW algorithm compresses.

A "Graphics Control Extension" (GCE) block controls the processing of the Table-Based Image Data or a Plain Text Extension, which directly follows it in the data stream. As shown in Figure 5.7, this block is of fixed format. Four bytes of data make up the content of the GCE. The first field of consequence is a packed bit field. Five of the 8 least significant bits of this bit field are currently utilized. Bits 3 through 5 control the "disposal method" for the GIF image; that is, how the display device is to be treated after the image is displayed. Four different disposal methods are defined. The value stored in the bit field determines which method is to be used, as follows:

Value	Function
0	Do nothing.
1	Leave the image in place on the display.
2	Repaint the portion of the display screen used to display the GIF image with the background color.
3	Restore the portion of the display screen used to display the GIF image to the content it had before the image was displayed.

Bit number 1 of the bit field is referred to as the "User input flag." If it is cleared, no user input is expected, so processing can continue immediately. If set, however, further processing will be suspended until user input is detected or a delay time has expired, whichever comes first. The delay time is specified in intervals of one-hundredth of a second. A value of zero for "Delay Time" turns the delay off.

The final bit in the bit field, bit 0, is the "Transparent color flag." If set, a "Transparent color index" is provided in byte 4 of the GCE. If this flag is cleared, byte 4 is a "don't care." When a transparency index is given, any pixel value that maps to that index is to remain unchanged on the display. Said another way, the color at every pixel position on the display of that index is not to be overwritten by the GIF image data but is to retain its original value. A single byte of zeros terminates the GCE subblock. This marker is referred to as a "block terminator" within the GIF specification.

A "Comment Extension" (CE) block is used to store textual information pertaining to a GIF image that is not itself a part of the graphics data. See the following discussion on the "Plain Text Extension" for an explanation of how to render textual information as part of the graphics image. A CE block can contain any noncontrol, nongraphics information. CE blocks can be ignored by a GIF reader or can be saved for later display or processing. The subblocks of comment data are terminated with a block terminator.

A "Plain Text Extension" (PTE) block is used to render textual information in graphics form on the display device, possibly over an existing graphics image. Text is taken from the plain text data subblocks a character at a time and rendered as 7-bit ASCII characters. Text is rendered onto a text grid defined by the PTE. The text grid contains an integral number of character cells of the specified width and height. The text grid itself is given a top and left edge position that locates where the text will be displayed. The text will be displayed from left to right and top to bottom, until either no more text is available or the text grid is fully occupied. A PTE requires a GCT because the text's foreground and background colors as specified in the PTE are in terms of indices into the GCT.

The final block type specified in the "89a" version of the GIF specification is called an "Application Extension" (AE). This block contains application-defined data. Using AEs, an application program can store within a GIF file any information it requires, in a manner consistent with the GIF specification. The ubiquitous "FRACTINT" program produced by the "Stone Soup Group," for example, uses AEs to store all of the information necessary to recreate the fractal image contained in a GIF file. The stored information includes the fractal type and all of the various parameters necessary to fully recreate the fractal. Normal GIF readers would skip the AE block and just display the fractal image in the GIF file. When the GIF file is loaded back into FRACTINT, which understands its AEs, the program can resume where the fractal creation left off. This is really quite handy.

The application-specific data contained within an AE depends on the application. The format of this data is not constrained by the GIF specification and is left up to the designer of the application program. Two fields within the AE are controlled by the GIF specification. The first field, the "Application identifier" (AI), is an 8-byte array of ASCII characters used to identify the application program that owns this AE. Application programs are asked to register their AI with CompuServe (in the PICS forum) in an attempt to make each AI unique. A second field in the AE is for a 3-byte "Application authentication code" (AAC). The contents of this field is used to further authenticate the AI. This can be a fixed tag or some kind of algorithmic process that further verifies that this AE truly belongs to an application program.

The final GIF block type is called the "Trailer block," and it indicates the end of the GIF file/data stream. This required block is a single byte in length and always contains the value 0x3B, the ASCII code for a semicolon. A GIF data stream is not properly formatted if it is not terminated with a Trailer block.

LZW Compression and Expansion

The preceding discussion has described the format of GIF files including the various block types and their required sequencing. With that behind us, we are halfway through the information necessary to completely understand GIF files. What is left is the discussion of LZW data compression. For many people, understanding LZW is difficult, and for most people, understanding LZW at the bit level is completely unnecessary. If you want to understand the operation of this clever algorithm in detail, read the following discussion.

LZW, like all data compression methods, takes advantage of repetition in the data to be compressed. Compression occurs when a block of repetitive data is identified and replaced by some symbol or symbol sequence that uses fewer bits than the original data. The size of the original data divided by the size of the compressed data results in a number referred to as the "compression ratio." To a point, the higher the compression ratio achieved, the better. A trade-off occurs with the amount of processing required to obtain the compression. For imaging applications, LZW compression/expansion is a good compromise between processing time and the compression achieved.

Until this point, we have referred to the compression algorithm used in GIF files as LZW. This is and is not entirely correct. Actually, the standard LZW algorithm is enhanced by the addition of:

1. Variable length output codes
2. The incorporation of a unique CLEARCODE code

Variable length output codes help to increase the compression ratio available with LZW compression. Please recall that compression occurs when a repetitive string of data is replaced by a single output code. The fewer the bits in the output code, the higher the compression. Initially, the LZW compressor uses 9-bit output codes, resulting in 512 unique string codes. Nine bits are needed because the pixel data being compressed is 8 bits wide. The additional bit makes 256 codes available for representation of strings of 8-bit pixel data. As more than 512 unique strings are identified in the input data stream, the number of bits used for the output codes is increased to 10 bits, then to 11 bits when needed, and finally to 12 bits. When the output codes reach 12 bits in width, 4,096 total string codes are available. For variable width output codes to work during LZW compression, the expansion process must be in tight synchronization and make the bit width transitions at exactly the same time when decoding its coded input data stream. If the two processes get out of sync, the expanded output data will look nothing like the data feed to the compressor; and hence the process will fail.

The other addition to LZW is the incorporation of a mechanism to clear the table of strings (referred to as the "string table," oddly enough) when no more bits are available to increase the output code size. As the number of bits used for the output codes increases from 9 to 12, the compression falls off as noted. When the 4,095th code is used, no more output codes are available with which to encode new strings of pixel data. These new strings would then be placed directly in the output data stream with no compression at all. To remedy the loss of compression, the compressor will output a CLEARCODE to the output code stream and then clear its string table. The process of building the string table from the input data stream then starts over at that point; no history of its previous content remains. An analogous operation occurs during the expansion process. The expander, on reception of the CLEARCODE, clears its string table at exactly the same position in the data stream that the compressor did. The expander then starts building the new string table again in synchronization with the compressor. When the terms LZW compression and expansion are used in the remainder of this discussion, they shall refer to the standard LZW algorithm plus these extensions.

LZW Compression. The LZW algorithm uses a string table during compression to keep track of strings of data in the input data stream and the code values used to represent them. We will defer our detailed discussion of the implementation and maintenance of the string table for a short time. For now, you just need to understand that a string table entry consists of a code and a character that represents a string of data. LZW compression proceeds as follows.

The first byte from the input data stream is read into the code variable. A while loop is then entered, each time reading a new byte of input data into the character variable. This code/character combination is looked up in the string table. If it is found, the code variable is updated with the code value representing this code/character combination and the process continues by reading the next byte of input data. If the code/character combination was not found in the string table, the value of code is sent to the output coded data stream and the code/character combination is added to the string table and assigned the next available output code value. The code variable is then set equal to the previous character value and the process continues. This loop repeats until no more input data is available for compression. At that time, the final code value is sent to the output coded data stream and the EOICODE follows it.

The only thing missing from this basic description is the discussion of the dynamic selection of output code bit widths. Every time a code/character combination (a new string) is added to the string table, it is assigned the next possible output code value. Following each of these assignments, a check is made to see if the output code just assigned is the maximum code value expressible in the current number of output bits. If it is the maximum code value, the compressor will check to see if the maximum number of output bits (12) is currently being used. If more output bits are available, the number of bits is increased by one and a new maximum code value is calculated. If, however, the output bits width is already at the maximum, a CLEARCODE is issued to the output coded data stream, the string table is reinitialized, and the process begins anew.

Finally, the code values sent to the output coded data stream must be bit-packed together, byte-blocked into the blocks required by the GIF specification, and then written to the output file or data stream. This is where some complex bit twiddling comes into play. This process is not trivial because the codes output by the compressor must first be masked to the correct output bit width (from 9 to 12 bits) before insertion in the output data stream at exactly the next free bit (not byte) position. See the function "OutCode" in the listing for the implementation details.

LZW Expansion. LZW expansion is just slightly more complex than LZW compression. The beauty and magic of the LZW algorithm is that the string table does not have to be passed from the compressor to the expander for the compressed data to be correctly expanded. The string table is built during the expansion process from the input coded data stream. This is possible because the compressor always outputs the string and character components of a coded value before the coded value is used in the data stream. The problem here is that a single special case exists in the LZW compression algorithm where certain strings of repeating characters cause the compressor to output a code value before the expander has had a chance to define it. Fortunately, since only a single special case exists, which is easily identifiable by the expander, an easy fix is possible. This condition is identified when the expander receives a code for which it does not yet have a string table entry. In this case, the expander expands the last valid code it received and appends the current character to the end of the expanded string. This combination is then entered into the string table and assigned the next code value, which is always equal to the undefined code that was previously received and that touched off the special case processing. With the special case noted, the basic expansion process moves ahead as follows.

The first code is read from the input coded data stream and sent directly to the output data stream. While there is coded input data available, the expander reads the new code value. If the new code is not yet defined in the string table (the special case), the expander builds an output string defined by old code and appends the current character onto it. If the new code was in the string table, the expander builds an output string defined by this new code. In either case, it outputs the string to the output data stream (in our case, it writes the pixel values to the display). The current character is then assigned the first character of the string just output. The old code and character are then added to the string table. The old code is assigned the value of the new code. This process continues until an EOICODE is found in the input coded data stream. Just as in the compressor, as each entry is made into the string table, a check is made on the code value assigned to it. If this code is the maximum code allowed for the current output bit width and more bits are available, the number of bits is increased by one and a new maximum code value is calculated. When a CLEARCODE is received by the expander, the string table is reinitialized and the process continues as before. *Note*: If the expander realizes that more bits are required for the input coded values but no more are available, it does not clear the string table of its own accord. Instead, it waits for the compressor to tell it what to do with the reception of the CLEARCODE. That way, the compressor and expander remain in synchronization.

The "InCode" function utilized by the expander performs a complimentary and analogous operation to the "OutCode" function described previously. InCode deblocks the coded image data from the input data stream and returns a code of the appropriate bit width to the expander. As the expander increases the bit width of the coded values, the bit width of the code returned by InCode also increases. Again, major amounts of bit manipulation are required to make this happen. See the listing.

Output Code Assignments. Throughout this discussion we have made many references to assigning codes to strings of data values. The codes that are assigned depend on the domain of the data being compressed. In our specific case, 8-bit pixel data is being compressed, which has a range of values from 0 to 255. Each single pixel value (values 0..255) is assigned a code equal to its value when it is placed in the string table. As a result, the first 256 code values are used up. Since the compression process begins using 9-bit codes, we initially have 512 code values at our disposal (0..511). Of these, the first 256 are already assigned as discussed. LZW requires two special code values for its use. These are the CLEARCODE, which is assigned a value of 256, and EOICODE, which is assigned a value of 257. The first code that can be assigned to a string of data will be 258. Therefore, 254 9-bit output codes are available for assignment to strings before the bit width must be increased.

String Table Implementation and Maintenance. The string table in this implementation is not a single entity, as has been implied throughout this discussion, but rather three associated arrays of values. These arrays are the "prefix_code" of type unsigned integer, the "append_character" array of type byte, and the "code_value" array of type integer. These three arrays interact to form the string table required for LZW compression and expansion. Throughout the remainder of this discussion, whenever we use the term "string table," we are referring to one or more of these arrays.

As discussed, all entries within the string table are in the form of a prefix_code (representing some previously compressed string of characters) and an append_character (a character that, when appended onto the end of the string defined by a prefix_code, makes a unique string and therefore a new string table entry). The code_value assigned to this new string table entry will be used to access this code/character combination. When the string table is initialized with a call to the "InitTable" function, all code_value entries are set equal to -1, indicating the entries are empty and available for use. During LZW compression, a hash function is used to determine if a specified code/character combination is contained within the string table. The function "FindMatch" performs the hashing. This function will return with either an index value that points to an empty string table entry found via the hash, or an index value that indicates the code/character combination searched for is already in the string table. If the code/character combination pre-existed, the code_value at the returned index is the code assigned to this string. If the code/character was not in the string table, then it is inserted at the returned index position as follows:

```
code_value[Index]       = NextCode++;
prefix_code[Index]      = Code;
append_character[Index] = Character;
```

You can see how the three associated arrays are used together to form the classic LZW string table.

During LZW expansion, only the "prefix_code" and "append_character" arrays are used for the string table. The "code_value" portion of the string table is not required because of the way the expansion process works. During expansion, the string table entries are added in strictly sequential order. That is, each code/character combination is added at the next empty slot in the string table and is indexed by the newly assigned code value.

The real work in the expansion process is performed by the "DecodeCodes" function. This function traverses the string table from prefix_code to prefix_code, building the string of append_characters that were represented by the initial code value passed to it. Expansion occurs as each code value is replaced by all of the code values it represented. This uncompressed string of codes (pixel values) is then written to the display in reverse order. The ordering is reversed because the first compressed value was expanded last. When the data is written out in reverse order, it then occurs in the order it was originally compressed in. This concept takes a little time to understand, so think about it while looking at the code for the "DecodeCodes" function.

The three arrays used for the string table are dynamically allocated within the "AllocMem" function. You must call the function "DeAllocMem" on program termination to free up the memory used by these arrays. Both the compression and expansion processes allocate and free these arrays; they are not allocated once and shared.

Overall GIF Function Library Operation

Due to the complexity of the functions contained in the GIF function library, we provide the following pseudocode to help make their operation clear. The pseudocode for the "WriteGIF-File" function (GIF file compression) and all of its required support functions appears first, followed by the pseudocode for the "DisplayGIFFile" (GIF file expansion) function and its support functions. Quoted items are function names within one of the libraries provided in this book.

Function WriteGIFFile

This function attempts to write a GIF file from the raster image currently being displayed on the computer's monitor. Only 256-color, noninterlaced GIF files containing a Global Color Table can be produced by this code.

```
Begin
  Allocate memory for the string table using "AllocMem"
  Write out an appropriate GIF file header by calling "WriteGIFHdr"
  Compress the image on the display in GIF format by calling "CompressFile"
  Write a trailer to the GIF file
  Close the GIF file
  Free up all allocated memory by calling "DeAllocMem"
End
```

Function WriteGIFHdr

This function opens the GIF file for output and writes the required GIF header, the Logical Screen Descriptor, the palette of 256 colors that makes up the Global Color Table, and the Image Descriptor. The file is then ready for the LZW compressed image data.

```
Begin
  Open specified file for binary write
  Write the GIF header to the file
  Build a Logical Screen Descriptor structure for the file
  Write the LSD to the file
  Read all 256 color register values from the DAC into the Global Color Table structure
  Scale values from 0..63 to 0.255
  Write the Global Color Table to the file
  Build an Image Descriptor for the file
  Write the ID to the file
End
```

Function CompressFile

This function performs the actual LZW compression of the raster data that is read directly from the computer's display.

```
Begin
  Initialize program variables
  Initialize string table by calling "InitTable"
  Output the bits/pixel value of 8 to the file
  Output the CLEARCODE to the output file using "OutCode"
  Get byte of pixel data into code variable
```

```
Do
  Get next byte of pixel data into character variable
  If not EOF then
    Search string table for code/character match using "FindMatch"
    If string in table then
      Code is code_value[Index] from table
    Else {code/character string not in string table}
      Output code to the output file using "OutCode"
      Assign next available code to this new string
      Put code/character string into string table at Index
      If output code requires more bits
        If more bits are available
          Bump number of bits used for output by one
        Else
          Output CLEARCODE to output file using "OutCode"
          Reinitialize string table using "InitTable"
        EndIf
      EndIF
      Code is now character
    EndIf
  Else
    break
  EndIf
EndDo
Output final code to output file using "OutCode"
Output EOICODE to output file using "OutCode"
Flush output file to disk by outputting FLUSHCODE to output file using "OutCode"
End
```

Function FindMatch

This is the hashing function. This code probes with a hash into the string table to see if the hashed entry is empty or if it is occupied. If the entry found with the hash is occupied, but not with the data we are looking for, then we will try again to find an empty slot by offsetting our search from the calculated hash value. An empty entry or an entry that contains our data will satisfy our search.

```
Begin
  Calculate hash index from code/character values passed in
  Do
    If entry in string table at hash index is empty
      return index
    EndIf
    If entry in string table at hash index is the code/character data
      return index
    EndIf
    Bump index and offset to probe string table again
    Force hash index to within the bounds of the string table.
  EndDo
End
```

Function OutCode

This function outputs a variable length code to the GIF file. This function packs the code value of the current number of bits into the compression buffer. When a full block of compressed data has been accumulated, it will be written to the disk file. When FLUSHCODE is detected, the data in the compression buffer is written to the disk in a somewhat smaller block.

```
Begin
  Calculate bit and byte position of code insertion in current bit stream
  If code to be output is not FLUSHCODE then
    If the code insertion point is byte aligned
      Insert the 8 LSBs of code into compression buffer at byte position
      Insert the 8 MSBs of code into compression buffer at byte position + 1
    Else {insertion point is not byte aligned—normal case}
      Create 32-bit merge word to merge code with data stream
      Merge 24 bits of merge word at byte position
    EndIf
    Add the current code size to next bit position
    If compression buffer is full or over full then
      Write buffer size to output file
      Write compression buffer to output file
      Adjust next insertion point because number of bits in compression buffer may have
        exceeded that just written to disk.
      Move extra bits past end of compression buffer to start of buffer
    EndIf
  Else {FLUSHCODE received}
    Adjust byte position by one if bits in next byte have been written
    Write size of final block of data in compression buffer to disk file
    Write valid compression buffer data to disk file
  EndIf
  Return no error status
End
```

The following pseudocode sequences describe the operation of the "DisplayGIFFile" function and its subordinates. These are the functions that read a GIF file and expand it for display on the computer monitor.

Function DisplayGIFFile

This function attempts to read and display the specified GIF file. Only 256-color, noninterlaced, 8-bit-per-pixel images can be displayed. Additionally, the GIF file must contain a Global Color Table for this code to work.

```
Begin
  Allocate memory for the string table using "AllocMem"
  Read GIF file header using "ReadGIFFileHdr"
  Read Image Descriptor from file
  If verbose mode then
    Display all ID information on the screen
  EndIF
```

```
    Check the image separator within the ID
    If not a comma then
      exit with error
    EndIf
    Verify image is not interlaced
    If interlaced then
      exit with error
    EndIf
    Verify presence of VESA graphics adapter using "CheckForVESA"
    Select appropriate video mode for image display using "SelectVideoMode"
    Scale color register values within the Global Color Table from 0..255 to 0..63
    Move color register values into the DAC using "SetAllColorRegs"
    Expand LZW image data from file using "ExpandFile"
    Read the image trailer
    If not a semicolon or Extension introducer then
      exit with error
    EndIf
    Close the GIF file
    Free up all allocated memory by calling "DeAllocMem"
End
```

Function ReadGIFFileHdr

This function attempts to read the GIF file header, logical screen descriptor, and color table from the specified GIF file. Various checks are performed to verify that the code in the GIF function library is capable of displaying the image. Any errors detected by these checks will terminate this function's operation and an error code describing the error condition will be returned.

```
Begin
  Open the GIF file for binary read
  Read the GIF header
  Verify GIF header
  If not GIF header then
    exit with error
  EndIf
  Read the Logical Screen Descriptor (LSD) from the file
  If verbose mode then
    Display all LSD information on the screen
  EndIf
  Check flag in LSD to verify presence of Global Color Table
  If no Global Color Table
    exit with error
  EndIf
  Verify image is 256 colors
  If not then
    exit with error
  EndIf
  Read the Global Color Table from the file
  return no error code
End
```

Function ExpandFile

This function performs the LZW expansion of the coded input data stream and writes the decoded pixel values to the display.

```
Begin
  Initialize program variables
  Read and discard bits/pixel value from file. Assume 8
  Initialize string table using "InitTable"
  Do
    Get new code from the file using "InCode"
    If new code is not EOICODE then
      If new code is the CLEARCODE then
        Reinitialize string table using "InitTable"
        Get old code from file using "InCode"
        If old code is EOICODE then
          break, we are done
        EndIf
        Set character to old code
        Output old code as pixel value to the display
        Continue
      EndIf
      If new code is greater than currently know codes-LZW special case
        Place character on decode stack as it will be final character output
        Traverse through string table starting at old code, stacking all append_characters
          using "DecodeCodes" function
      Else {new code is in string table-normal case}
        Traverse through string table starting at new code, stacking all append_characters
          using "DecodeCodes" function
      EndIf
      Character is now first code output as pixel value
      Output all pixel values from decode stack in reverse order
      Add old code/character to string table
      If code length exceeded and still more bits to go
        Increment bit count
        Calculate new max code value for this number of bits
      EndIf
      Old code is now new code
    EndIf
  EndDo
End
```

Function DecodeCodes

This function decodes a string from the string table, storing it in a stacklike buffer for eventual output in reverse order.

```
Begin
  While code values are found
    Push append_character @ code from string table onto the decode stack
    Get new code value @ code from string table for this code
    Check for overflow of decode stack, exit if error
```

```
   EndWhile
   Store final character (in code variable) onto the decode stack
   Return stack pointer
End
```

Function InitTable

This function initializes the code_value array portion of the string table and various variables necessary for the LZW compressor and expander. This function is called initially by both the compressor and expander and then whenever the CLEARCODE is output by the compressor or received by the expander.

```
Begin
  Initialize all string table code_value entries to -1 or empty
  Calculate number of bits to use initially (9), the next code value (258), and the
    maximum code value (512).
End
```

Function InCode

This function is used in LZW expansion to return the next "NumofBits" code from the input code stream. It handles the blocking utilized in the GIF specification. When the expansion buffer is depleted of data, this function reads in the next block from the disk.

```
Begin
  Calculate the code extraction point in the input code bit stream
  If extraction requires data not yet read from disk then
    Move final bytes of expansion buffer to beginning of buffer
    Fill remainder of expansion buffer from disk
    Calculate new extraction point at beginning of buffer
  EndIf
  Build 24-bit extraction word which is guaranteed to contain the code value to extract
  Shift right the number of bit positions to align to the extraction point
  Advance extraction point bit count
  Mask extraction word to the required code length
  Return the code
End
```

The GIF Function Library

The GIF function library consists of 15 functions, two of which are meant to be called externally by an application program. The other functions are utilized internally within the GIF function library. Figure 5.8 shows the external functions and gives a short description of their operation. The operation of the nonexternal functions in the library should be discernible from the comments in the listing (see Listing 5.4 on page 257) and from the pseudocode provided previously.

1. Display a GIF file on the VGA/SuperVGA graphics adapter.

Prototype:

     void DisplayGIFFile (char *FileName, int Verbose);

Where:
1.   FileName is a pointer to a NULL terminated ASCII filename.
2.   Verbose is a variable that determines whether detailed image information contained in various GIF data structures should be displayed. If TRUE, the image information will be displayed in textual form before the image is displayed. See the functions "ReadGIFFileHdr" and "Display-GIFFile" in the code listing for an idea of what GIF file information will be displayed.

Operation:
This function loads and displays a GIF image from a disk file. All parameters required for proper image display are taken from the data structures read from the GIF image file. The image data is taken directly from the file and placed onto the VGA/SuperVGA display; no intermediate image buffer is utilized. Any errors encountered in the execution of this function will terminate program operation and will provide an exit code to explain the error. The error codes are defined in the file "misc.h" on the companion disks and discussed in Chapter 1.

2. Write a GIF file from the image currently being displayed on the VGA/SuperVGA display.

Prototype:

     void WriteGIFFile(char *FileName,
                     unsigned ScreenWidth,   unsigned ScreenHeight
                     unsigned ImageWidth,   unsigned ImageHeight
                     unsigned ImageTop,   unsigned ImageLeft);

Where:
1.   FileName is a pointer to a NULL terminated ASCII filename.
2.   ScreenWidth and ScreenHeight represent the resolution of the display being used for the current image. In other words, they should always equal the resolution of the VGA/SuperVGA mode used to display the image. Within the GIF specification these values define the "logical screen" on which the image should be displayed.
3.   ImageWidth, ImageHeight, ImageTop, and ImageLeft define a portion of the logical screen from which the image should be captured. Since all values are defined in relation to the top left of the screen, ImageTop and ImageLeft values of zero, in conjunction with ImageWidth equal to ScreenWidth and ImageHeight equal to ScreenHeight, will result in the full screen image being captured and converted into a GIF file. Other values of these parameters will result in smaller images being captured.

Operation:
This function creates a GIF file from the image currently being displayed on the VGA monitor. The GIF file created can contain the complete displayed image or some specified subset thereof. This function writes out the GIF header, the Logical Screen Descriptor, a Global Color Table, an Image Descriptor, the LZW compressed image raster data, and finally a GIF trailer. The GIF file written complies with the "87a" version of the GIF specification. A single-plane, 8-bit-per-pixel format image is always used for the 256-color images dealt with in this book.

Figure 5.8   The GIF Function Library

The V256 PCX/GIF File Viewer Program

To illustrate the use of the PCX and GIF library functions in an application program, we have provided the V256 PCX/GIF File Viewer program. The purpose of this program is to allow the display of a properly formatted 256-color PCX or GIF image on a VGA/SuperVGA adapter. We found this example program very useful during the preparation of this book. It allows images to be displayed quickly for easy identification. You can also use this program in an "autoexec.bat" file on your PC to display an image for you every time you boot your computer. Listing 5.5 shows the code for this example program. The operation of the code should be discernible from the comments in the listing. The command line interface used by this program is similar to that described in Chapter 4, and we discussed the use of the PCX and GIF function libraries previously in this chapter.

Note: If your VGA/SuperVGA graphics adapter is not VESA compliant, the "v256.exe" program on the companion disks will not function correctly as supplied. You will have to modify the function "SelectVideoMode" in the VGA/SuperVGA function library of Chapter 1 to select the correct video modes for your VGA/SuperVGA graphics adapter. Once modified, all the code that makes up the "v256.exe" program will have to be compiled and relinked. See Chapter 1 for the details.

Please pay proper attention to the project make file "v256.prj" and the code file. These illustrate how any application program would interface to the PCX and the GIF function libraries. The files "v256.prj" and "v256.c" are available on the companion disks.

Listing 5.5 The V256 Program

The following describes the contents of the file "v256.prj" even though this file itself is not directly viewable outside of the Borland environment. To build the "v256" program, you must have access to the following C files (either in the current directory or by way of an explicit path): "vga.c," "pcx.c," "gif.c," and "v256.c." The include files "misc.h," "vga.h," "pcx.h," and "gif.h" must also be available. All of these files with the exception of "v256.c" have been shown and described previously. We show "v256.c" below.

The following is the contents of the file "v256.c."

```
/**********************************************************/
/***                    "v256.c"                       ***/
/***                 Special 256-Color                 ***/
/***        PCX and GIF File View Utility Program      ***/
/***     from the book, "Practical Ray Tracing in C"   ***/
/***           written in Borland/Turbo C 2.0          ***/
/***                       by                          ***/
/***                Craig A. Lindley                   ***/
/***                                                   ***/
/***       Vers: 1.0    Last Update: 12/28/91          ***/
/**********************************************************/

#include <stdio.h>
#include <process.h>
```

(continued)

Listing 5.5 *(continued)*

```c
#include <conio.h>
#include <dos.h>
#include <io.h>
#include <string.h>
#include "misc.h"
#include "vga.h"
#include "pcx.h"
#include "gif.h"

#define MAXFILENAMELENGTH 30 /* max supported length of filename */

extern struct PCX_File PCXData;

/* current revision level */
unsigned Ver = 1;
unsigned Rev = 0;

/*
This function provides help in the advent of operator error.
Program terminates after help is given
*/

void ShowHelp( void )  {
   printf("This program displays 256-color PCX and GIF images\n");
   printf("\nUsage: v256 [-v ?] filename[.pcx | .gif] <cr>\n");
   printf("  -v displays image file information\n");
   printf("  ? or -?  displays this help text\n");
   printf("  filename is name of 256-color PCX or GIF image file\n\n");
   exit(EBadParms);
}


void main(unsigned argc, char *argv[])   {

   unsigned Verbose = FALSE;
   unsigned FileNameCounter, ArgIndex, StrLength;
   char    *ImageFileName;
   char    FileName[MAXFILENAMELENGTH];
   char    PCXFileName[MAXFILENAMELENGTH];
   char    GIFFileName[MAXFILENAMELENGTH];

   clrscr();
   printf("V256 - 256-color PCX/GIF File Display Program. Ver: %d.%d\n",
          Ver,Rev);
   printf("from the book \"Practical Ray Tracing in C\"\n");
   printf("Code written by Craig A. Lindley\n\n");
   printf("The Graphics Interchange Format (c) is the Copyright property of\n");
   printf("CompuServe Incorporated. GIF (sm) is a Service Mark property of\n");
   printf("CompuServe Incorporated.\n\n");
```

```
/* parse all command line arguments */

FileNameCounter = 0;                    /* count of user-specified filenames */
for (ArgIndex=1; ArgIndex < argc; ArgIndex++)  {
  if (*argv[ArgIndex] != '-')  {    /* if not a cmd line switch */
                                    /* must be a filename */
    if (*argv[ArgIndex] == '?')     /* help requested ? */
      ShowHelp();
    if (FileNameCounter > 1)        /* only one filename allowed */
      ShowHelp();                   /* if more then error exit */
    ImageFileName = argv[ArgIndex]; /* save image filename */
    FileNameCounter++;              /* inc count for error check */
  }
  else  {                          /* it's a cmd line switch */
    switch (*(argv[ArgIndex]+1))  { /* parse the cmd line */
      case 'v':
      case 'V':
        Verbose = TRUE;
        break;
      case '?':
        ShowHelp();
        break;
      default:
        printf("Error - invalid cmd line switch encountered\n");
        ShowHelp();
    }
  }
}
if (FileNameCounter != 1)  {
  printf("Error: a single PCX or GIF filename must be specified\n");
  ShowHelp();
}

printf("Press the <Enter> key to terminate display\n\n\n");
delay(1000);
/*
Check for which type of file to display. This
sometimes means adding filename extensions if
one was not specified by the user.
*/
strupr(ImageFileName);                      /* Convert to uppercase */
if (strstr(ImageFileName,".PCX"))           /* does it have a .PCX ext ? */
   DisplayPCXFile(ImageFileName,Verbose); /* display PCX file */
else if (strstr(ImageFileName,".GIF"))      /* does it have a .GIF ext ? */
   DisplayGIFFile(ImageFileName,Verbose); /* display GIF file */
else  {
   strcpy(FileName,"");                     /* make storage empty */

   /* find filename length minus the extension */
   StrLength = strcspn(ImageFileName,".");
```

(continued)

Listing 5.5 *(continued)*

```
    if (StrLength == 0)                     /* no ext specified */
      strncat(FileName,ImageFileName,MAXFILENAMELENGTH); /* copy filename completely */
    else                                    /* an ext was specified */
      strncat(FileName,ImageFileName,StrLength); /* copy name only */
    /*
    Copy the processed filename to each of the
    filename storage areas and append the appropriate string.
    */
    strcpy(PCXFileName,FileName);
    strcat(PCXFileName,".PCX");
    strcpy(GIFFileName,FileName);
    strcat(GIFFileName,".GIF");
    /*
    Determine if files with these extensions really
    exist. If so, display with appropriate
    function.
    */
    if (access(PCXFileName,0) == 0)         /* does PCX file exist ? */
      DisplayPCXFile(PCXFileName,Verbose);/* yes then display */
    else if (access(GIFFileName,0) == 0)   /* does GIF file exist ? */
      DisplayGIFFile(GIFFileName,Verbose);  /* yes then display */
    else  {
      printf("Neither file %s nor %s found\n",
             PCXFileName,GIFFileName);
      exit(EFileNotFound);
    }
  }
  getchar();
  SetTextMode();
}
```

File Conversion Programs

It is inevitable that given the number and variety of graphics image file formats in current use, you will at some point be called on to write a conversion program. You will need to convert a file from some obscure file format into some other format so it can be manipulated with the tools you have to work with. If the format you will be converting from or converting to happens to be one of the formats discussed in this book, you are lucky and can probably modify some of the code provided to do the job quickly and easily. Even if the format is not something discussed in this book, the techniques discussed should help you figure out what needs to be done.

All graphics file formats have three things in common. First, most provide some information about the contained image in a header or other data structure(s). This embedded information allows the image and color palette data to be correctly interpreted. The second thing that all graphics files have in common is that they contain image data that is sometimes compressed and sometimes not. Finally, they contain color palette information needed to display the image in its intended colors.

The first step in the file conversion process is to utilize the image header information to figure out the dimensions of the contained image, the type, if any, of compression utilized, and the format (both the number of colors in the palette and their organization) of the color information stored in the file. With this information available, you then need to break down the image data into individual pixel values. These values are sometimes temporarily stored in a buffer, stored on the display device itself during the conversion process, or converted from one format to another on the fly (without buffering them at all). Whatever the method, once the individual pixel values from the input image are available, they can be converted to the output file format. Of course, the output file needs the same kind of treatment and consideration the input file was given. Specifically, the output header/data structures have to be written to the file in the proper format. Once the output data structures are written to the file, the image pixel data and the color palette information can be moved and/or converted from one format to the other and stored in the output file. This short explanation describes generally what is required for most any type of file conversion operation.

Graphics file conversions are sometimes required on proprietary file formats as well as end user file formats. Most likely, however, you will need a file conversion between end user formats. To show an example of how this might be accomplished, we present the "pcx2gif" program. This program has the ability to convert a 256-color PCX image into an equivalent GIF image. This is useful because, as we've discussed, a GIF file will be smaller than the equivalent PCX image file. This program was developed specifically to reduce the space taken up by images on a hard disk.

Actually, this program has two purposes. First, it is another example (the "v256" program was the first example) of how the PCX and the GIF function libraries are used together in an application program. The second purpose of this program is to show how simple a file conversion program of this type can be. Within this conversion program, a PCX image is first displayed on the screen of the PC using the "DisplayPCXFile" function from the PCX function library. After the PCX image is displayed, the width and the height of the image is ascertained from the PCX data structures. Some string manipulation is then performed to change the name of the file from filename.pcx to filename.gif. With this done, the function "WriteGIFFile" from the GIF function library is called to make a GIF file from the image on the screen. There—nothing to it. A "gif2pcx" program, which performs the opposite conversion function, could just as easily be developed. We will, however, leave that program for you.

The code for this example program is shown in Listing 5.6 and is included in the files "pcx2gif.prj" and "pcx2gif.c" on the companion disks. The operation of the code should be discernible from the comments in the listing. The command line interface used by this program was described in Chapter 4, and we discussed the use of the PCX and GIF function libraries previously in this chapter.

Listing 5.6   The PCX2GIF File Conversion Program

The following describes the contents of the file "pcx2gif.prj." To build the "pcx2gif" program, you must have access to the following C files (either in the current directory or by way of an explicit path): "vga.c," "pcx.c," "gif.c," and "pcx2gif.c." The include files "misc.h," "vga.h," "pcx.h," and "gif.h" must also be available. All of these files with the exception of "pcx2gif.c" have been shown and described previously. We show "pcx2gif.c" below.

The following is the contents of the file "pcx2gif.c."

```
/*************************************************************/
/***                    "pcx2gif.c"                      ***/
/***    A 256-color PCX to GIF File Conversion Program   ***/
/***       from the book "Practical Ray Tracing in C"    ***/
/***             written in Borland/Turbo C 2.0          ***/
/***                         by                          ***/
/***                  Craig A. Lindley                   ***/
/***                                                     ***/
/***         Vers: 1.0    Last Update: 01/06/92          ***/
/*************************************************************/

#include <stdio.h>
#include <stdlib.h>
#include <conio.h>
#include <string.h>
#include "misc.h"
#include "vga.h"
#include "pcx.h"
#include "gif.h"

/* Externals from the PCX function library */
extern unsigned ImageWidth;
extern unsigned ImageHeight;


void ShowHelp( void )  {

   printf("\nThis program converts 256-color PCX images to 256-color GIF images.\n");
   printf("It is invoked as follows:\n\n");
   printf("Usage: pcx2gif [-c -h -v] infilename[.pcx] <cr>\n");
   printf("  -c check new GIF file by displaying it.\n");
   printf("  -h or ? show help\n");
   printf("  -v displays program progress information\n");
   printf(" infilename is name of PCX file to be converted.\n");
   printf(" GIF file will be named \"infilename.gif\".\n\n");
   exit(1);
}

/* File conversion program */

void main(short argc, char *argv[])  {
```

```
unsigned FileNameCounter, ArgIndex;
unsigned Verbose, CheckGIF, StrLength;
char    *PCXFileName, GIFFileName[80];

clrscr();
printf("PCX2GIF -- 256-color PCX to GIF Image File Conversion Program.\n");
printf("from the book \"Practical Ray Tracing in C\"\n");
printf("Written by Craig A. Lindley\n\n");

/* install default options */
CheckGIF = FALSE;                      /* no checking of GIF file */
Verbose = FALSE;                       /* don't be wordy */

/* parse all command line arguments */

FileNameCounter = 0;                   /* count of user-specified filenames */
for (ArgIndex=1; ArgIndex < argc; ArgIndex++)  {
   if (*argv[ArgIndex] != '-')  {  /* if not a cmd line switch */
                                   /* must be a filename */
      if (*argv[ArgIndex] == '?')    /* help requested ? */
         ShowHelp();
      if (FileNameCounter > 1)       /* only one filename allowed */
         ShowHelp();                 /* if more then error exit */
      PCXFileName = argv[ArgIndex];  /* save input image filename */
      FileNameCounter++;             /* inc count for error check */
   }
   else  {                          /* it's a cmd line switch */
      switch (*(argv[ArgIndex]+1))  {/* parse the cmd line */
         case 'c':
         case 'C':
           CheckGIF = TRUE;
           break;
         case '?':
         case 'h':
         case 'H':
           ShowHelp();
           break;
         case 'v':
         case 'V':
           Verbose = TRUE;
           break;
         default:
           printf("Error - invalid cmd line switch encountered\n");
           ShowHelp();
      }
   }
}
if (FileNameCounter < 1)  {
   printf("Error - PCX filename required\n");
   ShowHelp();
}
```

(continued)

Listing 5.6 *(continued)*

```
printf("Press the <Enter> key to terminate display\n\n\n");
delay(1000);

/* Display the specified 256-color PCX file on the screen */
DisplayPCXFile(PCXFileName,Verbose);

/* Now make an equivalent GIF filename from the PCX filename */

strcpy(GIFFileName,"");                  /* make storage empty */

/* find filename length minus the extension */
StrLength = strcspn(PCXFileName,".");

if (StrLength == 0)                       /* no ext specified */
   strncat(GIFFileName,PCXFileName,30);  /* copy filename completely */
else                                      /* an ext was specified */
   strncat(GIFFileName,PCXFileName,StrLength); /* copy name only */

/* Now add the GIF extension */
strcat(GIFFileName,".GIF");

/* Now attempt to write a GIF file of image on screen */
WriteGIFFile(GIFFileName,ImageWidth,ImageHeight,
                        ImageWidth,ImageHeight,0,0);

/* Now, if requested, display the GIF file to see if conversion worked */
if (CheckGIF)
  DisplayGIFFile(GIFFileName,FALSE);

/* Wait for user to terminate the display */
getchar();
SetTextMode();
}
```

Conclusions

This chapter should have given you a good feel for the structure of the various image file formats utilized within this book. We first presented a short but thorough description of the "raw" and "dump" file formats. Following that, we provided a detailed description of the PCX and GIF file formats. You can now appreciate how much work it is to fully support any standard image file format. With the code presented in this chapter, you can save images of many varieties in standard formats that can be imported by other application programs. You also have the capability to read (a subset of) the image files produced by other application programs. Finally, you now also have components for image conversion programs that can load a PCX file, for example, and write out a GIF equivalent.

The "v256" program showed how you could combine all of the code into a coherent application program. This example program is also very handy as a stand-alone 256-color PCX and GIF viewer and file structure browser (using the -v command line switch). We will use this program extensively in the second part of this book when we view the results of our explorations into ray-traced imagery.

This chapter concludes Part One of this book, "The Science of Ray Tracing." Within Part One, we've given you a lot of background and information about ray-tracing theory. With the foundation provided in Part One, the artistic parts of ray tracing presented in Part Two will make much more sense. Hold on to your hats, the fun is about to begin!

PART TWO

THE ART OF RAY TRACING AND GALLERY OF IMAGES

However, there is still a great deal of satisfaction in knowing that although the moon is smaller than the earth, it is much further away!
—Jackson Wolfe

Introduction to Part Two

Well, here we are. If you read and understood Part One of this book, you are to be congratulated. Behind us in Part One are the theory of ray tracing, color quantization techniques, and graphics image file formats. In other words, we've explored the mechanics involved in the *production* of ray-traced images. In Part Two, our focus will change to the *design* of ray-traced imagery. This is where the fun truly begins. You really don't need to know the theory as described in Part One to put the techniques of ray tracing to work. Of course, a good theoretical and/or intuitive understanding of the important concepts will allow you to come up to speed faster. It will also help to make sense of what you see when your image doesn't turn out as you expected. The tools that we described in such detail in Part One will be used as regular DOS programs in Part Two without any fanfare. You will execute all of the tools from the DOS command line prompt just as you would execute a word processing program or spreadsheet. We will describe the complete image development process, which includes the use of the ray tracer and tools, from top to bottom.

The DKBTrace ray-tracing program used here utilizes a graphics scene description language of its own design to produce images. Images are described to DKBTrace using an English/computerlike language that resembles a traditional programming language in some respects.

If you are a nonprogrammer, don't worry; the language is very easy to understand and use. The tutorials provided will teach you this screen description language in small steps that we hope are intuitive. The teaching process will be "learn by example." In each of the tutorials, we provide a listing of the image model (the definition of the image in DKBTrace language terms) along with the image that the model produces. There is a color photograph of the output image for each of the tutorials in the "Gallery of Images." In addition to the model listing and the output image, we explain any new features of the ray tracer that have been utilized in the image model. In addition to the image models described in this text, many more (over 50) exist on the companion disks for your ray-tracing and viewing pleasure in the "\dkb\data" directory.

The tutorials start at the very beginning with the basic techniques and continue through the more complex topics. Because of the capabilities of the DKBTrace program, we can't cover all possible techniques; there are just too many. We hope that once you understand what is presented you can be guided by your own imagination and inquisitiveness.

Computer art produced with ray tracing uses a somewhat different process than traditional art produced with brush and canvas. In traditional painting (and in simplistic terms), the artist views the subject material first. Next, he or she formulates an approach or style to be used in painting the scene. This step also usually involves some kind of planning activity in which the artist determines how the scene is to be fit to the canvas. Finally, the technical skill of the artist comes into play when applying the paint to the canvas to produce the physical representation of what the artist visualized.

With ray tracing, a lot of time is spent visualizing and planning the imagery, but no time is spent by the artist in physically producing the artwork. The physical part of this process is carried out completely within the computer. It does not matter if the computer artist is even capable of drawing a straight line using a ruler. The computer handles all these issues and more. Ray tracing by definition takes care of such things as perspective, lighting, shadows, reflections, and highlights. These are factors a traditional painter would have to be aware of and mimic if the goal of the artwork were a realistic image or scene. In this respect, ray tracing allows people who never considered themselves artistic (because of a lack of physical skills) to produce some very interesting and complex imagery.

Because of this change in paradigm, it may take some time for you to develop an intuitive feel for the ray-tracing process. As with any new undertaking, practice is required. In the real estate business, they say three things are important for a home: location, location, and location. The three things required to become a proficient computer artist are practice, practice, and practice. With practice, you will be better able to model what you have envisioned in your mind on the first attempt. Please experiment. Some of your failures may turn out to be very interesting; they can even teach you new techniques you had not thought about before. As a wise man once said, "You learn nothing from your successes compared to what you learn from your failures."

We will start off in the tutorials with simple images meant to illustrate some basic techniques. Soon after, simple objects will give way to the use of Constructive Solid Geometry (CSG) for more complex shapes, and plain surface attributes will be enhanced with textures and bitmaps. These enhancements can give ray-traced images of your own design real zest. After we present the tutorials, we describe a few full-image models. You can use these as a sort of test to determine whether or not you understood the concepts in the tutorials. This part of the book also includes a section on the use of photography to capture your ray-traced images and some suggestions for use of these images.

DKBTrace and the
Image Development Process

Experience is a hard teacher.
She gives the test first and the lessons afterwards.
—Anonymous

In this chapter you will learn about:
- **The origins of the DKBTrace program**
- **How DKBTrace is executed and how it is controlled via command line parameters**
- **The image development process from start to finish**
- **Handy hints that will make the image development process easier and faster**
- **How photography can be used to capture your ray-traced images on film**
- **Some uses for your ray-traced imagery**

Introduction

In this chapter, we will describe the complete ray-traced image development process using DKBTrace. But first, you need some background. DKBTrace is a full-featured ray-tracing program written entirely in C by David Buck of Ontario, Canada. It supports general quadric surfaces, generalized quartic surfaces, constructive solid geometry, a very capable shading model supporting many surface attributes and textures, bounding volumes for performance enhancements, and anti-aliasing for increased image quality. It uses a scene description language to ease the burden of image model design and documentation. DKBTrace is capable of rendering ray-traced images of any resolution. The tools provided within this book to post process the image data are, however, limited to 1024 by 768 resolution at this time. See Chapter 4 for a detailed description of these tools.

The version of DKBTrace we will be using (and which is provided on the companion disks) is 2.12. As newer versions of this program are developed, they will be available via FTP at the Internet address specified in the preface of this book. DKBTrace is copyrighted by David Buck, but he has made the program freely distributable without cost or royalty. A group of programmers has taken over the development of DKBTrace from David Buck, added some enhancements, and renamed it "PoVRay" (PoV for "Persistence of Vision"). PoVRay has been placed in the public domain and is available from many sources. It is rumored that eventually it will have a graphics editor that will allow interactive placement of objects on the computer. This ability would be a welcome extension to DKBTrace.

The complete DKBTrace version 2.12 release package (excluding the miscellaneous utility programs) is on the companion disks. Included are executable versions of the code, documentation files including a user's manual, and a large number of user-donated image model files to experiment with. See the "Companion Disks" section of Part Three for information on the organization of the files on the companion disks. We recommend that you print out the user's manual (filename "dkb212.doc") and keep it available. It is the definitive guide to using DKBTrace. Some of the information presented in this chapter has been excerpted from the user's manual.

We chose DKBTrace for inclusion in this book because of its incredible versatility and ease of use. A person using DKBTrace is truly limited only by his or her imagination, as DKBTrace itself does not present many limits. DKBTrace is the most complete ray tracer available for the PC platform at this time. Versions of DKBTrace are also available for many other computers and computer environments. See the porting document in the DKBTrace area of the companion disks for more information.

DKBTrace Program Operation

DKBTrace is executed like any other DOS program, by typing the name of its executable file at the DOS prompt. Three different executable versions of DKBTrace exist, as have been mentioned:

1. dkbno87.exe. This version will run on IBM-compatible PCs (AT class and up) that do not have a numeric co-processor installed. In this case, a software emulation of the numeric co-processor is used to provide the required floating-point operations.
2. dkb.exe. This version will run on IBM-compatible PCs (also AT class and up) that have a numeric co-processor installed (8087, 80287, 80387, etc.).
3. dkbpro.exe. This is a protected-mode version of the program that can use all of a computer's extended memory. This version can be run only on a computer with a 286, 386, or 486 processor (both the DX or SX varieties of processors will do) and a numeric co-processor. *It will not run on other processors.* Please refer to the files "dkbpro.doc" and "dkbmod.doc" on the companion disks for more information about the requirements for running this version of DKBTrace.

Which of these programs you will want to use depends on the hardware configuration of your computer.

DKBTrace requires both an input image model file containing the description of the ray-traced image to render and command line parameters to control its operation (how it operates on the input image file). From these inputs, DKBTrace produces an output data file that contains the ray-traced image in numerical form. DKBTrace can optionally display a crude false-color version of the image on the computer screen as it is being generated. The image model is a pure ASCII file that contains the description of the image to be rendered in the scene description language DKBTrace understands. We will present the elements that make up this "language" in the next three chapters. There is also a good description of the language elements available in the DKBTrace user's manual previously mentioned.

DKBTrace uses parameters to control its operation. These parameters can come from four different sources and are collectively referred to as command line parameters. The four sources are as follows:

1. Parameters can be specified directly on the command line when DKBTrace is executed.
2. An environment variable called DKBOPT can contain command line parameters and therefore determine how DKBTrace will operate. See your DOS manual for information on how environment variables are set and inspected.
3. Command line parameters can be specified in an ASCII file called "trace.def." This file will be inspected by DKBTrace and the parameters utilized.
4. Parameters can be specified in an ASCII file of your choosing, and this file can be specified on the DKBTrace command line. This method of passing parameters to DKBTrace is used extensively throughout the remainder of this book. We will refer to these files of command line parameters as command files from now on.

Parameters can be specified in any order and may be repeated as many times as required. The final value assigned to a parameter will be the value used. The order of processing is as follows: First, the file "trace.def" is read, followed by the environment variable. After that, parameters manually entered on the command line and parameters contained in command files are processed in the order in which they are specified, left to right. The following are the important command line parameters understood by version 2.12 of DKBTrace. All command line parameters are described in the user's manual.

-a   This command line parameter turns anti-aliasing off.

+a[xxx] This command line parameter turns anti-aliasing on with the optional tolerance level (default 0.3) of xxx. See the DKBTrace user's manual for more information.

+c   This command allows a ray trace to be continued from where it was previously aborted. If for some reason a ray-trace session was aborted prematurely, this command is used to restart the session from where it previously concluded.

-d   This option tells DKBTrace not to display the image while ray tracing is being performed.

+d[x]   Tells DKBTrace to display the image while it is being generated using video mode x, where x can mean the following for an IBM-compatible video card:

    +d0   Autodetect (S)VGA type

    +d1   Standard VGA 320x200

    +d2   Simulated SVGA 360x480

    +d3   Tseng Labs 3000 SVGA 640x480

    +d4   Tseng Labs 4000 SVGA 640x480

    +d5   AT&T VDC600 SVGA 640x400

    +d6   Oak Technologies SVGA 640x480

    +d7   Video 7 SVGA 640x480

    +d8   Video 7 Vega (Cirrus) VGA 360x480

    +d9   Paradise SVGA 640x480

    +dA   Ahead Systems Ver. A SVGA 640x480

    +dB   Ahead Systems Ver. B SVGA 640x480

    +dC   Chips & Technologies SVGA 640x480

    +dD   ATI SVGA 640x480

    +dE   Everex SVGA 640x480

    +dF   Trident SVGA 640x480

    +dG   VESA Standard SVGA Adapter 640x480

-exxx   This command instructs DKBTrace to end the ray-tracing process at line number xxx.

-f   This parameter tells DKBTrace not to produce an output file.

+f[x]   Tells DKBTrace to produce an output file of type x, where x can be one of the following:

    +fd   Dump format as required by the tools in this book

    +fr   Raw format—three individual color files

    +ft   Uncompressed Targa-24 format

-hxxx   This parameter specifies the height of the image in pixels to be rendered.

-ifilename   This command line parameter tells DKBTrace the name of the file that contains the image model to be rendered. The default input filename of "object.dat" is used if no input filename is specified.

-lpath   This parameter is used to specify a path to search for data files, include files, and/or imagemap texture files. Up to ten -l options may be used to specify a search path. The current directory will be searched first, followed by the indicated library directories.

-ofilename   This command line parameter tells DKBTrace what to name the output image file. If no filename is specified, the name defaults to "data.dis" for dump mode, "data.r8," "data.g8," or "data.b8" for raw mode, and "data.tga" for Targa mode.

-p   This parameter tells DKBTrace that when finished with the ray trace it is performing to return to DOS without waiting for user interaction.

+p	This indicates that DKBTrace should beep when the ray tracing is completed and wait for the user to hit a key before clearing the screen of the displayed image and returning to DOS. This option gives the user time to admire the displayed image before it is erased.
-qx	This command line parameter controls the rendering quality. By default, maximum image quality (q9) is always used. To decrease rendering time, the image quality can be lowered. This is useful during image testing. The value of x determines the image quality as follows:

            0,1   Just show colors with ambient lighting
            2,3   Show diffuse and ambient lighting
            4,5   Render shadows
            6,7   Create surface textures
            8,9   Compute reflected, refracted, and transmitted rays

-sxxx	This command instructs DKBTrace to start ray tracing at line number xxx. This is useful for rendering part of an image to see what it looks like without having to render the whole thing.
-v	This turns verbose mode off.
+v	This turns the verbose mode of operation on, which prints out the scanline as it is rendered.
-wxxx	This parameter specifies the width of the image to be rendered in pixels.
-x	This command disallows a ray trace to be terminated prior to its finishing. In other words, DKBTrace is locked until finished. If DKBTrace is writing a file and the system "BREAK" is ON, then a ^C typed by the user will terminate program operation. ^C will not be recognized when files are not being accessed.
+x	This command unlocks DKBTrace such that it will terminate its operation when the user hits a key on the keyboard.

Executing DKBTrace without any command line parameters specified will cause a short help screen to be displayed before the program terminates. This help information is meant to remind you of the proper use of the command line parameters.

The Image Development Process

Some preparation is necessary before image development can begin. The first thing to do is to create a directory structure on your computer to contain the DKBTrace files. One way to organize these files is as follows:

\dkb	All DKBTrace files will exist under this subdirectory.
\dkb\code	The code subdirectory under dkb contains all executable files, all command files, the "shapes.dat," "textures.dat," and "colors.dat" include files, the color quantization programs "mquan.exe," "hquan.exe," and/or "oquan.exe," and the current image model being worked on.

\dkb\data   The data subdirectory will contain all image data files.

\dkb\docs   The docs subdirectory will contain all of the DKBTrace documentation files.

\dkb\src   This directory will contain all of the source code for the DKBTrace program.

You should expand the compressed files from the companion disks into these directories. See the "Companion Disks" section of Part Three for instructions on how this is done.

Next, it will be helpful to create a few command files to control the operation of DKB-Trace. These files will be specified on the command line when DKBTrace is executed. They control the resolution of the image to be ray traced, the generation of a dump format output file, the display of the image during the ray-tracing process, and numerous other facets of DKBTrace's operation. Listing 6.1 shows the contents and gives a short description of five command files that are useful for development.

To illustrate the complete image production process, we will go through the steps necessary to render, display, and save the image used in the first tutorial exercise of Chapter 7. The name of that image file is "exer1.dat." We will assume that the directory structure is set up as described earlier (meaning the exer1.dat file is in the code directory, which is also the current directory) and that the "dkb.exe" version of the DKBTrace executable file will be used.

Listing 6.1   DKBTrace Command Files

The following is the contents of the file "q." This file will cause DKBTrace to render an 80 by 50 pixel image of maximum image quality, to display the image during generation, to produce a dump format output file, to beep and pause when the image is completely rendered, to unlock the keyboard so that DKBTrace can be terminated by hitting a keyboard key, and to not use anti-aliasing. This file is called "q" for quick and is used to render a very quick image to check for object placement. Once satisfied with object placement, you can then render the image in higher resolution, which will take much more time.

```
-w80 -h50 -q9 +d1 +fd +p +x -a
```

The following is the contents of the file "t3x2." This file is identical in content and operation to the previous file in all aspects except that it produces a 320 by 200 image instead of the smaller 80 by 50 image.

```
-w320 -h200 -q9 +d1 +fd +p +x -a
```

The following is the contents of the file "t6x4." This file is also identical in function except it causes a 640 by 480 image to be produced.

```
-w640 -h480 -q9 +d1 +fd +p +x -a
```

The following is the contents of the file "t8x6." This file is also identical in function except it causes an 800 by 600 image to be produced.

```
-w800 -h600 -q9 +d1 +fd +p +x -a
```

The following is the contents of the file "t10x7." This file is also identical in function except it causes a 1024 by 768 image to be produced.

```
-w1024 -h768 -q9 +d1 +fd +p +x -a
```

First, to render a quick version of the image, type the following at the DOS prompt:

> dkb -iexer1.dat q <Enter>

This will produce an output file called "data.dis," which contains an 80 by 50 pixel image. The small image will also be displayed in pseudocolors on the screen while ray tracing is being performed. To view this image in its true colors, you must post process the output image file with a color quantizer program. Here we will use the median cut program "mquan.exe," although the other quantizer program of Chapter 4—"oquan.exe"—could also be used. To display the mini-image in its actual colors, type the following at the DOS prompt:

> mquan data.dis <Enter>

Hitting any keyboard key after the image is displayed will terminate the display and return the user to the DOS prompt. To render the highest possible resolution (1024 by 768) version of this same image, type the following:

> dkb -iexer1.dat -oexer1.dis t10x7 <Enter>

This will take considerably longer to produce than the small version of the image produced earlier. The dump format output file in this case will be called "exer1.dis," because that name was specified with the "-o" command line parameter. *Note*: Even though the image being rendered is high resolution, the image displayed on the screen during ray tracing will be low resolution. This is because the "+d1" option is specified in all of the command files defined above. If your VGA card is listed as one of those supported with the "d" parameter, you can change the "+d1" parameter entry in the command files for the higher-resolution images. This will make DKBTrace display the pseudocolor image on the screen in resolution greater than 320 by 200. This is a matter of personal preference and does not influence the output image produced by the ray tracer.

To display the image in quantized color and to save it as a GIF file for future use, you should type the following. *Note: Your SuperVGA card must be capable of displaying 1024 by 768 images in 256 colors for the color quantization program to work at this resolution*. Note also, the "hquan.exe" 32K-color quantizer program is limited to 640 by 480 and 800 by 600 resolution images. In other words, you cannot use it here instead of the "mquan.exe" program because the image is in 1024 by 768 resolution.

> mquan exer1.dis -g exer1 <Enter>

The "-g" parameter tells the mquan program to save the ray-traced image as a GIF file with the name "exer1.gif" after it is quantized and displayed.

With the image saved as a GIF file, you can use the "v256.exe" program of Chapter 5 to display it without having to go back through the color quantization process. This is done from the DOS prompt as follows:

> v256 exer1.gif <Enter>

Saving images as GIF or PCX files can save a considerable amount of disk space as compared to saving the output of the ray tracer directly (the "filename.dis" file). This is because GIF and PCX files are palettized and compressed. The dump file contains 24 bits of color information per pixel and can therefore take up a lot of room for high-resolution images.

If the images you produce need to be immortalized on film for all of posterity, the photographic techniques described later in this chapter can be useful. Having the images you wish to photograph available as GIF files allows them to be displayed quickly and easily during your photography session.

The actual image development process is best illustrated in the flow chart of Figure 6.1. As you can see, it is an iterative process of constant refinement that closely resembles the typical software development process. During the image design stage, the designer's ideas are translated into DKBTrace scene description language statements and edited into an ASCII image model file. The image file is then submitted to DKBTrace and a low-resolution image is produced to check on the design. Low-resolution images are used because they take a much shorter time to produce and can therefore be turned over quickly. Next, the output file produced by DKBTrace is color quantized and displayed to see what it really looks like. Most likely, some modifications will be required to make the produced image look like what was expected. This is accomplished by thinking out the changes and going back into the image model file with the editor and making them. This is the iterative part of the image development cycle. It continues until the image meets the expectations. When this point in the development process is reached, the image is rendered in high resolution with anti-aliasing (possibly) enabled and saved as a GIF or PCX file. This final image will take much longer to produce but needs to be done only once, so rendering time is not so important.

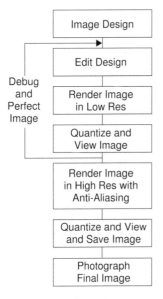

Figure 6.1   The Image Development Process Flow Chart

Handy Hints

This section contains some hints that will make your ray-tracing experience with DKBTrace more enjoyable. In general, any technique that speeds the process with which the images are rendered will make ray tracing more enjoyable. This is because the faster the images can be produced, the faster you'll arrive at the final image you want. So in one respect, the more powerful the computer you have, the shorter the image development time will be, and therefore the more you will enjoy the process.

The first technique for speeding the image development process is to use an editor that can remain in memory during the whole process. In other words, use an editor that does not need to be unloaded from memory when DKBTrace or the color quantization programs are executing. This can be accomplished by using a terminate and stay resident (TSR) editor like Borland's Sidekick, or by using some program (or DOS 5.0) that allows multiple DOS programs (including your favorite editor) to coexist in memory simultaneously. Being just a keystroke away from your editor with the image file already loaded makes for a very short editing time. If the editor must be reloaded every time a change is required to the image model file, a lot of time is wasted. Make sure that whatever editor you use for image model creation and editing does not embed control characters into the ASCII files. They have a propensity to confuse DKBTrace in the strangest ways.

Another technique that can save time is to render the smallest practical image you can during image development. Small images are fine for establishing object and/or viewpoint placement. You can then render larger images when you need to see the image detail. In conjunction with this technique, you can lower the rendering quality factor (command line parameter "q") to promote faster image generation time. Faster rendering times are thereby traded for lower-quality imagery—images without the visual effects that make ray-traced images so impressive. Still, lowering the quality during the image development process can speed things up substantially.

When developing complex scenes, you can save a lot of time by rendering only the portion(s) of the scene that are new (have not been proven before). You can do this by commenting out previously verified portions of the image file that are not needed to verify the new additions to the image. As the new additions are verified, they, too, can be commented out so their rendering time does not contribute to the image turnaround time. When all component parts of the image are verified, all comments can be removed and the complete image rendered. DKBTrace uses curly brackets {} to enclose comments. Any portions of an image file contained within these brackets are considered comments and will be ignored by the ray tracer.

Another way to save image development time that is probably obvious is not to use anti-aliasing except for the production of the final image. Anti-aliasing usually produces visually superior images, but at the expense of vastly increased processing times. By not using it when you are attempting to debug and/or perfect your ray-traced scene, you can save substantial time. For the highest-resolution images, it may not even be required.

Finally, you can save some typing within the image file by using DKBTrace's DECLARE statement to define quantities used repetitively. For example, if an elaborate texture is to be used over and over within an image file, it should be declared once and referenced throughout the file. For example, suppose the following texture definition is to be used in an image multiple times:

```
TEXTURE          { This is a cloud texture }
  TURBULENCE 0.5
  BOZO
  COLOR_MAP { transparent to transparent }
    [0.0 0.6   COLOR RED 1.0 GREEN 1.0 BLUE 1.0 ALPHA 1.0
               COLOR RED 1.0 GREEN 1.0 BLUE 1.0 ALPHA 1.0]
           { transparent to white }
    [0.6 0.8   COLOR RED 1.0 GREEN 1.0 BLUE 1.0 ALPHA 1.0
               COLOR RED 1.0 GREEN 1.0 BLUE 1.0]
             { white to gray }
    [0.8 1.001 COLOR RED 1.0 GREEN 1.0 BLUE 1.0
               COLOR RED 0.8 GREEN 0.8 BLUE 0.8]
  END_COLOR_MAP
  SCALE <0.4 0.08 0.4>
END_TEXTURE
```

You can type in this definition multiple times, or cut and paste it multiple times, or simply surround it with a declaration, as follows:

```
DECLARE Cloud_Texture =
  TEXTURE          { This is a cloud texture }
    TURBULENCE 0.5
    BOZO
    COLOR_MAP { transparent to transparent }
      [0.0 0.6   COLOR RED 1.0 GREEN 1.0 BLUE 1.0 ALPHA 1.0
                 COLOR RED 1.0 GREEN 1.0 BLUE 1.0 ALPHA 1.0]
             { transparent to white }
      [0.6 0.8   COLOR RED 1.0 GREEN 1.0 BLUE 1.0 ALPHA 1.0
                 COLOR RED 1.0 GREEN 1.0 BLUE 1.0]
               { white to gray }
      [0.8 1.001 COLOR RED 1.0 GREEN 1.0 BLUE 1.0
                 COLOR RED 0.8 GREEN 0.8 BLUE 0.8]
    END_COLOR_MAP
    SCALE <0.4 0.08 0.4>
END_TEXTURE
```

You can then use this texture any number of times after its definition by entering the following statement:

TEXTURE Cloud_Texture END_TEXTURE

You can see how much time and energy this can save. By the way, it also saves memory when DKBTrace executes.

The following list contains many items of information that are important to keep in mind while using DKBTrace. These pearls of wisdom were collected during extensive use of the program. Many of these will not make sense upon first reading, but will make sense after you use DKBTrace for a period of time. Please read this list before you attempt images of your own. File the information away in your mind so that you can retrieve it when needed. *Note*:

THE GALLERY OF IMAGES

The Gallery of Images contains a collection of imagery generated with the technology and tools provided in this book. All images were rendered in 1024 by 768 resolution and color quantized into 256 colors with the "mquan.exe" program, unless otherwise noted.

Image 1(a)
Image with gamma correction applied
data file: \gallery\torus3.dat

Image 1(b)
Image without gamma correction applied
data file: \gallery\torus3.dat

Image 2(a)
Image displayed with 256 colors and
quantized with the "mquan.exe" program
data file: \gallery\gradtst.dat

Image 2(b)
Image displayed with 32K colors and
quantized with the "hquan.exe" program
data file: \gallery\gradtst.dat

Image 3(a)
Image without anti-aliasing
640 by 480 resolution
data file: \gallery\pyr6.dat

Image 3(b)
Image with anti-aliasing
640 by 480 resolution
data file: \gallery\pyr6.dat

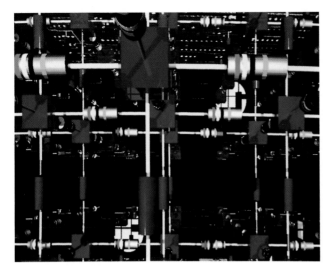

Image 4
Resistor Maze Image
Total rendering time: 27 hours
on a 33 MHz 486 PC

Image 5
Output from the TRACE Program
320 by 200 resolution in 256 colors
quantized with the "mquan.exe" program
without gamma correction

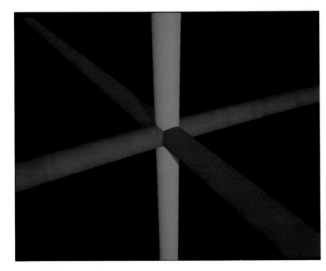

Image 6
Output from Tutorial Exercise One—
Getting Perspective
data file: exer1.dat

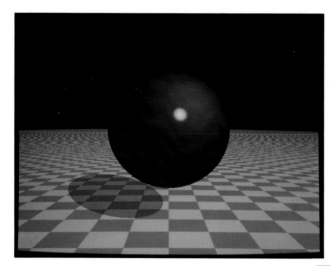

Image 7
Output from Tutorial Exercise Two—
A First Sphere
data file: exer2.dat

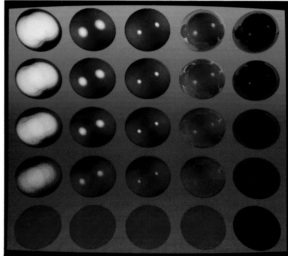

Image 8
Output from Tutorial Exercise Three—
Object Properties
data file: exer3.dat

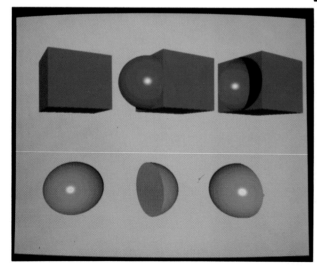

Image 9
Output from Tutorial Exercise Four—
Constructive Solid Geometry One
data file: exer4.dat

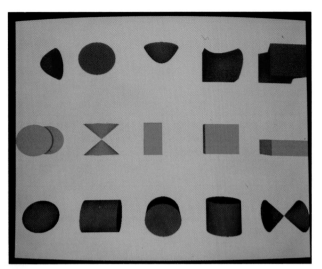

Image 10
Output from Tutorial Exercise Five—
The Quadric Family
data file: exer5.dat

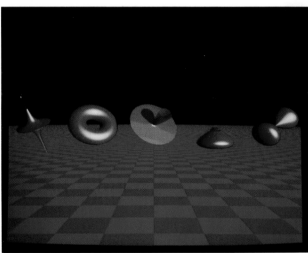

Image 11
Output from Tutorial Exercise Six—
The Quartic Family
data file: exer6.dat

Image 12
Output from Tutorial Exercise Seven—
Coloration Textures
data file: exer7.dat

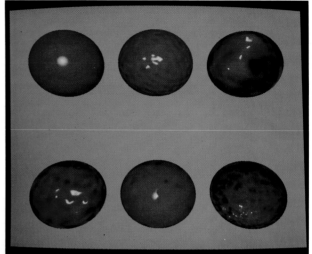

Image 13
Output from Tutorial Exercise Eight—
Surface Perturbation Textures
data file: exer8.dat

Image 14
Output from Tutorial Exercise Nine—
Constructive Solid Geometry Two
data file: exer9.dat

Image 15
Output from Tutorial Exercise Ten—
Constructive Solid Geometry Three
data file: exer10.dat

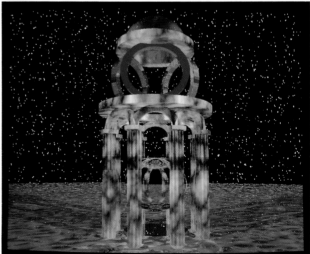

Image 16
Output from Tutorial Exercise Eleven—
Imagemaps
data file: exer11.dat

Image 17
Output from Tutorial Exercise Twelve—
Algorithmic Image Generation
data file: exer12.dat

Image 18
Image Model One—The Brake
data file: brake1.dat

Image 19
Image Model Two—The Maze
data file: maze6.dat

Image 20
Image Model Three—Advanced Imagemaps
data file: rt4.dat

Image 21
Image Model Four—The Desert
data file: cactus5.dat

The ordering of the items in this list is not an indication of their perceived importance. All items are important when you are having problems.

- All DKBTrace language elements must be specified in uppercase. User-assigned names can be in upper- or lowercase or a combination of both.
- The axes are defined as follows: the positive X axis is horizontal and to the right; the positive Y axis is vertical and upward; the positive Z axis is into the scene.
- The files "shapes.dat," "textures.dat," and "colors.dat" are usually included in each image file. They contain a basic set of definitions to make using DKBTrace easier.
- Always declare light sources centered at the origin <0 0 0> and translate them into their final position.
- Always specify the color of a light source both inside and outside of a texture block. The color specification outside the texture block is the color of the emitted light. The color specification within the texture block is what color the light source will have if it is directly viewable within a scene. Usually both colors would be specified the same.
- Three operations are possible with Constructive Solid Geometry (CSG): a UNION, which is a logical "or" of the surfaces; an INTERSECTION, which is the logical "and" of the surfaces; and DIFFERENCE, which is the subtraction of the second surface from the first surface.
- The basic shapes available within DKBTrace are quadrics, spheres, planes, triangles, smooth triangles, and quartics. More complex shapes can be fashioned using CSG.
- The optimized sphere shape cannot be scaled nonuniformly. If it is to be scaled, the scaling factors must be the same in the X, Y, and Z dimensions. A quadric sphere, however, can be scaled nonuniformly.
- All quadric shapes except the sphere and the ellipsoid are infinite in at least one direction. Scaling cannot be used to fit them into an image. They must be constrained using CSG to fit entirely within an image (and not extend outside of it).
- All shapes (except triangles) have an inside and an outside. A plane's outside is the side with the surface normal. The side of a plane opposite the normal is the inside. The concepts of inside and outside are important when using CSG.
- Composite objects are collections of simple or other composite objects that can be manipulated as a single object. Transformation applied to a composite object affects all the simple objects contained within it.
- The controllable surface attribute parameters within DKBTrace are ambient, diffuse, brilliance, reflection, refraction, IOR, Phong, Phong size, specular, and roughness.
- The sum of the ambient and diffuse parameters should never exceed 1.0; otherwise, strange things can happen.
- A colormap converts a number into a color using linear interpolation.
- The color of an object must be specified within a texture block when you are rendering high-quality images.
- A color with an ALPHA value of 1.0 is transparent. ALPHA values approaching 0.0 are more opaque.
- The colors displayed on the screen during the ray-tracing process are only rough approximations of the actual colors being generated. To see the image in its true color,

the data file output by DKBTrace must be post processed by one of the color quantization programs described in Part One of this book.

- The use of bounding objects is strongly recommended, as they can drastically decrease the image generation time.

- Transformations are always performed in relation to the origin. A sphere located at the origin that is rotated will show no visible displacement. A sphere first translated away from the origin and then rotated will spin like a planet in orbit around the origin.

- The "left-hand rule" is used to define the direction of rotation. When the thumb is pointed in the positive direction of the axis being rotated around, the fingers will curl in the direction of positive rotation.

- Use a RIGHT vector of < 1.333 0 0 > when rendering images in the 320 by 200 resolution 256-color VGA mode. This will compensate for the nonsquare pixels produced in this mode. You can change the RIGHT vector to < 1.0 0 0 > when rendering in resolutions that have square pixels. For SuperVGA, that is all 256-color modes above 640 by 400 in resolution.

- Two different types of textures exist within DKBTrace. They are coloration textures and surface perturbation textures. Examples of coloration textures include bozo, spotted, marble, wood, checker, checker_texture, granite, gradient, agate, and imagemap. Surface perturbation textures include waves, ripples, dents, bumps, and wrinkles.

- Textures are set up so as to produce approximately one feature change (color transition) across a sphere of radius one. Textures can be scaled to provide the appropriate number of feature changes needed within an image.

- By default, IMAGEMAP textures map into the XY plane in the range (0,0) to (1,1).

Photographic Hardcopy Techniques

Throughout this book we have seen how ray-traced images are designed, rendered, color quantized, and saved. Once we've saved them in a standard graphics file format, we have seen how the images can be displayed on a computer monitor using the "v256.exe" program. Also, once the ray-traced images are put into a standard file format they can be manipulated by desktop publishing programs and paint programs and can even be incorporated into animation sequences. Sometimes, however, it is necessary to make a hard copy of the images for use outside of the computer. Many of the programs that manipulate the standard graphics images can also print them, but with the current state of (affordable) color printer technology, the hard copy that results is usually less than optimal. Of course, if you have enough money to throw at the problem (either by purchasing or renting the printer or by using a color printer service available in some locations), you can gain access to a color printer capable of reproducing the full range and intensities of colors contained in a ray-traced image. Images printed with such a printer are truly beautiful. In this section, however, we will describe a hardcopy technique that is available to everyone at a reasonable cost and is extremely flexible in the images produced. The technique we are speaking about, of course, is photography.

By far, the highest-quality and lowest-cost method of producing hard copy of computer images is via photography. This is accomplished by displaying the desired image on a high-quality video monitor and subsequently photographing it. All of the imagery in this book was produced in this manner. After a high-quality photograph is taken, you can use standard darkroom techniques to enhance the image as required. For example, the image can be enlarged or reduced in size to fit the requirements of its application.

Talk of photography as a method of hardcopy production in this age of computers and laser printers probably borders on heresy. It is unfortunate that not all people have access to expensive color printers. Until a desktop-size, photograph-quality color printer is available for under a few hundred dollars, a properly taken photograph of a color monitor will probably have to suffice.

The techniques for color monitor photography are relatively simple and straightforward. They require the use of a 35mm camera set up for manual operation. If the camera to be used is fully automatic, it may still work if its light meter is accurate at low light levels. You may need to shoot a roll of film to know for sure. Remember, rolls of 12-exposure film are available and are ideal for experimental purposes such as this.

It is pretty hard to take a bad image if you are careful with the setup. Underexposure is one of the most common problems. If you use the following technique, you will have a high probability of success even on your first attempt.

1. Load your camera with either slide or print film depending on your needs. Kodak Kodachrome ASA 100 has been used successfully as has Ektar 25. The Ektar film is much more expensive to purchase and does not produce noticeably better results. ASA 100 slide or print film is recommended. If you plan on making enlargements of your images, you should shoot print film, as this makes the enlargements less expensive. *Note*: ASA 100 film is very forgiving in terms of exposure. If the exposure is anywhere close to what it should be, you will probably get a good photograph.

2. Use a zoom or telephoto lens on your 35mm camera. This will flatten out the curve of the monitor's screen. The photograph will appear flatter as a result. Make sure you remove any UV (ultraviolet) filters or polarizers that may be attached to the front of your telephoto lens. Clean the lens if necessary.

3. Mount your camera on a tripod for stability during the relatively long exposure intervals. Make sure your lens is positioned as perpendicular to the screen as possible in all directions. The plane of the film should be parallel to the plane of the monitor screen. Be careful of a tilted monitor.

4. Shoot in a dark room with the camera positioned at least 2 to 3 feet away from the monitor. Using the through-the-lens viewing capabilities of your camera, fill the complete field of view with your monitor's screen. Catching the edges of the monitor itself in the photographs is almost unavoidable. If you like, you can zoom into the image and miss the edges of the monitor completely, but this usually results in the loss of too much of the image itself. Do not worry if you catch a little of the monitor in your photographs. This can be removed in the enlargement and printing process.

5. Clean all fingerprints and smudges off the monitor's screen with an appropriate cleaner.

6. Turn down the brightness and contrast of the monitor to prevent glare in the photograph. Bright colors of high intensity will tend to bleed in the photograph.

7. When using ASA 100 film, set the shutter speed of the camera somewhere in the range of 1/8 to 1/2 of a second. With a 1/4-second shutter, start with the f-stop at f4 or f8. You do not want to use a shutter speed faster than 1/15 of a second because that is approaching the speed at which the monitor is refreshed. Too fast a shutter will produce images in which the interlace pattern is evident. This is manifested as a wide black horizontal bar partially obscuring the image on the screen. Be careful not to move the monitor and/or camera during exposure. Any movement with such a slow shutter speed will destroy the quality of the image being photographed. You can use a self-timer or a remote shutter to prevent camera movement.

8. Make sure the first few images photographed take up the full frame of the film. This is important because some film processing machines automatically locate the left edge of an image and assume it is the left edge of the print or slide. This can cause your slides or prints to be off-centered. Once some of these machines get off, they never recover, so your whole roll of film can be ruined. This is a quick and easy precaution that can prevent some stressful moments at the film processing center.

If you are fortunate enough to have a light meter that will work at low light levels, use it to determine the exact exposure required. In this case, the intensity of the computer monitor can be varied for each image photographed to maintain a constant light level at the camera. This will allow the use of constant shutter speeds and f-stops and will result in photographic prints and slides of consistent exposure.

For the best possible result, you should use the photographic technique of bracketing. That is, you should take several photographs of the monitor while adjusting the f-stop setting around the initial setting. This can use up a lot of film (e.g., three exposures per image) but will usually result in a slide or print of optimum exposure.

Once the images are photographed and processed, you have the problem of printing your images. Photographs of ray-traced images differ substantially from the normal photographs most film printing establishments are used to dealing with. Ray-traced images generally have a lot of black in them and contain lots of saturated colors. This can pose unique problems when printing. Usually a few units of density must be added when printing a ray-traced image to get a correct exposure. When you get a print of the correct exposure and color balance, you should note these parameters (they are usually printed on the back of machine-developed prints) so they can be reproduced. That way, whenever you take a negative back and ask for a print or enlargement, you can get reproducible results.

Many large photography stores have a Kodak machine that allows you to enlarge and print your own pictures. This machine is wonderful for printing ray-traced images because every print is custom and under your control. These machines allow you to control parameters such as enlargement size, cropping direction, image placement within the enlargement, density, and color balance. The great thing about these machines is that you can see what your print is going to look like (except for its density and color balance, unfortunately) on the attached color monitor before it is ever printed. When you are satisfied with the setup of the machine, you press a button and wait about five minutes for your custom print to be developed. These machines can produce enlargements up to 11 by 14 inches in size. Enlargements larger than this can certainly be made by other means (but not on these machines) but probably should be avoided. That is because the individual pixels in the ray-traced image start to become visible in such enlargements regardless of the resolution with which the image was originally rendered. This is a matter of personal taste. Some people like the look of images when the individual pixels can be discerned. It makes the image look more computerlike and somehow more unique.

By following the simple guidelines described in this section, you can produce and reproduce quality photographs of your ray-traced images in full color.

Uses of Ray-Traced Imagery

In commercial applications, ray tracing is sometimes used in mechanical CAD (Computer Aided Design) programs to make solid wire frame objects. This gives the objects a real appearance that is much easier for the brain to comprehend in three dimensions. The ability to view solid objects within a CAD program can, in some cases, prevent having to build the objects just to see what they look like. This can result in a substantial savings of both time and money. Ray tracing is also used in the video industry for special effects, still image backgrounds, and even short animation sequences (more on animation shortly). More and more computer graphics are also being used in the movie industry, especially in science-fiction movies. The use of advanced imaging techniques including ray tracing has reduced the amount of manual labor necessary to make an unreal scene look convincing. Specifically, computer graphics have reduced the need for matte painting, which is an expensive process.

One of the incredible things about ray tracing is that you can use it while letting your imagination run wild in the creation of art or you can use it to model something as exactly as possible. Examples of both types of images are shown in the "Gallery of Images." Then, of course, there is the full range of possibilities between the two extremes of realism and fantasy.

As this is a technical book and I am a technical author (and not an artist), I cannot presume to teach art or image composition or even how an artist should go about promoting his or her artwork (ray traced or otherwise). All I can suggest here are some uses of the imagery that have occurred to me. I am sure many more uses for these images exist and could be identified with a little effort.

In general, two primary uses of ray-traced imagery come to mind: ray-traced images can be used as documentation or for artistic/ornamentation purposes. Most applications of ray-traced imagery fall into one of these categories, although sometimes the distinctions are blurry.

In terms of documentation, ray-traced images can be incorporated into reports documenting new or proposed mechanical product designs, used to make solid images of arbitrary data to help with scientific visualization, used as a teaching tool in mathematics to show surfaces in three dimensions, used to produce unique company logos, and so on. The list could go on for a long time.

Once you've captured your images on film, there are many possible artistic uses for them, including:

- A personal collection of photographic prints of your images. If you get prints made of your images and put them into a small photo album you can carry them around with you to show your friends your new hobby. They will be dazzled by your technical prowess. After all, you got an impersonal personal computer to create such works of art. They will have no doubt about the kind of person you really are. Maybe you're not such a nerd after all.

- Framed enlargements make very nice gifts for friends and family because they are original and unique. Few people have seen ray-traced imagery before and are usually impressed when they do so. You'll find that 35mm negatives blow up nicely to 11- by 14-inch prints. These prints look especially nice if they are double matted and placed in 16- by 20-inch metallic (black or silver) frames. In addition to using them as gifts, you can also display and/or sell your framed enlargements at local art galleries as modern computer art.
- Various specialty photography stores will blow up your image negatives or slides to poster size. This might be fun to do with some of your best high-resolution images.
- Although we've already mentioned company logos, we can't stress them enough. Most logos are two-dimensional designs that show up on company stationery, company signs, memos, and so on. Using ray tracing to produce three-dimensional logos can add real visual impact. These small three-dimensional logos can then be used in place of the less eye-catching two-dimensional logos.
- Images of colorful and reflective spheres can make very nice custom holiday cards.
- Ray-traced images can be converted into unique, attention-getting business cards for people in the high-tech industries. It is very easy for someone to throw away an ordinary business card. It is much harder to throw one away that is an avant-garde piece of art. Many photo processing stores can make these unique business cards.
- Other uses of these images include coffee cups and T-shirts.

You can enhance your ray-traced images even further with other image processing techniques and programs. This is possible because, with the tools presented in this book, you can save your images in standard graphics file formats that other programs can import and manipulate. Importing a ray-traced image into a paint program would allow it to be captioned with text (personalized), be combined with other types of graphics information including scanned imagery or digitized video, have its coloration manipulated, or have portions of the image painted over for some interesting effects. Once the manipulations are complete, you can then photograph the screen or use the printing facilities of the paint program to produce hard copy.

You can also personalize your ray-traced images directly by incorporating ray-traced lettering within the image or incorporating scanned images as imagemap textures. See the "Gallery of Images" for examples of these techniques.

You can also use ray tracing to produce short animated movies. To do this, render each frame of the movie separately as a still ray-traced image. (This can take a very long time to do, even for a short movie, unless you have access to a supercomputer.) After each frame is rendered, you can dump it to a videotape with a hardware device called a VGA to NTSC video converter. (This must be done after the image has been color quantized.) Once on videotape, the movie can be played back at normal speed. Alternatively, several animation player programs exist for the PC that can also play back the individual frames of your animation in close to real time. Using this method, your short animated movie can be played back directly on your computer.

Producing a movie of this type requires much planning and preparation. Coordinating the movement of objects between the individual frames is very difficult and prone to error. To help with this task, a program called "RayScene" has been developed for use with DKBTrace. This program allows the use of variables within DKBTrace image model files that RayScene will manipulate on a frame-by-frame basis. The variables are used to control the motion of the user's viewpoint (basically the camera) and other objects within an image. A file is created that contains the values to be given to the variables for each frame. RayScene then generates the appropriate number of image model files, inserting the correct value of the variables into the proper place in each file. DKBTrace is then used to render each frame separately. If you're interested in obtaining RayScene, it is available over the Internet from tolsun.oulu.fi (128.214.5.6) in the directory /pub/rayscene or from iear.arts.roi.edu in the directory /pub/graphics/ray/rayscene. *Note*: "Temporal aliasing" can be a problem when using ray tracing to produce animation. See Chapter 2 for more information.

Another possible use for ray-traced images is as an attention getter for the public. We have all seen the computers in stores that continuously play some kind of advertisement or promotional material in the hopes of capturing people's attention. With the software given in this book, it is possible to construct a program that would continuously display one ray-traced image after another in random or sequential form. The unique qualities of ray-traced imagery displayed like this would surely attract people's attention, maybe even to the point where they would like to buy the demo or some of the individual images.

Conclusions

In this chapter, we have discussed the image development process using DKBTrace. Additionally, we discussed photographing your imagery from the computer monitor and certain uses of this imagery. With this chapter behind you, you are now prepared to begin ray tracing. In the final three chapters of this book, we present tutorials to teach you how to fully utilize DKBTrace. Learning will be done by example. Each tutorial exercise will be accompanied by a color image that shows the expected results (all images are shown in the "Gallery of Images"). Each tutorial will build on the information learned in the previous ones. When you fully understand all of the information contained in these tutorials, you will have learned how to use the DKBTrace ray tracer and will be better prepared to use other ray-tracing programs in the future.

7

Basic Ray-Tracing Techniques

An artist should concentrate on his technique so that he has a mastery of his craft. Then, when inspiration arrives, its expression will not be hampered by some lack of mastery of technique. Unless you know how to move your fingers on the piano, how to play the notes first, how can you make music?

—Mark Tobey

In this chapter you will learn:

- **The basic capabilities of the DKBTrace program**
- **How various surface attributes affect how a surface looks**
- **How to use Constructive Solid Geometry to combine simple shapes into more complex ones**
- **What the members of the quadric and quartic families of mathematical surfaces look like**
- **What coloration textures are supported by DKBTrace and what they look like when applied to surfaces**
- **What surface perturbation textures are supported by DKBTrace and what they look like when applied to surfaces**

Introduction

In this chapter, you will learn about the basic DKBTrace features and capabilities by way of example tutorial exercises. These tutorials will begin simply and progress toward the more complex. Each of these tutorials will build on the information presented in the previous ones.

The first tutorial will, by necessity, be longer and more in depth than the ones that follow it. That is because we must present and discuss a lot of basic information before even a simple image model will make sense. (An image model is an ASCII file of DKBTrace scene description statements that defines an image.) The desired result of both the basic and intermediate tutorials (presented in this and the following chapters) is a complete understanding of the scene description language used by DKBTrace along with a complete understanding of DKB-Trace's capabilities. Each tutorial will add an incremental amount of new information about DKBTrace to your total understanding.

Each tutorial presents an image model along with a complete textual explanation. The image represented by the image model is contained in the "Gallery of Images," so you can see it while reading about the image model. The immediate correlation between the visual image and the written word should make for quick understanding of the processes and techniques involved. So, without further ado, we'll begin.

Tutorial Exercise One—Getting Perspective

The purpose of this first tutorial exercise is to introduce most of the basic constructs of the DKBTrace scene description language. We will do this by describing on almost a line-by-line basis the image model file called "exer1.dat" and shown in Listing 7.1. This exercise is called "Getting Perspective" because it produces a three-dimensional rendition of the coordinate axes in three different colors to aid in understanding their spatial relationships. The X axis is shown as a red cylinder, the Y axis as a green cylinder, and the Z axis as a blue cylinder. As we discussed in Chapter 6, the X axis generally runs horizontally, the Y axis vertically, and the Z axis into and out of the scene. All objects within a scene, including light sources and viewpoints, are defined in the same coordinate system. Please refer to Listing 7.1 throughout the discussion to follow.

The first thing you will notice about this image model file is that it is an ASCII file and is somewhat self-documenting. The use of English and English-like words in the scene description language makes the intent of the model obvious. Other ray-tracing programs use files of numbers to define their models. All these numbers make for error-prone edits of those files and complete incomprehensibility after a day or two of not looking at them. Because the image model files here are plain ASCII, they can be edited, printed, and listed without problem. Please keep in mind that all keywords in the scene description language must be specified in uppercase; otherwise, DKBTrace will disavow any knowledge of their existence.

All modern programming languages allow the use of comments within source files for documentation purposes. DKBTrace is no different. Any ASCII text contained within curly braces { } is considered a comment and ignored by DKBTrace. Comments are used for and by the programmer; they are not used by DKBTrace. Nested comments are also allowed but generally unnecessary. Each of the tutorial image models has a block of text at the beginning of the file that describes its intent. This block of text is in the form of a comment and is therefore surrounded by curly braces. Having this introductory text is a good habit to get into for image model files and computer programming in general. *Note*: The date of the last update to the image model is included as part of this text. This helps keep tabs on the latest version of the image model. This, too, is optional but useful.

Listing 7.1 Tutorial Exercise One—Getting Perspective

The following is the contents of the file "exer1.dat."

```
{
  Ray-Traced Imaging - Tutorial Exercise One
  "Getting Perspective"
  from the book "Practical Ray Tracing in C" by Craig A. Lindley
  Last update to this image: 03/06/92

  This example image uses all of the basic elements needed to
  produce a ray-traced image including a viewpoint, a light
  source, and some objects to look at. In this case, cylinders
  are used to show the three-dimensional axes in three different
  colors. Red for the X axis, Green for the Y axis, and Blue for
  the Z axis. See the "Gallery of Images" for a look at what this
  image file produces.
}

INCLUDE "colors.dat"            { standard includes for color }
INCLUDE "shapes.dat"            { for shapes and }
INCLUDE "textures.dat"          { for textures }

VIEW_POINT                      { define the viewpoint }
  LOCATION < 0  0 -50 >
  DIRECTION < 0  0  1 >
  UP < 0  1  0 >
  RIGHT < 1.0  0  0 >
  ROTATE < 30  30  0 >
END_VIEW_POINT

OBJECT                          { define a light source }
  SPHERE < 0  0  0 > 2 END_SPHERE
  TRANSLATE <-30  50 -150 >
  TEXTURE
    COLOR White
    AMBIENT 1.0
    DIFFUSE 0.0
  END_TEXTURE
  COLOR White
  LIGHT_SOURCE
END_OBJECT

OBJECT              { X axis is Red }
  QUADRIC Cylinder_X
    SCALE < 1  2  2 >
  END_QUADRIC
  TEXTURE
   COLOR Red
  END_TEXTURE
END_OBJECT

OBJECT              { Y axis is Green }
```

```
QUADRIC Cylinder_Y
  SCALE < 2  1  2 >
END_QUADRIC
TEXTURE
 COLOR Green
END_TEXTURE
END_OBJECT

OBJECT                    { Z axis is Blue }
  QUADRIC Cylinder_Z
   SCALE < 2  2  1 >
  END_QUADRIC
  TEXTURE
   COLOR Blue
  END_TEXTURE
END_OBJECT
```

After the introductory text, you'll notice three INCLUDE statements which are followed by filenames. Includes allow the incorporation of other image model information from other files into the current file without having to physically copy it there. DKBTrace's include files function just as they do in most computer languages. When INCLUDE statements are encountered while DKBTrace is processing the main input file ("parsing the file," in computer language terminology), that processing is halted and processing of the first included file is begun. When completed, processing resumes in the main file. In our example, another INCLUDE is immediately found in the main file when its processing is resumed, so the cycle repeats itself.

Include files help in the organization of image model files. They keep the files uncluttered with information that is common to all image models. When all of the common information is moved to include files, the image model files contain only the unique information about the image and are therefore much more concise and understandable. In our example file, three files are included: "colors.dat" (Listing 7.2), "shapes.dat" (Listing 7.3), and "textures.dat" (Listing 7.4).

The file "colors.dat" contains color definitions. These definitions, when included in an image model, allow color names to be used to designate colors instead of having to specify all colors in terms of specific RGB values. It is much easier to understand what NavyBlue is than to recognize a color with RGB components of 0.137255, 0.137255, 0.556863 as Navy blue. All colors in this file are specified as:

DECLARE ColorName = COLOUR RED xx.xx COLOUR GREEN xx.xx COLOUR BLUE xx.xx

where all words in uppercase are DKBTrace language keywords, ColorName represents a user-defined identifier to reference the color, and the xx.xxs are floating-point numbers that indicate how much red, green, and blue make up the defined color. (Remember, all RGB components have a value in the range zero to one.) You will notice that the Canadian/British spelling of the word color is used in this file although the American spelling will work equally well. This reflects the fact that the author of the DKBTrace program, David Buck, is Canadian. After this definition is included in an image model, ColorName can be used as a symbolic name for the color as follows:

COLOR ColorName

This statement is equivalent to the longer and less easy to understand color specifications:

COLOR RED xx.xx COLOR GREEN xx.xx COLOR BLUE xx.xx

or

COLOUR RED xx.xx COLOUR GREEN xx.xx COLOUR BLUE xx.xx

Including the "colors.dat" file makes 73 predefined color names available within the image model. If other custom colors are required for an image, they can be defined in the main image model file as we've shown here. In other words, there is nothing special about the color definitions in the "colors.dat" file. Colors can be defined anywhere in an image model—in the main portion of the model or in an include file. Multiple files of color definitions could also be INCLUDEd within an image model. In the "RGB Color Tables" section of Part Three is another, more extensive, list of colors (in DKBTrace format) that can be used in your images. This list is included in the file "colors.rgb" on the companion disks.

As you will see, the DECLARE keyword is a very powerful language statement. It is used to declare a type of object with a certain description. This declaration is known to other portions of the image model but does not define an instance of the object. Rather, it is a prototype of the object. It is similar to a structure definition in C. A structure definition does not actually allocate space for a variable of that type. A variable of the structure's type must be declared to create an instance of the type. We will clarify this distinction throughout these tutorial exercises.

Listing 7.2 Color Definition File

The following is the contents of the file "colors.dat."

```
DECLARE Clear = COLOUR RED 1.0 GREEN 1.0 BLUE 1.0 ALPHA 1.0
DECLARE White = COLOUR RED 1.0 GREEN 1.0 BLUE 1.0
DECLARE Red = COLOUR RED 1.0
DECLARE Green = COLOUR GREEN 1.0
DECLARE Blue = COLOUR BLUE 1.0
DECLARE Yellow = COLOUR RED 1.0 GREEN 1.0
DECLARE Cyan = COLOUR BLUE 1.0 GREEN 1.0
DECLARE Magenta = COLOUR RED 1.0 BLUE 1.0
DECLARE Black = COLOUR RED 0.0 GREEN 0.0 BLUE 0.0
DECLARE Aquamarine = COLOUR RED 0.439216 GREEN 0.858824 BLUE 0.576471
DECLARE BlueViolet = COLOUR RED 0.62352 GREEN 0.372549 BLUE 0.623529
DECLARE Brown = COLOUR RED 0.647059 GREEN 0.164706 BLUE 0.164706
DECLARE CadetBlue = COLOUR RED 0.372549 GREEN 0.623529 BLUE 0.623529
DECLARE Coral = COLOUR RED 1.0 GREEN 0.498039 BLUE 0.0
DECLARE CornflowerBlue = COLOUR RED 0.258824 GREEN 0.258824 BLUE 0.435294
DECLARE DarkGreen = COLOUR RED 0.184314 GREEN 0.309804 BLUE 0.184314
DECLARE DarkOliveGreen = COLOUR RED 0.309804 GREEN 0.309804 BLUE 0.184314
DECLARE DarkOrchid = COLOUR RED 0.6 GREEN 0.196078 BLUE 0.8
DECLARE DarkSlateBlue = COLOUR RED 0.419608 GREEN 0.137255 BLUE 0.556863
DECLARE DarkSlateGray = COLOUR RED 0.184314 GREEN 0.309804 BLUE 0.309804
DECLARE DarkSlateGrey = COLOUR RED 0.184314 GREEN 0.309804 BLUE 0.309804
```

```
DECLARE DarkTurquoise = COLOUR RED 0.439216 GREEN 0.576471 BLUE 0.858824
DECLARE DimGray = COLOUR RED 0.329412 GREEN 0.329412 BLUE 0.329412
DECLARE DimGrey = COLOUR RED 0.329412 GREEN 0.329412 BLUE 0.329412
DECLARE Firebrick = COLOUR RED 0.556863 GREEN 0.137255 BLUE 0.137255
DECLARE ForestGreen = COLOUR RED 0.137255 GREEN 0.556863 BLUE 0.137255
DECLARE Gold = COLOUR RED 0.8 GREEN 0.498039 BLUE 0.196078
DECLARE Goldenrod = COLOUR RED 0.858824 GREEN 0.858824 BLUE 0.439216
DECLARE Gray = COLOUR RED 0.752941 GREEN 0.752941 BLUE 0.752941
DECLARE GreenYellow = COLOUR RED 0.576471 GREEN 0.858824 BLUE 0.439216
DECLARE Grey = COLOUR RED 0.752941 GREEN 0.752941 BLUE 0.752941
DECLARE IndianRed = COLOUR RED 0.309804 GREEN 0.184314 BLUE 0.184314
DECLARE Khaki = COLOUR RED 0.623529 GREEN 0.623529 BLUE 0.372549
DECLARE LightBlue = COLOUR RED 0.74902 GREEN 0.847059 BLUE 0.847059
DECLARE LightGray = COLOUR RED 0.658824 GREEN 0.658824 BLUE 0.658824
DECLARE LightGrey = COLOUR RED 0.658824 GREEN 0.658824 BLUE 0.658824
DECLARE LightSteelBlue = COLOUR RED 0.560784 GREEN 0.560784 BLUE 0.737255
DECLARE LimeGreen = COLOUR RED 0.196078 GREEN 0.8 BLUE 0.196078
DECLARE Maroon = COLOUR RED 0.556863 GREEN 0.137255 BLUE 0.419608
DECLARE MediumAquamarine = COLOUR RED 0.196078 GREEN 0.8 BLUE 0.6
DECLARE MediumBlue = COLOUR RED 0.196078 GREEN 0.196078 BLUE 0.8
DECLARE MediumForestGreen = COLOUR RED 0.419608 GREEN 0.556863 BLUE 0.137255
DECLARE MediumGoldenrod = COLOUR RED 0.917647 GREEN 0.917647 BLUE 0.678431
DECLARE MediumOrchid = COLOUR RED 0.576471 GREEN 0.439216 BLUE 0.858824
DECLARE MediumSeaGreen = COLOUR RED 0.258824 GREEN 0.435294 BLUE 0.258824
DECLARE MediumSlateBlue = COLOUR RED 0.498039 BLUE 1.0
DECLARE MediumSpringGreen = COLOUR RED 0.498039 GREEN 1.0
DECLARE MediumTurquoise = COLOUR RED 0.439216 GREEN 0.858824 BLUE 0.858824
DECLARE MediumVioletRed = COLOUR RED 0.858824 GREEN 0.439216 BLUE 0.576471
DECLARE MidnightBlue = COLOUR RED 0.184314 GREEN 0.184314 BLUE 0.309804
DECLARE Navy = COLOUR RED 0.137255 GREEN 0.137255 BLUE 0.556863
DECLARE NavyBlue = COLOUR RED 0.137255 GREEN 0.137255 BLUE 0.556863
DECLARE Orange = COLOUR RED 0.8 GREEN 0.196078 BLUE 0.196078
DECLARE OrangeRed = COLOUR RED 1.0 BLUE 0.498039
DECLARE Orchid = COLOUR RED 0.858824 GREEN 0.439216 BLUE 0.858824
DECLARE PaleGreen = COLOUR RED 0.560784 GREEN 0.737255 BLUE 0.560784
DECLARE Pink = COLOUR RED 0.737255 GREEN 0.560784 BLUE 0.560784
DECLARE Plum = COLOUR RED 0.917647 GREEN 0.678431 BLUE 0.917647
DECLARE Salmon = COLOUR RED 0.435294 GREEN 0.258824 BLUE 0.258824
DECLARE SeaGreen = COLOUR RED 0.137255 GREEN 0.556863 BLUE 0.419608
DECLARE Sienna = COLOUR RED 0.556863 GREEN 0.419608 BLUE 0.137255
DECLARE SkyBlue = COLOUR RED 0.196078 GREEN 0.6 BLUE 0.8
DECLARE SlateBlue = COLOUR GREEN 0.498039 BLUE 1.0
DECLARE SpringGreen = COLOUR GREEN 1.0 BLUE 0.498039
DECLARE SteelBlue = COLOUR RED 0.137255 GREEN 0.419608 BLUE 0.556863
DECLARE Tan = COLOUR RED 0.858824 GREEN 0.576471 BLUE 0.439216
DECLARE Thistle = COLOUR RED 0.847059 GREEN 0.74902 BLUE 0.847059
DECLARE Turquoise = COLOUR RED 0.678431 GREEN 0.917647 BLUE 0.917647
DECLARE Violet = COLOUR RED 0.309804 GREEN 0.184314 BLUE 0.309804
DECLARE VioletRed = COLOUR RED 0.8 GREEN 0.196078 BLUE 0.6
DECLARE Wheat = COLOUR RED 0.847059 GREEN 0.847059 BLUE 0.74902
DECLARE YellowGreen = COLOUR RED 0.6 GREEN 0.8 BLUE 0.196078
{ This color is new.  Works well with Polished_Metal texture }
DECLARE OldGold =  COLOUR RED   0.81 GREEN 0.71 BLUE  0.23
```

The next file that is typically included in an image model is "shapes.dat." This file, as the name implies, contains the definitions of many commonly used shapes. Again, the power of the DECLARE statement is used to allow reference to a shape name within an image model without having to specify the parameters of the shape explicitly. Take, for example, the definition of a cylinder along the X axis. As you will recall from the discussion in Chapter 2, all quadric shapes, including the cylinder, can be defined by ten parameters, A through J. For the cylinder along the X axis, the parameters A through J are:

A=0.0, B=1.0, C=1.0, D=0.0, E=0.0, F=0.0, G=0.0, H=0.0, I=0.0, and J=-1.0

The syntax used by DKBTrace for all quadric definitions is:

```
QUADRIC
    < A   B   C >
    < D   E   F >
    < G   H   I >
        J
END_QUADRIC
```

Within an image model file, an explicit definition of a cylinder along the X axis can thus be specified as:

```
QUADRIC
    < 0.0 1.0 1.0 >
    < 0.0 0.0 0.0 >
    < 0.0 0.0 0.0 >
        -1.0
END_QUADRIC
```

While this is a fairly concise definition, it is still tedious to retype every time a cylinder along the X axis is required in an image model. For this reason, an object of type Cylinder_X is DECLAREd as follows:

```
DECLARE Cylinder_X = QUADRIC
    < 0.0 1.0 1.0 >
    < 0.0 0.0 0.0 >
    < 0.0 0.0 0.0 >
        -1.0
END_QUADRIC
```

and referenced as:

```
QUADRIC Cylinder_X END_QUADRIC
```

This reference creates an instance of Cylinder_X in an image model. You can see how much easier this is to think about and use in practice. You no longer have to think in terms of the ten quadric parameters, you can think instead of Cylinder_X, which is much more descriptive.

Within the "shapes.dat" file there are 22 different shapes defined. Some are quadric shapes defined as discussed here while others use Constructive Solid Geometry (CSG) to define their shapes. We will discuss CSG in Tutorial Exercise Four, but for now, you must take these definitions on faith. *Note*: To create an instance of a quadric DECLAREd object type, use the procedure shown earlier. For the shapes defined using CSG of the form:

DECLARE ShapeName = INTERSECTION

.
.
.

END_INTERSECTION

an instance is created with the statement:

INTERSECTION ShapeName END_INTERSECTION

Definitions for a sphere, capped and uncapped cylinders along X, Y, and Z, cones along X, Y, and Z, planes along YZ, XZ, and XY, paraboloids along X, Y, and Z, a hyperbolic paraboloid (called a hyperboloid), a true hyperboloid, a cube, a tetrahedron, a hexagon, and a rhomboid are presented in the "shapes.dat" file. Please refer to Listing 7.3 for the exact definitions.

Listing 7.3   Shape Definition File

The following is the contents of the file "shapes.dat."

```
DECLARE Sphere = QUADRIC
  <1.0 1.0 1.0>
  <0.0 0.0 0.0>
  <0.0 0.0 0.0>
  -1.0
END_QUADRIC


DECLARE Cylinder_X = QUADRIC
  <0.0 1.0 1.0>
  <0.0 0.0 0.0>
  <0.0 0.0 0.0>
  -1.0
END_QUADRIC


DECLARE Cylinder_Y = QUADRIC
  <1.0 0.0 1.0>
  <0.0 0.0 0.0>
  <0.0 0.0 0.0>
  -1.0
END_QUADRIC


DECLARE Cylinder_Z = QUADRIC
  <1.0 1.0 0.0>
  <0.0 0.0 0.0>
  <0.0 0.0 0.0>
  -1.0
END_QUADRIC
```

(continued)

Listing 7.3 *(continued)*

```
DECLARE Cone_X = QUADRIC
  <-1.0 1.0 1.0>
  < 0.0 0.0 0.0>
  < 0.0 0.0 0.0>
    0.0
END_QUADRIC


DECLARE Cone_Y = QUADRIC
  <1.0 -1.0 1.0>
  <0.0  0.0 0.0>
  <0.0  0.0 0.0>
    0.0
END_QUADRIC


DECLARE Cone_Z = QUADRIC
  <1.0 1.0 -1.0>
  <0.0 0.0  0.0>
  <0.0 0.0  0.0>
    0.0
END_QUADRIC


DECLARE Plane_YZ = QUADRIC
  <0.0 0.0 0.0>
  <0.0 0.0 0.0>
  <1.0 0.0 0.0>
    0.0
END_QUADRIC


DECLARE Plane_XZ = QUADRIC
  <0.0 0.0 0.0>
  <0.0 0.0 0.0>
  <0.0 1.0 0.0>
    0.0
END_QUADRIC


DECLARE Plane_XY = QUADRIC
  <0.0 0.0 0.0>
  <0.0 0.0 0.0>
  <0.0 0.0 1.0>
    0.0
END_QUADRIC


{ y^2 + z^2 - x = 0 }
DECLARE Paraboloid_X = QUADRIC
```

```
   < 0.0   1.0   1.0>
   < 0.0   0.0   0.0>
   <-1.0   0.0   0.0>
     0.0
END_QUADRIC


{ x^2 + z^2 - y = 0 }
DECLARE Paraboloid_Y = QUADRIC
   <1.0   0.0   1.0>
   <0.0   0.0   0.0>
   <0.0  -1.0   0.0>
     0.0
END_QUADRIC


{ x^2 + y^2 - z = 0 }
DECLARE Paraboloid_Z = QUADRIC
   <1.0   1.0   0.0>
   <0.0   0.0   0.0>
   <0.0   0.0  -1.0>
     0.0
END_QUADRIC


{ y - x^2 + z^2 = 0 }
DECLARE Hyperboloid = QUADRIC
   < -1.0   0.0   1.0>
   <  0.0   0.0   0.0>
   <  0.0   1.0   0.0>
       0.0
END_QUADRIC


DECLARE Hyperboloid_Y = QUADRIC  { Vertical hyperboloid }
   <1.0 -1.0  1.0>            {                      }
   <0.0  0.0  0.0>            {            \   /      }
   <0.0  0.0  0.0>            { Like this:  ) (       }
   -1.0                       {            /   \      }
END_QUADRIC


DECLARE Cube = INTERSECTION
   PLANE < 0.0   0.0   1.0> 1.0 END_PLANE
   PLANE < 0.0   0.0  -1.0> 1.0 END_PLANE
   PLANE < 0.0   1.0   0.0> 1.0 END_PLANE
   PLANE < 0.0  -1.0   0.0> 1.0 END_PLANE
   PLANE < 1.0   0.0   0.0> 1.0 END_PLANE
   PLANE <-1.0   0.0   0.0> 1.0 END_PLANE
END_INTERSECTION
```

(continued)

Listing 7.3   *(continued)*

```
DECLARE Tetrahedron = INTERSECTION
   PLANE < 0.0 -1.0 0.0> 1.0 END_PLANE
   PLANE < 0.0  0.0 1.0> 1.0 ROTATE <-30.0   0.0    0.0> END_PLANE
   PLANE < 1.0  0.0 0.0> 1.0 ROTATE <  0.0  30.0   30.0> END_PLANE
   PLANE <-1.0  0.0 0.0> 1.0 ROTATE <  0.0 -30.0  -30.0> END_PLANE
END_INTERSECTION


DECLARE X_Disk = INTERSECTION          { Capped cylinder, Length in X axis }
   QUADRIC Cylinder_X END_QUADRIC
   PLANE <1.0 0.0 0.0> 0.0 INVERSE END_PLANE
   PLANE <1.0 0.0 0.0> 1.0 END_PLANE
END_INTERSECTION


DECLARE Y_Disk = INTERSECTION          { Capped cylinder, Length in Y axis }
   QUADRIC Cylinder_Y END_QUADRIC
   PLANE <0.0 1.0 0.0> 0.0 INVERSE END_PLANE
   PLANE <0.0 1.0 0.0> 1.0 END_PLANE
END_INTERSECTION


DECLARE Z_Disk = INTERSECTION          { Capped cylinder, Length in Z axis }
   QUADRIC Cylinder_Z END_QUADRIC
   PLANE <0.0 0.0 1.0> 0.0 INVERSE END_PLANE
   PLANE <0.0 0.0 1.0> 1.0 END_PLANE
END_INTERSECTION


DECLARE Hexagon = INTERSECTION          { Hexagonal Solid, axis along X }
   PLANE <0.0 0.0 1.0>  1.0 END_PLANE    { Rotate 90 in Z axis to stand up }
   PLANE <0.0 0.0 1.0>  1.0 ROTATE < 60.0 0.0 0.0> END_PLANE
   PLANE <0.0 0.0 1.0>  1.0 ROTATE <120.0 0.0 0.0> END_PLANE
   PLANE <0.0 0.0 1.0>  1.0 ROTATE <180.0 0.0 0.0> END_PLANE
   PLANE <0.0 0.0 1.0>  1.0 ROTATE <240.0 0.0 0.0> END_PLANE
   PLANE <0.0 0.0 1.0>  1.0 ROTATE <300.0 0.0 0.0> END_PLANE
   PLANE <1.0 0.0 0.0>  1.0 END_PLANE
   PLANE <1.0 0.0 0.0> -1.0 INVERSE END_PLANE
END_INTERSECTION

DECLARE Rhomboid = INTERSECTION  { Three-Dimensional 4-Sided Diamond }
   PLANE <-1.0  0.0   0.0>  1.0 ROTATE <0.0 0.0 -30.0> END_PLANE
   PLANE < 1.0  0.0   0.0>  1.0 ROTATE <0.0 0.0 -30.0> END_PLANE
   PLANE < 0.0  0.0   1.0>  1.0 END_PLANE
   PLANE < 0.0  0.0  -1.0>  1.0 END_PLANE
   PLANE < 0.0  1.0   0.0>  1.0 END_PLANE
   PLANE < 0.0 -1.0   0.0>  1.0 END_PLANE
END_INTERSECTION
```

Listing 7.4   Texture Definition File

The following is the contents of the file "textures.dat."

```
DECLARE Red_Marble = TEXTURE
    MARBLE
    TURBULENCE 1.0
    COLOUR_MAP
        [0.0 0.8   COLOUR RED 0.8 GREEN 0.8 BLUE 0.6
                   COLOUR RED 0.8 GREEN 0.4 BLUE 0.4]
        [0.8 1.001 COLOUR RED 0.8 GREEN 0.4 BLUE 0.4
                   COLOUR RED 0.8 GREEN 0.2 BLUE 0.2]
    END_COLOUR_MAP
END_TEXTURE

DECLARE White_Marble = TEXTURE
    MARBLE
    TURBULENCE 1.0
    COLOUR_MAP
        [0.0 0.3   COLOUR White COLOUR White]
        [0.3 0.7   COLOUR White COLOUR RED 0.6 GREEN 0.6 BLUE 0.6]
        [0.7 0.9   COLOUR RED 0.6 GREEN 0.6 BLUE 0.6
                   COLOUR RED 0.45 GREEN 0.45 BLUE 0.45]
        [0.9 1.001 COLOUR RED 0.45 GREEN 0.45 BLUE 0.45
                   COLOUR RED 0.3 GREEN 0.3 BLUE 0.3]
    END_COLOUR_MAP
END_TEXTURE

DECLARE Black_Marble = TEXTURE
    MARBLE
    TURBULENCE 1.0
    COLOUR_MAP
        [0.0 0.3   COLOUR RED 0.3 GREEN 0.3 BLUE 0.3
                   COLOUR RED 0.45 GREEN 0.45 BLUE 0.45]
        [0.3 0.7   COLOUR RED 0.45 GREEN 0.45 BLUE 0.45
                   COLOUR RED 0.6 GREEN 0.6 BLUE 0.6]
        [0.7 0.9   COLOUR RED 0.6 GREEN 0.6 BLUE 0.6
                   COLOUR White]
        [0.9 1.001 COLOUR White COLOUR White]
    END_COLOUR_MAP
END_TEXTURE

DECLARE Blue_Agate = TEXTURE
    AGATE
    COLOUR_MAP
        [0.0 0.5   COLOUR RED 0.30 GREEN 0.30 BLUE 0.50
                   COLOUR RED 0.30 GREEN 0.30 BLUE 0.50]
        [0.5 0.55  COLOUR RED 0.30 GREEN 0.30 BLUE 0.50
                   COLOUR RED 0.20 GREEN 0.20 BLUE 0.30]
        [0.55 0.6  COLOUR RED 0.20 GREEN 0.20 BLUE 0.30
                   COLOUR RED 0.25 GREEN 0.25 BLUE 0.35]
        [0.6 0.7   COLOUR RED 0.25 GREEN 0.25 BLUE 0.35
```

(continued)

Listing 7.4 *(continued)*

```
                      COLOUR RED 0.15 GREEN 0.15 BLUE 0.26]
        [0.7 0.8    COLOUR RED 0.15 GREEN 0.15 BLUE 0.26
                      COLOUR RED 0.10 GREEN 0.10 BLUE 0.20]
        [0.8 0.9    COLOUR RED 0.10 GREEN 0.10 BLUE 0.20
                      COLOUR RED 0.30 GREEN 0.30 BLUE 0.50]
        [0.9 1.001 COLOUR RED 0.30 GREEN 0.30 BLUE 0.50
                      COLOUR RED 0.10 GREEN 0.10 BLUE 0.20]
    END_COLOUR_MAP
END_TEXTURE

DECLARE Brown_Agate = TEXTURE
    AGATE
    COLOUR_MAP
        [0.0 0.5    COLOUR RED 1.0 GREEN 1.0 BLUE 1.0
                      COLOUR RED 0.9 GREEN 0.7 BLUE 0.6]
        [0.5 0.6    COLOUR RED 0.9 GREEN 0.7 BLUE 0.6
                      COLOUR RED 0.9 GREEN 0.7 BLUE 0.4]
        [0.6 1.001 COLOUR RED 0.9 GREEN 0.7 BLUE 0.4
                      COLOUR RED 0.7 GREEN 0.4 BLUE 0.2]
      END_COLOUR_MAP
END_TEXTURE

DECLARE Jade = TEXTURE
    MARBLE
    TURBULENCE 1.0
    COLOUR_MAP
        [0.0 0.8    COLOUR RED 0.1 GREEN 0.6 BLUE 0.1
                      COLOUR RED 0.0 GREEN 0.3 BLUE 0.0]
        [0.8 1.001 COLOUR RED 0.1 GREEN 0.6 BLUE 0.1
                      COLOUR RED 0.0 GREEN 0.2 BLUE 0.0]
    END_COLOUR_MAP
END_TEXTURE


DECLARE Sky = TEXTURE
    BOZO
    TURBULENCE 0.3
    COLOUR_MAP
       [0.0 0.5    COLOUR RED 0.25 GREEN 0.25 BLUE 0.5
                      COLOUR RED 0.25 GREEN 0.25 BLUE 0.5]
       [0.5 0.6    COLOUR RED 0.25 GREEN 0.25 BLUE 0.5
                      COLOUR RED 0.7 GREEN 0.7 BLUE 0.7]
       [0.6 1.001 COLOUR RED 0.7 GREEN 0.7 BLUE 0.7
                      COLOUR RED 0.3 GREEN 0.3 BLUE 0.3]
    END_COLOUR_MAP
END_TEXTURE

DECLARE Cloud_Sky = TEXTURE
    BOZO
    TURBULENCE 0.5
```

```
    COLOUR_MAP
        [0.0 0.5   COLOUR RED 0.5 GREEN 0.5 BLUE 1.0
                   COLOUR RED 0.5 GREEN 0.5 BLUE 1.0]
        [0.5 0.6   COLOUR RED 0.5 GREEN 0.5 BLUE 1.0
                   COLOUR RED 1.0 GREEN 1.0 BLUE 1.0]
        [0.6 1.001 COLOUR RED 1.0 GREEN 1.0 BLUE 1.0
                   COLOUR RED 0.5 GREEN 0.5 BLUE 0.5]
    END_COLOUR_MAP
END_TEXTURE


DECLARE Cherry_Wood = TEXTURE
    WOOD
    TURBULENCE 0.2
    COLOUR_MAP
        [0.0 0.8   COLOUR RED 0.666 GREEN 0.312 BLUE 0.2
                   COLOUR RED 0.666 GREEN 0.312 BLUE 0.2]
        [0.8 1.01  COLOUR RED 0.4 GREEN 0.133 BLUE 0.066
                   COLOUR RED 0.2 GREEN 0.065 BLUE 0.033]
    END_COLOUR_MAP
END_TEXTURE

DECLARE Pine_Wood = TEXTURE
    WOOD
    TURBULENCE 0.2
    COLOUR_MAP
        [0.0 0.8   COLOUR RED 1.0 GREEN 0.71875 BLUE 0.25
                   COLOUR RED 1.0 GREEN 0.71875 BLUE 0.25]
        [0.8 1.01  COLOUR RED 0.5 GREEN 0.5 BLUE 0.066
                   COLOUR RED 0.4 GREEN 0.4 BLUE 0.033]
    END_COLOUR_MAP
END_TEXTURE

DECLARE Dark_Wood = TEXTURE
    WOOD
    TURBULENCE 0.2
    COLOUR_MAP
        [0.0 0.8   COLOUR RED  0.42857 GREEN 0.23810 BLUE 0.04762
                   COLOUR RED  0.42857 GREEN 0.23810 BLUE 0.04762]
        [0.8 1.01  COLOUR RED 0.4 GREEN 0.333 BLUE 0.066
                   COLOUR RED 0.2 GREEN 0.033 BLUE 0.033]
    END_COLOUR_MAP
END_TEXTURE

DECLARE Tan_Wood = TEXTURE
    WOOD
    TURBULENCE 0.1
    COLOUR_MAP
        [0.0 0.8   COLOUR RED 0.888 GREEN 0.600 BLUE 0.3
                   COLOUR RED 0.888 GREEN 0.600 BLUE 0.3]
        [0.8 1.01  COLOUR RED 0.6 GREEN 0.4 BLUE 0.2
```

(continued)

Listing 7.4   *(continued)*

```
                      COLOUR RED 0.4 GREEN 0.3 BLUE 0.2]
      END_COLOUR_MAP
END_TEXTURE

DECLARE White_Wood = TEXTURE
    WOOD
    TURBULENCE 0.6
    COLOUR_MAP
        [0.0 0.8  COLOUR RED 0.93 GREEN 0.71  BLUE 0.532
                  COLOUR RED 0.98 GREEN 0.81  BLUE 0.6]
        [0.8 1.01 COLOUR RED 0.6  GREEN 0.333 BLUE 0.266
                  COLOUR RED 0.7  GREEN 0.6   BLUE 0.23]
      END_COLOUR_MAP
END_TEXTURE

DECLARE Tom_Wood = TEXTURE
    WOOD
    TURBULENCE 0.31
    COLOUR_MAP
        [0.0 0.8   COLOUR RED 0.7 GREEN 0.3 BLUE 0.0
                   COLOUR RED 0.7 GREEN 0.3 BLUE 0.0]
        [0.8 1.01  COLOUR RED 0.5 GREEN 0.2 BLUE 0.0
                   COLOUR RED 0.4 GREEN 0.1 BLUE 0.0]
      END_COLOUR_MAP
END_TEXTURE


DECLARE Dull = TEXTURE
    PHONG 0.5
    PHONGSIZE 1
END_TEXTURE

DECLARE Shiny = TEXTURE
    PHONG 1.0
    PHONGSIZE 50
END_TEXTURE

DECLARE Mirror = TEXTURE
    AMBIENT 0.0
    DIFFUSE 0.0
    REFLECTION 1.0
END_TEXTURE

DECLARE Luminous = TEXTURE
    AMBIENT 1.0
    DIFFUSE 0.0
END_TEXTURE

DECLARE Glass = TEXTURE
    COLOR RED 1.0 GREEN 1.0 BLUE 1.0 ALPHA 1.0
```

```
      AMBIENT 0.0
      DIFFUSE 0.0
      REFLECTION 0.2
      REFRACTION 1.0
      IOR 1.2
      PHONG 0.3
      PHONGSIZE 60
END_TEXTURE

DECLARE Metal = TEXTURE
      REFLECTION 0.2
      BRILLIANCE 6.0
      PHONG 1.0
      PHONGSIZE 60
END_TEXTURE

DECLARE Glass2 = TEXTURE
      COLOR RED 1.0 GREEN 1.0 BLUE 1.0 ALPHA 1.0
      AMBIENT 0.0
      DIFFUSE 0.0
      REFLECTION 0.5
      REFRACTION 0.85
      IOR 1.5
      PHONG 0.3
      PHONGSIZE 60
END_TEXTURE

DECLARE Pearl = TEXTURE   { You need to supply a COLOUR with ALPHA...}
      AMBIENT 0.4
      DIFFUSE 0.6
      BRILLIANCE 8.0
      REFLECTION 0.75
      REFRACTION 0.25
      IOR 2.5
      PHONG 1.0
      PHONGSIZE 30.0
END_TEXTURE

DECLARE Polished_Metal = TEXTURE { You need to supply a COLOUR...}
      AMBIENT 0.3
      DIFFUSE 0.7
      BRILLIANCE 8.0
      REFLECTION 0.5
      PHONG 1.0
      PHONGSIZE 90
END_TEXTURE

DECLARE Brass = TEXTURE
      COLOUR RED 1.0 GREEN 1.0  { Yellow }
      REFLECTION 0.75
      BRILLIANCE 8.0
```

(continued)

Listing 7.4   *(continued)*

```
   PHONG 1.0
   PHONGSIZE 90
END_TEXTURE

DECLARE Iron = TEXTURE
   AGATE
   TURBULENCE 0.3
   COLOUR_MAP
       [0.0 0.5   COLOUR RED 0.21 GREEN 0.1  BLUE 0.1
                  COLOUR RED 0.25 GREEN 0.25 BLUE 0.01]
       [0.5 0.6   COLOUR RED 0.25 GREEN 0.25 BLUE 0.01
                  COLOUR RED 0.3  GREEN 0.1  BLUE 0.1]
       [0.6 1.001 COLOUR RED 0.15 GREEN 0.1  BLUE 0.1
                  COLOUR RED 0.15 GREEN 0.1  BLUE 0.1]
   END_COLOUR_MAP
   BRILLIANCE 2.0
   PHONG 0.75
   PHONGSIZE 50
END_TEXTURE


DECLARE Candy_Cane = TEXTURE
   GRADIENT < 1.0 1.0 0.0 >
   COLOUR_MAP
       [0.00 0.25  COLOUR RED 1.0 GREEN 0.0 BLUE 0.0
                   COLOUR RED 1.0 GREEN 0.0 BLUE 0.0]
       [0.25 0.75  COLOUR RED 1.0 GREEN 1.0 BLUE 1.0
                   COLOUR RED 1.0 GREEN 1.0 BLUE 1.0]
       [0.75 1.001 COLOUR RED 1.0 GREEN 0.0 BLUE 0.0
                   COLOUR RED 1.0 GREEN 0.0 BLUE 0.0]
   END_COLOUR_MAP
END_TEXTURE

DECLARE Y_RGB_Gradient = TEXTURE
   GRADIENT < 0.0 1.0 0.0 >
   COLOUR_MAP
       [0.00 0.33  COLOUR RED 1.0 GREEN 0.0 BLUE 0.0
                   COLOUR RED 0.0 GREEN 0.0 BLUE 1.0]
       [0.33 0.66  COLOUR RED 0.0 GREEN 0.0 BLUE 1.0
                   COLOUR RED 0.0 GREEN 1.0 BLUE 0.0]
       [0.66 1.001 COLOUR RED 0.0 GREEN 1.0 BLUE 0.0
                   COLOUR RED 1.0 GREEN 0.0 BLUE 0.0]
   END_COLOUR_MAP
END_TEXTURE

DECLARE X_RGB_Gradient = TEXTURE
   GRADIENT < 1.0 0.0 0.0 >
   COLOUR_MAP
       [0.00 0.33  COLOUR RED 1.0 GREEN 0.0 BLUE 0.0
                   COLOUR RED 0.0 GREEN 0.0 BLUE 1.0]
```

```
       [0.33 0.66  COLOUR RED 0.0 GREEN 0.0 BLUE 1.0
                   COLOUR RED 0.0 GREEN 1.0 BLUE 0.0]
       [0.66 1.001 COLOUR RED 0.0 GREEN 1.0 BLUE 0.0
                   COLOUR RED 1.0 GREEN 0.0 BLUE 0.0]
    END_COLOUR_MAP
END_TEXTURE
```

The final include file to be examined is "textures.dat." This file contains a collection of coloration textures that can be used within your image models. Remember, any parameter that changes the appearance of a surface but doesn't change its defined shape is a texture. Coloration textures are derived textures in that they are derived from the coloration textures contained within DKBTrace. In all, there are 26 textures in this file at your disposal. We will take up the use of coloration textures in earnest in Tutorial Exercise Seven. The DKBTrace intrinsic coloration textures are BOZO, SPOTTED, MARBLE, WOOD, CHECKER, CHECKER_TEXTURE, GRANITE, GRADIENT, AGATE, and IMAGEMAP. The derived textures contained in the "textures.dat" file include Red_Marble, White_Marble, Black_Marble, Blue_Agate, Brown_Agate, Jade, Sky, Cloud_Sky, Cherry_Wood, Pine_Wood, Dark_Wood, Tan_Wood, White_Wood, Tom_Wood, Dull, Shiny, Mirror, Luminous, Glass, Metal, Glass2, Pearl, Polished_Metal, Brass, Iron, Candy_Cane, Y_RGB_Gradient, and X_RGB_Gradient. As before, the DECLARE statement is used extensively in this file to give the names listed above to the derived textures. Any of the textures defined as:

    DECLARE TextureName = TEXTURE
                .
                .
                .
    END_TEXTURE

can be used within an image model by declaring an instance of the texture as follows:

    TEXTURE TextureName END_TEXTURE

As before, the use of the DECLARE statement to name a texture can hide much of the complexity of the texture's definition while leaving the image model file easy to read and understand. We will cover the use of textures in depth in the tutorial exercises described later. Now, back to the image model for Tutorial Exercise One.

The next entry in the image model is the definition of the VIEW_POINT. The VIEW_POINT determines where the viewer's eye is in relation to the objects in the three-dimensional scene. The four main vectors that define the VIEW_POINT (as described in Chapter 2) are LOCATION, DIRECTION, UP, and RIGHT. In this specific case, the location of the eye is 50 units (units can have any dimension you desire: microns, inches, meters, miles, etc.) back on the negative Z axis (away from the objects in the scene). The direction the eye is looking is straight down the positive Z axis. Up in the image is directly overhead and aligned with the positive Y axis. Finally, the right in the image corresponds to the positive X axis.

Each of these values is specified by a vector described by three floating-point numbers enclosed in angle brackets <>.

The placement of the VIEW_POINT as just defined above is then modified by rotating it 30 degrees around first the X axis and then the Y axis. This is accomplished with the ROTATE statement. The vector following the ROTATE keyword indicates how much rotation is to be applied in the X, Y, and Z directions, respectively. All rotations are in relation to the coordinate system origin and happen around the specified axes. If multiple direction rotations are specified in a single ROTATE statement (as is the case here), the rotations are applied in X, Y, then Z order. The left-hand rule is used to determine the direction of positive rotation, as described in Chapter 6. A VIEW_POINT rotation is performed in this image model to give a better view of the three coordinate axes modeled with cylinders in this example. Keep in mind that the rotation of the VIEW_POINT in a specified direction(s) is equivalent to a rotation of the objects being viewed in the opposite direction(s). That is because the eye's position is always brought to the center of the view plane (the center of the computer's monitor) regardless of where in space it is positioned or how it is rotated. Shifting the rotated VIEW_POINT to the center of the screen causes the objects in the scene to move in the opposite direction(s). Think about it for a moment and it will make sense.

Finally, the RIGHT vector specified in the VIEW_POINT definition assumes that square pixels are going to be used to display the resulting image. The aspect ratio correction capability available with the RIGHT vector, and described in Chapter 2, is not used. Therefore, the ray-traced image produced by this image model must be displayed in a graphics mode that supports square pixels, otherwise spatial distortion will result. The VIEW_POINT used in this example image model is typical of those used in all image models in this chapter.

Next comes the definition of the first OBJECT in the scene. In this case, however, the object is a light source that provides illumination for the objects in the scene. The definition of light source objects is remarkably similar to the definition of other objects, except light sources include the DKBTrace keyword LIGHT_SOURCE.

All object definitions are enclosed by the OBJECT, OBJECT_END keywords. When defined this way, an instance of the object is immediately created. Objects can be DECLAREd also, but as before, an instance of the declared object is not created until the object type is later instantiated. Object definitions usually contain information on the shape of the object and its coloration and texture. In the case of the light source in the image model, the light is a SPHERE, centered at the origin and having a 2-unit radius. DKBTrace supports two special shapes, the SPHERE and the PLANE. These are not treated as regular QUADRIC shapes but are highly optimized for speed in calculations. The use of the optimized SPHERE is shown here. The use of the optimized PLANE will be shown later. You should use these optimized shapes whenever possible to increase DKBTrace's performance. An equivalent sphere could have been defined using the regular QUADRIC method, as follows:

```
QUADRIC Sphere
    SCALE < 2 2 2 >
END_QUADRIC
```

SCALEing of the sphere is required because all quadrics defined within DKBTrace have a radius of 1. A radius of 2 is required to be identical to the SPHERE definition used in the image model. SCALEing equally by 2 in all dimensions creates the larger sphere shape that is required. The optimized SPHERE and the QUADRIC sphere are identical in all respects except one, and that has to do with SCALEing. An optimized SPHERE cannot be scaled non-uniformly, whereas the QUADRIC sphere can. Said another way, optimized SPHEREs can be scaled as long as they are scaled equally in all dimensions. A QUADRIC sphere, in contrast, can be scaled disproportionally in any direction to create an ellipsoid from the sphere. This shows that the optimized SPHERE is not quite as flexible as the QUADRIC sphere—a classic trade-off of flexibility for performance.

The light source definition in the image model shows one very important thing about defining and using light sources; that is, *light sources must be defined at the origin of the coordinate system and then TRANSLATEd to their final position.* A translation is a movement of an object in three dimensions by the amounts stipulated in the TRANSLATE statement. A single TRANSLATE statement can specify movement in up to three directions. The three numbers in the statement specify the amount of movement in the X, then Y, then Z directions, respectively. If LIGHT_SOURCEs are not TRANSLATEd to their final destination, they will not work as you would expect. Light will not come from the position you wanted it to. Please keep this fact in mind when designing images of your own. In this image model, the light source (Z = -150) is positioned behind the viewer's position (Z = -50) so it won't be visible in the image.

Next, a TEXTURE, END_TEXTURE block is defined to give DKBTrace some information about the light source. In this case, the color of the light will be white, and by convention, the LIGHT_SOURCE object will have all AMBIENT and no DIFFUSE lighting components. You will notice that the color of the LIGHT_SOURCE is specified both inside and outside the TEXTURE, END_TEXTURE block. This is necessary because of the way DKBTrace works. The color specification inside the TEXTURE block determines what color the light source will be if it is visible within a scene. The color specification outside the TEXTURE block determines what color the light is that leaves the LIGHT_SOURCE and impinges on other objects within a scene. Normally, these two color specifications should be the same, but they do not have to be.

Finally, in this image model, three cylindrical OBJECTs are defined on the coordinate axes to show the position and orientation of these axes from the viewer's (VIEW_POINT) perspective. The first OBJECT defined is a red cylinder along the X axis. As indicated in Chapter 2, all quadric shapes except the sphere and the ellipsoid are infinite in one dimension. In the case of a Cylinder_X type, the infinite length is in the X dimension. Also, by definition, all cylinders (regardless of orientation) have a radius of 1. The SCALEing performed within the QUADRIC, END_QUADRIC block scales the Cylinder_X by 1 in the X direction and by 2 in both the Y and Z directions. Scaling in the X direction does not do anything because scaling infinity by any number is still infinity. *Note: You must never scale by zero, as numeric overflow will most definitely occur and your computer will most certainly crash.* Scaling by 2 in the Y and Z directions produces a circular cylinder along the X axis with a radius of 2. If the Y and Z scaling factors were not equal, the cylinder would be stretched or flattened in one direction, resulting in a noncircular cylinder. Finally, a TEXTURE, END_TEXTURE block is used to give this Cylinder_X the color of red to distinguish it from the other two cylindrical OBJECTs yet to be defined.

What is not shown in this TEXTURE block but is equally important are the default values of the surface attributes that DKBTrace assigns to all objects. See both the discussion in Chapter 2 and the DKBTrace user's manual for more information about surface attributes. Unless expressly overwritten by parameters specified within the TEXTURE block, all surfaces by default have the following characteristics:

COLOR	= Black
REFLECTION	= 0.0
REFRACTION	= 0.0
IOR	= 1.0 (Index of Refraction)
AMBIENT	= 0.3
DIFFUSE	= 0.7
BRILLIANCE	= 1.0
SPECULAR	= 0.0
ROUGHNESS	= 0.05
PHONG	= 0.0
PHONGSIZE	= 50

In the case of the Cylinder_X object, only the color attribute is overwritten within the TEXTURE block. All of the other default specifications remain as shown.

The second and third cylinder OBJECTs, representing the Y and Z axes, are defined in exactly the same way. In these cases, however, Cylinder_X is replaced with Cylinder_Y and Cylinder_Z, respectively, and the assigned color is changed.

When this image model file is rendered with DKBTrace, you will see the three infinite cylinders meeting in the middle of the image and going off the screen in their respective directions. Because of the rotation in the VIEW_POINT you will see the green Y axis in the vertical direction, the red X axis traversing the screen from lower left to upper right, and the blue Z axis traversing from upper left to lower right. You can also see the effects of perspective in this image; the portions of the cylinders closer to the viewer are larger and the portions farther away are smaller.

We gave detailed directions on how to submit this image model file to DKBTrace for rendering in Chapter 6. Please follow them now and render this example image. The image that you should expect to see is in the "Gallery of Images" (see Image 6).

Tutorial Exercise Two—A First Sphere

The purpose of this tutorial exercise is to introduce more of the basic constructs of the DKB-Trace scene description language and to show how diffuse illumination, specular highlights, and shadows can increase the realism of an image. What this image model produces is a "classical," but dated, ray-traced image. It is classical, in that most early ray-traced images contained only spheres because they were easy to understand and model (see Chapter 2). Many of the early images also had checkered or tiled floors, as this image has. Images of this type are dated, however, because modern ray-tracing programs like DKBTrace can model many complex shapes and are thus not limited to spheres anymore. The image model file for this tutorial is called "exer2.dat" and is shown in Listing 7.5. This tutorial is appropriately called "A First Sphere."

Listing 7.5 Tutorial Exercise Two—A First Sphere

The following is the contents of the file "exer2.dat."

```
{
  Ray-Traced Imaging - Tutorial Exercise Two
  "A First Sphere"
  from the book "Practical Ray Tracing in C" by Craig A. Lindley
  Last update to this image: 03/06/92

  This is an image of a sphere with specular highlights located
  at the origin of the coordinate system floating above a
  checkered floor. The use of a sphere and a checkered floor
  make this a classical (although dated) ray-traced image. The
  purpose of this image is to show how highlights and shadows
  increase the realism of images. See the "Gallery of Images"
  for a look at what this image file produces.
}

INCLUDE "colors.dat"               { standard includes for color }
INCLUDE "shapes.dat"               { for shapes and }
INCLUDE "textures.dat"             { for textures }

VIEW_POINT                         { define the viewpoint }
  LOCATION < 0  0 -50 >
  DIRECTION < 0  0  1 >
  UP < 0  1  0 >
  RIGHT < 1  0  0 >
END_VIEW_POINT

OBJECT                             { define a light source }
  SPHERE < 0  0  0 > 2 END_SPHERE
  TRANSLATE < 60  70 -150 >
  TEXTURE
    COLOR White
    AMBIENT 1.0
    DIFFUSE 0.0
  END_TEXTURE
  COLOR White
  LIGHT_SOURCE
END_OBJECT

OBJECT                { Definition of the sphere }
  SPHERE < 0  0  0 > 10 END_SPHERE
  TEXTURE
    COLOR Red
    PHONG 1.0
    PHONGSIZE 90.0
    BRILLIANCE 10.0
  END_TEXTURE
END_OBJECT
```

(continued)

Listing 7.5 *(continued)*

```
OBJECT                    { Definition of the floor }
  PLANE < 0  1  0 > -20 END_PLANE
  TEXTURE
    CHECKER COLOR Green COLOR Yellow
    SCALE < 7.5  7.5  7.5 >
  END_TEXTURE
END_OBJECT
```

Much of this image model is identical to that presented in the last tutorial exercise. The model starts off with the comment block enclosed in curly braces, includes the three standard include files "colors.dat," "shapes.dat," and "textures.dat," sets up a VIEW_POINT, which is actually simpler than in the previous example, and then creates a single white LIGHT_SOURCE translated into its final position above, to the right, and behind the viewer. The new material in this tutorial is contained within the two objects that are now defined.

The first OBJECT is another optimized SPHERE centered at the origin with a radius of 10 units. Nothing new here. The TEXTURE block contains some new material, however. Inside the TEXTURE block, the sphere is made the color red, and is assigned the PHONG, PHONGSIZE, and BRILLIANCE surface attributes that give it its "realness." See the DKB-Trace user's manual "dkb212.doc" for a description of what these attributes are. Briefly, PHONG controls the amount of specular highlights on an object calculated via the Phong model. Specular highlights, as you will recall, show up as a bright spot of light on an object's surface from each light source in a scene. The smoother the object's surface, the tighter (smaller) the highlight. The value for PHONG can range from zero to one, with zero meaning no highlights and one meaning the highlights are exclusively the color of the light source at their center and fade to the object's color at the periphery of the highlight. PHONGSIZE indicates how smooth the surface is. The values can range from 1.0, which is very dull, to 100 or more, which indicates a very highly polished surface. BRILLIANCE controls the tightness of the diffuse illumination on an object. A BRILLIANCE value of four to ten will give an object a more metallic appearance.

The final OBJECT defined in this image model can be thought of as the floor of the image. In actuality, it is a plane that lies underneath the sphere floating at the coordinate system origin. This plane has a coloration texture mapped to it that makes it resemble a tiled or checkered floor. The specifics are as follows.

This OBJECT uses the optimized PLANE shape mentioned previously. As was the case with the optimized SPHERE, a plane can also be defined with the QUADRIC construct, although the use of the optimized PLANE speeds calculations. An optimized PLANE is fully defined by a vector that describes the direction of its surface normal and a floating-point value that specifies how far from the coordinate system axes along the normal the PLANE is located. The PLANE defined for this object has a normal in the positive Y direction (making it an infinite plane in the XZ directions), located a negative 20 units from the origin. In this case, then, the PLANE is 20 units below the origin and separated from the SPHERE by 10 units.

The CHECKER keyword within the TEXTURE block for this object is what causes the checkered pattern to be mapped onto the PLANE. The parameters within the CHECKER statement determine the colors to be used in the alternating pattern. In this case, the colors alternate between green and yellow, as seen in the image. Remember, these color names were established by including the file "colors.dat" in this image model. Finally, the checkered pattern is SCALEd uniformly in all directions to enlarge the size of the tile. SCALEing was done purely for aesthetic purposes.

When you look at the image produced by this image model in the "Gallery of Images" (see Image 7), you will see the red sphere with its specular highlight up and to the right of the sphere's center. You will also see the diffuse illumination as increased brightness up and to the right of the specular highlight. This diffuse illumination makes the surface of the sphere appear to glow. You will also see the shadow of the sphere cast onto the checkered floor with the orientation you would expect with the positioning of the single light source illuminating the scene. The floor is positioned beneath the sphere a small distance away.

Tutorial Exercise Three—Object Properties

This tutorial exercise is designed to show how changes in various textural attributes of a surface are reflected in changes in the appearance of the surface. Twenty-five spheres of differing surface attributes are used to illustrate these changes. These spheres are arranged in five rows of five spheres each in the image. In the horizontal direction from left to right, the spheres are given attributes that model dull, semi-shiny, very shiny, reflective, and refractive surfaces. In the vertical direction from top to bottom, the ALPHA factor of each row of spheres is increased. ALPHA controls how transparent a color is. An ALPHA of 0 indicates the color is totally opaque. An ALPHA of 1.0 means the color is fully transparent. Therefore, the spheres closer to the bottom of the image become more and more transparent while retaining the glossiness attributes established from left to right. Also shown in this tutorial exercise are the incorporation of multiple light sources, a color gradient background, and the use of the DECLARE statement to define OBJECTs. The image model file for this tutorial is called "exer3.dat" and is shown in Listing 7.6. This tutorial is titled "Object Properties."

This image model begins just like the other image models previously discussed. The first real difference is the definition of a second light source. As you can see in the listing, the second light source is defined exactly like the first light source; the only difference is in the positioning. The first light source is TRANSLATEd to a final position of <200 100 -200>, whereas the second light source is TRANSLATEd to <-200 -100 -200>. The first light source is above, behind, and to the far right of the viewer, while the second is below, behind, and to the far left of the viewer. Two light sources within a scene can result in two specular highlights on an object if the properties of the object's surface support specular reflection. The same is true of diffuse illumination. There is no practical limit on the number of light sources that can be contained in an image. The time it takes to render an image increases, however, with the addition of each new light source.

Listing 7.6 Tutorial Exercise Three—Object Properties

The following is the contents of the file "exer3.dat."

```
{
  Ray-Traced Imaging - Tutorial Exercise Three
  "Object Properties"
  from the book "Practical Ray Tracing in C" by Craig A. Lindley
  Last update to this image: 03/06/92

  This image contains many spheres that illustrate various
  surface attributes that objects can be assigned. In the
  horizontal direction, various glossiness factors are tried
  out, and in the vertical direction, various levels of
  transparency. The mapping is as follows:
```

Dull	Semi-Shiny	Very Shiny	Reflective	Refractive	
○	○	○	○	○	ALPHA 0.0
○	○	○	○	○	ALPHA 0.25
○	○	○	○	○	ALPHA 0.50
○	○	○	○	○	ALPHA 0.75
○	○	○	○	○	ALPHA 1.0

```
  Also illustrated in this model are multiple light sources,
  a color gradient background, and parameter substitution.
  See the "Gallery of Images" for a look at what this image file
  produces.
}

INCLUDE "colors.dat"              { standard includes for color }
INCLUDE "shapes.dat"              { for shapes and }
INCLUDE "textures.dat"            { for textures }

VIEW_POINT                        { define the viewpoint }
  LOCATION < 0  0 -62 >
  DIRECTION < 0  0  1 >
  UP  < 0  1  0 >
  RIGHT < 1.0  0  0 >
END_VIEW_POINT

OBJECT                            { light source 1 }
  SPHERE  < 0 0 0 > 2 END_SPHERE
  TRANSLATE  < 200 100 -200>
  TEXTURE
    COLOR White
    AMBIENT 1.0
    DIFFUSE 0.0
```

```
    END_TEXTURE
    COLOR White
    LIGHT_SOURCE
END_OBJECT

OBJECT                              { light source 2 }
    SPHERE   < 0 0 0 > 2 END_SPHERE
    TRANSLATE   <-200 -100 -200>
    TEXTURE
      COLOR White
      AMBIENT 1.0
      DIFFUSE 0.0
    END_TEXTURE
    COLOR White
    LIGHT_SOURCE
END_OBJECT


{ Add a background plane with color gradient for contrast }
OBJECT
    PLANE < 0  0  -1 > -10 END_PLANE
    TEXTURE
      Y_RGB_Gradient
      AMBIENT 1.0
      DIFFUSE 0.0
      SCALE < 1  150  1 >
      TRANSLATE < 0 -50  0 >
    END_TEXTURE
END_OBJECT

{ Define a variable called SphereColor }
DECLARE SphereColor =
    COLOR Red

{ Declare all of the 25 spheres }

DECLARE Sphere1 = OBJECT
    SPHERE < 0  0  0 > 5 END_SPHERE
    TEXTURE
      PHONG 1.0
      PHONGSIZE 1.0
      BRILLIANCE 5.0
      COLOR SphereColor ALPHA 0.0
    END_TEXTURE
END_OBJECT

DECLARE Sphere2 = OBJECT
    SPHERE < 0  0  0 > 5 END_SPHERE
    TEXTURE
      PHONG 1.0
      PHONGSIZE 20
      BRILLIANCE 5.0
```

(continued)

Listing 7.6   *(continued)*

```
      COLOR SphereColor ALPHA 0.0
    END_TEXTURE
END_OBJECT

DECLARE Sphere3 = OBJECT
  SPHERE < 0   0   0 > 5 END_SPHERE
  TEXTURE
      PHONG 1.0
      PHONGSIZE 100
      BRILLIANCE 5.0
      COLOR SphereColor ALPHA 0.0
    END_TEXTURE
END_OBJECT

DECLARE Sphere4 = OBJECT
  SPHERE < 0   0   0 > 5 END_SPHERE
  TEXTURE
      REFLECTION 0.5
      BRILLIANCE 5.0
      PHONG 0.3
      PHONGSIZE 50
      COLOR SphereColor ALPHA 0.0
    END_TEXTURE
END_OBJECT

DECLARE Sphere5 = OBJECT
  SPHERE < 0   0   0 > 5 END_SPHERE
  TEXTURE
      AMBIENT 0.0
      DIFFUSE 0.0
      REFLECTION 0.5
      IOR 1.54
      REFRACTION 0.85
      BRILLIANCE 5.0
      PHONG 0.3
      PHONGSIZE 50
      COLOR White ALPHA 0.0
    END_TEXTURE
END_OBJECT

DECLARE Sphere6 = OBJECT
  SPHERE < 0   0   0 > 5 END_SPHERE
  TEXTURE
      PHONG 1.0
      PHONGSIZE 1.0
      BRILLIANCE 5.0
      COLOR SphereColor ALPHA 0.25
    END_TEXTURE
END_OBJECT
```

```
DECLARE Sphere7 = OBJECT
  SPHERE < 0  0  0 > 5 END_SPHERE
  TEXTURE
    PHONG 1.0
    PHONGSIZE 20
    BRILLIANCE 5.0
    COLOR SphereColor ALPHA 0.25
  END_TEXTURE
END_OBJECT

DECLARE Sphere8 = OBJECT
  SPHERE < 0  0  0 > 5 END_SPHERE
  TEXTURE
    PHONG 1.0
    PHONGSIZE 100
    BRILLIANCE 5.0
    COLOR SphereColor ALPHA 0.25
  END_TEXTURE
END_OBJECT

DECLARE Sphere9 = OBJECT
  SPHERE < 0  0  0 > 5 END_SPHERE
  TEXTURE
    REFLECTION 0.5
    BRILLIANCE 5.0
    PHONG 0.3
    PHONGSIZE 50
    COLOR SphereColor ALPHA 0.25
  END_TEXTURE
END_OBJECT

DECLARE Sphere10 = OBJECT
  SPHERE < 0  0  0 > 5 END_SPHERE
  TEXTURE
    AMBIENT 0.0
    DIFFUSE 0.0
    REFLECTION 0.5
    IOR 1.54
    REFRACTION 0.5
    BRILLIANCE 5.0
    PHONG 0.3
    PHONGSIZE 50
    COLOR White ALPHA 0.25
  END_TEXTURE
END_OBJECT

DECLARE Sphere11 = OBJECT
  SPHERE < 0  0  0 > 5 END_SPHERE
  TEXTURE
    PHONG 1.0
    PHONGSIZE 1.0
```

(continued)

Listing 7.6   *(continued)*

```
      BRILLIANCE 5.0
      COLOR SphereColor ALPHA 0.5
   END_TEXTURE
END_OBJECT

DECLARE Sphere12 = OBJECT
   SPHERE < 0  0  0 > 5 END_SPHERE
   TEXTURE
      PHONG 1.0
      PHONGSIZE 20
      BRILLIANCE 5.0
      COLOR SphereColor ALPHA 0.5
   END_TEXTURE
END_OBJECT

DECLARE Sphere13 = OBJECT
   SPHERE < 0  0  0 > 5 END_SPHERE
   TEXTURE
      PHONG 1.0
      PHONGSIZE 100
      BRILLIANCE 5.0
      COLOR SphereColor ALPHA 0.5
   END_TEXTURE
END_OBJECT

DECLARE Sphere14 = OBJECT
   SPHERE < 0  0  0 > 5 END_SPHERE
   TEXTURE
      REFLECTION 0.5
      BRILLIANCE 5.0
      PHONG 0.3
      PHONGSIZE 50
      COLOR SphereColor ALPHA 0.5
   END_TEXTURE
END_OBJECT

DECLARE Sphere15 = OBJECT
   SPHERE < 0  0  0 > 5 END_SPHERE
   TEXTURE
      AMBIENT 0.0
      DIFFUSE 0.0
      REFLECTION 0.5
      IOR 1.54
      REFRACTION 0.5
      BRILLIANCE 5.0
      PHONG 0.3
      PHONGSIZE 50
      COLOR White ALPHA 0.5
   END_TEXTURE
END_OBJECT
```

```
DECLARE Sphere16 = OBJECT
  SPHERE < 0  0  0 > 5 END_SPHERE
  TEXTURE
    PHONG 1.0
    PHONGSIZE 1.0
    BRILLIANCE 5.0
    COLOR SphereColor ALPHA 0.75
  END_TEXTURE
END_OBJECT

DECLARE Sphere17 = OBJECT
  SPHERE < 0  0  0 > 5 END_SPHERE
  TEXTURE
    PHONG 1.0
    PHONGSIZE 20
    BRILLIANCE 5.0
    COLOR SphereColor ALPHA 0.75
  END_TEXTURE
END_OBJECT

DECLARE Sphere18 = OBJECT
  SPHERE < 0  0  0 > 5 END_SPHERE
  TEXTURE
    PHONG 1.0
    PHONGSIZE 100
    BRILLIANCE 5.0
    COLOR SphereColor ALPHA 0.75
  END_TEXTURE
END_OBJECT

DECLARE Sphere19 = OBJECT
  SPHERE < 0  0  0 > 5 END_SPHERE
  TEXTURE
    REFLECTION 0.5
    BRILLIANCE 5.0
    PHONG 0.3
    PHONGSIZE 50
    COLOR SphereColor ALPHA 0.75
  END_TEXTURE
END_OBJECT

DECLARE Sphere20 = OBJECT
  SPHERE < 0  0  0 > 5 END_SPHERE
  TEXTURE
    AMBIENT 0.0
    DIFFUSE 0.0
    REFLECTION 0.5
    IOR 1.54
    REFRACTION 0.5
    BRILLIANCE 5.0
    PHONG 0.3
```

(continued)

Listing 7.6 *(continued)*

```
    PHONGSIZE 50
    COLOR White ALPHA 0.75
  END_TEXTURE
END_OBJECT

DECLARE Sphere21 = OBJECT
  SPHERE < 0  0  0 > 5 END_SPHERE
  TEXTURE
    PHONG 1.0
    PHONGSIZE 1.0
    BRILLIANCE 5.0
    COLOR SphereColor ALPHA 1.0
  END_TEXTURE
END_OBJECT

DECLARE Sphere22 = OBJECT
  SPHERE < 0  0  0 > 5 END_SPHERE
  TEXTURE
    PHONG 1.0
    PHONGSIZE 20
    BRILLIANCE 5.0
    COLOR SphereColor ALPHA 1.0
  END_TEXTURE
END_OBJECT

DECLARE Sphere23 = OBJECT
  SPHERE < 0  0  0 > 5 END_SPHERE
  TEXTURE
    PHONG 1.0
    PHONGSIZE 100
    BRILLIANCE 5.0
    COLOR SphereColor ALPHA 1.0
  END_TEXTURE
END_OBJECT

DECLARE Sphere24 = OBJECT
  SPHERE < 0  0  0 > 5 END_SPHERE
  TEXTURE
    REFLECTION 0.5
    BRILLIANCE 5.0
    PHONG 0.3
    PHONGSIZE 50
    COLOR SphereColor ALPHA 1.0
  END_TEXTURE
END_OBJECT

DECLARE Sphere25 = OBJECT
  SPHERE < 0  0  0 > 5 END_SPHERE
  TEXTURE
```

```
     AMBIENT 0.0
     DIFFUSE 0.0
     REFLECTION 0.5
     IOR 1.54
     REFRACTION 0.5
     BRILLIANCE 5.0
     PHONG 0.3
     PHONGSIZE 50
     COLOR White ALPHA 1.0
  END_TEXTURE
END_OBJECT

{
Declare instances of the defined spheres and translate
them into the desired position.
}

OBJECT Sphere1  TRANSLATE <-24 24 0 > END_OBJECT
OBJECT Sphere2  TRANSLATE <-12 24 0 > END_OBJECT
OBJECT Sphere3  TRANSLATE <  0 24 0 > END_OBJECT
OBJECT Sphere4  TRANSLATE < 12 24 0 > END_OBJECT
OBJECT Sphere5  TRANSLATE < 24 24 0 > END_OBJECT

OBJECT Sphere6  TRANSLATE <-24 12 0 > END_OBJECT
OBJECT Sphere7  TRANSLATE <-12 12 0 > END_OBJECT
OBJECT Sphere8  TRANSLATE <  0 12 0 > END_OBJECT
OBJECT Sphere9  TRANSLATE < 12 12 0 > END_OBJECT
OBJECT Sphere10 TRANSLATE < 24 12 0 > END_OBJECT

OBJECT Sphere11 TRANSLATE <-24  0 0 > END_OBJECT
OBJECT Sphere12 TRANSLATE <-12  0 0 > END_OBJECT
OBJECT Sphere13 TRANSLATE < 0  0 0 > END_OBJECT
OBJECT Sphere14 TRANSLATE < 12  0 0 > END_OBJECT
OBJECT Sphere15 TRANSLATE < 24  0 0 > END_OBJECT

OBJECT Sphere16 TRANSLATE <-24 -12 0 > END_OBJECT
OBJECT Sphere17 TRANSLATE <-12 -12 0 > END_OBJECT
OBJECT Sphere18 TRANSLATE <  0 -12 0 > END_OBJECT
OBJECT Sphere19 TRANSLATE < 12 -12 0 > END_OBJECT
OBJECT Sphere20 TRANSLATE < 24 -12 0 > END_OBJECT

OBJECT Sphere21 TRANSLATE <-24 -24 0 > END_OBJECT
OBJECT Sphere22 TRANSLATE <-12 -24 0 > END_OBJECT
OBJECT Sphere23 TRANSLATE <  0 -24 0 > END_OBJECT
OBJECT Sphere24 TRANSLATE < 12 -24 0 > END_OBJECT
OBJECT Sphere25 TRANSLATE < 24 -24 0 > END_OBJECT
```

The next new concept in this image model is the use of a color gradient for background coloring. A color gradient can provide almost infinite variations in color over an object's surface. The range of colors in the gradient is controlled by the COLORMAP associated with the gradient. We will take up COLORMAPs in later tutorials, but for now, we will be using a derived coloration texture (from the file "textures.dat") called Y_RGB_Gradient. This gradient provides a full, repeating spectrum of colors that vary in the Y, or top to bottom, direction. The portion of the color gradient's spectrum that is applied to an object's surface is controlled by SCALEing and TRANSLATEing the gradient texture. In this image model, the color gradient is applied to a PLANE used as a backdrop behind the 25 spheres. This PLANE has a surface normal pointing in the minus Z direction, toward the viewer (it is an XY plane), and is located 10 units behind the coordinate axes and 10 units behind the center of the spheres, also. By SCALEing and TRANSLATEing the gradient's texture, the backdrop changes in color from green/blue at the top, through blue in the middle, and on toward pink at the bottom of the image. All in all, it's very pleasing to look at. Notice that an AMBIENT value of 1.0 and a DIFFUSE value of 0.0 are assigned to this PLANE. This indicates that the illumination of the PLANE (the light with which the color gradient is seen) should be from ambient lighting only, with no contribution from any of the light sources. What this means practically is that the spheres in the foreground will not cast shadows on the backdrop if they happen to be in the way of a light source.

Next, a constant SphereColor is DECLAREd and given the value of red. All 25 spheres in this image have a color of SphereColor and are therefore rendered in red. DECLAREing a constant in this manner is a convenient thing to do, because if you wish to change the color of all of the spheres in the image, only a single line edit is required. If you changed SphereColor to gold and rendered the image, all of the 25 spheres would be gold instead of red. This is much easier than to have to edit the definition of each of the defined spheres individually.

Finally, all 25 of the spheres are DECLAREd as OBJECTs instead of being defined as OBJECTs. As mentioned, DECLAREd OBJECTs are nothing more than templates or prototypes of the actual objects. They resemble type definitions more than anything else. Instances of these sphere OBJECTs will be created at the end of the model file when the spheres are TRANSLATEd into their final position from their original position at the coordinate origin.

In total, five spheres (Spheres 1, 6, 11, 16, and 21) will have a dull surface appearance. This is accomplished with the following surface parameters:

```
PHONG       = 1.0
PHONGSIZE   = 1.0
BRILLIANCE  = 5.0
```

The semi-shiny spheres' (Spheres 2, 7, 12, 17, and 22) surface parameters are:

```
PHONG       = 1.0
PHONGSIZE   = 20.0
BRILLIANCE  = 5.0
```

The very shiny spheres' (Spheres 3, 8, 13, 18, and 23) surface parameters are:

```
PHONG       = 1.0
PHONGSIZE   = 100.0
BRILLIANCE  = 5.0
```

The reflective spheres' (Spheres 4, 9, 14, 19, and 24) surface parameters are:

```
PHONG        = 0.3
PHONGSIZE    = 50.0
BRILLIANCE   = 5.0
REFLECTION   = 0.5
```

And finally, the refractive spheres (Spheres 5, 10, 15, 20, and 25) have surface parameters that attempt to simulate glass and are:

```
PHONG        = 0.3
PHONGSIZE    = 50.0
BRILLIANCE   = 5.0
REFLECTION   = 0.5
REFRACTION   = 0.85
IOR          = 1.54
AMBIENT      = 0.0
DIFFUSE      = 0.0
```

The ALPHA values used are 0.00, 0.25, 0.50, 0.75, and 1.00 for sphere rows one through five.

After all of the 25 spheres are defined, instances of each are created and TRANSLATEd into final position. The translations involve movement of the spheres in the X and Y directions to form the five rows of five spheres each. No translation is performed in the Z direction (i.e., the center of all spheres lies in the plane Z = 0).

Two interesting observations can be made by looking at the image produced by this image model. First, the specular highlighting effect diminishes in sharpness with increasing ALPHA, and second, the sphere at the lower right corner shows how light bends because of a nonunity IOR (Index of Refraction).

Tutorial Exercise Four—Constructive Solid Geometry One

The purpose of this tutorial exercise is to show how more complex and therefore more interesting and useful object shapes can be created by using Constructive Solid Geometry (CSG). CSG provides three operations for combining primitive shapes: UNION, INTERSECTION, and DIFFERENCE. As stated in Chapter 6, a UNION is the logical "or" of some number of surfaces, an INTERSECTION is the logical "and" of the surfaces, and DIFFERENCE is the subtraction of one or more surfaces from another. In all cases, a new indivisible shape is formed as a result of these CSG operations. The new shape is a whole; that is, it is no longer made up of its primitive parts. This new shape, therefore, can be manipulated just as if it were a primitive shape known to DKBTrace. In practical terms, a UNION forms a new shape that is the sum of its component shapes. An INTERSECTION creates a new shape where the component shapes overlap. Finally, a DIFFERENCE forms a new shape from the difference between the component shapes. The image in this tutorial exercise shows CSG in operation. The image model file is called "exer4.dat" and is shown in Listing 7.7. We will present two other tutorial exercises having to do with CSG in Chapter 8. Each of these will expand on the concepts presented here.

Listing 7.7   Tutorial Exercise Four—Constructive Solid Geometry One

The following is the contents of the file "exer4.dat."

```
{
  Ray-Traced Imaging - Tutorial Exercise Four
  "Constructive Solid Geometry One"
  from the book "Practical Ray Tracing in C" by Craig A. Lindley
  Last update to this image: 03/06/92

  The purpose of this exercise is to illustrate the concept of
  constructive solid geometry (CSG). On the left of this image is a
  cube (itself generated with CSG) and a sphere that will be
  used to demo CSG techniques. Middle top shows a UNION of the
  two shapes, middle bottom the INTERSECTION. Right top is a
  DIFFERENCE of the two shapes; in this case cube-sphere. Right
  bottom is a DIFFERENCE also, but this time it's sphere-cube.
  CSG will again be taken up in more advanced exercises.

  See the "Gallery of Images" for a look at what this image file
  produces.
}

INCLUDE "colors.dat"              { standard includes for color }
INCLUDE "shapes.dat"              { for shapes and }
INCLUDE "textures.dat"            { for textures }

VIEW_POINT                        { define the viewpoint }
  LOCATION <  0  0 -5.0 >
  DIRECTION < 0  0  1 >
  UP  < 0  1  0 >
  RIGHT < 1.0  0  0 >
  LOOK_AT < 0  0  0 >
END_VIEW_POINT

OBJECT                            { define a light source }
  SPHERE  < 0 0 0 > 2 END_SPHERE
  TRANSLATE  < 0 0 -20 >
  TEXTURE
    COLOR White
    AMBIENT 1.0
    DIFFUSE 0.0
  END_TEXTURE
  COLOR White
  LIGHT_SOURCE
END_OBJECT

{ Add a background plane for contrast }
OBJECT
  PLANE < 0  0  -1 > -10 END_PLANE
  TEXTURE
    AMBIENT 1.0
```

```
      DIFFUSE 0.0
      COLOR LightGray
    END_TEXTURE
END_OBJECT

{ Define a basic cube shape centered at origin 1 unit on a side }
DECLARE ACube = INTERSECTION
    PLANE <-1   0   0 > 0.5 END_PLANE
    PLANE < 1   0   0 > 0.5 END_PLANE
    PLANE < 0  -1   0 > 0.5 END_PLANE
    PLANE < 0   1   0 > 0.5 END_PLANE
    PLANE < 0   0  -1 > 0.5 END_PLANE
    PLANE < 0   0   1 > 0.5 END_PLANE
END_INTERSECTION

DECLARE ACubeShape = OBJECT
    INTERSECTION ACube END_INTERSECTION
    TEXTURE
      Shiny
      COLOR MediumBlue
    END_TEXTURE
END_OBJECT

DECLARE ASphere = UNION
    SPHERE < 0   0   0 > 0.5 END_SPHERE
END_UNION

DECLARE ASphereShape = OBJECT
    UNION ASphere END_UNION
    TEXTURE
      Shiny
      COLOR MediumForestGreen
    END_TEXTURE
END_OBJECT

DECLARE AUnion = OBJECT
    UNION
      INTERSECTION ACube
        TRANSLATE < 0.25   0   0 >
      END_INTERSECTION
      UNION ASphere
        TRANSLATE <-0.25   0   0 >
      END_UNION
    END_UNION
    TEXTURE
      Shiny
      COLOR MediumBlue
    END_TEXTURE
END_OBJECT

DECLARE AIntersection = OBJECT
    INTERSECTION
```

(continued)

Listing 7.7 *(continued)*

```
    INTERSECTION ACube
      TRANSLATE < 0.25   0   0 >
    END_INTERSECTION
    UNION ASphere
      TRANSLATE <-0.25   0   0 >
    END_UNION
  END_INTERSECTION
  TEXTURE
    Shiny
    COLOR MediumForestGreen
  END_TEXTURE
END_OBJECT

DECLARE ADifference1 = OBJECT
  DIFFERENCE
    INTERSECTION ACube
      TRANSLATE < 0.25   0   0 >
    END_INTERSECTION
    UNION ASphere
      TRANSLATE <-0.25   0   0 >
    END_UNION
  END_DIFFERENCE
  TEXTURE
    Shiny
    COLOR MediumBlue
  END_TEXTURE
END_OBJECT

DECLARE ADifference2 = OBJECT
  DIFFERENCE
    UNION ASphere
      TRANSLATE <-0.25   0   0 >
    END_UNION
    INTERSECTION ACube
      TRANSLATE < 0.25   0   0 >
    END_INTERSECTION
  END_DIFFERENCE
  TEXTURE
    Shiny
    COLOR MediumForestGreen
  END_TEXTURE
END_OBJECT

{ Instances of all of the objects }
OBJECT ACubeShape     ROTATE < 0 -30 0 > TRANSLATE <-1.5  1  0 > END_OBJECT
OBJECT ASphereShape   ROTATE < 0 -30 0 > TRANSLATE <-1.5 -1  0 > END_OBJECT
OBJECT AUnion         ROTATE < 0 -30 0 > TRANSLATE < 0.0  1  0 > END_OBJECT
OBJECT AIntersection  ROTATE < 0 -30 0 > TRANSLATE < 0.0 -1  0 > END_OBJECT
OBJECT ADifference1   ROTATE < 0 -30 0 > TRANSLATE < 1.5  1  0 > END_OBJECT
OBJECT ADifference2   ROTATE < 0 -30 0 > TRANSLATE < 1.5 -1  0 > END_OBJECT
```

By examining Listing 7.7, you can see that this image model starts out the same way as all of the previous image models. We will not discuss the similarities with previous image models here, only the differences. The first difference in this image model is the incorporation of a LOOK_AT vector in the VIEW_POINT specification. The vector specified by LOOK_AT is the position that the viewer's eye should always see centered in the middle of the ray-traced image, regardless of the other VIEW_POINT parameters. DKBTrace will manipulate the VIEW_POINT parameters to make sure the LOOK_AT point is always in the forefront. This is a convenient way of moving the VIEW_POINT around within a scene (as if panning a camera) and keeping the specified LOOK_AT position always in sight. This is especially handy for animation. As an example of its usefulness, consider a sphere located at the origin of the coordinate system. With the standard VIEW_POINT specification, the LOCATION would be somewhere on the negative Z axis and the DIRECTION would be down the positive Z axis. Under these conditions, the sphere would be visible in the exact center of this image. If the LOCATION of the VIEW_POINT were raised vertically and the DIRECTION not changed, the sphere would become invisible because we would be looking over the top of it. To compensate, of course, a slightly negative Y component of the DIRECTION vector could bring the sphere back into the field of view, but this would be a trial and error process to get it centered once more in the view plane. If a LOOK_AT position of < 0 0 0 > were specified in the VIEW_POINT definition, as the LOCATION was raised, the DIRECTION vector would automatically be modified by DKBTrace to place position < 0 0 0 > directly in the middle of the view plane. You can see the benefit of this.

For this image model, a PLANE is again used as a backdrop behind the foreground objects. This PLANE has a surface normal pointing toward the viewer in the negative Z direction and is located 10 units behind the coordinate system origin. It is given a light gray color and full ambient lighting to prevent shadowing from the foreground objects that would distract from the information presented in the image.

The first shape constructed here with CSG is a cube. This cube is 1 unit on a side and centered at the coordinate system origin. The cube is constructed using the INTERSECTION operator and six planes, each located half a unit from the origin. Remember, an INTERSECTION forms a new shape where the component shapes overlap. This is where the concept of the inside and outside of shapes comes into play. As you will recall from previous discussions, the side of a plane that has the surface normal is the outside. The inside is therefore the side without the normal. Notice how the INTERSECTION type ACube is formed. First, a PLANE is defined that is located a negative half unit along the X axis. (Yes, this description is correct. The distance specified from the origin for the PLANE is along the normal, so a positive half unit displacement along the negative X axis is really a negative half unit displacement for the PLANE. Darn, more things to think about.) The PLANE has a surface normal pointing down the negative X axis. The inside of this PLANE is therefore in the positive X direction. Next, a PLANE is defined with a surface normal pointing in the positive X direction and located half a unit along the positive X axis. The inside of this PLANE is along the negative X axis. With just these two PLANEs in INTERSECTION, we have created a new plane 1 unit thick in the X direction but still infinite in the Y and Z directions. The next two PLANEs that are defined cap this new plane in the ± Y directions.

The INTERSECTION of these four PLANEs results in a rectangular beam 1 unit wide, 1 unit tall, infinite in the Z direction, and located at the origin. The incorporation of the final two PLANEs, then, results in our ACube located at the origin and 1 unit in each dimension. We have just used CSG to create a new shape. This is one of the shapes that we will use to illustrate the other CSG operations.

Because ACube was DECLAREd, no real instance of the ACube was created. We want to create an instance of this shape to show what it looks like in the image model. Toward this end, an OBJECT is DECLAREd called ACubeShape which defines an instance of the ACube type and gives it a shiny blue coloring. In reality, an actual instance of ACube has still not been created, but it will be when an instance of ACubeShape is created.

Next, another DECLAREd type called ASphere is created. It is declared as a UNION, but it is just a single optimized SPHERE located at the origin with a radius of half a unit. ASphere is made a UNION so it can easily be incorporated within other CSG operations. As a UNION, it can be used repeatedly in other parts of the image model. Then, if a change, say, in the radius of the SPHERE were required, the change could be made in the definition of ASphere and it would ripple through the whole image model. This is a good programming technique that will help prevent errors during image model development and update.

For the same reasons mentioned earlier, we want to define an unmodified ASphere for display in our image. Like before, we DECLARE an ASphereShape type, give it the ASphere shape, and provide it with a coat of shiny medium forest green paint. An instance of this type will be created later in the image model file.

To illustrate the primary intended use of the UNION CSG operator, we next DECLARE an AUnion type, which is the UNION of the ACube and the ASphere slightly offset from one another. This UNION creates a new shape from these two other shapes. This new OBJECT with its new shape will be given the color of medium blue.

We next create another new shape type called AIntersection to illustrate CSG INTERSECTION. The same two shapes offset in the same manner are intersected and given the medium forest green color.

Finally, two DIFFERENCE shapes are created from the ACube and the ASphere. ADifference1 is the result of subtracting the ASphere shape from the ACube shape. This new shape is given the color of medium blue. ADifference2 is just the opposite and is the result of subtracting ACube from ASphere. Again, we use the medium forest green paint for this OBJECT.

The last operation performed in this image model is the creation, orientation, and placement of the various OBJECTs within the ray-traced image. All instances of these OBJECTs are ROTATEd in the negative Y direction so they can be better seen in the image. As each OBJECT is instantiated, it is ROTATEd and TRANSLATEd into its final orientation and position.

Looking at the image produced by this image model, you can see the results of the CSG operations. The ACube cube is shown in the upper left of the image and is itself a creation of CSG. Below it, the ASphereShape sphere is located. These are the two shapes with which the other four constructions in the image were created. In the upper middle of the image, the UNION of these two shapes is presented. As you can see, the result is a cube with a sphere sticking out the side. Below that, the INTERSECTION of the two shapes is shown. The resulting half sphere represents the only portions of the two component shapes that overlapped. In the upper right of the image, the first DIFFERENCE is shown. In this case, the sphere shape was subtracted from the cube shape, resulting in a spherical depression in the side of the cube.

The other DIFFERENCE, shown on the lower right, illustrates how a half sphere object can be created by subtracting away its other half.

Although the image produced with this image model is not very exciting, it does show how CSG can be used to create more complex objects than are inherently available with DKBTrace. Later CSG tutorials will create more interesting imagery, I promise.

Tutorial Exercise Five—The Quadric Family

The intent of this tutorial exercise is to show the various members of the quadric family of shapes. Quadric shapes are defined with second-order quadratic equations. CSG, as described in the last exercise, is needed to bound these shapes because all are, with the exceptions of the sphere and ellipsoid, infinite in one direction or another. Seven different quadric shapes, including the sphere, the cylinder, the cone, the plane, the paraboloid, the hyperbolic parabo-loid, and the hyperboloid, are included. These are all shapes defined in the DKBTrace include file "shapes.dat" discussed at the beginning of this chapter. With the many orientations of each quadric shape provided, a total of 15 shapes are contained in this image model. The image model file is called "exer5.dat" and is shown in Listing 7.8.

Listing 7.8 Tutorial Exercise Five—The Quadric Family

The following is the contents of the file "exer5.dat."

```
{
    Ray-Traced Imaging - Tutorial Exercise Five
    "The Quadric Family"
    from the book "Practical Ray Tracing in C" by Craig A. Lindley
    Last update to this image: 03/06/92

    The purpose of this exercise is to show many of the quadric
    shapes. Constructive Solid Geometry (CSG) is used to
    bound many of the shapes as only the sphere and the ellipsoid
    are self-bounding. This is a top view looking down on the
    various shapes. The shapes are arranged as follows:

    Para in X   Para in Y   Para in Z   HyperP    Hyper in Y
    Cone in Y   Cone in Z   Plane YZ    Plane XZ  Plane XY
    Sphere      Cyl in X    Cyl in Y    Cyl in Z  Cone in X

    where: Para=Paraboloid; Hyper=Hyperboloid; Cyl=Cylinder
           HyperP=Hyperbolic Paraboloid

    A small amount of color dithering is added to objects to
    increase detail. See the "Gallery of Images" for a look at
    what this image file produces.
}
```

(continued)

Listing 7.8   *(continued)*

```
INCLUDE "colors.dat"              { standard includes for color }
INCLUDE "shapes.dat"              { for shapes and }
INCLUDE "textures.dat"            { for textures }

VIEW_POINT                        { define the viewpoint }
  LOCATION <  0  0  -17 >
  DIRECTION < 0   0  1 >
  UP  < 0  1  0 >
  RIGHT < 1.0  0  0 >
  ROTATE < 90  0  0 >
END_VIEW_POINT

OBJECT                            { define a light source }
  SPHERE   < 0 0 0 > 2 END_SPHERE
  TRANSLATE  < 0  20  0 >
  TEXTURE
    COLOR White
    AMBIENT 1.0
    DIFFUSE 0.0
  END_TEXTURE
  COLOR White
  LIGHT_SOURCE
END_OBJECT

{ Add a floor plane for contrast }
OBJECT
  PLANE < 0  1  0 > -10 END_PLANE
  TEXTURE
    AMBIENT 1.0
    DIFFUSE 0.0
    COLOR LightGray
  END_TEXTURE
END_OBJECT


{ Define the basic shapes centered at origin 1 unit on a side }

DECLARE ASphere = OBJECT
  QUADRIC Sphere END_QUADRIC
  TEXTURE
    0.25
    COLOR Red
  END_TEXTURE
END_OBJECT

DECLARE Cyl_X = OBJECT
  INTERSECTION
    QUADRIC Cylinder_X END_QUADRIC
    PLANE <-1  0  0 > 1 END_PLANE
    PLANE < 1  0  0 > 1 END_PLANE
  END_INTERSECTION
```

```
    TEXTURE
      0.25
      COLOR Red
    END_TEXTURE
END_OBJECT


DECLARE Cyl_Y = OBJECT
    INTERSECTION
      QUADRIC Cylinder_Y END_QUADRIC
      PLANE < 0 -1  0 > 1 END_PLANE
      PLANE < 0  1  0 > 1 END_PLANE
    END_INTERSECTION
    TEXTURE
      0.25
      COLOR Red
    END_TEXTURE
END_OBJECT


DECLARE Cyl_Z = OBJECT
    INTERSECTION
      QUADRIC Cylinder_Z END_QUADRIC
      PLANE < 0  0 -1 > 1 END_PLANE
      PLANE < 0  0  1 > 1 END_PLANE
    END_INTERSECTION
    TEXTURE
      0.25
      COLOR Red
    END_TEXTURE
END_OBJECT


DECLARE Con_X = OBJECT
    INTERSECTION
      QUADRIC Cone_X END_QUADRIC
      PLANE <-1  0  0 > 1 END_PLANE
      PLANE < 1  0  0 > 1 END_PLANE
    END_INTERSECTION
    TEXTURE
      0.25
      COLOR Red
    END_TEXTURE
END_OBJECT


DECLARE Con_Y = OBJECT
    INTERSECTION
      QUADRIC Cone_Y END_QUADRIC
      PLANE < 0 -1  0 > 1 END_PLANE
      PLANE < 0  1  0 > 1 END_PLANE
    END_INTERSECTION
    TEXTURE
      0.25
      COLOR Green
    END_TEXTURE
END_OBJECT
```

(continued)

Listing 7.8   *(continued)*

```
DECLARE Con_Z = OBJECT
  INTERSECTION
    QUADRIC Cone_Z END_QUADRIC
    PLANE < 0   0 -1 > 1 END_PLANE
    PLANE < 0   0  1 > 1 END_PLANE
  END_INTERSECTION
  TEXTURE
    0.25
    COLOR Green
  END_TEXTURE
END_OBJECT


DECLARE ACube = INTERSECTION
  PLANE <-1   0   0 > 1 END_PLANE
  PLANE < 1   0   0 > 1 END_PLANE
  PLANE < 0  -1   0 > 1 END_PLANE
  PLANE < 0   1   0 > 1 END_PLANE
  PLANE < 0   0  -1 > 1 END_PLANE
  PLANE < 0   0   1 > 1 END_PLANE
END_INTERSECTION


DECLARE Pln_YZ = OBJECT
  INTERSECTION
    INTERSECTION ACube END_INTERSECTION
    QUADRIC Plane_YZ END_QUADRIC
  END_INTERSECTION
  TEXTURE
    0.25
    COLOR Green
  END_TEXTURE
END_OBJECT

DECLARE Pln_XZ = OBJECT
  INTERSECTION
    QUADRIC Plane_XZ END_QUADRIC
    INTERSECTION ACube END_INTERSECTION
  END_INTERSECTION
  TEXTURE
    0.25
    COLOR Green
  END_TEXTURE
END_OBJECT

DECLARE Pln_XY = OBJECT
  INTERSECTION
    QUADRIC Plane_XY END_QUADRIC
    INTERSECTION ACube END_INTERSECTION
  END_INTERSECTION
```

```
    TEXTURE
      0.25
      COLOR Green
    END_TEXTURE
END_OBJECT

DECLARE Para_X = OBJECT
  INTERSECTION
    QUADRIC Paraboloid_X END_QUADRIC
    INTERSECTION ACube END_INTERSECTION
  END_INTERSECTION
  TEXTURE
    0.25
    COLOR Blue
  END_TEXTURE
END_OBJECT

DECLARE Para_Y = OBJECT
  INTERSECTION
    QUADRIC Paraboloid_Y END_QUADRIC
    INTERSECTION ACube END_INTERSECTION
  END_INTERSECTION
  TEXTURE
    0.25
    COLOR Blue
  END_TEXTURE
END_OBJECT

DECLARE Para_Z = OBJECT
  INTERSECTION
    QUADRIC Paraboloid_Z END_QUADRIC
    INTERSECTION ACube END_INTERSECTION
  END_INTERSECTION
  TEXTURE
    0.25
    COLOR Blue
  END_TEXTURE
END_OBJECT

DECLARE HyperP = OBJECT
  INTERSECTION
    QUADRIC Hyperboloid END_QUADRIC
    INTERSECTION ACube END_INTERSECTION
  END_INTERSECTION
  TEXTURE
    0.25
    COLOR Blue
  END_TEXTURE
END_OBJECT
```

(continued)

Listing 7.8 *(continued)*

```
DECLARE Hyper_Y = OBJECT
  INTERSECTION
    QUADRIC Hyperboloid_Y END_QUADRIC
    INTERSECTION ACube END_INTERSECTION
  END_INTERSECTION
  TEXTURE
    0.25
    COLOR Blue
  END_TEXTURE
END_OBJECT


DECLARE Row_1_Objects = COMPOSITE
  OBJECT ASphere   TRANSLATE <-7    0  0 > END_OBJECT
  OBJECT Cyl_X     TRANSLATE <-3.5  0  0 > END_OBJECT
  OBJECT Cyl_Y                             END_OBJECT
  OBJECT Cyl_Z     TRANSLATE < 3.5  0  0 > END_OBJECT
  OBJECT Con_X     TRANSLATE < 7    0  0 > END_OBJECT
END_COMPOSITE

DECLARE Row_2_Objects = COMPOSITE
  OBJECT Con_Y     TRANSLATE <-7    0  0 > END_OBJECT
  OBJECT Con_Z     TRANSLATE <-3.5  0  0 > END_OBJECT
  OBJECT Pln_YZ                            END_OBJECT
  OBJECT Pln_XZ    TRANSLATE < 3.5  0  0 > END_OBJECT
  OBJECT Pln_XY    TRANSLATE < 7    0  0 > END_OBJECT
END_COMPOSITE

DECLARE Row_3_Objects = COMPOSITE
  OBJECT Para_X    TRANSLATE <-7    0  0 > END_OBJECT
  OBJECT Para_Y    TRANSLATE <-3.5  0  0 > END_OBJECT
  OBJECT Para_Z                            END_OBJECT
  OBJECT HyperP    TRANSLATE < 3.5  0  0 > END_OBJECT
  OBJECT Hyper_Y   TRANSLATE < 7    0  0 > END_OBJECT
END_COMPOSITE

COMPOSITE Row_1_Objects TRANSLATE < 0  0 -5 > END_COMPOSITE
COMPOSITE Row_2_Objects END_COMPOSITE
COMPOSITE Row_3_Objects TRANSLATE < 0  0  5 > END_COMPOSITE
```

Because of the number of individual objects that need to be included in this image model, we need a new approach to viewing. This new approach is a view from directly above all of the objects looking straight down onto them. This view is necessary to prevent perspective from distorting the view as it would if the objects were viewed directly from the front. The objects are organized into three rows of five objects each. The resulting image shows paraboloids in the X, Y, and Z directions, followed by a hyperbolic paraboloid and then a hyperboloid in the top row; cones in the Y and Z directions, followed by planes in the YZ, XZ, and XY orientations in the middle row; a sphere, then cylinders in the X, Y, and Z directions, followed by a cone in the X direction in the bottom row. The view from directly above the quadric objects is accomplished by ROTATEing the standard VIEW_POINT 90 degrees in the positive direction around the X axis. So instead of being directly in front of the rows of objects, the VIEW_POINT is directly overhead and looking down.

A light gray backdrop is placed under the objects to accentuate the objects' shape and color. This backdrop is actually a PLANE with XZ orientation; that is, it has a surface normal in the positive Y direction. This PLANE is located 10 units under the coordinate system origin.

The definition of the quadric OBJECTs begins with the ASphere. The ASphere type is DECLAREd and given the color red, as are all OBJECTs in the bottom row of the image. You will notice the number 0.25 included within the TEXTURE block. This number (which is not tagged by a DKBTrace keyword) adds a small amount of randomness to the color applied to this OBJECT. In other words, it causes the color to be dithered (modified a small amount in a random fashion), which gives additional character to the coloring. All OBJECTs in this image model have dithered coloring.

Next, the cylinders in three orientations are defined. You will notice the CSG INTER-SECTION operation is required to limit the infinite length of the cylinders to something that can be contained within the image. The resulting cylinders have a radius of 1 (by default) and a length of 2 (by design). Two PLANEs are used to limit the length. Picture these planes with their normals sticking out both ends of the cylinders. The shape that results, the length limited or capped cylinder, is formed from the overlap of the insides of the three shapes.

Following the cylinders, the cones are defined. Cones are also infinite shapes. They have an apex at the origin but fan out as cones will toward infinity. They also have a symmetrical counterpart on the opposite side of the origin that progresses toward the infinite. Two PLANEs are used here to contain the cones to a usable size. The cone in the X direction, which is contained in the bottom row of the image, is colored red, the cones in the Y and Z directions, residing in the middle row, are given the green color.

To aid in bounding the quadric shapes yet to be discussed, another ACube INTERSEC-TION is defined like that discussed in the last tutorial exercise. When an ACube is subsequently used in an INTERSECTION with a quadric shape, the resulting OBJECT can never be larger than the ACube, which is 2 units in size in each dimension. This is not the most optimal form of bounding to use for the quadric shapes, but it is the easiest and it always works no matter what direction the quadric shape is infinite in. *Note*: The use of the word bounding in this context is different than bounding volumes, which we will describe in the next tutorial exercise. Here, bounding is used to limit the size or extent of some other quadric shape. Bounding volumes are used as a performance enhancement technique within DKBTrace (more on this in the next tutorial).

The first use of ACube bounding is within the definitions of the planes. ACube bounding works the same regardless of the orientation of the plane being bounded. All three plane OBJECTs are bound using the ACube. All three are also colored green. Further, all remaining quadric shapes in this image model also use the ACube for bounding. Finally, all OBJECTs that make up the top row within the image are colored blue.

The next new DKBTrace language construct to be presented is the COMPOSITE,

END_COMPOSITE block. A COMPOSITE object is made up of OBJECTs and/or other COMPOSITE objects. OBJECTs defined together within a COMPOSITE block are manipulated as a single OBJECT. Any transformations or rotations applied to the COMPOSITE are applied to each component OBJECT as well. A COMPOSITE block is similar to a CSG UNION, except that a UNION is generally just a shape without texture while OBJECTs within a COMPOSITE have both shape and texture. As shown in the listing, COMPOSITE objects can be DECLAREd just as all other items in the DKBTrace scene description language can. Instances of all OBJECTs contained within a COMPOSITE object are created when an instance of the COMPOSITE object is created. Instantiation and translation of COMPOSITE objects is the final operation performed in this image model.

Please remember when viewing this image model in the "Gallery of Images" that you are looking straight down on the objects from directly overhead. Otherwise, the stated orientations of the objects will appear to be in error.

Tutorial Exercise Six—The Quartic Family

The second major family of mathematical shapes supported by DKBTrace is the quartic family. Quartic shapes are fourth-order shapes encompassing spectacular variety. Because of their higher order, quartic shapes are both more complex to describe and slower to render. In addition, this implementation of quartic shapes has some bugs because it is a relatively new addition to the DKBTrace program. These bugs will probably be fixed in a new version of DKBTrace (if and when that ever happens), but for now, we must live with them. These minor problems aside, quartic shapes are fun to experiment with because they can produce a wide variety of uniquely bizarre shapes. Five of the more common quartic shapes—the quartic cylinder, the torus, the folium, the piriform, and the lemniscate—are illustrated in this tutorial exercise. If you're interested in experimenting with other mathematical shapes, you must see the book *The CRC Handbook of Mathematical Curves and Surfaces*, written by David Von Seggern. See the "Further Reading" section of Part Three for the details. The image model file for this tutorial is called "exer6.dat" and is shown in Listing 7.9.

This image model defines five quartic shapes of approximately the same size, color, and texture floating in a single row above a blue/midnight blue checkered floor. The only new information provided in this image model is on the creation of the quartic shapes and on the use of bounding volumes. This is where we will focus our discussion.

As you recall, quadric shapes were defined by the proper selection of ten parameters. By varying these parameters, you can create all quadric shapes at any location and with any orientation. If 10 parameters scared you, consider the quartic definition, which uses 35 different parameters, A_0 through A_{34}, to define a surface. By varying these parameters, you can create all quartic shapes at any location and with any orientation. (As an aside, you can also create all third-order and second-order surfaces with proper parameter selection.) The trick is knowing how to select the appropriate parameter values. The DKBTrace user's manual has some information on quartic surfaces and parameter selection, as does David Von Seggern's book. Defining quartic surfaces is, however, beyond the scope of this discussion and will not be pursued. What we will discuss here is the syntax used within DKBTrace to define the quartic surfaces.

Listing 7.9 Tutorial Exercise Six—The Quartic Family

The following is the contents of the file "exer6.dat."

```
{
  Ray-Traced Imaging - Tutorial Exercise Six
  "The Quartic Family"
  from the book "Practical Ray Tracing in C" by Craig A. Lindley
  Last update to this image: 03/06/92

  The purpose of this exercise is to show a few of the quartic
  shapes. Constructive Solid Geometry (CSG) is used to bound
  many of the shapes because they are not self-bounding.

  See the "Gallery of Images" for a look at what this image file
  produces.
}

INCLUDE "colors.dat"              { standard includes for color }
INCLUDE "shapes.dat"              { for shapes and }
INCLUDE "textures.dat"           { for textures }

VIEW_POINT                        { define the viewpoint }
  LOCATION < 0  0 -17 >
  DIRECTION < 0  0  1 >
  UP  < 0  1  0 >
  RIGHT < 1.0  0  0 >
END_VIEW_POINT

OBJECT                            { define a light source }
  SPHERE  < 0 0 0 > 2 END_SPHERE
  TRANSLATE  < 20  0 -25 >
  TEXTURE
    COLOR White
    AMBIENT 1.0
    DIFFUSE 0.0
  END_TEXTURE
  COLOR White
  LIGHT_SOURCE
END_OBJECT

{ Add a tiled floor for contrast }
DECLARE Floor = OBJECT
  PLANE < 0  1  0 > -2.5 END_PLANE
  TEXTURE
    CHECKER COLOR Blue COLOR MidnightBlue
    AMBIENT 0.9
    DIFFUSE 0.1
  END_TEXTURE
END_OBJECT

{ Define a texture for all quartic shapes }
DECLARE QuarticTex =
```

(continued)

Listing 7.9   *(continued)*

```
TEXTURE
  COLOR Red
  SPECULAR 0.85
  ROUGHNESS 0.05
END_TEXTURE

{ Quartic Cylinder - A Space Needle or Top? }
DECLARE QuarticCyl = OBJECT
  QUARTIC
    < 0.0    0.0    0.0    0.0    1.0    0.0    0.0    0.0    0.0    0.01
      0.0    0.0    0.0    0.0    0.0    0.0    0.0    0.0    0.0    0.0
      0.0    0.0    0.0    1.0    0.0    0.0    0.0    0.0    0.0    0.0
      0.0    0.0    0.01   0.0   -0.01 >
  END_QUARTIC
  BOUNDED_BY
    SPHERE < 0   0   0 > 2 END_SPHERE
  END_BOUND
  TEXTURE
    QuarticTex
  END_TEXTURE
END_OBJECT

{ Torus having major radius sqrt(40), minor radius sqrt(12) }
DECLARE Torus = OBJECT
  QUARTIC
    < 1.0    0.0    0.0    0.0    2.0    0.0    0.0    2.0    0.0 -104.0
      0.0    0.0    0.0    0.0    0.0    0.0    0.0    0.0    0.0    0.0
      1.0    0.0    0.0    2.0    0.0   56.0    0.0    0.0    0.0    0.0
      1.0    0.0 -104.0    0.0  784.0 >
  END_QUARTIC
  BOUNDED_BY
    SPHERE < 0   0   0 > 10 END_SPHERE
  END_BOUND
  TEXTURE
    QuarticTex
  END_TEXTURE
  SCALE < 0.15 0.15 0.15 >
END_OBJECT

{ Folium }
DECLARE Folium = OBJECT
  INTERSECTION
    QUARTIC
      < 0.0    0.0    0.0    0.0  0.0  0.0    0.0    0.0    0.0  2.0
        0.0    0.0   -3.0    0.0  0.0  0.0    0.0   -3.0    0.0  0.0
        0.0    0.0    0.0    0.0  0.0  1.0    0.0    0.0    0.0  0.0
        0.0    0.0    1.0    0.0  0.0 >
      TEXTURE
        QuarticTex
      END_TEXTURE
    END_QUARTIC
```

```
    SPHERE < 0  0  0 > 10
      TEXTURE
        COLOR Clear
      END_TEXTURE
    END_SPHERE
  END_INTERSECTION
  BOUNDED_BY
    SPHERE <0 0 0> 11 END_SPHERE
  END_BOUND
  SCALE < 0.15 0.15 0.15 >
END_OBJECT

{ Piriform - looks like a candy kiss }
DECLARE Piriform = OBJECT
  INTERSECTION
    QUARTIC
      < 4.0    0.0    0.0   -4.0  0.0   0.0   0.0   0.0   0.0  0.0
        0.0    0.0    0.0    0.0  0.0   0.0   0.0   0.0   0.0  0.0
        0.0    0.0    0.0    0.0  0.0   1.0   0.0   0.0   0.0  0.0
        0.0    0.0    1.0    0.0  0.0 >
    END_QUARTIC
    { This intersection is necessary because of discontinuity }
    { in Piriform at apex }
    PLANE <-1   0   0 > -0.1 END_PLANE
  END_INTERSECTION
  BOUNDED_BY
    SPHERE < 0   0   0 > 2 END_SPHERE
  END_BOUND
  TEXTURE QuarticTex END_TEXTURE
  SCALE < 1.6 1.6 1.6 >
END_OBJECT

{ Lemniscate of Gerono }
DECLARE Lemniscate = OBJECT
  QUARTIC
    < 1.0    0.0    0.0    0.0  0.0   0.0   0.0   0.0   0.0 -1.0
      0.0    0.0    0.0    0.0  0.0   0.0   0.0   0.0   0.0  0.0
      0.0    0.0    0.0    0.0  0.0   1.0   0.0   0.0   0.0  0.0
      0.0    0.0    1.0    0.0  0.0 >
  END_QUARTIC
  BOUNDED_BY
    SPHERE < 0   0   0 > 2 END_SPHERE
  END_BOUND
  TEXTURE
    QuarticTex
  END_TEXTURE
  SCALE < 1.6 1.6 1.6 >
END_OBJECT
```

(continued)

Listing 7.9   *(continued)*

```
{ Now define the whole scene in a composite structure }
DECLARE Scene = COMPOSITE
  OBJECT Floor END_OBJECT
  OBJECT QuarticCyl
    ROTATE <-30 20 0>
    TRANSLATE <-7  0  0 >
  END_OBJECT
  OBJECT Torus
    ROTATE <-60 -30  0>
    TRANSLATE <-3.5  0  0 >
  END_OBJECT
  OBJECT Folium
    ROTATE < 0  50  45 >
    TRANSLATE < 0  0  0 >
  END_OBJECT
  OBJECT Piriform
    ROTATE < 0  0 -90 >
    TRANSLATE < 3.5 0  0 >
  END_OBJECT
  OBJECT Lemniscate
    ROTATE < 0 -45  0 >
    ROTATE < -45  0  0 >
    TRANSLATE < 7  0  0 >
  END_OBJECT
END_COMPOSITE

{ Render the whole scene }
COMPOSITE Scene END_COMPOSITE
```

The quartic syntax is similar to that used for quadric surfaces. In the quartic case, the DKBTrace keyword QUARTIC is followed by 35 floating-point numbers enclosed in angled brackets <>. The parameters are coefficients in the equation:

$$
\begin{aligned}
&a00\,X^4 &&+\,a01\,X^3\,Y &&+\,a02\,X^3\,Z &&+\,a03\,X^3 &&+\,a04\,X^2\,Y^2 &&+ \\
&a05\,X^2\,Y\,Z &&+\,a06\,X^2\,Y &&+\,a07\,X^2\,Z^2 &&+\,a08\,X^2\,Z &&+\,a09\,X^2 &&+ \\
&a10\,X\,Y^3 &&+\,a11\,X\,Y^2\,Z &&+\,a12\,X\,Y^2 &&+\,a13\,X\,Y\,Z^2 &&+\,a14\,X\,Y\,Z &&+ \\
&a15\,X\,Y &&+\,a16\,X\,Z^3 &&+\,a17\,X\,Z^2 &&+\,a18\,X\,Z &&+\,a19\,X &&+ \\
&a20\,Y^4 &&+\,a21\,Y^3\,Z &&+\,a22\,Y^3 &&+\,a23\,Y^2\,Z^2 &&+\,a24\,Y^2\,Z &&+ \\
&a25\,Y^2 &&+\,a26\,Y\,Z^3 &&+\,a27\,Y\,Z^2 &&+\,a28\,Y\,Z &&+\,a29\,Y &&+ \\
&a30\,Z^4 &&+\,a31\,Z^3 &&+\,a32\,Z^2 &&+\,a33\,Z &&+\,a34
\end{aligned}
$$

which defines all quartic surfaces. These 35 coefficient parameters are specified to DKBTrace as follows:

```
QUARTIC
   < a00  a01  a02  a03  a04  a05  a06  a07  a08  a09
     a10  a11  a12  a13  a14  a15  a16  a17  a18  a19
     a20  a21  a22  a23  a24  a25  a26  a27  a28  a29
     a30  a31  a32  a33  a34 >
END_QUARTIC
```

The sets of parameters used for the five quartic surfaces in this image model are shown in the listing. Once the quartic surface is defined, it can be manipulated with the same ease as any of the quadric surfaces.

Because of their complexity, the calculations of quartic/ray intersections and the calculations of quartic surface normals take quite a bit of time to perform. In fact, the quartic calculations take somewhere in the order of ten times as long to execute as the quadric calculations do. For this reason, when you use quartic shapes within ray-traced images, you should surround them by bounding volumes to speed image rendering time. We described the concepts behind bounding volumes in Chapter 2. Briefly, for review, the idea is to place simple shapes, called bounding volumes, around the more complex shapes within an image. The ray tracer will first check to see if a ray pierces the simpler bounding volume before checking to see if the ray pierces the more complex shape. If the ray does not pierce the bounding volume it cannot possibly intersect the contained complex shape, so you do not have to perform the complex and time-consuming intersection calculation. If, of course, the bounding volume is pierced, then you will indeed have to perform the complex intersection calculations, resulting in a small performance penalty.

Within DKBTrace, bounding volumes are declared in a BOUNDED_BY, END_BOUND block. Any shape can be used for the bounding volume, but the simpler the shape the better. Spheres, being the simplest of all shapes, should be used whenever practical. In this image model, all of the quartic surfaces are bounded by spheres to decrease the image rendering time. To get a feel for the difference in rendering time that bounding volumes make, comment out the BOUNDED_BY blocks in this image model and render it again. The difference is amazing.

In this image model, a COMPOSITE object called Scene is DECLAREd, which encompasses all of the OBJECTs within the whole scene except the LIGHT_SOURCE. Within this COMPOSITE object, all of the individual quartic OBJECTs are ROTATEd into viewing position and then TRANSLATEd to their final location. An instance of the complete scene is created with the statement:

```
COMPOSITE Scene END_COMPOSITE
```

located at the end of the image model.

The piriform quartic needs further mention. If you look closely at the image produced by this image model in the "Gallery of Images" (see Image 11), the piriform is the object that resembles a chocolate candy kiss. If you look closely at the piriform, you will see some aberration of its surface and a small, single-pixel-width line shooting off from its left side. This is a problem with the quartic implementation within DKBTrace. Now examine the piriform definition in the listing. You will see that it had to be bounded using a PLANE and an INTERSECTION to keep it fairly well behaved. For some reason, numerous discontinuities exist near the apex of the piriform that cause strange behavior during rendering. The PLANE/piriform INTERSECTION used in the piriform definition does get rid of most of the problem, leaving only the little bit that shows up in the image. That also could have been avoided by moving the position of the PLANE within the INTERSECTION, but such a move would have resulted in a flat-topped piriform, not one shaped like a candy kiss.

Tutorial Exercise Seven—Coloration Textures

The purpose of this tutorial exercise is to acquaint you with some of the coloration textures available with DKBTrace. As you will recall from previous discussions, textures come in two varieties: coloration textures and surface perturbation textures. Coloration textures, as illustrated in this tutorial exercise, change the color of surfaces without changing the apparent shape or geometry of the surface. Surface perturbation textures, however, as illustrated in the next tutorial exercise, appear to change the shape of a surface instead of directly changing its color. Surface perturbation textures do sometimes change the color or shading of surfaces because of their manipulation of surface geometry. This, however, is a side effect of their primary purpose. But we are getting ahead of ourselves. We'll have more on surface perturbation textures shortly.

Textures are one of DKBTrace's biggest strengths. Use of texture(s) within ray-traced images adds character to the images as well as realism. The coloration texture possibilities available with DKBTrace are almost infinite. DKBTrace allows two kinds of coloration textures. The first I refer to as intrinsic textures and are those textures built directly into the DKBTrace program and always available for use. The second variety I call derived textures and are those textures built from the intrinsic textures with the addition of TURBULENCE functions, color dithering, COLORMAPs, and the manipulation of other surface attributes. The include file "textures.dat," which has been included in all image models and shown at the beginning of this chapter, contains all of the derived textures used here. These textures are available for use in any image model that includes this file. An imagemap is a special form of intrinsic coloration texture that allows bit-mapped imagery to be mapped to an object's surface. We will take up imagemaps in the tutorial exercises in Chapter 8. To make things even more interesting, you can apply multiple layers of textures to a surface. With this feature, for example, it is possible to create a wood grain/cloud texture, in addition to many other textures equally esoteric. You can find much more information on textures in the DKBTrace user's manual.

In this image model, 18 different coloration textures are shown. Each is mapped onto a simple sphere to show the effect. All spheres are identical in size and are organized into three rows of five textures each and one row of three textures. The textures illustrated are the following:

Red Marble	Black Marble	Jade	Blue Agate	Brown Agate
Wood	Tan Wood	Dark Wood	Tom Wood	White Wood
Spotted	Granite	Brass	Iron	Pearl
	Candy Cane	Checker	Y_RGB_Gradient	

Additionally, this image model defines two light sources and a backdrop PLANE for showcasing the coloration textures. The image model file for this tutorial is "exer7.dat" and is shown in Listing 7.10.

Listing 7.10 Tutorial Exercise Seven—Coloration Textures

The following is the contents of the file "exer7.dat."

```
{
  Ray-Traced Imaging - Tutorial Exercise Seven
  "Coloration Textures"
  from the book "Practical Ray Tracing in C" by Craig A. Lindley
  Last update to this image: 03/06/92

  The purpose of this exercise is to illustrate many of
  the coloration texture possibilities available with
  DKBTrace. This image contains both intrinsic and
  derived textures. All textures are mapped to spheres.
  The arrangement of textures are as follows:

  Red Marble  Black Marble  Jade       Blue Agate Brown Agate
  Wood        Tan Wood      Dark Wood  Tom Wood   White Wood
  Spotted     Granite       Brass      Iron       Pearl
              Candy Cane    Checker    Y_RGB_Gradient

  See the "Gallery of Images" for a look at what this image
  file produces.
}

INCLUDE "colors.dat"           { standard includes for color }
INCLUDE "shapes.dat"           { for shapes and }
INCLUDE "textures.dat"         { for textures }

VIEW_POINT                     { define the viewpoint }
  LOCATION < 0  0 -60 >
  DIRECTION < 0  0  1 >
  UP  < 0  1  0 >
  RIGHT < 1.0  0  0 >
END_VIEW_POINT

OBJECT                         { define a light source }
  SPHERE  < 0  0  0 > 2 END_SPHERE
  TRANSLATE  < 200 150 -200>
  TEXTURE
    COLOR White
    AMBIENT 1.0
    DIFFUSE 0.0
  END_TEXTURE
  COLOR White
  LIGHT_SOURCE
END_OBJECT

OBJECT                         { define a 2nd light source }
  SPHERE  < 0  0  0 > 2 END_SPHERE
  TRANSLATE  <-200 -150 -200>
  TEXTURE
    COLOR White
```

(continued)

Listing 7.10 *(continued)*

```
      AMBIENT 1.0
      DIFFUSE 0.0
   END_TEXTURE
   COLOR White
   LIGHT_SOURCE
END_OBJECT


{ Add a background plane for contrast }
OBJECT
  PLANE < 0  0 -1 > -300 END_PLANE
  TEXTURE
     COLOR MediumForestGreen
     AMBIENT 1.0
     DIFFUSE 0.0
  END_TEXTURE
END_OBJECT

{ Coloration Textures }
DECLARE Sphere1 = OBJECT
  SPHERE < 0  0  0 > 5 END_SPHERE
  TEXTURE
     Red_Marble
     SPECULAR 0.45
     ROUGHNESS 0.01
     SCALE < 5  7  6 >
  END_TEXTURE
END_OBJECT

DECLARE Sphere2 = OBJECT
  SPHERE < 0  0  0 > 5 END_SPHERE
  TEXTURE
     Black_Marble
     SPECULAR 0.45
     ROUGHNESS 0.01
     SCALE < 7  7 15 >
  END_TEXTURE
END_OBJECT

DECLARE Sphere3 = OBJECT
  SPHERE < 0  0  0 > 5 END_SPHERE
  TEXTURE
     Jade
     SPECULAR 0.45
     ROUGHNESS 0.01
     SCALE < 6  8.5  3 >
  END_TEXTURE
END_OBJECT

DECLARE Sphere4 = OBJECT
  SPHERE < 0  0  0 > 5 END_SPHERE
```

```
   TEXTURE
     Blue_Agate
     SPECULAR 0.45
     ROUGHNESS 0.01
     SCALE < 9.5  6.1  9 >
   END_TEXTURE
END_OBJECT

DECLARE Sphere5 = OBJECT
   SPHERE < 0  0  0 > 5 END_SPHERE
   TEXTURE
     Brown_Agate
     SPECULAR 0.45
     ROUGHNESS 0.01
     SCALE < 5  7  6 >
   END_TEXTURE
END_OBJECT

DECLARE Sphere6 = OBJECT
   SPHERE < 0  0  0 > 5 END_SPHERE
   TEXTURE
     0.15
     WOOD
     SPECULAR 0.45
     ROUGHNESS 0.01
     SCALE < 3  9  7 >
   END_TEXTURE
END_OBJECT

DECLARE Sphere7 = OBJECT
   SPHERE < 0  0  0 > 5 END_SPHERE
   TEXTURE
     0.15
     Tan_Wood
     SPECULAR 0.45
     ROUGHNESS 0.01
     SCALE < 3  9  7 >
   END_TEXTURE
END_OBJECT

DECLARE Sphere8 = OBJECT
   SPHERE < 0  0  0 > 5 END_SPHERE
   TEXTURE
     0.15
     Dark_Wood
     SPECULAR 0.45
     ROUGHNESS 0.01
     SCALE < 3  9  7 >
   END_TEXTURE
END_OBJECT
```

(continued)

Listing 7.10 *(continued)*

```
DECLARE Sphere9 = OBJECT
   SPHERE < 0  0  0 > 5 END_SPHERE
   TEXTURE
      0.15
      Tom_Wood
      SPECULAR 0.45
      ROUGHNESS 0.01
      SCALE < 3  9  7 >
   END_TEXTURE
END_OBJECT

DECLARE Sphere10 = OBJECT
   SPHERE < 0  0  0 > 5 END_SPHERE
   TEXTURE
      0.15
      White_Wood
      SPECULAR 0.45
      ROUGHNESS 0.01
      SCALE < 3  9  7 >
   END_TEXTURE
END_OBJECT

DECLARE Sphere11 = OBJECT
   SPHERE < 0  0  0 > 5 END_SPHERE
   TEXTURE
      SPOTTED
      SPECULAR 0.45
      ROUGHNESS 0.01
      SCALE < 3  3  7 >
   END_TEXTURE
END_OBJECT

DECLARE Sphere12 = OBJECT
   SPHERE < 0  0  0 > 5 END_SPHERE
   TEXTURE
      GRANITE
      SPECULAR 0.45
      ROUGHNESS 0.01
      SCALE < 3  9  7 >
   END_TEXTURE
END_OBJECT

DECLARE Sphere13 = OBJECT
   SPHERE < 0  0  0 > 5 END_SPHERE
   TEXTURE
      Brass
   END_TEXTURE
END_OBJECT
```

```
DECLARE Sphere14 = OBJECT
  SPHERE < 0  0  0 > 5 END_SPHERE
  TEXTURE
    Iron
  END_TEXTURE
END_OBJECT

DECLARE Sphere15 = OBJECT
  SPHERE < 0  0  0 > 5 END_SPHERE
  TEXTURE
    Pearl
    COLOR White ALPHA 0.75
  END_TEXTURE
END_OBJECT

DECLARE Sphere16 = OBJECT
  SPHERE < 0  0  0 > 5 END_SPHERE
  TEXTURE
    Candy_Cane
    SPECULAR 0.45
    ROUGHNESS 0.01
  END_TEXTURE
END_OBJECT

DECLARE Sphere17 = OBJECT
  SPHERE < 0  0  0 > 5 END_SPHERE
  TEXTURE
    CHECKER COLOR Blue COLOR MidnightBlue
    SPECULAR 0.45
    ROUGHNESS 0.01
  END_TEXTURE
END_OBJECT

DECLARE Sphere18 = OBJECT
  SPHERE < 0  0  0 > 5 END_SPHERE
  TEXTURE
    Y_RGB_Gradient
    SPECULAR 0.45
    ROUGHNESS 0.01
    SCALE < 1  10  1 >
    TRANSLATE < 0 -5  0 >
  END_TEXTURE
END_OBJECT

DECLARE Scene = COMPOSITE
  OBJECT Sphere1  TRANSLATE <-24  18  0 > END_OBJECT
  OBJECT Sphere2  TRANSLATE <-12  18  0 > END_OBJECT
  OBJECT Sphere3  TRANSLATE <  0  18  0 > END_OBJECT
  OBJECT Sphere4  TRANSLATE < 12  18  0 > END_OBJECT
  OBJECT Sphere5  TRANSLATE < 24  18  0 > END_OBJECT
```

(continued)

Listing 7.10   *(continued)*

```
  OBJECT Sphere6  TRANSLATE <-24   6   0 > END_OBJECT
  OBJECT Sphere7  TRANSLATE <-12   6   0 > END_OBJECT
  OBJECT Sphere8  TRANSLATE <  0   6   0 > END_OBJECT
  OBJECT Sphere9  TRANSLATE < 12   6   0 > END_OBJECT
  OBJECT Sphere10 TRANSLATE < 24   6   0 > END_OBJECT

  OBJECT Sphere11 TRANSLATE <-24  -6   0 > END_OBJECT
  OBJECT Sphere12 TRANSLATE <-12  -6   0 > END_OBJECT
  OBJECT Sphere13 TRANSLATE <  0  -6   0 > END_OBJECT
  OBJECT Sphere14 TRANSLATE < 12  -6   0 > END_OBJECT
  OBJECT Sphere15 TRANSLATE < 24  -6   0 > END_OBJECT

  OBJECT Sphere16 TRANSLATE <-12 -18   0 > END_OBJECT
  OBJECT Sphere17 TRANSLATE <  0 -18   0 > END_OBJECT
  OBJECT Sphere18 TRANSLATE < 12 -18   0 > END_OBJECT
END_COMPOSITE

COMPOSITE Scene END_COMPOSITE
```

It should be apparent, from the image produced by this image model, how much textures can contribute to ray-traced imagery. This simple image of the 18 spheres, each with different textures, is much more visually interesting and exciting than the images produced by previous tutorial exercises. By careful application of textures, you can simulate such materials as granite, agate, marble, glass, wood, clouds, metal, plastic, rubber, and so on. The textures used in this tutorial barely scratch the surface of the textural possibilities offered by DKBTrace.

An important point to realize about DKBTrace textures is that they are three-dimensional textures. This means that the texture is not just mapped at the surface of an object, it extends through the object as well. It is just like the veins of coloring that extend through rocks, or grains that extend through wood. If a section of a textured object is removed via CSG, there will be texture underneath. This underlying texture will not be a copy of what was on the surface but will be unique to that portion of the object, just as in nature. If you are interested in knowing how textures are implemented, please refer to Chapter 2.

Realistic looking textures take some amount of skill and finesse to produce. The textures usually require three-dimensional scaling and/or translation before they appear correctly on an object's surface (the image model shows many examples of this type of manipulation). In some cases, you may need a custom COLORMAP to accurately model the color transitions required of a texture. In other cases, you may need to alter other surface attributes to get the look you want. Generally, a lot of experimentation is required before you will be satisfied with the result. But, as this tutorial exercise shows, you can have a lot of fun with the built-in textures. Future tutorial exercises will show many other texture possibilities.

Other than the use of the coloration textures, we convey no other new information in this tutorial and, therefore, no further discussion of this image model is necessary.

Tutorial Exercise Eight—Surface Perturbation Textures

The final tutorial exercise in this chapter illustrates the use of the surface perturbation textures offered by DKBTrace. Unlike its support of the coloration textures discussed in the previous tutorial, DKBTrace supports only intrinsic surface perturbation textures. That is, additional surface perturbation textures cannot be defined by the user. Fortunately, five different controllable surface perturbation textures exist within DKBTrace. These textures are controllable to the extent that a single floating-point number controls the degree of effect obtained. A value of 0 results in no effect, whereas a value of 1.0 is a drastic effect. You can use these textures in conjunction with coloration textures to produce many, many different surfaces to use in your ray-traced imagery. Surface perturbation textures, like the coloration textures, can also be scaled and translated to fit your needs. Additionally, two of the surface perturbation textures, WAVES and RIPPLES, respond to PHASE and FREQUENCY parameters, which further increase their flexibility. See the DKBTrace user's manual for more information.

This image model is relatively simple. It consists of a single light source, a background PLANE, and six spheres, each with a different surface perturbation. The six spheres model a normal shiny surface, a surface with bumps, one with ripples, one with dents, one with waves, and one with wrinkles. As you can see from the resulting image, the surfaces definitely look perturbed. In other words, it looks as if the surface of the spheres has actual roughness—not just color, but actual texture.

The image model file for this tutorial is "exer8.dat" and is shown in Listing 7.11. Other than the use of surface perturbation textures, no other new information is conveyed in this tutorial exercise.

Listing 7.11   Tutorial Exercise Eight—Surface Perturbation Textures

The following is the contents of the file "exer8.dat."

```
{
  Ray-Traced Imaging - Tutorial Exercise Eight
  "Surface Perturbation Textures"
  from the book "Practical Ray Tracing in C" by Craig A. Lindley
  Last update to this image: 03/06/92

  The purpose of this exercise is to illustrate the
  various surface perturbation textures available with
  DKBTrace. The textures in this image are organized as
  follows:
          Normal      Ripples     Waves
          Bumps       Dents       Wrinkles

  See the "Gallery of Images" for a look at what this image
  file produces.
}
```

(continued)

Listing 7.11   *(continued)*

```
INCLUDE "colors.dat"              { standard includes for color }
INCLUDE "shapes.dat"              { for shapes and }
INCLUDE "textures.dat"            { for textures }

VIEW_POINT                        { define the viewpoint }
  LOCATION < 0  0 -40 >
  DIRECTION < 0  0  1 >
  UP  < 0  1  0 >
  RIGHT < 1.0  0  0 >
END_VIEW_POINT

OBJECT                            { define a light source }
  SPHERE  < 0  0  0 > 2 END_SPHERE
  TRANSLATE  < 0  0 -200 >
  TEXTURE
    COLOR White
    AMBIENT 1.0
    DIFFUSE 0.0
  END_TEXTURE
  COLOR White
  LIGHT_SOURCE
END_OBJECT


{ Add a background plane for contrast }
OBJECT
  PLANE < 0  0 -1 > -300 END_PLANE
  TEXTURE
    COLOR MediumForestGreen
    AMBIENT 1.0
    DIFFUSE 0.0
  END_TEXTURE
END_OBJECT


DECLARE Sphere1 = OBJECT
  SPHERE < 0  0  0 > 5 END_SPHERE
  TEXTURE
    Shiny
    COLOR Red
  END_TEXTURE
END_OBJECT

DECLARE Sphere2 = OBJECT
  SPHERE < 0  0  0 > 5 END_SPHERE
  TEXTURE
    Shiny
    COLOR Red
    RIPPLES 0.90
    FREQUENCY 10
```

```
      SCALE < 10 10 10 >
    END_TEXTURE
END_OBJECT

DECLARE Sphere3 = OBJECT
  SPHERE < 0   0   0 > 5 END_SPHERE
  TEXTURE
    Shiny
    COLOR Red
    WAVES 0.90
    FREQUENCY 10
    SCALE < 10 10 10 >
  END_TEXTURE
END_OBJECT

DECLARE Sphere4 = OBJECT
  SPHERE < 0   0   0 > 5 END_SPHERE
  TEXTURE
    Shiny
    COLOR Red
    BUMPS 0.90
  END_TEXTURE
END_OBJECT

DECLARE Sphere5 = OBJECT
  SPHERE < 0   0   0 > 5 END_SPHERE
  TEXTURE
    Shiny
    COLOR Red
    DENTS 0.90
  END_TEXTURE
END_OBJECT

DECLARE Sphere6 = OBJECT
  SPHERE < 0   0   0 > 5 END_SPHERE
  TEXTURE
    Shiny
    COLOR Red
    WRINKLES 0.90
  END_TEXTURE
END_OBJECT


{ Instances of all of the objects }
OBJECT Sphere1  TRANSLATE <-12  10  0 > END_OBJECT
OBJECT Sphere2  TRANSLATE <  0  10  0 > END_OBJECT
OBJECT Sphere3  TRANSLATE < 12  10  0 > END_OBJECT

OBJECT Sphere4  TRANSLATE <-12 -10  0 > END_OBJECT
OBJECT Sphere5  TRANSLATE <  0 -10  0 > END_OBJECT
OBJECT Sphere6  TRANSLATE < 12 -10  0 > END_OBJECT
```

Conclusions

In this chapter, we have presented the basic aspects of ray-traced imaging using DKBTrace. Through the eight tutorials in this chapter, you have been taught about the scene description language utilized by DKBTrace. By now, it should read almost like English to you. The scene description language should be easy to learn because it has a very structured syntax and easily understood semantics.

Probably more important than making you immediately fluent in the scene description language is to try and impress upon you how capable DKBTrace really is. You have seen how simple objects are declared and used, how these simple objects can be combined into more complex objects using CSG, what the second-order quadric and the fourth-order quartic shapes look like, and finally, how the surface properties can be manipulated to simulate many different materials and textures. In the next chapter, we will present even more complex and more interesting tutorial exercises.

You now have the background to begin experimenting on your own. Try modifying some of the tutorial image models presented here and see if you get the results you anticipate. If not, don't feel bad. It can sometimes take a while before what you think should happen agrees with what DKBTrace produces. That is half the fun!

Intermediate Ray-Tracing Techniques

What is mystery, after all, other than what we don't know?
—Gerald Asher

In this chapter you will learn:

- **How to use Constructive Solid Geometry to create lettering and Roman-like structures with columns and domes**
- **How noise can be used to create realistic looking clouds and starry night skies**
- **How bit-mapped images can be imported into DKBTrace and applied to surfaces**
- **How other computer programs can generate image models for DKBTrace to render**

Introduction

This chapter will explore intermediate and advanced DKBTrace features with the aid of tutorial exercises. In addition, these tutorial exercises will attempt to enhance your ray-tracing abilities by illustrating techniques you may not yet have thought about. Each of the tutorial exercises in this chapter is built on what you learned in the last chapter. Old information will not be repeated here; we will discuss only new information, as the image models in this chapter are much longer than those previously presented. As before, you can find the images that result from each of the image models in the "Gallery of Images."

The image models in this chapter are different from those in the last in that they try to illustrate important concepts using interesting images—not the mundane examples used in

Chapter 7. In viewing these new images, you should begin to get a feeling for what is possible with ray tracing. By the time you have read and digested all of the information contained in the text and image models of this chapter, you will be prepared to ray trace anything you can visualize. You will have mastered your apprentice ray-tracing training.

Tutorial Exercise Nine—Constructive Solid Geometry Two

The purpose of this image model is to show you how to use CSG to create simple lettering that can be incorporated into your ray-traced images. This technique has applications in the production of company logos, organizational signs, and so on. The image produced from this image model has the letters of the author's last name, Lindley, floating above a ringed sphere or planet. The complete image is surrounded by clouds for a very pleasing effect. The clouds are produced with noise in conjunction with DKBTrace COLORMAPs. The scene is illuminated with three different light sources. Please refer to Listing 8.1 throughout the discussion to follow.

Listing 8.1   Tutorial Exercise Nine—Constructive Solid Geometry Two

The following is the contents of the file "exer9.dat."

```
{
  Ray-Traced Imaging - Tutorial Exercise Nine
  "Constructive Solid Geometry Two"
  from the book "Practical Ray Tracing in C" by Craig A. Lindley
  Last update to this image: 03/06/92

  The purpose of this image model is to show how constructive
  solid geometry (CSG) can be used to create simple letters. In
  this image model, the author's last name "Lindley" is made to
  float around a ringed planet. The ring itself is produced
  with CSG also. Also illustrated is the use of noise to produce
  a blue sky filled with very realistic clouds. Three light
  sources are used to illuminate this scene. See the "Gallery
  of Images" for a look at what this image file produces.
}

INCLUDE "colors.dat"              { standard includes for color }
INCLUDE "shapes.dat"              { for shapes and }
INCLUDE "textures.dat"            { for textures }

{ Define some colors not in "colors.dat" file }
DECLARE Copper = COLOR RED 0.84 GREEN 0.04 BLUE 0.15
DECLARE Silver = COLOR RED 0.80 GREEN 0.80 BLUE 0.80

VIEW_POINT                        { define the viewpoint }
  LOCATION < 0 -50 -240 >
  DIRECTION < 0 0.3 1 >
  UP  < 0  1  0 >
```

```
  RIGHT < 1.0   0   0 >
END_VIEW_POINT

OBJECT                          { define light source 1 }
  SPHERE  < 0   0   0 > 2 END_SPHERE
  TRANSLATE  < 100 75 -210 >
  TEXTURE
    COLOR White
    AMBIENT 1.0
    DIFFUSE 0.0
  END_TEXTURE
  COLOR White
  LIGHT_SOURCE
END_OBJECT

OBJECT                          { define light source 2 }
  SPHERE  < 0   0   0 > 2 END_SPHERE
  TRANSLATE  <-100 75 -210 >
  TEXTURE
    COLOR White
    AMBIENT 1.0
    DIFFUSE 0.0
  END_TEXTURE
  COLOR White
  LIGHT_SOURCE
END_OBJECT

OBJECT                          { define light source 3 }
  SPHERE  < 0   0   0 > 2 END_SPHERE
  TRANSLATE  < 0 -75 -290 >
  TEXTURE
    COLOR White
    AMBIENT 1.0
    DIFFUSE 0.0
  END_TEXTURE
  COLOR White
  LIGHT_SOURCE
END_OBJECT

{ Add the cloudy sky to the picture }
DECLARE Sky = OBJECT
  SPHERE < 0 0 0 > 300 END_SPHERE
  TEXTURE
    COLOR RED 0.5  GREEN 0.5  BLUE 1.0
    AMBIENT 0.8
    DIFFUSE 0.0
    TURBULENCE 0.5
    BOZO
    COLOR_MAP
      [0.0 0.6   COLOR RED 0.40 GREEN 0.40 BLUE 1.00
                 COLOR RED 0.40 GREEN 0.40 BLUE 1.00]
```

(continued)

Listing 8.1 *(continued)*

```
      [0.6 0.8   COLOR RED 0.40 GREEN 0.40 BLUE 1.00
                 COLOR RED 1.00 GREEN 1.00 BLUE 1.00]
      [0.8 1.001 COLOR RED 1.00 GREEN 1.00 BLUE 1.00
                 COLOR RED 0.85 GREEN 0.85 BLUE 0.85]
    END_COLOR_MAP
    SCALE < 100.0  20.0  100.0 >
  END_TEXTURE
END_OBJECT


{ These define the color, surface texture, and depth of the letters }
DECLARE LetterColor =
  COLOR Silver

DECLARE LetterTexture =
  TEXTURE
    Polished_Metal
    SPECULAR 1.0
    ROUGHNESS 0.009
    REFLECTION 0.5
  END_TEXTURE

DECLARE LetterDepth = 10

{ The Sphere and Ring }
DECLARE RingedSphere =
  COMPOSITE                      { define the planet }
    OBJECT
      SPHERE < 0  0  0 > 80 END_SPHERE
      TEXTURE
        COLOR Copper
        REFLECTION 0.75
        BRILLIANCE 20.0
        PHONG 0.9
        PHONGSIZE 100
      END_TEXTURE
    END_OBJECT                   { and the ring around it }
    OBJECT
      INTERSECTION
        QUADRIC Cylinder_Y SCALE < 105  105  105 > END_QUADRIC
        QUADRIC Cylinder_Y SCALE <  95   95   95 > INVERSE END_QUADRIC
        PLANE < 0  1  0 > -18 END_PLANE
        PLANE < 0 -1  0 >  22 END_PLANE
      END_INTERSECTION
      TEXTURE LetterTexture COLOR LetterColor END_TEXTURE
    END_OBJECT
  END_COMPOSITE
```

```
{
Now define the letters. Note: these letters have their origin
at the middle bottom front of the character. See text for
details.
}

DECLARE LetterL = OBJECT
  UNION
    INTERSECTION
      PLANE <-1   0    0 > 10 END_PLANE
      PLANE < 1   0    0 > 10 END_PLANE
      PLANE < 0  -1    0 >  0 END_PLANE
      PLANE < 0   1    0 >  5 END_PLANE
      PLANE < 0   0   -1 >  0 END_PLANE
      PLANE < 0   0    1 > LetterDepth END_PLANE
    END_INTERSECTION
    INTERSECTION
      PLANE <-1   0    0 > 10 END_PLANE
      PLANE < 1   0    0 > -5 END_PLANE
      PLANE < 0  -1    0 >  0 END_PLANE
      PLANE < 0   1    0 > 40 END_PLANE
      PLANE < 0   0   -1 >  0 END_PLANE
      PLANE < 0   0    1 > LetterDepth END_PLANE
    END_INTERSECTION
  END_UNION
  BOUNDED_BY
    INTERSECTION
      PLANE <-1   0    0 > 10 END_PLANE
      PLANE < 1   0    0 > 10 END_PLANE
      PLANE < 0  -1    0 >  0 END_PLANE
      PLANE < 0   1    0 > 40 END_PLANE
      PLANE < 0   0   -1 >  0 END_PLANE
      PLANE < 0   0    1 > LetterDepth END_PLANE
    END_INTERSECTION
  END_BOUND
  TEXTURE LetterTexture COLOR LetterColor END_TEXTURE
END_OBJECT

DECLARE Letteri = OBJECT
  UNION
    INTERSECTION
      PLANE <-1   0    0 >  2.5 END_PLANE
      PLANE < 1   0    0 >  2.5 END_PLANE
      PLANE < 0  -1    0 >  0 END_PLANE
      PLANE < 0   1    0 > 20 END_PLANE
      PLANE < 0   0   -1 >  0 END_PLANE
      PLANE < 0   0    1 > LetterDepth END_PLANE
    END_INTERSECTION
    INTERSECTION
      QUADRIC Cylinder_Z
        SCALE < 2.5 2.5 10 >
```

(continued)

Listing 8.1   *(continued)*

```
        TRANSLATE < 0 27.5 0 >
      END_QUADRIC
      PLANE < 0    0  -1 >  0 END_PLANE
      PLANE < 0    0   1 > LetterDepth END_PLANE
    END_INTERSECTION
  END_UNION
  BOUNDED_BY
    INTERSECTION
      PLANE <-1   0   0 >  2.5 END_PLANE
      PLANE < 1   0   0 >  2.5 END_PLANE
      PLANE < 0  -1   0 >  0 END_PLANE
      PLANE < 0   1   0 > 30 END_PLANE
      PLANE < 0   0  -1 >  0 END_PLANE
      PLANE < 0   0   1 > LetterDepth END_PLANE
    END_INTERSECTION
  END_BOUND
  TEXTURE LetterTexture COLOR LetterColor END_TEXTURE
END_OBJECT

DECLARE Lettern = OBJECT
  UNION
    INTERSECTION
      PLANE <-1   0   0 > 10 END_PLANE
      PLANE < 1   0   0 > -5 END_PLANE
      PLANE < 0  -1   0 >  0 END_PLANE
      PLANE < 0   1   0 > 20 END_PLANE
      PLANE < 0   0  -1 >  0 END_PLANE
      PLANE < 0   0   1 > LetterDepth END_PLANE
    END_INTERSECTION
    INTERSECTION
      PLANE <-1   0   0 > -5 END_PLANE
      PLANE < 1   0   0 > 10 END_PLANE
      PLANE < 0  -1   0 >  0 END_PLANE
      PLANE < 0   1   0 > 10 END_PLANE
      PLANE < 0   0  -1 >  0 END_PLANE
      PLANE < 0   0   1 > LetterDepth END_PLANE
    END_INTERSECTION
    INTERSECTION
      QUADRIC Cylinder_Z
        SCALE < 10 10 10 >
        TRANSLATE < 0 10 0 >
      END_QUADRIC
      QUADRIC Cylinder_Z
        SCALE < 5 5 10 >
        TRANSLATE < 0 10 0 >
        INVERSE
      END_QUADRIC
      PLANE < 0  -1   0 > -10 END_PLANE
      PLANE < 0   0  -1 >   0 END_PLANE
      PLANE < 0   0   1 > LetterDepth END_PLANE
```

```
      END_INTERSECTION
    END_UNION
    BOUNDED_BY
      INTERSECTION
        PLANE <-1   0   0 > 10 END_PLANE
        PLANE < 1   0   0 > 10 END_PLANE
        PLANE < 0  -1   0 >  0 END_PLANE
        PLANE < 0   1   0 > 20 END_PLANE
        PLANE < 0   0  -1 >  0 END_PLANE
        PLANE < 0   0   1 > LetterDepth END_PLANE
      END_INTERSECTION
    END_BOUND
    TEXTURE LetterTexture COLOR LetterColor END_TEXTURE
END_OBJECT

DECLARE Letterd = OBJECT
  UNION
    INTERSECTION
      QUADRIC Cylinder_Z
        SCALE < 10 10 10 >
        TRANSLATE < 0 10 0 >
      END_QUADRIC
      QUADRIC Cylinder_Z
        SCALE < 5 5 10 >
        TRANSLATE < 0 10 0 >
        INVERSE
      END_QUADRIC
      PLANE < 0   0  -1 >  0 END_PLANE
      PLANE < 0   0   1 > LetterDepth END_PLANE
    END_INTERSECTION
    INTERSECTION
      PLANE <-1   0   0 > -5 END_PLANE
      PLANE < 1   0   0 > 10 END_PLANE
      PLANE < 0  -1   0 >  0 END_PLANE
      PLANE < 0   1   0 > 40 END_PLANE
      PLANE < 0   0  -1 >  0 END_PLANE
      PLANE < 0   0   1 > LetterDepth END_PLANE
    END_INTERSECTION
  END_UNION
  BOUNDED_BY
    INTERSECTION
      PLANE <-1   0   0 > 10 END_PLANE
      PLANE < 1   0   0 > 10 END_PLANE
      PLANE < 0  -1   0 >  0 END_PLANE
      PLANE < 0   1   0 > 40 END_PLANE
      PLANE < 0   0  -1 >  0 END_PLANE
      PLANE < 0   0   1 > LetterDepth END_PLANE
    END_INTERSECTION
  END_BOUND
  TEXTURE LetterTexture COLOR LetterColor END_TEXTURE
END_OBJECT
```

(continued)

Listing 8.1   *(continued)*

```
{
NOTE no bounding volume is declared for the letter l because
the bounds check is just as expensive as the object check.
}
DECLARE Letterl = OBJECT
  INTERSECTION
    PLANE <-1   0    0 >  2.5 END_PLANE
    PLANE < 1   0    0 >  2.5 END_PLANE
    PLANE < 0  -1    0 >  0 END_PLANE
    PLANE < 0   1    0 > 40 END_PLANE
    PLANE < 0   0   -1 >  0 END_PLANE
    PLANE < 0   0    1 > LetterDepth END_PLANE
  END_INTERSECTION
  TEXTURE LetterTexture COLOR LetterColor END_TEXTURE
END_OBJECT

DECLARE Lettere = OBJECT
  UNION
    INTERSECTION
      QUADRIC Cylinder_Z
        SCALE < 10 10 10 >
      END_QUADRIC
      QUADRIC Cylinder_Z
        SCALE < 5 5 10 >
        INVERSE
      END_QUADRIC
      PLANE < 0  -1   0 >  0 END_PLANE
      PLANE < 0   0  -1 >  0 END_PLANE
      PLANE < 0   0   1 > LetterDepth END_PLANE
    END_INTERSECTION
    INTERSECTION
      QUADRIC Cylinder_Z
        SCALE < 10 10 10 >
      END_QUADRIC
      QUADRIC Cylinder_Z
        SCALE < 5 5 10 >
        INVERSE
      END_QUADRIC
      PLANE < 0  -1   0 >  0 END_PLANE
      PLANE < 0   0  -1 >  0 END_PLANE
      PLANE < 0   0   1 > LetterDepth END_PLANE
      ROTATE < 0  0 135 >
    END_INTERSECTION
    INTERSECTION
      PLANE <-1   0   0 >  7.5 END_PLANE
      PLANE < 1   0   0 >  7.5 END_PLANE
      PLANE < 0  -1   0 >  0   END_PLANE
      PLANE < 0   1   0 >  2.5 END_PLANE
      PLANE < 0   0  -1 >  0   END_PLANE
```

```
            PLANE < 0    0    1 > LetterDepth END_PLANE
        END_INTERSECTION
      END_UNION
      BOUNDED_BY
        INTERSECTION
          PLANE <-1    0    0 > 10 END_PLANE
          PLANE < 1    0    0 > 10 END_PLANE
          PLANE < 0   -1    0 > 10 END_PLANE
          PLANE < 0    1    0 > 10 END_PLANE
          PLANE < 0    0   -1 >  0 END_PLANE
          PLANE < 0    0    1 > LetterDepth END_PLANE
        END_INTERSECTION
      END_BOUND
      TEXTURE LetterTexture COLOR LetterColor END_TEXTURE
      TRANSLATE < 0 10 0 >
END_OBJECT

DECLARE Lettery = OBJECT
    INTERSECTION
      UNION
        INTERSECTION
          PLANE <-1    0    0 > 2.5 END_PLANE
          PLANE < 1    0    0 > 2.5 END_PLANE
          PLANE < 0   -1    0 > 30 END_PLANE
          PLANE < 0    1    0 > 30 END_PLANE
          PLANE < 0    0   -1 >  0 END_PLANE
          PLANE < 0    0    1 > LetterDepth END_PLANE
          ROTATE < 0  0 -20 >
        END_INTERSECTION
        INTERSECTION
          PLANE <-1    0    0 >  2.5 END_PLANE
          PLANE < 1    0    0 >  2.5 END_PLANE
          PLANE < 0   -1    0 >  0 END_PLANE
          PLANE < 0    1    0 > 30 END_PLANE
          PLANE < 0    0   -1 >  0 END_PLANE
          PLANE < 0    0    1 > LetterDepth END_PLANE
          ROTATE < 0  0  20 >
        END_INTERSECTION
      END_UNION
      PLANE < 0 -1 0 > 20 END_PLANE
      PLANE < 0  1 0 > 20 END_PLANE
    END_INTERSECTION
    BOUNDED_BY
      INTERSECTION
        PLANE <-1    0    0 > 10 END_PLANE
        PLANE < 1    0    0 > 10 END_PLANE
        PLANE < 0   -1    0 > 20 END_PLANE
        PLANE < 0    1    0 > 20 END_PLANE
        PLANE < 0    0   -1 >  0 END_PLANE
        PLANE < 0    0    1 > LetterDepth END_PLANE
```

(continued)

Listing 8.1   *(continued)*

```
    END_INTERSECTION
  END_BOUND
  TEXTURE LetterTexture COLOR LetterColor END_TEXTURE
END_OBJECT

{
Now translate and rotate the Lindley lettering into place.
The letters are first brought directly forward and up to line up
with the outer edge of the ring and then they are rotated
into final position.
}

DECLARE Lettering = COMPOSITE
  OBJECT LetterL
    TRANSLATE < 0 -15 -105 >
    ROTATE < 0  40.0  0 >
  END_OBJECT
  OBJECT Letteri
    TRANSLATE < 0 -15 -105 >
    ROTATE < 0  26.67  0 >
  END_OBJECT
  OBJECT Lettern
    TRANSLATE < 0 -15 -105 >
    ROTATE < 0  13.33  0 >
  END_OBJECT
  OBJECT Letterd
    TRANSLATE < 0 -15 -105 >
  END_OBJECT
  OBJECT Letterl
    TRANSLATE < 0 -15 -105 >
    ROTATE < 0 -13.33  0 >
  END_OBJECT
  OBJECT Lettere
    TRANSLATE < 0 -15 -105 >
    ROTATE < 0 -26.67  0 >
  END_OBJECT
  OBJECT Lettery
    TRANSLATE < 0 -15 -105 >
    ROTATE < 0 -40.0  0 >
  END_OBJECT
END_COMPOSITE

{ Create instances of all objects in the scene }
OBJECT    Sky           END_OBJECT
COMPOSITE RingedSphere END_COMPOSITE
COMPOSITE Lettering     END_COMPOSITE
```

The image model begins, as all image models presented so far, with the inclusion of the three files "colors.dat," "shapes.dat," and "textures.dat." Definitions contained within these files are used throughout this image model. Next, two new colors are DECLAREd—Copper and Silver. These are defined here because their definitions were not contained in the "colors.dat" file. Next, a VIEW_POINT and the three light sources are defined. Nothing new here yet. Notice, however, that as required, all light source spheres are defined at the origin and TRANSLATEd into their final positions.

The first new concept presented in this image model is shown when we DECLARE the Sky OBJECT. Here, a sphere is defined that contains the whole scene including the light sources, the viewer, and the objects within the scene. Everything is inside this sphere, of radius 300. The clouds will be mapped onto the inside of this sphere, making them visible in all directions, even behind the viewer. The reflective lettering and planet within the scene shows the presence of the clouds behind the viewer. The clouds are visible as reflections in those objects.

To create the clouds, we used the BOZO coloration texture (noise function) and a COLORMAP. The noise is defined for every point in space, as we discussed in Chapter 2. If two points are physically close together, their noise values will be similar. If far apart, however, the two noise values are only randomly related. The BOZO function returns a floating-point number (for the point being shaded) in the range 0.0 to 1.0, which is then used by the COLORMAP to define a color for that point. The TURBULENCE value specified in the TEXTURE block determines how the noise function behaves. With low values for TURBULENCE, the noise function produces slowly changing noise values. With high TURBULENCE values, the noise become more chaotic.

The COLORMAP establishes the mapping of the noise value to color. In the case of the Sky OBJECT, three ranges of noise values are established and processed by the COLORMAP. In general, a range of values is specified as:

```
[From_Value To_Value Color1 Color2]
```

When a noise value falls into the range From_Value to To_Value, it is processed by this portion of the COLORMAP. The color given to the point is the linear interpolation of the noise value from Color1 to Color2. For example, if the noise value is 90% of the To_Value, the color given that point will be 90% Color2 and only 10% Color1. If the noise value equaled the From_Value, the color returned would be Color1. If the noise value equaled the To_Value, the color returned would be Color2. In the COLORMAP for our image model, the first range is specified as:

```
[0.0 0.6 COLOR RED 0.40 GREEN 0.40 BLUE 1.00
       COLOR RED 0.40 GREEN 0.40 BLUE 1.00]
```

This indicates that all noise values in the range 0.0 to 0.6 should be given the color of a blue sky and that the color should not change over this range of values. The next color range in the COLORMAP:

```
[0.6 0.8 COLOR RED 0.40 GREEN 0.40 BLUE 1.00
       COLOR RED 1.00 GREEN 1.00 BLUE 1.00]
```

indicates that for this range of noise values, the color should change from the blue sky value to white (R=G=B=1.0). This forms the white, lacy portions of the clouds. The final range in the COLORMAP:

```
[0.8 1.001 COLOR RED 1.00 GREEN 1.00 BLUE 1.00
          COLOR RED 0.85 GREEN 0.85 BLUE 0.85]
```

says that for this narrow range of noise values, the clouds should change in color from white to gray (R=G=B=0.85), simulating the moisture-carrying portions of the clouds. All in all, it makes for a very nice cloud simulation.

To get the clouds shaped properly and dispersed within a scene, you must scale the cloud texture. The scaling values are determined experimentally because they depend on the distance between the surface being mapped with the clouds and the viewer. In this case, scaling factors of 100, 20, and 100 are applied in the X, Y, and Z directions, respectively. For very calm days, a TURBULENCE value of 0.2 might be used. As the value of TURBULENCE is raised, the day becomes more and more stormy.

Within our image model we now turn our attention to the definition of the lettering used in the image. Three DECLARE statements are used: "LetterColor," to control the color of the lettering; "LetterTexture," to control the surface properties of the lettering; and "LetterDepth," to control the depth of the lettering. In this image model, the lettering will be silver in color, will be highly polished and reflective, and will have a depth of 10 units. By changing the LetterDepth definition, you can make the lettering any depth. You can use a large value of LetterDepth to make the letters trail off to infinity or any depth in between. A LetterDepth of 10 makes the letters fit nicely above the ring around the planet, as the ring also has a depth of 10 units.

Next, the ringed planet is defined. This COMPOSITE OBJECT is comprised of a sphere located at the origin with radius 80 that is copper colored, highly polished, and highly reflective. Surrounding it is a ring of the color and texture of the letters. This ring is formed using CSG with two vertical, or Cylinders_Y, shapes and two PLANES. Notice the definition of the ring in the listing. It is an INTERSECTION of these four surfaces. The first cylinder, of type Cylinder_Y, determines the outer diameter of the ring. The second cylinder determines the inside diameter of the hole in the ring, where the planet goes. As you will recall, the INTER-SECTION forms a new surface where the "insides" of the component surfaces overlap. The inside of a cylinder is between its origin and its outer surface. By using the INVERSE keyword with the second cylinder definition, you effectively reverse its inside and outside. The INTERSECTION of these two cylinders is then the ring seen in the image. The two PLANEs (both are XZ planes) within this intersection control the vertical height of the ring and, in this case, where the ring is located in space. The top of the ring is located at 18 units below the X axis, while the bottom is at 22 units below the X axis. In this case, then, the ring is 5 units high and is centered at location < 0 -20 0 >.

Recall from the previous discussions of planes that the number to the right of the normal vector in the plane definition determines how many units along the normal the plane is from the coordinate axes. The definition:

```
PLANE < 0 1 0 > -18 END_PLANE
```

defines a plane with a normal pointing in the positive Y direction (hence it is an XZ plane) a negative 18 units along the normal. A negative displacement along a normal is a displacement in the negative direction. Therefore, this plane is located at Y equals negative 18. The second PLANE:

PLANE < 0 -1 0 > 22 END_PLANE

has a normal pointing in the negative Y direction (downward) and is located 22 units from the origin. Since the displacement is positive, the plane is located on the same side of the origin as its normal is pointing. Since the inside of a plane is the side away from the normal, the INTERSECTION of these two planes is the space between them, which is 5 units thick. The intersection of this 5-unit-thick infinite rectangular volume with the nested cylinders described above results in the ring that we desire. This information about plane placement and intersection is very important in the definitions of the lettering to be discussed next. Make sure you understand it before proceeding with this discussion.

All of the lettering used in this image model is defined with simple shapes. In fact, the only shapes involved are planes and cylinders. By necessity, the lettering is a very simple block font. More complex fonts could surely be generated, but they would require a lot of work to design and would take a long time to render. If more complex fonts are required, it would probably be best to generate their definitions algorithmically with a computer program instead of manually. We show an example of algorithmic image generation in Tutorial Exercise Twelve, later in this chapter. For now, this simple font is more than adequate for our needs. We will also use this simple font in Image Model Three, in Chapter 9.

As shown in Figure 8.1, letters in this simple font are constructed within a 60 by 20 by LetterDepth rectangular volume. All of the characters except the y character are contained within the upper portion of the volume. That is, they are above the Y equals zero plane that is considered the baseline of the characters. The character y has a descending portion that crosses the baseline into the bottom of the volume. All of the characters are constructed such that their origin is at the baseline in the middle and the front of the character. When you move these characters about within a scene, their origin is most important. All positioning is relative to the character's origin.

In this figure, we show the geometry used to construct four of the characters. All characters are formed in a similar manner, so once you understand how one is formed, you should easily understand the others. Because of its relative complexity, we will discuss the construction of letter "n."

The letter n is comprised of three pieces referred to as segments. Segment one is the vertical upright box on the left, segment two is the smaller upright box on the right, and segment three is the cylindrical portion in the middle. These three segments taken together make up the letter n. The three individual segments are easily discernible in the listing. Each is an individual INTERSECTION concatenated together into a CSG UNION, which makes up the complete character. As seen in Figure 8.1, letter n is lowercase and is completely contained within a volume delineated by X=-10, X=+10, Y=0, Y=+20, Z=0, and Z=LetterDepth. The first and second segments are formed by the INTERSECTION of six planes positioned as shown in the listing. The cylindrical third segment is made up of nested Cylinder_Z surfaces translated 10 units above the origin and cut in half vertically. This is the same technique used to form the ring discussed earlier. This half-cylindrical surface aligned in the Z direction forms the curved portion of the n character.

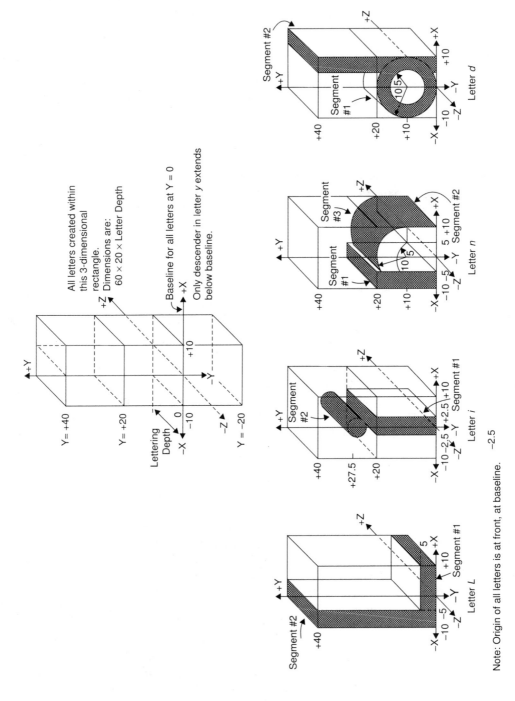

Note: Origin of all letters is at front, at baseline.

Figure 8.1   Lettering Information and Formation

398

Because of the complexity of the geometry that makes up the letters, each is surrounded by a bounding volume as a performance enhancement. For each of the letters, an INTERSECTION of six planes is used as the bound. These bounding volumes tightly surround the letters, thereby limiting the number of ray intersection tests that need to be performed for each letter. Of course, you must adjust the configuration of the bounding volume for the character being bounded. You can see how this is done in the listing. After the bounding volume for each character is defined, the letter is given the LetterTexture and LetterColor. This makes all of the letters silver, highly polished, and reflective.

After all of the lettering is defined, a COMPOSITE object called Lettering is DECLAREd that defines how the individual letters that make up the name "Lindley" are to be placed. Each letter of the name is processed slightly differently because of its final position. Since Lindley has an odd number of characters, the middle character, "d," will be positioned directly in front of the viewer while all other characters will be rotated around the circumference of the planet. This manipulation is performed in a two-step process. First, the individual letter is brought down and directly forward toward the viewer. It is brought down so that it sets directly above the ring. It is brought forward so that the letter's baseline lines up with the forward edge of the ring. Then, depending on which letter is being manipulated, the letters are rotated into their final position. The name Lindley spans a total of 80 degrees of arc around the planet. Each letter, except the "d" (d faces the viewer directly), is rotated accordingly to make that happen.

The final operation performed within this image model is the creation of instances for the Sky, the RingedSphere, and the Lettering objects. As you will recall, this causes the objects to be actually rendered. The declaration statements used previously in this image model only defined the objects. These last three statements cause the defined objects to be rendered.

Take a look in the "Gallery of Images" at what this image model produces (see Image 14). As an exercise, you should attempt to construct the letters that make up your own name and place them into this image. A personalized image of this type makes a very nice picture to hang on your office wall to let people know who you are and whose office it is. It's much nicer than a little plastic nameplate on the wall or desk, don't you agree?

Tutorial Exercise Ten—Constructive Solid Geometry Three

Before beginning the discussion of this image model, take a moment to look at the resulting image in the "Gallery of Images" (see Image 15). Notice the details within this image: the structure, the supporting columns, the various attributes of the surfaces, the coloration and the textures, the stars in the midnight-black sky, and the realistic ocean complete with ripples and waves. It is amazing to think all of this was created with a computer, based only on the relatively simple image model shown in Listing 8.2. Herein lies the beauty and the fascination of ray tracing.

While simple ray-traced images with spheres and planes can be interesting, it seems that the more complex the shapes involved, the more interesting and eye-catching the imagery becomes. As we saw in Tutorial Exercise Nine, using CSG is the way to create complex shapes from simpler ones. The purpose of this tutorial exercise is to refine your CSG skills further so you will be better prepared to model the objects that you visualize. Within this image model, we will first create a Cyl QUADRIC. We will then sweep these in a circle to create a column. We will then add a pad to the top of the column and bound the whole COMPOSITE object. Next, we will create a cylindrical base and various donutlike rings that will be used in the structure. An Arch OBJECT, which will span from column to column, is then defined from nested cylinders along the Z axis. From these individual objects, the first floor of the structure is built. The Floor1 COMPOSITE object is also bounded to help with ray-tracing performance.

Next, the definitions of the objects that make up the second floor of the structure, called Floor2, are defined. First, a RingSupport INTERSECTION type is defined which will be used to hold up the top of the second-floor structure. Three different colors of RingSupport are then defined. One each of the three different colored RingSupports will be used within this image. The second-floor structure also has a donutlike ring that rests on top of the RingSupports and supports the half-spherical Dome that forms the top of the second-floor structure. Floor2 is declared to be a COMPOSITE object that contains the three different color RingSupports, the support ring, and the Dome. The Floor2 COMPOSITE is then bounded for performance. The final DECLARE statement in the image model defines the whole Scene to be a COMPOSITE object containing the NightSky OBJECT, the Ocean COMPOSITE object, the Floor1 COMPOSITE object, the Floor2 COMPOSITE object, and a mirrored sphere thrown in for fun. The last statement in the image model creates an instance of the COMPOSITE Scene object, thereby causing it to be rendered. That is the condensed version of the explanation. We will provide the details shortly.

As with the other image models described earlier, we will discuss only the information that is important in this new context. If some portion of the explanation seems to be lacking here, it is probably covered in one of the previous tutorial exercises or elsewhere in the book. Consult the Index for the topic you are looking for. You will probably find a pointer there to where your topic is discussed.

This image model begins like all others, with the incorporation of the three include files. Three colors are then defined, which are used for the RingSupports previously mentioned. These colors are defined here because they are not defined in the standard "colors.dat" DKBTrace include file. Following the includes, a VIEW_POINT and two light sources are defined identical to what we have seen before. The first new item in this image model is the use of BOZO noise to create stars. The night sky is mapped onto an XY PLANE located 75 units behind the coordinate system origin. Stars are created with the same process used for clouds in Tutorial Exercise Nine. In this case, however, the COLORMAP that is used maps all values of noise from 0.00 to 0.99 to the color black and the noise values in the small range 0.99 to 1.001 to the color white. With this COLORMAP and the appropriate scaling, we can create a decent starry sky. We can vary the value used for TURBULENCE along with the scaling to control the number and size of the stars produced. Some experimentation with these values is always required to get the effect you desire.

The definition of the Ocean COMPOSITE object requires some explanation. The ocean effect is actually achieved using two PLANEs, as shown in the listing. The topmost plane is colored a semitransparent white, given optical properties resembling glass, and then perturbed with the RIPPLES surface perturbation texture. It is the underlying blue PLANE, located 10.5 units below the white PLANE, that gives the Ocean the blue coloring. The combination of these two PLANEs gives the Ocean a realistic appearance. The top PLANE of the Ocean is located half a unit above the coordinate system origin.

Listing 8.2   Tutorial Exercise Ten—Constructive Solid Geometry Three

The following is the contents of the file "exer10.dat."

```
{
  Ray-Traced Imaging - Tutorial Exercise Ten
  "Constructive Solid Geometry Three"
  from the book "Practical Ray Tracing in C" by Craig A. Lindley
  Last update to this image: 03/09/92

  The purpose of this exercise is again to use constructive solid
  geometry to create even more complex shapes. In this image model,
  a Roman-like structure with columns is created from simple cylinders
  and planes. Many different types of surface colorings and textures
  are applied to the constructed structure. The Roman structure
  appears to be floating on a lake and surrounded by a night-
  time sky filled with stars. Noise is used to make the starry
  night. See the "Gallery of Images" for a look at what this image
  file produces.
}

INCLUDE "colors.dat"            { standard includes for color }
INCLUDE "shapes.dat"            { for shapes and }
INCLUDE "textures.dat"          { for textures }

{ Colors not defined in "colors.dat" }
DECLARE Copper  = COLOR RED 0.84 GREEN 0.04 BLUE 0.15
DECLARE Orange2 = COLOR RED 1.00 GREEN 0.35 BLUE 0.00
DECLARE Purple1 = COLOR RED 0.87 GREEN 0.00 BLUE 1.00

VIEW_POINT                      { define the viewpoint }
  LOCATION < 0   5 -19 >
  DIRECTION < 0   0.15  1 >
  UP < 0   1   0 >
  RIGHT < 1.0   0   0 >
END_VIEW_POINT

OBJECT                          { define light source 1 }
  SPHERE < 0   0   0 > 2 END_SPHERE
  TRANSLATE < 40   25  -40 >
  TEXTURE
    COLOR White
    AMBIENT 1.0
    DIFFUSE 0.0
  END_TEXTURE
  COLOR White
  LIGHT_SOURCE
END_OBJECT

OBJECT                          { define light source 2 }
  SPHERE < 0   0   0 > 2 END_SPHERE
  TRANSLATE <-40   25  -40 >
```

(continued)

Listing 8.2 *(continued)*

```
    TEXTURE
      COLOR White
      AMBIENT 1.0
      DIFFUSE 0.0
    END_TEXTURE
    COLOR White
    LIGHT_SOURCE
END_OBJECT

{ Define night-time sky with stars }
DECLARE NightSky = OBJECT
  PLANE < 0  0 -1 > -75 END_PLANE
  TEXTURE
    COLOR Black
    AMBIENT 1.0
    DIFFUSE 0.0
    BOZO
    TURBULENCE 0.3
    COLOR_MAP
      [0.0   0.99  COLOR Black COLOR Black ]
      [0.99  1.001 COLOR Black COLOR White ]
    END_COLOR_MAP
    SCALE < 0.3 0.55 0.4 >
  END_TEXTURE
END_OBJECT

{ Define the ocean surface with two planes }
DECLARE Ocean = COMPOSITE
  OBJECT
    PLANE < 0  1  0 > 0.5 END_PLANE
    TEXTURE
      COLOR White ALPHA 0.75
      REFRACTION 0.85
      REFLECTION 0.65
      IOR 1.54
      RIPPLES 20.0
      TURBULENCE 0.5
      FREQUENCY 750
      SCALE < 1000 1000 1000 >
      AMBIENT 0.2
      DIFFUSE 0.6
      PHONG 0.3
      PHONGSIZE 60
    END_TEXTURE
  END_OBJECT
  { Another plane under the ocean's surface colored blue }
  OBJECT
    PLANE < 0  1  0 > -10.0 END_PLANE
    TEXTURE
      COLOR Blue
    END_TEXTURE
```

```
   END_OBJECT
END_COMPOSITE

{ Define the color and texture of surfaces in this image }

DECLARE RockTexture = TEXTURE
   GRANITE
   SCALE < 5 7 4 >
   REFLECTION 0.3
   PHONG 0.5
   PHONGSIZE 50
   BRILLIANCE 10
   AMBIENT 0.5
   DIFFUSE 0.5
END_TEXTURE

{ This texture is for the RingSupports }
DECLARE ShinyTexture = TEXTURE
   REFLECTION 0.65
   BRILLIANCE 20.0
   PHONG 0.9
   PHONGSIZE 100
END_TEXTURE

{ Define the basic column }

{ This cylinder is replicated and rotated to form a column }
DECLARE Cyl = QUADRIC
   Cylinder_Y
   SCALE < 0.12  1  0.12 >
   TRANSLATE < 0   0 -0.3 >
END_QUADRIC

{ This is a basic column without header }
DECLARE Column = OBJECT
   INTERSECTION
     UNION
       QUADRIC Cyl END_QUADRIC
       QUADRIC Cyl ROTATE < 0    45  0 > END_QUADRIC
       QUADRIC Cyl ROTATE < 0    90  0 > END_QUADRIC
       QUADRIC Cyl ROTATE < 0   135  0 > END_QUADRIC
       QUADRIC Cyl ROTATE < 0   180  0 > END_QUADRIC
       QUADRIC Cyl ROTATE < 0   225  0 > END_QUADRIC
       QUADRIC Cyl ROTATE < 0   270  0 > END_QUADRIC
       QUADRIC Cyl ROTATE < 0   315  0 > END_QUADRIC
     END_UNION
     PLANE < 0 -1  0 > 0.0 END_PLANE
     PLANE < 0  1  0 > 7.5 END_PLANE
   END_INTERSECTION
   TEXTURE RockTexture END_TEXTURE
END_OBJECT
```

(continued)

Listing 8.2 *(continued)*

```
{ This is a header for the top of the column }
DECLARE Pad = OBJECT
  INTERSECTION
    PLANE <-1  0   0 > 0.50 END_PLANE
    PLANE < 1  0   0 > 0.50 END_PLANE
    PLANE < 0 -1   0 > 0.00 END_PLANE
    PLANE < 0  1   0 > 0.25 END_PLANE
    PLANE < 0  0  -1 > 0.50 END_PLANE
    PLANE < 0  0   1 > 0.50 END_PLANE
  END_INTERSECTION
  TEXTURE
    RockTexture
  END_TEXTURE
END_OBJECT

{ This is the complete definition of a single column }
DECLARE FullColumn = COMPOSITE
  OBJECT Pad TRANSLATE < 0  7.50  0 > END_OBJECT
  OBJECT Column END_OBJECT
  BOUNDED_BY
    INTERSECTION
      QUADRIC
        Cylinder_Y
        SCALE < 0.55 1 0.55 >
      END_QUADRIC
      PLANE < 0 -1  0 > 0.0 END_PLANE
      PLANE < 0  1  0 > 7.75 END_PLANE
    END_INTERSECTION
  END_BOUND
  { Column is moved forward so it can be rotated in the image }
  TRANSLATE < 0   0 -3 >
END_COMPOSITE

{ This is a circular piece of material located between the columns }
DECLARE Base = OBJECT
  INTERSECTION
    QUADRIC
      Cylinder_Y
      SCALE < 2.0  1  2.0 >
    END_QUADRIC
    PLANE < 0 -1  0 > 0.50 END_PLANE
    PLANE < 0  1  0 > 0.75 END_PLANE
  END_INTERSECTION
  TEXTURE
    ShinyTexture COLOR Copper
  END_TEXTURE
END_OBJECT
```

```
{ This is the horizontal ring at the top of the first floor }
{ It rests on the arches and supports the second floor }
DECLARE Ring1 = OBJECT
  INTERSECTION
    QUADRIC
      Cylinder_Y
      SCALE < 3.6  1  3.6 >
    END_QUADRIC
    QUADRIC
      Cylinder_Y
      SCALE < 2  1  2 >
      INVERSE
    END_QUADRIC
    PLANE < 0 -1  0 > -9.07382 END_PLANE
    PLANE < 0  1  0 >  9.57382 END_PLANE
  END_INTERSECTION
  TEXTURE
    RockTexture
  END_TEXTURE
END_OBJECT

{ Semicircular vertical rings that rest on the columns and support }
{ the horizontal ring }
DECLARE Arch = OBJECT
  INTERSECTION
    QUADRIC
      Cylinder_Z
      SCALE < 1.34805  1.34805  1 >
    END_QUADRIC
    QUADRIC
      Cylinder_Z
      SCALE < 0.94805  0.94805  1 >
      INVERSE
    END_QUADRIC
    PLANE < 0 -1  0 > 0.0 END_PLANE
    PLANE < 0  0 -1 > 0.2 END_PLANE
    PLANE < 0  0  1 > 0.2 END_PLANE
  END_INTERSECTION
  TEXTURE
    RockTexture
  END_TEXTURE
  { The arch is raised to the proper vertical position and }
  { brought forward so it can be replicated and rotated into place. }
  TRANSLATE < 0  7.75 -2.77164 >
END_OBJECT

{ This is the definition of the first floor of the Roman structure }
DECLARE Floor1 = COMPOSITE
  OBJECT Base END_OBJECT
```

(continued)

Listing 8.2 *(continued)*

```
COMPOSITE FullColumn END_COMPOSITE
COMPOSITE FullColumn ROTATE < 0  45  0 > END_COMPOSITE
COMPOSITE FullColumn ROTATE < 0  90  0 > END_COMPOSITE
COMPOSITE FullColumn ROTATE < 0 135  0 > END_COMPOSITE
COMPOSITE FullColumn ROTATE < 0 180  0 > END_COMPOSITE
COMPOSITE FullColumn ROTATE < 0 225  0 > END_COMPOSITE
COMPOSITE FullColumn ROTATE < 0 270  0 > END_COMPOSITE
COMPOSITE FullColumn ROTATE < 0 315  0 > END_COMPOSITE
OBJECT Arch ROTATE < 0  22.5  0 > END_OBJECT
OBJECT Arch ROTATE < 0  67.5  0 > END_OBJECT
OBJECT Arch ROTATE < 0 112.5  0 > END_OBJECT
OBJECT Arch ROTATE < 0 157.5  0 > END_OBJECT
OBJECT Arch ROTATE < 0 202.5  0 > END_OBJECT
OBJECT Arch ROTATE < 0 247.5  0 > END_OBJECT
OBJECT Arch ROTATE < 0 292.5  0 > END_OBJECT
OBJECT Arch ROTATE < 0 337.5  0 > END_OBJECT
OBJECT Ring1 END_OBJECT
BOUNDED_BY
  INTERSECTION
    QUADRIC
      Cylinder_Y
      SCALE < 4.25  1  4.25 >
    END_QUADRIC
    PLANE < 0 -1  0 > 0.5 END_PLANE
    PLANE < 0  1  0 > 9.57382 END_PLANE
  END_INTERSECTION
END_BOUND
ROTATE < 0  22.5  0 >
END_COMPOSITE

{ Define the second floor of the structure }
{ Ring supports rest on the top of the first-floor ring and support }
{ the second-floor ring. Three different colors are defined. }

DECLARE RingSupport = INTERSECTION
  QUADRIC
    Cylinder_Z
    SCALE < 2.0  2.0  1 >
  END_QUADRIC
  QUADRIC
    Cylinder_Z
    SCALE < 1.6  1.6   1 >
    INVERSE
  END_QUADRIC
  PLANE < 0  0 -1 > 0.0 END_PLANE
  PLANE < 0  0  1 > 0.4 END_PLANE
  TRANSLATE < 0  11.57382 -2.0 >
END_INTERSECTION
```

```
DECLARE CopperRingSupport = OBJECT
  INTERSECTION RingSupport END_INTERSECTION
  TEXTURE
    ShinyTexture COLOR Copper
  END_TEXTURE
END_OBJECT

DECLARE Purple1RingSupport = OBJECT
  INTERSECTION RingSupport END_INTERSECTION
  TEXTURE
    ShinyTexture COLOR Purple1
  END_TEXTURE
END_OBJECT

DECLARE Orange2RingSupport = OBJECT
  INTERSECTION RingSupport END_INTERSECTION
  TEXTURE
    ShinyTexture COLOR Orange2
  END_TEXTURE
END_OBJECT

{ This is a smaller horizontal ring that supports the dome }
DECLARE Ring2 = OBJECT
  INTERSECTION
    QUADRIC
      Cylinder_Y
      SCALE < 2.5  1  2.5 >
    END_QUADRIC
    QUADRIC
      Cylinder_Y
      SCALE < 1.75  1  1.75 >
      INVERSE
    END_QUADRIC
    PLANE < 0 -1  0 > -13.57382 END_PLANE
    PLANE < 0  1  0 >  14.07382 END_PLANE
  END_INTERSECTION
  TEXTURE
    RockTexture
  END_TEXTURE
END_OBJECT

{ The Dome is at the top of the structure }
DECLARE Dome = OBJECT
  INTERSECTION
    SPHERE < 0  0  0 > 2.0 END_SPHERE
    PLANE  < 0 -1  0 > 0.0 END_PLANE
  END_INTERSECTION
  TEXTURE
    ShinyTexture COLOR Copper
  END_TEXTURE
  TRANSLATE < 0  14.07382  0 >
END_OBJECT
```

(continued)

Listing 8.2 *(continued)*

```
{ This is the second-floor definition }
DECLARE Floor2 = COMPOSITE
  OBJECT Purple1RingSupport END_OBJECT
  OBJECT CopperRingSupport  ROTATE < 0  120   0 > END_OBJECT
  OBJECT Orange2RingSupport ROTATE < 0 -120   0 > END_OBJECT
  OBJECT Ring2 END_OBJECT
  OBJECT Dome  END_OBJECT
  BOUNDED_BY
    INTERSECTION
      QUADRIC
        Cylinder_Y
        SCALE < 2.9  1  2.9 >
      END_QUADRIC
      PLANE < 0 -1  0 > -9.57382 END_PLANE
      PLANE < 0  1  0 > 16.07382 END_PLANE
    END_INTERSECTION
  END_BOUND
END_COMPOSITE

{ This is a mirrored sphere thrown in for fun. It resides between }
{ the columns above the rock base. }
DECLARE Ball = OBJECT
  SPHERE < 0  4.0  0 > 2 END_SPHERE
  TEXTURE
    Mirror
  END_TEXTURE
END_OBJECT


{ The definition of the complete scene }
DECLARE Scene = COMPOSITE
  OBJECT NightSky  END_OBJECT
  COMPOSITE Ocean  END_COMPOSITE
  COMPOSITE Floor1 END_COMPOSITE
  COMPOSITE Floor2 END_COMPOSITE
  OBJECT Ball      END_OBJECT
END_COMPOSITE

{ This creates an instance of the scene for rendering }
COMPOSITE Scene END_COMPOSITE
```

Two textures are defined next for use within the image. The RockTexture specifies both the coloring (GRANITE) and the surface attributes of the rock surfaces. Most of the objects within this image model use this texturing. The rock is made to be glossy and reflective. Also, because of its rather dark nature, the AMBIENT value for the rock is increased. This causes all of the rock surfaces within the image to have increased illumination levels, making them easier to see. The other texture that is defined, ShinyTexture, is used for the colored RingSupports. This texture is very shiny and very reflective, as you can see from the image.

How the component pieces of the structure are designed should be obvious from the listing. We will, however, discuss each one so no mysteries remain. There is a definite, specific reason for every statement within these definitions, and you should strive to understand each and every one of them.

The columns within this image model are made from a collection of small vertical cylinders arranged in a circle. The Cyl QUADRIC defines these basic vertical cylinders. As designed, Cyls are initially positioned along the Y axis, are 0.12 units in radius, and are infinite in length in the Y direction. The Cyl is then translated 0.3 units in the negative Z direction from the origin (toward the viewer's position) in preparation for being rotated into position when a Column is formed.

A Column is an OBJECT formed from the INTERSECTION of a UNION and two PLANEs. As mentioned, Cyls are used to create the Column. Eight Cyl QUADRICs are rotated into place around the Y axis on a circle of radius 0.3 units. The Cyls are 45 degrees apart. These eight Cyls comprise the UNION portion of the INTERSECTION. The two PLANEs that form the other part of the INTERSECTION limit the length of the eight infinite cylinders. The INTERSECTION causes the Column to have a lower end at Y=0 and an upper end at Y=7.5 units. This is effective beginning at just below the Ocean level and continuing upward. The whole Column is given the RockTexture described earlier.

No column with any self-respect would be without a rectangular pad at its top. The Pad OBJECT defined next fulfills this need. It is constructed as an INTERSECTION of six planes and given the RockTexture. The Pad is 1 unit square in the X and Z directions, with its bottom located at Y=0. The Pad is 0.25 units high. The FullColumn COMPOSITE object defined next permanently attaches a Pad to the top of each Column and throws a bounding volume around the whole thing.

The Base OBJECT defined next is another cylindrical object. It is defined in place to extend out of the ocean between the FullColumns that make up the bottom floor, Floor1, of the complete structure. There is nothing special about the definition of this object.

Ring1 is a cylindrical ring in the Y direction with an outside radius of 3.6 units and an inside radius of 2.0 units. This ring rests on the Arch supports (described next) and is the highest member of the Floor1 structure. As such, it supports the Floor2 portion of the complete structure. This ring is formed by the INTERSECTION of two Cylinder_Y QUADRICs and two PLANEs. The first and larger of the two Cylinder_Y QUADRICs is defined normally, whereas the second and smaller is defined as an INVERSE. As you will recall, this is what effectively cuts the smaller cylinder's area out from the larger cylinder, leaving a whole in the middle. Because the cylinders are still infinite in the Y direction, they must be trimmed to fit. In this case, the two PLANEs slice the cylindrical ring into a piece 0.5 units thick located 9.07382 units up the Y axis. In essence, this is where the ring resides in the structure. *Note*: The slice could alternatively have been made at Y=0.25 and Y=-0.25, resulting in the same thickness piece, but the ring would then have to be translated upward into its final position in the structure. Either way works fine.

Arches are fun. The Arch object defined in this image model is made from the INTERSECTION of two QUADRICs and three PLANEs. The QUADRICs are cylinders in the Z direction with an outside radius of 1.34805 units and an inside radius of 0.94805 units. We did not pick these numbers out of the air; they resulted from the geometry of the structure. With the eight columns that make up the Floor1 structure positioned 45 degrees apart and located on a radius of 3 units, the straight-line distance between the columns is, from trigonometry, 2.29610 units, or the radius of 3 units times the sine of 22.5 degrees. This makes the radius of the Arch one-half that, or 1.14805 units. If we want the Arch surface to be 0.4 units thick, the defining radii will work out as stated above; that is, 1.14805 ± 0.2 units. Finally, the Arch is translated vertically to be of the correct height for placement and brought forward by 2.77164 units (three times the cosine of 22.5 degrees) in preparation for rotation into final position.

With all of its component parts defined, the Floor1 COMPOSITE object is defined. It consists of a single instance of Base, eight FullColumns rotated into position, eight Arch OBJECTs also rotated into position, and a single Ring1 OBJECT. A bounding volume is placed around the complete Floor1 structure.

The OBJECTs and COMPOSITE objects that make up the Floor2 COMPOSITE object are defined in the exact same style. A bounding volume is also placed around the Floor2 COMPOSITE. Following the definition of Floor2, a mirrored sphere called Ball is DECLAREd. This OBJECT is included in this image model just for fun; it does not serve any real purpose other than to set off some of the colors in the image. The sphere is positioned at < 0 4 0 > and has a radius of 2 units. Its texture is Mirror. The final DECLARE statement in this image model collects all of the objects together into the one COMPOSITE Scene. The instance of Scene declared in the last statement causes the NightSky, the Ocean, Floor1, Floor2, and the Ball to be rendered, thus completing this image model.

Tutorial Exercise Eleven—Imagemaps

This short tutorial deals with the use of the imagemap coloration texture. This is a special kind of texture that allows bit-mapped images to be imported into DKBTrace and then mapped to the surfaces of objects within a ray-traced image. As you might imagine, this feature has almost unlimited usefulness in ray tracing. Any bit-mapped image available in dump format, GIF format, or IFF (a Commodore Amiga-specific) format can be brought into DKBTrace and used. In the image model presented here, a picture of Guess Who? is mapped to both a sphere in the center of the image and to a plane that forms the floor of the image. Elsewhere in this scene are many multicolored, highly reflective spheres in which the reflection of the bit-mapped image can be seen clearly. A backdrop plane, which is given the Blue_Agate coloration texture, finishes up this image. The scene is illuminated by two light sources, hence the two specular highlights seen on most of the objects within this scene. Listing 8.3 shows the image model that is contained in the file "exer11.dat" on the companion disks. The "Gallery of Images" has a picture of the image this image model produces (see Image 16).

Except for the incorporation of the IMAGEMAP textures, this image model is basically the same as the other image models previously discussed. The first use of the IMAGEMAP texture is in the definition of the PLANE OBJECT that functions as the floor within the image. As you can see in the listing, the PLANE has its normal pointing in the positive Y direction, making it an XZ plane, and is located 50 units under the coordinate system origin. (Remember the negative displacement discussion in Tutorial Exercise Ten.) The IMAGEMAP usage is declared within the TEXTURE block. The general format for an IMAGEMAP statement is as follows:

IMAGEMAP [<gradient>] FileType "Filename" [ONCE]

where the items in brackets are optional. IMAGEMAP is the DKBTrace keyword that must be specified in uppercase letters. The gradient is a vector that tells DKBTrace the direction in which the bit-mapped image is to be applied to a surface. By default, DKBTrace will map the bit-mapped image into the XY plane in the range (0.0, 0.0) to (1.0, 1.0). That is to say, the imported image will be addressed with these coordinates regardless of size. If you wish to change the orientation of the image mapping, you must specify a gradient. A gradient consists of three numbers, one of which must be zero, one of which must be +1, and one that must be -1. The ordering of these numbers within the vector determines how the image will be mapped; the vector is specified as < X Y Z >. The position of the +1 within the vector indicates which direction the local X axis of the image will be aligned with. The position of the -1 determines which of the axes the Y axis of the image will be aligned with. The default mapping of IMAGEMAPs into the XY plane could be specified (if required) by a vector of < 1 -1 0 >. This would make the local image X axis line up with DKBTrace's X axis and make the local image Y axis line up with DKBTrace's Y axis. In this image model, however, we would like the bit-mapped image to be mapped onto the PLANE forming the floor. Since this PLANE is an XZ plane, a gradient of < 1 0 -1 > is specified. This makes the image left/right, line up with DKBTrace's left/right, while making the local Y axis of the image line up with the positive Z axis in the scene. This effectively lays the image down on its back.

The FileType indicates to DKBTrace the format of the bit-mapped image file that is to be read. The supported file types are DUMP, GIF, and IFF. Filename specifies the path and the filename of the bit-mapped image file. The specified filename must be enclosed in double quotes.

The final and optional field is the ONCE designator. If ONCE is specified, the image will be mapped onto the surface once, and all portions of the surface not covered by the image will be considered transparent. Transparency will allow underlying textures to show through. If the ONCE keyword is not specified, the image will be mapped onto the surface continuously with no empty space on the surface remaining.

After the bit-mapped image is read in, it must be scaled to the correct size and positioned on the surface. Remember, the image is mapped into the range (0.0, 0.0) to (1.0, 1.0) as it is read in. It must be scaled so as to be visible and to fit on the surface on which it is to be mapped. In this image model, the image is scaled by 50 in each direction and then is translated a negative 25 in each direction. This results in the bit-mapped image being centered at the coordinate system origin. As shown in this listing, other surface attributes can also be assigned to the surface on which a bit-mapped image resides. In this case, the BRILLIANCE of the surface and its AMBIENT and DIFFUSE lighting characters are altered.

The next item DECLAREd in the image model is the "SphereTex" texture. This texture is used for all of the spheres within this image model. This texture makes the spheres very smooth and very reflective. The colors assigned to each sphere are determined within the individual sphere definitions.

Listing 8.3   Tutorial Exercise Eleven—Imagemaps

The following is the contents of the file "exer11.dat."

```
{
  Ray-Traced Imaging - Tutorial Exercise Eleven
  "Imagemaps"
  from the book "Practical Ray Tracing in C" by Craig A. Lindley
  Last update to this image: 03/06/92

  In this tutorial exercise a simple use of imagemap coloration
  textures will be shown. This image is made up of many multi-
  colored spheres floating in space. A backdrop plane with
  Blue_Agate coloring is used to set off the spheres. In the
  center of this image, a bit map of the author's face is mapped
  onto a sphere and the same bit-mapped image is mapped onto a
  plane defining the "floor" of the image. Two light sources
  illuminate this scene. See the "Gallery of Images" for a look
  at what this image file produces.
}

INCLUDE "colors.dat"           { standard includes for color }
INCLUDE "shapes.dat"           { for shapes and }
INCLUDE "textures.dat"         { for textures }

{ These are colors not contained in the file "colors.dat" }
DECLARE Copper  = COLOR RED 0.84 GREEN 0.04 BLUE 0.15
DECLARE Orange1 = COLOR RED 1.00 GREEN 0.16 BLUE 0.00
DECLARE Orange2 = COLOR RED 1.00 GREEN 0.35 BLUE 0.00
DECLARE Purple1 = COLOR RED 0.87 GREEN 0.00 BLUE 1.00
DECLARE Purple3 = COLOR RED 0.82 GREEN 0.00 BLUE 0.82
DECLARE Green1  = COLOR RED 0.45 GREEN 0.91 BLUE 0.00

VIEW_POINT                          { define the viewpoint }
  LOCATION  < 0  -5 -110 >
  DIRECTION < 0 -0.05  1 >
  UP  < 0  1  0 >
  RIGHT < 1.0  0  0 >
END_VIEW_POINT

OBJECT                              { define light source 1 }
  SPHERE  < 0.0  0.0  0.0 > 20 END_SPHERE
  TRANSLATE  < 200  200 -200 >
  TEXTURE
    COLOR White
    AMBIENT 1.0
    DIFFUSE 0.0
  END_TEXTURE
  COLOR White
  LIGHT_SOURCE
END_OBJECT

OBJECT                              { define light source 2 }
```

```
  SPHERE  < 0.0  0.0  0.0 > 20 END_SPHERE
  TRANSLATE  <-260  100 -200 >
  TEXTURE
    COLOR White
    AMBIENT 1.0
    DIFFUSE 0.0
  END_TEXTURE
  COLOR White
  LIGHT_SOURCE
END_OBJECT

{ Add the backdrop to the picture }
OBJECT
   PLANE < 0 0 -1 > -200 END_PLANE
   TEXTURE
     Blue_Agate
     SCALE < 60 80 70 >
     AMBIENT 0.75
     DIFFUSE 0.25
     BRILLIANCE 1.0
   END_TEXTURE
END_OBJECT

{ Define the floor of the image }
OBJECT
  PLANE < 0 1 0 > -50 END_PLANE
  TEXTURE
    IMAGEMAP < 1  0 -1 > DUMP "craig.dis"
    SCALE < 50 50 50 >
    TRANSLATE <-25 -25 -25 >
    BRILLIANCE 20
    AMBIENT 0.75
    DIFFUSE 0.25
  END_TEXTURE
END_OBJECT

{ All spheres will have the same texture }
DECLARE SphereTex = TEXTURE
  REFLECTION 0.65
  BRILLIANCE 20.0
  PHONG 0.9
  PHONGSIZE 100
END_TEXTURE

{ Now define all of the spheres in this image }
{ The spheres are defined in place, that is they are not }
{ translated into their final position in three-dimensional }
{ space. Also, the sphere object instances are created directly }
{ instead of being DECLAREd now and instances created later. }

OBJECT { Sphere 1 }
  SPHERE < 0 0 0 > 25 END_SPHERE
```

(continued)

Listing 8.3 *(continued)*

```
  TEXTURE
    IMAGEMAP DUMP "craig.dis"
    SCALE < 30 30 30 >
    TRANSLATE <-15 -15 -15 >
    PHONG 0.5
    PHONGSIZE 100
    AMBIENT 0.75
    DIFFUSE 0.25
  END_TEXTURE
END_OBJECT

OBJECT { Sphere 2 }
  SPHERE < -37.5 -30 -15.5 > 20 END_SPHERE
  TEXTURE
    SphereTex
    COLOR MediumForestGreen
  END_TEXTURE
END_OBJECT

OBJECT { Sphere 3 }
  SPHERE < 52.5 -17.5 -18 > 20 END_SPHERE
  TEXTURE
    SphereTex
    COLOR Orange1
  END_TEXTURE
END_OBJECT

OBJECT { Sphere 4 }
  SPHERE <-57.5 12.5 0 > 15 END_SPHERE
  TEXTURE
    SphereTex
    COLOR Copper
  END_TEXTURE
END_OBJECT

OBJECT { Sphere 5 }
  SPHERE < 12.5 -32.5 -14 > 15 END_SPHERE
  TEXTURE
    SphereTex
    COLOR Copper
  END_TEXTURE
END_OBJECT

OBJECT { Sphere 6 }
  SPHERE < 47.5 17.5 20 > 15 END_SPHERE
  TEXTURE
    SphereTex
    COLOR Purple1
  END_TEXTURE
END_OBJECT
```

```
OBJECT { Sphere 7 }
  SPHERE <-32.5 32.5 35 > 15 END_SPHERE
  TEXTURE
    SphereTex
    COLOR Green1
  END_TEXTURE
END_OBJECT


OBJECT { Sphere 8 }
  SPHERE < 17.5 30 47.5 > 20 END_SPHERE
  TEXTURE
    SphereTex
    COLOR Gold
  END_TEXTURE
END_OBJECT


OBJECT { Sphere 9 }
  SPHERE < 62.5 0 -77.5 > 20 END_SPHERE
  TEXTURE
    SphereTex
    COLOR Blue
  END_TEXTURE
END_OBJECT


OBJECT { Sphere 10 }
  SPHERE < 0 -30 -100 > 20 END_SPHERE
  TEXTURE
    SphereTex
    COLOR Red
  END_TEXTURE
END_OBJECT


OBJECT { Sphere 11 }
  SPHERE <-62.5 0 -77.5 > 20 END_SPHERE
  TEXTURE
    SphereTex
    COLOR Green
  END_TEXTURE
END_OBJECT


OBJECT { Sphere 12 }
  SPHERE <-45 -18.5 0 > 15 END_SPHERE
  TEXTURE
    SphereTex
    COLOR Orange2
  END_TEXTURE
END_OBJECT


OBJECT { Sphere 13 }
  SPHERE <40 -18.5 0 > 15 END_SPHERE
  TEXTURE
```

(continued)

Listing 8.3 *(continued)*

```
    SphereTex
    COLOR Purple3
  END_TEXTURE
END_OBJECT

OBJECT { Sphere 14 }
  SPHERE <-75 100 -50 > 40 END_SPHERE
  TEXTURE
    SphereTex
    COLOR Orange2
  END_TEXTURE
END_OBJECT
```

The first sphere defined in this image model is also given an IMAGEMAP texture of the same smiling face. You'll notice that in this case, a gradient is not specified, because the default directional mapping of the IMAGEMAP suits the requirements of the sphere. The scaling and translations applied to this instance of the IMAGEMAP texture are different than those used previously because of the distances of the viewer from the objects given the IMAGEMAP textures. The values used for scaling and translation are found via experimentation and are chosen by the viewer's preferences.

Thirteen other spheres are then defined within this image model. Many are assigned different colors, though all have the same SphereTex texture. All of the sphere OBJECTs are defined in place (instances are created immediately) instead of being DECLAREd in one spot and later referenced.

You may be interested in how I got a picture of myself into dump format for use in this image. Actually, this is beyond the scope of this discussion, but I will say that I utilized the video digitizer developed in my last book, *Practical Image Processing in C*. Once I had a digitized color image available (the color image was close to black and white in this case), some custom software allowed me to cut my face out of the whole digitized image and save only that portion of the image as a dump file. That file is included on the companion disks as "craig.dis." Professional image scanners will sometimes include software to cut out portions of scanned images and save them in a standard file format. If the format is GIF, you are home free. If not, you may have to write a file conversion utility program of the kind discussed in Chapter 5 to get the image data into a format that DKBTrace will accept.

As mentioned, the use of IMAGEMAP textures is wide open. Besides placing your face into an image, you could also digitize or scan in pictures of grass or granite rock or a brick wall and apply them to objects within your ray-traced images. That would provide very life-like textures. Another interesting use of IMAGEMAP textures is the importation of fractal images. See the discussion of Image Model Three in Chapter 9 for details.

Tutorial Exercise Twelve—Algorithmic Image Generation

As you have seen in this chapter, some image models can be very complex and therefore time-consuming to design. After a certain point of complexity is reached, it becomes almost impossible to design and input an image model manually. This can be because of the tedious nature of the calculations involved in designing the model, because of the vast amounts of typing required to input the model, because of the accuracy that must be kept, or just because of the sheer number of surfaces involved. We can all envision ray-traced objects and images we would like to create, but the complexity of some of these will prohibit us from attempting to do so. Elaborate three-dimensional fonts are an example of an image element that would be nice to include in a ray-traced image but very difficult to design manually. The simple block font used in Tutorial Exercise Nine was difficult enough to figure out. A script font would be next to impossible to do manually. Fortunately, some of the tasks that humans consider tedious computers excel at. And when it comes to repetitive calculations, nothing beats a computer.

The idea then is instead of laboring over the meticulous details required by a complex image model or image element, you could simply write a computer program instead. The computer program would perform the repetitive calculations and provide as its output an image model file in the scene description language that DKBTrace understands. In other words, one computer program would write code for another computer program, DKBTrace, to interpret. The time spent in developing the complex image is spent in developing the computer program and not spent calculating and typing, as would be required if the image model were developed manually.

The purpose of this tutorial exercise, as you have probably guessed by now, is to show how this process can be made to work. Specifically, a computer program called "mount.c" is written that generates land mass and mountain shapes built from triangular surfaces utilizing fractal data. In total, over 7,600 triangles are generated to simulate the land mass. The output of the mountain-building program is an ASCII file called "mount.inc," in DKBTrace scene description language, which contains the triangle data. This file is INCLUDEd in the very short image model program called "exer12.dat" shown in Listing 8.4. When this image model file is ray traced, the result is a crude, but somewhat lifelike, piece of land surrounded by an ocean and a sky with clouds. You can dramatically alter the characteristics of the land by using parameters in the "mount.c" program. The land can be made to resemble rolling hills or can be made as jagged as the Grand Tetons. We'll have more on the generation of the land data later in this discussion.

A word of caution should be given at this point: You should realize that 7,600 objects within a scene makes for a very complex image. Ray tracing all of these objects takes an extremely long time on a PC. On a 33 MHz 486 computer with 8 megabytes of RAM, ray tracing this image model and producing the image seen in the "Gallery of Images" required over 30 hours. To even attempt to ray trace this image model requires the use of the protected-mode version of DKBTrace, which must run on a 286 processor or better. There is not enough room in the 640K bytes of DOS memory that the real-mode versions of DKBTrace have access to, to handle an image of this complexity. The protected-mode version of DKBTrace and a minimum of 2 megabytes of extended memory are absolutely required. Enough said. Now, please refer to Listing 8.4 during the discussion of the image model to follow.

Listing 8.4   Tutorial Exercise Twelve—Algorithmic Image Generation

The following is the contents of the file "exer12.dat."

```
{
  Ray-Traced Imaging - Tutorial Exercise Twelve
  "Algorithmic Image Generation"
  from the book "Practical Ray Tracing in C" by Craig A. Lindley
  Last update to this image: 03/06/92

  The purpose of this exercise is to show how computer programs
  can generate image model data that can be incorporated into
  DKBTrace image models. The program "mount.exe" discussed in the
  text generates fractal data in the form of triangles that can
  be used to simulate land masses. This image model sets up the
  viewpoint, a light source, a background sky, and a simulated ocean
  to be displayed with the land mass. It then includes the file
  "mount.inc" produced by the "mount.exe" program which contains
  the land mass data. Because "mount.inc" is an ASCII file, you
  can look at it with your editor. See the "Gallery of Images" for
  a look at what this image file produces.

  NOTE: ray tracing this image at 1024 by 768 resolution on a 33 MHz
  486 computer took approximately 30 hours because of the number of
  triangular objects (approx. 7600 ) used to simulate the land mass.
  To even attempt to render this scene, you must be running the
  protected-mode version of DKBTrace and have a lot of extended
  memory. Attempt rendering this scene on your own computer at
  your own risk.
}

INCLUDE "colors.dat"             { standard includes for color }
INCLUDE "shapes.dat"             { for shapes and }
INCLUDE "textures.dat"           { for textures }

VIEW_POINT                       { define the viewpoint }
  LOCATION < 0  0 -40000 >
  DIRECTION < 0  0  1 >
  UP  < 0  1  0 >
  RIGHT < 1.0  0  0 >
  ROTATE < 0 -15 0 >
  ROTATE < 40  0  0 >
END_VIEW_POINT

OBJECT                           { define a light source }
  SPHERE  < 0 0 0 > 2 END_SPHERE
  TRANSLATE  < 25000 30000 -25000 >
  TEXTURE
    COLOR White
    AMBIENT 1.0
    DIFFUSE 0.0
  END_TEXTURE
  COLOR White
```

```
  LIGHT_SOURCE
END_OBJECT

{ Add a backdrop cloudy sky for contrast }
OBJECT
  PLANE < 0  0 -1 > -12000 END_PLANE
  TEXTURE
   Cloud_Sky
   SCALE < 10000 4504 30456 >
   AMBIENT 1.0
   DIFFUSE 0.0
  END_TEXTURE
END_OBJECT

{ Add a perturbed blue ocean in the foreground }
OBJECT
  PLANE < 0  1  0 > 10 END_PLANE
  TEXTURE
   COLOR NavyBlue
   WAVES 0.1
   FREQUENCY 50
   SCALE < 2000 3000 2000 >
   REFLECTION 0.4
   PHONG 0.75
   PHONGSIZE 50
  END_TEXTURE
END_OBJECT

{ Now include the mountain data generated by the "mount.exe" program }
{ Note: path to file "mount.inc" may change depending on your development }
{ environment. }

INCLUDE "mount.inc"
```

Not much is different about this image model than previous ones except for the scale of the objects involved. The mountain-building program (to be discussed) was given parameters that cause it to generate a mountain object approximately the size and shape of Pike's Peak. That is, the land data contains at least one peak that will be 14,440 feet tall. For this reason, the positions of the VIEW_POINT and the single light source illuminating the scene have been altered to the same relative scale. You can see this in the listing. A PLANE with mapped sky and clouds is positioned behind the MOUNTAIN object for effect. This time, instead of defining our own COLORMAP to produce the clouds from the BOZO noise texture, we will incorporate the Cloud_Sky texture contained in the "texture.dat" file for the same effect. Finally, another PLANE simulating an ocean is defined, which will show through all portions of the land mass at the 10-foot height or below. This creates lakes where surrounded by land and oceans outside of the land mass. The WAVES surface perturbation texture is used to create oceanlike waves on the surface of the water.

The final operation performed by this image model is to include the file "mount.inc," which contains the definition of the land mass in terms of triangles. Since this is a very large file, it will not be listed here. If you are curious about what this file looks like, compile and run the "mount.c" program on the companion disks. It will produce a "mount.inc" file that is identical to the one that produced the image in the "Gallery of Images." As you can see if you examine this file, it is very structured and readable because the "mount.c" program that generated it made it that way. The readability is important when trying to debug an algorithmic image generation program of this type. Readability is unnecessary, of course, from DKBTrace's point of view.

As should now be obvious, the majority of the effort involved in the creation of the land mass data and the image model is performed in the "mount.c" program shown in Listing 8.5. This rather lengthy program creates fractal data with user-specified parameters using the "Mid-PointFM2D" algorithm from the book *The Science of Fractal Image* published by Springer-Verlag New York, Inc. This algorithm creates fractal data in a square two-dimensional array called Elevations, entries of which contain the elevation of points on the synthesized surface of the land. After the fractal data is created, the "mount.c" program does the following:

1. It constrains and scales the data contained in the Elevations array so that it all resides between sea level (Y=0) and a maximum height of 14,440 feet.

2. It creates the output file "mount.inc" in which to store the scene description of the MOUNTAIN COMPOSITE object. All data written to this file consists of DKBTrace keywords and corresponding parameters. The first things written to the output file are the strings Str0 and Str1, which as shown in the listing are first a comment to identify the Fractal Mountain Object followed by a DECLARE statement declaring a Mountain to be a COMPOSITE object.

3. The program then traverses the Elevations array, creating two triangle objects from each four data points in the array. This process is illustrated in Figure 8.2. These triangles are then converted into DKBTrace scene description language statements and written to the output file.

4. When the complete Elevations array has been processed and all of the triangles written to the output file, the program finishes the definition of the Mountain COMPOSITE object, a bounding volume for the Mountain is written to the output file, and finally a statement is written to the file that, when executed, will cause an instance of the Mountain object to be created and translated into final position. The "mount.inc" file is then closed and the "mount.c" program terminates.

We will fill in the details involved in this process in the following discussion. Please refer to Listing 8.5 at this time.

The "mount.c" listing begins with many #define statements that control its operation. The first important definition is GRIDSIZE, which controls the size of the Elevations array. The next two definitions are derived from GRIDSIZE and are used in the definition of the Elevations array. GRIDSIZE directly determines how many triangles this program will produce. You should never use values greater than six unless you have a supercomputer on which to render the scene. As mentioned, 7,600 triangles are produced with a GRIDSIZE of six.

SNOWFACTOR determines at what altitude on the land/mountain data the snow line should begin. In this case, the snow will begin at 90% of the mountain's total height, and tree line, controlled by TREEFACTOR, will be at 80% of the mountain's height. These elevation distinctions are used to control the color assigned to the land mass data.

This figure illustrates how the land mass data is converted
into triangle data for rendering with DKBTrace.
Two triangles are formed from each four data points.
The elevation of each data point (Y value) is stored in Elevations array.

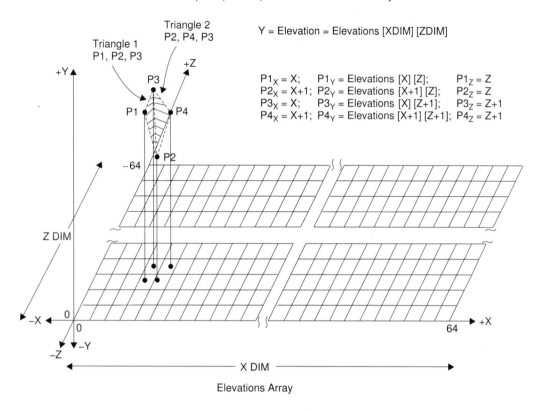

Y = Elevation = Elevations [XDIM] [ZDIM]

$P1_X = X;$ $\quad$ $P1_Y$ = Elevations [X] [Z]; $\quad$ $P1_Z = Z$
$P2_X = X+1;$ $\quad$ $P2_Y$ = Elevations [X+1] [Z]; $\quad$ $P2_Z = Z$
$P3_X = X;$ $\quad$ $P3_Y$ = Elevations [X] [Z+1]; $\quad$ $P3_Z = Z+1$
$P4_X = X+1;$ $\quad$ $P4_Y$ = Elevations [X+1] [Z+1]; $\quad$ $P4_Z = Z+1$

Elevations Array

Notes: With GRIDSIZE = 6, XDIM = ZDIM = 65. With no optimizations,
8192 triangles would be formed. With sea level triangle elimination,
7600+ triangles are produced. Other optimization techniques
could further reduce the number of triangles.

Figure 8.2   Generation of Land Mass Data

The constants MWIDTHRATIO and MDEPTHRATIO control the proportions of the
mountain data in relation to the height of the mountain. In this case, the mountain terrain will
span three times the mountain's height and will have a depth two-and-one-half times the
height. The steepness of the terrain will be used to partially control the color assigned to the
terrain. The constant THRESHOLDRATIO is used to determine what this program considers
steep. Any portion of the image data that has a gradient greater than THRESHOLDRATIO
times the PeakHeight is considered steep. The next three constants determine the colors to be
assigned to the snow, the rock, and the forest portions of the land mass, respectively.

Listing 8.5   Tutorial Exercise Twelve C Code—Algorithmic Image Generation Continued

The following is the contents of the file "mount.c."

```
/*************************************************************/
/***                      "mount.c"                     ***/
/***    Fractal Mountain Building Program for DKBTrace   ***/
/***             part of tutorial exercise 12           ***/
/***          Based on Algorithm MidPointFM2D from      ***/
/***            "The Science of Fractal Images"         ***/
/***     edited by Heinz-Otto Peitgen and Dietmar Saupe ***/
/***                                                    ***/
/***      from the book "Practical Ray Tracing in C"    ***/
/***            written in Borland/Turbo C 2.0          ***/
/***                        by                          ***/
/***                 Craig A. Lindley                   ***/
/***         Ver: 1.0    Last Update: 03/01/92          ***/
/*************************************************************/

#include <stdio.h>
#include <stdlib.h>
#include <math.h>
#include <string.h>
#include <conio.h>
#include "misc.h"

#define NRAND     4               /* used in Gauss calculation */
#define GRIDSIZE 6                /* controls size of grid of elevation data */
#define XDIM   ((1<<GRIDSIZE)+1) /* dimensions of the grid */
#define ZDIM   ((1<<GRIDSIZE)+1) /* dimensions of the grid */
#define SNOWFACTOR 0.90           /* snow starts at this % of peak height */
#define TREEFACTOR 0.80           /* tree line at this % of peak height */
#define MWIDTHRATIO (3.0)         /* ratio of mountain width to height */
#define MDEPTHRATIO (2.5)         /* ratio of mountain depth to height */
#define THRESHOLDRATIO 0.15       /* gradients ratio */
#define THRESHOLD   (PeakHeight*THRESHOLDRATIO) /* gradients over this are considered
                                               steep */

#define SNOWCOLOR    "White"
#define ROCKCOLOR    "Brown"
#define FORESTCOLOR "ForestGreen"


/* Global Data Declarations */

static unsigned Ver = 1;
static unsigned Rev = 0;

static double   Elevations[XDIM][ZDIM]; /* The mountain data */
static double   GaussAdd, GaussFac;
static unsigned PeakHeight;
static double   SnowLine;
static double   TreeLine;
static double   GradientThreshold;
```

```
static double   Texture;
static double   TotalMWidth;
static double   TotalMDepth;
static unsigned NumOfTriangles;
static char     LineBuf[256];
static char     NumBuf[80];

/*
Color array is used to select land colors based upon elevation and
steepness (gradient). It is set up from lower to higher elevations.
At low elevations FORESTCOLOR is used unless land is very steep in
which case ROCKCOLOR is used. Above treeline, use SNOWCOLOR unless
very steep then use ROCKCOLOR. Above snowline, always use SNOWCOLOR.
*/
static char *Colors[] =  {
  FORESTCOLOR,ROCKCOLOR,
  SNOWCOLOR,ROCKCOLOR,
  SNOWCOLOR,SNOWCOLOR
};

/*
Strings used in this program. The spaces in the strings
help keep the output file "mount.inc" formatted readably.
*/
static char *Str0  = "{ Fractal Mountain Object }\n";
static char *Str1  = "DECLARE Mountain = COMPOSITE\n";
static char *Str2  = "  OBJECT\n";
static char *Str3  = "  END_OBJECT\n";
static char *Str4  = "    UNION\n";
static char *Str5  = "    END_UNION\n";
static char *Str6  = "      TRIANGLE ";
static char *Str7  = "END_TRIANGLE\n";
static char *Str8  = "    TEXTURE\n";
static char *Str9  = "    END_TEXTURE\n";
static char *Str10 = "      COLOR ";
static char *Str11 = "END_COMPOSITE\n";
static char *Str12 = "\n\nCOMPOSITE Mountain TRANSLATE < ";
static char *Str13 = "< ";
static char *Str14 = " > ";
static char *Str15 = "\n";
static char *Str16 = "  BOUNDED_BY\n";
static char *Str17 = "  END_BOUND\n";
static char *Str18 = "    INTERSECTION\n";
static char *Str19 = "    END_INTERSECTION\n";
static char *Str20 = "      PLANE ";
static char *Str21 = "      END_PLANE\n";

/*
The following is the name given to output data file. This file
will be included in the DKBTrace image model "exer12.dat."
*/
static char *FileName  = "mount.inc";
```

(continued)

Listing 8.5 *(continued)*

```c
/* Begin Program Code */

/*
Functions to calculate and process the elevation data that will
become the mountain. See the "Science of  Fractal Images" for
additional information.
*/

void InitGauss (unsigned Seed)  {

   register double Arand;

   Arand = pow (2L,15L) - 1;
   GaussAdd = sqrt((double)(3.0 * NRAND));
   GaussFac = 2 * GaussAdd/(NRAND * Arand);
   srand(Seed);
}


double Gauss (void)  {

   register double Sum;
   register int  I;

   Sum = 0;
   for (I=0;  I < NRAND;  I++)
      Sum += rand();

   return (GaussFac * Sum - GaussAdd );
}


double Ave3 (double delta, double X1, double X2, double X3)  {

   return ((X1 + X2 + X3)/3.0 + delta * Gauss());
}


double Ave4 (double delta, double X1, double X2, double X3, double X4)  {

   return ((X1 + X2 + X3 + X4)/4.0 + delta * Gauss());
}

/*
The following is the algorithm that calculates the mountain elevation
data. It implements the midpoint displacement algorithm in two dimensions.
*/
void MidPointFM2D (double Data [][ZDIM], int MaxLevel,
                   double Sigma,          double H,
                   int   Addition,        unsigned Seed)  {
```

```
unsigned Stage,x,y,D,d,N;
double   Delta;

InitGauss(Seed);
N = pow(2L,MaxLevel);
Delta = Sigma;

/* Set the initial random corners */
Data[0][0] = Delta * Gauss();
Data[0][N] = Delta * Gauss();
Data[N][0] = Delta * Gauss();
Data[N][N] = Delta * Gauss();

D = N;
d = N/2;
for (Stage = 0; Stage < MaxLevel; Stage ++)  {
   /* going from type 1 to type 2 grid */
   Delta *= pow((double) 0.5,(double)(0.5 * H));

   /* interpolate and offset points */
   for (x = d; x <= N-d; x +=D)
      for (y = d; y <= N-d; y +=D)
         Data[x][y] = Ave4(Delta,Data[x+d][y+d],
                                 Data[x+d][y-d],
                                 Data[x-d][y+d],
                                 Data[x-d][y-d]);

   if (Addition)
   for (x = 0; x <= N; x += D)
      for (y = 0; y <= N; y += D)
          Data[x][y] += (Delta * Gauss());

   /* going from type 2 to type 1 grid */
   Delta *= pow((double) 0.5,(double)(0.5 * H));

   /* interpolate and offset boundary points */
   for (x = d; x <= N-d; x +=D)  {
      Data[x][0] = Ave3(Delta,Data[x+d][0],
                              Data[x-d][0],
                              Data[x][d]);
      Data[x][N] = Ave3(Delta,Data[x+d][N],
                              Data[x-d][N],
                              Data[x][N-d]);
      Data[0][x] = Ave3(Delta,Data[0][x+d],
                              Data[0][x-d],
                              Data[d][x]);
      Data[N][x] = Ave3(Delta,Data[N][x+d],
                              Data[N][x-d],
                              Data[N-d][x]);
   }
```

(continued)

Listing 8.5 *(continued)*

```
/* interpolate and offset interior points */
for (x = d; x <= N-d; x +=D)
   for (y = D; y <= N-d; y +=D)
      Data[x][y] = Ave4(Delta,Data[x][y+d],
                              Data[x][y-d],
                              Data[x+d][y],
                              Data[x-d][y]);

for (x = D; x <= N-d; x +=D)
  for (y = d; y <= N-d; y +=D)
      Data[x][y] = Ave4(Delta,Data[x][y+d],
                              Data[x][y-d],
                              Data[x+d][y],
                              Data[x-d][y]);

if (Addition)  {
   for (x = 0; x <= N; x += D)
      for (y = 0; y <= N; y += D)
         Data[x][y] += (Delta * Gauss());

   for (x = d; x <= N-d; x += D)
      for (y = d; y <= N-d; y += D)
         Data[x][y] += (Delta * Gauss());
   }
   D = D/2;
   d = d/2;
   }
}
/*
The purpose of this function is to:
  1. Make a pass through the elevation data setting entries
     with negative elevation to zero elevation.
  2. Make two more passes over the data setting the elevation at
     the boundaries of the elevation grid to zero.
*/
void ConstrainElevation (void)  {

   register unsigned x,z;
   double   ThisElevation;

   /*
   Make a pass through the elevation data to find any negatives
   amplitude. Set those to zero.
   */
   for (x = 0; x < XDIM; x++)
      for (z = 0; z < ZDIM; z++)  {
         ThisElevation = Elevations[x][z];
         Elevations[x][z] = (ThisElevation < 0.0) ? 0.0:ThisElevation;
      }
   /*
```

```
      Now make more passes through the data and make sure all edges have
      an amplitude of zero so the mountain starts at ground level and not
      somewhere in midair.
   */
   for (x = 0; x < XDIM; x++)  {
      Elevations[x][0] = 0.0;
      Elevations[x][ZDIM-1] = 0.0;
   }
   for (z = 0; z < ZDIM; z++)  {
      Elevations[0][z] = 0.0;
      Elevations[XDIM-1][z] = 0.0;
   }
}
/*
Scale the elevation data so it is of the required height of PeakAmp.
*/

void ScaleElevation (unsigned PeakAmp)  {

   register unsigned x,z;
   double   MaxAmpl, ThisElevation, ScaleFactor;

   /*
   First make a pass through the elevation data to find the max
   amplitude. MaxAmpl has the peak value.
   */
   MaxAmpl = 0;                     /* find largest elevation in data */
   for (x = 0; x < XDIM; x++)
      for (z = 0; z < ZDIM; z++)  {
         ThisElevation = Elevations[x][z]; /* get current point data */
         MaxAmpl = (ThisElevation > MaxAmpl) ? ThisElevation:MaxAmpl;
      }
   /*
   Now make another pass through and scale the data to the
   requested height.
   */
   ScaleFactor = (double) PeakAmp / MaxAmpl;
   for (x = 0; x < XDIM; x++)
      for (z = 0; z < ZDIM; z++)
         Elevations[x][z] *= ScaleFactor;
}
/*
Given the coordinates of three points which will define a triangle,
calculate from the elevation data the maximum slope or gradient of
the triangle. This gradient will be used to help select the color
assigned to the triangle when it is rendered.
*/

double CalcGradient( unsigned X1, unsigned Z1,
                     unsigned X2, unsigned Z2,
                     unsigned X3, unsigned Z3)    {
```

(continued)

Listing 8.5   *(continued)*

```
  double Diff1, Diff2, Diff3, MaxDiff;

  /* Calculate the elevation differences */
  Diff1 = fabs(Elevations[X1][Z1] - Elevations[X2][Z2]);
  Diff2 = fabs(Elevations[X1][Z1] - Elevations[X3][Z3]);
  Diff3 = fabs(Elevations[X2][Z2] - Elevations[X3][Z3]);

  /* Select the largest gradient for return */
  MaxDiff = Diff1;
  MaxDiff = (Diff2 > MaxDiff) ? Diff2:MaxDiff;
  MaxDiff = (Diff3 > MaxDiff) ? Diff3:MaxDiff;
  return(MaxDiff);
}


/*
Given the coordinates of three points which will define a triangular
patch of land, calculate the peak elevation of this land. From
this assign zone 0 for under treeline, zone 1 for land between treeline but
below snowline and zone 2 for snowline and above. The zone will be used
to establish the color of the triangle when it is rendered.
*/
unsigned CalcZone ( unsigned X1, unsigned Z1,
                    unsigned X2, unsigned Z2,
                    unsigned X3, unsigned Z3)    {

  double PeakElevation;
  unsigned Zone;

  /* Calculate peak elevation of this triangular patch of land */
  PeakElevation = Elevations[X1][Z1];
  PeakElevation = (Elevations[X2][Z2] > PeakElevation) ? Elevations[X2][Z2]:PeakElevation;
  PeakElevation = (Elevations[X3][Z3] > PeakElevation) ? Elevations[X3][Z3]:PeakElevation;

  /* Assign zones from the peak elevation */
  if (PeakElevation < TreeLine)
    Zone = 0;
  else if ((PeakElevation >= TreeLine) && (PeakElevation < SnowLine))
    Zone = 1;
  else
    Zone = 2;

 return(Zone);
}
/*
This function uses the Zone and the elevation gradient to calculate
the actual color to be assigned to the land. An index is returned into
the Colors array for the name of the color to be assigned.
*/
unsigned CalcColor( unsigned Zone, unsigned ColorOffset)    {
```

```c
unsigned Index;

switch(Zone)    {
  case 0:   Index = 0;      /* temperate zone */
            break;
  case 1:   Index = 2;      /* alpine zone */
            break;
  case 2:   Index = 4;      /* arctic zone */
            break;
  }
  if (ColorOffset)
    Index++;                /* if terrain is steep bump one color */

  return (Index);           /* index is the color to use */
}


/*
The following routines write strings to the output file. Handle
is the file handle of the ASCII output file. All strings in the
output file are in a format understandable by DKBTrace. In other
words, this program produces an image model in DKBTrace's scene
description language.
*/

/*
This function writes the string pointed at by Str to the
ASCII output file.
*/
int WriteToFile(FILE *Handle, char *Str)  {

  if (fwrite(Str, strlen(Str), 1, Handle) != 1)
    return(EWrtOutFile);
  else
    return(NoError);
}
/*
This function writes a DKBTrace vector of the form < X Y Z >
to the output file. The values for X, Y, and Z are passed into
this function.
*/
int WriteVector(FILE *Handle, double X, double Y, double Z)   {

  static char TmpBuf[80];

  TmpBuf[0] = '\0';              /* make buf empty */
  strcat(TmpBuf,Str13);          /* < */
  sprintf(NumBuf,"%8.2f ",X);/* double -> Ascii */
  strcat(TmpBuf,NumBuf);         /* Ascii # into LineBuf */
  sprintf(NumBuf,"%8.2f ",Y);/* double -> Ascii */
  strcat(TmpBuf,NumBuf);         /* Ascii # into LineBuf */
```

(continued)

Listing 8.5 *(continued)*

```
    sprintf(NumBuf,"%8.2f ",Z);/* double -> Ascii */
    strcat(TmpBuf,NumBuf);     /* Ascii # into LineBuf */
    strcat(TmpBuf,Str14);      /* > */
    return(WriteToFile(Handle,TmpBuf)); /* return ptr to buffer */
}

/*
All triangular patches of land of the same color will be concatenated
together with a UNION into a OBJECT. Calling this function begins
the definition of a new OBJECT.
*/
void BeginObjDef (FILE *Handle)  {

  WriteToFile(Handle,Str2);  /* OBJECT */
  WriteToFile(Handle,Str4);  /* UNION */
}
/*
This function is called to end a UNION OBJECT. This happens every time
a new triangle is defined that is of a different color than those collected
into this UNION OBJECT. This function ends the UNION, defines a texture
block for assigning color to the OBJECT, and finally ends the OBJECT's
definition.
*/
void EndObjDef (FILE *Handle, unsigned ColorIndex)  {

  WriteToFile(Handle,Str5);  /* END_UNION */
  WriteToFile(Handle,Str8);  /* TEXTURE */
  if (Texture != 0.0)   {
     sprintf(NumBuf,"%8.2f ",Texture); /* double -> Ascii */
     WriteToFile(Handle,NumBuf);
     WriteToFile(Handle,Str15); /* ret */
  }
  WriteToFile(Handle,Str10); /* COLOR */
  WriteToFile(Handle,Colors[ColorIndex]);  /* color name */
  WriteToFile(Handle,Str15); /* ret */
  WriteToFile(Handle,Str9);  /* END_TEXTURE */
  WriteToFile(Handle,Str3);  /* END_OBJECT */
}
/*
This function is called when all of the elevation or mountain data
has been formatted and written to the output file. This function
writes out a BOUNDED_BY block containing an INTERSECTION of PLANEs
which forms the boundaries of the mountain. It then terminates the
COMPOSITE object's definitions, defines an instance of Mountain, and
finally translates the mountain so as to center it at the origin.
*/
void EndMountainDef (FILE *Handle)  {

  WriteToFile(Handle,Str16);  /* BOUNDED_BY */
  WriteToFile(Handle,Str18);  /* INTERSECTION */
```

```
   WriteToFile(Handle,Str20);   /* PLANE */
   WriteVector(Handle,-1.0,0.0,0.0);
   WriteToFile(Handle," 0.0");
   WriteToFile(Handle,Str21);   /* END_PLANE */
   WriteToFile(Handle,Str20);   /* PLANE */
   WriteVector(Handle,1.0,0.0,0.0);
   sprintf(NumBuf,"%8.2f ",TotalMWidth); /* double -> Ascii */
   WriteToFile(Handle,NumBuf);
   WriteToFile(Handle,Str21);   /* END_PLANE */

   WriteToFile(Handle,Str20);   /* PLANE */
   WriteToFile(Handle,Str13);   /* < */
   WriteToFile(Handle," 0.0 -1.0  0.0 > 0.0");
   WriteToFile(Handle,Str21);   /* END_PLANE */
   WriteToFile(Handle,Str20);   /* PLANE */
   WriteVector(Handle,0.0,1.0,0.0);
   sprintf(NumBuf,"%8.2f ",(double) PeakHeight); /* double -> Ascii */
   WriteToFile(Handle,NumBuf);
   WriteToFile(Handle,Str21);   /* END_PLANE */

   WriteToFile(Handle,Str20);   /* PLANE */
   WriteVector(Handle,0.0,0.0,-1.0);
   WriteToFile(Handle,"0.0");
   WriteToFile(Handle,Str21);   /* END_PLANE */
   WriteToFile(Handle,Str20);   /* PLANE */
   WriteVector(Handle,0.0,0.0,1.0);
   sprintf(NumBuf,"%8.2f ",TotalMDepth); /* double -> Ascii */
   WriteToFile(Handle,NumBuf);
   WriteToFile(Handle,Str21);   /* END_PLANE */

   WriteToFile(Handle,Str19);   /* END_INTERSECTION */
   WriteToFile(Handle,Str17);   /* END_BOUND */

   WriteToFile(Handle,Str11);   /* END_COMPOSITE */
   WriteToFile(Handle,Str12);   /* COMPOSITE Mountain TRANSLATE < */
   sprintf(NumBuf,"%8.2f ",-TotalMWidth/2.0); /* double -> Ascii */
   WriteToFile(Handle,NumBuf);
   WriteToFile(Handle," 0.0 ");
   sprintf(NumBuf,"%8.2f",-TotalMDepth/2.0); /* double -> Ascii */
   WriteToFile(Handle,NumBuf);
   WriteToFile(Handle,Str14);   /* > */
   WriteToFile(Handle,Str11);   /* END_COMPOSITE */
   WriteToFile(Handle,Str15);   /* ret */
   WriteToFile(Handle,Str15);   /* ret */
}
/*
This function writes out a definition for the triangle defined
by the parameters passed to it. The definition begins with the
keyword TRIANGLE and is followed by three vectors defining the
triangle. Following the vectors, END_TRIANGLE is written to the
output file. Finally, the statistic for the number of triangles
processed thus far is updated on the display.
*/
```

(continued)

Listing 8.5 *(continued)*

```
void WriteTriangle( FILE *Handle,
                    double X1, double Y1, double Z1,
                    double X2, double Y2, double Z2,
                    double X3, double Y3, double Z3)   {

  unsigned CurX, CurY;

  LineBuf[0] = '\0';          /* make line buf empty */
  strcat(LineBuf,Str6);       /* TRIANGLE */
  strcat(LineBuf,Str13);      /* TRIANGLE < */

  sprintf(NumBuf,"%8.2f ",X1); /* double -> Ascii */
  strcat(LineBuf,NumBuf);      /* Ascii # into LineBuf */
  sprintf(NumBuf,"%8.2f ",Y1); /* double -> Ascii */
  strcat(LineBuf,NumBuf);      /* Ascii # into LineBuf */
  sprintf(NumBuf,"%8.2f ",Z1); /* double -> Ascii */
  strcat(LineBuf,NumBuf);      /* Ascii # into LineBuf */
  strcat(LineBuf,Str14);       /* TRIANGLE < X Y Z > */

  strcat(LineBuf,Str13);       /* < */
  sprintf(NumBuf,"%8.2f ",X2); /* double -> Ascii */
  strcat(LineBuf,NumBuf);      /* Ascii # into LineBuf */
  sprintf(NumBuf,"%8.2f ",Y2); /* double -> Ascii */
  strcat(LineBuf,NumBuf);      /* Ascii # into LineBuf */
  sprintf(NumBuf,"%8.2f ",Z2); /* double -> Ascii */
  strcat(LineBuf,NumBuf);      /* Ascii # into LineBuf */
  strcat(LineBuf,Str14);       /* < X Y Z > */

  strcat(LineBuf,Str13);       /* < */
  sprintf(NumBuf,"%8.2f ",X3); /* double -> Ascii */
  strcat(LineBuf,NumBuf);      /* Ascii # into LineBuf */
  sprintf(NumBuf,"%8.2f ",Y3); /* double -> Ascii */
  strcat(LineBuf,NumBuf);      /* Ascii # into LineBuf */
  sprintf(NumBuf,"%8.2f ",Z3); /* double -> Ascii */
  strcat(LineBuf,NumBuf);      /* Ascii # into LineBuf */
  strcat(LineBuf,Str14);       /* < X Y Z > */
  strcat(LineBuf,Str7);        /* END_TRIANGLE ret */

  NumOfTriangles++;            /* bump the count */

  CurX = wherex();             /* write the current count */
  CurY = wherey();
  printf("%u",NumOfTriangles);
  gotoxy(CurX,CurY);

  WriteToFile(Handle,LineBuf); /* write the triangle definition to file */
}
```

```
/* The following is the mountain building program */

void main( void )  {

    FILE    *OutFile;
    double Gradient;
    double X1, Y1, Z1, X2, Y2, Z2, X3, Y3, Z3, X4, Y4, Z4;
    unsigned Zone, ColorIndex, OldColorIndex, ColorOffset;
    unsigned X, Z, TriangleWritten;

    clrscr();
    printf("Fractal Mountain Generation Program for DKBTrace -- Ver: %d.%d\n",
            Ver,Rev);
    printf("From the book \"Practical Ray Tracing in C\"\n");
    printf("Written by: Craig A. Lindley\n\n");

    /* These are the operator entered parameters. */
    PeakHeight = 14440;            /* mountain is Pike's Peak */
    Texture = 0.15;               /* texture of surface */

    /* Calculate variables */
    SnowLine = PeakHeight * SNOWFACTOR;
    TreeLine = PeakHeight * TREEFACTOR;
    TotalMWidth = PeakHeight * MWIDTHRATIO;
    TotalMDepth = PeakHeight * MDEPTHRATIO;
    GradientThreshold = THRESHOLD;

    /* Give the user some information about the mountain being created */
    printf("Program Parameters:\n");
    printf("\tOutput filename: %s\n",FileName);
    printf("\tPeakHeight = %d  SnowLine = %8.2f  TreeLine = %8.2f\n",
            PeakHeight, SnowLine, TreeLine);
    printf("\tMountain width = %8.2f  Mountain depth = %8.2f\n",
            TotalMWidth, TotalMDepth);
    printf("\tGradient Threshold = %8.2f\n",GradientThreshold);
    printf("\tTexture Value = %6.2f\n\n",Texture);
    printf("Writing Triangle:  ");

    /*
    Calculate and scale the fractal mountain data. The parameters to the
    MidPointFM2D function can be varied to give different characteristics
    to the terrain.
    */
    MidPointFM2D(Elevations,GRIDSIZE,-100.671,0.75,1,49311U);
    ConstrainElevation();
    ScaleElevation(PeakHeight);

    /*
    Now prepare to output the mountain as a series of
    DKBTrace triangle objects. Begin by opening the output
    file.
```

(continued)

Listing 8.5   *(continued)*

```
*/
if ((OutFile = fopen(FileName,"wt")) == NULL)
    exit(EOpeningFile);

NumOfTriangles = 0;                /* none written yet */
OldColorIndex = 0xFFFF;            /* bogus color index so 1st triangle */
                                   /* will be written */
WriteToFile(OutFile,Str0);         /* tag the mountain data */
WriteToFile(OutFile,Str1);         /* begin mountain definition */
BeginObjDef(OutFile);              /* beginning of 1st triangle definition */
TriangleWritten = FALSE;           /* new set of triangles */
/*
Traverse the Elevation data array converting the elevations into
triangles and writing them to the output file.
*/
for (Z=0; Z < ZDIM-1; Z++)
  for (X=0; X < XDIM-1; X++)    {

    /*
    Get the vertices for all points on the grid. These will
    be converted into two triangles each time through this
    loop. X and Z dimensions are converted to the scale of
    the mountain. Elevation has already been converted.
    */
    X1 = ((double) X / (double) XDIM      * TotalMWidth;
    Z1 = ((double) Z / (double) ZDIM      * TotalMDepth;
    Y1 = Elevations[X][Z];

    X2 = ((double) (X+1) / (double) XDIM) * TotalMWidth;
    Z2 = ((double) Z / (double) ZDIM      * TotalMDepth;
    Y2 = Elevations[X+1][Z];

    X3 = ((double) X / (double) XDIM      * TotalMWidth;
    Z3 = ((double) (Z+1) / (double) ZDIM) * TotalMDepth;
    Y3 = Elevations[X][Z+1];

    X4 = ((double) (X+1) / (double) XDIM) * TotalMWidth;
    Z4 = ((double) (Z+1) / (double) ZDIM) * TotalMDepth;
    Y4 = Elevations[X+1][Z+1];

    /* Triangle Number 1 */
    Gradient = CalcGradient(X,Z,X+1,Z,X,Z+1);
    ColorOffset = (Gradient > GradientThreshold) ? 1:0;
    Zone = CalcZone(X,Z,X+1,Z,X,Z+1);
    ColorIndex = CalcColor(Zone,ColorOffset);

    /* If triangle has no elevation, no need to write it out */
    if ((Y1!=0.0) || (Y2!=0.0) || (Y3!=0.0)) {
```

```
            if ((ColorIndex != OldColorIndex) && TriangleWritten)    {
              EndObjDef(OutFile,OldColorIndex);
              BeginObjDef(OutFile);
            }
            WriteTriangle(OutFile,X1,Y1,Z1,X2,Y2,Z2,X3,Y3,Z3);
            TriangleWritten = TRUE;
            OldColorIndex = ColorIndex;
          } else  {
            /*
            If this triangle was not written, previous definition
            must be finished.
            */
            if (TriangleWritten)  {
              EndObjDef(OutFile,OldColorIndex);
              BeginObjDef(OutFile);
              TriangleWritten = FALSE;
            }
          }

          /* Triangle Number 2 */
          Gradient = CalcGradient(X+1,Z,X+1,Z+1,X,Z+1);
          ColorOffset = (Gradient > GradientThreshold) ? 1:0;
          Zone = CalcZone(X+1,Z,X+1,Z+1,X,Z+1);
          ColorIndex = CalcColor(Zone,ColorOffset);

          if ((Y2!=0.0) || (Y3!=0.0) || (Y4!=0.0)) {
            if ((ColorIndex != OldColorIndex) && TriangleWritten)    {
              EndObjDef(OutFile,OldColorIndex);
              BeginObjDef(OutFile);
              OldColorIndex = ColorIndex;
            }
            WriteTriangle(OutFile,X2,Y2,Z2,X4,Y4,Z4,X3,Y3,Z3);
            TriangleWritten = TRUE;
            OldColorIndex = ColorIndex;
          } else  {
            if (TriangleWritten)  {
              EndObjDef(OutFile,OldColorIndex);
              BeginObjDef(OutFile);
              TriangleWritten = FALSE;
            }
          }
        }
      }
  /*
  Finish up last defined triangle and end mountain definitions. Close
  the output file as the last step.
  */
  EndObjDef(OutFile,OldColorIndex);
  EndMountainDef(OutFile);
  fclose(OutFile);
}
```

"Colors" is an array that is used during color assignment for the land. The first two entries control the colors assigned to the land that is less than tree line in elevation. The first of these two colors is the color assigned to the land of mild grade. The second is the color assigned to the land considered steep. For example, FORESTCOLOR will be assigned to all land from sea level to tree line in elevation except the land that is considered steep, which will be assigned ROCKCOLOR under the assumption that vegetation does not grow on steep rock surfaces. The second two entries in this array control the color assignments for the land between tree line and snow line using the same reasoning. The final two entries are for the land above snow line. In this case, SNOWCOLOR is assigned regardless of the slope or steepness of the land.

Following the definition of the Colors array, numerous strings of ASCII scene description statements are defined. These will be written to the output file as the fractal data is converted into DKBTrace language statements.

The first C functions within this program—"InitGauss," "Gauss," "Ave3," "Ave4," and "MidPointFM2D"—are involved in the generation of the fractal data. The parameters passed to the MidPointFM2D function control the characteristics of the data produced. An explanation of how these functions generate the fractal data is beyond the scope of this discussion and is best left to the original authors. We will just use these functions to generate our data assuming they work the way they are supposed to.

The function "ConstrainElevation" makes a pass through the Elevations array after it has been filled with the fractal data and sets all negative entries to zero. All zero entries will correspond to sea level when the elevation data is rendered. This function also sets all of the elevation data located at the periphery of the array to zero value so that the land appears to start at sea level instead of magically appearing in space. The "ScaleElevation" function, which is called next in sequence by main, scales the fractal data in the Elevations array to the height specified by PeakHeight. This results in the highest point in the terrain data being set to an elevation of 14,440 feet, and all other elevations scaled accordingly.

The "CalcGradient" function accepts the Elevations array coordinates of three points, which define a triangular area in the land data, and calculates the maximum slope over that triangle. The value returned by this function represents the maximum difference in elevation among the three points that make up the vertices of the triangle. This value is used to determine if the land represented by this triangle is considered steep. "CalcZone" also accepts the coordinates of a triangular area, calculates the peak elevation of any part of the triangle, and assigns a climatic zone number to the maximum elevation. A zone assignment of zero represents an elevation of less than tree line. A zone of one represents land between tree line and snow line. A zone of two indicates a maximum elevation that extends above snow line. These zones roughly correspond to the temperate, alpine, and arctic zones. The calculated zone number is returned by this function. A related function "CalcColor" accepts a zone number and another number that indicates whether the triangle is to be considered steep and returns an Index into the Colors array that defines what color the triangular land mass area should be assigned in the ray-traced image.

The next few functions are used to write ASCII strings of characters to the output file.

These strings represent DKBTrace keywords and statements. The parameters needed to accompany these keywords are filled in on the fly by this program. The "WriteToFile" function writes the character string passed to it to the output file. This is the lowest-level output function, and it is called by all of the other higher-level string output functions described next. The "WriteVector" function forms a DKBTrace vector from the X, Y, and Z floating-point numbers passed to it and writes the properly formed vector to the output file.

All triangles written to the output file that have the same assigned color are concatenated with a CSG UNION into an OBJECT definition. The "BeginObjDef" function writes the strings associated with these DKBTrace keywords to the output file. This function is called every time a new triangular object is defined. That happens every time a run of triangles of the same color is followed by a new triangle of a different color. The old triangle definition must be completed by a call to "EndObjDef," and a new definition is begun by calling "BeginObjDef." When "EndObjDef" is executed, it terminates the UNION definition by writing an END_UNION keyword to the output file. It then opens a TEXTURE block where the texture value specified by the user is written, followed by the color to be assigned to this UNION OBJECT. The color value is fetched from the "Colors" array as mentioned, using the color index value calculated by the "CalcColor" function. The rather involved function "EndMountainDef" is called once during program execution after all triangle data has been processed to terminate the definition of the Mountain COMPOSITE object. It establishes a bounding volume around the mountain data, declares an instance of the Mountain, and translates it so it is centered on the Y axis.

The next string output function, "WriteTriangle," writes a correctly formatted DKBTrace triangle definition to the output file. The values to be assigned to the triangle vertices are passed into this function. After the triangle is written to the output file, the count of total triangles created is updated and displayed to the user.

The main function is where the operation of the "mount.c" program is coordinated. Upon execution, a message is displayed to the user along with the values of the parameters the program will be using to generate the land mass data. Shortly thereafter, the "MidPointFM2D" function is called to generate the fractal data and place it into the Elevations array. The functions of the parameters passed to "MidPointFM2D" are described in the original text. Suffice it to say that as these parameters are varied, the characteristics of the generated terrain data also change. You can experiment with these values to get different looking land masses.

After the data is generated, it is constrained and scaled as previously discussed. After some overhead operations are performed, the Elevations array is traversed, converting the data into triangles and writing the triangles to the output file. The operation of the code should be apparent from the listing and the previous discussions. After all of the Elevations data is processed, the output file is closed and the "mount.c" program terminates.

You will have to place the file produced by this program's execution—"mount.inc"—in the same directory where the ray tracing is to be performed, or else you will have to modify the image model to include a complete path to where this file can be found. When the image model is ray traced, the result will be as shown in the "Gallery of Images" (see Image 17).

Conclusions

We chose the tutorial exercises within this chapter to illustrate a wide range of concepts. We attempted to make the images used in this chapter interesting to look at in addition to being informative. You should now have a firm grasp of the capabilities provided with Constructive Solid Geometry, the uses of noise and colormaps within ray-traced imagery, how bit-mapped images can be imported into image models and mapped to surfaces of all orientations, and finally, how computer programs can be written that algorithmically create image models. With the techniques presented in this chapter you should be ready to strike out on your own and create some unique images of your own design. Experiment as much and as often as possible. Some of your mistakes may prove to be very interesting. You can start small if desired, by modifying portions of the image models supplied and seeing the results. Or you can be bold and start from scratch and see what happens. The image models discussed in the next and final chapter of this book illustrate some of the experimentation performed by the author.

Image Model Discussions

Don't be afraid to take a big step if one is indicated.
You can't cross a chasm in two small jumps.
—David Lloyd George

In this chapter you will learn about:

- **How the various ray-tracing techniques presented in the previous chapters can be integrated together into more complex image models**
- **A few new techniques and ideas**
- **The use of multiple IMAGEMAP textures within a single image**
- **The wide range of imaging possibilities available with the tools and techniques presented in this book**

Introduction

In this chapter, you will learn more about DKBTrace and about ray tracing in general by examining complete and relatively complex image models. We will not provide a lot of explanation because the concepts used in these image models have all been seen and discussed before. In fact, we have used almost all of the techniques in the previous tutorial exercises. Where new techniques are employed, they will be discussed. We hope that by reviewing the image model code along with the resulting ray-traced image, ray-tracing techniques will become more firmly cemented in your mind. It is also possible that the imagery itself will give you ideas for images of your own.

The first image model that we show is a "pseudo" scale model of a heavy-duty truck brake. We have included this image model here because it illustrates an industrial application of ray tracing: the use of ray tracing for the rendering of mechanical parts. The second image model, called the "maze," illustrates how you can use mirrored planes to increase perceived image complexity with very little increase in effort. The third image model shows how multiple bit-mapped images can be used as IMAGEMAP textures within a single image. Finally, we have provided the "desert" scene to widen out the scope of the images this book—from the mere mechanical to a more organic image.

Image Model One—The Brake

As mentioned, we have included this image model to show an industrial application of ray-tracing techniques. In this image, a heavy-duty truck disc brake assembly is modeled, complete with axle, wheel bearings, and grease cups. All component parts of this image are modeled to scale, in relation to each other. A rendering of this type would be used by mechanical designers to "see" what their new brake assembly design looked like before going to the time and expense of building the actual item. Correcting mistakes that may be visually apparent in a design at the early stages of development is much less expensive than doing so later in the manufacturing process after the tooling (to be used to create the brake assemblies) has been built.

This image model, shown in Listing 9.1 and included on the companion disks in the file "brake1.dat," is another study in the use of constructive solid geometry. CSG is used to create all of the component parts that make up the disc brake assembly. As you can see from the listing, extensive use is made of bounding volumes to help with the rendering performance. There are no new techniques in this image model.

Listing 9.1   Image Model One—The Brake

The following is the contents of the file "brake1.dat."

```
{
  Ray Traced Imaging - Image Model One
  "The Brake"
  from the book "Practical Ray Tracing in C" by Craig A. Lindley
  Last update to this image: 03/06/92

  This image model produces a rendering of a truck brake. This shows
  how ray tracing is used in industrial applications. See the "Gallery
  of Images" for a look at what this image file produces.
}

INCLUDE "colors.dat"              { standard includes for color }
INCLUDE "shapes.dat"              { for shapes and }
INCLUDE "textures.dat"            { for textures }

VIEW_POINT
  LOCATION < 0 6.0 -15 >
  DIRECTION < 0 0 1 >
```

```
  UP  < 0 1 0 >
  RIGHT < 1.333 0 0 >
  SKY < 0.2 0.8 0 >
  LOOK_AT < 0   0   0 >
END_VIEW_POINT

OBJECT
  SPHERE  < 0 0 0 > 2 END_SPHERE
  TRANSLATE  < 40 20 -25 >
  TEXTURE
    COLOR White
    AMBIENT 1.0
    DIFFUSE 0.0
  END_TEXTURE
  COLOR White
  LIGHT_SOURCE
END_OBJECT

{ Add a background plane for contrast }
OBJECT
  PLANE < 0 0 -1 > -300 END_PLANE
  TEXTURE
    COLOR BlueViolet
    AMBIENT 1.0
     DIFFUSE 0.0
  END_TEXTURE
END_OBJECT

{Define the axle }
DECLARE Axle = OBJECT
  QUADRIC Cylinder_Y
    SCALE < 0.725 0.725 0.725 >
  END_QUADRIC
  TEXTURE
    Polished_Metal
    COLOR Silver
  END_TEXTURE
END_OBJECT

{ Define the misc. parts of the brake assembly }
DECLARE Cap = OBJECT
  INTERSECTION
    QUADRIC Cylinder_Y
      SCALE < 1.5 1.5 1.5 >
    END_QUADRIC
    QUADRIC Cylinder_Y
      INVERSE
    END_QUADRIC
    PLANE < 0 -1  0 > 0.2 END_PLANE
    PLANE < 0  1  0 > 0.2 END_PLANE
  END_INTERSECTION
```

(continued)

Listing 9.1   *(continued)*

```
  TEXTURE
    Dull
    COLOR Black
  END_TEXTURE
END_OBJECT

DECLARE Ring = OBJECT
  INTERSECTION
    QUADRIC Cylinder_Y
      SCALE < 1.2 1.2 1.2 >
    END_QUADRIC
    QUADRIC Cylinder_Y
      INVERSE
    END_QUADRIC
    PLANE < 0 -1  0 > 0.1 END_PLANE
    PLANE < 0  1  0 > 0.1 END_PLANE
  END_INTERSECTION
  TEXTURE
    Dull
    COLOR Black
  END_TEXTURE
END_OBJECT

{ Define the parts of the bearing }
DECLARE Roller = OBJECT
  INTERSECTION
    QUADRIC Cylinder_Y
      SCALE < 0.20 0.20 0.20 >
    END_QUADRIC
    PLANE <0 -1  0 > 0.2 END_PLANE
    PLANE <0  1  0 > 0.2 END_PLANE
  END_INTERSECTION
  TEXTURE
    Polished_Metal
    COLOR Silver
  END_TEXTURE
END_OBJECT

DECLARE BearingHousing = OBJECT
  INTERSECTION
    QUADRIC Cylinder_Y END_QUADRIC
    QUADRIC Cylinder_Y
      SCALE < 0.85 0.85 0.85 >
      INVERSE
    END_QUADRIC
    PLANE < 0 -1  0 > 0.375 END_PLANE
    PLANE < 0  1  0 > 0.375 END_PLANE
  END_INTERSECTION
  TEXTURE
    Iron
```

```
    END_TEXTURE
END_OBJECT

DECLARE Bearing = COMPOSITE
  OBJECT BearingHousing END_OBJECT
  OBJECT Roller TRANSLATE < 0 0 0.925 > END_OBJECT
  OBJECT Roller TRANSLATE < 0 0 0.925 > ROTATE < 0  45 0 > END_OBJECT
  OBJECT Roller TRANSLATE < 0 0 0.925 > ROTATE < 0  90 0 > END_OBJECT
  OBJECT Roller TRANSLATE < 0 0 0.925 > ROTATE < 0 135 0 > END_OBJECT
  OBJECT Roller TRANSLATE < 0 0 0.925 > ROTATE < 0 180 0 > END_OBJECT
  OBJECT Roller TRANSLATE < 0 0 0.925 > ROTATE < 0 225 0 > END_OBJECT
  OBJECT Roller TRANSLATE < 0 0 0.925 > ROTATE < 0 270 0 > END_OBJECT
  OBJECT Roller TRANSLATE < 0 0 0.925 > ROTATE < 0 315 0 > END_OBJECT
END_COMPOSITE


{ Define the parts of the disc brake }
DECLARE MainPlate = OBJECT
  INTERSECTION
    QUADRIC Cylinder_Y
      SCALE < 6 6 6 >
    END_QUADRIC
    PLANE < 0 -1  0 > 0.125 END_PLANE
    PLANE < 0  1  0 > 0.125 END_PLANE
  END_INTERSECTION
  TEXTURE
    Metal
    COLOR Silver
    AMBIENT 0.2
    DIFFUSE 0.8
  END_TEXTURE
END_OBJECT

DECLARE Spacer = OBJECT
  INTERSECTION
    QUADRIC Cylinder_Y
      SCALE < 0.10 0.10 0.10 >
    END_QUADRIC
    PLANE <0 -1  0 > 0.626 END_PLANE
    PLANE <0  1  0 > 0.626 END_PLANE
  END_INTERSECTION
  TEXTURE
    Polished_Metal
    COLOR Silver
  END_TEXTURE
END_OBJECT


DECLARE MainBrake = COMPOSITE
  OBJECT MainPlate TRANSLATE < 0  0.5 0 > END_OBJECT
  OBJECT MainPlate TRANSLATE < 0 -0.5 0 > END_OBJECT
```

(continued)

Listing 9.1   *(continued)*

```
OBJECT Spacer
  TRANSLATE < 0   0 -5.75 >
END_OBJECT
OBJECT Spacer
  TRANSLATE < 0   0 -5.75 >
  ROTATE < 0   10   0 >
END_OBJECT
OBJECT Spacer
  TRANSLATE < 0   0 -5.75 >
  ROTATE < 0   20   0 >
END_OBJECT
OBJECT Spacer
  TRANSLATE < 0   0 -5.75 >
  ROTATE < 0   30   0 >
END_OBJECT
OBJECT Spacer
  TRANSLATE < 0   0 -5.75 >
  ROTATE < 0   40   0 >
END_OBJECT
OBJECT Spacer
  TRANSLATE < 0   0 -5.75 >
  ROTATE < 0   50   0 >
END_OBJECT
OBJECT Spacer
  TRANSLATE < 0   0 -5.75 >
  ROTATE < 0   60   0 >
END_OBJECT
OBJECT Spacer
  TRANSLATE < 0   0 -5.75 >
  ROTATE < 0   70   0 >
END_OBJECT
OBJECT Spacer
  TRANSLATE < 0   0 -5.75 >
  ROTATE < 0   80   0 >
END_OBJECT
OBJECT Spacer
  TRANSLATE < 0   0 -5.75 >
  ROTATE < 0   90   0 >
END_OBJECT
OBJECT Spacer
  TRANSLATE < 0   0 -5.75 >
  ROTATE < 0   100   0 >
END_OBJECT
OBJECT Spacer
  TRANSLATE < 0   0 -5.75 >
  ROTATE < 0   110   0 >
END_OBJECT
OBJECT Spacer
  TRANSLATE < 0   0 -5.75 >
  ROTATE < 0   120   0 >
END_OBJECT
```

```
OBJECT Spacer
  TRANSLATE < 0   0 -5.75 >
  ROTATE < 0   130   0 >
END_OBJECT
OBJECT Spacer
  TRANSLATE < 0   0 -5.75 >
  ROTATE < 0   140   0 >
END_OBJECT
OBJECT Spacer
  TRANSLATE < 0   0 -5.75 >
  ROTATE < 0   150   0 >
END_OBJECT
OBJECT Spacer
  TRANSLATE < 0   0 -5.75 >
  ROTATE < 0   160   0 >
END_OBJECT
OBJECT Spacer
  TRANSLATE < 0   0 -5.75 >
  ROTATE < 0   170   0 >
END_OBJECT
OBJECT Spacer
  TRANSLATE < 0   0 -5.75 >
  ROTATE < 0 -10   0 >
END_OBJECT
OBJECT Spacer
  TRANSLATE < 0   0 -5.75 >
  ROTATE < 0 -20   0 >
END_OBJECT
OBJECT Spacer
  TRANSLATE < 0   0 -5.75 >
  ROTATE < 0 -30   0 >
END_OBJECT
OBJECT Spacer
  TRANSLATE < 0   0 -5.75 >
  ROTATE < 0 -40   0 >
END_OBJECT
OBJECT Spacer
  TRANSLATE < 0   0 -5.75 >
  ROTATE < 0 -50   0 >
END_OBJECT
OBJECT Spacer
  TRANSLATE < 0   0 -5.75 >
  ROTATE < 0 -60   0 >
END_OBJECT
OBJECT Spacer
  TRANSLATE < 0   0 -5.75 >
  ROTATE < 0 -70   0 >
END_OBJECT
OBJECT Spacer
  TRANSLATE < 0   0 -5.75 >
  ROTATE < 0 -80   0 >
```

(continued)

Listing 9.1 *(continued)*

```
END_OBJECT
OBJECT Spacer
  TRANSLATE < 0   0 -5.75 >
  ROTATE < 0 -90   0 >
END_OBJECT
OBJECT Spacer
  TRANSLATE < 0   0 -5.75 >
  ROTATE < 0 -100   0 >
END_OBJECT
OBJECT Spacer
  TRANSLATE < 0   0 -5.75 >
  ROTATE < 0 -110   0 >
END_OBJECT
OBJECT Spacer
  TRANSLATE < 0   0 -5.75 >
  ROTATE < 0 -120   0 >
END_OBJECT
OBJECT Spacer
  TRANSLATE < 0   0 -5.75 >
  ROTATE < 0 -130   0 >
END_OBJECT
OBJECT Spacer
  TRANSLATE < 0   0 -5.75 >
  ROTATE < 0 -140   0 >
END_OBJECT
OBJECT Spacer
  TRANSLATE < 0   0 -5.75 >
  ROTATE < 0 -150   0 >
END_OBJECT
OBJECT Spacer
  TRANSLATE < 0   0 -5.75 >
  ROTATE < 0 -160   0 >
END_OBJECT
OBJECT Spacer
  TRANSLATE < 0   0 -5.75 >
  ROTATE < 0 -170   0 >
END_OBJECT
OBJECT Spacer
  TRANSLATE < 0   0 -5.75 >
  ROTATE < 0 -180   0 >
END_OBJECT
BOUNDED_BY
  INTERSECTION
    QUADRIC Cylinder_Y
      SCALE < 6.1 6.1 6.1 >
    END_QUADRIC
    PLANE < 0  -1   0 > 0.75 END_PLANE
    PLANE < 0   1   0 > 0.75 END_PLANE
  END_INTERSECTION
```

```
      END_BOUND
END_COMPOSITE

DECLARE Hub = OBJECT
  INTERSECTION
    QUADRIC Cone_Y
      SCALE < 1.0 2.0 1.0 >
      TRANSLATE < 0   6.0 0 >
    END_QUADRIC
    PLANE < 0 -1  0 > 0.0 END_PLANE
    PLANE < 0  1  0 > 1.5 END_PLANE
  END_INTERSECTION
  TEXTURE
    Metal
    COLOR Silver
    AMBIENT 0.2
    DIFFUSE 0.8
  END_TEXTURE
END_OBJECT

DECLARE AxleHousing = OBJECT
  DIFFERENCE
    INTERSECTION
      QUADRIC Cylinder_Y
        SCALE < 1.5 1.5 1.5 >
      END_QUADRIC
      QUADRIC Cylinder_Y
        SCALE < 1.0 1.0 1.0 >
        INVERSE
      END_QUADRIC
      PLANE < 0 -1  0 > 0.0 END_PLANE
      PLANE < 0  1  0 > 2.0 END_PLANE
    END_INTERSECTION
    INTERSECTION
      PLANE <-1  0  0 > 1.0 END_PLANE
      PLANE < 1  0  0 > 1.0 END_PLANE
      PLANE < 0 -1  0 > 0.1 END_PLANE
      PLANE < 0  1  0 > 0.7 END_PLANE
      PLANE < 0  0 -1 > 1.6 END_PLANE
      PLANE < 0  0  1 > 1.6 END_PLANE
    END_INTERSECTION
    ROTATE < 0 45 0 >
  END_DIFFERENCE
  BOUNDED_BY
    INTERSECTION
      QUADRIC Cylinder_Y
        SCALE < 1.5 1.5 1.5 >
      END_QUADRIC
      PLANE < 0 -1  0 > 0.0 END_PLANE
      PLANE < 0  1  0 > 2.0 END_PLANE
    END_INTERSECTION
  END_BOUND
```

(continued)

Listing 9.1   *(continued)*

```
  TEXTURE
    Metal
    COLOR Silver
    AMBIENT 0.2
    DIFFUSE 0.8
  END_TEXTURE
END_OBJECT


DECLARE BrakeAssembly = COMPOSITE
  COMPOSITE Bearing TRANSLATE < 0 4.75 0 > END_COMPOSITE
  OBJECT Ring        TRANSLATE < 0 5.75 0 > END_OBJECT
  OBJECT Cap         TRANSLATE < 0 6.75 0 > END_OBJECT
  COMPOSITE Bearing TRANSLATE < 0 -7.75 0 > END_COMPOSITE
  OBJECT Cap         TRANSLATE < 0 -9.75 0 > END_OBJECT
  OBJECT Axle        END_OBJECT
  COMPOSITE MainBrake END_COMPOSITE
  OBJECT Hub TRANSLATE < 0 0.625 0 > END_OBJECT
  OBJECT Hub ROTATE < 0  0  180 > TRANSLATE < 0 -0.625 0 > END_OBJECT
  OBJECT AxleHousing TRANSLATE < 0 2.125 0 > END_OBJECT
  OBJECT AxleHousing ROTATE < 0  0  180 > TRANSLATE < 0 -2.125 0 > END_OBJECT
END_COMPOSITE

COMPOSITE BrakeAssembly ROTATE < -10 0 0 > END_COMPOSITE
```

Image Model Two—The Maze

This image model simulates a nearly infinite matrix of connected geometric objects. The image resembles something that might possibly be seen in a refinery, although it was not created for that reason. This image model uses four mirrored planes to create an almost infinite depth effect. The planes are placed such that the viewer is looking through the maze structure at the mirrors regardless of the direction he or she is looking. The viewer then sees the structure itself and its reflection in the mirrors. For a completely infinite effect, an additional mirror could be placed behind the viewer's position and the image could be rendered again. This experiment, however, is left for you. *Note*: This image takes a very long time to render in high resolution. If you attempt it, make sure you do not have other needs for your computer; it will be tied up for quite a while.

The majority of the image model is taken up with the definition of a three-dimensional motif called a "Deck." A Deck is one instance of a brass colored MidSphere, a green Left-Beam, an orange RightBeam, a red FrontBeam, a blue RearBeam, four midnight-blue Cubes, a green vertical beam called a VertBeam, and two green diagonal CrossBeams. Most of the surfaces within this image model are given a shiny but nonreflective texture. The MidSphere, however, is shiny and highly reflective, as you can see in the picture.

The Deck motif is instantiated a total of 48 times within the image model. Each of these instances of a Deck is translated such that they all seem to interconnect. That is, they seem to form one continuous structure. The total matrix of Deck objects is arranged in three rows of four instances, each four levels deep. The reflective property of the mirrors multiplies the depth effect many times. You may want to remove the mirrored planes from the image model and render it again to see what effect the mirrors provide.

The maze image model is shown in Listing 9.2 and is available on the companion disks in the Chapter 9 file under the name "maze6.dat." Have fun experimenting with this image and its derivatives.

Listing 9.2 Image Model Two—The Maze

The following is the contents of the file "maze6.dat."

```
{
  Ray-Traced Imaging - Image Model Two
  "The Maze"
  from the book "Practical Ray Tracing in C" by Craig A. Lindley
  Last update to this image: 03/13/92

  This image model produces a complex maze of three-dimensional
  pipes, boxes, and spheres. It illustrates how cleverly placed
  mirrors within a scene can increase perceived image complexity
  without actually increasing it. See the "Gallery of Images" for
  a look at what this image file produces.
}

INCLUDE "colors.dat"
INCLUDE "shapes.dat"
INCLUDE "textures.dat"

VIEW_POINT
  LOCATION < 100 -40 -35>
  DIRECTION < 0  -0.05  1 >
  UP  < 0  1  0 >
  RIGHT < 1.0  0  0 >
  ROTATE < 0  22  0 >
END_VIEW_POINT

{ Define a light source }
OBJECT
  SPHERE  <0.0  0.0  0.0> 2.0 END_SPHERE
  TRANSLATE   <0 -25  -100>
  TEXTURE
    COLOR White
```

(continued)

Listing 9.2 *(continued)*

```
      AMBIENT 1.0
      DIFFUSE 0.0
   END_TEXTURE
   COLOR White
   LIGHT_SOURCE
END_OBJECT

DECLARE LeftBeam = OBJECT
   INTERSECTION
      QUADRIC Cylinder_Z
         SCALE <2.5 2.5 110>
      END_QUADRIC
      PLANE <0 0 -1>   0 END_PLANE
      PLANE <0 0  1> 110 END_PLANE
   END_INTERSECTION
   TEXTURE Shiny COLOR Green END_TEXTURE
   TRANSLATE <-25 0 -55>
END_OBJECT

DECLARE RightBeam = OBJECT
   INTERSECTION
      QUADRIC Cylinder_Z
         SCALE <2.5 2.5 110>
      END_QUADRIC
      PLANE <0 0 -1>   0 END_PLANE
      PLANE <0 0  1> 110 END_PLANE
   END_INTERSECTION
   TEXTURE Shiny COLOR Orange END_TEXTURE
   TRANSLATE <25 0 -55>
END_OBJECT

DECLARE FrontBeam = OBJECT
   INTERSECTION
      QUADRIC Cylinder_X
         SCALE <100 2.5 2.5>
      END_QUADRIC
      PLANE <-1 0 0>   0 END_PLANE
      PLANE < 1 0 0> 100 END_PLANE
   END_INTERSECTION
   TEXTURE Shiny COLOR Red END_TEXTURE
   TRANSLATE <-50 0 -27.5>
END_OBJECT

DECLARE RearBeam = OBJECT
   INTERSECTION
      QUADRIC Cylinder_X
         SCALE <100 2.5 2.5>
      END_QUADRIC
      PLANE <-1 0 0>   0 END_PLANE
      PLANE < 1 0 0> 100 END_PLANE
   END_INTERSECTION
```

```
   TEXTURE Shiny COLOR Blue END_TEXTURE
   TRANSLATE <-50 0 27.5>
END_OBJECT

DECLARE CrossBeam = OBJECT
  INTERSECTION
    QUADRIC Cylinder_Z
      SCALE <1 1 150>
    END_QUADRIC
    PLANE <0 0 -1>  0    END_PLANE
    PLANE <0 0  1> 77.77 END_PLANE
  END_INTERSECTION
  TRANSLATE <0 0 -38.9>
  TEXTURE 0.5 Shiny COLOR Green END_TEXTURE
END_OBJECT

DECLARE VertBeam = OBJECT
  INTERSECTION
    QUADRIC Cylinder_Y
      SCALE <2.5 100 2.5>
    END_QUADRIC
    PLANE <0  1 0>  55 END_PLANE
    PLANE <0 -1 0>   0 END_PLANE
  END_INTERSECTION
  TRANSLATE <0 -27.5 0>
  TEXTURE Shiny COLOR Green END_TEXTURE
END_OBJECT

DECLARE Cube = OBJECT
   INTERSECTION
      PLANE <0.0 0.0 1.0>  7.5 END_PLANE
      PLANE <0.0 0.0 1.0> -7.5 INVERSE END_PLANE
      PLANE <1.0 0.0 0.0>  5 END_PLANE
      PLANE <1.0 0.0 0.0> -5 INVERSE END_PLANE
      PLANE <0.0 1.0 0.0>  5 END_PLANE
      PLANE <0.0 1.0 0.0> -5 INVERSE END_PLANE
   END_INTERSECTION
   TEXTURE Dull COLOR MidnightBlue END_TEXTURE
END_OBJECT

DECLARE MidSphere = OBJECT
   SPHERE < 0 0 0 > 10 END_SPHERE
   TEXTURE Brass END_TEXTURE
END_OBJECT

DECLARE Deck = COMPOSITE
  OBJECT MidSphere END_OBJECT
  OBJECT LeftBeam  END_OBJECT
  OBJECT RightBeam END_OBJECT
  OBJECT FrontBeam END_OBJECT
  OBJECT RearBeam  END_OBJECT
```

(continued)

Listing 9.2   *(continued)*

```
   OBJECT Cube TRANSLATE <-25 0  27.5> END_OBJECT
   OBJECT Cube TRANSLATE < 25 0  27.5> END_OBJECT
   OBJECT Cube TRANSLATE <-25 0 -27.5> END_OBJECT
   OBJECT Cube TRANSLATE < 25 0 -27.5> END_OBJECT
   OBJECT VertBeam END_OBJECT
   OBJECT CrossBeam ROTATE <0  45 0> END_OBJECT
   OBJECT CrossBeam ROTATE <0 -45 0> END_OBJECT
   BOUNDED_BY
    INTERSECTION
       PLANE <0.0 0.0 1.0>  55   END_PLANE
       PLANE <0.0 0.0 1.0> -55   INVERSE END_PLANE
       PLANE <1.0 0.0 0.0>  50   END_PLANE
       PLANE <1.0 0.0 0.0> -50   INVERSE END_PLANE
       PLANE <0.0 1.0 0.0>  27.5 END_PLANE
       PLANE <0.0 1.0 0.0> -27.5 INVERSE END_PLANE
    END_INTERSECTION
   END_BOUND
END_COMPOSITE

COMPOSITE Deck                      END_COMPOSITE
COMPOSITE Deck TRANSLATE <100 0 0> END_COMPOSITE
COMPOSITE Deck TRANSLATE <200 0 0> END_COMPOSITE
COMPOSITE Deck TRANSLATE <300 0 0> END_COMPOSITE

COMPOSITE Deck TRANSLATE <  0 0 110> END_COMPOSITE
COMPOSITE Deck TRANSLATE <100 0 110> END_COMPOSITE
COMPOSITE Deck TRANSLATE <200 0 110> END_COMPOSITE
COMPOSITE Deck TRANSLATE <300 0 110> END_COMPOSITE

COMPOSITE Deck TRANSLATE <  0 0 220> END_COMPOSITE
COMPOSITE Deck TRANSLATE <100 0 220> END_COMPOSITE
COMPOSITE Deck TRANSLATE <200 0 220> END_COMPOSITE
COMPOSITE Deck TRANSLATE <300 0 220> END_COMPOSITE

COMPOSITE Deck TRANSLATE <  0 0 330> END_COMPOSITE
COMPOSITE Deck TRANSLATE <100 0 330> END_COMPOSITE
COMPOSITE Deck TRANSLATE <200 0 330> END_COMPOSITE
COMPOSITE Deck TRANSLATE <300 0 330> END_COMPOSITE

COMPOSITE Deck TRANSLATE <  0 -55 0> END_COMPOSITE
COMPOSITE Deck TRANSLATE <100 -55 0> END_COMPOSITE
COMPOSITE Deck TRANSLATE <200 -55 0> END_COMPOSITE
COMPOSITE Deck TRANSLATE <300 -55 0> END_COMPOSITE

COMPOSITE Deck TRANSLATE <  0 -55 110> END_COMPOSITE
COMPOSITE Deck TRANSLATE <100 -55 110> END_COMPOSITE
COMPOSITE Deck TRANSLATE <200 -55 110> END_COMPOSITE
COMPOSITE Deck TRANSLATE <300 -55 110> END_COMPOSITE
```

```
COMPOSITE Deck TRANSLATE <   0 -55 220> END_COMPOSITE
COMPOSITE Deck TRANSLATE <100 -55 220> END_COMPOSITE
COMPOSITE Deck TRANSLATE <200 -55 220> END_COMPOSITE
COMPOSITE Deck TRANSLATE <300 -55 220> END_COMPOSITE

COMPOSITE Deck TRANSLATE <   0 -55 330> END_COMPOSITE
COMPOSITE Deck TRANSLATE <100 -55 330> END_COMPOSITE
COMPOSITE Deck TRANSLATE <200 -55 330> END_COMPOSITE
COMPOSITE Deck TRANSLATE <300 -55 330> END_COMPOSITE

COMPOSITE Deck TRANSLATE <   0 -110 0> END_COMPOSITE
COMPOSITE Deck TRANSLATE <100 -110 0> END_COMPOSITE
COMPOSITE Deck TRANSLATE <200 -110 0> END_COMPOSITE
COMPOSITE Deck TRANSLATE <300 -110 0> END_COMPOSITE

COMPOSITE Deck TRANSLATE <   0 -110 110> END_COMPOSITE
COMPOSITE Deck TRANSLATE <100 -110 110> END_COMPOSITE
COMPOSITE Deck TRANSLATE <200 -110 110> END_COMPOSITE
COMPOSITE Deck TRANSLATE <300 -110 110> END_COMPOSITE

COMPOSITE Deck TRANSLATE <   0 -110 220> END_COMPOSITE
COMPOSITE Deck TRANSLATE <100 -110 220> END_COMPOSITE
COMPOSITE Deck TRANSLATE <200 -110 220> END_COMPOSITE
COMPOSITE Deck TRANSLATE <300 -110 220> END_COMPOSITE

COMPOSITE Deck TRANSLATE <   0 -110 330> END_COMPOSITE
COMPOSITE Deck TRANSLATE <100 -110 330> END_COMPOSITE
COMPOSITE Deck TRANSLATE <200 -110 330> END_COMPOSITE
COMPOSITE Deck TRANSLATE <300 -110 330> END_COMPOSITE

OBJECT PLANE <0 0 1> 385    END_PLANE TEXTURE Mirror END_TEXTURE END_OBJECT
OBJECT PLANE <1 0 0> 350    END_PLANE TEXTURE Mirror END_TEXTURE END_OBJECT
OBJECT PLANE <0 1 0> 27.5   END_PLANE TEXTURE Mirror END_TEXTURE END_OBJECT
OBJECT PLANE <0 1 0> -137.5 END_PLANE TEXTURE Mirror END_TEXTURE END_OBJECT
```

Image Model Three—Advanced Imagemaps

This image model produces a striking image of a glasslike sphere with a fractal mapped onto its surface floating in midair between a floor and two walls, which are also covered with different fractal patterns. The words that make up the title of this book are modeled with a simple block font and a black marble coloration texture and are placed conspicuously in the scene. This image model is an excellent example of how simple concepts such as lettering, IMAGEMAP textures, and simple shapes can be used in combination to produce images that appear very complex. This image model is contained in the file "rt4.dat" on the companion disks and is shown in Listing 9.3. The four fractals used within this image (as IMAGEMAP textures) are called "fract1.gif" through "fract4.gif"and are on the companion disks also. As with all images described in this book, you have everything you need to recreate this image (on your computer) on the companion disks.

Listing 9.3   Image Model Three—Advanced Imagemaps

The following is the contents of the file "rt4.dat."

```
{
  Ray-Traced Imaging - Image Model Three
  "Advanced Imagemaps"
  from the book "Practical Ray Tracing in C" by Craig A. Lindley
  Last update to this image: 03/14/92

  This image model shows how multiple imagemaps can be incorporated
  into a single image with dramatic effect. In total four fractal
  images in GIF format are imported. The fractal images were generated
  using the shareware FRACTINT program. Lettering is also used within
  this image. See the "Gallery of Images" for a look at what this
  image file produces.
}

INCLUDE "colors.dat"
INCLUDE "shapes.dat"
INCLUDE "textures.dat"

VIEW_POINT
  LOCATION < 0   3 -8 >
  DIRECTION < 0   0  1 >
  UP < 0   1   0 >
  RIGHT < 1.333   0   0 >
  LOOK_AT < 0   1   0 >
END_VIEW_POINT

OBJECT { a light source }
  SPHERE < 0   0   0 > 1 END_SPHERE
  TRANSLATE < 10 12 -20 >
  TEXTURE
    COLOR White
    AMBIENT 1.0
    DIFFUSE 0.0
  END_TEXTURE
  COLOR White
  LIGHT_SOURCE
END_OBJECT

DECLARE LeftWall = OBJECT
  PLANE < 0   0   -1 > 0 END_PLANE
  TEXTURE
    IMAGEMAP GIF "fract1.gif"
    SCALE < 40 40 40 >
    TRANSLATE < 0 -20 -20 >
    AMBIENT 1.0
    DIFFUSE 0.0
  END_TEXTURE
  ROTATE < 0 -45   0 >
  TRANSLATE <-50   0   0 >
```

```
END_OBJECT

DECLARE RightWall = OBJECT
  PLANE <-1  0  0 > 0 END_PLANE
  ROTATE < 0 -45  0 >
  TRANSLATE < 50  0  0 >
  TEXTURE
    IMAGEMAP GIF "fract2.gif"
    SCALE < 30 30 30 >
    TRANSLATE < 0 -15 -15 >
    AMBIENT 1.0
    DIFFUSE 0.0
  END_TEXTURE
END_OBJECT

DECLARE Floor = OBJECT
  PLANE < 0  1  0 > -10 END_PLANE
  TEXTURE
    AMBIENT 1.0
    DIFFUSE 0.0
    IMAGEMAP < 1  0  -1 > GIF "fract3.gif"
    SCALE < 15 15 15 >
    TRANSLATE <-7.5  -7.5  7.5 >
  END_TEXTURE
END_OBJECT

DECLARE TheSphere = OBJECT
  SPHERE < 0  1.5  0 > 2 END_SPHERE
  TEXTURE
    IMAGEMAP GIF "fract4.gif"
    SCALE < 3 3 3 >
    TRANSLATE <-1.5  -1.5  -1.5 >
    AMBIENT 0.3
    DIFFUSE 0.7
    BRILLIANCE 8.0
    REFLECTION 0.5
    PHONG 1.0
    PHONGSIZE 90
  END_TEXTURE
END_OBJECT

{ This defines the surface texture of the letters }
DECLARE LetterTexture =
  TEXTURE
   Black_Marble
   SCALE < 7 13 9 >
   AMBIENT 0.2
   DIFFUSE 0.8
   PHONG 0.25
  END_TEXTURE
```

(continued)

Listing 9.3 *(continued)*

```
{
Define the letters. Note: these letters have their origin
at the middle bottom front of the character. These characters
are on a 40x20 grid.
}

{ PSegment is used within the letters R and P }
DECLARE PSegment =
  INTERSECTION
    QUADRIC Cylinder_Z
      SCALE < 12.0 12.0 12.0 >
    END_QUADRIC
    QUADRIC Cylinder_Z
      SCALE < 7.0 7.0 12.0 >
      INVERSE
    END_QUADRIC
    PLANE < 0  -1   0 >    3 END_PLANE
    PLANE < 0   0  -1 >    0 END_PLANE
    PLANE < 0   0   1 >   10 END_PLANE
  END_INTERSECTION

DECLARE LetterP = OBJECT
  UNION
    INTERSECTION
      PLANE <-1   0   0 > 10 END_PLANE
      PLANE < 1   0   0 > -5 END_PLANE
      PLANE < 0  -1   0 >  0 END_PLANE
      PLANE < 0   1   0 > 40 END_PLANE
      PLANE < 0   0  -1 >  0 END_PLANE
      PLANE < 0   0   1 > 10 END_PLANE
    END_INTERSECTION
    INTERSECTION PSegment
      ROTATE < 0  0  -90 >
      TRANSLATE < -2  28   0 >
    END_INTERSECTION
  END_UNION
  BOUNDED_BY
    INTERSECTION
      PLANE <-1   0   0 > 10 END_PLANE
      PLANE < 1   0   0 > 10 END_PLANE
      PLANE < 0  -1   0 >  0 END_PLANE
      PLANE < 0   1   0 > 40 END_PLANE
      PLANE < 0   0  -1 >  0 END_PLANE
      PLANE < 0   0   1 > 10 END_PLANE
    END_INTERSECTION
  END_BOUND
  TEXTURE LetterTexture END_TEXTURE
END_OBJECT
```

```
DECLARE Letterr = OBJECT
  UNION
    INTERSECTION
      PLANE <-1    0    0 > 10 END_PLANE
      PLANE < 1    0    0 > -5 END_PLANE
      PLANE < 0   -1    0 >  0 END_PLANE
      PLANE < 0    1    0 > 20 END_PLANE
      PLANE < 0    0   -1 >  0 END_PLANE
      PLANE < 0    0    1 > 10 END_PLANE
    END_INTERSECTION
    INTERSECTION
      QUADRIC Cylinder_Z
        SCALE < 10 10 10 >
        TRANSLATE < 0 10 0 >
      END_QUADRIC
      QUADRIC Cylinder_Z
        SCALE < 5 5 10 >
        TRANSLATE < 0 10 0 >
        INVERSE
      END_QUADRIC
      PLANE < 0   -1    0 > -10 END_PLANE
      PLANE < 0    0   -1 >   0 END_PLANE
      PLANE < 0    0    1 >  10 END_PLANE
    END_INTERSECTION
  END_UNION
  BOUNDED_BY
    INTERSECTION
      PLANE <-1    0    0 > 10 END_PLANE
      PLANE < 1    0    0 > 10 END_PLANE
      PLANE < 0   -1    0 >  0 END_PLANE
      PLANE < 0    1    0 > 20 END_PLANE
      PLANE < 0    0   -1 >  0 END_PLANE
      PLANE < 0    0    1 > 10 END_PLANE
    END_INTERSECTION
  END_BOUND
  TEXTURE LetterTexture END_TEXTURE
END_OBJECT

DECLARE Lettera = OBJECT
  UNION
    INTERSECTION
      QUADRIC Cylinder_Z
        SCALE < 10 10 10 >
        TRANSLATE < 0 10 0 >
      END_QUADRIC
      QUADRIC Cylinder_Z
        SCALE < 5 5 10 >
        TRANSLATE < 0 10 0 >
        INVERSE
      END_QUADRIC
      PLANE < 0    0   -1 >  0 END_PLANE
      PLANE < 0    0    1 > 10 END_PLANE
    END_INTERSECTION
```

(continued)

Listing 9.3 *(continued)*

```
      INTERSECTION
        PLANE <-1   0    0 > -5 END_PLANE
        PLANE < 1   0    0 > 10 END_PLANE
        PLANE < 0  -1    0 >  0 END_PLANE
        PLANE < 0   1    0 > 10 END_PLANE
        PLANE < 0   0   -1 >  0 END_PLANE
        PLANE < 0   0    1 > 10 END_PLANE
      END_INTERSECTION
    END_UNION
    BOUNDED_BY
      INTERSECTION
        PLANE <-1   0    0 > 10 END_PLANE
        PLANE < 1   0    0 > 10 END_PLANE
        PLANE < 0  -1    0 >  0 END_PLANE
        PLANE < 0   1    0 > 20 END_PLANE
        PLANE < 0   0   -1 >  0 END_PLANE
        PLANE < 0   0    1 > 10 END_PLANE
      END_INTERSECTION
    END_BOUND
    TEXTURE LetterTexture    END_TEXTURE
  END_OBJECT

{ HalfSegment used within the letters c and g }
DECLARE HalfSegment =
  INTERSECTION
    QUADRIC Cylinder_Z
      SCALE < 10 10 10 >
    END_QUADRIC
    QUADRIC Cylinder_Z
      SCALE < 5 5 10 >
      INVERSE
    END_QUADRIC
    PLANE < 0  -1    0 >  0 END_PLANE
    PLANE < 0   0   -1 >  0 END_PLANE
    PLANE < 0   0    1 > 10 END_PLANE
  END_INTERSECTION

DECLARE Letterc = OBJECT
  UNION
    INTERSECTION HalfSegment
      ROTATE < 0  0  90 >
      TRANSLATE < 0  10  0 >
    END_INTERSECTION
    INTERSECTION HalfSegment
      ROTATE < 0  0  45 >
      TRANSLATE < 0  10  0 >
    END_INTERSECTION
    INTERSECTION HalfSegment
      ROTATE < 0  0  135 >
      TRANSLATE < 0  10  0 >
    END_INTERSECTION
```

```
      END_UNION
      BOUNDED_BY
        INTERSECTION
          PLANE <-1   0    0 > 10 END_PLANE
          PLANE < 1   0    0 > 10 END_PLANE
          PLANE < 0  -1    0 >  0 END_PLANE
          PLANE < 0   1    0 > 20 END_PLANE
          PLANE < 0   0   -1 >  0 END_PLANE
          PLANE < 0   0    1 > 10 END_PLANE
        END_INTERSECTION
      END_BOUND
      TEXTURE LetterTexture END_TEXTURE
    END_OBJECT

    DECLARE Lettert = OBJECT
      UNION
        INTERSECTION { long stem }
          PLANE <-1   0    0 > 2.5 END_PLANE
          PLANE < 1   0    0 > 2.5 END_PLANE
          PLANE < 0  -1    0 > -6.25 END_PLANE
          PLANE < 0   1    0 > 40 END_PLANE
          PLANE < 0   0   -1 >  0 END_PLANE
          PLANE < 0   0    1 > 10 END_PLANE
        END_INTERSECTION
        INTERSECTION { curl bottom }
          QUADRIC Cylinder_Z
            SCALE < 6.25 6.25 6.25 >
          END_QUADRIC
          QUADRIC Cylinder_Z
            SCALE < 1.25 1.25 6.25 >
            INVERSE
          END_QUADRIC
          PLANE < 0   1    0 >  0 END_PLANE
          PLANE < 0   0   -1 >  0 END_PLANE
          PLANE < 0   0    1 > 10 END_PLANE
          TRANSLATE < 3.75  6.25  0 >
        END_INTERSECTION
        INTERSECTION { dash in middle }
          PLANE <-1   0    0 >  5 END_PLANE
          PLANE < 1   0    0 >  5 END_PLANE
          PLANE < 0  -1    0 > -20 END_PLANE
          PLANE < 0   1    0 > 25 END_PLANE
          PLANE < 0   0   -1 >  0 END_PLANE
          PLANE < 0   0    1 > 10 END_PLANE
        END_INTERSECTION
      END_UNION
      BOUNDED_BY
        INTERSECTION
          PLANE <-1   0    0 > 10 END_PLANE
          PLANE < 1   0    0 > 10 END_PLANE
          PLANE < 0  -1    0 >  0 END_PLANE
          PLANE < 0   1    0 > 40 END_PLANE
```

(continued)

Listing 9.3   *(continued)*

```
          PLANE < 0    0  -1 >  0 END_PLANE
          PLANE < 0    0   1 > 10 END_PLANE
      END_INTERSECTION
    END_BOUND
    TEXTURE LetterTexture END_TEXTURE
END_OBJECT

DECLARE Letteri = OBJECT
  UNION
    INTERSECTION
        PLANE <-1   0    0 >  2.5 END_PLANE
        PLANE < 1   0    0 >  2.5 END_PLANE
        PLANE < 0  -1    0 >  0 END_PLANE
        PLANE < 0   1    0 > 20 END_PLANE
        PLANE < 0   0   -1 >  0 END_PLANE
        PLANE < 0   0    1 > 10 END_PLANE
      END_INTERSECTION
    INTERSECTION
      QUADRIC Cylinder_Z
        SCALE < 2.5 2.5 10 >
        TRANSLATE < 0 27.5 0 >
      END_QUADRIC
      PLANE < 0    0   -1 >  0 END_PLANE
      PLANE < 0    0    1 > 10 END_PLANE
    END_INTERSECTION
  END_UNION
  BOUNDED_BY
    INTERSECTION
        PLANE <-1   0    0 >  2.5 END_PLANE
        PLANE < 1   0    0 >  2.5 END_PLANE
        PLANE < 0  -1    0 >  0 END_PLANE
        PLANE < 0   1    0 > 30 END_PLANE
        PLANE < 0   0   -1 >  0 END_PLANE
        PLANE < 0   0    1 > 10 END_PLANE
      END_INTERSECTION
    END_BOUND
    TEXTURE LetterTexture    END_TEXTURE
END_OBJECT

DECLARE Letterl = OBJECT
  INTERSECTION { long stem }
      PLANE <-1   0    0 > 2.5 END_PLANE
      PLANE < 1   0    0 > 2.5 END_PLANE
      PLANE < 0  -1    0 >  0 END_PLANE
      PLANE < 0   1    0 > 40 END_PLANE
      PLANE < 0   0   -1 >  0 END_PLANE
      PLANE < 0   0    1 > 10 END_PLANE
    END_INTERSECTION
  BOUNDED_BY
    INTERSECTION
        PLANE <-1   0    0 >  2.5 END_PLANE
```

```
      PLANE < 1    0    0 >  2.5 END_PLANE
      PLANE < 0   -1    0 >   0 END_PLANE
      PLANE < 0    1    0 > 40 END_PLANE
      PLANE < 0    0   -1 >   0 END_PLANE
      PLANE < 0    0    1 > 10 END_PLANE
    END_INTERSECTION
  END_BOUND
  TEXTURE LetterTexture END_TEXTURE
END_OBJECT


DECLARE LetterR = OBJECT
  UNION
    INTERSECTION
      PLANE <-1    0    0 > 10 END_PLANE
      PLANE < 1    0    0 > -5 END_PLANE
      PLANE < 0   -1    0 >   0 END_PLANE
      PLANE < 0    1    0 > 40 END_PLANE
      PLANE < 0    0   -1 >   0 END_PLANE
      PLANE < 0    0    1 > 10 END_PLANE
    END_INTERSECTION
    INTERSECTION PSegment
      ROTATE < 0  0  -90 >
      TRANSLATE < -2  28  0 >
    END_INTERSECTION
    INTERSECTION
      PLANE <-1    0    0 > 2.5 END_PLANE
      PLANE < 1    0    0 > 2.5 END_PLANE
      PLANE < 0   -1    0 >   0 END_PLANE
      PLANE < 0    1    0 > 20 END_PLANE
      PLANE < 0    0   -1 >   0 END_PLANE
      PLANE < 0    0    1 > 10 END_PLANE
      ROTATE < 0   0   15 >
      TRANSLATE < 7.5  0   0 >
    END_INTERSECTION
  END_UNION
  BOUNDED_BY
    INTERSECTION
      PLANE <-1    0    0 > 10 END_PLANE
      PLANE < 1    0    0 > 10 END_PLANE
      PLANE < 0   -1    0 >   0 END_PLANE
      PLANE < 0    1    0 > 40 END_PLANE
      PLANE < 0    0   -1 >   0 END_PLANE
      PLANE < 0    0    1 > 10 END_PLANE
    END_INTERSECTION
  END_BOUND
  TEXTURE LetterTexture   END_TEXTURE
END_OBJECT


DECLARE Lettery = OBJECT
  INTERSECTION
    UNION
```

(continued)

Listing 9.3 *(continued)*

```
      INTERSECTION
        PLANE <-1    0    0 > 2.5 END_PLANE
        PLANE < 1    0    0 > 2.5 END_PLANE
        PLANE < 0   -1    0 > 30 END_PLANE
        PLANE < 0    1    0 > 30 END_PLANE
        PLANE < 0    0   -1 >  0 END_PLANE
        PLANE < 0    0    1 > 10 END_PLANE
        ROTATE < 0 0 -20 >
      END_INTERSECTION
      INTERSECTION
        PLANE <-1    0    0 >  2.5 END_PLANE
        PLANE < 1    0    0 >  2.5 END_PLANE
        PLANE < 0   -1    0 >  0 END_PLANE
        PLANE < 0    1    0 > 30 END_PLANE
        PLANE < 0    0   -1 >  0 END_PLANE
        PLANE < 0    0    1 > 10 END_PLANE
        ROTATE < 0 0 20 >
      END_INTERSECTION
    END_UNION
    PLANE < 0 -1 0 > 20 END_PLANE
    PLANE < 0  1 0 > 20 END_PLANE
  END_INTERSECTION
  BOUNDED_BY
    INTERSECTION
      PLANE <-1    0    0 > 10 END_PLANE
      PLANE < 1    0    0 > 10 END_PLANE
      PLANE < 0   -1    0 > 20 END_PLANE
      PLANE < 0    1    0 > 20 END_PLANE
      PLANE < 0    0   -1 >  0 END_PLANE
      PLANE < 0    0    1 > 10 END_PLANE
    END_INTERSECTION
  END_BOUND
  TEXTURE LetterTexture   END_TEXTURE
END_OBJECT

DECLARE LetterT = OBJECT
  UNION
    INTERSECTION
      PLANE <-1    0    0 >  2.5 END_PLANE
      PLANE < 1    0    0 >  2.5 END_PLANE
      PLANE < 0   -1    0 >  0 END_PLANE
      PLANE < 0    1    0 > 40 END_PLANE
      PLANE < 0    0   -1 >  0 END_PLANE
      PLANE < 0    0    1 > 10 END_PLANE
    END_INTERSECTION
    INTERSECTION
      PLANE <-1    0    0 >  10 END_PLANE
      PLANE < 1    0    0 >  10 END_PLANE
      PLANE < 0   -1    0 > -35 END_PLANE
      PLANE < 0    1    0 >  40 END_PLANE
      PLANE < 0    0   -1 >   0 END_PLANE
      PLANE < 0    0    1 >  10 END_PLANE
```

```
      END_INTERSECTION
    END_UNION
    BOUNDED_BY
      INTERSECTION
        PLANE <-1   0   0 > 10 END_PLANE
        PLANE < 1   0   0 > 10 END_PLANE
        PLANE < 0  -1   0 >  0 END_PLANE
        PLANE < 0   1   0 > 40 END_PLANE
        PLANE < 0   0  -1 >  0 END_PLANE
        PLANE < 0   0   1 > 10 END_PLANE
      END_INTERSECTION
    END_BOUND
    TEXTURE LetterTexture   END_TEXTURE
END_OBJECT

DECLARE Letterr = OBJECT
  UNION
    INTERSECTION
      PLANE <-1   0   0 > 10 END_PLANE
      PLANE < 1   0   0 > -5 END_PLANE
      PLANE < 0  -1   0 >  0 END_PLANE
      PLANE < 0   1   0 > 20 END_PLANE
      PLANE < 0   0  -1 >  0 END_PLANE
      PLANE < 0   0   1 > 10 END_PLANE
    END_INTERSECTION
    INTERSECTION
      QUADRIC Cylinder_Z
        SCALE < 10 10 10 >
        TRANSLATE < 0 10 0 >
      END_QUADRIC
      QUADRIC Cylinder_Z
        SCALE < 5 5 10 >
        TRANSLATE < 0 10 0 >
        INVERSE
      END_QUADRIC
      PLANE < 0  -1   0 > -10 END_PLANE
      PLANE < 0   0  -1 >   0 END_PLANE
      PLANE < 0   0   1 >  10 END_PLANE
    END_INTERSECTION
  END_UNION
  BOUNDED_BY
    INTERSECTION
      PLANE <-1   0   0 > 10 END_PLANE
      PLANE < 1   0   0 > 10 END_PLANE
      PLANE < 0  -1   0 >  0 END_PLANE
      PLANE < 0   1   0 > 20 END_PLANE
      PLANE < 0   0  -1 >  0 END_PLANE
      PLANE < 0   0   1 > 10 END_PLANE
    END_INTERSECTION
  END_BOUND
  TEXTURE LetterTexture   END_TEXTURE
END_OBJECT
```

(continued)

Listing 9.3 *(continued)*

```
DECLARE Lettern = OBJECT
  UNION
    INTERSECTION
      PLANE <-1   0   0 > 10 END_PLANE
      PLANE < 1   0   0 > -5 END_PLANE
      PLANE < 0  -1   0 >  0 END_PLANE
      PLANE < 0   1   0 > 20 END_PLANE
      PLANE < 0   0  -1 >  0 END_PLANE
      PLANE < 0   0   1 > 10 END_PLANE
    END_INTERSECTION
    INTERSECTION
      PLANE <-1   0   0 > -5 END_PLANE
      PLANE < 1   0   0 > 10 END_PLANE
      PLANE < 0  -1   0 >  0 END_PLANE
      PLANE < 0   1   0 > 10 END_PLANE
      PLANE < 0   0  -1 >  0 END_PLANE
      PLANE < 0   0   1 > 10 END_PLANE
    END_INTERSECTION
    INTERSECTION
      QUADRIC Cylinder_Z
        SCALE < 10 10 10 >
        TRANSLATE < 0 10 0 >
      END_QUADRIC
      QUADRIC Cylinder_Z
        SCALE < 5 5 10 >
        TRANSLATE < 0 10 0 >
        INVERSE
      END_QUADRIC
      PLANE < 0  -1   0 > -10 END_PLANE
      PLANE < 0   0  -1 >   0 END_PLANE
      PLANE < 0   0   1 >  10 END_PLANE
    END_INTERSECTION
  END_UNION
  BOUNDED_BY
    INTERSECTION
      PLANE <-1   0   0 > 10 END_PLANE
      PLANE < 1   0   0 > 10 END_PLANE
      PLANE < 0  -1   0 >  0 END_PLANE
      PLANE < 0   1   0 > 20 END_PLANE
      PLANE < 0   0  -1 >  0 END_PLANE
      PLANE < 0   0   1 > 10 END_PLANE
    END_INTERSECTION
  END_BOUND
  TEXTURE LetterTexture   END_TEXTURE
END_OBJECT

DECLARE Letterg = OBJECT
  UNION
    INTERSECTION HalfSegment
      TRANSLATE < 0  10  0 >
    END_INTERSECTION
```

```
      INTERSECTION HalfSegment
        ROTATE < 0   0   180 >
        TRANSLATE < 0   10   0 >
      END_INTERSECTION
      INTERSECTION HalfSegment
        ROTATE < 0   0   180 >
        TRANSLATE < 0  -10   0 >
      END_INTERSECTION
      INTERSECTION
        PLANE <-1    0    0 > -5 END_PLANE
        PLANE < 1    0    0 > 10 END_PLANE
        PLANE < 0   -1    0 > 10 END_PLANE
        PLANE < 0    1    0 > 10 END_PLANE
        PLANE < 0    0   -1 >  0 END_PLANE
        PLANE < 0    0    1 > 10 END_PLANE
      END_INTERSECTION
    END_UNION
    BOUNDED_BY
      INTERSECTION
        PLANE <-1    0    0 > 10 END_PLANE
        PLANE < 1    0    0 > 10 END_PLANE
        PLANE < 0   -1    0 > 20 END_PLANE
        PLANE < 0    1    0 > 20 END_PLANE
        PLANE < 0    0   -1 >  0 END_PLANE
        PLANE < 0    0    1 > 10 END_PLANE
      END_INTERSECTION
    END_BOUND
    TEXTURE LetterTexture    END_TEXTURE
END_OBJECT


DECLARE PracticalLettering = COMPOSITE
  OBJECT LetterP
    TRANSLATE <-100 0 0 >
  END_OBJECT
  OBJECT Letterr
    TRANSLATE <-75 0 0 >
  END_OBJECT
  OBJECT Lettera
    TRANSLATE <-50 0 0 >
  END_OBJECT
  OBJECT Letterc
    TRANSLATE <-25 0 0 >
  END_OBJECT
  OBJECT Lettert
  END_OBJECT
  OBJECT Letteri
    TRANSLATE < 25 0 0 >
  END_OBJECT
  OBJECT Letterc
    TRANSLATE < 50 0 0 >
  END_OBJECT
  OBJECT Lettera
    TRANSLATE < 75 0 0 >
```

(continued)

Listing 9.3 *(continued)*

```
    END_OBJECT
    OBJECT Letterl
      TRANSLATE < 100 0 0 >
    END_OBJECT
END_COMPOSITE

DECLARE RayTracingLettering = COMPOSITE
    OBJECT LetterR
      TRANSLATE <-125 0 0 >
    END_OBJECT
    OBJECT Lettera
      TRANSLATE <-100 0 0 >
    END_OBJECT
    OBJECT Lettery
      TRANSLATE <-75 0 0 >
    END_OBJECT

    OBJECT LetterT
      TRANSLATE <-25 0 0 >
    END_OBJECT
    OBJECT Letterr { middle of word Ray_Tracing }
    END_OBJECT
    OBJECT Lettera
      TRANSLATE < 25 0 0 >
    END_OBJECT
    OBJECT Letterc
      TRANSLATE < 50 0 0 >
    END_OBJECT
    OBJECT Letteri
      TRANSLATE < 75 0 0 >
    END_OBJECT
    OBJECT Lettern
      TRANSLATE < 100 0 0 >
    END_OBJECT
    OBJECT Letterg
      TRANSLATE < 125 0 0 >
    END_OBJECT
END_COMPOSITE

DECLARE in_CLettering = COMPOSITE
    OBJECT Letteri
      TRANSLATE <-37.5 0 0 >
    END_OBJECT
    OBJECT Lettern
      TRANSLATE <-12.5 0 0 >
    END_OBJECT
    OBJECT Letterc
      SCALE < 2.5 2.5 1 >
      TRANSLATE < 37.5  0  0 >
    END_OBJECT
END_COMPOSITE
```

```
{ Create instances of the lettering and place it accordingly }
COMPOSITE
  PracticalLettering
  ROTATE < 0  0  3 >
  TRANSLATE < 485  0  0 >
  SCALE < 0.085 0.085 0.085 >
  ROTATE < 0 -45   0 >
  TRANSLATE <-40 5.5  0 >
END_COMPOSITE

COMPOSITE
  RayTracingLettering
  ROTATE < 0  0  -5 >
  TRANSLATE <-500  0  0 >
  SCALE < 0.085 0.085 0.085 >
  ROTATE < 0  45  0 >
  TRANSLATE < 40 5.5  0 >
END_COMPOSITE

COMPOSITE
  in_CLettering
  TRANSLATE < 0  0  -5 >
  SCALE < 0.025 0.025 0.025 >
  ROTATE < 90  0  0 >
  TRANSLATE < 0  0 -4.35 >
END_COMPOSITE

{ Create instances of the objects within the scene }
OBJECT Floor     END_OBJECT
OBJECT LeftWall  END_OBJECT
OBJECT RightWall END_OBJECT
OBJECT TheSphere END_OBJECT
```

All of the fractals used in this image were created with the FRACTINT shareware program, available from the Stone Soup Group directly, with the book *Fractal Creations* by Timothy Wegner and Mark Peterson and published by the Waite Group Press, or from many sources over Internet. The FRACTINT program is highly recommended for generating many kinds of fractal data and images. Be warned, however; you can spend a lot of time playing with this program and get nothing else done whatsoever. The fractals, after being generated by the FRACTINT program, were saved in a GIF file format. You can, of course, import GIF files directly into DKBTrace as IMAGEMAP textures just as we imported the dump format image in Chapter 8. In total, four different fractal image files were imported to produce this image. *Note*: You must be running the protected-mode version of DKBTrace to have access to enough memory to import four GIF files of this size simultaneously. You will run out of memory if you use the real-mode versions of DKBTrace.

When the GIF bit-mapped image files are imported into this image model, they are scaled and translated into position on the surfaces on which they are mapped. Some of the mappings (the Floor object, for example) require the use of a GRADIENT statement (as described in Chapter 8) to orient the bit-mapped image correctly on the object's surface.

In addition to using IMAGEMAPs in this image model, we have modeled the words "Practical Ray Tracing in C" in the block font described in Chapter 8 and rendered in this image. As in Chapter 8, we have given all of the lettering a single texture, which in this case is called LetterTexture. The lettering itself is modeled using the same techniques as discussed in Chapter 8, except in this case, we have defined two primitive shapes called PSegment and HalfSegment, which aid in the generation of the R/P and c/g letters, respectively. See the image model listing for examples of their use.

Besides the use of multiple IMAGEMAP textures in a single image, we convey no other significant new information within this image model. The letters defined in this image model do add to the collection of letters defined in Chapter 8, however. Completing the alphabet, both upper- and lowercase, will be left as an exercise for you. Modeling the numerals zero through nine would also be a useful addition to your ray-tracing bag of tricks. Having a complete collection of letters and numbers would allow you to create images with lettering quickly and effortlessly. Previously defined lettering is extremely convenient for the production of business logos and/or signs, for example. You could place all of the lettering in a separate file to be included in your image models when lettering was required. That would keep your image model files uncluttered and easy to understand. The letters would be instantiated, scaled, and then translated in their final positions as required in your design.

Image Model Four—The Desert

The final image model we will present is a desert scene. This is the only image model in this book that attempts to model something organic, although it does so in a highly stylized way. Within this scene are two different types of cactus (Saguaro and prickly pear), a well made from wildly colored desert rock, and a starry nighttime sky. Long shadows cast from unseen cactuses onto the desert sand dominate the scene. The shadows are from what little light is left in the desert as nightfall approaches. The image model that creates this desert scene is called "cactus5.dat" and is shown in Listing 9.4. As usual, this image model is available on the companion disks.

There is nothing really new about the concepts presented in this image model. We included this image more for aesthetic reasons than for technical ones. Again, constructive solid geometry is used extensively to create "pieces" of the cactuses individually. The cactuses are then defined as composite objects made up of all of the individual pieces. The cactuses are given a CactusTex texture to more accurately depict a real cactus, which is generally full of holes and imperfections. After both the Saguaro and prickly pear cactuses are defined, many instances of each are created within the image model. Some are placed into the field of view to be seen, while others are placed behind the viewer so as to cast their long shadows into the field of view. It is the long shadows that add visual interest to this image. The well is created by the intersection of nested spheres and planes. The well is given the Brown_Agate coloration texture. The desert floor is a plane with the coloring of sand that has a RIPPLES surface perturbation texture. This simulates a windblown surface on the sand. All in all, this is a very interesting image that somehow conveys the emptiness and stillness of the desert at night.

Listing 9.4   Image Model Four—The Desert

The following is the contents of the file "cactus5.dat."

```
{
  Ray-Traced Imaging - Image Model Four
  "The Desert"
  from the book "Practical Ray Tracing in C" by Craig A. Lindley
  Last update to this image: 03/06/92

  This image model uses many of the effects shown in the tutorial
  exercises to produce an image of a desert scene complete with
  a well, two kinds of cactus, desert sand, and a starry night. See
  the "Gallery of Images" for a look at what this image file produces.
}

INCLUDE "colors.dat"
INCLUDE "shapes.dat"
INCLUDE "textures.dat"

{ Define the color Sand as it is not in "colors.dat" }
DECLARE Sand = COLOR RED 1.00 GREEN 0.66 BLUE 0.20

VIEW_POINT
  LOCATION <-5  11.4 -25>
  DIRECTION < 0 -0.15  1 >
  UP < 0  1  0 >
  RIGHT < 1.0  0  0 >
END_VIEW_POINT

{ Add a light source }
OBJECT
  SPHERE <0.0 0.0 0.0> 1.0 END_SPHERE
  TRANSLATE < 55  50 -200 >
  TEXTURE
    COLOR White
    AMBIENT 1.0
    DIFFUSE 0.0
  END_TEXTURE
  COLOR White
  LIGHT_SOURCE
END_OBJECT

{ Define space with stars }
OBJECT
  PLANE < 0 0 1> 50000 END_PLANE
  TEXTURE
    COLOR Black
    BOZO
    TURBULENCE 0.3
    COLOR_MAP
      [0.0 0.9   COLOR Black COLOR Black ]
      [0.9 1.001 COLOR Black COLOR White ]
```

(continued)

Listing 9.4 *(continued)*

```
      END_COLOR_MAP
      SCALE < 100 200 300 >
    END_TEXTURE
END_OBJECT

{ Define the desert floor }
OBJECT
  PLANE < 0 1 0 > 0 END_PLANE
  TEXTURE
    0.05  { This value dithers the colors }
    COLOR Sand
    AMBIENT 0.3
    DIFFUSE 0.7
    RIPPLES 0.75
    FREQUENCY 2000.0
    SCALE <5000.0 50000.0 5000.0>
  END_TEXTURE
END_OBJECT

{ Start definition of Saguaro cactus }

{ This is the texture all cactus will have }
DECLARE CactusTex = TEXTURE
  ROUGHNESS 0.75
  COLOR LimeGreen
  BOZO
  TURBULENCE 0.3
  COLOR_MAP
    [0.0 0.9   COLOR LimeGreen COLOR LimeGreen ]
    [0.9 1.001 COLOR LimeGreen COLOR Black ]
  END_COLOR_MAP
  SCALE < 1 2 3 >
END_TEXTURE


DECLARE LargeCap = OBJECT
  INTERSECTION
    SPHERE <0.0 0.0 0.0>  1 END_SPHERE
    PLANE  <0.0 -1.0 0.0> 0 END_PLANE
  END_INTERSECTION
  TEXTURE CactusTex END_TEXTURE
END_OBJECT

DECLARE SmallCap = OBJECT
  INTERSECTION
    SPHERE <0.0 0.0 0.0>  0.75 END_SPHERE
    PLANE  <0.0 -1.0 0.0> 0.0 END_PLANE
  END_INTERSECTION
  TEXTURE CactusTex END_TEXTURE
END_OBJECT
```

```
DECLARE Trunk = OBJECT
  INTERSECTION
    QUADRIC Cylinder_Y SCALE < 1 27 1 > END_QUADRIC
    PLANE <0.0  1.0 0.0> 27.0 END_PLANE
    PLANE <0.0 -1.0 0.0>  0.0 END_PLANE
  END_INTERSECTION
  TEXTURE CactusTex END_TEXTURE
END_OBJECT

DECLARE Arm = OBJECT
  INTERSECTION
    QUADRIC Cylinder_X SCALE < 3.75 0.75 0.75 > END_QUADRIC
    PLANE <-1.0  0.0 0.0> 0.0 END_PLANE
    PLANE < 1.0  0.0 0.0> 3.75 END_PLANE
  END_INTERSECTION
  TEXTURE CactusTex END_TEXTURE
END_OBJECT

DECLARE Joint = OBJECT
  SPHERE < 0 0 0 > 0.75 END_SPHERE
  TEXTURE CactusTex END_TEXTURE
END_OBJECT

DECLARE LeftUpright = OBJECT
  INTERSECTION
    QUADRIC Cylinder_Y SCALE < 0.75 11.0 0.75 > END_QUADRIC
    PLANE <0.0  1.0 0.0> 11.0 END_PLANE
    PLANE <0.0 -1.0 0.0>  0.0 END_PLANE
  END_INTERSECTION
  TEXTURE CactusTex END_TEXTURE
END_OBJECT

DECLARE RightUpright = OBJECT
  INTERSECTION
    QUADRIC Cylinder_Y SCALE < 0.75 13.0 0.75 > END_QUADRIC
    PLANE <0.0  1.0 0.0> 13.0 END_PLANE
    PLANE <0.0 -1.0 0.0>  0.0 END_PLANE
  END_INTERSECTION
  TEXTURE CactusTex END_TEXTURE
END_OBJECT

DECLARE Cactus = COMPOSITE
  OBJECT Trunk                                   END_OBJECT
  OBJECT LargeCap      TRANSLATE <0.0    27.0 0.0 > END_OBJECT
  OBJECT Arm           TRANSLATE <-3.75   9.0 0.0 > END_OBJECT
  OBJECT Arm           TRANSLATE < 0.0   12.0 0.0 > END_OBJECT
  OBJECT Joint         TRANSLATE <-3.75   9.0 0.0 > END_OBJECT
  OBJECT Joint         TRANSLATE < 3.75  12.0 0.0 > END_OBJECT
  OBJECT LeftUpright   TRANSLATE <-3.75   9.0 0.0 > END_OBJECT
  OBJECT RightUpright  TRANSLATE < 3.75  12.0 0.0 > END_OBJECT
  OBJECT SmallCap      TRANSLATE <-3.75  20.0 0.0 > END_OBJECT
  OBJECT SmallCap      TRANSLATE < 3.75  25.0 0.0 > END_OBJECT
  BOUNDED_BY
```

(continued)

Listing 9.4   *(continued)*

```
      INTERSECTION
        QUADRIC Cylinder_Y SCALE < 4.6 40.0 4.6 > END_QUADRIC
        PLANE <0.0  1.0 0.0> 28.0 END_PLANE
        PLANE <0.0 -1.0 0.0>  0.0 END_PLANE
      END_INTERSECTION
    END_BOUND
END_COMPOSITE

{ Start definition of Prickly Pear cactus }
DECLARE Leaf = OBJECT
  INTERSECTION
    QUADRIC
      Sphere SCALE < 0.57 1.17 0.57 >
             TRANSLATE < 0 1.17 0 >
    END_QUADRIC
    PLANE < 0 0 -1 > 0.05 END_PLANE
    PLANE < 0 0  1 > 0.05 END_PLANE
  END_INTERSECTION
  TEXTURE
    COLOR MediumForestGreen
    WRINKLES 0.3
  END_TEXTURE
END_OBJECT

DECLARE Flower = OBJECT
  SPHERE < 0 2.33 0 > 0.19 END_SPHERE
  TEXTURE COLOR OrangeRed END_TEXTURE
END_OBJECT

DECLARE WholeLeaf = COMPOSITE
  OBJECT Leaf END_OBJECT
  OBJECT Flower END_OBJECT
END_COMPOSITE

DECLARE PricklyPear = COMPOSITE
  OBJECT Leaf END_OBJECT
  COMPOSITE WholeLeaf ROTATE < 0 0  45 > END_COMPOSITE
  COMPOSITE WholeLeaf ROTATE < 0 0 -45 > END_COMPOSITE
  BOUNDED_BY
    SPHERE < 0 1.5 0 > 1.75 END_SPHERE
  END_BOUND
END_COMPOSITE

{ Define the well }
OBJECT
  INTERSECTION
    SPHERE < 0  0  0 > 5.32 END_SPHERE
    SPHERE < 0  0  0 > 4.56 INVERSE END_SPHERE
    PLANE  < 0  1  0 > 3.42 END_PLANE
```

```
      PLANE  < 0 -1  0 > 0.0 END_PLANE
   END_INTERSECTION
   BOUNDED_BY
     SPHERE <0.0 0.0 0.0> 5.33 END_SPHERE
   END_BOUND
   TEXTURE
     Brown_Agate
     SCALE < 10.0 10.0 10.0 >
     ROUGHNESS 0.2
     DIFFUSE 0.7
     AMBIENT 0.3
     TRANSLATE < 0 0.0 4.56>
   END_TEXTURE
END_OBJECT


{ Define the whole scene }

COMPOSITE Cactus TRANSLATE < 10.84 0.0 0 > END_COMPOSITE
COMPOSITE Cactus TRANSLATE < 0 0.0 -28 > END_COMPOSITE
COMPOSITE Cactus TRANSLATE <-15 0.0 -28 > END_COMPOSITE
COMPOSITE Cactus TRANSLATE < -5 0.0 30.24> END_COMPOSITE
COMPOSITE Cactus ROTATE <0 180 0> TRANSLATE <24 0.0 34.56 > END_COMPOSITE
COMPOSITE Cactus ROTATE <0 40 0> TRANSLATE <-30.98 0.0 34.56 > END_COMPOSITE
COMPOSITE Cactus ROTATE <0 -30 0> TRANSLATE <24 0.0 70 > END_COMPOSITE
COMPOSITE Cactus ROTATE <0  60 0> TRANSLATE <-30.98 0.0 80 > END_COMPOSITE
COMPOSITE Cactus ROTATE <0 -30 0> TRANSLATE <50 0.0 100 > END_COMPOSITE
COMPOSITE Cactus ROTATE <0  60 0> TRANSLATE <-65 0.0 100 > END_COMPOSITE
COMPOSITE Cactus ROTATE <0 -80 0> TRANSLATE <100 0.0 200 > END_COMPOSITE
COMPOSITE Cactus ROTATE <0  75 0> TRANSLATE <-120 0.0 200 > END_COMPOSITE

COMPOSITE Cactus TRANSLATE < 0 0.0 -228 > END_COMPOSITE
COMPOSITE Cactus TRANSLATE < -75 0.0 230.24> END_COMPOSITE
COMPOSITE Cactus ROTATE <0 180 0> TRANSLATE <124 0.0 234.56 > END_COMPOSITE
COMPOSITE Cactus ROTATE <0 40 0> TRANSLATE <-130.98 0.0 234.56 > END_COMPOSITE
COMPOSITE Cactus ROTATE <0 -30 0> TRANSLATE <240 0.0 270 > END_COMPOSITE
COMPOSITE Cactus ROTATE <0  60 0> TRANSLATE <-300.98 0.0 280 > END_COMPOSITE
COMPOSITE Cactus ROTATE <0 -30 0> TRANSLATE <50 0.0 300 > END_COMPOSITE
COMPOSITE Cactus ROTATE <0  60 0> TRANSLATE <-165 0.0 300 > END_COMPOSITE
COMPOSITE Cactus ROTATE <0 -80 0> TRANSLATE <200 0.0 300 > END_COMPOSITE
COMPOSITE Cactus ROTATE <0  75 0> TRANSLATE <-180 0.0 300 > END_COMPOSITE

COMPOSITE PricklyPear ROTATE < 0 45 0 >
 TRANSLATE <-3.42 0.0 -2.56 > END_COMPOSITE
COMPOSITE PricklyPear TRANSLATE <-9.12 0.0 -2.00 > END_COMPOSITE

COMPOSITE PricklyPear ROTATE < 0 65 0 >
 TRANSLATE <6.42 0.0 18 > END_COMPOSITE

COMPOSITE PricklyPear ROTATE < 0 -45 0 >
 TRANSLATE <-12.42 0.0 4.56 > END_COMPOSITE
```

(continued)

Listing 9.4 *(continued)*

```
COMPOSITE PricklyPear ROTATE < 0  45 0 >
 TRANSLATE <-12.42 0.0 12.56 > END_COMPOSITE

COMPOSITE PricklyPear ROTATE < 0 -45 0 >
 TRANSLATE <-32.42 0.0 40 > END_COMPOSITE

COMPOSITE PricklyPear ROTATE < 0  45 0 >
 TRANSLATE <-60.42 0.0 50 > END_COMPOSITE
```

A whole series of unique desert scenes are possible by reorganizing the component parts contained in this image model. Consider also the addition of a full moon, a road leading to nowhere, and other types of desert flora and possibly fauna when expanding upon this image model.

Conclusions

In this, the final chapter of this book, you have been exposed to some rather complex image models. We hope you now understand that complex image models are nothing more than combinations of simpler image components. These simpler components can be developed separately and combined into a more complex image model only after being thoroughly debugged on their own. This is an important concept, because as the number of objects within an image model increases, so does the time required to ray trace the image. By starting out simply and rendering each image component in a piecemeal fashion, you can develop complex imagery in a much shorter amount of time. As you develop custom objects (such as lettering, for example), custom colors, or custom textures, you can put them into library files to be included in your image models when you need them. In this way, you can quickly bring together a large collection of imaging ideas when creating new imagery.

This concludes the information on ray tracing provided in this book. We hope that you are now as excited about the possibilities of ray tracing as we are. Ray tracing is a fascinating subject, and ray-traced images are among the most spectacular imagery that can be produced on a personal computer. With the tools and techniques presented in this book, along with an IBM or compatible personal computer, you should now be able to create exciting imagery of your own—imagery to be proud of even if you do not consider yourself artistic and even if you are not capable of drawing a straight line with the aid of a ruler. Anything that you can visualize can be ray traced in some form or another. Your imagination and your motivation are your only limits.

Part Three

ADDITIONAL INFORMATION

Any sufficiently advanced technology is indistinguishable from magic.
—Arthur C. Clarke

The scientific theory I like best is that the rings of Saturn are composed entirely of lost airline luggage.
—Mark Russell

Further Reading

Books: Image Processing, Graphics, and Mathematics

Angel, Edward. *Computer Graphics*. Reading, MA: Addison-Wesley Publishing Company, 1990. ISBN 0-201-13548-5.

Angell, Ian O. *High Resolution Computer Graphics Using C*. New York: Halsted Press Book, John Wiley & Sons, Inc., 1990. ISBN 0-470-21634-4.

CONRAC Division, CONRAC Corp. *Raster Graphics Handbook*. Covina, CA: CONRAC Corp., 1980. ISBN 0-9604972-0-X.

Glassner, Andrew S., ed. *An Introduction to Ray Tracing*. New York: Academic Press, Inc., Harcourt Brace Jovanovich, Publishers, 1989. ISBN 0-12-286160-4.

____, ed. *Graphic Gems* Vol. 1. New York: Academic Press, Inc., Harcourt Brace Jovanovich, Publishers, 1990. ISBN 0-12-286165-5.

Holzmann, Gerald J., and AT&T Bell Labs Staff. *Beyond Photography: The Digital Darkroom*. Englewood Cliffs, NJ: Prentice-Hall, 1988. ISBN 0-13-074410-7.

Joy, Kenneth I., Charles W. Grant, Nelson L. Max, and Lansing Hatfield, eds. *Computer Graphics: Image Synthesis*. Washington, DC: IEEE Computer Society Press, 1988. ISBN 0-8186-8854-8.

Lindley, Craig A. *Practical Image Processing in C*. New York: John Wiley & Sons, Inc., 1991. ISBN 0-471-54377-2.

Newman, W.M., and R.F. Sproull. *Principles of Interactive Computer Graphics*. New York: McGraw-Hill, 1979. ISBN 0-07-046337-9.

Peitgen, Heinz-Otto, and Dietmar Saupe, eds. *The Science of Fractal Images*. New York: Springer-Verlag, 1988. ISBN 0-387-96608-0.

Perlin, Ken. *An Image Synthesizer*. SIGGRAPH Conference Proceedings, 1984.

Thomas, George B., Jr. *Calculus and Analytic Geometry*. 2d ed. Reading, MA: Addison-Wesley Publishing Company, 1968.

VanDam, A., and J.D. Foley. *Fundamentals of Interactive Computer Graphics*. Reading, MA: Addison-Wesley Publishing Company, 1983. ISBN 0-201-14468-9.

Von Seggern, David. *The CRC Handbook of Mathematical Curves and Surfaces*. Boca Raton, FL: CRC Press, 1992. ISBN 0-8493-0196-3.

Wegner, Timothy, and Mark Peterson. *Fractal Creations*. Mill Valley, CA: Waite Group Press, 1991. ISBN 1-878739-05-0.

Books: Programming Reference

Borland International, Inc. *Borland C++ User's Guide, Borland C++ Programmer's Guide*, and *Borland C++ Library Reference*. Scotts Valley, CA: Borland International, Inc., 1991.

IBM Corp. *Personal System/2 and Personal Computer BIOS Interface Technical Reference*. IBM Corp., 1988. 68X2341, S68X-2341-00.

Intel Corp. *iAPX 86/88, 186/188 User's Manual, Programmer's Reference*. CA: Intel Corp., 1986.

Morgan, Christopher L., and Mitchell Waite. *8086/8088 16-Bit Microprocessor Primer*. Peterborough, NH: BYTE/McGraw-Hill, 1982. ISBN 0-672-22024-5.

Video Electronics Standards Association. *Super VGA Standard*. Standard #VS911022. San Jose, CA: Video Electronic Standards Association, 1991.

Willen, David C., and Jeffrey I. Krantz. *8088 Assembler Language Programming: The IBM PC*. Indianapolis: Howard W. Sams and Co., Inc., 1983. ISBN 0-672-22024-5.

Articles

Apiki, Steve. "Lossless Data Compression" from the column "Some Assembly Required." *BYTE* (March 1991).

Ericsson, Bo. "VESA VGA BIOS Extensions." *Dr. Dobbs Journal* (April 1990).

Gervautz, Michael, and Werner Purgathofer. "A Simple Method for Color Quantization." *Graphic Gems* 1.

Glassner, Andrew S. "Ray Tracing for Realism." *BYTE* (December, 1990).

Heckbert, Paul. "Color Image Quantization for Frame Buffer Display." *ACM Computer Graphics Journal* 16, no. 3 (July 1982).

_____. "Survey of Texture Mapping." *IEEE Computer Graphics and Applications* (November 1986).

Howard, Christopher A. "Super VGA Programming." *Dr. Dobbs Journal* (July 1990).

Kliewer, Bradley Dyck. "VGA to the Max." *BYTE* (December 1990).

Lyke, Daniel. "Ray Tracing." *Dr. Dobbs Journal* (September 1990).

Nelson, Mark R. "LZW Data Compression." *Dr. Dobbs Journal* (October 1989).

Nicholls, Bill. "Is It Really Super?" *BYTE* IBM Special Edition (Fall 1989).

Pomerantz, Dave. "A Few Good Colors." *Computer Language* (August 1990).

Regan, Shawn M. "LZW Revisited." *Dr. Dobbs Journal* (June 1990).

Schore, Michael. "Octree Method of Color Matching." *The C User's Journal* (August 1991).

Welsh, Terry A. "A Technique for High Performance Data Compression." *Computer Magazine* (June 1984).

Wilton, Richard. "Programming the Enhanced Graphics Adapter." *BYTE* IBM Special Edition (Fall 1985).

_____. "PS/2 Video Programming." *BYTE* IBM Special Edition (Fall 1987).

_____. "VGA Video Modes." *BYTE* IBM Special Edition (Fall 1988).

Glossary

The following is a list of some common terms used in the computer graphics and imaging industries along with their definitions.

Adaptive tree depth. A technique to limit the depth of a ray tree based on the significance of the contribution of individual rays.

Aliasing. Undesirable artifacts in a ray-traced image that result from an insufficient sampling rate. Visual aberrations that can result from aliasing include jaggy lines and small missing objects and object detail.

Ambient illumination. Light in a ray-traced scene that is used to simulate diffuse interobject reflections because these reflections are so difficult to model. Ambient light seems to come from everywhere and illuminates all objects equally.

Animation. Computer animation is the creation of a motion picture using a computer with a graphics device. Quickly changing the image displayed on the graphics device gives the appearance of motion.

Anti-aliasing. Techniques for combating aliasing artifacts. An example is smoothing out the jagged appearance of edges in an image on a raster display. Anti-aliasing is generally accomplished in ray tracing by using super sampling techniques that cast multiple rays per pixel.

APA. All Points Addressable. The expression is used with raster displays and printers. It implies graphics capabilities in which every element is individually controllable.

Argument. Data passed to a function or a program.

Aspect ratio. The ratio of width to height of a single pixel on a display. If a display has an aspect ratio of one, it is said to have square pixels.

Assembler language. The mnemonic codes that are converted into machine language by an assembler program. Assembler language is the only language a computer can execute directly.

BIOS. A set of ROM-based firmware functions that control the resources of an IBM-compatible computer system. BIOS stands for Basic Input Output System.

Bit map. A memory image of a portion of a display area. The size of a bit map depends on display resolution and the number of supported colors.

Byte map. A type of image in which each pixel is defined by 1 byte of storage (8 bits). The byte is capable of storing up to 256 levels of gray, with 0 as black (typically) and 255 as white. A color image that utilizes a palette for display can also be considered byte-mapped.

Casting or type casting. A method for forcing a compiler to convert a variable's value from one type to another.

Chrominance. The color portion of a video signal.

Clip. To eliminate a portion of the image outside a specified boundary.

Color separation. The process of separating color images into the three primary color components: red, green, and blue.

Command line arguments or switches. Arguments passed into a program when it is run from the DOS command line. These are the string of arguments that follow a DOS command, including the command to initiate the execution of an application program.

Compression. Various techniques used by imaging devices and software to reduce image-storage requirements, usually without affecting the appearance of the image. RLE compression is used within PCX graphics files, LZW compression is used within GIF files.

Constructive Solid Geometry (CSG). A technique using INTERSECTIONs, UNIONs, and DIFFERENCEs to combine simple object shapes into more complex shapes that can be manipulated as a whole.

Contrast. The difference between the light and dark regions of an image.

CRT. Cathode Ray Tube; the display device for a computer monitor or TV.

Default. An assumed value that exists if no other value is assigned.

Diffuse reflection. A light transport mechanism in which incident light is absorbed by a surface and reradiated equally in all directions.

Diffuse transmission. A light transport mechanism in which incident light is absorbed by one side of a surface, transmitted (but attenuated) through the surface, and reradiated in all directions on the opposite side.

Digital image processing. Digital image processing deals with arrays of numbers (samples) that represent an image. Various algorithms are used to manipulate the image samples to obtain some desired result. After processing is completed, the modified samples are used to reconstruct the image for viewing.

Digital to Analog Converter (DAC). An electronic device that converts digital numerical values into a corresponding analog signal.

Display or graphics adapter. Electronic circuitry designed to interface a display (monitor) to a computer system. It is usually located on a printed circuit card, but not always.

Dithering. A technique for displaying gray-scale images on a monochrome output device (monitor or printer) by carefully distributing the location of OFF and ON pixels. It is also used as a term to mean a small, random variation of coloring.

Dot. The smallest controllable element on an APA device. It is often referred to as a pixel, picture element, or a pel.

Dynamic range. The ratio between the brightest and dimmest light level (pixel-intensity values).

Electron beam. A moving beam of electrons that creates an image on a raster display screen.

Exhaustive ray tracing. A brute-force ray-tracing technique that tests for intersection between every generated ray and every object within a scene. This is the simplest technique to use in ray tracing, but it is also the most expensive in computer resource terms.

Eye ray. A ray that starts at the location of the viewer's eye, proceeds in the direction the viewer is looking, pierces the view plane, and continues on into object space. The eye ray will be tested for intersection with some or all of the objects defined within the scene being ray traced.

Filter. A device, method, or program that separates data, signals, or material based on a specified criteria.

Fractal. A fractal is a mathematical collection or set of numbers that has a definite structure regardless of how closely the numbers are examined. In common usage, the term fractal refers to the computer-generated image of this data.

Frustum. The pyramidlike volume that contains all objects within a viewer's field of view. The viewer's eye is placed at the apex of the pyramid.

Geometric optics. An area of physics that is concerned with the study of light.

Graphics mode. A mode of the display adapter in which all pixels are independently controllable. This is opposed to text mode, where only predefined characters can be displayed.

Highlight. Refers to specular highlights that appear as bright spots of reflected light on object surfaces when they have the required glossiness.

Hue. Refers to the name of a color, such as red, green, or blue. The hue of a color is its dominant wavelength.

Illumination. The sum total of all light (conveyed by all light transport modes) impinging on an object's surface.

Include files. Files that are temporarily inserted into a source code file during the compilation process, usually containing identifiers that are referenced in the source file. They are used to ensure consistency of identifiers across an application program.

Index of Refraction (IOR). A number, pertinent to the material that makes up a surface, that is the ratio of angles of incidence to refraction when light enters the material from a vacuum.

Interpolation. The process of determining a new value that lies between other values with known attributes. This new value depends on the attributes surrounding it and on its proximity to these other values. The new value is calculated by a mathematical function that considers these factors.

Lambert's law. The law that states that the intensity of diffusely reflected light is proportional to the intensity of the light, the reflective properties of the surface, and the cosine of the angle between the incident light ray and the surface normal.

Luminance. The black and white or brightness portion of a video signal.

Machine dependent code. Code that relies on some feature of a particular computer.

Machine independent code. Code that can be made to work on any computer because it does not rely on any particular features of any one computer.

Mapping. The mathematical conversion of one set of numbers into a different set based on some transformation.

Mask. A technique for eliminating certain bits within a number, leaving only the bits of interest.

Memory model. A designation that tells a compiler where code and data are located and how they are to be referenced.

Monitor. Another term for CRT or display.

Object space. That portion of the three-dimensional universe in which the objects in a ray-traced image reside.

Palette. A set or collection of colors available simultaneously for display of an image.

Pel. *Pi*cture *el*ement. The smallest area of an image display device capable of being addressed and switched between the visible and the invisible states.

Penumbra. Shadows with soft edges that are caused by a light source with finite size, not a point light source.

Picture. A collection of pixels or pels that form a recognizable image when visually represented together.

Pixel. Element of an image on a logical and conceptual level.

Quadric surfaces. A family of surfaces that is defined by second-order quadratic equations of three variables: X, Y, and Z. Quadric spheres include spheres, cones, cylinders, and so on.

Quantization. In hardware terms, quantization is the process by which an A-to-D converter maps the instantaneous brightness and/or color values of analog signals into discrete integer samples. Color quantization, as used in this book, refers to a collection of software techniques that can reduce the large gamut of colors in an image down to a minimum set necessary for accurate display of the image.

Quartic surfaces. A family of surfaces that is defined by fourth-order equations of three variables: X, Y, and Z. A torus, a piriform, and a lumniscate are all quartic surfaces, for example.

Raster. A predetermined pattern of lines that provides uniform coverage of a display space.

Ray. A line segment defined by an origin and a direction. A ray is infinite in length along its direction.

Recursive shading. A technique that attempts to figure out shading at a point on a surface by the summation of contributions made to the point by reflected and refracted light rays. The process is recursive because any illumination contributions made by reflected or refracted rays at level N are directly influenced by the contributions of reflected and refracted rays at all deeper levels.

Resolution. The number of discernible points in a given field of view. The density of the sampling points affects the amount of detail visible in an image. The greater the image detail, the higher the required resolution.

RGB. An additive color model that forms colors by mixing various ratios of the red, green, and blue color components. Lack of color contributions (R=G=B=0.0) results in black, whereas full contribution of each color component (R=G=B=1.0) results in white.

Rotation. A three-dimensional process that alters an object's position in three-dimensional space by rotating it around the coordinate axes.

Sampling. The selection of a set of points over the field of observation. Only the values at those points will be used in further processing. All values in between are discarded.

Saturation. Designates the purity of a color or how much the color is diluted by white. Red is a highly saturated color. Pink has the same hue but a lower saturation.

Scaling. A three-dimensional process for adjusting the size of objects.

Scanline. A single row of display data.

Shading. The process by which the color of a surface at some point is determined. The surface color is a function of the light sources within a scene and the material of which the surface is constructed. In ray tracing, shading calculations are usually performed as a recursive process.

Shadow. Portions of an object's surface not directly illuminated by a light source.

Snell's law. The law of refraction that specifies how light is bent when traveling through different, transparent mediums.

Spatial resolution. The density of sample points.

Specular reflection. A directional form of light transport where light reflects off a surface (instead of being absorbed and reradiated) in generally the same plane in which it strikes the surface. The angle of light reflected off the surface depends on the angle at which the light struck the surface—the incident angle.

Specular transmission. A light transport mechanism where light travels through a surface and is emitted on the opposite side of the surface.

Surface normal. A unit-length vector that points away from a surface and is perpendicular to the surface at some point.

Texturing. A process to enhance an object's surface detail without modeling the detail as part of the object's shape.

Translation. A three-dimensional process used to transpose an object's position in three-dimensional space.

Vector. A directed line segment.

View plane. An imaginary window in space through which the viewer sees the objects in a ray-traced image. It can be pictured as a grid of pixels floating in space through which a scene is viewed. To display a ray-traced image, the view plane is mapped to the screen of the computer's monitor.

Viewpoint. The position in space where the viewer's eye is located when viewing a three-dimensional scene. In the context of this book, the viewpoint is a data structure comprised of four vectors that determine what the viewer will see. These are the LOCATION, DIRECTION, UP, and RIGHT vectors.

The Companion Disks

The companion disks contain all of the code described and listed in this book along with a selection of ray-trace image models and images for your experimentation and viewing pleasure. The companion disks are packaged with this book. If they are missing, please bring it to the attention of your retailer. The use of the companion disks will save hours of typing and program debugging caused by typing errors. As noted in the text, absolutely no program development is required to begin experimenting with ray tracing. This is because we have provided executable versions of the important programs on the companion disks. The only possible exception to this rule will be mentioned shortly.

All files on the companion disks are in compressed format. This was necessary because of the large amount of source code, executable files, images, and documentation provided. To use these files, you must first decompress them with the "lharc.exe" program provided on the disks. To decompress the files contained in the "GALLERY.LZH" file, for example, use the following command:

    lharc x gallery.lzh <enter>

If you type this command at the DOS command prompt, it will decompress the files into the current directory. Because the disks are tightly packed, you may have to copy the file(s) you wish to decompress onto a different disk before decompressing.

Two types of viewable image files are included on the companion disks in the "GALLERY.LZH" file. These are GIF files (".GIF") and an autodisplay (".COM") file. Image files in GIF format require the "v256.exe" program or any other GIF viewing program to display. Autodisplay files will display themselves on a VGA-equipped computer when you type their filename at the DOS command prompt. *Note*: If your graphics card is not VESA compatible, you will have to modify the "v256.exe" program before it will work. Also, your Super-VGA card will need 1 megabyte of RAM to display 1024 by 768 images in 256 colors. See Chapter 5 for the details of what is involved in making these modifications.

All of the C code provided is directly compilable by Borland C/C++ version 2.0. Some code changes will be required for use with other C compilers. Chapter 1 discusses code porting briefly.

The following table describes the types of files found on the companion disks. The file "readme.doc" on the disks describes last-minute changes to the code that did not make it into the printing of this book. Please read this file carefully if it exists on your companion disks.

Filename Extension	Type/Content of File
".ASM"	assembler language source code files
".C"	C source code files
".COM"	directly executable autodisplay image files
".DAT"	DKBTrace image model data files
".DIS"	DKBTrace dump files
".DOC"	documentation files
".EXE"	directly executable program files
".GIF"	GIF format image files—use "v256.exe" to view
".H"	C header (include) files
".MAK"	traditional make files
".PCX"	PCX format image files—use "v256.exe" to view
".PRJ"	Borland C's "project make" files

Content of the Companion Disks

All files from this book have been compressed into separate chapter files. A chapter file contains all of the code described within a chapter. Use the following lists to find out which compressed chapter file contains the file(s) you are interested in. Decompress those chapter files as instructed earlier. You will then have access to the decompressed files you require.

Companion Disk One—The DKBTrace Disk

```
File: README.DOC    Last-minute information file (ASCII)

File: LHARC.EXE     File compression/decompression program

File: DKB212DA.LZH  Compressed DKBTrace image model files
      The following image model files are included:

      ALPHATS2.DAT, ALPHATST.DAT, ARCHES.DAT, CAR.DAT, CHECKER2.DAT, CHESS.DAT,
      COLORS.DAT, COLORTES.DAT, COLORTES.DOC, COLORTES.GIF, COLORTES.KEY, DATAFILE.TXT,
      DESK.DAT, DEVIL.DAT, DISH.DAT, DKB211.GIF, EIGHT.DAT, FISHX.DAT, FOLIUM.DAT,
      GLASS3.GIF, HYPTORUS.DAT, ILLUM1.DAT, ILLUM2.DAT, IMAGE13.DAT, KSCOPE.DAT, LAMP.DAT,
      LEMNISC2.DAT, LEMNISCA.DAT, LILY1.DAT, LPOPS1.DAT, LPOPS2.DAT, MAZE.IFF, MERRY.INC,
      MONKEY.DAT, NTREAL.DAT, NUMBER.IFF, PACMAN.DAT, PARTORUS.DAT, PENCIL.DAT,
      PIRIFORM.DAT, PLANET.DAT, POOL.DAT, POOLBALL.DAT, QUARCYL.DAT, QUARPARA.DAT,
      READ.ME, ROMAN.DAT, ROOM.DAT, ROSETEST.DAT, SHAPES.DAT, SKYVASE.DAT, SPLINE.DAT,
      STARS.GIF, STONEWAL.DAT, SUNSET.DAT, SUNSET1.DAT, TCUBIC.DAT, TETRA.DAT,
      TEXTURES.DAT, TOMB.DAT, TORUS.DAT, TROUGH.DAT, TWISTER.INC, WATERBOW.DAT,
      WEALTH.DAT, WINDOW.DAT, WITCH.DAT
```

File: DKB212DO.LZH   Compressed DKBTrace documentation files
        The following documentation files are included:

        12TO20.DOC, 25TO210.DOC, DKB212.DOC, PRESSREL.TXT, READ.ME, TGA2DUMP.DOC, WHATS.NEW

File: DKB212SR.LZH   Compressed DKBTrace source code files
        The following source code files are included:

        AMIGA.C, AMIGA.MAK, AMIGACON.H, COLOUR.C, CSG.C, DKBPROTO.H, DUMP.C, FRAME.H, GIF.C,
        GIFDECOD.C, IBM.C, IBM.LNK, IBM.MAK, IBMCONF.H, IBMTC.LNK, IBMTC.MAK, IFF.C, LIGHT-
        ING.C, MAC.C, MACCONF.H, MATRICES.C, OBJECTS.C, PARSE.C, PLANES.C, PORTS.DOC,
        PRIOQ.C, QUADRICS.C, QUARTICS.C, RAW.C, RAY.C, READ.ME, RENDER.C, SPHERES.C,
        TARGA.C, TEXTURE.C, THEICON, TOKENIZE.C, TRACE.C, TRIANGLE.C, UNIX.C, UNIX.MAK,
        UNIXCONF.H, VAX.C, VAXBUILD.COM, VAXCONF.H, VECT.C, VECTOR.H, VIEWPNT.C, WITHFILE,
        XWIN.C

File: DKB212IB.LZH   Compressed DKBTrace executable code files
        The following files are included:

        DKB.EXE, DKBNO87.EXE, READ.ME, TRACE.DEF

File: DKB212PR.LZH   Compressed DKBTrace protected-mode executable code files
        The following files are included:

        DKBMOD.DOC, DKBMOD.EXE, DKBPRO.DOC, DKBPRO.EXE

Companion Disk Two—The Tools Disk

File: README.DOC Last-minute information file (ASCII)

File: LHARC.EXE File compression/decompression program

File: CHAP1.LZH
  GAMMA.C   A code fragment to generate GAMMA tables
  HICOLOR.C   32K-color support code for the ET-4000 chip set
  HICOLOR.H   Include file for above
  MISC.H   A file of miscellaneous defines and error codes
  VESA.C   VESA experimentation program
  VESA.PRJ   A Borland project make file for the above program
  VGA.C   VGA function library code
  VGA.H   Include file for above
  VGAGRAPH.ASM   Direct video memory access code in assembler
  VGAGRAPH.C   Direct video memory access code in C

File: CHAP2.LZH
  VECTORS.H   Vector manipulation macros

File: CHAP3.LZH
  ATTRIB.C   Surface attribute code for simple ray tracer
  BTRACE.PRJ   Borland C project make file
  ERRORS.H   Miscellaneous defines and error codes
  LIGHT.C   Code dealing with light sources and rays
  LINKLIST.C   Code to handle singly linked lists
  MYMEM.H   Include to allow compilation with Microsoft C
  OUTPUT.C   Code that writes the output dump file
  PLANE.C   Code for planes

RAYS.C	Code for generation of rays
SPHERE.C	Code for spheres
STRUCT.H	General data structures used in ray tracer
TRACE.C	Scene description file
TRACE.DAT	DKBTrace image model file for image produced by trace.c
TRACE.H	Function prototypes for ray tracer
TRACE.MAK	Make file for ray tracer
TTRACE.PRJ	Turbo C project make file
VECTORS.H	Vector manipulation macros

File: CHAP4.LZH

HQUAN.C	32K-color quantization code
HQUAN.EXE	Executable version
HQUAN.PRJ	Borland project make file
IMAGECOM.ASM	Autodisplay program assembler source
MQUAN.C	Median cut 256-color quantization code
MQUAN.EXE	Executable version
MQUAN.PRJ	Borland project make file
OQUAN.C	Octree 256-color quantization code
OQUAN.EXE	Executable version
OQUAN.PRJ	Borland project make file

File: CHAP5.LZH

COMPRESS.ASM	PCX RLL compressor assembler code
DUMPIO.C	Dump image file format I/O code
DUMPIO.PRJ	Borland project make file for test harness
GIF.C	GIF function library code
GIF.H	Include file for above
PCX.C	PCX function library code
PCX.H	Include file for above
PCX2GIF.C	PCX to GIF file conversion utility code
PCX2GIF.PRJ	Borland project make file
V256.C	256-color PCX and GIF file viewing program code
V256.EXE	Executable version of above
V256.PRJ	Borland project make file

File: CHAP6.LZH

Q	80 by 50 pixel resolution DKBTrace command file
T3X2	320 by 200 pixel resolution DKBTrace command file
T6X4	640 by 480 pixel resolution DKBTrace command file
T8X6	800 by 600 pixel resolution DKBTrace command file
T10X7	1024 by 768 pixel resolution DKBTrace command file

File: CHAP7.LZH

EXER1.DAT	Tutorial Exercise 1 DKBTrace image model file
EXER2.DAT	Tutorial Exercise 2 DKBTrace image model file
EXER3.DAT	Tutorial Exercise 3 DKBTrace image model file
EXER4.DAT	Tutorial Exercise 4 DKBTrace image model file
EXER5.DAT	Tutorial Exercise 5 DKBTrace image model file
EXER6.DAT	Tutorial Exercise 6 DKBTrace image model file
EXER7.DAT	Tutorial Exercise 7 DKBTrace image model file
EXER8.DAT	Tutorial Exercise 8 DKBTrace image model file

```
File: CHAP8.LZH
  CRAIG.DIS       Bit map file of author's face in dump format
  EXER9.DAT       Tutorial Exercise 9 DKBTrace image model file
  EXER10.DAT      Tutorial Exercise 10 DKBTrace image model file
  EXER11.DAT      Tutorial Exercise 11 DKBTrace image model file
  EXER12.DAT      Tutorial Exercise 12 DKBTrace image model file
  MOUNT.C         Tutorial Exercise 12 C code for mountain generation

File: CHAP9.LZH
  BRAKE1.DAT      DKBTrace image model of truck brake
  CACTUS5.DAT     DKBTrace image model of desert scene
  FRACT1.GIF      Fractal IMAGEMAP file for use with RT4.DAT
  FRACT2.GIF      Fractal IMAGEMAP file for use with RT4.DAT
  FRACT3.GIF      Fractal IMAGEMAP file for use with RT4.DAT
  FRACT4.GIF      Fractal IMAGEMAP file for use with RT4.DAT
  MAZE6.DAT       DKBTrace image model of infinite maze (cover image)
  RT4.DAT         DKBTrace image model using IMAGEMAPs

File: MISC.LZH
  COLORS.RGB      Extended color definitions from Part Three

File: GALLERY.LZH
  BRAKE1.GIF      GIF file of truck brake 1024 by 768 in 256 colors
  CACTUS5.GIF     GIF file of desert scene 1024 by 768 in 256 colors
  EXER9.GIF       GIF file of lettering 1024 by 768 in 256 colors
  GRADTST.DAT     Image model to create gradient data for showing 256 colors versus 32K colors
  MAZE6.GIF       GIF file of infinite maze of pipes and spheres
  PYR6.DAT        Image model of pyramids used to illustrate anti-aliasing
  TORUS3.DAT      Image model of interwoven tori used to illustrate nongamma versus gamma
                  correction
  TRACE.COM       Autodisplay file of image produced by simple ray tracer of Chapter 3.
```

Note: Only a few of the images in the "Gallery of Images" have a corresponding GIF file in this compressed chapter file. The image files are just too large for floppy disks, compressed or not. You can recreate all of the Gallery images, however, by submitting the image model data files (".DAT") to DKBTrace for rendering. That way, you can recreate the Gallery images at a resolution your computer can support.

RGB Color Tables

Following is an enhanced list of colors that you can use in place of or in conjunction with DKBTrace's "colors.dat" include file. All colors are defined in RGB format.

The following is the contents of the file "colors.rgb."

```
{ These are various shades of the color white }
DECLARE AntiqueWhite   = COLOR RED 0.9804 GREEN 0.9216 BLUE 0.8431
DECLARE Azure          = COLOR RED 0.9412 GREEN 1.0000 BLUE 1.0000
DECLARE Bisque         = COLOR RED 1.0000 GREEN 0.8941 BLUE 0.7686
DECLARE BlanchedAlmond = COLOR RED 1.0000 GREEN 0.9216 BLUE 0.8039
DECLARE Cornsilk       = COLOR RED 1.0000 GREEN 0.9725 BLUE 0.8627
DECLARE Eggshell       = COLOR RED 0.9900 GREEN 0.9000 BLUE 0.7900
DECLARE FloralWhite    = COLOR RED 1.0000 GREEN 0.9804 BLUE 0.9412
DECLARE Gainsboro      = COLOR RED 0.8627 GREEN 0.8627 BLUE 0.8627
DECLARE GhostWhite     = COLOR RED 0.9725 GREEN 0.9725 BLUE 1.0000
DECLARE Honeydew       = COLOR RED 0.9412 GREEN 1.0000 BLUE 0.9412
DECLARE Ivory          = COLOR RED 1.0000 GREEN 1.0000 BLUE 0.9412
DECLARE Lavender       = COLOR RED 0.9020 GREEN 0.9020 BLUE 0.9804
DECLARE LavenderBlush  = COLOR RED 1.0000 GREEN 0.9412 BLUE 0.9608
DECLARE LemonChiffon   = COLOR RED 1.0000 GREEN 0.9804 BLUE 0.8039
DECLARE Linen          = COLOR RED 0.9804 GREEN 0.9412 BLUE 0.9020
DECLARE MintCream      = COLOR RED 0.9608 GREEN 1.0000 BLUE 0.9804
DECLARE MistyRose      = COLOR RED 1.0000 GREEN 0.8941 BLUE 0.8824
DECLARE Moccasin       = COLOR RED 1.0000 GREEN 0.8941 BLUE 0.7098
DECLARE NavajoWhite    = COLOR RED 1.0000 GREEN 0.8706 BLUE 0.6784
DECLARE OldLace        = COLOR RED 0.9922 GREEN 0.9608 BLUE 0.9020
DECLARE PapayaWhip     = COLOR RED 1.0000 GREEN 0.9373 BLUE 0.8353
DECLARE PeachPuff      = COLOR RED 1.0000 GREEN 0.8549 BLUE 0.7255
DECLARE Seashell       = COLOR RED 1.0000 GREEN 0.9608 BLUE 0.9333
DECLARE Snow           = COLOR RED 1.0000 GREEN 0.9804 BLUE 0.9804
DECLARE Thistle        = COLOR RED 0.8471 GREEN 0.7490 BLUE 0.8471
```

```
DECLARE TitaniumWhite     = COLOR RED 0.9900 GREEN 1.0000 BLUE 0.9400
DECLARE Wheat             = COLOR RED 0.9608 GREEN 0.8706 BLUE 0.7020
DECLARE White             = COLOR RED 1.0000 GREEN 1.0000 BLUE 1.0000
DECLARE WhiteSmoke        = COLOR RED 0.9608 GREEN 0.9608 BLUE 0.9608
DECLARE ZincWhite         = COLOR RED 0.9900 GREEN 0.9700 BLUE 1.0000

{ These are various shades of the color gray }
DECLARE ColdGray          = COLOR RED 0.5000 GREEN 0.5400 BLUE 0.5300
DECLARE DimGray           = COLOR RED 0.4118 GREEN 0.4118 BLUE 0.4118
DECLARE Gray              = COLOR RED 0.7529 GREEN 0.7529 BLUE 0.7529
DECLARE LightGray         = COLOR RED 0.8275 GREEN 0.8275 BLUE 0.8275
DECLARE SlateGray         = COLOR RED 0.4392 GREEN 0.5020 BLUE 0.5647
DECLARE SlateGrayDark     = COLOR RED 0.1843 GREEN 0.3098 BLUE 0.3098
DECLARE SlateGrayLight    = COLOR RED 0.4667 GREEN 0.5333 BLUE 0.6000
DECLARE WarmGray          = COLOR RED 0.5000 GREEN 0.5000 BLUE 0.4100

{ These are various shades of the color black }
DECLARE Black             = COLOR RED 0.0000 GREEN 0.0000 BLUE 0.0000
DECLARE IvoryBlack        = COLOR RED 0.1600 GREEN 0.1400 BLUE 0.1300
DECLARE LampBlack         = COLOR RED 0.1800 GREEN 0.2800 BLUE 0.2300

{ These are various shades of the color red }
DECLARE AlizarinCrimson   = COLOR RED 0.8900 GREEN 0.1500 BLUE 0.2100
DECLARE Brick             = COLOR RED 0.6100 GREEN 0.4000 BLUE 0.1200
DECLARE CadmiumRedDeep    = COLOR RED 0.8900 GREEN 0.0900 BLUE 0.0500
DECLARE Coral             = COLOR RED 1.0000 GREEN 0.4980 BLUE 0.3137
DECLARE CoralLight        = COLOR RED 0.9412 GREEN 0.5020 BLUE 0.5020
DECLARE DeepPink          = COLOR RED 1.0000 GREEN 0.0784 BLUE 0.5765
DECLARE EnglishRed        = COLOR RED 0.8300 GREEN 0.2400 BLUE 0.1000
DECLARE Firebrick         = COLOR RED 0.6980 GREEN 0.1333 BLUE 0.1333
DECLARE GeraniumLake      = COLOR RED 0.8900 GREEN 0.0700 BLUE 0.1900
DECLARE HotPink           = COLOR RED 1.0000 GREEN 0.4118 BLUE 0.7059
DECLARE IndianRed         = COLOR RED 0.6900 GREEN 0.0900 BLUE 0.1200
DECLARE LightSalmon       = COLOR RED 1.0000 GREEN 0.6275 BLUE 0.4784
DECLARE MadderLakeDeep    = COLOR RED 0.8900 GREEN 0.1800 BLUE 0.1900
DECLARE Maroon            = COLOR RED 0.6902 GREEN 0.1882 BLUE 0.3765
DECLARE Pink              = COLOR RED 1.0000 GREEN 0.7529 BLUE 0.7961
DECLARE PinkLight         = COLOR RED 1.0000 GREEN 0.7137 BLUE 0.7569
DECLARE Raspberry         = COLOR RED 0.5300 GREEN 0.1500 BLUE 0.3400
DECLARE Red               = COLOR RED 1.0000 GREEN 0.0000 BLUE 0.0000
DECLARE RoseMadder        = COLOR RED 0.8900 GREEN 0.2100 BLUE 0.2200
DECLARE Salmon            = COLOR RED 0.9804 GREEN 0.5020 BLUE 0.4471
DECLARE Tomato            = COLOR RED 1.0000 GREEN 0.3882 BLUE 0.2784
DECLARE VenetianRed       = COLOR RED 0.8300 GREEN 0.1000 BLUE 0.1200

{ These are various shades of the color brown }
DECLARE Beige             = COLOR RED 0.6400 GREEN 0.5800 BLUE 0.5000
DECLARE Brown             = COLOR RED 0.5000 GREEN 0.1647 BLUE 0.1647
DECLARE BrownMadder       = COLOR RED 0.8600 GREEN 0.1600 BLUE 0.1600
DECLARE BrownOchre        = COLOR RED 0.5300 GREEN 0.2600 BLUE 0.1200
DECLARE Burlywood         = COLOR RED 0.8706 GREEN 0.7216 BLUE 0.5294
DECLARE BurntSienna       = COLOR RED 0.5400 GREEN 0.2100 BLUE 0.0600
```

```
DECLARE BurntUmber     = COLOR RED 0.5400 GREEN 0.2000 BLUE 0.1400
DECLARE Chocolate      = COLOR RED 0.8235 GREEN 0.4118 BLUE 0.1176
DECLARE DeepOchre      = COLOR RED 0.4500 GREEN 0.2400 BLUE 0.1000
DECLARE Flesh          = COLOR RED 1.0000 GREEN 0.4900 BLUE 0.2500
DECLARE FleshOchre     = COLOR RED 1.0000 GREEN 0.3400 BLUE 0.1300
DECLARE GoldOchre      = COLOR RED 0.7800 GREEN 0.4700 BLUE 0.1500
DECLARE GreenishUmber  = COLOR RED 1.0000 GREEN 0.2400 BLUE 0.0500
DECLARE Khaki          = COLOR RED 0.9412 GREEN 0.9020 BLUE 0.5490
DECLARE KhakiDark      = COLOR RED 0.7412 GREEN 0.7176 BLUE 0.4196
DECLARE LightBeige     = COLOR RED 0.9608 GREEN 0.9608 BLUE 0.8627
DECLARE Peru           = COLOR RED 0.8039 GREEN 0.5216 BLUE 0.2471
DECLARE RosyBrown      = COLOR RED 0.7373 GREEN 0.5608 BLUE 0.5608
DECLARE RawSienna      = COLOR RED 0.7800 GREEN 0.3800 BLUE 0.0800
DECLARE RawUmber       = COLOR RED 0.4500 GREEN 0.2900 BLUE 0.0700
DECLARE Sepia          = COLOR RED 0.3700 GREEN 0.1500 BLUE 0.0700
DECLARE Sienna         = COLOR RED 0.6275 GREEN 0.3216 BLUE 0.1765
DECLARE SaddleBrown    = COLOR RED 0.5451 GREEN 0.2706 BLUE 0.0745
DECLARE SandyBrown     = COLOR RED 0.9569 GREEN 0.6431 BLUE 0.3765
DECLARE Tan            = COLOR RED 0.8235 GREEN 0.7059 BLUE 0.5490
DECLARE VanDykeBrown   = COLOR RED 0.3700 GREEN 0.1500 BLUE 0.0200

{ These are various shades of the color orange }
DECLARE CadmiumOrange   = COLOR RED 1.0000 GREEN 0.3800 BLUE 0.0100
DECLARE CadmiumRedLight = COLOR RED 1.0000 GREEN 0.0100 BLUE 0.0500
DECLARE Carrot          = COLOR RED 0.9300 GREEN 0.5700 BLUE 0.1300
DECLARE DarkOrange      = COLOR RED 1.0000 GREEN 0.5490 BLUE 0.0000
DECLARE MarsOrange      = COLOR RED 0.5900 GREEN 0.2700 BLUE 0.0800
DECLARE MarsYellow      = COLOR RED 0.8900 GREEN 0.4400 BLUE 0.1000
DECLARE Orange          = COLOR RED 1.0000 GREEN 0.5000 BLUE 0.0000
DECLARE OrangeRed       = COLOR RED 1.0000 GREEN 0.2706 BLUE 0.0000
DECLARE YellowOchre     = COLOR RED 0.8900 GREEN 0.5100 BLUE 0.0900

{ These are various shades of the color yellow }
DECLARE AureolineYellow     = COLOR RED 1.0000 GREEN 0.6600 BLUE 0.1400
DECLARE Banana              = COLOR RED 0.8900 GREEN 0.8100 BLUE 0.3400
DECLARE CadmiumLemon        = COLOR RED 1.0000 GREEN 0.8900 BLUE 0.0100
DECLARE CadmiumYellow       = COLOR RED 1.0000 GREEN 0.6000 BLUE 0.0700
DECLARE CadmiumYellowLight  = COLOR RED 1.0000 GREEN 0.6900 BLUE 0.0600
DECLARE Gold                = COLOR RED 1.0000 GREEN 0.8431 BLUE 0.0000
DECLARE Goldenrod           = COLOR RED 0.8549 GREEN 0.6471 BLUE 0.1255
DECLARE GoldenrodDark       = COLOR RED 0.7216 GREEN 0.5255 BLUE 0.0431
DECLARE GoldenrodLight      = COLOR RED 0.9804 GREEN 0.9804 BLUE 0.8235
DECLARE GoldenrodPale       = COLOR RED 0.9333 GREEN 0.9098 BLUE 0.6667
DECLARE LightGoldenrod      = COLOR RED 0.9333 GREEN 0.8667 BLUE 0.5098
DECLARE Melon               = COLOR RED 0.8900 GREEN 0.6600 BLUE 0.4100
DECLARE NaplesYellowDeep    = COLOR RED 1.0000 GREEN 0.6600 BLUE 0.0700
DECLARE Yellow              = COLOR RED 1.0000 GREEN 1.0000 BLUE 0.0000
DECLARE YellowLight         = COLOR RED 1.0000 GREEN 1.0000 BLUE 0.8784

{ These are various shades of the color green }
DECLARE Chartreuse          = COLOR RED 0.4980 GREEN 1.0000 BLUE 0.0000
DECLARE ChromeOxideGreen    = COLOR RED 0.4000 GREEN 0.5000 BLUE 0.0800
```

```
DECLARE CinnabarGreen        = COLOR RED 0.3800 GREEN 0.7000 BLUE 0.1600
DECLARE CobaltGreen          = COLOR RED 0.2400 GREEN 0.5700 BLUE 0.2500
DECLARE EmeraldGreen         = COLOR RED 0.0000 GREEN 0.7900 BLUE 0.3400
DECLARE ForestGreen          = COLOR RED 0.1333 GREEN 0.5451 BLUE 0.1333
DECLARE Green                = COLOR RED 0.0000 GREEN 1.0000 BLUE 0.0000
DECLARE GreenDark            = COLOR RED 0.0000 GREEN 0.3922 BLUE 0.0000
DECLARE GreenPale            = COLOR RED 0.5961 GREEN 0.9843 BLUE 0.5961
DECLARE GreenYellow          = COLOR RED 0.6784 GREEN 1.0000 BLUE 0.1843
DECLARE LawnGreen            = COLOR RED 0.4863 GREEN 0.9882 BLUE 0.0000
DECLARE LimeGreen            = COLOR RED 0.1961 GREEN 0.8039 BLUE 0.1961
DECLARE Mint                 = COLOR RED 0.7400 GREEN 0.9900 BLUE 0.7900
DECLARE Olive                = COLOR RED 0.2300 GREEN 0.3700 BLUE 0.1700
DECLARE OliveDrab            = COLOR RED 0.4196 GREEN 0.5569 BLUE 0.1373
DECLARE OliveGgreenDark      = COLOR RED 0.3333 GREEN 0.4196 BLUE 0.1843
DECLARE PermanentGreen       = COLOR RED 0.0400 GREEN 0.7900 BLUE 0.1700
DECLARE SapGreen             = COLOR RED 0.1900 GREEN 0.5000 BLUE 0.0800
DECLARE SeaGreen             = COLOR RED 0.1804 GREEN 0.5451 BLUE 0.3412
DECLARE SeaGreenDark         = COLOR RED 0.5608 GREEN 0.7373 BLUE 0.5608
DECLARE SeaGreenMedium       = COLOR RED 0.2353 GREEN 0.7020 BLUE 0.4431
DECLARE SeaGreenLight        = COLOR RED 0.1255 GREEN 0.6980 BLUE 0.6667
DECLARE SpringGreen          = COLOR RED 0.0000 GREEN 1.0000 BLUE 0.4980
DECLARE SpringGreenMedium    = COLOR RED 0.0000 GREEN 0.9804 BLUE 0.6039
DECLARE TerreVerte           = COLOR RED 0.2200 GREEN 0.3700 BLUE 0.0600
DECLARE ViridianLight        = COLOR RED 0.4300 GREEN 1.0000 BLUE 0.4400
DECLARE YellowGreen          = COLOR RED 0.6039 GREEN 0.8039 BLUE 0.1961

{ These are various shades of the color cyan }
DECLARE Aquamarine           = COLOR RED 0.4980 GREEN 1.0000 BLUE 0.8314
DECLARE AquamarineMedium     = COLOR RED 0.4000 GREEN 0.8039 BLUE 0.6667
DECLARE Cyan                 = COLOR RED 0.0000 GREEN 1.0000 BLUE 1.0000
DECLARE CyanWhite            = COLOR RED 0.8784 GREEN 1.0000 BLUE 1.0000
DECLARE Turquoise            = COLOR RED 0.2510 GREEN 0.8784 BLUE 0.8157
DECLARE TurquoiseDark        = COLOR RED 0.0000 GREEN 0.8078 BLUE 0.8196
DECLARE TurquoiseMedium      = COLOR RED 0.2824 GREEN 0.8196 BLUE 0.8000
DECLARE TurquoisePale        = COLOR RED 0.6863 GREEN 0.9333 BLUE 0.9333

{ These are various shades of the color blue }
DECLARE AliceBlue            = COLOR RED 0.9412 GREEN 0.9725 BLUE 1.0000
DECLARE Blue                 = COLOR RED 0.0000 GREEN 0.0000 BLUE 1.0000
DECLARE BlueLight            = COLOR RED 0.6784 GREEN 0.8471 BLUE 0.9020
DECLARE BlueMedium           = COLOR RED 0.0000 GREEN 0.0000 BLUE 0.8039
DECLARE Cadet                = COLOR RED 0.3725 GREEN 0.6196 BLUE 0.6275
DECLARE Cobalt               = COLOR RED 0.2400 GREEN 0.3500 BLUE 0.6700
DECLARE Cornflower           = COLOR RED 0.3922 GREEN 0.5843 BLUE 0.9294
DECLARE Cerulean             = COLOR RED 0.0200 GREEN 0.7200 BLUE 0.8000
DECLARE DodgerBlue           = COLOR RED 0.1176 GREEN 0.5647 BLUE 1.0000
DECLARE Indigo               = COLOR RED 0.0300 GREEN 0.1800 BLUE 0.3300
DECLARE ManganeseBlue        = COLOR RED 0.0100 GREEN 0.6600 BLUE 0.6200
DECLARE MidnightBlue         = COLOR RED 0.0980 GREEN 0.0980 BLUE 0.4392
DECLARE Navy                 = COLOR RED 0.0000 GREEN 0.0000 BLUE 0.5020
DECLARE Peacock              = COLOR RED 0.2000 GREEN 0.6300 BLUE 0.7900
DECLARE PowderBlue           = COLOR RED 0.6902 GREEN 0.8784 BLUE 0.9020
```

```
DECLARE RoyalBlue          = COLOR RED 0.2549 GREEN 0.4118 BLUE 0.8824
DECLARE SlateBlue          = COLOR RED 0.4157 GREEN 0.3529 BLUE 0.8039
DECLARE SlateBlueDark      = COLOR RED 0.2824 GREEN 0.2392 BLUE 0.5451
DECLARE SlateBlueLight     = COLOR RED 0.5176 GREEN 0.4392 BLUE 1.0000
DECLARE SlateBlueMedium    = COLOR RED 0.4824 GREEN 0.4078 BLUE 0.9333
DECLARE SkyBlue            = COLOR RED 0.5294 GREEN 0.8078 BLUE 0.9216
DECLARE SkyBlueDeep        = COLOR RED 0.0000 GREEN 0.7490 BLUE 1.0000
DECLARE SkyBlueLight       = COLOR RED 0.5294 GREEN 0.8078 BLUE 0.9804
DECLARE SteelBlue          = COLOR RED 0.2745 GREEN 0.5098 BLUE 0.7059
DECLARE SteelBlueLight     = COLOR RED 0.6902 GREEN 0.7686 BLUE 0.8706
DECLARE TurquoiseBlue      = COLOR RED 0.0000 GREEN 0.7800 BLUE 0.5500
DECLARE Ultramarine        = COLOR RED 0.0700 GREEN 0.0400 BLUE 0.5600

{ These are various shades of the color magenta }
DECLARE BlueViolet          = COLOR RED 0.5412 GREEN 0.1686 BLUE 0.8863
DECLARE CobaltVioletDeep    = COLOR RED 0.5700 GREEN 0.1300 BLUE 0.6200
DECLARE Magenta             = COLOR RED 1.0000 GREEN 0.0000 BLUE 1.0000
DECLARE Orchid              = COLOR RED 0.8549 GREEN 0.4392 BLUE 0.8392
DECLARE OrchidDark          = COLOR RED 0.6000 GREEN 0.1961 BLUE 0.8000
DECLARE OrchidMedium        = COLOR RED 0.7294 GREEN 0.3333 BLUE 0.8275
DECLARE PermanentRedViolet  = COLOR RED 0.8600 GREEN 0.1500 BLUE 0.2700
DECLARE Plum                = COLOR RED 0.8667 GREEN 0.6275 BLUE 0.8667
DECLARE Purple              = COLOR RED 0.6275 GREEN 0.1255 BLUE 0.9412
DECLARE PurpleMedium        = COLOR RED 0.5765 GREEN 0.4392 BLUE 0.8588
DECLARE UltramarineViolet   = COLOR RED 0.3600 GREEN 0.1400 BLUE 0.4300
DECLARE Violet              = COLOR RED 0.5600 GREEN 0.3700 BLUE 0.6000
DECLARE VioletDark          = COLOR RED 0.5804 GREEN 0.0000 BLUE 0.8275
DECLARE VioletRed           = COLOR RED 0.8157 GREEN 0.1255 BLUE 0.5647
DECLARE VioletRedMedium     = COLOR RED 0.7804 GREEN 0.0824 BLUE 0.5216
DECLARE VioletRedPale       = COLOR RED 0.8588 GREEN 0.4392 BLUE 0.5765
```

It ain't over 'til it's over.
—Yogi Berra

It's over.
—Craig A. Lindley

Index

G